ISBN 978-1-331-32175-0
PIBN 10174068

English
Français
Deutsche
Italiano
Español
Português

www.forgottenbooks.com

THE

DUBLIN REVIEW.

VOL. XVI. NEW SERIES.

JANUARY——JULY,

MDCCCLXXI.

LONDON:

BURNS, OATES, & CO., 17 & 18, PORTMAN STREET,
AND 63 PATERNOSTER ROW.
DERBY: RICHARDSON & SONS.
DUBLIN: JAMES DUFFY; W. B. KELLY.
1871.

THE

DUBLIN REVIEW.

JANUARY, 1871.

Art I.—PIUS IX. AND THE REVOLUTION.

Pontificate of Pius the Ninth (being the third edition of *Rome and its Ruler*). By JOHN FRANCIS MAGUIRE, M.P. London: Longmans, Green, & Co.

TWO centuries, we think, have passed since some ancient ruins, the existence of which had for long ages been forgotten, were discovered in Spain, and among them the inscription which has since become celebrated through the world, and which had put on everlasting record the gratitude of the province to the Roman Emperor, for having "abolished the name of Christian." Some fifteen hundred years before that inscription had been voted by the municipal rulers, the marble had been laboriously dug from the quarry, and carefully polished with all the skill of a highly-civilized age, and cunning workmen had wrought at the letters, chipping away one fragment after another with the model of the inscription before them. Emperor and Empire, Proconsul, Duumviri and Decuriones, nay the very stonecutters and quarrymen, were then all of one mind, that at least that hateful name of Christian would never more be borne by living man. Yet when the stone was discovered, not only the emperor but the empire had for ages passed away. The names of the municipal and proconsular rulers were no more remembered than those of the men who cut the marble by their order. The civilized province of Spain, although by its position so happily inaccessible to any enemy, because he could not even reach it until he should have conquered either Gaul or Africa, had for centuries been possessed by barbarian tribes, in whose mouths the name of Roman was the foulest term of reproach. One thing only remained of all that had existed upon the earth fifteen hundred years before, and that one thing was the "Christian Name" and the Catholic Church, to which, alike when the monument was erected and when its ruins were discovered, that Name belonged. The Catholic king of Spain, in whose dominions it was found, although lord of an empire upon which the sun never set, regarded that Name as his proudest title. It was spread over "regions Cæsar never knew," and was as little likely ever to be "abolished" as the eternal hills themselves or the unchangeable ocean.

And yet, not once, but over and over again, in that long period, the world had boasted of its victory and of the final overthrow of its rival and enemy. Its attempts had been renewed, age after age, in forms ever varying, but with the same instinctive hatred. The persecution of Diocletian was materially different from that of Nero—that of Julian from his. Mahommed again had been different from all. At one period the avowed object was to crush the Church, at another to divide it. One age directed its fury at the sacred books, another specially at the successors of Peter; but behind all these changes of outward appearance, there had all along been the same power directed by the craft and malice of the same great enemy; the hosts of wicked men and evil spirits, carrying with them unhappily in each age men of whom we may sorrowfully say "they know not what they do"; but all, in one age as in the other actuated and directed by the "god of this world."

Little indeed then would be our wisdom if we allowed ourselves to be astonished that in our own age the immediate object of attack is not exactly the same as in ages past—still less our faith, if we suffered ourselves to be fearful, because, at one time or another, it seems as if the enemy had gained some signal advantage. Nothing can overthrow that society which is the Church, the Body, "the very Self below," of the Eternal Son, the King of Kings and Lord of Lords. Its existence in the world to this day is, as S. Augustine says, the strongest proof of its Divine origin. For if human power or the revolutions of human society could have affected it, it must have perished ages back.

The peculiar form taken by the assaults of the enemy during the last century has been that of an attack on the visible Head of the Church, the Vicar of Christ. No wonder then that the men most eager in carrying it on are so careful to disclaim any enmity to the Church; just as, three centuries ago, when the great attack was made upon the Church, the assailants were equally earnest in declaring that their enmity was not against the Gospel but against the Church only. What is before us who can tell? In our own day, as in every former period of the history of the Church, there are good and wise men, fully persuaded that the end is very near at

hand, that the troubles upon which they see her entering are
those which are to immediately usher in her final victory, and
that the Lord, for whose coming we are all waiting, will
almost immediately be seen among us. That such should be
the attitude of His expectant Church in every successive age
seems to have been His Divine will and purpose; and accordingly, ever since He went away from her into Heaven, she
has been pleading His words, "Surely I come quickly," and
crying out with His beloved Apostle, "Even so come Lord
Jesus." Yet, as man cannot judge what is in His sight a long
time or a short, it is not really inconsistent with hearty faith
in His promise, nor with this desire and prayer, that others
should incline to the opinion that possibly there may still be
before us many centuries of struggles and conflicts, and that
the time may come when believing men shall look back to
those of our own time, as we ourselves do to those of the
early martyrs,—nay, when Pius IX. shall be classed in the
memory of Christians with Cornelius and Stephen, Gregory
and Innocent, as one of those who, in the earlier ages of the
Church, carried on, each in his day, the great battle against
the kingdom of this world. Should this be the will of God,
however much may be coming which we are quite unable to
foresee, there are still things of which we may be sure beforehand: one is, that every succeeding age will be marked by its
own special evils and dangers, against which the Church will
have to contend, and the other, that in each successive period
these special evils will not only be different from those of
former periods, but that the men against whom the battle will
then have to be waged will admit, nay boast, that in the earlier
stages of the conflict the right was on the side of the Church,
even while they are most strenuous in denouncing her attitude
in their own days. Thus the generation which denied and
slew the Lord of the prophets, themselves built the sepulchres
of the prophets whom their fathers had slain, and protested,
"If we had been in the days of our fathers we would not have
been sharers with them in the blood of the prophets."

Should the time ever come when men thus look back upon
the present age, its special character surely will be, that it is
the age of revolution. Already for eighty years the repose of
the old system in which civilized Europe was reposing has
been broken by successive shocks, as of some mighty earthquake; and although to foretell the future is not given to
man, we can hardly err in saying that the earthquake is not
yet over, and that seasons of peace enjoyed by this generation
are but intervals between its shocks. Men are sure to accom-
modate themselves, in the course of years, to any conditions,

however intolerable they may at first appear ; as the sensitive plant droops its leaves when first shaken, but, if the shaking continues, gradually raises them, and even renews its alarm when it suddenly ceases. Thus the European nations are already building and planting, marrying and giving in marriage, over the yet trouble dearth, as men have often done in the valley beneath Vesuvius. But those who look back will regard the whole reign of Pius IX. as one during which the earthquake still lasted.

It is most natural that we should figure to ourselves a condition of lasting peace as that most to be desired for the Church. We read of her sufferings during the persecutions, and can hardly persuade ourselves, that when they have passed they will not be followed, through a sort of poetical justice, by a time of peace and prosperity, in which she is to discharge, without let or hindrance, the work of mercy for which she has been planted among men. But all history bears witness, that however desirable this may seem to human judgment, it is not that which has been chosen for her by Him who orders her lot, and to Whom is given all power in Heaven and on earth. We must not then esteem as less highly favoured a man called by God to sit enthroned in his Church upon earth, because his lot has been to be born just when this great convulsion was beginning, and to have his whole life disturbed by its repeated throes; and such has been the lot of our Holy Father. His birth almost exactly coincided with the commencement of the first great revolution ; his earlier years were disturbed by its overflow into his native country : he was summoned, when only twenty years of age, to do homage to the principle of revolution embodied and enthroned in the person of the great usurper and conqueror ; his succession to the Chair of S. Peter was the signal for that great outbreak all over Europe which marked the middle of the nineteenth century; and if his dying bed should be shaken by some other mighty commotion, it will be but one more example of what we have already seen, in one form or another, in the history of many most highly favoured saints. The last words heard from the dying lips of the great S. Gregory VII. were, "I have loved righteousness and hated iniquity, therefore I die an exile." Yet the Church has never thought of him as of an unsuccessful man.

Nor must we expect that the result effected by the life-long testimony of our Holy Father against the evils of his age will be seen in his own time or in ours—

> Christ only of God's messengers to man
> Finished the work of Grace which He began.

His sentence even upon his most favoured servants is—

> Christ will avenge His Church ; yea, even now
> Begins the work ; and thou
> Shalt spend in it thy strength, but ere He save,
> Thy lot shall be the grave.

For it is no there that the servants of God either take their rest or receive their wages.

Painful then, as it must ever be to stand by and witness a triumph of force and fraud over right such as has just been exhibited at Rome, we are not surprised, and assuredly even less alarmed at it. On the contrary, we knew beforehand that such things must needs be; and the cry of triumph which has been raised over it seems to us only one more repetition of that which, seventeen hundred years ago, celebrated the utter extinction of the Christian name. If we needed anything to put us in good heart, we should find it in the past history of the Papacy. No less than five-and-forty Popes have, at one time or another of their reigns, been exiled from Rome either by the outrages of feudal nobles, or the aggressions of neighbouring sovereigns, or the uprising of a disorderly mob. Nor need we go back to distant times.

The outrages of which Pius IX. and Pius VII. have been the objects have almost obliterated from the minds of this generation the history of Pius VI., the first of those Pontiffs against whom the waves of the revolution broke in their full fury. But it is not well that such things should be forgotten. Assuredly, in 1799, it must have appeared that the power of the Pope had come to an end, to all except those who saw with the eye of faith that the strength of the Church and of the successor of S. Peter was not in the possession of armies, not even in the obedience and devotion of nations (though this is their best earthly possession), but in the presence of Him who is pleased to make His people His Own dwelling-place on earth; and none of them so manifestly as His Vicar, nor even him at any other season so assuredly as when both faithful and suffering for his fidelity. This, and not any confidence in the merely human principle that a popular reaction may be expected on behalf of innocent sufferers, was ever the real meaning of the maxim, that "the blood of the martyrs is the seed of the Church." And the moment when the heathen most furiously raged was ever that at which those who saw things as they really are, were most confident that the time was near at hand when it would appear to all men that He that sitteth in the Heavens had laughed them to scorn—"the Lord had had them in derision." Pius VI. passed away, and again his successor stood alone against the whole power of Napoleon I. Napoleon had on his side all the power of this earth, and once again the Head of the Church was for years an exile and a prisoner. But the time appointed for the fall of the French Emperor came; he fell by the hands, not of man but of God. A new world, as different from that which had existed under Napoleon as from that which it superseded was constituted, and lasted for a generation of men, and the successor of S. Peter was once more its leading feature. Then came, in 1848, a new outbreak of universal revolution; and once more he was an exile. In 1870, so far as man can see, there is every assurance that we are entering upon another new epoch. The French army, so long the terror of Europe, has been crushed in a day. The second Empire has been swept away like leaves before the blast of autumn. What is to follow, it baffles the most confident prophets to predict. Russia judges that its time is come, and threatens once more to involve the whole world in blood. Nearer home a new Empire of Germany is in the act of forming itself, with powers far more real, and in hands more efficient than the world has seen for ages. In the midst of the confusion of this death-struggle between the greatest nations of the earth, Rome, so often coveted and so often seized, has once more been invaded. This time, however, there are two circumstances which distinguish the act of the aggressor from all which have come before it. He has invaded the patrimony of S. Peter without any pretence of grievance, and without the form of proclaiming war; in this respect, at least, departing from the precedents set both by the French Revolutionists and by Napoleon I., who always took care both to make a proclamation of war before invading the dominion of a neighbour, and to found it upon some pretence of wrongs received, although generally much like those by which the wolf justified his attack upon the lamb. And, moreover, the excuse urged for him by others is that unless he forcibly seized the thrones of his neighbours, his own would undoubtedly have been over-thrown by the Revolution. There is certainly nothing in these circumstances to suggest the fear that a spasmodic outrage like this is likely to end in the permanent possession of a prize so often coveted and seized by the greatest powers of the earth, but which none has as yet been able to keep. We are assured, indeed, that the temporal dominion of the Pope has fallen never again to rise. But this is not by any means the first time we have been told so. In 1806, when the object was to intimidate Pius VII., Napoleon I. formally announced to the Nuncio at Paris that if he once annexed the States of the Church to the French Empire, they could never by any change be released from his grasp. He had, at least, this appearance of truth on his side, that he spoke in the name of that great nation one of whose leading characteristics it is to account it a portent and a sacrilege terrible and portentous in the sight of heaven and earth, that any province once by any means annexed to herself should ever be wrested from her. No man ever understood better than Napoleon the greatness and the littleness of that great nation, or more skilfully availed himself of his knowledge. Pius VII., however, replied to this threat, "His Majesty may very easily believe this, and may persuade himself of it; but I frankly reply, that if his Majesty has a right to be confident that power is on his side, I, for my part, know that, above all monarchs, there reigns a God, the avenger of justice and innocence, before Whom every human power must bend." The event proved that Pius, not Napoleon, was the true prophet; and in the solitude of St. Helena Napoleon acknowledged it as his great mistake that he had entered into the contest with the Pope. He had, not unnaturally, been dazzled by the blaze of earthly glory, by which he had for so many years been encompassed. It was not his to do violence to the loud remonstrances of conscience merely at the bidding of craven fear. This is the avowed reason of the present aggression; and it is not easy to believe that a power which was the conqueror when it stood, calm and fearless, unsupported and alone, engaged for life or death in a close contest against Napoleon I., is likely to be permanently swept away by a poor, trembling, hesitating profligate, driven to strike by the fear of man, and yet able only to strike unsteadily with a hand trembling for fear of God; and who, as the *Spectator* says, "having acquired Rome, looks at it much as a child looks at the cold bath for which it has been crying; standing there stripped, on the edge, to inquire ten times over whether the water feels warm." It is hardly by such poor creatures as this that great and permanent changes in the face of the world have ever been made. Those who would gain advantages in a contest with the Church are perhaps most likely to succeed, in proportion as they adopt the principles of the mightiest of all its enemies in these later centuries, and persuade themselves, with Martin Luther, to refer to the direct action of the devil any and every compunctious remonstrance of conscience, against any sin of whatever kind, however monstrous, voluntary, habitual, or dominant.* The price at

---

* See a Lecture by Mr. Baring Gould, published in the "Church Review" of December 3, 1870.

which such men obtain their success reminds one of the stories
of men, who, for worldly gain, have deliberately sold themselves to the devil. Victor Emmanuel (if we may believe
any account which was ever given of him, whether by friend
or foe) is not one of these consistent Lutherans; he is a
sound Lutheran only in practice, but in faith a Catholic; and
this explains the perpetual uncertainty and vacillation of his
conduct. "The double-minded man is unstable in all his
ways"; and it is not by unstable men that states are erected
which defy the power of political antagonists and ripen
instead of decaying by time.

The time, God be praised, has not yet come for a complete
history of the Pontificate of Pius IX. Long may it be delayed.
Yet, we are indebted to Mr. Maguire for giving us in a convenient
shape the materials for a history of, at least, the three most
important crises of an eventful reign. The zeal of a faithful
son, with which he has always written, has not been allowed
to divert him from collecting all the materials in his reach for
a dispassionate judgment. And if any one should fear that a
fair account of these events could hardly be given, except by
one whose feelings were those of complete impartiality to one
and the other party of whom he wrote, it can only be replied
that, in that case, it would be simply impossible that the
Pontificate of Pius IX., or indeed that any momentous period
in the Church's history, should ever be satisfactorily recorded;
for, by those who do not love and reverence the Vicar of
Christ, for the very same reasons whether they know it or
not, he is hated with a virulence which blinds their eyes more
effectually than the most earnest zeal.

Mr. Maguire's volume, founded upon his former work,
"Rome and its Ruler," but containing much very important
additional matter, is one which we can heartily recommend to
every Catholic, and to all, even though not Catholics, who
desire to see the events which have been going on at Rome
for the last quarter of a century, as they were, not distorted by
prejudice and coloured by an atmosphere of outrageous falsehood. It begins with the personal history of Pius IX.; and
even this has been misrepresented; for although it would have
been no disgrace to him if he had been a soldier before he devoted himself to the priesthood, the facts were not so. He is
remarkable as the first of all the successors of S. Peter who has
set his foot on the shores of the New World, having been sent
there on a mission by Leo XII. After having been successively
Archbishop of Spoleto and Bishop of Imola, he was elected
Pope, June 17, 1846, after a conclave which had lasted only for
forty-eight hours, and to which he had been summoned after

the death of Gregory XVI., by a messenger who found him engaged in a spiritual retreat with the clergy of his diocese.

It was well that the Pope against whom the revolution was to break with all its fury was no defender of abuses, no lover of obsolete institutions unsuited to modern times, but one who, of his own free choice, made his accession the signal for a multitude of reforms, against none of which indeed anything could reasonably be urged, but which at the time seemed dangerous to those who think (as many always do) that to make any change, however reasonable in itself, is to open the door to revolution. Those who are old enough to remember the years 1846 and '47 can hardly have forgotten the strange sympathy with which the reforming Pope was greeted by English Protestants; with their usual inability to understand Catholics, they took for granted, that a Pope who was so zealous in reforming abuses, and was the most formidable enemy of all jobs, whether in the hospitals, in the prisons, in the barracks, in the police, in the ecclesiastical or civil courts, could not fail to be at heart a good Protestant; for it was simply self-evident to the English mind, that of all abuses which he could possibly have to remove or reform, the most obvious and undeniable, as well as the most fatal, was Popery. The new Pope, some time after his accession, issued a Pastoral letter, in which he expressed (as a Catholic much less fervent than Pius IX. would assuredly have done) his devotion to the Blessed Sacrament and to the most Holy Mother of God; and the writer well remembers that when it appeared, religious and well-intentioned Protestants, who had watched all his former proceedings with hearty sympathy, complained, with surprise as well as with regret, " So, after all, this liberal Pope is really a papist." This, we presume, was one of those purely English feelings, which are as mysterious to continental Protestants as to Catholics themselves; and every such peculiarity, when sincere, as in this case it certainly was, is worth putting on record.

These were the short sunny days of the Pontificate of Pius IX. That he should even then be without grave anxiety was, of course, out of the question. But he at least felt that he had the opportunity of conferring much happiness and of doing, as he hoped, lasting good. He was wont to walk freely and safely through the streets, " clad in a plain garb and sparingly attended. Sorrow had not then robbed his cheek of its freshness nor dimmed the mild lustre of his eye." There is something inexpressibly touching in such a memento of what was to follow. " As he passed, an almost adoring populace received with ecstasy the benediction of the Pontiff, and the sweet smiles of their ruler and their father. Children ran to him with eagerness, and artlessly made known to him their wishes, which were ever sure of being complied with." Mr. Maguire gives many touching anecdotes, which we have no room to copy, in illustration of the details of the political and social reforms introduced during this part of his reign. Among them was a general amnesty for all crimes against the State, committed in the revolutionary attempts which had been made in past years. Those condemned to imprisonment were set free. Those who had fled were invited to return. Those condemned to police surveillance, or made incapable of holding offices, were restored to their full rights as subjects. All processes actually in course of proceeding were quashed, except that, with true delicacy, the accused were allowed, if they so pleased, to demand the continuation of their trials, in order to enable themselves to prove their innocence. The only exceptions from this general amnesty were a very small number of ecclesiastics, or persons in different employments under government. These, however, were not excluded from hope, for it was added, " with regard to these, we reserve our decision until we shall have obtained information as to their particular position." The amnesty, of course, did not extend " to ordinary offences." The only condition required of the political offenders who availed themselves of it was to sign a declaration, in which each of them "pledged himself, upon his word of honour, not in any way, nor at any time, to abuse this act of the sovereign clemency of his lawful sovereign, and moreover to fulfil in future all the duties of a loyal subject."

This amnesty was received by the Roman people at large with genuine southern enthusiasm. " Vivas rent the air; blessings and prayers followed the steps of Pius; flowers were thrown beneath his feet." The people proceeded with music and banners through the streets of Rome to the palace of their sovereign, to give vent to an enthusiasm which appeared to know no limits and could hardly find suitable utterance. " Peal after peal of frenzied shouts burst from the crowded mass when the Pope, yielding to the fond importunity of his subjects, came out on the balcony of the Quirinal, and with fatherly gesture imparted to them his apostolical benediction."

Very many of the political prisoners, who soon flocked into Rome, not content with signing the pledge of honour—the only condition imposed by the terms of the amnesty—added of their own free accord such gratuitous vows as these—" I swear by my head, and the heads of my children, that I will be faithful to the death to Pius IX."—" I swear to shed all my blood for Pius IX."—" I renounce my share of Paradise if ever I betray the oath of honour which binds me to Pius IX."

There were Italians, as there certainly would, in a like case, have been Englishmen, who suspected that these gentlemen did " protest too much." An allowance must, of course, be made for national modes of expression, though it was not possible that Pius IX. should forget, what he well knew, the prevalence in Italy of secret societies, banded to obtain the overthrow not only of all government, of property and social institutions, but of all religion. When he deliberately made up his mind to reform all that gave to his subjects real and solid ground for complaint, he knew better than any one else, that there was everywhere in Italy a class resolved, if possible, to make use of his concessions for the purposes of anarchy and revolution.

And although his plan did not succeed, we believe that he judged right. It is well known that he acted upon no sudden feeling of kindliness, such as might naturally take possession of a man so genial, who suddenly found himself made absolute governor of his native country. He had long deliberately believed that extensive reforms ought to be made. He knew that the power to make them had been given to himself by God. In making them he did not aim (as many people in England easily took for granted) at obtaining mere popular applause, but acted for God, as one " ever in his great Task-master's eye." That amidst difficulties such as beset his attempt, it failed of full success, does not in any degree prove even that it was made without the necessary caution and prudence; for who can say that, if he had made no changes, the revolution of 1848 would not equally have carried all before it. As things were, he had at least the satisfaction of feeling, that, if he had not succeeded in averting revolution, he had at least removed all reasonable excuse for it. The difficulties which he must have foreseen arose from the unworthiness of his subjects. Among them, as in many other countries, there was, as we have already said, a party resolved to overthrow all order, government, and even property, and which received the Pope's favours with the deliberate purpose of employing for the subversion of his government whatever power he might allow them.

It is most important that well-intentioned men should know what the so-called party of progress in Italy really is, and what a " Secret Society," of which we hear men talking, really means. We sit over our breakfast-table, and read in the *Times* articles so smooth and plausible that we might easily

· be tempted to imagine that the question between the secret societies and the governments was merely political, that they are perhaps imprudent politicians; who risk the peace and order of society by their too forward zeal for progress. We shall miserably deceive ourselves if we forget that they really are, as most important extracts given by Mr. Maguire from papers written by Mazzini and others of their leaders (to which we would especially direct the attention of our readers), would suffice to prove beyond all possibility of doubt, if any had existed, a party bent upon the destruction not of monarchy only, but of all established order, of property, and finally, most of all; of Christianity; and that the means by which they keep their machine in motion consist of secret assassination and the dread of it.

As an example of the practical working of this mainspring, we need hardly remind our readers that the invasion of Italy by Napoleon III. was believed universally, and we have no doubt truly, to have been caused by the threat of assassination brought to bear upon the Emperor through Orsini.

When, however, we spoke of the real difficulty which Pius IX. had to overcome in his attempts to benefit his subjects, we did not so much mean from the outrageous wickedness of these secret societies as from the unworthiness of the great mass of the population, which detested their principles and acts. Had this majority been ready to purge their country of the secret societies at all risks to themselves, there would really have been nothing to fear. God forbid we should suppose that the number of men so utterly detestable was very large. But we fear it must be admitted that the mobs whose evil deeds drove the Holy Father from Rome in November, 1848, were in very large measure a brute inert mass, of which they were the moving principle. That there were among the Roman people a number actually large who were ready to sacrifice themselves for their country and their Faith, we do not doubt. But we do not see how to avoid the conclusion that they were comparatively few, and their influence upon the mass hardly discernible. The great majority, we fear, must have been content to shrug their shoulders and give to the Holy Father their best wishes, but to stay in-doors when there was any chance of fighting in the streets. Nor does this seem to have been the case only with the lower class. The overwhelming majority of the Roman nobles were thoroughly on His side. Yet what did they do? We can answer for the truth of an anecdote which gives the explanation as to one of the chief of them. He was strongly expressing to an English priest, who had never known what fear meant, his conviction of the absolute loyalty of the great majority of the Roman people. The priest asked, " Why, then, do not you and your fellow-nobles, who feel with you, put yourselves at the head of those whom you know and can trust, and put down the small minority who are bringing shame upon the Roman name as well as insult and wrong upon the Holy Father and the Church ? " " Oh," replied the nobleman, "you don't see what that implies." " What ? " inquired the priest. " Why, if I were to put a gun on my shoulder, and go out into the street, how could I be sure that I might not get shot myself? " A question certainly not to be answered.

The Holy Father is commonly reported to have said that the mass of the Roman people were not wicked but cowardly; whether so severe a sentence really passed from those charitable lips we do not know. We feel no doubt that it might most truly have been pronounced.

Should any one ask whether such a character could have been formed without some degree of fault, not indeed of Pius IX., but of his predecessors, by whom they had so long been governed, it must be remembered, that the States of the Church were never the whole of Italy, and that for nearly 400 years the whole nation had been placed in circumstances unfavourable to the development of manly qualities. Had it been the sole object of the Popes to cultivate those qualities in their subjects, they would have found it difficult. Nor is it to be expected that a paternal government should make its subjects, in this respect, a contrast to all the surrounding peoples of the same race and language. A small state, even though neutralized, if placed in the middle of England, France, or Germany, would have abundant opportunities of developing great military and political talents among its subjects. It was not therefore so much the peculiar character of the ecclesiastical government, as its position in the centre of Italy, which made it almost hopeless that great qualities should be called out among the lay portion of its subjects. Of course a paternal government does not tend to produce them when all surrounding influences work in an opposite direction. And among the Roman people these things had produced their effect. The courage and energy of the ecclesiastics had not been diminished. They had been taught from the beginning that they aspired to be " Priests to Him Who the world's forfeit bore," and that the " good Shepherd giveth His life for the sheep." That this spirit was not extinct was manifested in the example of Cardinal Altieri, who left his place at Rome, second only to that of the Holy Father, the moment he heard that cholera had broken out at Albano, and ministered amongst his flock, with the vigour of youth as well as the charity of an aged priest, and then cheerfully met among them the death he had expected and braved. Had anything of the same spirit prevailed among those of the Roman laity, whose hearts were faithful to the Holy Father, there would have been nothing to fear from revolution. As it was, they would have done more for him than for any other cause on earth, only, unfortunately, they would do nothing worth doing, either for him or even for themselves. Indeed, they looked to him to do everything for them. A friend of the writer, a man absolutely trustworthy, had been taking a vigorous swim out to sea at Porto d'Antio. When he had returned to shore, an Italian gentleman congratulated him upon his swimming, and then went on to blame, of all things in the world, the Roman Government, that neither he himself nor any of his friends could swim a stroke. He evidently supposed, not perhaps that Queen Victoria herself personally gave lessons in swimming, but at least that she and her ministers took care that all her subjects should one way or another learn it. Another Roman gentleman, a young lawyer, declared, with indignation to an Englishman with whom he had made an accidental acquaintance, as a charge against the government, that he had been in practice for several years, and had a wife and three children, and yet that his professional income would not suffice for his support if he had not, fortunately, been possessed of some private fortune.

Such was the people whom Pius IX., well knowing the difficulty of the task, set himself to raise. It is difficult to see what he could have done, more than he did, in reforming every department of the practical administration, and especially throwing open to laymen the great mass of offices and employments under government. This difficulty he must very clearly have foreseen, knowing as he did both the schemes and arts of the revolutionists, and the character of the people with whom he had to do. But the chief cause of the explosion by which his reforms and his government were swept away together in 1848, he could not have foreseen, and had no reason to expect. This was the fall of the French Government. All the world knows that a revolution in France has long been a revolution in Europe, and the waves set rolling by the sudden overthrow of the throne of Louis Philippe spread revolution on every side. Those who are old enough to recollect that year will remember, that for many weeks Englishmen used to open their *Times* and look to see what new revolution had broken out, much as they have turned during the last autumn to the war telegrams, and that they thought it almost as flat when none was reported, as

they now do when everything has remained the same "extra
Iliacos muros et intra." Revolutions broke out in almost every
state of Germany and Italy. Rome of course was under circumstances of peculiar difficulty, because its sovereign, whether introducing changes unasked, as in the earlier months of his reign,
or conceding political liberty to the demands of his subjects,
was always bound to keep in view not merely their political
and material interests, but also those of the Catholic Church,
of which he was the ruler. His difficulties were increased
by the attempts made by the Austrian Government, the year
before the French Revolution, to put down by force the free
institutions which Pius IX. had voluntarily introduced. The
demand that he should make war against Austria—a demand
which he met as Pius VII. had met the demands of Napoleon I.,
that he should join in his war against England—occasioned
the first expression of discontent on the part of his subjects
against him. In 1848 he called to the post of his prime
minister the Count Rossi, a layman who was not only faithful
to himself, but perhaps more likely than any other man to
combine the preservation of peace with the establishment
of as much freedom as the Roman people could use. Nothing
could be so fatal as this to the hopes of the Mazzinian
faction and of the secret societies. Accordingly, on the 15th of
November, 1848, Rossi was assassinated at noonday, at the
door of the Quirinal.

This event, and those which immediately followed, were
described in a letter addressed to his Government by the
Duke d'Harcourt, the ambassador of France, dated the next
day, and laid before the French Chamber of Representatives,
of which our author gives us a translation.

He was justly horrified that neither the populace nor the
police took the least notice of the murder; and that the
Chamber of Deputies, who were sitting when it was committed
on the steps of their hall of meeting, went on with their routine
business as if nothing had happened, while the murderers were
allowed to parade the streets with music in a triumphal procession. He expressly says: "It is generally thought that
there were only a few hundred plotters who had laid the plan
of this conspiracy."

Mr. Maguire adds further particulars from "a gentleman,
then correspondent of the *Daily News*, whose communications
to that journal excited the greatest attention at the time." The
mob, part of whom were soldiers, "went first to the Chamber
of Deputies, and insisted on several members accompanying
them, as their organ and mouthpiece, to the palace of the
Pope. To his eternal honour, the insulted Sovereign declared,

in spite of the hoarse and savage shouts which reached his ears, that 'he would not grant anything to intimidation.' This was his reply to the second demand made by the dishonoured Deputies, in the name of a frenzied mob." At last he gave way, after the cannon had been pointed, and the leaders had declared that, if their demands were not granted, "they would break into the Quirinal and put to death every inmate thereof, with the sole and single exception of the Pope himself."

This was on November 16th, 1848. On the 24th the Holy Father made his escape, by the assistance of the French ambassador. It was apparently to represent him in a degrading light that it was stated in the London papers that he sat on the box of the carriage disguised as a footman. As a matter of fact he was dressed as a simple priest. Count Spaur, the Bavarian minister, was on the box, the Holy Father, the countess, her son, and a Bavarian priest inside.

Thus sadly closed what we may call the first act of his Pontificate. Immediately the cry arose, "Pius IX. has seen the last of Rome ; the republic is erected on the ruins of the throne of the Popes, which the shout of all Europe and the maledictions of the people and the spirit of the Gospel have trampled in the dust." Mr. Maguire shows that the *Times* wrote words which, for its own sake, not for that of the Holy Father, it is just to preserve. "At a crisis when every other constituted authority has been more or less shaken, and every other institution tried, the Romish hierarchy has, in all countries where it exists, extended its influence and more displayed its power." And it attributed this remarkable fact to the personal character of Pius IX. Meanwhile a triumvirate, of whom Mazzini was the first, tyrannized over Rome. One remarkable characteristic of their rule, mentioned by Mr. Maguire, is in exact agreement with what we have heard on independent authority, as being carried out both at Rome and all other places which have come into the hands of Victor Emmanuel. The attempt has been deliberately made to undermine the morals of the people, those who have the power knowing (Q. by their own experience) that nothing is so efficacious in weaning Catholics from the Pope and the Church as vicious morals.

The Quirinal had been converted into an hospital by the republicans ; and there, as at San Spirito and other hospitals, abandoned women were sent by the infidels on purpose to excite evil desires in the minds of the sick. The Pope, in his Allocution of December 8, 1849, addressed from Portici to the archbishops and bishops of Italy, thus refers to these infamies :—"Even the miserable sick, struggling with death, deprived of all aids of religion, were compelled to yield up their souls in the midst of the wanton solicitations of lewd harlots."

It is no part of our object to tell in detail the outrages which marked the short reign of the Triumvirate. Those who wish may see some account of the systematic plunder, and the permitted if not authorized murders, especially of ecclesiastics, which went on " at Rome, Ancona, Sinigaglia, Bologna, and throughout the Papal States"; or how the glorious shrine of S. Peter's was desecrated, a suspended priest being set to usurp the place of the Vicar of Christ by offering the sacrifice on Christmas Day. It is curious that "Lord Palmerston, then Foreign Minister, assured those who successively waited upon him on behalf of the Roman republic, that it was advisable to come to terms with the Pope, for that it was certain he would be restored in spite of all opposition." When the republic had gained a temporary success, he repeated the advice even more strongly, assuring them "that, no matter what might be the form of government in France, even should it be a red republic, still France would restore the Pope to his dominions under some title, name, or colour."

All the world knows that this prediction was fulfilled; most people, however, imagine that it was to Napoleon III. that its fulfilment was due. It was done, as Mr. Maguire shows, not only before he attained supreme power, but against his opinion as a member of the assembly by which it was voted. The French entered Rome July 2nd, 1849, and the Pope returned April 12th, 1850. Mr. Maguire, with a good deal of skill, brings in immediately after this restoration of his reign an account of the daily life of the Holy Father, and of the religious and charitable institutions of Rome, especially those in which Pius IX. has shown the greatest interest. This occupies nearly two hundred and fifty pages of the present edition, over which we must pass lightly. It would, we think, be hardly possible that any one, even of those who, as a general rule, least like parental government (and, in a country like England, for instance, we should heartily agree with them), to doubt that Rome, for the last twenty years, has afforded the best possible specimen of that government.* We cannot doubt either that, taking the Romans as they are, parental

---

* Upon this subject Mr. Maguire publishes in an appendix an invaluable document, the report made on the subject of the Roman government to the French Minister for Foreign Affairs by the Count de Rayneval, the French envoy at Rome, in May 1856. We have already referred to it, and would wish to direct to it the attention of all our readers.

government gives them far more of happiness, and even of substantial liberty, than they could enjoy under any other system, or that parental government could, under no circumstances, be more successfully carried out than under the Papal government, with Pius IX. upon the throne of S. Peter. One would have thought that the most daring political economist would be glad that there should be one city on earth in which institutions such as foundling hospitals, refuges, &c., which he dislikes in theory, might be tried by actual experiment. The institutions of Rome are designed, for instance, to take away all temptation to the dreadful crime of infanticide. It hardly becomes the members of a nation in which it is so miserably prevalent to condemn them, at least without examining their working. It is also curious, if nothing more, that we have here in full operation a government in which the Sovereign, living in the most majestic palace in the world, and uncontrolled by a House of Commons, calculates his own personal expenses at half a crown a day. On this subject Mr. Maguire says :—

There is one item of expenditure to which I cannot avoid making special allusion. It consists of a sum of 600,000 scudi, or about £120,000. With this sum, not an extraordinary income for an English nobleman, the following expenses are defrayed :—The support of the Holy Father, the College of Cardinals, the ecclesiastical congregations, the offices of the Secretaries of State, the diplomatic body, religious ceremonies, maintenance of the Government palaces, the museums and libraries connected with them, and the pensions of the Papal court, besides making provision for casual expenses.

A general idea prevails that the priests absorbed all the offices of the State, and had the entire administration of the country in their hands. But what is the fact? The proportion of ecclesiastics to laymen, taking into account every department of public administration, was not greater than one ecclesiastic to *eighty* laymen. M. de Rayneval, in his despatch, makes the following statement on this subject :—

" But here a curious fact presents itself to our consideration. The provinces administered by laymen, amongst others those of Ferrara and Camerino, are sending deputation upon deputation to the Government for permission to have a PRELATE appointed. The people are not accustomed to lay delegates. They refuse obedience and respect to these latter. They accuse them of confining their interest to their own families ; and there is nothing, even to their wives, which does not give rise to questions of precedence and etiquette. In a word, the Government, which, to satisfy this pretended desire of the population to be presided over by laymen, preserved a certain number of places for them, finds this disposition opposed by the population themselves."

Mr. Maguire adds that the desire was so strong that Ferrara, Camerino, and Orvieto had obtained their petition, and that in 1859 Fermo was pressing for the same favour. Dr. Tait's visit, which we earnestly hope may be useful to his own health, may suggest to the Italians that there are countries in which great offices might be intrusted even to ecclesiastics without avoiding the danger of which they complain under lay governors.

Another subject well worthy of consideration is, the religious effect which has already been produced by the ease with which in modern times Rome is accessible, and by the multitudes of all religions who are attracted thither year by year. As to the ease with which access to the Pope by letter is allowed, we may mention an instance which has lately come to our knowledge. A youth in England who believed that he had a vocation, but who had no means of obtaining a priest's education, resolved in his perplexity to write personally to the Holy Father, explaining his difficulties and asking his aid, or at least his advice. The letter was received and read. The Pope of course could not possibly be sure that the vocation was real; but he wrote to England and caused inquiry to be made into the circumstances of the case. The result was, that the writer of the letter is now a priest. But the real effect of the personal influence of the Vicar of Christ is seen in those who are able to visit Rome. We can hardly imagine that any one with the faith of a Catholic in his heart, can listen to one whom he knows to be the successor of Peter and the Vicar of Christ, or receive his blessing, without feeling himself in some degree a different man for the rest of his life. We need not add that the effect is increased beyond our estimate by the power of attaching men personally to himself which is one of the gifts of Pius IX.

Passing over, with these few words, as nearly as possible one half of the book before us, and in some respects the most valuable half, inasmuch as it puts on record a number of facts as to the state of Rome which the friends of the usurping government and of the revolution are sure to conceal, if not absolutely to deny, we pass to the year 1859. The Holy Father had now reigned, since his return from Gaeta, for nine years. The peace of his dominions had been guarded by a French garrison. But war became necessary, if not to France, to the Emperor. A gentleman who visited the captive Prince Louis Napoleon the day after he had been taken prisoner at Strasbourg relates that he tried to make him see, that even if he had succeeded in obtaining possession of the French government, he would find his difficulties only beginning, for the

real difficulty had long been to govern France. The Prince
replied, " I do not believe it would be at all difficult to govern
France. All it needs is to give it a war every three years."
No one can watch the course of the Emperor without seeing
that although he did not measure the period exactly by the
almanac but by his own necessities, he kept the principle
steadily in view from the first day of his power to the last.
Besides, there is nothing which so completely dazzles the imagination of all Frenchmen as the annexation of a province; and
we now know that Savoy and Nice were to be the bait to the
Emperor Napoleon for carrying out the plans of Cavour. Accordingly, war was declared, the battles of Magenta and Sol-
ferino were fought, France was intoxicated with *la gloire,*
peace was suddenly made, Victor Emmanuel got Lombardy,
and, in due time, Napoleon III. got Savoy and Nice.

Our concern is with Cavour and the revolution. How far
the Emperor was the dupe of Cavour, how far his accomplice,
is a subject upon which we need not enter. Cavour well
understood that the effect of the war was pretty sure to be a
general confusion, in which Piedmont would gain something.
Mr. Maguire shows that he had long been dealing underhand
with the revolutionists in the dominions of all his master's
Italian allies, and that the ambassadors commissioned to the
several courts were the tools whom he employed for this
purpose.

The British Government had been informed of this alliance
by Mr. Scarlett, Her Majesty's representative at Florence. It
is now made plain to all men by the publication of Cavour's
correspondence with Admiral Persano, the commander of the
Piedmontese fleet, which has been given to the world in the
present year, as part of the admiral's private diary. Cavour
wrote to La Farina, the President of the National Society,
" You are not a minister, and you can act freely; but learn
that if I am interrogated I shall repudiate you." To the
admiral he wrote :—" The problem we have to solve is this—
help the revolution, but in such a way that it may appear in
the eyes of Europe to have been a spontaneous act." Meanwhile he was always ready to intervene ostensibly for the purpose of putting down the revolutions which he had himself
" helped " really to gain for them any advantage he could.

The attacks made by the government of Victor Emmanuel
and its agents upon the States of the Church took place at
four distinct periods. We would gladly give a detailed account
of each of these, nor do we think it in any degree needless,
because, although the main events of each were notorious
enough at the time, the details, we fear, have long ago faded

from the memory even of those who took the trouble to master them. Our space, however, forbids us to enter upon any of them except the last, which took place in the autumn of 1870. We will therefore only mention the main characters by which each of these distinct outrages was marked, and the result which attended it.

In 1859, the first of these periods, Cavour took advantage of Napoleon's war in Italy, and of the vacillation of the emperor (if indeed it was nothing worse than vacillation, as we hope and are inclined to believe) to gain possession of all the northern portion of the States of the Church, which, before the war, had been occupied by the Austrians, for the purpose of putting down the revolutionists. This portion included Ferrara, Rimini, Bologna, &c. For the strangely tangled web of falsehood and fraud by which this acquisition was made we must refer to Mr. Maguire.

The second period was 1860. On this occasion Cavour pretended to interfere in consequence of revolutionary movements which endangered the peace of Italy. This, we need hardly say, was seen even at the time to be a false pretence. His papers, now published, prove that he wrote beforehand:—

"In order to prevent the revolution extending into our own kingdom, there is but one resource, *i.e.*, to make ourselves masters, without delay, of Umbria and the Marches. The Government is decided to attempt this arduous enterprise, whatever may be the consequences. To this end the following programme has been agreed upon:—An insurrectionary movement will be got up in these provinces from between the 8th to the 12th of September. Whether it be suppressed or not, we will interfere. General Cialdini will enter the Marches, and make immediately for Ancona. But he cannot hope to get possession of that city unless he be energetically seconded by our squadron. You will let me know immediately what you deem necessary for the successful issue of this undertaking. I would indeed be proud if I, as Minister of the Marine, could declare you the conqueror of Ancona."

The Pope's forces, commanded by General de la Moricière, a man as distinguished for Catholic piety as for daring and military skill, could easily have put down these movements, but the forces of Piedmont poured in with overwhelming numbers, crushed his army at Castelfidardo, and afterwards bombarded Ancona. The day before this a brave band of Irish, under Major O'Reilly, had been overpowered by numbers in the same manner at Spoleto. On this occasion Victor Emmanuel seized all the rest of the Marches and Umbria, leaving to the Holy Father only Rome and the patrimony of

S. Peter. This was an open act of unprovoked violence, while the acquisitions of the preceding year had been managed by fraud, without open invasion. The Emperor Napoleon had distinctly declared, that if the States of the Church were invaded by Piedmont, he would resist the invasion by force, but he did not fulfil his word. The Emperor of Austria was on the point of interfering, but was held back by the fear of once more bringing the French into Italy. In this same year Victor Emmanuel also obtained Naples, as it was pretended at the time, by means of a private invasion of Garibaldi, undertaken against the will of his Government. The papers now made public, and which are quoted by Mr. Maguire, prove, what every one supposed at the time, that the whole plot was arranged by Cavour.

In 1862 (Cavour having died the year before) Garibaldi tried to make an attack on Rome without securing the connivance and approval of the Government, and was easily put down, his band being dispersed, and himself wounded at Aspromonte.

In 1864 the convention was made, at the desire and proposal of the Florentine Government, by which it bound itself not to invade the states remaining in the hands of the Pope, not to oppose or complain of his maintaining foreign Catholic soldiers for his defence ; and, moreover, to put down, by force if necessary, all attempts of the revolutionists to enter his dominions. France, on her part, agreed to withdraw her garrison from Rome, and this was finally executed in 1866.

In September, 1869, the ministers of Victor Emmanuel, in perfidious violation of this convention, and this time, as it soon appeared, without the secret permission of Napoleon, again made use of Garibaldi, as before nominally against their consent, to enter the Papal States at the head of revolutionary forces, which the officers and men of the royal army were freely allowed to join. This time there was no open invasion of the Pope's dominions by the army of Piedmont. But the collusion of the Government was so evident, that after the overpowering numbers of the Garibaldian bands had been most gallantly resisted for a whole month by the brave little army of the Holy Father (in which the Zouaves, under the gallant Charette, were specially distinguished), France declared the convention violated, and sent a small body of men, which shared with them the final victory of Mentana.

That this attempt was made in opposition to the wishes of the Roman people was admitted by the revolutionary papers.

The *Reforma* thus describes the Roman population, and their profound indifference to their liberators :—"It must be spoken out, in order that there may be no illusion on the subject in future. All these populations are so brutish, that they care nothing about Italy, or unification, or liberty ; nothing about the cause which the volunteers are supporting, and the Florence Government is abandoning. For what, for whom is it, that we are getting ourselves shot down ? When we entered Mentana not one cry of rejoicing or encouragement greeted us. , During the struggle no hand was held out to help us ; and, after it was over, no one of the inhabitants administered a word of consolation over our discomfiture."

This extract so thoroughly admits the truth—the actual state of feeling among the Roman populations with regard to their regenerators—that it renders the accumulation of proof unnecessary. Hundreds of passages from speeches and newspaper articles spoken and written in the same spirit of indignant disgust and disappointment, might be quoted. (p. 443.)

It may be worth notice that Mr. Disraeli represents the Pope taking refuge from this invasion in the Castle of S. Angelo. It is the advantage of the mode of writing he adopts, that if any statement is contradicted, he can always say it was not meant to be historical, being in a novel, and yet that ninety-nine out of a hundred readers will believe that a man in the position of an ex-premier to Queen Victoria would not make a statement against a well-known living man, if it were not true. What would he say if Mr. Gladstone had described him in a novel as taking a bribe from the enemies of his country ? He may doubtless plead, with justice, that. Mr. Gladstone's statements would carry more weight than any he could make. Be this as it may, the statement is an invention. An eyewitness gives the most striking testimony to the supernatural calmness of Pius IX. at periods of the greatest danger. He himself explained its source :—

"If the cabinets of Europe have their politics, I have mine," said the Pope to a distinguished personage, who spoke to him of the difficulties of his position.

"Could you, Holy Father, inform me of yours ? " inquired the statesman.

"Willingly, my son," replied the Pope, and then raising his eyes to Heaven, repeated in a voice of the most solemn emotion, the words, "Our Father, who art in Heaven, hallowed be Thy name ; Thy kingdom come, Thy will be done on earth as it is in Heaven." Then he added—"You now know my policy, my son ; be sure it will triumph."

Only two persons were executed after this dangerous outbreak. It was for blowing up the barracks of the Zouaves. Our readers will not be surprised, that those who thought it quite right that a Fenian should be executed for trying to blow up Clerkenwell Prison, were loud in their reproaches of the Pope for allowing the execution of these wretched men, who, in the very same way, had murdered some thirty of his faithful defenders.

Now passing three years, to the autumn of 1870, we reach the fourth attack of Victor Emmanuel's Government upon the States of the Church. The success of the two first had enabled him to seize at least three-fourths of the Papal States, the third had been baffled at Mentana; the fourth was made under circumstances widely different.

The gallant French army had fallen into a state of undisciplined disorder. The vacancies in its ranks had been supplied by men who existed only on paper. Such were to unhappy France some among the benefits of personal rule. The necessity of maintaining the popularity of the dynasty had induced the Emperor to declare an unjust war, in which that army, so long overladen with all martial glory, was in an hour crushed.

On the 2nd of August, 1870, the day on which Napoleon's son (to secure whose future prospects this war was no doubt made) received his well-known " baptism of fire," the French Foreign Minister announced to the Government of Florence that Napoleon would withdraw his troops from Civita Vecchia, relying on "the declarations made by the Cabinet of Florence, and the high tone taken recently in the Italian Parliament," which had " given a guarantee that it admitted the engagements which bind Italy with regard to us." Thus he said—

"The two governments were replaced on the basis of the Convention of September, in virtue of which Italy engages not to attack, and in case of need to defend against all aggression, the Pontifical territory. Restoring to their original vigour the several clauses of this act, the two cabinets have given it a new ratification, which reinstates its authority, and henceforth, as we recognize anew the obligations which it imposes on France, so we rest fully assured of the vigilance and firmness with which Italy will carry out all arrangements falling within the scope of her own duties." (p. 468.)

To this the Prime Minister of Victor Emmanuel replied, "The King's Government, in all that concerns itself, will comply exactly with all the obligations resulting to it from the stipulations of 1864."

Accordingly, on the 6th of August (the same day on which France received the first terrible blow at Wörth) the French garrison quitted the Roman states. As Mr. Maguire adds, " What secret understanding there may have been, time will disclose;" but it is obvious that in undertaking so terrible a war, although its greatness was not as yet in any degree anticipated, it was of importance to France to have Italy as an ally, or at least in a "benevolent neutrality." This, however, does not alter the fact, that the Government of Florence voluntarily renewed its engagements as late as August, 1870. Even after the French garrison had been withdrawn, the Italian Ministers continued to make the same professions. On the 19th of August the chief Minister declared that, "even if there were no convention, the Roman States ought to be respected in virtue of the common law of nations." On the 24th he indignantly repudiated the idea of aggression, adding,

"Such a course must have at least two very serious inconveniences. It is in contradiction with our declared policy, and it places us in antagonism with the public opinion of the whole of Europe. There is no one, I am sure, in this house, who is prepared to urge such a course on the Government." (p. 469.)

Time may probably show exactly what the worthy successors of Cavour were privately writing and preparing at the moment when they made these public professions. Only four days later, August 30th, "a note was published, in which the Government laboured to make out a justification of the course on which they had determined, and again proposed conditions which they knew the Holy Father never could accept."

Nine days more (only fifteen days since the idea of any attack on Rome had been so indignantly repudiated) the now celebrated letter to the Holy Father was signed by Victor Emmanuel, and dispatched by the Count di San Martino. It was that which has been known as the "Kiss of Judas," and which began—"Most Holy Father, with the affection of a son, with the faith of a Catholic, with the sentiments of an Italian, I address myself again, as I have formerly done, to the heart of your Holiness." Then speaking of the danger of revolution, which threatened "both the monarchy and the papacy," he went on—

"I know, most Holy Father, that the greatness of your soul would not fall below the greatness of events; but for me, a Catholic king, and an Italian king, and as such guardian and surety, by the dispensation of Divine Providence and by the will of the nation, of the destinies of all Italians, I feel the duty of taking, in the face of Europe and of all Catholicity, the responsibility of maintaining order in the Peninsula and the security of the Holy See. Now, Most Holy Father, the state of mind of the populations governed by your Holiness, and the presence among them of foreign troops, coming from different places with different intentions, are a source of agitation and perils evident to all. Chance and the effervescence of passions may lead to violence and to an effusion of blood, which it is my duty and yours, most Holy Father, to avoid and prevent. I see the indefeasible necessity, for the security of Italy and the Holy See, that my troops, already guarding the frontiers, should advance and occupy the positions which shall be indispensable to the security of your Holiness and to the maintenance of order. Your Holiness will not see a hostile act in this measure of precaution. My Government and my forces will restrict themselves absolutely to an action conservative and tutelary of the rights, easily reconcilable, of the Roman population, with the independence of the Sovereign Pontiff, and of his spiritual authority and with the independence of the Holy See. If your Holiness, as I do not doubt, and as your sacred character and as the goodness of your soul give me a right to hope, is inspired with a wish equal to mine of avoiding all contact and escaping the danger of violence, you will be able to take with the Count Ponza di San Martino, who presents you with this letter, and who is furnished with the necessary instructions by my Government, those measures which shall best conduce to the desired end. Will your Holiness permit me to hope still that the present moment, as solemn for Italy as for the Church and for the Papacy, will give occasion to the exercise of that spirit of benevolence which has never been extinguished in your heart towards this land, which is also your own country, and of those sentiments of reconciliation which I have always studied with an indefatigable perseverance to translate into acts, in order that while satis-fying the national aspirations, the chief of Catholicity, surrounded by the devotion of the Italian populations, might preserve on the banks of the Tiber a glorious seat independent of all human sovereignty. Your Holiness, in delivering Rome from the foreign troops, in freeing it from the continued peril of being the battlefield of subversive parties, will have accomplished a marvellous work, given peace to the Church, and shown to Europe, shocked by the horrors of war, how great battles can be won and immortal victories achieved by an act of justice and by a single word of affection. I beg your Holiness to bestow on me your apostolical benedic-tion, and I send to your Holiness the expression of my profound respect. Your Holiness's most humble, most obedient, and most devoted son, VICTOR EMMANUEL."*

It will be observed that this letter only professes that Victor Emmanuel proposed that his troops should enter the States of the Church for the purpose of preventing revolution and pre-serving order. As far as words went, it implied no more than an intention of doing what France had done until 1864 with the same object, and it especially disclaimed any hostile intention. Even persons accustomed to the public papers of Cavour and

---

* There are several expressions of which we suspect that the transla-tion does not give the full force.

his school must have been taken by surprise, when Victor Emmanuel was made to appeal, in proof of his amicable intentions, to his past acts. How, he pleads, could the Holy Father, knowing as he did the king's past acts, suspect that in " occupying the positions indispensable to the security of his Holiness and the maintenance of order," he could have any hostile object. " I have always studied to put into acts my sentiments of conciliation." " I address myself now, as formerly, to the heart of your Holiness," as if he would say, " if any one doubts why my troops are entering the States of the Pope, let him remember why they did so in 1859, in 1860, and 1867."

Mr. Maguire learned the substance of what passed in the interview accorded to the Count di San Martino from one to whom the Holy Father described it a few days later. He says the Pope went through every particular of the letter, exposing its falsehood in detail, giving to each proposition an emphatic " Never, never, never." " He would make no terms with revolution and robbery, he would resist their demand to the last."

It has been asserted, and in all probability with truth, that the Holy Father employed these awful words of condemnation : " In the name of Jesus Christ I tell you that you are all whited sepulchres." . . .

Cardinal Antonelli, in the official protest issued on the 20th of September, on which day Rome was forcibly entered, thus refers to the result of Count di San Martino's mission :—

" Your Excellency may readily imagine the profound grief and lively indignation which the Holy Father felt in consequence of this strange declaration. Nevertheless, immovable in the accomplishment of his sacred duties, and fully confiding himself to Divine Providence, he resolutely repelled every proposal, considering that he ought to preserve intact his sovereignty as it had been transmitted to him by his predecessors."

On the 11th the Holy Father replied personally:—" To the King Victor Emmanuel. Your Majesty. The Count Ponza di San Martino has put into my hands a letter which your Majesty has been pleased to address to me; but it is not a letter worthy of an affectionate son who glories in the profession of the Catholic religion, and who prides himself on the due observance of kingly faith. I do not enter into the details of the letter itself, because I would not renew the grief which its first perusal caused me. I adore my God, who has permitted your Majesty to add to the bitterness of the latter days of my life.

"In conclusion, I cannot admit the demands advanced in your letter, nor can I give any adhesion to the principles contained in it. I once more pray to the Lord, and I place my cause in His hands, because it is wholly His own. I pray Him that He would grant abundant graces to your Majesty, that He would deliver you from all dangers, and bestow upon you those favours of which you have need.—From the Vatican, September 11th, 1870."

On the same day this announcement appeared in the *Official Gazette* of Florence :—" The King, upon the proposition of the Council of Ministers, has this day issued his commands to the army to enter the Roman provinces." (p. 474.)

It is somewhat perplexing to try to account for the extreme suddenness of the change in the conduct of Victor Emmanuel's government. Their evident policy would have seemed to be to wait until they had once more stirred up revolutionary movements in the states of the Holy Father, and to have made then an excuse for marching in to restrain them. We can hardly help thinking that this must have been their intention. It was probably abandoned in consequence of the extreme suddenness and rapidity of the successes of the Germans after August 2nd, until they culminated in the surrender of all that remained in the field of the French army on September 2nd. If there was, as can hardly be doubted, any secret understanding with Napoleon, which was to have been carried out in a few months, by keeping the Pope's states in a perpetual state of confusion and bloodshed (as in 1869) until they could plead that intervention had become a matter of urgent necessity, it is easy to see that such a plan would have been effectually frustrated if peace had been made, as all the world then expected, at the latest as soon as the German armies could reach Paris. Who could say that in such a case France itself (by whomsoever it might be administered) might not refuse to recognize any secret understanding with the Emperor, and have demanded the exact fulfilment of the convention by which the ministers of Victor Emmanuel, as late as August 24th, had publicly admitted themselves to be bound? Disastrous as the first month of the war had been, the strength of France was not yet exhausted, and peace would at once have restored her armies to their liberty. Her fleet was intact. Nothing was more certain than that she could, without difficulty, compel Victor Emmanuel to observe his engagements, few things more likely than that she would. Besides, who could say that the conqueror in that short struggle, who was already believed to aspire to the imperial throne, would allow Victor Emmanuel, under the pretence of fearing the revolution, which he was using as his tool, to take possession of Rome? It is easy to understand that such considerations may have frightened the Government of Florence into taking sudden measures early in September, which possibly they did not contemplate even in the latter part of August. They might reckon it their best chance that when peace came it should find the seizure of Rome a *fait accompli*.

Be this as it may, without waiting for any appearance of revolutionary movement in the States of the Church, " 60,000 men of all arms, thoroughly equipped and provided with every necessary engine of warfare," marched into them (the Roman Zouaves, under the gallant Colonel Charette, falling back before them), and reached the walls of Rome on September 19th. The correspondent of the *Times*, who will not be suspected of taking the side of the Pope, writes : " It is certain that the native troops had been very much worked upon during the last three or four weeks by Italian emissaries. Fine promises were made to them and tempting baits offered. It is even rumoured that the officers are certain of retaining their military rank. It would be easy for me to name some of those who succeeded in entering the town, and carrying on their intrigues, in spite of the vigilance of the police." But nothing came of these intrigues : as to the populace, " it is admitted, in journals far from friendly to the Papal interest, that, on the whole, the Italians did not find the welcome which they expected; that, on the contrary, they were " much discouraged" by the silence and coldness of those on whom they had to confer the blessings of a stern rule and crushing taxation " (p. 476).

The Holy Father had given orders to General Kanzler, who commanded his army, that resistance should be made only just long enough

" to testify the violence done to us, and nothing more; in other words, that negotiations shall be opened so soon as a breach shall have been made.

" At a moment when the whole of Europe is mourning over the numerous victims of the war now in progress between two great nations, never let it be said that the Vicar of Christ, however unjustly assailed, had to give his consent to a great shedding of blood. Our cause is the cause of God, and we put our whole defence in His hands. From my heart, General, I bless you and your whole army.—From the Vatican, September 19th." (p. 480.)

Accordingly, at five in the morning of the 20th of September, 1870, fire was opened by the army of Victor Emmanuel on the walls of Rome; " in a few moments a terrific fire blazed from the whole Italian line."

At seven o'clock that morning the Pope said his usual Mass in his private chapel of the Vatican, and after the Sacrifice of the Altar, the Litany of the Blessed Virgin was sung, the voice of the Holy Father being as clear, as sweet, and full as ever. The roar of cannons and the crash of bursting shells formed a strange accompaniment to these words of praise

and supplication. By ten or half-past ten, after several buildings had been
set on fire, batteries had been dismounted, barricades shattered, and wide
breaches effected in walls of ancient date and little strength, the signal of
surrender was made, and resistance was at an end. The firing ceased along
the whole Italian line soon after the signal of surrender was made,
but while the negotiations for the capitulation were being made, the
enemy marched, or rather rushed in, and took possession of the city.
Strangely enough, the Italian troops entered with shouts of "Savoy,
Savoy!" forgetting that the king, whose uniform they wore, had ten
years before bartered away for a consideration the cradle of his race and
the home of his ancestors. (p. 492.)

There was no fight, no hand-to-hand encounter at gate or breach.
The white flag prevented any conflict of that nature * * *

With the troops of the victors entered some thousand of the worst
spirits of Italy, who, fraternizing with the lowest rascaldom of Rome,
added to their numbers by flinging open the cells of prisons and giving
liberty to hundreds of malefactors, who, some days after, had to be
relegated to their unwelcome solitude. Violence and murder, outrage and
brutality, were in the ascendant in the emancipated city. The streets,
hitherto so quiet and orderly, were filled with raging, yelling mobs,
whose excesses were either encouraged or could not be controlled. In the
prostituted name of liberty, wounded men were set upon, hunted down and
slain. Even the revolutionary journals admit this to have been the case.
The *Soluzione* of Naples, writing of the Zouaves, says, "These praises of the
Italie enable people to judge of the barbarity, the infamy, and the vileness
of those who tracked them after the entry of our troops, and hunted them
with as much savagery as if they had been wolves." (p. 481.)

The same paper itself said of the Zouaves :—

"Modest and brave, they did their duty as heroes know how to do it,
and the defence of Rome, as far as they were concerned, was short, it is
true, but most courageous and brilliant. They would have allowed themselves to be cut to pieces, if the Holy Father had not ordered them to surrender." A writer in the other journal says, "One thing must be admitted
and never can be denied—the Zouaves fought like brave and noble soldiers.
They gave full proof of that at the Porta Pia and the Villa Buonaparte,
where I saw them with my own eyes."

Next day, September 21st, the Holy Father—

Took his farewell of his faithful soldiers, who were massed in the square
of S. Peter's. From a window in the Vatican the aged Pontiff presented
himself to that devoted army ; and as that beloved countenance was beheld,
a great cry, expressive at once of love and reverence, rage and sorrow, rose
like thunder from their ranks. . . . Never were their hearts more wholly
his than in that moment of anguish and bitterness of soul. Cries of *Viva il
Papa, Viva il Rê, Viva Pio Nono*, rang again and again through the

vast piazza. The Pope was sublimely affected, and as he raised his arms
to heaven and called down God's choicest blessings upon those who would
willingly have died for his cause, his attitude, his look, his voice struck
the imagination with awe. (p. 481.)

The soldiers then left the city by the Porta Angelica, and
laid down their arms in the garden of a villa. The manner in
which their surrender was witnessed by the Italian troops was
honourable to both parties. Unhappily the noble prisoners
were treated with dastardly insults by the authorities.
A letter, signed "Charles Woodward, Arthur Vansittart,
Walter Maxwell, Charles Lynch, Wm. Watts Russell, John G.
Kenyon," shows that, in violation of the terms of the capitulation, they were "thrust into prison, fed on bread and water for
twenty hours, kept under lock and key for six days, and
exposed to all the hardships of ordinary prisoners."

The number of troops who thus laid down their arms was 9,500. Of the
entire army of the Pope but one-third was foreign, the rest were Italian.
(p. 483.)

There is no need to say that the French Zouaves (who
exceeded in numbers those of any one other nation) carried to
the defence of their country in her extremest need the swords
which were, for the time, discharged from the service of the
Church, and continuing, by the permission of M. Gambetta,
to wear their old Roman uniform, have on every occasion been
discriminated among the thousands of gallant men composing
the army of the Loire for their especial valour and good conduct.
While we write, all who feel any sympathy with high personal
qualities derived from noble ancestors and worthily devoted
to the noblest cause, are awaiting with deep anxiety definite
intelligence of their commander Charette, who is reported to
have fallen wounded from his horse in the great action of
December 4.

The army of Victor Emmanuel entered Rome, as we have
seen, under pretences which, if they meant anything, meant
that it came to support the temporal as well as spiritual
authority of the Holy Father, objecting merely to his employment of foreign Catholic soldiers, to which, however, the king
had specially engaged not to object in the convention renewed
a month before. Yet, on October 1st, only ten days later, the
Roman people were called to declare by a plebiscite (in the true
Napoleon fashion) whether or not they chose to be annexed
to his kingdom. Rome was still "in possession of an overwhelming armed force, thousands of vengeful revolutionists

from all parts of the Italian Peninsula, and a mob composed
of the worst elements of disorder." The Holy Father had
expressed his wish that loyal subjects should not vote either
way, and any one who was so absurd as to say that those of the
Romans who desired the continuance of his rule would have
shown it by their votes, must explain why it was, that when
Count Rossi was assassinated at the door of the Chamber of
Deputies, the Chamber went on with the routine business of the
day without in any way alluding to the incident. It will hardly
be said that every individual in that body sympathized with it.
As to this plebiscite, reports have been published of multitudes
sent in from a distance to vote. The only improbability is
that it hardly seemed worth the trouble. It has been shown in
the *Tablet* that it is physicially impossible that under the
arrangements made, one half of the votes officially declared
could have been given in the time allowed. The only thing
which surprises us is that the official report should give more
than 1,500 noes. By whom can these have been given? The
Spectator remarks they are too few for the purpose, as the
clergy, who are admitted to have been against annexation, must
have numbered more than that. Is it possible that a few of
Victor Emmanuel's creatures were required to vote " no," lest
the *plebiscite* should be a manifest farce?

The next step was that a deputation waited upon the king,
who accepted the act.

Of all that has since gone on at Rome it is too soon to speak.
We must own ourselves, so far, surprised that the outrages
committed against religion should have been so open and so
numerous as are reported. We incline to think a man as
crafty as Cavour would have been careful to make it appear
that the religious liberty, both of the clergy and people, was
left without interference. But perhaps it was feared that the
revolutionists would resent any appearance of fairness in this
matter. In one respect the policy adopted in Rome in 1848
and in the other Italian cities which have, at different times,
been subject to Victor Emmanuel, has been carefully followed.
Indecent and disgusting books and prints, such as Lord
Campbell's Act would not allow to be exposed in London, are
everywhere to be seen. In this we incline to think the invaders " wise in their generation "; for if the object is to set
Catholics against the Church and the Pope, there is nothing
so likely to be efficacious as the corruption of their morals.
We do not think it equally wise to set a Jew to efface from
the gateway of the Collegio Romano the initials of the sacred
name. The Roman people are not far enough advanced for
that. They ought, for some considerable time, to have been

accustomed to indecent prints before that was ventured upon. They were sure to consider it a judgment that the wretched man fell to the ground and died of the injury.

Meanwhile Victor Emmanuel has only ventured to pay a flying visit to Rome, but his agents have seized the Quirinal, and even the private property of Pius IX. It is most characteristic, and we are assured that it is attested by one who was present, that when his ministers were urging him to take immediate possession, and assured him that they would undertake to guarantee him before all the governments of Europe, the wretched king replied—" Yes; but who will guarantee me before the devil?" It is sad, but most certain, that there are men with enough of religion to make them heartily afraid of the devil, although not to make them love God; who have faith enough to be a real obstacle to their success in the world seen, though not enough to be any security to them in that which is unseen.

Meanwhile it is worth notice that on September 20th, the very day on which Rome was taken by force, the *Times* published an official paper, stating in detail how the Italian Government engaged to act. It is important, as showing the principles which the statesmen of the school of Cavour thought it necessary to profess in order to obtain the support of the English people. We need hardly say they were never intended to be acted upon. Still they are hardly less important on that account.

The Sovereign Pontiff preserves the dignity, inviolability, and all the other prerogatives of sovereignty, and also the privileges towards the king and other sovereigns which are established by custom. The title of prince and corresponding honours are conceded to the Roman cardinals of the Church.

The Leonine city remains under the full jurisdiction and sovereignty of the Pontiff.

The Italian Government guarantees on its territory :—

a. The liberty of communication by the Sovereign Pontiff with foreign states, clergy, and peoples.

b. The diplomatic immunity of the Pontifical nuncios or legates to foreign powers, and of foreign representatives to the Holy See.

The Italian Government engages to preserve all the institutions, offices, and ecclesiastical bodies, and their officials, existing at Rome, but it does not recognise the civil or penal jurisdiction.

The Government engages to preserve entire, and without subjecting them to special taxes, all the ecclesiastical properties whose revenues belong to ecclesiastical charges, offices, corporations, institutes, and bodies having their seat at Rome or in the Leonine city.

The Government has no interference in the interior discipline of ecclesiastical bodies at Rome.

The bishops and priests of the kingdom in their respective dioceses and parishes shall be free from all interference of the Government in the exercise of their spiritual ministry.

His Majesty renounces in favour of the Church all right of royal patronage over the smaller or larger ecclesiastical benefices of the city of Rome.

The Italian Government grants to the Holy See and the Sacred College a fixed and unalterable revenue of a value not inferior to that actually assigned them in the budget of the Pontifical State.

The royal Government preserves their rank, salaries, and precedence to the civil and military servants of the Pontifical State who are Italians.

These articles would be considered a public bi-lateral contract, and would form the subject of an agreement with the powers having Catholic subjects.

Italy is to-day still ready to adopt the same bases of a solution.

Florence, August 29th, 1870.

This was meant of course to express, more in detail, Cavour's professed principle of "a free Church in a free State." How they intended to act upon it they have already shown. The Holy Father has issued an Encyclical to the prelates of the Catholic Church, publishing the sentence of excommunication which the law of the Church enacts against all concerned in the seizure of Rome. To make the sentence more pointed, he pronounces it "against all, be their dignity what it may, even although it should most demand special mention." What this means of course no one can doubt. It is a rule that persons against whom the greater excommunication has been pronounced must be avoided by all Christians; and as Christian subjects might be involved in persecution if they should observe this rule in the case of an absolute monarch, it is further provided that they shall not be bound to observe it unless he is excommunicated by name. Pius IX. therefore, by the form of words in which his sentence is pronounced, expresses as clearly as possible that Victor Emmanuel is excommunicated as before the Church and Her Lord, but that his servants and others are not bound to take cognizance of the sentence.

The Pontiff by whom this sentence is deliberately promulgated is living unguarded in the Vatican, while Rome is held by the soldiers of the man against whom he pronounces it— by lawless banditti, far more ready to avenge him by murder than were the Norman knights of our Henry II.—and by all the lawless spirits of Italy, and, indeed, of all nations. We doubt whether the history of the Church exhibits a nobler instance of Apostolic courage than the deliberate publication of this Encyclical, marked, as it is, with every precaution to prevent persecution from falling upon the head of any except the Holy

Father himself. For not only was the sentence worded in a manner designed expressly to prevent any danger to the servants and courtiers of the king; but to shelter the printer of the Encyclical from danger, it was printed at Geneva. The scene which followed in Italy was described by the Archbishop of Westminster in the late meeting on behalf of the Holy Father. It was expected that the Catholic paper of Florence, the *Unità Cattolica*, would publish the document; and accordingly, to carry out the principles of a free State and a free Church, the emissaries of Victor Emmanuel were on the watch to seize every copy. They effected the seizure, but not completely. A packet got out. The anti-Catholic papers republished the Encyclical, with many expressions of scorn towards the Holy Father for so needlessly having it printed at Geneva; and at the *Unità*, for having denied that the press in Italy is free. The same day they were all seized themselves, and a fierce contest has arisen between them and the Government as to its right to seize them for publishing the Pope's Encyclical.

This is the last incident, as yet made public, in illustration of the freedom of religious action which the Holy Father would enjoy in the kingdom of Victor Emmanuel. And here, for the present, we bring our narrative to a close. We regret that our narrow limits forbid our doing more than touch one or two points of a subject of surpassing interest. We have as yet spoken not of the real reign of Pius IX., of the objects in which his heart has been engaged, but only of those political events by which he has been tried and hindered in carrying out great objects in themselves widely different. We would gladly have spoken of his internal government, of his care for every work of mercy, spiritual or temporal, of which Mr. Maguire has written much and well; of his zealous solicitude for all the Churches in every land in which any one of the first twelve ever preached, and in multitudes of which they never heard; of the increase of the Episcopate during his administration, in which he has erected twenty archiepiscopal sees (five of them never before the seat of a bishop), 112 episcopal sees, besides 22 apostolic delegations, 2 vicariates, and 11 prefectures, of which most of the occupants are of episcopal rank. Among these we need hardly say are numbered the new hierarchies of England and Holland, and the greater part of the episcopal sees in the United States. We would gladly have spoken of the action of the Church under his government in heathen lands, of its "new glories," the martyrs of his reign, and of his sentence of canonization in the case of those who received the crown before his own day. Specially we would gladly have spoken of that august assemblage the General Council of the Vatican, the meeting of which has invested the reign of Pius IX., with a dignity unknown to that of any of his predecessors for three centuries. But each of these subjects alone might fill more than our space.

In conclusion, therefore, we will only say, that of all the assaults of which the Roman See has ever been the object, we doubt whether there has been one which bore upon its face so evidently as this, the note of an ephemeral outrage.

At a moment when the greatest powers of Christendom are unhappily engaged in a death-struggle, and when the rest are occupied with the pretensions of Russia to be free from all bonds of law or treaty, a thief, relying on the general disturbance, has seized the dominions of the Holy Father. When peace may come, God only knows. There are not wanting, we fear, but too many indications that, before it comes, the hideous plague of war may be yet farther extended. Neither can any one forget the danger which exists, lest revolutionists as well as kings may avail themselves of the opportunity to spread confusion even more widely. But peace, thank God, will have its turn. Does any one suppose that when it arrives, the nations of Europe, which, even amid the wildest crash of arms, have been astounded because the Czar claimed, of his own authority, to set aside a treaty made sixteen years ago, which limited his natural power, by forbidding him to fortify his southern harbours and launch a navy on the Black Sea, will allow Victor Emmanuel, equally on his own authority, to set aside a convention renewed only a month before, in order to seize the dominions of an inoffensive neighbour, that neighbour being moreover the Vicar of Christ?

Art. II.—GRIGNON DE MONTFORT AND HIS DEVOTION.

Life and Select Writings of the Venerable Servant of God, Louis-Marie Grignon de Montfort. Translated from the French by a Secular Priest. London : Richardson. 1870.

A Treatise on True Devotion to the Blessed Virgin, by the Venerable Servant of God Louis-Marie Grignon de Montfort. Translated from the French by F. W. Faber, D.D. London : Burns & Lambert. 1863.

A Treatise on True Devotion to the Blessed Virgin Mary, by the Venerable Servant of God Louis-Marie Grignon de Montfort. Approved by his Grace the Archbishop of Dublin. London : Richardson. 1864.

WE are most grateful to this " Secular Priest," for his very important contribution to Catholic literature. The name of Grignon de Montfort is in England associated, not by Protestants only but by several Catholics, with no other idea than that of a strange and almost idolatrous devotion to the Mother of God; and it is very desirable that all our English brethren in the Faith should be made aware of what is notorious among foreign Catholics, his heroic saintliness. As to his writings, the highest authority in the Church has formally and finally proclaimed—and that with a view to his prospective canonization—that they " contain nothing contrary to faith or morals, nor any new doctrine contrary to the Church's common sentiment and practice." Yet, not seculars alone have assailed them, but an excellent religious has gone out of her way, to accuse him of " exaggerated and preposterous expressions " in regard to our Blessed Lady. The biography, to which we refer as written by that religious, is so singularly beautiful, and its subject is so noble and saintly a person, that we feel ourselves more especially bound to protest against a statement, which will come before a large number of readers as invested with such persuasive authority.*

Our main purpose in this article is briefly to consider the

---

* It is not only the Venerable Grignon de Montfort, but a canonized Saint —S. Alphonsus—who is charged in the same passage with " exaggerated and preposterous expressions."

We do not for a moment deny—in a few pages later we expressly affirm— that it is most possible for a saintly writer to *express* inaccurately thoughts which *in themselves* are orthodox ; and we should rejoice to think that no particular devotion, which Montfort has so emphatically advocated, and which has exposed him to charges so serious. As to his personal history, our contemporary the "Month" gives the following interesting analysis of the French biography :—

Louis Marie Grignon de la Bacheleraie, called De Montfort, was born in 1673, in the little Breton town of Montfort-la-Canne. He himself exchanged his family name for that of his birthplace, as a sign that he had broken off the ties of flesh. At twelve years old he was sent to the Jesuit College at Rennes, where he was soon at the head of his class, and an example to the other boys in conduct and attention to the rules. He was also one of the foremost in the Congregation of our Lady, and used to frequent the house of an excellent priest in Rennes, who gathered the best of the collegians about him for familiar conferences, and afterwards sent them to serve the sick in the hospitals, &c. The only amusement Louis allowed himself was drawing, which afterwards helped him in the decoration of the churches he frequented in his missions. A Breton lady gave him the means of entering the Seminary of St. Sulpice, which he did in 1695. Before doing so he lived for a year in a small community of students of M. de la Barmondière. Here the already severe discipline was not austere enough for young De Montfort, and he added, with his director's leave, sharp discipline, chains, girdles, and watches beside the dead for the whole night, when he never tasted the food or wine provided. At the end of two years M. de Barmondière died, and De Montfort went for another year to a second private community, where the food and lodging were even worse than before. The bad living nearly destroyed his life, and being likely to die he was sent to the priests' ward in the Hôtel Dieu. Just as he was apparently about to breathe his last he recovered, and as he was now pretty well known, the directors gladly received him into the Little Seminary of St. Sulpice. In the Seminary, De Montfort was not popular, and it is evident that his superiors, as well as the students, thought his devotions and habits constrained. In the classes at the Sorbonne, he used to go and kneel down alone in a corner to pray, to walk bareheaded in the streets out of devotion to the presence of God, and to wear a rosary hung outside his cassock. He was scarcely ever known to speak of anything but religion. His director discouraged and tried him severely, but at last was obliged to tell the superior that he had humbled him to the very last, and that he had never seen De Montfort either the least sullen or angry. He was ordained priest in 1700, and having been appointed chaplain to the hospital, or rather hospice, at Poitiers, he gave himself up wholly to good works, especially loving and cherishing the sick and little children. In 1703, De Montfort chose out eighteen or twenty poor girls of the hospice and began

more than this is intended in the passage which we criticise : but such certainly is not its obvious sense.

As for F. Newman, to whom the said passage refers, the case is most simple. Until he read the "Eirenicon," he had never even heard of Montfort's name ; and he expressed himself as certain that Dr. Pusey misunderstood that holy writer.

to form them into a congregation. This was the first stone of the " Daughters of Wisdom." In 1706 De Montfort went to Rome, when he was made Missionary Apostolic by Clement XI., who enjoined him by all means to combat the errors of Jansenism. During the course of several years of fervent missionary labours in Brittany, the ·'Daughters of Wisdom" were established at La Rochelle in 1715, but after stirring up many other priests to devote themselves to home missions with him, De Montfort himself died in 1716, at Saint-Laurent-sur-Sèvre, in the middle of a mission he was giving. As the weeping and sobbing people pressed around his bed for his last blessing, the dying priest collected all his strength and sung a verse of one of his own hymns—

> Allons mes chers amis,
> Allons en Paradis ;
> Quoiqu'on gagne en ces lieux,
> Le Paradis vaut mieux.

The " Secular Priest " thus comments in his preface on the general current of Montfort's life :—

Although he has been sometimes compared to such saints as St. Simon Salo and St. Philip Neri, there is very little of what is extraordinary to be met with in his life. When we think of St. Philip's strange procession from San Girolamo to the Chiesa Nuova ; or of his reading light books before his Mass ; or of his playing with the flowers upon the altar to distract him from the thought of God ; or of that last wonderful Mass of his, when he who seldom sang burst forth into almost unearthly song at the angel's hymn of the " Gloria in Excelsis," or of St. Simon Salo praying in his marvellous humility that his body might be possessed by the evil one, and of God taking him at his word ;--how trifling seem the few extraordinary things, if indeed they can be called extraordinary, or even the singularities, which are related of de Montfort. Wearing his rosary suspended from his girdle, while as yet a seminarist at St. Sulpice ; kneeling down in the corner of the class-room to implore God's light upon his studies ; always walking with his hat off, or at times, when he thought he was not seen, lying prostrate on the ground out of respect to the ever-present Majesty of God ; carrying some poor tired-out lay-brother upon his shoulders ; or lifting from the ground some beggar covered with ulcers, and bearing him tenderly in his arms to the door of the mission-house, crying out, " Open for Jesus Christ " ; throwing his rosary round the necks of sinners, and taking them prisoners, as he called it, for the love of Christ ; refusing to preach when he thought that persons had come to hear him out of curiosity ; abstaining from visiting his earthly father or mother, when engaged in the business of his Father who was in heaven ; forcing with a holy violence his companions in a passage-boat to say the rosary ; interfering for the love of God and his neighbour in some soldiers' drunken brawl ; walking to prison with as much joy as if he were taking part in some procession of the Church ;—what are these, after all, but the actions of a man who has realized to the full that the only realities in this world are the love of God and of his neighbour in God, and the thought of God's Presence ; and that every action and every circumstance in the river of life may be made a stepping-stone to heaven ? What are all these but simply that "foolishness and weakness of God which is wiser and stronger than men" ? Alas ! let us confess with the author of this work, that "the saints have passed their life in the light, while we require the torch of death to enlighten us." One or two combats with the evil one ; here and there a prophecy ; a few visions of the unseen world ; such are the chief of the extraordinary things which happened during his lifetime to this zealot of Mary's name. (pp. xvi.-xviii.)

If, however, there were "few extraordinary things" in Montfort's life, one must not for a moment understand that it was other than one ceaseless exhibition of heroic sanctity. "His entire life," says F. Faber,—

was such an exhibition of the holy folly of the Cross, that his biographers unite in always classing him with St. Simon Salo and St. Philip Neri. Clement XI. made him a missionary-apostolic in France, in order that he might spend his life in fighting against Jansenism, so far as it affected the salvation of souls.

He was at once persecuted and venerated everywhere. His amount of work, like that of St. Antony of Padua, is incredible, and indeed inexplicable.

He founded two religious congregations— one of men and one of women— which have been quite extraordinarily successful ; and yet he died at the age of forty-three, in 1716, after only sixteen years of priesthood. (Preface, pp. vi., vii.)

On this head we will add no more than to quote one single passage from the Life ; a passage recounting his visit to Montfort, his birth-place, and which reads like a kind of parable :—

He therefore left Rennes for Montfort his birth-place, where he arrived on the feast of All Saints, but so as not to be discovered ; for he wished to owe everything to charity, and nothing to personal consideration. He even avoided entering the town, and stopped at a little village about a quarter of a league distant. It was his intention to lodge with a poor woman who had been his nurse. He sent Brother Mathurin to beg of her, in charity, to give shelter to a poor priest and his companion ; a proposal which was not to the taste of the good woman. Montfort presented himself at two or three other houses, and asked, for the love of our Lord, for a little straw for himself and his companion. Everywhere he met only with refusals. At last, he asked, who was the poorest person in the village ; the cabin of a poor old man, named Pierre Balin, was pointed out to him, and he presented himself at the door. "Welcome !" joyfully exclaimed the old man, "I have only a little bread and water to give you, and a little straw for your bed. Had I anything better, I would gladly offer it you ; but, at any rate, I will willingly share with you the little which I have." Never was an offer more willingly made', nor more thankfully received. The servant of God was filled with joy, to see himself in an out-of-the-way place, which recalled so well to his mind the stable of Bethlehem. The old man however earnestly regarded him, and at last recognised in his new guest the son of M. Grignon de la Bacheleraie. The next day, the news soon spread through the village ; and then every one hastened to the relief of the holy priest. Amongst other things, a blanket, mattress, sheets, and pillow-case, were brought to him ; but, instead of making use of them, he gave them away to a poor man in the neighbour-hood, observing that such conveniences " were not suitable to a wretched man like himself, but only to the true poor of Jesus Christ." Those who had pre-viously refused him now testified their sorrow. His poor nurse especially was inconsolable ; she threw herself at his feet, shed a torrent of tears, asked a thousand pardons, and begged of him not to refuse to come and take at least a meal in her house. He consented ; and, as the poor woman, full of joy, was putting herself to great trouble concerning him, he said to her, less by way of reproach, than to enlighten her charity, " Andrée, Andrée, you have taken great care of me ; but you have not been charitable. Forget Montfort, he is nothing. Think of Jesus Christ, He is everything ; and it is He whom you must always regard in the poor " (pp. 108–109.)

But if his life were in some sense common-place, dis-tinguished by no very special characteristics from that of other heroically saintly men, it is far otherwise as regards his writings. Here again we cannot do better than quote the " Secular Priest."

I do not think I am wrong in saying, that more light is thrown upon his character by his writings than by his life. With most men their written are more guarded than their spoken words ; but it is otherwise with De Montfort. In his writings, and even in his letters, he seems to pour forth his whole soul without restraint, as if the Spirit of the Lord were upon him constraining him to write. His shrinking humility seems to give way to a holy boldness, and he writes as " a man full of faith and the Holy Ghost." His pen is " the pen of one who writeth swiftly the good things uttered by his heart." There is an undercurrent of prophecy running through almost all his writings ; and he seems to catch, as it were, somewhat of the spirit of the elder prophets, when speaking of the latter times. And when we read his burning words, we feel that God had heard his own earnest prayer, and allowed him to dip his pen in the unction of the Holy Ghost, while the very pen which he used seems to have been formed out of the Cross of Christ. Whether in his Treatise on Divine Wisdom, or in his letter to the Friends of the Cross, or in his prayer for those fiery missionaries of the Holy Ghost and of Mary, whom he foresees God will raise up in the latter days, and whom he addresses as if they were already born into the world, he seems to be writing under a mightier influence than that of his own spirit ; while in his Treatise on True Devotion to the Blessed Virgin and in the Secret of Mary, he speaks to us as if he had been carried up by the Spirit of God to the foot of Mary's throne in heaven, and had heard " secret words which it is not granted to a man to utter." (pp. xviii.—xx.)

So much for Montfort's writings in general. Turning to the particular treatise which has excited the severest animadversion, —his " True Devotion to the Blessed Virgin,"—two English translations of this treatise appeared within a year of each other; F. Faber's in England, and another in Ireland " approved " by Cardinal (then Archbishop) Cullen, and guaranteed by the " nihil obstat " of F. Curtis, the then Jesuit Provincial. This latter translator (p. 1) holds, that " it were perhaps difficult to find a book so concise and so suited to general circulation, in which " Marian devotion "is advocated with more solidity, or with more cogent reasons. The saintly author," adds the translator, " declares that he had read almost every book that had ever been written on the subject, and seems to have culled from all much of what is most excellent in reference to it." And as to the special devotion which Montfort recommends, F. Faber does not hesitate to say (Preface, p. x.) that he " cannot think of a higher work or a broader vocation than the simple spreading of it." He proceeds to speak of " the transformations which it causes in the soul," and its " almost incredible efficacy as a means for the salvation of men." What then precisely is this devotion, and what are its advantages ?

First of all, we must inquire how far the Catholic's liberty of criticising this devotion is restrained, by the general ecclesiastical approval of Montfort's writings which we have already cited. It has been decided that these writings " contain nothing contrary to faith or morals, nor any new doctrine contrary to the Church's common sentiment and practice." This implies a great deal : in fact, in the case of S. Alphonsus, it has been authoritatively decided that, for the precise reason of his works having received this approbation, a priest is at liberty to act in every single case on the Saint's opinion, in matters of Moral Theology. In like manner then, as the " Secular Priest " admirably observes (p. xxviii.), " although no one is bound to accept " Montfort's various writings " as *true*," yet, on the other hand, " no one is at liberty to condemn them as *unsound*. Admitting then that any one, who finds them out of harmony with his mind or unsuited to his devotion, has the most perfect liberty not to use them; still it must also be admitted, that no one has a right to condemn or find fault with those who do."

One qualification of this however seems to us in this par-

ticular case especially called for. A saintly man, as such, has
no exemption from incorrectness of reasoning and language;
nay, the very fervour of feeling with which he contemplates
spiritual Objects—a fervour which reasonable men so admire
and revere—is not favourable to (though by no means inconsistent with) philosophical accuracy in their treatment. It is
abundantly possible then, that here and there a sentence may
occur, which by no means faithfully represents its author's
meaning; a sentence which, if taken isolatedly and uninter-
preted by the context, it may be impossible to reconcile with
sound theology, nay and with what the writer may have elsewhere emphatically stated. The Church has understood his
meaning, not from individual sentences, but from the general
drift and bearing of the whole; and it would be absurd to
suppose that mere inaccuracy of language is a bar to canonization. We speak of Montfort's *individual sentences:* it
is *the general drift and bearing of his works,* considered each
as a whole, in regard to which (as we understand the matter)
it has been authoritatively pronounced, that they are sullied
by no taint of theological unsoundness or doctrinal novelty.

No Catholic then is at liberty to call in question the lawful-
ness and permissibleness of that particular devotion, which
Montfort so earnestly recommends. It of course however is a
different question, and a perfectly open one, how far that devotion is suited to men's spiritual needs and really calculated to
promote solid piety. This question we are now very briefly to
consider; and while doing so, we shall implicitly show in
every particular instance—what Catholics will of course have
already taken for granted—that the devotion contains nothing
in any respect divergent from sound doctrine.

There is one devotional view indeed, which must be
encountered at starting; for undoubtedly, if accepted, it
would overthrow Montfort's fabric from its very foundation.
It has been thought by some Catholics, that the Marian cultus,
as practised in the Church and commended by authority, has
comparatively little concern with what is strictly personal and
primary in religion; nay, it has apparently been held that,
were the case otherwise, Catholics might justly be accused of
interposing the creature as a kind of veil or barrier between
the soul and its Creator. We are not a little surprised that any
Catholic can have so thought. We must really maintain it to
be evident on the surface, that those who have been most
known and trusted in their worship of Mary, cherish that
worship precisely because of its intimate bearing on what is
most strictly personal and primary; because of the invaluable help it gives them, towards growing in the love of God,

in piety and self-mastery.   But it is worth while pointing out,
how closely connected with the interior life are those addresses
to our Blessed Lady, which are especially commended by the
Church to her faithful children.   The following prayers then
have been indulgenced; we quote them from F. St. John's
admirable translation of the "Raccolta," and we italicize one
or two expressions :—

When at length my hour is come, then do thou, Mary, *my hope,* be thyself
my aid in those great troubles wherewith my soul will be encompassed.
Strengthen me, that I may not despair when the enemy sets my sins before
my face.   Obtain for me at that moment grace *to invoke thee often,* so that I
may breathe forth my spirit with *thine own sweet name and that of thy most
holy Son upon my lips.* (p. 183.)

In thee let the Holy Church find safe shelter; protect it, and be its sweet
asylum, its tower of strength, impregnable against every inroad of its enemies.
Be thou *the road leading to Jesus;* be thou *the channel whereby we receive
all graces needful for our salvation.*   Be thou our help in need, our comfort
in trouble, *our strength in temptation, our refuge in persecution,* our aid in
all dangers ; but especially *in the last struggle of our life,* at the moment of
our death, when all hell shall be unchained against us to snatch away our
souls,—in that dread moment, that hour so terrible, *whereon our eternity
depends,* ah, yes, most tender Virgin, do thou, then, make us feel how great
is the sweetness of thy Mother's Heart, and the power of thy might with the
Heart of Jesus, by *opening for us a safe refuge* in the very fount of mercy
itself, that so one day we too may join with thee in Paradise in praising that
same Heart of Jesus for ever and for ever. (p. 179.)

I would I had a greater love, a more tender love : this thou must gain for
me, since *to love thee is a great mark of predestination,* and a grace which God
grants to those who shall be saved. (p. 185.)

Thou, Mary, art *the stewardess of every grace which God vouchsafes to give
us sinners,* and therefore did He make thee so mighty, rich, and kind, that
thou mightest succour us.   I will that I may be saved : in thy hands I place
my eternal salvation, to thee I consign my soul.   I will be associated with
those who are thy special servants ; reject me not.   *Thou goest up and down
seeking the wretched to console them.*   Cast not away, then, a wretched sinner
who has recourse to thee.   Speak for me, Mary ; thy Son grants what thou
askest. (pp. 186–7.)

My Queen ! my Mother ! *I give thee all myself;* and to show my devotion
to thee, *I consecrate to thee this day my eyes, ears, mouth, heart, myself wholly,
and without reserve.*   Wherefore, O loving Mother, as I am thine own, keep
me, defend me, *as thy property, and thy own possession.*

Ejaculation in any Temptation.

My Queen, my Mother ! *remember I am thine own.*

Keep me, defend me, as *thy property, thy own possession.* (p. 197.)

Accept what we offer, grant us what we ask, *pardon us what we fear;* for
thou art the sole hope of sinners.   Through thee we hope for the forgiveness
of our faults : and in thee, most blessed one, is the hope of our reward.

Holy Mary, succour the wretched, help the faint-hearted, comfort the sorrowful, pray for the people, shield the clergy, intercede for the devout female sex, let all feel thy help who celebrate thy holy commemoration. *Be thou at hand, ready to aid our prayers, when we pray;* and return to us *laden with the answers we desire.* Make it thy care, blessed one, to intercede ever for the people of God—thou who didst deserve to bear the Redeemer of the world, who liveth and reigneth for ever and ever. (p. 199.)

O Joseph, help us with thy prayers to be of the number of those who, *by the merits of Jesus and his Virgin Mother,* shall be partakers of the resurrection to glory. (pp. 274-5.)

O Joseph, obtain for us, that, *being entirely devoted to the service of Jesus and Mary,* we may live and die for them alone. (p. 275.)

O Joseph, obtain for us, that, having our hearts freed from idle fears, we may enjoy the peace of a tranquil conscience, *dwelling safely with Jesus and Mary, and dying at last in their arms.* (p. 275.)

No Catholic then—so much we think must really be admitted by every one who will look facts in the face—no Catholic can consistently hold the opinion which we mentioned above; the opinion, that to connect most intimately the worship of Mary with the worship of Jesus, is to interpose a barrier or veil between the soul and its Creator. But what reply should be made to *Protestants*, who are ever forward in urging this opinion almost as a kind of first principle? One reply " ad homines " was put forth in our number for July, 1866—with immediate reference to Dr. Pusey's Eirenicon—and ran as follows :—Take any argument you please which purports to show, that the constantly and habitually turning to Mary—for pardon of sin, for spiritual strength, for abundant supplies of grace—obscures the thought of God's presence and sole sovereignty. We maintained that such argument, if consistently carried out, would no less efficaciously show, that prayer to *Jesus Christ* for these blessings must produce the very same disastrous effect (pp. 150-157). We maintained in fact (p. 157) that the same line of thought, which vindicates against Deists the worship of Jesus, vindicates no less triumphantly against Anglicans the worship of Mary.

This method of reply, which we still believe to be irrefragably cogent, was impugned by an opponent, on the obvious ground that Jesus Christ is God; and that the thought of *Him* therefore cannot possibly interpose a barrier or veil between the soul and its Creator. We had already met this objection by implication; but we explicitly replied as follows. Dr. Pusey's argument may be thus expressed. "Love of God and of Jesus is the highest of spiritual perfections. But the constant thought of Mary is greatly prejudicial to this love, by drawing men's minds from the Creator to the creature;

and a proof of this is, that when a pious Roman Catholic is in trouble, he far more spontaneously turns to Mary than to her Son." Now a Unitarian may use an argument most strikingly analogous, against belief in the Incarnation. Thus. "Love of God, for the sake of His Divine Excellences, is the highest of spiritual perfections. But the constant thought of Christ is greatly prejudicial to this perfection, as leading men to love God, not for the sake of His Necessary *Divine* Excellences, but for the sake of those *human* excellences which (according to Trinitarian doctrine) He has freely assumed. And a proof of this is, that a pious Trinitarian, when in trouble, very far more spontaneously turns to the Second Person than to the First. The *Divine* Excellences appertain to *Both ;* if therefore it were for *them* that he loved God, the Father would be quite as frequently in his thoughts as the Son." Undoubtedly, every devout Trinitarian sees that this argument is monstrously fallacious; and in like manner, every devout Roman Catholic sees that *Dr. Pusey's* argument is monstrously fallacious : but we must really maintain that the one is quite as plausible as the other.

We were not content however with this negative defence of the Catholic Marian devotion ; we set forth positively, to the best of our abilities, the invaluable assistance which it confers on the soul struggling towards perfection. Our argument in substance was this. Over and above the singular advantage, in apprehending our Lord's mysteries, derived from contemplating them in sympathy with His Mother—there is another different consideration altogether. The mind has a most real capacity for apprehension and love of the Infinite : but however intensely that capacity be exercised, there still remains a very large residue of affection for finite objects. Now it is the Church's end, that the heart of her children be anchored in the invisible world; that they measure all earthly things by a heavenly standard. This great end then is most inadequately promoted, unless their love for the finite, as well as for the Infinite, find great scope in their religious exercises. And more particularly it is of inestimable value, that that unspeakably tender and powerful feeling—a child's love towards its mother—be allowed a hearty vent on such a being as Mary. Lastly, their love of finite heavenly persons reacts most powerfully on, and indefinitely intensifies, their love of God; and gives to that love an otherwise untasted quality of tenderness and passionate devotion.

It being seen then, how earnestly the unintermittent worship of Mary is recommended by the Church, and how unspeakably efficacious it has been found by experience towards fostering the love of God,—our way is open to consider the particular *form* of that worship so emphatically counselled by Montfort. We will refer chiefly for its exposition to his little work called " The Secret of Mary," contained in the newly-published volume ; because, as the " Secular Priest " mentions (p. 391, note), it surpasses his larger treatise in clearness of arrangement. And we begin with observing, that he calls his devotion a " slavery " : " the slavery of Jesus in Mary " being his common description of it. Objection was raised against this phrase in England, on the ground that man's service of God should be no " slavery," but " a free and reasonable service." Montfort however had anticipated this objection. " There are three kinds of slavery, " he had said :—

> The first is the slavery of nature ; all men, good and bad, are the slaves of God in this sense. The second is the slavery of constraint ; the devils and the damned are slaves of God in this second sense. The third is the slavery. of *love and of the will ; and it is in this sense that we ought to consecrate ourselves to God by Mary,* as being the most perfect way in which a creature can possibly give itself to its Creator. (p. 402.)

Why then does he use the term " slavery "? Because, as he at once proceeds to explain, " a *servant* is free to leave his master when he likes ; a *slave* cannot justly leave his master, but belongs to him his whole life long." Thus, as the " Secular Priest " points out (p. xxxiii.), S. Paul calls himself " the slave of Jesus Christ " ; and the same may be added of S. James. Moreover, S. Paul tells Christians that they have become " slaves to God ; " and elsewhere that they are " slaves of Christ " (p. xxxiv.) : while the Tridentine Catechism speaks of the faithful as under a strict obligation of consecrating themselves as *slaves* to their Redeemer and Lord (p. xxxv.). The same general fact had been pointed out by F. Knox, of the London Oratory, in some very interesting letters on Montfort, which the Catholic papers published towards the beginning of 1866.

Sometimes however undoubtedly Montfort uses the phrase " slaves of *Mary*." No one who reads what he has said, can doubt for a moment what he intended to express by this phrase. " This dedication is made to her," says the Dublin Editor (p. 2), " as a secondary personage, and merely that we may be more perfectly and completely devoted to the service of her Divine Son, who Alone is the primary Object of our servitude." Moreover, as has been already seen, the Church has indulgenced a prayer, in which the Christian entreats Mary that she will " keep him and defend him as her *property*, her own *possession*." Still, on the whole, we think M. Tronson's advice was very judicious, that the phrase should not be com_monly used.

Now in what devotional exercises is this "slavery" exhibited and realized? They may perhaps with sufficient accuracy be reduced to two. Firstly, those who practise it "leave the entire disposal of their prayers, their alms, and their mortifications to the Holy Virgin"; they leave at her disposal "all the value, satisfactory and impetratory, of their good works" (p. 401). And the full meaning of this surrender will be better understood by the following passages : —

> After we have made the oblation, although without any vow, we are no longer masters of any of the good we do ; the most Holy Virgin may apply it, at one time for the relief and deliverance of a soul in Purgatory, at another for the conversion of some poor sinner.
>
> We give her all our prayers and good works, so far as they are impetratory and satisfactory, to distribute and apply them to whom she pleases ; and if, after having thus consecrated ourselves to the Holy Virgin, we desire to relieve some soul in Purgatory, to save some sinner, to help some one of our friends by our prayers, our alms, our mortifications, or our sacrifices, *we must ask it of her humbly, and leave everything to her good pleasure and determination,* without knowing anything about it, being fully persuaded that the value of our actions, being dispensed by the same hand of which God makes use to distribute to us His graces and gifts, it cannot fail to be applied to His greatest glory. (pp. 401-402.)

It will be seen at once, that prayers for *our own* well-being, spiritual or temporal, are in no way affected by this pious practice. But one impression might be derived from a hasty perusal of the passage just quoted, which its more careful study will entirely correct. It might be thought that Montfort would establish our Blessed Lady's arbitrary will as the final disposer of things natural and supernatural. But it is not so. It is because " she knows what is for the greatest glory of *God* " (p. 401), that he would place men's congruous merits and prayers in her hands. Moreover it is an elementary Catholic doctrine, that in her every act she simply conforms herself to God's Preference ; and accordingly, as F. Newman excellently expresses it (Letter to Dr. Pusey, p. 111), " she intercedes *according to His will.* He wills indeed according to her prayer, but then she prays *according to His will.*"

What is really involved then in this part of Montfort's devotion is, that those who practise it abdicate all practice of praying or of offering their congruous merits and satisfactions in behalf of others, for any one gift spiritual or temporal, except so far as it may conduce according to God's Preference to His greater glory. This is indeed, as it has been most truly called, an "heroic sacrifice": but we incline to think that the number of Catholics is not so very small, who have the full moral strength to make it; while the number is of course much greater, who would *acquire* such strength gradually by due faithfulness to present grace. Every one may see its vast efficacy in purging the soul from inordinate human attachments, and fixing the heart undividedly on God; nor are we aware of any objection which can be raised, except one admitting a very easy reply. It may be said that a devout Catholic has various relations, friends, benefactors, &c., who have in some sense a claim on his intercessory prayer; and that he should not defraud them of that benefit. But it is obvious, that He who disposes all things powerfully and sweetly, can advance His own greater glory by this or that means, according to His will; and can thus satisfy every reasonable claim on His servant's intercession, without injury to the "heroic sacrifice." And this is the answer suggested by Montfort himself, in a sentence which we have italicized; where he speaks of "asking" some favour "humbly, and leaving every thing to Mary's good pleasure and determination." On the whole then, speaking with all diffidence, we incline to follow Montfort in this part of his doctrine; viz., in thinking that all who enjoy a high spiritual vocation, will derive a very important help in their noble enterprise, by such a surrender as he recommends of their various congruous merits, satisfactions, and impetrations.

The other practice of devotion which he suggests, we may suppose him to defend by some such consideration as the following:—It is admitted, he may say, by all reasonable theists, that men are more *perfect*,—more adequately pursue the end of their existence—in proportion as they more simply conform themselves to God's Preference, in their various acts, words, and thoughts. The Christian adds to this statement, that help is given to them of inestimable value for the *achievement* of their great enterprise, the more habitually they unite the thought of God with the thought of Jesus Christ the God Incarnate. And in like manner the Catholic may further allege, that an invaluable additional assistance is afforded in the same direction, if the thought of Jesus is indissolubly connected with the thought of Mary His Mother.

So far we follow him unreservedly; the question to our mind turns entirely on his practical application of this principle. He recommends (p. 409), that "we *never* go to our Lord except in Mary, through her intercession and power with Him; we must never be alone,"—i.e. as we understand him, without the explicit remembrance of Mary,—"when we

pray to Him.   Nor can there be," he beautifully adds, " any
possibility of Mary obscuring the soul from God:" for " far from
her detaining in herself the soul which casts itself upon her
bosom, she on the contrary casts it immediately upon God, and
unites it to Him with so much the more perfection as the
soul is more united to her.   Mary is the *marvellous echo of God,*
who answers only ' God' when we say ' Mary'; who glorifies
only God, when with S. Elizabeth we call her Blessed."   And
the kind of practical result which Montfort desires to secure,
is perhaps nowhere more clearly illustrated than in his beautiful
practice for Communion.   The following extract will explain
what we mean :—

After Holy Communion, while you are inwardly recollected and holding
your eyes shut, you will introduce Jesus into the heart of Mary.   You will
give Him to his Mother, who will receive Him lovingly, will place Him
honourably, will adore Him profoundly, will love Him perfectly, will embrace
Him closely, and will render to Him, in spirit and in truth, many homages
which are unknown to us in our thick darkness.   Or else you will keep yourself profoundly humbled in your heart, in the presence of Jesus residing in
Mary.   Or you will sit like a slave at the gate of the king's palace, where he
is speaking with the queen ; and while they talk one to the other without
need of you, you will go in spirit to heaven and over all the earth, praying
all creatures to thank, adore, and love Jesus and Mary in your place :
" Venite, adoremus, venite."   Or else you shall yourself ask of Jesus, in union
with Mary, the coming of His kingdom on earth, through His holy Mother ;
or you shall sue for the Divine wisdom, or for Divine love, or for the pardon
of your sins, or for some other grace ; but always *by* Mary and *in* Mary,
saying, while you look aside at yourself, " Ne respicias, Domine, peccata
mea,"—" Lord, look not at my sins " ; " Sed oculi tui videant æquitates
Mariæ,"—" But let your eyes look at nothing in me but the virtues and
merits of Mary " : and then, remembering your sins, you shall add, " Inimicus
homo hoc fecit,"—" It is I who have committed these sins " ; or you shall
say, " Ab homine iniquo et doloso erue me"; or else, "Te oportet crescere,
me autem minui,"—"My Jesus, you must increase in my soul, and I must
decrease ; Mary, you must increase within me, and I must be still less than I
have been."   " Crescite et multiplicamini,"—"O Jesus and Mary, increase
in me, and multiply yourselves outside in others also."

There are an infinity of other thoughts which the Holy Ghost furnishes,
and will furnish you, if you are thoroughly interior, mortified, and faithful
to this grand and sublime devotion which I have been teaching you.   But
always remember that the more you leave Mary to act in your Communion,
the more Jesus will be glorified.   The more you leave Mary to act for Jesus,
and Jesus to act in Mary, the more profoundly you will humble yourself, and
will listen to them in peace and silence, without putting yourself in trouble
about seeing, tasting, or feeling : for the just man lives throughout on faith ;
and particularly in Holy Communion, which is an action of faith.—(Faber's
translation, pp. 188-190.)

Now we heartily follow Montfort in holding, that never was there such a mere bugbear as the Protestant fear, lest the worship of Mary should keep God from shining in the whole heart. We further heartily follow him, in regarding it as an unspeakable blessing to the soul, that it should deeply feel its interior dependence, not on Jesus alone, but also on Mary. Again, due meditation on our Lord and on His Mother, on their mutual relations and their respective offices, will doubtless establish so close a connection between the two in a Catholic's mind, that the thought of one will be ever *implicitly* accompanied by thought of the other. But it is quite a further statement, that the union of the two Objects should be always *explicitly* maintained; and that it would be generally advantageous never to address Jesus except through Mary. On this proposal—which we understand to be Montfort's —with profound diffidence we would make the following remarks :—

1. He would himself of course admit, that there is a considerable number of men who have grown old in the practice of prayer on a different basis from his own ; nor do we suppose for a moment that he would wish *them* to give a sudden and violent wrench to their religious habits. He can only mean, that those who are new in piety and have their devotional practices to form, or again who are dissatisfied with their existing usages, would derive great benefit from acting on his method.

2. Further he would, we fancy, also admit—certainly it is undeniable—that there is a large multitude possessing ordinary and (so to speak) common-place vocations, whom no one would dream of inviting to such a practice.

3. On the other hand, neither (it would seem) can it admit of doubt, that there are *some* who derive vast spiritual benefit from Montfort's rule. He himself did so ; and one sees no reason for accounting him singular in this respect.

4. The real question then seems to be this :—Can it be truly said that all, who are called to the heights of spiritual perfection, would be importantly assisted in their noble course, did they adopt the habit of never praying to Jesus except through Mary ; nor meditating on the former except in relation with the latter? Doubtless it is of immense benefit that such prayer and meditation should be very frequently practised ; but the question is, whether every *other* kind of prayer and meditation towards our Lord should be avoided. Our own humble impression would be strongly on the negative side. There is no more marked characteristic of the Church's dealing with souls, than the inex-

haustible variety of devotions, among which she would have
individuals choose according to their several necessities and
tastes.* And we are not at all disposed to believe, without much
greater evidence than to our knowledge exists, that holy men
of every various temperament and character would all do well
to take up so stringent and gratuitous a rule as the one in
question. It may be an excellent rule for certain individuals ;
but we can see no reason for wishing it universally adopted.
Speaking generally, if addresses to the Eternal Father are
often most conducive to holiness though containing no mention
of His Incarnate Son,—surely also many prayers to Jesus
may be of invaluable benefit though they make no reference
to His Mother.

At the same time, though we cannot follow Montfort in the
universality of his recommendation, we are the very last to
undervalue or disparage the books which contain it. The
"Treatise on True Devotion," and another smaller work now
first translated, abound in exquisitely beautiful and true
thoughts, and are quite singularly calculated to promote the
Catholic's love both to Mary and her Son.

These works contain in themselves the explanations of a fact,
which has greatly perplexed Dr. Pusey. Montfort earnestly
desires that there should arise in the Church an immense

---

* This is expressed by F. Newman with his customary felicity of language
in his letter to Dr. Pusey :—"The faith is everywhere one and the same ;
but a large liberty is accorded to private judgment and inclination in matters
of devotion. Any large church, with its collections and groups of people,
will illustrate this. The fabric itself is dedicated to Almighty God, and
that, under the invocation of the Blessed Virgin, or some particular Saint ;
or again, of some mystery belonging to the Divine Name or to the Incarnation, or of some mystery associated with the Blessed Virgin. Perhaps there
are seven altars or more in it, and these again have their several Saints.
Then there is the Feast proper to the particular day ; and during the celebration of Mass, of all the worshippers who crowd around the Priest, each
has his own particular devotions, with which he follows the rite. No one
interferes with his neighbour ; agreeing, as it were, to differ, they pursue
independently a common end, and by paths, distinct but converging, present
themselves before God. Then there are Confraternities attached to the
church,—of the Sacred Heart, of the Precious Blood ; associations of prayer
for a good death, or the repose of departed souls, or the conversion of the
heathen ; devotions connected with the brown, blue, or red scapular ;—not to
speak of the great ordinary Ritual through the four seasons, the constant Presence of the Blessed Sacrament, its ever-recurring rite of Benediction, and its
extraordinary forty hours' Exposition. Or, again, look through some such
manual of prayers as the _Raccolta_, and you at once will see both the number
and the variety of devotions, which are open to individual Catholics to choose
from, according to their religious tastes and prospect of personal edification "
(pp. 30–31).

increase of devotion to the Blessed Virgin ; * and Dr. Pusey can only regard this as a wish for a still larger substitution of Mary for Jesus than even now (as he thinks) exists. Yet consider. Montfort thinks it desirable, that the latter Object should never be approached in prayer or meditation except through the former. But take any ordinary book of prayer and meditation: who can possibly say that this practice is carried forward therein to one hundredth part of that extent, which is most

---

* The following extracts in illustration are taken from F. Faber's edition of his treatise :—

All the rich among the people shall supplicate thy face from age to age, and *particularly at the end of the world ;* that is to say, the greatest Saints, the souls richest in graces and virtues, shall be the most assiduous in praying to our Blessed Lady, and in having her always present as their perfect model to imitate, and their powerful aid to give them succour.

I have said that this would come to pass, particularly at the end of the world, and indeed presently, because *the Most High with His holy Mother* has to form for Himself great Saints, *who shall surpass most of the other Saints in sanctity, as much as the cedars of Lebanon outgrow the little shrubs,* as has been revealed to a holy soul, whose life has been written by a great servant of God.

These great souls, full of grace and zeal, shall be chosen to match themselves against the enemies of God, who shall rage on all sides ; and they shall be *singularly devout to our Blessed Lady,* illuminated by her light, nourished by her milk, led by her spirit, supported by her arm, and sheltered under her protection, so that they shall fight with one hand and build with the other. With one hand they shall fight, overthrow, and crush the heretics with their heresies, the schismatics with their schisms, the idolaters with their idolatries, and the sinners with their impieties. With the other hand *they shall build the temple of the true Solomon, and the mystical city of God ; that is to say, the most holy Virgin,* called by the holy Fathers the temple of Solomon and the city of God. By their words and by their examples *they shall bend the whole world to true devotion to Mary*. This shall bring upon them many enemies ; but it shall also bring many victories and much glory for God alone. It is this which God revealed to S. Vincent Ferrer, the great apostle of his age, as he has sufficiently noted in one of his work. (pp. 25–7).

God, then, wishes to *reveal and discover* Mary, the masterpiece of His hands, *in these latter times* (p. 28).

It is necessary, then, for the greater knowledge and glory of the Most Holy Trinity, that Mary *should be more known than ever.*

Mary must *shine forth more than ever* in mercy, in might, and in grace, *in these latter times* (p. 29).

The power of Mary over all the devils will especially break out in the latter times, when Satan will lay his snares against her heel : that is to say, her humble slaves and her poor children, whom she will raise up to make war against him (p. 33).

God wishes that His holy Mother should be at present *more known, more loved, more honoured, than she has ever been.* This no doubt will take place, if the presdestinate enter, with the grace and light of the Holy Ghost, into the interior and perfect practice which I will disclose to them shortly (p. 33).

readily imaginable? It was Montfort's strong opinion, that the time was come when this should be vigorously done. No Catholic is called upon to *agree* with this opinion if it displeases him; but the notion of its disparaging our Blessed Lord is simply preposterous.

It may be observed however by the way, that even those who do not follow Montfort in the particular devotion which we have been discussing, may nevertheless, for various reasons, both desire and expect a large increase of Marian devotion within the Church. As an instance of what we mean, there is hardly any title of our Blessed Lady which has received more unequivocal sanction from the Church, than that of " co-redemptress." Yet the various doctrines involved in that name are very far, as yet, from being adequately embedded in Catholic popular devotion; and for ourselves, we earnestly hope that an improvement in this direction may speedily set in. There is a sign of this, in F. Jeanjacquot's beautiful little work on the " Co-operation of the Blessed Virgin "; which was most emphatically praised by our contemporary "The Month," and to which we ourselves also drew prominent attention last January (p. 225).

In intimate connection with Mary's office as co-redemptress, stands the doctrine that she did not sin in Adam; that she never incurred the debitum proximum of contracting original sin. We cannot but eagerly desire that the attention of theologians should be strongly fixed on this doctrine; because it seems to us undeniable, that almost all the arguments, which establish the Apostolicity of the Immaculate Conception, establish no less conclusively the Apostolicity of this farther doctrine. See our number for October, 1866, pp. 476-489.*

Then consider the widely-spread desire which has recently been exhibited among Catholics, that her *Assumption* be de-

---

* We believe that Catholic theologians of this day would be almost unanimous in their advocacy of this doctrine, were it not for the difficulty of reconciling it with the indubitable verity, that Christ redeemed His Mother by His Passion and Death. On this head we make, with all diffidence, the following suggestion. We hold, with many theologians, that God's decree of creating Mary depended on His prevision of the fall; that had Adam remained sinless, the Son would not have become incarnate nor Mary called into existence. We submit then that God firstly (in order of nature) decreed the Son's Incarnation, Passion, and Death; then, secondly, resolved to create Mary. Moreover that, in resolving to create her, He redeemed her, by His Son's foreseen Passion and Death, from the debitum proximum of contracting original sin. And this is most truly a " redemption "; nay, a higher redemption than any other : she was " redeemed " or " purchased back," by her Son's foreseen death, from a sentence which every other carnal descendant of Adam incurred.

fined as a dogma of the Faith. This fact alone seems to imply, that there is a great stirring of heart just now on the various mysteries which concern the Mother of God.

Lastly Pius IX. has now solemnly placed the whole Church under the patronage of S. Joseph. Can it be doubted that one result of this will be increased devotion to that Holy Family, called by pious writers "the earthly Trinity"?

But we will not pursue further a line of thought which, however tempting, draws us away from our immediate theme. We proceed therefore finally to one or two doctrinal statements of Montfort, which have most groundlessly given some offence. Thus in his "Secret of Mary" he speaks of her *presence in the soul* as one special fruit of the devotion which he recommends. Now so far as the mere *phrase* is concerned, the "Secular Priest" (p. xliv.) points out that it has received the Church's express sanction; because an indulgenced prayer supplicates her "that she would *come down again* and be *reborn* spiritually *in our souls."* But it is quite a mistake to understand Montfort as implying any real presence of Mary in the soul. He refers, as we understand him, to two things. On the one hand to the *implicit thought* of Mary, which he considers will never be absent from the mind of one who faithfully practises the devotion. On the other hand, and as it were by way of requital, Mary exercises (so Montfort thinks) a very special influence, and practises a very special watchfulness, over such a faithful servant. He touches her with his heart, and she in return (so to speak) touches *him.* The "Secular Priest" with quite extraordinary aptness cites a passage (pp. xliv.-xlvi.) from the Life of F. Ravignan, which we cannot do better than reproduce.

From the very beginning the blessed Saint (Ignatius) responded to the affection of his son, but their hearts went on to closer and closer union. I cannot mention precisely at what time this closer union began ; but from repeated confidential communications, I know that for the latter years of his life, he enjoyed, not mere distant affection, but direct immediate intercourse ; and from this period F. de Ravignan dealt with the saint with all the familiarity of a child. On the one side there was unceasing invocation ; for long hours together spent in prayer he spoke with his heart rather than his lips, repeating "Father ! Father." On the other side there was sensible assistance and a *presence almost real.* "I do not see him," said F. de Ravignan, "*I do more, I feel him ; he is there, and I touch him by my heart."* Again, when asked on his death-bed whether S. Ignatius was still, as formerly, *always present* to his soul, he answered, "The thought of my Father, S. Ignatius, never leaves me night or day. . . . I received a great grace last night ! I asked my Blessed Father whether this sickness would lead to my death. He gave me an answer in the *depth of my heart,* with a clearness and distinctness

which fill me at this moment with the most absolute certainty, accompanied
with the greatest joy and peace. Surely, then, what the presence of his
Father S. Ignatius was to F. de Ravignan, the presence of Mary was to Ven.
Grignon de Montfort. Nothing less, perhaps something more, even as S.
Ignatius is less than his glorious Queen. And it is, although no doubt in an
inferior degree, this intimate union of soul with soul and spirit with spirit,
which the servant of God promises, not to every one, but to him who shall
be faithful in the practice of. his devotion to our Blessed Lady. O happy,
happy lot, if to any one who reads this Life the day should ever come when
Mary may speak to him as S. Ignatius spoke to his faithful son, and when
he may feel her and touch her by his heart !

Did F. Ravignan then believe in the *real presence* of
S. Ignatius in his (F. Ravignan's) soul?   The notion is preposterous.   "O happy, happy lot," says the "Secular Priest"
—and we heartily sympathize,—"if to any one who reads
this Life the day should ever come when Mary speaks to him
as S. Ignatius spoke to his faithful son, that he may feel and
touch her by his heart!"
There is another class of expressions, which recur in the
"True Devotion" : such as that "elect souls are born of God
and Mary"; that "the Holy Ghost and Mary jointly form
Jesus in the heart "; that "the Holy Ghost brings into fruitfulness His action by her; producing in her and by her Jesus
Christ in His members." The "Secular Priest" has admirably
defended these expressions from p. liv. to p. lix.: for ourselves
we shall be contented with reproducing the analysis of them
which we gave in July, 1866.
These extracts then refer, one and all, to an analogy, which
to some may seem far-fetched, but which to us appears
singularly beautiful; an analogy between that joint office, on
the one hand, whereby the Holy Ghost and Mary produced
Christ Himself, and that joint office, on the other hand,
whereby they form Christ in the individual soul. The
paragraphs are not very distinctly expressed; but there can
be no doubt as to the general doctrine which they contain.
Certain souls permit Mary to "strike her roots" in them;
i.e., to produce in them, by her watchful vigilance and unre-
mitting intercession, a real though imperfect image of herself.
When the Holy Ghost sees that Mary *has* thus taken root;—
or (to use the author's expression), when he sees Mary in
those souls;—He flies to them, and, in conjunction with
Mary, performs the "startling wonder" (p. 20) of forming
Christ within them. In other words, sanctity in its germs is
specially attributed by the author to Mary's intercession. In
its maturity however, it is described as the formation of Jesus
Christ in the soul, through the joint agency of the Holy Ghost

and Mary. She watchfully intercedes; He puts forth His highest efficacy in training and nurturing the soul; and so the complete image of her Son is more and more effectually produced within it.

We should further add, what is a first principle in theology, that the Holy Ghost differs from the other Divine Persons, in that he has no *Divine* Fecundity. The Father generates the Son; the Father and Son, by one undivided spiration, produce the Holy Ghost; but He produces no Divine Person. It is only, therefore, in acting on created things that His Fecundity exists. "The Holy Ghost therefore brings into fruitfulness His action by her; producing in her and by her Jesus Christ in His members."

We must not entirely omit a matter, which has afforded theme for some controversy; though, as the "Secular Priest" observes, it is in no way essential to Montfort's particular devotion. We refer to his recommending the wearing of *little chains*, to indicate that profession of *slavery* to Christ on which he lays so much stress; whereas a decree of the Holy Office abolished the use of those chains, at least in the case of confraternities. The "Secular Priest" treats this question with exemplary moderation, from p. lxiv. to p. lxix.; suggesting that in practice "a simple rosary or scapular worn round the neck" should rather be adopted. But a still fuller and more complete exposition of the controversy was given by F. Knox, in his three letters of 1866 which we have already mentioned.

In concluding our very imperfect review of the "Secular Priest's" volume, we must again express our sense of his admirable qualifications for the work which he has undertaken. He writes throughout in a singularly loving and Christian spirit; while he has exhibited in an unusual degree at once great accuracy and fairness of thought and a keen apprehension of ascetical truth. In his judgment of Montfort he is appreciative and sympathetic; in his judgment of others, guarded and moderate. He has given us a volume calculated to produce a most salutary effect on the Catholic's devotional spirit, and we heartily hope that it will be generally studied by English Catholics.

Art. III.—DEAN STANLEY ON WESTMINSTER ABBEY.

Historical Memorials of Westminster Abbey. By Arthur Penrhyn
Stanley, D.D. Third Edition. London: Murray. 1869.

SIR CHARLES BELL, an eminent surgeon in the last
generation, wrote a book which he entitled "The
Anatomy of Expression." His object was to show, from a
point of view semi-artistic, semi-physiological, what particular
muscles were called into play by the development of human
passions on their index, the human face. Fear, hope, joy,
anger, courage, envy, pain, contempt, had each its appropriate
muscular tension. But then comes the

> Last scene of all,
> That ends this strange eventful history,
> Is second childishness, and mere oblivion;
> Sans teeth, sans eyes, sans taste, sans everything.

This, too, has its anatomy of expression in the powerfully
illustrated book we have quoted, as it has in nature. The
fallen jaw, the muscles all relaxed, with eyeball dimmed and
inexpressive lips, combine in one solemn demonstration that
the soul has fled. We have accompanied the pilgrim of life
through the various disturbing causes that have swept and
agitated his spirit, awaking now one chord of emotion, now
another: at length, we have reached the point where the
strings have snapped, and the harp itself lies broken. We
are standing by a corpse.

Such is ever the feeling which accompanies us, as we wander
through the aisles of our old national cathedrals. They retain the
general form and outline that betokens the religion they were
built to serve, even as the "subject" from which Sir Charles
Bell sketched the anatomy of death retained the lineaments
of humanity. There are the features, minus the life. The
purpose for which they existed has ceased to animate them.
No muscles, play no emotions vary the chill and dead monotony. Where once processions moved with their banners,
where the sanct-bell tolled the moment of consecration to
the city that nestled round the minster, and to husbandmen
working in fields and crofts and granges far away, out of

sight, not out of mind, there the hollow footfall of the tourist, and the perfunctory drawl of the showman, waking the dismal silence, do but intensify the sadness of hearts which feel that the life is fled, and the inheritance in the hand of strangers.

Of strangers and of aliens in faith; though near in blood, and to our interest and our yearnings most dear. If there is a lesson which our cathedrals teach, it is the utter futility of the claims put forth by well-meaning Anglicans, of being the direct spiritual descendants and successors of those who reared the ancient structures, endowed them, served them, worshipped in them. Canterbury and Cologne, York and Amiens, Lichfield and Rouen, Westminster and Notre Dame; each are sisters to each, amid distinctions such as consist with a prevailing family likeness. The essential difference is, that Canterbury is dead, while Cologne is alive. The relics of S. Thomas have been scattered to the winds, while those of the Three Kings are enshrined by the high altar; an Archbishop of Canterbury has expressed his wish to be rid of the Athanasian Creed, and an Archbishop of Cologne, within our memory, has gone to prison for the Catholic faith; the one would and did, and the other didn't and wouldn't, present himself at the Vatican Council. In all that constitutes the idea and stamps the character of a cathedral, beyond the mere architectural features that survive because they are physically indestructible, Canterbury and Cologne are to each other as night to day. If a communion table differs from an altar, and lawn and black apron from chasuble and pectoral cross, and candles that must not be lighted till dusk from candles that must be lighted under pain of mortal sin, and "the black rubric" from the directions of the missal, and "When the wicked man" from "Jube, domne, benedicere"; then is Cologne to Canterbury as the light and life of Catholicity to the dark death of a faith denied, and a devotion sunk and smothered in its ashes.

The absolute change, indeed, of our cathedrals, from the past to the present phase of their existence, from shrines of devotion to national repositories of the monuments of celebrated men, is naïvely acknowledged by Dean Stanley :—

The reign of Elizabeth brings with it the first distinct recognition of the Abbey as a Temple of Fame. It was the natural consequence of the fact that amongst her favourites so many were heroes and heroines (!) Not only does Poet's Corner now leap into new life, but the counsellors and warriors, who in the long preceding reigns had dropped in here and there, according to the uncertain light of court favour, suddenly close round upon us, and the vacant chapels are thronged, as if with the first burst of national life and independence. Now also that life and indepen-

dence are seen *in forms peculiar to the age, when the old traditions of Christendom gave way* before that epoch of revolution. The royal monuments,
though changed in architectural decoration, still preserved the antique
attitude and position, and hardly interfered with the outline of the sacred
edifice. But the taste of private individuals at once *claimed its new liberty,*
and opened the way to that extravagant latitude of monumental innova-
tion which prevailed throughout Europe, and in our own day has roused
a reaction against the whole sepulchral fame of the Abbey. The gorgeous
dames are for the most part recumbent. But, as we have seen, they have
trampled on the ancient altars in their respective chapels. The Duchess
of Suffolk still faces the east; but the Duchess of Somerset and the
Countess of Hertford, dying thirty or forty years later, lie north and
south. Then follow, in the same chapel, Sir R. Pecksall, with his two
wives, drawn hither by the attraction of the contiguous grave of Sir
Bernard Brocas, from whom, through his mother, he inherited the post of
Master of the Buckhounds to the Queen.—*Westminster Abbey,* pp. 217, 218.

We remember an inscription in the Roman catacombs which
records that a Christian, dying after persecution had ceased,
was laid, according to the pious desire of those early days, as
near as possible to the bodies of the martyrs whose relics
hallowed the spot—"in crypta nova retro sanctos." The
juxtaposition of these two quotations would be weakened, we
think, by any word of comment.

It will be evident, that between Dean Stanley and ourselves,
the only point at issue is the interpretation given to this
plain difference which separates the Catholic from the post-
Reformation Abbey. But that difference is diametrical. He
reads us backwards, or we him. Hebrew, read in European
fashion, would form a senseless jargon. And we listen to our
author's sounding periods in much the same state of mind.
What he rejoices in as a Temple of Fame is, with us, the
statue of the heathen intruded into the sanctuary. The new
life into which Poet's Corner leaps is the quenching of the
sacred fire before the shrine: we hear the rush of the angels'
wings as they depart with " Let us go hence." His first burst
of national life and independence is, to our reading of English
history, the sere and yellow leaf into which the May of
England's moral life had fallen, or the leaf itself dropping
from the tree. The old traditions of Christendom did truly
give way before that epoch of revolution; and if the Dean and
ourselves meant the same thing by the words, we could here
heartily adopt his definition. We fear we are hopelessly at
cross purposes as to the meaning of terms. And we comment
thus on the first of our quotations from him, because this
diametric opposition to the Catholic idea of an Abbey runs
throughout his very interesting volume. As one who has

cultivated the literature and history of his country to no ordinary degree, Dean Stanley could not fail to give us a fascinating work. His groupings are admirable, his quotations much to the point. But, as we read on, and remember what the Abbey was in its spiritual life, what it has now become in its spiritual death, we feel that we are following a blind guide, and must beware of the ditch of a wide historical and literary blunder. We cannot but recall what Johnson said of Goldsmith's "Animated Nature" before it appeared, an anecdote which we here find reproduced (p. 327). "Goldsmith, sir, will give us a very fine book on this subject; but if he can distinguish a cow from a horse, that, I believe, is the extent of his knowledge of natural history."

The following passage on the Abbey monuments shows considerable power in grouping the facts of, at least, literary history: we should cordially enjoy it, if it were written of a mere Valhalla :—

We have seen how, by a gradual but certain instinct, the main groups have formed themselves round particular centres of death : how the Kings ranged themselves round the Confessor; how the Princes and Courtiers clung to the skirts of the Kings; how out of the graves of the Courtiers were developed the graves of the Heroes; how Chatham became the centre of the Statesmen, Chaucer of the Poets, Purcell of the Musicians; Casaubon of the Scholars; Newton of the Men of Science; how, even in the exceptional details, natural affinities may be traced; how Addison was buried apart from his brethren in letters, in the royal shades of Henry VII.'s Chapel, because he clung to the vault of his own loved Montague; how Ussher lay beside his earliest instructor, Sir James Fullerton, and Garrick at the foot of Shakespeare, and Spelman opposite his revered Camden, and South close to his master Busby, and Stephenson to his fellow-craftsman Telford, and Grattan to his hero Fox, and Macaulay beneath the statue of his favourite Addison. These special attractions towards particular graves and monuments may interfere with the general uniformity of the Abbey, but they make us feel that it is not a mere dead museum, that its cold stones are warmed with the life-blood of human affections and personal partiality (pp. 362, 363).

We could hardly pause on anything more illustrative of the thought we began with, that the Abbey, as to its supernatural life, is dead and buried. If High Mass is ever sung again under its solemn ancient vaultings, it will be by a distinct resurrection : it will be "life from the dead." Such an act would substitute one religion for another, as when the statue of Jupiter was toppled from the Roman Capitol, and the fat of victims gave place to the incense of the thurifer in Ara Coeli. For here, in the glowing language of an enthusiast, and with the detail of an historical student, we have a grouping which strikes on us with a pagan impression like the Olympus of Homer. It is the apotheosis of Hercules, the cultus of Minerva and the Muses. True, it is a paganism not gross, but thoughtful and refined, not popular merely, but esoteric and philosophical, as might have been the worship of Æscula-pius in the mind of Socrates. But not therefore the less is it the *dulia* of intellect to mere intellect and force of will. Here is Christianity dethroned, though fragments of its throne and incoherent portions of its utterance may remain; great men in the natural order usurping the altar of the Most High, and "the abomination of desolation standing in the holy place." "Gorgeous dames," as the Dean tells us, "have trampled on the ancient altars in their respective chapels." We will venture, though with as much hault courtesy as Sir Kingsley himself, to suppose these high ladies to be a little out of place. For a moment, let us reverse the rule of *place aux dames;* let their marble ruffs and farthingales disappear. We are going, indeed, to attempt a dissolving view.

Our camera is prepared: it is to be a glance at Westminster Abbey, present and past. For the first and actual view, the Abbey as we know it to-day, the museum through whose statue galleries vergers and visitors range, showing and being shown, let us cast into the focus the strongest and clearest light we can borrow from the history of England's literature, of England's statesmanship and brave achievements. We are in no sense concerned to ignore or to undervalue these things. "Every best gift, and every perfect gift, is from above, coming down from the Father of lights." So, too, gifts less good, less perfect, inasmuch as they are of nature, not of grace, are yet good in themselves, are still of God, and are better than themselves or their first beginnings, in proportion as they are sanctified and spiritualized in the receiver. To follow the Dean in his glimpse into Valhalla; we can glow at the eloquence of Chatham, and wish him free from uncatholic self-reliance; we could enjoy the vigour of Chaucer, were he purged of his uncatholic grossness and irreligion; we freely admire Newton's genius, while smiling at the uncatholic bombast which would announce that

Existence saw him spurn her bounded reign ;*

and Ussher's learning, though wishing it a better employment

---

* Words, however, which were first written of Shakspeare, though we think they have been applied to Newton.

than the upholding the Anglican schism; and Garrick's versatility in the exposition of human nature, wherever it was employed to elevate, not to worsen, the nature to which he so deftly fitted his plastic mask; and Macaulay's brilliancy, even though his shafts be barbed and winged by all the hereditary or personal prejudice and blindness of a partisan. Last, and greatest name, the Bard of Avon, or rather of mankind, is in no danger of being refused, by the Catholic cognisant of our country's literature, that tribute which is, within its own range, unapproachably his. Our Shakespeare—we love to think of him as responsible alone for what he actually wrote; guiltless and pure of the vile daubings with which (we fondly believe) later playwrights may have overlaid him. This sweet singer and untaught sage, learned in the wisdom of an intuition into his fellow-creatures, could report of " airs from heaven," though editors, perchance, have inspired into his dead lips " blasts from hell." Shakespeare, in this ideal,—may it hereafter prove to have been the truth about him—is a Catholic poet, and only in the measure of his reader's catholicity can he be valued.

So much by way of showman's preface. Our camera is not to depreciate England's true worthies, nor their affectionate and solemn association in the tomb, except by comparison with what is nobler still. " Be zealous for the better gifts. And I yet show to you a more excellent way." Let us adjust the lantern.

(I.) Westminster actual, in the nineteenth century. Within the circle of light thrown from our lens is the concentrated history of three hundred years of intellectual and martial power. Names that will live as household words, so long as an English-speaking man, in the Old World or the New, shall breathe, think, or remember, are presented before us. They survive in the imperishable marble that gives them to us with a life-like vividness of the noblest though not always the most Christian art, and is only less enduring than the fame they have achieved. They are grouped, nay, they overcrowd one another, with a superabundance of national wealth, within the too contracted casket of a narrow Benedictine Abbey.* " The tall statue " of Sir George Holles " stands,

---

* " Already, in the eighteenth century, the alarm was raised that the Abbey was ' loaded with marbles '; a ' Petition from Posterity ' was presented to the Dean and Chapter, to entreat that their case might be considered; and a French traveller remarked that ' le peuple n'est pas plus serré dans les rues de Londres qu'à Westminster, célèbre Abbaye, demeure des monuments funèbres de toutes les personnes illustres de la nation ' " (p. 373).

not, like that of Vere, modestly apart from the wall, but on
the site of the altar once dedicated to the Confessor's favourite
Saint *—*the first in the Abbey that stands erect;* the first that
wears, not the costume of the time, but that of a Roman
general; the first monument which, in its sculpture, repro-
duces the events in which the hero was engaged—the battle
of Nieuport. . . . Deeper yet into these chapels the Flemish
trophies penetrate. Against the wall, which must have held
the altar of the Chapel of S. Andrew, is the mural tablet of
John de Burgh, who fell in boarding a Spanish ship" (p. 229).
"In the vaults lies the beautiful Duchess of Richmond of
Charles II.'s time, . . . whose effigy was, by her own special
request, placed close by after her death, 'as well done in wax
as could be,' 'under crown glass and none other,' in the robes
she wore at the coronation of Queen Anne, and with a parrot
which had 'lived with her grace for forty years, and survived
her only a few days' (p. 234). Buckingham, 'the friend of
Laud, the pillar of the High Church party, nevertheless from
his tomb asserts and reasserts his claim to the name—in our
own times by their followers so vehemently repudiated—of
'Protestant'; and the allegorical figures are *the first wanton
intruders* into the imagery (now so dear to the school of Laud)
which adorns that ancient chapel" (pp. 237–8). One of these
allegories was "Fame even bursting herself and trumpets to
tell the news of his so sudden fall." . . . "In St. Paul's
Chapel is Sir Francis (afterwards Lord) Cottington. Look at
his face, as he lifts himself up on his elbow; . . . and think
of the quaint caustic humour which he must have diffused
through those three strange English reigns" (James I. to
Charles II.) (p. 240). "In Henry VII.'s Chapel . . . was
magnificently buried (1649) the learned Isaac Dorislaus, advocate at the king's trial. Under the Commonwealth he was
ambassador at the Hague, where he was·assassinated 'one
evening, by certain highflying Royalist cut-throats, Scotch
most of them: a man of heavy, deep-wrinkled, elephantine
countenance, pressed down with the labours of life and law.
The good ugly man here found his quietus'"† (p. 244).
Admiral Blake's public funeral in the same chapel was "the
first distinct claim of a burial in Westminster Abbey as an

---

* S. John the Apostle and Evangelist, to the plea of whose name
S. Edward granted every petition for charity. The beautiful legend of the
Confessor giving away his royal ring to the Saint under the guise of a
beggar, and having it restored to him as a token of his approaching death,
is well known.

† Quoted from Carlyle's *Cromwell*, i. 311.

incentive to heroic achievements, and it came well through the ruler [Cromwell] from whose reign ' the maritime glory of the Empire may first be traced in a track of continuous light ' " (p. 264).

Like his two princely kinswomen in the Chapels of St. Edmund and St. Nicholas, his [Hunsdon's] interment was signalized by displacing the altar of the Chapel of St. John the Baptist. The monument was remarkable, even in the next century, as "most magnificent," and is, in fact, the loftiest in the Abbey (p. 221). Edward [Norris] alone survived his father and brothers ; and, accordingly, he alone is represented, not, as the others, in an attitude of prayer, but looking cheerfully upwards " (p. 231). On [the monument of Holles, Duke of Newcastle] the sculptor Gibbs staked his immortality ; and by the figures of " Prudence" and " Sincerity," which stand on either side, set the example of the allegorical figures which, from that time, begin to fill up the space equally precious to the living and the dead (p. 257).

This would be incomplete, did we not take in a view of the Abbey monuments in general, propounded in Strype's edition of " Stow's Survey " (last edition, 1755), quoted in the Dean's Appendix, p. 648. •

I shall now pass by a number of rude Gothic monuments, which, instead of adorning, really encumber the church. . . . The principal figure [of Vere's monument] is in the old Gothic taste, flat on his back, and, of consequence, not to be relished. . . . Just opposite this is a martial figure, representing one of the Hollises, and, till that of Mr. Craggs was put up, was the only erect one in the Abbey : an attitude I am far from discouraging, for it is my opinion statues should always represent life and action, and not languor and insensibility. It is particularly happy when applied to soldiers and heroes, *who ought never to be supposed at rest*, and should have their characters represented as strong as possible.

We will remember this dictum if hereafter we should notice the other great statuary shop, St. Paul's. But let us shift the lens a little, till we catch a different portion of the Abbey.

The variety of the monuments, in country and in creed, as well as in tastes and in politics, is a proof that the successive chiefs [*i.e.* deans] who have held the keys of S. Peter's Abbey have, on the whole, risen to the greatness of their situation, and have endeavoured to embrace, within the wide sympathy of their consecrated precincts, those whom a narrow and sectarian spirit might have excluded, but whom the precepts of their common Master, no less than the instincts of their common humanity, should have bid them welcome (p. 366).

For instance :—

Courayer, the foreign latitudinarian ; Ephraim Chambers, the sceptic

of the humbler, and Sheffield, the sceptic of the higher ranks, were
buried with all respect and honour by the "college of priests," at
Westminster, who thus acknowledged that the bruised reed was not to be
roken, nor the smoking flax quenched.   Even the yet harder problem of
high intellectual gifts, united with moral infirmity or depravity, has on
the whole here met with *the only solution which on earth can be given.*
If Byron was turned from our doors, many a one as questionable as
Byron has been admitted.   Close above the monument of the devoted
Granville Sharpe is the monument of the epicurean St. Evremond.   Close
beneath the tablet of the blameless Wharton lies the licentious Congreve.
The godlike gift of genius was recognised—the baser earthly part was left
to the merciful judgment of its Creator.   So long as Westminster Abbey
maintains its hold on the affections of the English Church and nation,
so long will it remain a standing proof that there is in the truest feelings
of human nature, and in the noblest aspirations of religion, something
deeper and broader than the partial (!) judgments of the day, and the
technical distinctions of sects,—even than the just, *though for the moment
misplaced*, indignation against the errors and sins of our brethren
(pp. 366, 367).

The italics, and the astonishment, are all our own.   With
the Dean there is no astonishment, and no emphasis, but a
smooth, complacent assurance that what he is saying is
grounded in the very essence of things.   ·This is holding the
keys of S. Peter's Abbey with a vengeance ; and, as befits a
good Protestant dean, holding them without any reference to
the keys of S. Peter.   "Bruised reeds ? " but such miserable
men, who have ".died and made no sign," were remorseless
clubs in the hand of the evil one, to bruise, to crush, to shatter
souls.   "Smoking flax?" but they were firebrands of de-.
struction, to widen the conflagration of Gehenna.   "Technical distinctions of sects?" but here is the broad question
of teaching the observance, or the violation, of the Deca-
logue.   "Misplaced indignation?"   We confine our own
within bounds, and will simply remark that the zeal of the
Lord's house is not the zeal of Westminster Abbey.   When
next the Dean reads the public service, let him skip such texts
as Psalm cxxxviii. 21, 22,* and S. Matthew xxi. 13, S. John

---

* "Have I not hated them, O Lord, that hated Thee ; and pined away
because of Thy enemies?   I have hated them with a perfect hatred : and
they are become enemies to me."   On which the comment is : "Not with
a hatred of malice, but a zeal for the observance of God's command-
ments ; which he saw were despised by the wicked, who were to be considered enemies to God."—*Douay Bible.*

"My house shall be called the house of prayer : but you have made it a
den of thieves."

"And His disciples remembered that it was written : The zeal of Thy
house hath eaten me up."

iii. 17 ; or let him expound their modern application, and the authority of their context, by a *distinguo* from the "Essays and Reviews," or his own "Essays on Church and State."

This single passage, which hovers between mischievous sense and splendid nonsense, appears to us to interpret the whole tone of the "Memorials." It justifies, too, the title we have already assigned to them, as an apotheosis of the mere natural and pagan qualities of man, apart from his relations with the Giver of all intellect, the Author of all revelation, the Judge of all words and deeds. But there is a Book, still, by a happy accident, read under the vaults of Westminster Abbey, though its sacred words re-echo from the tablets of Sheffield, Congreve, and others, who scoffed at its precepts while living, and have been scrutinized by them in their death-hour. And the whole tone of that Book, which is the upholding of God's unalterable law against the sophisms of man's pride and sensuality, as well as some of its most special and solemn passages, we commend to the earnest consideration of such as are led away by the paganism of our modern times. Let us here but offer two of them. "Woe to you that call evil good, and good evil; that put darkness for light, and light for darkness ; that put bitter for sweet, and sweet for bitter." Or, coming from the prophet to the Apostle, "If thou . . . restest in the law, and makest thy boast of God, and knowest His will, and approvest the things that are more profitable, being instructed by the law, art confident that thou thyself art a guide of the blind, a light of them that are in darkness, an instructor of the foolish, a teacher of infants, having the form of knowledge and of the truth in the law. . . . Thou that sayest men should not commit adultery,"—hast the amiable weakness to admit such men to their repose among the Saints and just, because they wrote well, though against their Creator, and sang melodiously, luring other souls into the pit.—"Thou that abhorrest idols, committest sacrilege." We would we could express our meaning in terms less emphatic ; but these are our Master's words, not ours.

(II.) It is now time to roll back the wheels of centuries, and find ourselves for a while in the Westminster Abbey of its Catholic past. For the external features that would have there met our view, about the period when Henry VIII. went to his account, we may (as far as he professes to go) trust our author's accuracy. Into their meaning he cannot penetrate, except in vague speculation, and with the interest of an historian and an archæologist. The inner things, which those outward features betoken, are to him *tolerabiles ineptiæ.* These we must supply in our own thoughts ; and reawaken that dead

past, till the curse that has lain on the place these three long
hundred years has vanished, and the royal Benedictine Abbey
lives again.

We ask in vain for the peculiarities of the several chapels which
sprang up round the shrine, or for the general appearance of the worship.
The faint allusions in Abbot Ware's rules reveal, here and there, the
gleam of a lamp burning at this or that altar, or at the tomb of Henry III.,
and of the two Saxon Queens, or in the four corners of the cloisters, or in
the chapter-house. We see at certain times the choir hung with ivy,
rushes, and mint. We detect at night the watchers with lights by their
sides, sleeping in the church. A lofty crucifix met the eyes of those
who entered through the north transept ; another rose above the high
altar ; another, deeply venerated, in the chapel of S. Paul. We catch
indications of altars of S. Thomas of Canterbury, of S. Helena, of the
Holy Trinity, and of the Holy Cross, of which the very memory has
perished. The altar of S. Faith stood in the revestry ; the chapel and
altar of S. Blaize in the south transept. The relics given by Henry III.
and Edward I. have been already mentioned ; the phial of the Sacred
Blood, the girdle of the Virgin, the tooth of S. Athanasius, the head of S.
Benedict. And we have seen their removal from place to place, as the
royal tombs encroached upon them ; how they occupied first the place
of honour eastward of the Confessor's shrine ; then, in order to make
way for Henry V.'s chantry, were transported to the space between the
shrine and the tomb of Henry III., whence they were again dislodged,
or threatened to be dislodged, by the intended tomb of Henry VI.

Then follows an interesting account of Egelric, successively
Bishop of York and of Durham, who was driven out of both
sees, back to his monastery in Peterborough. Afterwards, on
a doubtful plea, let us hope for " suspicion of treasonable ex-
communications at Peterborough," such as might have attached
to S. Thomas, he was, in 1069, arrested by order of the Conqueror, and imprisoned during two years in Westminster. He
there acquired a reputation for sanctity, and on his death, in
1072, was buried in the porch of the chapel of S. Nicholas,
" ordering his fetters to be buried with him, *to increase* " (says
the Dean) " *his chance of a martyr's glory.*" A strange expression, and no more accurate than if we were to say
that the *ungulæ,* the *scorpiones, plumbatæ,* and other instruments of torture, found in the graves of the early martyrs,
contributed to their aureola. They were, indeed, buried with
them by a beautiful appropriateness ; they were laid by the
survivors in the same *loculi* which contained the relics, as
having been instruments in breaking up the mortal tabernacle
for a while; and sending the freed spirit to God. They were
thus laid up for the affectionate veneration of after-times. But

it would be a misuse of terms, if it did not imply a confusion of thought, to speak of them as Dean Stanley speaks of the aforesaid fetters. It is, indeed, remarkable how he stumbles occasionally in his English, even when with the best intentions he is describing Catholic things ; as, for example, in this very passage, where he uses " sanctified " for " saintly." And here, as critics, we must own, once for all, to some disappointment in the literary merits of the book. Dean Stanley's high university reputation, equalled, indeed, by few, had prepared us for more than we here find ; whether we regard accuracy of thought or precision of style. His sophisms are astonishingly transparent, as may be seen by the quotations, few out of the catena of proof, we have inserted in this article. His language has about it a certain poetical character, which vanishes, like the waters of the mirage, when viewed more closely, and leaves us on the waste sands. These " Memorials " are the first of his works on which we have bestowed the degree of attention necessarily implied in a review ; nor have we ever had the advantage of being among the Dean's congregation in the Abbey. But we can imagine the popular style of his preaching from what we read in his pages ; which strike us as precisely what a ready shorthand writer would take down of a specious, and not very profound, address in public. * This is hardly enough to satisfy the requirements of a literature which is to survive ; but the Dean so completely swims with the actual current, that we are not surprised to find his volume already in the third edition.

To finish the quotation :—

> The grave which, seventy years after, was honoured by the vows and prayers of pilgrims, is therefore probably under the southern wall of the Abbey ; and it is an interesting thought, that in the stone coffin recently found near the spot we may perhaps have. seen the skeleton of the sanctified prisoner Egelric.

If Cicero had known English, and had sat down to the task of retranslating into Latin some passage rendered into English from Petavius or De Lugo, he would probably have done it smoothly, and also inaccurately. Not from failure in style, but from being unable to seize the thoughts and principles which had led to the selection of terms. Our traditional Church-Latin seems comparatively rude, because it is terse ; it wastes no time on balanced periods, but goes right at its mark ; says what it has to say, and has done with it. For the *ore rotundo* we might turn from the treatise " De Deo Trino et Uno," to " De Naturâ Deorum," and from " De Peccatis " or " De Legibus " to " De Officiis." But, after all, when the old

Academician had executed his task, we should be compelled
to say to him :—"You have done extremely well, considering
that the special ideas were foreign to you, though the general
language was familiar. We recognise the grace and the
facility; dearly bought, as they are, at the expense of the
teaching which those sentences were meant by their author to
convey. The polish is great: only too great, for you have
rubbed away the sequence of truths."

When Dean Stanley "asks in vain for the peculiarities" of
the several chapels which sprang up round the shrine, or for
the general appearance of the worship, we cannot but contrast this meagreness and blank oblivion with the fulness of
detail and living interest with which he gives us everything
in literature, art, science, statesmanship, and soldiership, from
Elizabeth downwards. "Where your treasure is," not to say
it of him personally, but of the spirit of the age he represents,
" there will your heart be also." The world loves its own.
Meanwhile, we will endeavour to reproduce something of those
peculiarities bygone. Our author shall help us to one principal
feature, as far as he can. He acknowledges it is not very far.

> The Confessor's shrine was, of course, the chief object. But no Chaucer
> has told us of the pilgrimages to it, whether few or many ; no record reveals
> to us *the sentiments which animated* the inmates of the convent, or the con-
> gregations who worshipped within its walls, towards the splendid edifice
> of which it was the centre (p. 454).

Did any one expect that the monastic records, or "Abbot
Ware's rules," would contain the *sentiments* of the worshippers, sorted and classified, docketed, labelled, and furnished with an index? We know of no such compilation,
literary or religious, unless we except the manuscript sermons
of a worthy divine of the Church of England, which he left
behind him, and which were found to contain marginal directions, to remind himself at what point of the discourse he was
to exhibit a moderate and decorous emotion; where he was to
wave his handkerchief, and cry a little. The Dean has "gotten
to his English," as our Scottish neighbours say, when any one
north of the Tweed indulges in a high-sounding strain. We
will not bring him severely to book for what seems to us to
border (as the sublime so often does) on the grotesque. That
the sentiment which he finds written in no cramped, clerkly
hand on parchment faded with age, was widely felt and influential in merry England notwithstanding, he himself attests
at the close of the same passage :—

> The Bohemian travellers in the fifteenth century record the admiration

inspired by the golden sepulchre of "S. Keuhard," or "S. Edward,"
"the ceiling more delicate and elegant than they had seen elsewhere";
"the musical service lovely to hear"; and, above all, the unparalleled
number of relics, "so numerous that two scribes writing for two weeks
could hardly make a catalogue of them." At the eastern end of the shrine
two steps still remain, *deeply hollowed out* by the knees of the successive
pairs of pilgrims who knelt at that spot (p. 455).

This is a record in stone, if ever there was one. We will
supply another peculiarity or two.

Say that it is five or six o'clock in the morning. The grey
light comes in through the high and pointed windows of the
Benedictine choir; tinted, not by a London fog, for the monks
of Tynemouth Priory have not worked their coal extensively.
But it is still a dim, religious light in its passage through
some "storied" pane with saintly effigy. Each outline, on
glass alike and in stone, conveys a message from the unseen
eternal world, to those who have hearts to read it. We are
merely, however, to observe, not to suggest. What is observable is, that at each of from twelve to twenty altars * a monk,
with the close tonsure of S. Benedict, with amice covering his
cowl over the chasuble, stands to offer the Most Holy Sacrifice.
He is served by a lay brother of the community. Let it be
under the abbacy of Langham, 1349-62, a man whose "stern
and frugal administration in Westminster"—he was afterwards
Bishop of Ely, and thence removed to Canterbury—"if it
provoked some enmity from the other monks, won for him
the honour of a second founder of the monastery" (p. 391).
We will suppose his sternness to have consisted in such observance of the Benedictine rule as sustained his community
in something like their primitive fervour. Some Cistercian
guests, entertained with brotherly hospitality in the Abbey,
have also a precedence in saying Mass. You may know them
by their white habit appearing beneath the alb, in contradis-
tinction to the sable garb of S. Benedict's children.† The

---

* Those of the Most Holy Trinity, Holy Cross, Our Lady, S. John the
Baptist, S. John the Evangelist, S. Michael, S. Andrew, S. Paul, S.
Edward, S. Benedict, S. Thomas of Canterbury, S. Edmund, S. Nicolas,
S. Blaize, S. Erasmus, S. Helena and S. Faith.

† Along the whole length of the southern cloister extended the refectory
of the convent, as distinguished from that of the abbot's hall in his own
palace. There were here, as in the other great monasteries, guest chambers.
The rules for the admission of guests show how numerous they were. They
were always to be hospitably received, mostly with a double portion of
what the inmates had, and were to be shown over the monastery as soon
as they arrived. All Benedictines had an absolute claim on their brother
Benedictines, and it was a serious complaint that on one occasion *a crowd*

guests in the Abbey, or the more privileged faithful of the
laity, are hearing Mass at the several altars, as their devotion may lead them.   The body of the faithful attend a low
mass at an altar, perhaps a temporary one, in front of the
choir screen.   Others of the community are employed in the
confessionals.   When these low masses are over—and, from
the number of the celebrants, they will last some time—the
hour will approach for High Mass, at which all the choir
religious will assist.   It will be sung by the abbot or prior,
especially if the day on which we are peering through the
vista of five hundred years be a high day—the Feast of
S. Peter's Chains, or the Translation of S. Edward.   After
the Gospel, a Benedictine priest ascends " the old mediæval
platform,"* turns to the crowded nave, through which the

---

of disorderly Cistercian guests (!) led to the improper exclusion of the
abbots of Boxley and Bayham, and the Precentor of Canterbury.   The
refectory was a magnificent chamber, of which the lower arcades were of
the time of the Confessor, or of the first Norman kings ; the upper story,
which contained the hall itself, of the time of Edward III.   It was approached by two doors, which still remain in the cloister. . . . . The
regulations for the behaviour of the monks at dinner are very precise.
No monk was to speak at all, no guest above a whisper.   Laymen of low
rank were not to dine in the refectory, except on the great exceptional
occasions when, as we have seen, the fisherman—the successor of Edric—
came with his offering of salmon to S. Peter.   The prior sate at the high
table, with a small hand-bell (skylla) beside him, and near him sate the
greater guests.   No one but abbots or priors of the Benedictine order
might take his place, especially no abbot of the rival Cistercians, and no
bishop (p. 425).

* " The successive pulpits of the Abbey, if not equally expressive of the
changes which it has witnessed, *carry on the sound of many voices* (!) heard
with delight and wonder in their time.   No vestige remains of the old
mediæval platform, whence the abbots urged the reluctant court of
Henry III. to the Crusades.   But we have still the fragile structure from
which Cranmer must have preached at the coronation and funeral of his
royal godson ; and the more elaborate carving of that which resounded
with the passionate appeals, at one time of Baxter, Howe, and Owen, at
other times of Haylin, Williams, South, and Barrow.   That from which
was poured forth the oratory of the deans of the eighteenth century, from
Atterbury to Horsley, is now in Trotterscliffe church, near Maidstone.
The marble pulpit in the nave, given in 1859 to commemorate the beginning of the Special Services, through which Westminster led the way in
re-animating the silent naves of so many of our cathedrals, has thus been
the chief vehicle of the varied teaching of those who have been well called
' the people's preachers :' ' Vox quidem dissona, sed una religio ' " (S.
Jerome, Opp. i. p. 82).—*Westminster Abbey*, pp. 580, 581.   This cool
enlistment of S. Jerome into the service of latitudarian wideness of belief,
reminds us irresistibly of the way in which the Thirty-nine Articles try
their best to make that great Latin doctor speak un-Catholic language on
the subject of the "Apocrypha."   "The other books, *as Hierome saith,*" &c.
How far would either the Dean or the Articles stand by S. Jerome's language, or train of thought, in his Epistle to Pope S. Damasus ?

procession will soon pass with hymns and waving banners, and delivers his "postil" on some topic of Catholic faith and practice. Then comes that word of significance and power, which sends a thrill through every heart that has once apprehended its meaning—*Credo*. It rises, as if on angel's wings, floats a moment on the half-note of the Gregorian cadence, then is caught up and borne onward through the distinct, successive utterances in which the Church unfalteringly and changelessly reports, aye enforces, the revelation of her Lord.

Now, when we remember *what* every Catholic believes of the merits and graces of each Mass offered; that every Mass of all those daily sacrifices offered through long centuries on the twenty altars of Catholic Westminster was a "true, proper, and propitiatory sacrifice for the living and the dead," the oblation of the Lamb of God who taketh away the sins of the world: and that living and dead alike have been despoiled of their inheritance in this "unspeakable gift" for three hundred years; then, inded, the marble effigies and high-sounding inscriptions of the desecrated Abbey look on us, not with mere unconscious apathy, but with the malignity of a phantom, and the set *rictus* of a skull. We "seek the living among the dead"; but the dead have buried their dead. We turn from poet to statesman, and from statesman to dramatist, and back to Elizabethan warriors, then to later heroes whose grandsons are alive, and to the Palmerston and Thackeray of our day; and we find great glorification everywhere, reality and comfort nowhere. The Dean comes in to expound the rarities of his museum, and does his best to console us. We feel grateful for his good intentions. There is a something soothing in his tone; he discourses of brotherhood and great England, of the Augustan age of Elizabeth or of Anne, of mighty men of literature, thought, and action, of Mars, Apollo, and Mercury, of large-hearted comprehensiveness, merging of differences, the vanishing of creeds; of the amalgamation of all sorts and conditions of men in his Valhalla. He sets up this great golden image—this *Idolon Tribûs*, as Bacon would say—like that of Babylon the elder, to a multifarious Dutch concert; to the "sound of the trumpet, and of the flute, and of the harp, of the sackbut, and of the psaltery, and of the symphony, and of all kinds of music." He invites us to fall down and adore; " quotes Puffendorf and Grotius, and proves from Vatel exceedingly well "—stay: are we nodding off under these dulcet strains? or does there come indeed a sardonic smile from the marble lips of Canning, from his station in the Abbey, to modify the Dean's persuasives?

> Come, little drummer boy ; here are some books for you ;
> Nice clever books by Tom Paine, the philanthropist !
> Reason, philosophy, fiddledum, diddledum ;
> Peace and fraternity, higgledy, piggledy :
> Higgledy, piggledy, fiddledum, diddledum.*

No ; there is only one formula in which we can adequately put our sense of this portentous fallacy. It is a formula severe, trenchant, uncompromising, because it is Truth and Revelation. The words come over us irresistibly, as we stand within walls once ˙consecrated to the Eternal, which in the Dean's eyes has become transitory—built to rebuke and to subdue the transitory in man, which to our author, by a strange travesty, seems the Eternal :— †

> Love not the world, nor those things which are in the world. If any
> man love the world, the love of the Father is not in him. For all that is
> in the world is the concupiscence of the flesh, and the concupiscence of the
> eyes, and the pride of life : which is not of the Father, but is of the world.
> And the world passeth away, and the concupiscence thereof. But he that
> doeth the will of God abideth for ever.‡

We can hardly persuade ourselves that a man of Dean Stanley's perception, and one whose personal earnestness would surely prevent his becoming an easy-minded optimist, a mere *theologus umbratilis,* sitting under his vine or under his fig-tree, could write as follows. As we read his easy-chair rhetoric, we ask ourselves : Of what country, and of what city, is he writing ? Is it the broad England, is it the vast multitudinous London, as we know them to-day ? Is it England, out of whose ten thousand parishes such proofs of rustic

---

* Poetry of the " Anti-Jacobin," by George Canning.

† 1 S. John ii. 15-17.

‡ " The design of the new screen and altar, erected in 1867, has united the ancient forms of the fifteenth century with the simpler and loftier faith of the nineteenth. And now the contrast of its newness and youth with the venerable mouldering forms around it, is but the contrast of the perpetual growth of the soul of religion with the stationary or decaying memories of its external accompaniments. We sometimes think that it is the Transitory alone which changes—the Eternal which stands still. Rather, the Transitory stands still, fades, and falls to pieces ; the Eternal continues, by changing its form in accordance with the movement of advancing ages " (p. 580). So that what is permanent is therefore unstable, and Proteus outlasts everybody and everything, and the surest way to perpetuate a substance is to evaporate it. By this process of evaporation and so of immortalizing or rather eternizing, the old Westminster Confession of 1643 has developed into the new of 1869, when Socinian and Churchman, under the Dean's inspiration, knelt side by side at that " altar " in the most solemn rite of religion which they knew.

ignorance, such stains of rustic immorality, only await the notice of the first inquirer? Is it London of "the Seven Curses?" Is it London of our *literati* and freethinkers? Truly, the walls of the deanery must be impervious to sounds from without, and the study of its occupant an absorbingly pleasant place. For, hear his complacent voice from their recesses. After a graceful expression of humility, he says :—

Comparing the abbots with the deans and head masters of Westminster, the monks with the prebendaries, and with the scholars of the College — the benefits which have been conferred on the literature and the intelligence of England since the Reformation may fairly be weighed in the balance against the architectural prodigies which adorned the ages before.

No doubt: to build up the soul of man, in intelligence and sanctity, is a nobler work than to rear the stateliest minster; and to substitute the one for the other would be to give him stones for bread. But how have these three centuries, in Westminster or elsewhere in England, built up man's soul?

The English and Scottish Confessions of 1561 and 1643, the English Prayer-Book of 1662, and the American Prayer-Book of 1789—which derive their origin, in part at least, from our Precincts—have, whatever be their defects, a more enduring and lively existence than any result of the mediæval Councils of Westminster (p. 576).

He shall analyse one of these into its constituent elements.

Doubtless in the choir of the Abbey, on July 1, 1643, the Assembly met. There were the 121 divines, including four actual and five future bishops. Some few only of these attended, and "seemed the only Nonconformists for their conformity, whose gowns and canonical habits differed from all the rest." The rest were Presbyterians, with a sprinkling of Independents, "dressed in their black cloaks, scull-caps, and Geneva bands." There were the thirty lay assessors, "to overlook the clergy . . . just as when the good woman puts a cat into the milkhouse to kill a mouse, she sends her maid after the cat—lest the cat should eat up the cream." (*Selden's Table-Talk.*) So august an assembly had not been in the Abbey since the Conference which ushered in the re-establishment of the Protestant Church under Elizabeth (p. 507).

Without difficulty, one may abstain from coveting these neighbour's goods. We are not cats after that cream. But will the Dean summarize for us, in a new edition, merely the heads (not to ask too much) of the canons enacted in the mediæval Councils of Westminster?

We must give ourselves another dip or two into his pages
by way of further illustration :—

Goldsmith found "in Westminster Abbey several new monuments
erected to the memory of several great men. . . . Alas! alas! cried I;
such monuments as these confer honour not on the great men, but on little
Roubiliac" (p. 277). "Long Sir Thomas Robinson . . . was a man of the
world, or rather of the town, and a great pest to persons of high rank, or
in office. . . . His epitaph commemorates his successful career in Barbadoes,
and 'the accomplished woman, agreeable companion, and sincere friend'
he found in his wife" (p. 276). Sir John Fleming erected a monument
"to the memory of his uncle and his best of friends" (p. 277).

So we might go on, ranging up and down, and encounter at
every turn the absence of a "theology," and the presence of
a deism. All is cold, as to any heavenly ray, even as the marble
that gives us statue and epitaph. There is not even the
Egyptian globe and wings, to testify to a belief in such immortality as was dwelt upon in Carnac and Thebes; there is not
even Memnon, catching warmth on his rigid lips as he turns
to the rising sun; nor Horus presiding over judgment; nor
the soul weighed in the balance; nor the ferry over the dark
river; nor so much as the dog-faced Anubis holding the key
of paradise. All is airy and transitory; Horatian, Pompeian,
Epicurean. There is "Rutili pus atque venenum" in the
satiric writer; there is "non præter solitùm levis" in the
licentious poet and dramatist; "parcus deorum cultor et in-
frequens" in the wit and the infidel; and

> Exegi monumentum ære perennius
> Regalique sitù pyramidum altius,

in the warrior, bearded like a pard, seeking the bubble reputation at the cannon's mouth, who rushes on, in the uniform of
the Royal Buffs, or of a colonel of sepoys; while Fame, or the
Muse of British History, is dropping her trumpet to receive his
soul.

Alas! alas! we may exclaim with Goldsmith, that such
great men as these, and little Roubiliac, should divide our
desecrated shrine between them. We are not fond of saying
strong things. But, in all plainness of speech, we hardly know
a more exact fulfilment of the prophecy of Daniel than Westminster Abbey. It is a representative church, as the Dean has
truly said or implied. What it represents is, emphatically, the
abomination that maketh desolate. The desolation, the abomination, is this intrusion of paganisms into what was once
the Holy of holies. The desolation yet more harrowing, the

abomination yet more desolating, is the substitution of communion table for altar, of " service " for the Holy Sacrifice, of a
distribution of bread and wine—we pause. There are parallels
and contrasts that are best left for the heart to mourn and
pray over, not for the lips to utter or to bewail. Dean Stanley
himself shall be our chronicler and interpreter. We will first
give a note of his, then the text to which it is appended. The
note runs thus : we leave it to the meditations of some of our
high Anglican friends.

The communion table in Westminster Abbey is the only one in England which has any authoritative claim to the popular name of " Altar."
The word is nowhere so applied in the Liturgy or Articles. But it is used
of the table of Westminster Abbey in the Coronation Service issued by
order of the Privy Council at the beginning of each reign. It is there preserved with other antique customs which have disappeared everywhere else.
In no other place, and on no other occasion, could the word be applied so
consistently with the tenor of the Reformed Liturgy. If an altar be a
place of sacrifice, and if (as is well known) the only sacrifices acknowledged in the English Prayer-book are those of praise and thanksgiving,
and still more emphatically of human hearts and lives—then there is a
certain fitness in this one application of the name of altar. For here it
signifies the place and time in which are offered up the sacrifice of the
prayers and thanksgivings of the whole English nation, and the sacrifice
of the highest life in this church and realm, to the good of man and the
honour of God (pp. 578, 579).

A graceful text for the next time the Dean preaches before
the Court. What strikes us, before we pass on, is a similarity in the tone, and the very language, of this and other
passages in the book, to the writings of an older friend of ours,
late Canon and Archdeacon of Westminster, now reposing,
not in marble, but in lawn. We encountered Dr. Wordsworth
in single combat six long years ago : and if we despoiled him
then of some rags and tags of " splendid purple," which looked
fair enough, as Horace says, *at a distance*, the shreds have
fallen on the shoulders of Dean Stanley; who has better rai-
ment of his own, if he would only wear it. But to his text.

The history of the " Altar " of Westminster Abbey is almost the history
of the English Church. The monuments and chapels have remained comparatively unchanged, except by the natural decay of time. The Holy
Table and its accompaniments alone have kept pace with the requirements of each succeeding period. The simpler feeling of the early Middle
Ages was represented in its original position, when it stood, as in most
churches of that time, at the eastern extremity. In the changes of the
thirteenth century, which so deeply affected the whole framework of
Christian doctrine——

We hardly know when we have read so few words containing so marvellous a hazarding of utter mis-statement. With
a flourish of his pen the Dean commits himself to a grave
assertion, which, without asking much, we may call on him to
substantiate or to retract. It would demand an article in
detail from us, which shall be forthcoming, whenever so much
as a lengthened note from him shall expound his reasons for
what he here asserts without rhyme or reason. What he
means, without proving, is plain. Hyperdulia to our Lady
and the cultus of the Saints received at that period, according
to him, some unexplained development, unknown to previous
ages. In the process of these " changes,"

> The new veneration for the local saint and for the Virgin Mother, whilst
> it produced the Lady Chapel and the Confessor's Shrine, thrust forward
> the High Altar to its present place in front of S. Edward's Chapel.

Why, bless the Dean ! Has he never heard of Sancta Maria
ad Nives, called *Major* from the days of Pope Liberius, for the
reason that other churches under the invocation of our Lady
existed already, from *S. Maria trans Tiberim* downwards ?
Did he never hear of the shrines of the martyrs in the Roman
catacombs—" local Saints," every one of them—or of the body,
aye, and *translation* of the body, of S. Peter in and to the
Vatican Hill ? What is the meaning of S. Laurence beyond
the Walls, S. Agnes, S. Clement, and a host of others ? To
come from the Eternal City homewards, why does S. Alban's
supplant old Verulam, but that the spot where our proto-martyr
shed his blood, and where his relics repose, became the point
of attraction away from the heathen city, and so grew into his
shrine ? The instances of this principle crowd upon us, and
each precludes our noticing the others. The veriest tyro in
history would tell how long the majority of them were in existence before the thirteenth century. And a neophyte in theology would answer, that the Sacrifice consummated on the
high altar was not intrinsically *higher,* though surrounded with
more solemnity, than that at our Lady's altar, or at S. Edward's
shrine. It was in every case the same adorable Mass, though
" *localized,*" if you like so to speak, according to local circumstances. There was, therefore, no irreverence, even had the
thirteenth century been the first (which it was not, by many)
to " thrust," as the Dean says, the high altar into a new position, to make room for a local Saint. He might as well quarrel
with the Church for displacing a feast which is *simplex* or
semiduplex, to make way for a fresh canonization of a higher
class. But we must follow him in his passage from the altar
to the communion table.

The foreign art of the period left its trace in the richly-painted frontal, the only remnant of the gorgeous mediæval altar. When, in the fifteenth century, reflecting the increasing divisions and narrowing tendencies of Christendom,—

The subject of a second chapter, let us hope, in his future *Apologia,*

Walls of partitions sprung up everywhere across the churches of the West, the screen was erected which parted asunder the altar from the whole eastern portion of the Abbey. At the Reformation, and during the Commonwealth, the wooden movable table, which was brought down into the body of the Church, reproduced, though by a probably undesigned conformity, the primitive custom both of East and West.

Was ever anything more absurdly said ? Even in our haste to conclude this article, we pause a moment.

> Quamquam festinas, non est mora longa, licebit
> Injecto ter pulvere curras.

Three pinches of dust, then, if no more, to cast upon these outlandish assertions. The Genevan and Puritan custom of setting the table lengthways in the middle of the chancel area, was not a reproduction, even undesigned, of primitive practice, but a direct antagonism to it :—for (1), the primitive system did, the Genevan system did not, recognise the Sacrifice of the altar, and a transelementated, objective, and therefore adorable Presence. (2.) The person who ministered at the Genevan table would have shrunk with horror, and would forthwith have " protested," if you had told him he was a sacrificing priest : the celebrant at a primitive altar would have been equally horrified (the sanity of the speaker being supposed) to be told that he was not. (3.) The posture of those who assisted at each respective act testified to the diversity of their beliefs : they who surrounded the primitive altar *stood up*, after the manner of the *orantes* of their day, especially on the Lord's day, and festivals ; the communicants at the Genevan table *sat down*, as is the fashion of men who are partaking of a supper.

So much dust for our Archytas : we will, moreover, give him a spadeful at once by saying, that even a candid and learned man, starting with an unconscious prejudice, is like a bowl with a concealed bias—the further and the more forcibly he trundles, the wider he goes of the mark.

Even as we write, our eyes fall upon the report of Mr. Voysey's trial, and the use he is enabled to make of Dean Stanley's name. We should greatly desire to see either a

categorical refutation of his words and inferences, or at least such an explanation as would amount to it. It may be hoping against hope. He quotes, with approval, Tillotson's words:—
"The account given of Athanasius's Creed appears to me nowise satisfactory. I wish we were well rid of it." Elsewhere the Dean says:—"The elaborate anathemas which were once appended to the Nicene Creed, even the fierce denunciations which are still the very bone and marrow of the Athanasian Creed, are, indeed, interesting only as the dreary records of a sulphurous flame, which has long ceased to burn in the better heart of Christendom."—*Essays on Church and State*, p. 10. Mr. Voysey then quotes four other passages from Dr. Stanley to the same effect; the two last of them being:—"It is a Creed without authority—constantly and necessarily misunderstood—and involving the Church which continues to enforce it in endless anomalies and contradictions." Again: "It is unquestionable, therefore, that, with all the advantages which this Creed may possess, it has been a burden and a scandal far beyond any use which even its most devoted admirers may claim for it."

Certainly, if his own sense of the following words were true, Dean Stanley might be said to have amply fulfilled the requirements of the office he holds. He gives in a note, p. 577, one clause of a "Prayer at the Installation of a Dean or a Canon," which runs: "That those things which he hath promised, and which his duty requires, he may faithfully perform, to the praise and glory of the Name of God, and the *enlargement* of His Church." On which he comments:—"What is yet in store for the Abbey, none can say. Much, assuredly, remains to be done to place it on a level with the increasing demands of the human mind, with the changing wants of the English people, with the never-ending 'enlargement of the Church,' for which every member of the Chapter is on his installation pledged to labour."

What remains to be done? we ask ourselves. Enlargement might be thought to have reached its limits in the communion, to which we have already referred, at those same altar rails. Shall it be now a hymn to Voltaire, sung by a pilgrim band of American Know-nothings around the tomb of his friend Congreve? or Sir Jamsetjee Jejeebhoy, or Baboo Keshub Chunder Sen, heading a deputation of intelligent Brahmins to venerate in the marble bust of Warren Hastings an avatar of Siva the Destroyer?* Christianity goes to-morrow; deism

---

* Baboo Keshub Chunder Sen, as our readers may remember, preached on theism in Mr. Martineau's chapel in Little Portland-street, on the 11th

is too strict and bigoted for the day after:—*Ça ira!* down
with the altar! down with the screen! No pulpit! Pulpits
imply dogma. Nothing finally in the Abbey but the Pantheon
inscription: "*Aux grands hommes la Patrie reconnaissante!*"
This will come, on Dean Stanley's principles, when the requirements of the age have, in the prophet's words, enlarged
themselves like hell, and are like death, and are never satisfied.

On the whole, there are passages in this book which are
specious, and fall harmoniously on the ear. But in the light
of faith they signify absolutely nothing, or worse: "mere
sound," though not "fury." Certainly not sense, unless we
are content to return to Paganism in one of the earliest forms
of its developments—an idealized hero-worship. If, indeed, we
are prepared to mean: Truth is that which each man troweth,
and Christianity is what each one with a Christian name may
opine, or say, so that it be not atheistic, immoral, or self-evidently
absurd; why, then, long live the Dean's idealities. Long live
Professor Huxley's recent distinction between "religion"
and "theology." "Vox quidem dissona," says S. Jerome
travestied, "sed una religio." Then does Poet's Corner
indeed "leap into new life," and more than one writer and
statesman, among those whom old-world notions had considered by no means satisfactory characters, comes forward,
somewhat to his own astonisment, to deliver in his quota of
instruction, and illustrate his country's faith :—

Miraturque novos frondes, et non sua poma.

---

of last April. He is, as we mentioned in two earlier numbers, the leader
of the Brahmo Samaj, a society of Hindoo reformers who have renounced
idol-worship without embracing Christianity. So far, it must be acknowledged, his visit to the bust of Warren Hastings would be out of place,
though he would probably fraternize heartily with us on the irreligious
character of the Abbey monuments. One passage, at least, of his discourse, may be not inappropriately referred to. He spoke of "thousands
of nominal theists, who boasted of having given up idolatry, but beneath
their boasted theological scholarship there lurked unbelief in its milder
but not less insidious forms."

A limit to this enlargement, however, has really been found, if the
same journal is accurate in reporting a conference held in the Social Science
Rooms on the 6th inst. (Dec.) "The object of the Church Reform Union
. . . . as stated by . . . . the Dean of Westminster, and others, in this
matter of preaching, is to open the pulpits of the National Church not
only to Protestant Dissenters, but to men like the Archbishop Lycurgus,
Father Hyacinthe, and others. The Dean said, *some regulations would be
necessary to prevent such a scandal as a Mormon preaching in St. Paul's
Cathedral, for example.*" Poor Brigham Young! It strikes us as rather
hard. Would they have excluded Archbishop Whately, who was inclined to allow polygamy among converts from heathenism? *Quis tulerit
Gracchos de seditione querentes ?*

Thus, of Congreve :

> His burial in the Abbey was justified by the fame which attracted the visit of Voltaire to him, as to the chief representative of English literature ; which won from Dryden the praise of being next to Shakespeare ; from Steele the homage of "Great sir, great author," whose "awful name was known" by barbarians ; and from Pope, the dedication of the Iliad, and the title of "*Ultimus Romanorum*" (pp. 312, 313).

This is hardly religion, and would not satisfy even Professor Huxley. We confess to have looked twice at the passage before we accepted it as coming from one so personally respectable as Dean Stanley. A visit paid to a licentious poet from the chief, perhaps, of all the haters of our Lord who ever ran a course of impiety on earth, and whose war-cry against the Christianity on which he gnashed his teeth, as one tormented before his time, we will not repeat—this seems a strange reason, from a Very Reverend author, why the said poet should be interred within a Christian shrine. After such a passage, it is tame to remark on his mode of treatment when the stage and its votaries are in question. Of Anne Oldfield, to whom a monument had been refused, he says (p. 333) : "Her extraordinary grace of manner drew a veil over her many failings;" and proceeds to quote the "Tatler" on the subject, finishing with Pope's well-known lines about her being buried in Brussels lace, after having been rouged on her death-bed. We confess to a feeling that these indications are not of the pleasantest.

So much for "religion" and the religious ἦθος. As to more special "theology" (to return to the Huxleian distinction) we are not, of course, surprised to find Dean Stanley among the broadest. To give illustrations of what we mean, further than those we have given, would be almost to quote *passim* from his book : it would at least be summarizing its whole intention. On a minor point, however, we will reproduce a passage, cited from Hackett, regarding a conference held in Westminster College Hall, in the reign of James I. The interlocutors were, the Lord Keeper (Dean Williams) and "a French abbot, 'but a gentleman that held his abbacy in a lay capacity.'" We may imagine the man, without much effort. He is the spiritual ancestor of those French abbés, laymen many of them, and some of them who had much better have remained so, of whom the type is the Abbé de Rancé, before —not after—his conversion. We notice this, because not to attend to the distinction would lead to a false estimate of such a move towards "the reunion of Christendom." It might be supposed that "the Abbot" was some learned and venerable superior of a community, Dom Placidus say, of Solesme or S. Omer, who after deep research had been led to recognise in the Lord Keeper a true successor to the departed Feckenham, last Abbot of Westminster. Whereas, he might have been a polite Frenchman, with spade-beard and doublet, who had never once shaken his love-locks over the essential difference between "the Churches."

In it [the gallery] we must conceive the conversation, as carried on between the Lord Keeper and "his brother abbot," on the comparison, suggested by what the Frenchman had seen, between the Church of England and the continental Churches, both Roman Catholic and Protestant. Let them part with the concluding remark of the Lord Keeper :— "I use to say it often, that there ought to be no secret antipathies in divinity or in Churches *for which no reason can be given*." [We pass by the truism.] "But let every house sweep the dust from their own door. We have done our endeavour, God be praised, in England, to model a churchway which is not afraid to be searched into by the sharpest critics for purity and antiquity. But, as Pacatus said in his panegyric in another case, *Parum est quando cœperit, terminum non habebit.* Yet I am confident it began when Christ taught upon earth, and I hope it shall last till He comes again." "I will put my attestation thus far to your confidence," said the Abbot, "that I think you are not far from the kingdom of Heaven." So, with mutual smiles and embraces, they parted (p. 495).

Such visions of unreality are shared by Dean Stanley. In a passage so inflated and rhetorical, that in another man we should think he was talking loud and "tall," to inspire himself with confidence in what he was saying, he winds up his "Memorials" in the following strain. With the first of his sentences, of course, we cordially agree; from the second, in the sense of the author, we must dissent; the third we can partly adopt, *exceptis excipiendis;* and the rest appears to us describable only by a word in Aristophanes, well known to the Dean—τὸ φλαττοθραττοφλαττοθραττοφλαττοθράττ—a very Marathonian flourish of trumpets :—

Not surely in vain did the architects of successive generations raise this consecrated edifice in its vast and delicate proportions, more keenly appreciated in this our day than in any other since it first was built ; designed, if ever were any forms on earth, to lift the soul heavenward to things unseen. Not surely in vain has our English language grown to meet the highest ends of devotion with a force which the rude native dialect and barbaric Latin of the Confessor's age could never attain. Not surely for idle waste has a whole world of sacred music been created, which no ear of Norman or Plantagenet ever heard, nor skill of Saxon harper or

Celtic minstrel ever conceived. Not surely for nothing has *the knowledge of the will of God almost steadily increased* (!) century by century, through the better understanding of the Bible, of history, and of nature. Not in vain, surely, has the heart of man kept its freshness whilst the world is waxing old, and the most restless and inquiring intellects clung to the belief that "the everlasting arms are still beneath us," and that "prayer is the potent inner supplement of noble outward life." Here, if anywhere, the Christian worship of England may labour to meet both the strength and weakness of succeeding ages, to *inspire new meaning into ancient forms* [as *e. g.* in the late communion of Socinians with Churchmen within these consecrated walls], and embrace within itself each rising aspiration after all greatness, human and divine (p. 523).

He is writing, not of England, but of Dreamland. The actual men are *non Angeli, sed Angli,* spite of whatsoever theories would spiritualize or heroize them. And, until vague declamation by cathedral authorities gives place to fixed religious principles, until professors learn that theology and religion occupy the same sphere, until the masses of this great Babylon, high and low, who are living without God in the world, discover that more is needed to enlighten and save their souls than a little Sunday pastime around the pulpit of a "special service," so long, *surely in vain,* has this chief among our desecrated shrines been surrendered to a system from whose stammering, incoherent utterances men of thought are daily falling into sheer and mere infidelity.

Art. IV.—CHAMPAGNY'S CÆSARS OF THE THIRD CENTURY.

Etudes sur l'Empire Romain. Les Césars du Troisième Siècle. Par le Comte de Champagny, de l'Académie Française. Paris. Ambroise Bray. 1870. 3 vols.

IN the three volumes before us M. de Champagny completes à great work, undertaken many years ago; and to the earlier part of which we have already called the attention of our readers.* It is to any man no small blessing to have been led to select as his own some undertaking the achievement

---

* See number for April, 1866.

of which is, in itself, important, and for which he is adapted by his position, talents, and attainments. It is a greater blessing still when, after having selected it with judgment, he has not been diverted from it either by human frailty or mutability, or by the distractions and accidents with which in every age the life of man is beset. His happiness is greater still, if the great task, wisely undertaken and perseveringly pursued, is not broken off unfinished by the shortness of human life. This accumulation of happiness, denied to so many great thinkers in every age, has been conceded to few of those, who, in our own, have devoted themselves to a subject of which a thoughtful mind can hardly become wearied, although its extent may alarm any ordinary diligence,—the history of the Eternal City, which shines with a double glory, as the centre and metropolis of all that is great, first in the natural order, and subsequently in the kingdom of God Himself upon earth.

The great work in which the History of the Rise of Rome was illustrated by the genius and learning of Niebuhr, was cut short by his death before he had begun the narrative of the Second Punic War. Arnold left the history of that war nearly ended. Gibbon was spared to finish a gigantic work. His record of its commencement and its completion contrasts, as might be expected, so sadly with the language of M. de Champagny that it may be worth while to compare the two. "It was at Rome, on the 15th of October, 1764, as I sat musing amidst the ruins of the Capitol, while the barefooted friars were singing vespers in the Temple of Jupiter, that the idea of writing the Decline and Fall of the city first entered into my mind." "It was on the day, or rather night, of the 27th of June, 1787, between the hours of eleven and twelve, that I wrote the last lines of the last page, in a summer-house in my garden. After laying down my pen, I took several turns in a *berceau*, or covered walk, of acacias, which commands a prospect of the country, the lake, and the mountains. The air was temperate, the sky was serene, the silver orb of the moon was reflected from the waters, and all nature was silent. I will not dissemble the first emotions of joy on the recovery of my freedom, and, perhaps, the establishment of my fame. But my pride was soon humbled, and a sober melancholy was spread over my mind, by the idea that I had taken an everlasting leave of an old and agreeable companion, and that, whatsoever might be the future fate of my history, the life of the historian must be short and precarious. * * * The rational pride of an author may be offended rather than flattered by vague indiscriminate praise, but he cannot, he should not be indifferent to the fair testimonies of private and public esteem. Even his moral sympathy may be gratified by the idea, that now, in the present hour, he is imparting some degree of amusement or knowledge to his friends in a distant land, and that one day his mind will be familiar to the grand-children of those who are yet unborn." *

To the self-styled philosopher—" Myself "—" my posthumous fame," is all in all; the highest thought to which he soars is that of the amusement of friends in a distant land. Now turn to M. de Champagny.

Thirty years ago he wrote—

Such an undertaking cannot be the work of a few days. As the Apostle teaches us, " We know not what shall be on the morrow," and we ought to say, " If the Lord will, and if we live we will do this or that."—(*Cæsars*, vol. i. xxii.)

He now ends—

Here I bring to a conclusion, not without emotion, these labours [*Etudes*] upon the Roman Empire, which have occupied more than forty years of my life, and which, by God's help, have supported and consoled me through the trials of private life, and through the revolutions of our national life, the former very bitter, the last, whatever else they may have been, full of suffering. * * * *

In following the course of history from Julius Cæsar to Constantine, I have travelled through twelve generations of men, before whose eyes was carried out the greatest revolution, intellectual, moral, and social, which the history of the world exhibits ; a revolution which has no equal in the past, and which, I fear not to pronounce, will have none in the future—the revolution which made the world Christian. Whence did it come, and how was it brought about ?

Whence did it come ? I have several times touched this question, and it has been discussed by others, with much more of completeness and eloquence than I could pretend to. On one side are records, ancient, clear, simple, positive, which, until the last few centuries, have been understood literally by all mankind, and which, literally understood, give, in a single word, the full and complete solution of this revolution—the intervention of God in the course of this world. On the other side, there are theories, ingenious no doubt, profound we are assured, supported by a mighty armament of learning, learning accumulated from every quarter, and still more by a mighty power of imagination, by a self-confident criticism which throws scorn upon ordinary men, and rather lays down the law to them than aims at convincing them. These theories, while in other respects divergent and contradictory, agree only in accounting for this great event by causes of which it is not always easy to give any account. Between this record, so simply historical and

---

* Gibbon, Miscellaneous Works, vol. i. pp. 129 and 170.

literal, on the one side, and these theories so unintelligible and conflicting on the other, each man can judge for himself; not to say that the controversy does not exactly form part of my subject.

But as to the second question, how was this revolution brought about? That it has been the whole object of my labours to explain.

After all, was there any need of so much labour? Is there not one fact, as plain as the day, and of which nothing can get rid—one fact notorious even to those whose knowledge of history is the most elementary? At the death of Augustus there was not so much as one Christian in the world; at the death of Constantine, three hundred and twenty-three years later, more than half the world was Christian.

And was this change brought about by material force, by the authority of princes, or by the insurrection of peoples against their princes? There may no doubt be a question whether or not this or that emperor was a persecutor, and to what point the persecution was carried; whether it was made chiefly by the authorities or chiefly by the multitude; whether it was chiefly political or chiefly popular. It is possible, with Dodwell, to reduce the number of martyrs to the lowest possible estimate, or with others to count them by millions. There are questions of detail, upon which discussion is possible; and legends which may, rightly or wrongly, be considered apocryphal. But what is certain is this—that all through these three centuries, force, whenever and in whatever degree it was employed, was always employed against and never in support of Christianity. Force, whether that of the emperor or of the people, the executioner or the rioter, all along acted a part which, if not constant, was at least habitual. The mild Marcus Aurelius himself speaks of the Christians as a set of people accustomed to go to death, from which it follows that it was an habitual practice to lead them to it. The one thing certain is that persecution, more or less violent, now and then suspended, but soon renewed, was the legal condition of the Roman Empire. Christianity was all along a thing proscribed, to which some emperors, more humane than the rest, now and then allowed a short respite; but always a thing proscribed, against which the proscription was never long in resuming its course.

And what force was it that resisted the force thus exerted against Christianity? Where is there any mention of an insurrection, a league, or a riot among the Christians? Here was no league of Smalkalde, no conspiracy of Amboise, no "oath of the tennis-court" (*serment du jeu de paume, June* 20, 1789), no one of the ordinary circumstances of a revolution. Those who were proscribed concealed themselves, or fled; those who were arrested suffered death without resistance. That is all that can be said. And this is repeated thousands of times (no one, not Dodwell himself, denies that), and each succeeding age saw it repeated more frequently. Every time that force resolved to destroy, it found a greater number to be destroyed, and those whom it destroyed were more numerous. Insomuch that, at last, this war, in which the one party only inflicted death and never suffered it, while the other only suffered and never inflicted it, ended in the triumph of that party which died over that which slew. The sword fell shivered against breasts which offered themselves to it.

And this event stands by itself in the history of the world. This universal resignation, this courage so heroically so constantly passive, and still more this triumph won only by dying, has no single parallel in history. People try to persuade themselves that the sword cannot triumph over ideas. For the honour of the human race one would gladly have it so, but it is a delusion. Ideas, doctrines, and religions have been conquered by the sword. Budhism was resisted by force, and was driven out of India, the land of its birth. The religion of Zoroaster was extirpated in Persia by the sword of the Mahommedans. Druidism was swept away out of the Gauls and Britain ; nor did it find any place of refuge elsewhere.

Sometimes, no doubt, ideas have overcome force, but only when they have employed force in their turn ; when, being persecuted by the sword, they have, rightly or wrongly, taken up the sword to resist. Mahommedanism was victorious because it took up the sword. Protestantism has reigned in Europe because it has met fire and sword with fire and sword. Both one and the other may have had its missioners, but neither would ever have triumphed, if it had not also had its soldiers. No sect, no religion has ever encountered the sword with the absolute passiveness which was the characteristic of the primitive Christians, or if there has been any one which ever practised it, that one has been crushed. Christianity alone, so far as I can learn, has ever submitted itself in this manner ; Christianity alone, most unquestionably, has ever gained such a victory by so submitting itself.

Is it not clear that it was only by a Divine power that this triumph over all human power could have been won? The question as to the origin of Christianity is solved by the other question of the means by which it accomplished its victory. It was victorious here below, only because it had its origin from above.

This conclusion is so evident, and the facts on which it rests so incontestable, that if I had only to prove it I need not have undergone so much labour, nor traced so many historical facts, nor raised so many questions. But my object in writing was not merely to give a proof of Christianity but to kindle the love of it.

Consider well this point. Our age honours with the name of ideas, many interests and many passions ; and with the name of questions of principle, many mere questions of fact. Most of the objects on which it is occupied are things merely transitory—human institutions not Divine laws, —facts which pass away not truths which abide. But the great, the eternal question, turns upon higher truths. Slighted, treated as if they were forgotten, systematically thrown into the shade, and only spoken of in vague terms—all this they may be. But they come back, they force themselves on men's notice. Then men are compelled to resort to an utter, brutal, absolute denial of God, of truth, of themselves, and they will more and more be compelled to do so.

More and more decidedly will two things confront each other, leaving in obscurity all that lies between them. On one side atheism the most cynical and radical ; on the other, Christianity the most strictly practical. To make a decision and take part with one or the other will be a matter of necessity, no middle position will any longer be tenable.

While then this, the great struggle of our age is in progress, how can any man, however powerless or obscure, be content not to bring his humble aid ? To speak more strictly, while the great labour of all ages for the building up of truth in the heart of man is in progress, woe to him who, having the truth in his heart, does not labour in her cause, and contribute his little grain of sand to that monument built up of human thought of which the builder is God. In proportion to the limited degree of power vouchsafed to my intellect, and to the goodwill which I have been able (however wavering) to maintain in my heart, I have striven to contribute to this labour. It has almost occupied my life, and I regret that it has not occupied it more entirely. In the midst of the discouragements of human life mental labour is a great consolation and a great support ; but even mental labour itself becomes weary, distasteful, burdensome to the soul, except when it is undertaken in the cause of good, of truth, of God.—(Vol. iii. pp. 485 *et seq.*)

It was to exhibit the contrast of our author's tone with that of Gibbon that we began our notice of his work by this long quotation from its conclusion. But we do it not without misgivings, for, taken alone, it would give an unjust as well as inadequate notion of that work. It might not unreasonably lead a reader to expect merely a history or estimate of the progress of Christianity in the empire. The fact, however, is so much the opposite, that he may read whole volumes without having the idea directly suggested to him. Confident of the divine origin of Christianity, M. de Champagny has never been tempted to doubt that any picture of the age in which it was first given to mankind, and of those during which it was gradually working its way from obscurity to universal dominion, will best illustrate it, in proportion as the account itself is most true and lifelike. And hence, although it may, and no doubt was, from first to last, the cherished motive of his inmost heart to illustrate the struggles and the triumph of the Church, yet the means by which he has sought that object are none others than unusual fidelity and life in his picture of the history and manners of the first three centuries. His desire has evidently been that expressed by the illustrious Niebuhr. " Would that I could write history so vividly, that I could so discriminate what is fluctuating and uncertain, and so develop what is confused and intricate, that every one, as soon as he heard the name of a Greek of the age of Thucydides or Polybius, or of a Roman of the days of Cato or Tacitus, might be able to form a clear and adequate idea of what he was." Nothing could more strikingly illustrate the contrast between history as it is in our own day and as it was a century ago, than that men should now propose to themselves such an object. That it should be fully attained is, no doubt, impossible ; but M. de Champagny has at least aimed at the highest excellence, and if he has in any degree fallen short of it, he has more nearly succeeded than any writer known to us.

It might, no doubt, be suspected that a man who wrote the history of the heathen empire, with the Church ever nearest to his heart, would be under a strong temptation to sacrifice truth to his own prejudices. To this it would be an easy and true reply, that every man who has been brought into any relations with Christianity must of necessity either love or hate it ; and that hatred is even more inconsistent than love with historical impartiality. In truth, however, there is much more to be said. The great difficulty of historians, in every age, is to give a picture, in any degree expressive and true, of the people and the times of which they write, not a mere record of their disasters and wars, and of the fortunes and disputes, triumphs and conquests, of their emperors and kings. Oh how precious would have been the information which the least imaginative of the ancient writers could have given us, if only he had been able to foresee that the whole fabric of society as he saw it was about to be swept away, and that times would come when the heirs of a new civilization, unlike that of his own day as well as distinct from it, would, above all things, prize lively pictures of the daily habits of the men of the world that has passed away ; and would labour assiduously to piece together, at the best very imperfectly, out of chance fragments collected here and there, from poems, histories, orations, letters, and philosophical treatises, a sort of Mosaic, which, after all, would by no means equal the picture that might have been given in a few pages by any writer under the Roman Empire, who possessed, even in the most moderate degree, that talent for observation and word-painting by which many writers of our own times have been distinguished. Unfortunately one of the main difficulties of the historian of the Roman Empire, is not merely the inferior quality but the absolute dearth of materials. The periods for which we have any contemporary writer, or even one who, though not contemporary, commands belief by his accuracy and truthfulness, are quite the exception. Every now and then there is a period upon which exceptional light is thrown by some happy accident, like that which enables us to read the whole history of the last agony of the Republic, in the letters, speeches, and philosophical works of Cicero. But these are few and far between ; and there are cases in which we are able to infer that a particular period must have been marked by important changes, rather from the results which they produced than from any positive record of them. There are parts even of the reign of Augustus himself about which very little is

known. Above all, even when we know most of the historical
events of any period, we have at best very poor and disjointed
scraps of information about the life and manners of the mass
of the people. And the little we have of this sort is chiefly
in the Christian writings. The Acts of the Apostles give
us a much better idea than any other book how people lived
in the Greek provinces of the Empire under Nero—how the
population was mixed of Jews and Greeks—how many of the
Greeks, especially the more religious of both sexes, had already
been attracted by the pure theism of the Jews—how some
had actually submitted to circumcision, and had become
proselytes, while many more devoutly worshipped the One God
without feeling themselves bound (as it is plain they were not)
to put on the yoke of the law of Moses. Then, again, as to
the relations of the populace, and of the municipal magistrates,
to the Roman governors; the practical use of the privileges of
the Roman citizen; the appeal from the sentence of a local
judge to the Roman people, at that time represented by
Cæsar—what heathen writer of the same age gives us, in so
small a compass, so much real and lifelike historical information? The same is true of later periods. The letters of S.
Cyprian, for instance, unveil to us much of the under working
of society in Roman Africa at a period in many respects of
great interest, and about which we are most scantily supplied
with any professed history. He became Bishop of Carthage
A.D. 248 (the fourth year of the Emperor Philip), and was
martyred A.D. 258 (the fifth year of Valerian). Yet Gibbon
writes the history of those times without so much as alluding
either to Cyprian himself or to the persecutions, from one of
which he hid himself, continuing the administration of the
Church in letters which have been preserved to us, while in
another he received the crown of martyrdom. In a later
volume, no doubt, he relates, in his own scornful tone, the
history of S. Cyprian, in his well-known chapter on "the
conduct of the Roman Government towards the Christians
from the reign of Nero to that of Constantine," but only
for the purpose of proving how slight, even in the times of
most violent persecution, was the danger of the Christians;
and how great the moderation and forbearance of the
persecutors. It can hardly be doubted that if any collection of
letters had been preserved, written by and to the leader in
any one school of heathen philosophy at that period, Gibbon
would have seen that it gave him an opportunity of throwing
upon the scanty remains of its history an unexpected gleam
of real light. But Cyprian he could not bring himself to for-
give for being a Christian, a bishop, a saint, and a martyr,

and his name was therefore passed over in the history.   And
the chapters in which mention is made of Church affairs
are so little connected with the rest of his work, that a well-
meaning editor, some forty years back (Bowdler), thought he
should in no degree lessen the historical value of Gibbon's
work by leaving them out altogether.   He has, therefore, presented us with a history of the Roman Empire in which no
mention at all is made of the very names of any of the great
Christian heroes, although they were not only the most remarkable men of those times, but also the men of whom most is
known.   Yet to Gibbon at least he really has done no injustice ;
for Gibbon was as unconscious as himself that their lives,
actions, and deaths formed any part of the history of those
times.   It would not be easy to find a stronger instance of
the injurious effects of anti-religious prejudice, even upon the
literary powers of a really great writer.

M. de Champagny, on the contrary, invests his volumes
with the most lively interest, by mixing the narrative of the
Church—its spread, its contests, its sufferings, its martyrdoms
—with the secular history of the decaying Pagan Empire. No
other work with which we are acquainted does this to the
same degree.   We have histories of the Cæsars, and we have
ecclesiastical histories ; but none which blends the two subjects
into one, like the volumes before us. The political and military
history is as carefully drawn out as if it were the only subject
of the book ; and yet the relations of the Empire to the
Church, the sufferings, perils, and conquests of the divine
kingdom, the heresies which strove to corrupt it, and the
labours of the saints by whom they were encountered, are all
given in their place.   The result is, that we not only see the
gradual growth of the " kingdom of heaven," from the time
when it was sown as a grain of mustard seed until its branches
overshadowed the whole earth, but we see also its connection
with the events of each succeeding generation, and especially
how its peace and its sufferings depended upon the varying
characters of the different inheritors of the power of Augustus
and Tiberius.

Another circumstance, to which his hatred of the Church and
of Christianity necessarily blinded the eyes of Gibbon, and
which, as far as we remember, has passed unobserved, even by
our latest English historian of the Cæsars (who could, not without
gross injustice, be classed with him), is that to which we called
attention in our notice of the earlier portion of M. de Champagny's book, but which naturally becomes more prominent
as we proceed further with the history—the leavening even
of heathen manners and legislation, and, still more, of the

best heathen philosophers, by the ever-increasing influence of Christian faith and morals. As a tide, silently filling up some wide-spreading inland harbour, surrounds and covers, or else bears upon its bosom every object which it finds there, so was Christianity insinuating itself into every province, every city, every family of the great heathen Empire; and penetrating, or sweeping before it every established institution. At last a time came when, although there were still many heathens, there was probably not one who had not all his life been in intercourse with companions, friends, instructors, sisters, mother, by whom the great principles of Christian religion and morality were taken for granted rather than maintained. It was impossible that such a state of society should not modify, silently but profoundly, the thoughts and maxims of every heathen who aspired to anything higher than a mere animal life. Many of them, indeed, had an intense hatred for the Christian religion. That could not but be. But even those who hated it most could not shut their eyes to the truth and beauty of its moral and social principles. So great is the power of sympathy, that any man who lives for years in familiar intercourse with those who assume, as first principles, maxims which he rejects when formally stated—nay, which in his conscience and reason he feels to be false and evil—will yet try in vain to keep himself wholly uninfluenced by them. This is the great danger experienced by those who, while they · deliberately intend to serve God above all things, are obliged, or induced, to live for years with persons in many respects perhaps attractive, but who take for granted that the practical objects to be aimed at in life are worldly pleasures, or honours, or material prosperity, or (even if their pursuits are higher than these) mere intellectual cultivation. The same again is the cause of the danger to which, in our own country especially, Catholics are exposed from the tone of the periodical press. There is no fear of their finding in the *Times* or the *Saturday Review* arguments which, as mere reasoning, could be formidable to their faith; for they can hardly fail to see that the writers (however on other subjects well-informed as well as able) are quite ignorant what Catholics really believe, and unable to understand the grounds on which they believe it. And yet their spiritual health is gradually undermined, as if by living long in an unwholesome atmosphere. An infection like this, combined with the natural voice of conscience, gradually produced an exactly opposite effect upon thoughtful heathens, who were surrounded by Christians. No man, for instance, hated Christianity more than Julian the Apostate; yet the great object of his reign was to introduce into the notions and manners of the heathen, and especially of the heathen priests, as much as possible of Christian theology and morality.* And, doubtless, the feeling of the most respectable heathens, however they may have shared his hatred of the Christian religion, must have been one of regret that so many men and women, in other respects estimable and even admirable, should unfortunately be Christians. Thus it came to pass, all through the first three centuries, as Christians became more and more numerous and better known, and their influence more widely spread, that, although the old heathen religion was dying out, and the military, political, and social aspect of the Roman Empire was one of progressive decline, there was still, in one respect, a constant advance. The moral and religious principles which approved themselves to the thoughtful heathen in each generation, were higher than those of the age before. To adopt, in a most real and worthy sense, one of the most unmeaning terms of our day, there was a constant " progress."

We have, happily, unusual means of tracing this progress; for it pleased God that just before Christianity was given to the world there was exhibited to it a living example of the highest wisdom and virtue which heathenism could attain, in a man whose exalted station attracted to him the eyes of all his contemporaries; and whose prominent literary and oratorical talents have placed his letters, philosophical treatises, and orations among the most highly-prized of the comparatively scanty remains of ancient literature which have come down to our own day. We know Cicero as we can hardly know any one of our own countrymen, except those with whom we have spent our lives in habits of intimate familiarity. We are, therefore, able

---

* " Julian beheld with envy the wise and humane regulations of the Church, and he very frankly confesses his intention to deprive the Christians of the applause as well as advantage which they had acquired by the exclusive practice of charity and beneficence. The same spirit of imitation might dispose the emperor to adopt several ecclesiastical institutions, the use and importance of which were approved by the success of his enemies. But if these imaginary plans of reformation had been realized, the forced and imperfect copy would have been less beneficial to Paganism than honourable to Christianity."—Gibbon, chap. xxiii. " As to his theology," Gibbon says, chap. xxii., " it contained the sublime and important principles of natural religion. The pious emperor acknowledged and adored the eternal Cause of the universe, to whom he ascribed all the perfections of an infinite nature, invisible to the eyes and inaccessible to the understanding of feeble mortals. The Supreme God had created—or rather, in the Platonic language, had generated—the gradual succession of dependent spirits, of gods, of demons, of heroes, and of men, and every being which derived its existence immediately from the First Cause received the inherent gift of immortality."

to compare his knowledge and acceptance of the great principles of moral and social duty, with those of men, in all
other respects his inferiors, two centuries later. Our author,
when speaking of Marcus Aurelius, thus sums up the comparison :—

> Beyond a doubt a new progress has taken place. From Cicero to Seneca,
> from Seneca to Epictetus, from Epictetus to Marcus Aurelius, the light has
> been gradually increasing. Assuredly it was not that the philosophical ideas
> of those who came later were either higher, or clearer, or more true ; in them
> the theory of philosophy was always either poor or wanting. In this respect
> Cicero could have taught much to those who came later than himself. But
> this spontaneous drawing towards virtue, independent of the metaphysical
> ideas which in this respect are more frequently an incumbrance than an
> assistance, this taste for what is good, which already showed itself through all
> the impurity of Seneca, which shone out in Musonius, which was so strongly
> marked in Epictetus, is seen more clearly still in Marcus Aurelius. It is
> evident that in the course of something more than a hundred years the con-
> science of the human race has been awakened. Hence is all the merit of these
> men, all their glory. They have, to speak truly, no other philosophy than
> this sentiment of right developed and perfected. Marcus Aurelius, for his
> part, carries it to the very verge of Christianity. If not quite humility there
> is modesty, and something that goes beyond modesty ; if not charity there
> is beneficence ; if not Christian mercy there is mildness ; if not the love of
> the neighbour there is at least love of mankind ; if not the prayer of the
> Christian there is the prayer of the philosopher. The soul has put off
> Paganism although not yet clothed with Christianity.—*Antonines*, vol. iii.
> p. 15.

Marcus Antoninus was the latest of the heathen philosophers
whom M. de Champagny was at liberty in this passage to
contrast with Cicero. But the case would have been stronger
still, if he could have gone later, and contrasted him with
Porphyry. Porphyry no doubt has, very justly, a bad name
among Christians, because, living as he did immediately before
the final victory of Christianity, and having been, to say the
least, brought into close contact with it, he not only remained
a heathen, but published a work in thirteen books against the
Christians. These things, naturally and justly, tell against the
man ; but in his case, as in that of Julian, they give us a more
striking example of the gradually increasing influence of
Christianity, as it became better known, even upon these
philosophers by whom it was least loved.

> The idea of God, One, Supreme, and Lord of all those inferior beings,
> which were still by a sort of courtesy styled gods—that idea which we have
> already found in so many of the heathen philosophers who were contemporary
> with Christianity—is more distinct than ever in Porphyry, who came later,

and was more familiar with Christian thought. He pronounces a sentence laconically energetic and containing in itself a complete demonstration of the existence of God. "The One must of necessity come before the many."* The idea of the purely incorporeal Being, which was so often obscured by clouds in the phraseology of the Greek philosophers, stands out here in a clear light. He conceives of God—or, if you will, of the first God—as unchangeable, without parts ; present everywhere, because He is not anywhere present corporally. The relations of man to God, the supernatural life, the communication of the soul with the Divine Being by a pure act of the mind and without recourse to *theurgia ;* † prayer offered in a generous and pure spirit almost unknown to heathen prayers, nothing of this is unknown to Porphyry. He is indignant at the merely earthly and material character of Pagan piety and Pagan thought. "That prayer which is accompanied by evil actions is not pure, and cannot be accepted by God. The wise man is the only priest, the only religious man, the only one who knows how to pray." What follows seems quite Christian. "Religion has four principal foundations : Faith, Truth, Hope, Love. Faith is necessary because there is no salvation save for him who turns himself towards God. It is necessary to give all diligence to apply oneself wholly to know the truth with regard to God. When He is known, it is necessary that He should be loved. When He is loved, it is necessary to feed the soul with noble hopes."

Porphyry again, after many other philosophers, no doubt, but in a manner much more distinct than they, requires that the soul should break the links which bind her to the body, separating herself from the passions and from the slavery of the body. The body is a burden which is ever weighing us downwards. The body is not oneself. " I am not this tangible being which is the object of the senses, I am a being very different from my body, without colour, without shape, not to be apprehended by human hands, but only to be apprehended by the thoughts." But if I allow myself to be ruled by this appendage alien from my being, and which is no more myself than the chaff is the grain ; if I cleave to the senses which, like an iron nail, fasten together two things so different—the flesh and the spirit—I no longer know how to live my proper life. Unless I know how to put off this vestment of the flesh and its affections, so as to run free and unimpeded the course of life, I am lost. Even after death, the soul which has loved the body is weighed down towards low places, and lives a life degraded and gross ; but the soul which has subjugated the body, and separated herself from it, which it is the mark of the philosopher to do, that soul will live a celestial life. The former is charged with gross vapours, and, drawn down by their weight, its habitation will be hell—that is ignorance, childishness, and eternal darkness ; the latter, free, disengaged, will mount on high with the spirit

---

* Πρὸ τῶν πολλῶν ἀνάγκη εἶναι τὸ "Ἑν.

† Theurgia, St. Augustine says (De Civitate Dei, x. 9), is distinguished by the heathen philosophers from göetia :—" Conantur ista discernere, et illicitis artibus deditos, alios damnabiles, quos et maleficos vulgus appellat, hos enim ad *göetiam* pertinere dicunt ; alios autem laudabiles videri volunt, quibus *theurgiam* deputant." He condemns both as magical and unlawful.

($\pi\nu\epsilon\tilde{\upsilon}\mu\alpha$) which she has received from on high, and which no burden will weigh down, she will mount higher than the stars, she will live in a divine sphere and in an ethereal body.

Porphyry, in fact, understood that man is a fallen creature ; and that the soul of man, united to his body under the conditions in which that union actually exists, no longer lives in its original dignity. We must needs live after the spirit ; and we are in some measure condemned, as if by force, to live after the flesh. "We have fallen from an higher abode, to which we must return by raising ourselves upon two wings absolutely necessary to us—resistance to things of earth, and desire for things divine. We are exiles who would fain return to our country, to that invisible and spotless abode which was once ours by right."

And to mount thither, Porphyry well knows, suffering is necesssary. "We cannot return by running the race of pleasure. Mountains are not climbed without fatigue or without danger. The path which leads to the summit is none other than vigilance, and the remembrance of the fall which has thrown us down so low as we are."—(Vol. iii. p. 198.)

To any man at all conversant with the works even of the best and greatest of heathen philosophers, the only difficulty in reading these words is to remember that they were not written by a Christian, and in consequence he naturally judges of them by a standard far more severe than he would think of applying to any merely heathen philosopher. For in them we are struck to find any point on which they have attained the knowledge of religious truth, while in Porphyry there is so much that is purely Christian, that our minds instinctively turn rather to the points on which he falls short of Christian teaching, and contradicts it : for instance, no one who believed that the Word has been made Flesh, would regard the body, as he did, as in itself evil. It is here that the strictest Christian asceticism is divided by a broad line from Gnosticism.

But to say nothing on this subject, let us observe that the facts of history are quite inconsistent with any explanation which would account for this gradual elevation of the religious teaching of the heathen philosophers of the first three centuries by anything else than the gradually increasing, though unacknowledged, influence of Christianity with which in each succeeding generation they were brought more and more closely into contact. It cannot be attributed to the natural progress and advancement of the human mind during a period of high civilization. For beyond a doubt the three centuries between Augustus and Constantine were not a period of intellectual and social development, but of decline. And again, this solution is contrary to facts ; for the Christian thinkers and teachers during the same period, so far from improving upon the principles of their first teachers, made it their highest ambition not to fall below, them. This, indeed, was only to be expected by those who know that Christianity was not invented and matured by men, but revealed by God. How it can be accounted for by those who deny its Divine origin one does not see. Such, however, was the fact. During three centuries there stood side by side, in the Roman Empire, acting mutually on each other, two rival systems of religion and morals ; on the one side Christian faith and grace, originating and taking root among classes overlooked and despised by the wise men of the age, and only gradually, as they became more prominent, forcing themselves upon their attention ; on the other, the theology and philosophy which had already been developed to the highest excellence which its nature admitted, by the genius and labours of all the greatest minds of the civilized world, from the day when Socrates began to teach at Athens to the day when Cicero held out his head to the satellites of the Triumvirs. And the result was, that the teaching of the despised and unrefined Galileans, although, at a later period, some of the greatest and most gifted minds that ever existed on earth devoted all their energies to cultivate and promote it, never attained to anything higher than had been taught by the unlettered men who first propagated it ; while that which, before this period began, had engrossed all the greatest men of the world during many centuries, which had already long passed the age of growth, and which promised nothing but decay, gradually admitted into itself many principles before unknown to it, each of which had been from the beginning a first principle of the rival system, and more and more of which were adopted by the philosophers, exactly as the society in which they lived became more and more deeply imbued with that system. Could anything more strongly prove that the improvement of the systems of the philosophers was due, not to any principle of internal growth and development, but to the external influence iof Christianity ?

In mere notions of religion, also, considerable advance seems to have been made from the same cause, even by men who so far from becoming Christians were among the vilest of heathens. Such at least is the opinion of our author, and it seems to us well-founded. Heathens of old times had always been ready to admit new gods. "The policy of the emperors and the Senate," says Gibbon, in words often quoted, "so far as it concerned religion, was happily seconded by the reflections of the enlightened, and by the habits of the superstitious part of their subjects. The various modes of worship which prevailed in the heathen world, were all considered by the people as equally true, by the philosopher as equally false, and by the magistrates as equally useful. And thus toleration produced not only mutual indulgence but even religious concord." That is, of course, that the worshipper of the gods of Rome had no feeling that he did anything inconsistent, in offering sacrifice or worship according to the rites of other nations to the gods whom they worshipped. This was the fundamental principle of heathenism, and, so far as we know, it was only among the Hebrew people that the idea of one religion exclusively true ever existed in the ancient world. But late in the history of heathen Rome, one emperor conceived and attempted to carry out the idea of one supreme god, and one universal religion. He did not indeed deny the existence or forbid the worship of other gods, but he made them all subordinate to the one supreme Syrian god, to whom he had been priest before he attained the Empire, and whom he installed at Rome. The vile moral degradation of this young tyrant, and his doubtful sanity, have induced most writers to suppose that this was merely a wanton freak of the Emperor Elagabalus. M. de Champagny is inclined to think that there may have been in it something deeper.

Under all this, may there not have been a thought in some degree serious⸮ —some degree of belief in the rites practised ? Not in the boy Cæsar, of course, in whom rottenness had come before ripeness, corruption before manhood. But in his mother, perhaps, or in some of those around him, the project existed of uniting in the worship of the god of Edessa, all the worships of the Empire. His temple was the dominant temple in which were to meet, directly or indirectly, the prayers and homage of collective humanity. Whatever Rome had of venerated symbols, of sacred and mysterious talismans, was unpityingly summoned to surrender to it. The Emperor-Priest caused himself to be affiliated to all the priesthoods, in order to learn their secret emblems, and to bring their gods to the feet of his god. [The enumeration which follows is striking and picturesque, but we have not room for it.] His idea, or that of those by whom he was directed, was the fusion into one of all the Pagan religions. "He said," says Lampridius, "that all gods were only the servants of his god, some of them his chamberlains, some his guards, some his ministers. It was not merely the religion of Rome that he desired to abolish, it was throughout the whole world that he would have his god Elagabalus alone and everywhere the object of worship."

Nothing probably could appear to a heathen a stronger sign of madness than this desire to unite all mankind in one religion. But the wretched youth who conceived it had been brought up in Syria, and the religion of the Jews and Christians had unquestionably some attraction for him. We are expressly told that he resolved to unite in one, not only all the heathen religions, but "that he would bring to his

temple of Mount Palatine the religion of the Samaritans, that of
the Jews, and that of the Christians, that so the priesthood of
Elagabalus might hold in possession the secrets of all the
religions of the world." He even submitted to circumcision,
and abstained from pork—strange notion for a youth who
knew not what abstinence from anything meant. But there is
positive testimony that his mother's sister, if not actually a
Christian (which is one account), had received instruction in
Christianity; and there seems little doubt that it was the
Christian idea of one God and one Church for all nations, of
which he had laid hold, and which he corrupted as he did all
else that he touched.

We have devoted a disproportionate space to the development of M. de Champagny's estimate of the indirect and unacknowledged influence of Christianity on the Roman Empire,
both because we think that he most clearly establishes the fact ;
because, so far as we have observed, he is the first writer upon
those times by whom it has been brought out; and because,
moreover, it gives to this portion of the history of the Roman
Empire the interest which it wants in the hands of other historians. Nothing can be more dreary than the narrative of mere
decay and corruption—a ruin physical and moral. From Gibbon's picture of the period between the accession of Commodus
and the accession of Constantine, we cannot help turning with a
disgust almost unrelieved. That the barbarians were like wolves
baying round a mountain village on some winter night is really
the only redeeming feature in it, for it is the only one which
presents the hope of some better in the distant future. M. de
Champagny, with surprising skill, has contrived to make
this period interesting and attractive. This is in great measure
because he keeps constantly before us the blessed truth, that
this Empire, slowly dying away, not of any external dangers
or assaults, but of its deep, internal corruption, held within it a
life distinct from its own, which was daily increasing in strength,
and preparing to take possession of the new world which
was to succeed when the wretchedness of the old world should
no longer be endured by God or by man. We are reminded
of the ceremonial so often mentioned in these volumes, and
which formed a standing part of the funeral rites of an
emperor. At the moment when the pile by which his body
was to be consumed was kindled, an eagle, which had been concealed within it, was released, and soared away through the sky.
Like it, the Christian Church was in but not of, the decaying
Roman Empire : and its freedom and power began with the
utter destruction of the Empire. M. de Champagny agrees
with all other historians in regarding this period as one of

mere decay. He divides the history of the Empire into three. The first period, that of the Cæsars, ending with Nero (the last emperor allied by blood to Augustus or Julius) gives us the working out of the system invented and established by Tiberius. Then (after a few months of civil confusion, in which the purple was worn by three puppets, whom Tacitus compares to those actors who for a few hours present on the stage a royal character) came a succession of wise and good rulers—from Vespasian to Marcus Aurelius, under whom the Roman world, for more than a century, enjoyed a remarkable degree of peace and repose, except during the few years of the tyranny of Domitian. This is the period of which M. de Champagny treated in his last work, " The Antonines," to which we have already called the attention of our readers. It is regarded by him as an interval during which the decay of the empire was suspended but not arrested; during which the wisest and most humane emperor could not help feeling that he might be succeeded by a Nero or a Caligula, but during which, as a matter of fact, the material prosperity of the free portion, at least, of the population of the Empire, was greater than at any other period of heathen history, although not to be compared with that of modern Italy, even at its least prosperous times; a fact which he is careful to prove by details, because the anti-Christian writers of the eighteenth century have delighted to exaggerate the period of the Antonines into a sort of millennium, in order to depreciate, by comparison, the condition of Christian nations. With the death of the Emperor Marcus Aurelius, which took place anno Domini 180, this period ended. Many subsequent emperors, indeed, took the name of Antoninus, and some degree of confusion has been introduced by the inscriptions on their monuments bearing the well-remembered name (for the practice of distinguishing from each other, by numbers, rulers who bore the same name did not exist in the ancient world), but it was disgraced by their monstrous vices and tyranny, and history has refused to accord it to them. Thus each of the emperors who have ever since been known only as Carcalla and Elagabalus styled himself Marcus Aurelius Antoninus.

The three volumes now before us take up the history, where it was left by the last volume of the " The Antonines," at the death of Marcus Aurelius, and the accession of his son Commodus. This imposed on the author the necessity of devoting all the rest of his work to the most calamitous and ignominious part of Roman history. This fact was so strongly on our minds when we took up the first volume, that we felt almost disinclined to read it. But so skilfully has M. de

Champagny performed his task, that he has given us a work, with regard to which the only difficulty we have found has been to lay it down.   It is one, moreover, quite essential to the full enjoyment of the volumes which have preceded it, and without which, indeed, many things in them would have been incomplete.   For instance, one main subject of Roman history must ever be that of the relations of the Empire to the Christian Church.   Of the blessed influence of the Church upon the Empire we have already spoken.   The history of the action of the Empire towards the Church, on the other hand, is little more than the history of the persecutions.   It is a subject little attractive to an un-Christian writer, for he has to record much against his will, that great phenomenon stated by M. de Champagny, in the extract with which we began the present article, that every inch of ground traversed by the Church, in her triumphal progress of victory over the heathen world, was won for her and secured to her by the blood of her martyrs. The subject, however distasteful, could not be avoided even by Gibbon. He was compelled to treat it, whether he would or not, and the result is his well-known sixteenth chapter, in which, professing to tell " the conduct of the Roman Government towards the Christians from the reign of Nero to that of Constantine," he labours, as far as possible, to explain away and palliate the persecutions which he could not wholly deny ; while he throws as much doubt as possible upon every fact connected with them, lessens as much as possible the number of the martyrs, and especially sets himself to engage the interest and sympathies of his readers on the side of the high-minded, philosophical, enlightened men who, no doubt under a mistaken view of the facts, felt it their painful duty to pronounce sentence, and against the score or two of vulgar, wrongheaded, seditious fanatics, whom he admits to have suffered death as Christians at one time or other, and in different provinces of the vast Empire.   It is hardly necessary to say that the subject is treated very differently by M. de Champagny.   As a critic and a member of the French Academy we cannot suspect him of any tendency to neglect a scrupulous examination of the evidence by which different martyrdoms are proved.   But in each successive persecution he gives us the most striking and well-attested records of the sufferings of those whom he loves and reverences as his own brethren and fathers in the common faith ; by whose blood and self-sacrifice it has pleased God to preserve to us those blessings which He originally gave us by the Blood and Sacrifice of His Eternal Son.   Thus he begins his notice of the last general persecution :—

It is, indeed, the æra of 'martyrs. They meet us more abundantly than ever. Already, pressed by our space, we have often abridged the narrative of the persecutions, lest we should weary the reader by the constant repetition of the same cruelties and the same heroism. In future we shall be compelled to abridge them still more. The harvest is so abundant that it is impossible to gather it ear by ear, or even sheaf by sheaf. We shall only cast our eyes over the plain on which the executioners are the mowers, and the angels those who gather in the harvest. We shall pass in silence over many names which the Church has recorded in her annals ; many of the most celebrated names, and of the most popular records. May we be forgiven by these holy ones, if we see in them only the members of the Holiest of Holies, of Him in whom we are all one.—(Vol. iii. p. 330.)

Here is the true Catholic tone. Among Catholics, thank God, there is little ground for the reproach addressed to his countrymen by a poet contemporary with Gibbon.

> Patriots have toiled, and in their country's cause
> Bled nobly ; and their deeds, as they deserve,
> Receive proud recompense.   *   *
> But martyrs struggle for a brighter prize,
> And win it with more pain. Their blood is shed
> In confirmation of our noblest claim—
> Our claim to feed upon immortal Truth,
> To walk with God, to be divinely free,
> To soar and to anticipate the skies.
> Yet few remember them. They lived unknown
> Till persecution dragged them into fame,
> And chased them up to Heaven. Their ashes flew
> No marble tells whither. With their names
> No bard embalms and consecrates his song ;
> And history, so warm on meaner themes,
> Is cold on this.

A most true estimate, alas ! of the general tone of English literature. Nor could there be a more just comparison between the popular feeling of a Protestant and a Catholic people than one between it and that of our author. In these volumes he goes through the whole period of the heathen persecutions in the old world. Their character was quite different in the later and in the earlier portion of it. At first Christians for the most part were, like their Lord, reluctantly given over to the fury of a popular cry by judges who even in condemning them could not refrain from asking "what evil have they done?" Under Nero they were thrown to the populace maddened by the burning of Rome. Under Domitian they were confused with the philosophers who had incurred his jealousy. At a still earlier period they had been involved in a momentary jealousy against Jews. Pliny reported to Trajan that he could find nothing criminal in them except their obstinacy. Thus, in the periods included in M. de Champagny's former series, persecution, though far from unfrequent, was little more than accidental. The power of the magistrate was so absolute, that no set of men could be safe against whom suspicion was once excited, and in them there was at all times peculiarity enough to excite suspicion. Above all, in times of pestilence (and no age of the world was more severely afflicted with that scourge than that which began with Marcus Aurelius), or when famine threatened, or even when strange portents in the sky alarmed the people, according to the well-known passage of Tertullian—" If the Tiber rises to the walls, or if the Nile does not rise over the fields; if the heaven hath stood still, or the earth hath moved; if there is any famine, if any pestilence "—the cry was still, " the Christians to the lion." Such was persecution down to the beginning of the period of which these volumes treat. The reign of the Emperor Severus, which marked in many other respects a new era in Roman history, is selected by our author as the first in which persecution was a deliberate act of Roman policy.

> The persecution of Severus may be called the first which was a solemn, spontaneous, political act of Roman authority. Nero had given the signal for persecution, but chiefly at Rome and from accidental circumstances. Domitian had been led to proscribe the Christians rather for financial motives than as part of a proclaimed policy. Trajan, Hadrian, Marcus Aurelius himself, had permitted persecution rather than persecuted, maintaining, of course, the legal principle which condemned Christianity, but not always urging its execution, and allowing it to be active or inactive, according to the fanaticism or the indifference of the different peoples, the weakness or wisdom of the Proconsuls. Severus was the first of whom we are told that by a formal, public, dated act, he forbid that Christians should exist, thus rendering the persecution not merely legal but obligatory, not merely possible here and there, but necessary everywhere. He first gave the signal for one of those single combats hand to hand, between authority and the Church, which the world was to see many times renewed in the course of this age, always to the disgrace of idolatrous tyranny, and to the glory of Christian patience. This combat was fierce and of long continuance. We have a work of Tertullian, written after the death of Severus, and at least ten years later than the commencement of the persecution, from which it appears that it had not yet been given up. The Church was not in numbers what it was later ; and the administration of the Cæsars reconstituted by Severus, had a power of action which afterwards steadily diminished. The struggle, therefore, though not more violent, was of longer duration, than those which followed.—(Vol. i. p. 259.)

It was in this persecution that several of the blessed saints whose names we still daily honour in the canon of the Mass, received their crowns—the slave Felicitas, and the noble lady Perpetua, whose martyrdoms, which no one can weary of reading, are given by our author in full detail. How little thought those humble martyrs that, age after age, when the very name of Severus should be known only to students, and when the Empire itself should have passed away, their contest and their names should be watchwords in the Christian fight to millions in every clime, men and women of all nations and all languages, wherever the " world-encircling sun " looks down upon the habitations of men.

It is impossible to read any of these soul-stirring narratives without being strongly impressed by a sense of the wholly fragmentary character of our knowledge, not only of the history of the martyrs, but of ancient times as a whole. Here and there we have the " genuine acts " of some martyr whose fame is thus preserved in the Church, while we cannot but feel that there must have been many more, in our judgment quite as well worth preserving, which are known only to God. The saints and martyrs would be, of all men, the first to say, " even so, Father, for so it hath seemed good in Thy sight." What to them the applause even of their brethren in the Church, in comparison with the praise of Him for whom they lived, and fought the good fight, and died. " Receperunt mercedem suam, vani vanum," says S. Augustine * of the successful candidates for posthumous fame. But so it is ; our acquaintance for instance with the details of the persecution in Carthage, under Decius and Valerian, we owe merely to what, speaking in human language, we must call the chance which has preserved to us the letters of S. Cyprian ; our knowledge of the martyrdoms at Lyons and Vienne, to a similar chance which has preserved the letters in which they were reported to the Christians of the East. Who can doubt that many documents as valuable, many narratives as thrilling, must have been wrecked as they floated down the stream of time, set thick as it was with rocks upon which have been lost so many of the most precious relics of ancient literature, whether sacred or secular ?

With regard to the later persecutions, they seem to have partaken, each more decidedly than that which came before it, of the same character of deliberate acts of the central government rather than of popular outbreaks like those of the earlier days. M. de Champagny points out also that in the

---

* Quoted, Champagny, vol. ii. p. 140,

last and most terrible of all, that under Diocletian, there does not seem to have been any of the old popular demand for deeds of blood and cruelty. Christianity had already become so far known as to make it quite impossible that the mass of the people should any longer believe the calumnies against it, as they did in earlier days.

This persecution had much less than those which went before it the support of popular passion. Very seldom on this occasion did the people interfere to denounce, excite, or complain of the backwardness of the magistrates. Sometimes, on the contrary, it did interfere to express sorrow and pity for the victims, and to demand their pardon. Heathenism had lost ground, not only in the number of its adherents, but in its power over their minds. The heathen populace was no longer that of the preceding century. The Christians had lived in the midst of it in too great numbers, and too publicly not to be better understood. Many minds, indifferent or tolerant, had come to think that the worship of God and the worship of the gods (as Tertullian somewhere expresses it) might live side by side. Their reason inclined to the former, although their corrupt hearts shrunk from it. The few sincere heathens there were, were a part of the common people, without much reflection or knowledge, in whose eyes the offence of the Christians (whom in other respects they thought worthy people) was to have too much knowledge and too much reflection. Is not that in truth at this very day the offence of Christians in the eyes of the great mass of people who do not wish to know or to reflect ?"—(Vol. iii. p. 346.)

The most important change was in the popular estimate of Christian morality. Time was, when strange and horrible stories of monstrous and unutterable impurity practised by the Christians in their secret assemblies were really believed, not merely by the vulgar, but even by educated men. This suspicion could not but be fostered by the care with which Christian reverence compelled them to conceal the real nature of that great act which has at all times formed the principal part of Christian worship. By degrees, however, the popular estimate had become so much modified, that it became the general feeling that Christians, whatever else there might be to say against them, were at least more pure than any one else. Thus, when a woman named Afra, who was well known to have been an harlot, was brought before the heathen magistrate at Iconium, charged with being a Christian, and admitted the charge, he said, "You a Christian! you are not worthy of Christ. It is in vain for you to call Him your God, for He will never acknowledge you as His." A still more remarkable case is given by M. de Champagny.

An immodest woman came into a nursery-garden belonging to one Serenus, at an unbecoming hour, professing that she wished to walk there. He reproached her for her boldness, and turned her out. She had a duped husband, who was a favourite servant of the prince, and she complained of having been insulted, and caused Serenus to be summoned before the magistrate. He related what had happened in a simple manner, exposing the artifice of the wretched woman. She was silenced, and her indignant husband took her out of the court. " But," said the judge to Serenus, " who are you? who but a Christian would have had such a scruple?" " I am a Christian." " How then have you escaped our pursuit? Have not you sacrificed to the gods?" " As long as it was the will of God, he kept me out of notice. I was like the stone which the builders rejected. Now He is pleased to make use of me, and I am ready." And the Christian suffered death.—(Vol. iii. p. 396.)

The disappearance of this old prejudice was the sign that the long æra of persecution was drawing to an end. We cannot help thinking that a similar symptom gives us good hope for our own country. No one who knows England now, and can remember what it was fifty years ago, can fail to observe the great change that has taken place. Then the notion of respectable men was that Catholics were a race morally degraded. Now they are disliked by many people, but on the whole it is on the ground of needless strictness. God forbid that any who bear the honoured name should give them reason to think that Catholic men and Catholic women are much the same as other men and women of their own class of society, except that on Sundays they hear Mass instead of going to the Established Church. No doubt there is always some danger of this, when the fear of persecution has passed away. If the Dioclesian persecution found Christians so well prepared, it was because the Church had been sifted and purified by those of Decius, Valerian, and Aurelian in the preceding half century. When the first of these broke out—

At the first moment the triumph of the emperor's will seemed complete. The Christians had been sleeping calmly, for the persecution had been suspended for eight-and-thirty years, and had come to regard it only as a heroical tradition of times gone by. They had accustomed themselves to a life, easy, soft, and in some cases half heathen. At the sound of the edict of persecution they started up in terror. The faith which they had received from their fathers, and which they had been carelessly holding, did not seem to them a treasure so precious as their property or their life. They flocked in crowds before the Proconsul. Those who held public offices (for the Christians had begun to enter into such offices), because their rank exposed them to more notice, and in some sense called on them to make a decision; those who had pagan brothers or kindred, because they were urged to it by their kinsfolk; others because they were cited to appear; others because they were in a shameful hurry to apostatise. They were led before the idols and sacrificed. Some were pale, trembling, distracted between fear of man and fear of God.   These timid souls, who had not courage either for martyrdom or for apostasy, were a little laughed at by the heathen populace. Others, more firm in appearance, with an unabashed forehead and a confident voice, shamelessly denied that they had ever been Christians.   They said true : these, says S. Dionysus of Alexandria, were those of whom our Lord foretold that their salvation would be difficult.   Some went still further in their ardour for apostasy.   They proclaimed that they had sacrificed to the gods— that they had sacrificed without compulsion ; they obtained from the judge a written certificate of their baseness ; they hastened to their shame with an affected joy ; they prevailed on their neighbours to come ; they brought their children and got the idol's wine poured over their innocent lips.   Sometimes when put off to the next day by a magistrate too busy to receive apostasies, they begged and implored.—(Vol. iii. p. 290.)

What picture would the Catholic Church in England present, if persecution should suddenly return upon us? Doubtless there would be many martyrs.   It is from the letters of S. Cyprian, the martyr Archbishop of Carthage, that this description of what he had seen go on before his own eyes is drawn.   But would none be found " asleep "? none " whom the roar of the edicts would startle up in terror " ?   none accustomed to a " life easy and soft," half Protestant? and if so, might not London as well as Carthage * see many " fallen "?

We have left ourselves no space to follow M. de Champagny's narrative through what may be called the secular part of his history.   In this we feel that we have done him less than justice, because, as we have already said, it is the blending of the two elements together that gives to his volumes their special charm.   He has been as conscientiously diligent in one as in the other, and the secular history, although we may not have prepared the reader to expect it, occupies more than two-thirds of the volumes before us.   As a French writer living under the Second Empire he could hardly refrain himself from following, with especial care, the history of the fall of Rome under the Cæsars, if it were only that he might expose the peculiar corruptions against which his own country had most need to be warned.   He is strongly impressed with a truth most certain and momentous, and not less necessary to be urged upon England than upon France ; that the ruin of nations is brought on, not by material or even by political, but by social and moral causes.   It is, therefore, the social and moral bearing of political changes, which has always the greatest attraction for our author.   With this thought before him, he

---

* · S. Cyprian says : Aspice totum orbem pene vastatum et ubique jacere dejectorum reliquias et ruinas.

weighs and estimates the new system introduced into the
Roman Empire by Severus, which is indeed the beginning of
the political history of the three volumes before us, and the
effect produced both upon his family and his successors, as well
as upon the public interests, by the new supremacy given by
him to the soldier. He estimates in the same way the object
and effects of the change introduced by Caracalla, when he admitted the whole world to the citizenship of Rome. In another
part of the work we have a most interesting account of the
growth of the Roman law, and of the circumstances to which
it owes its peculiar characteristics. Lastly, he considers the
new system introduced by Diocletian. Upon all these things
we designed, when we commenced our work, to enter at some
length. But our space is filled, and we have not touched
them. We regret this the less, because we think the extracts
we have given will suffice to direct the attention of our readers
to the volumes of M. de Champagny himself. He is a writer
whose chief characteristic it is that it is impossible to read
him without being set thinking. In words which, in our
notice of his former works, we quoted from a French critic,
" Le plus beau privilége des écrivants qui pensent c'est de
faire penser ceux qui les lisent. M. de Champagny fait penser." The remark is as applicable to this work as to those
which preceded it.

We will conclude with a single example of the skill of our
author in setting vividly before his readers a picture of the
men and manners of times in many respects so unlike our own,
as far as decency allows, a qualification which, in striking
contrast to Gibbon, he never forgets.

Well, then, let us go into that villa of Laurentum, in which, sick of
empire, having signed in a heap twenty edicts, and having written at the
foot of a letter the single word *farewell*, the son of Marcus Aurelius is
resting himself in the shade of the bays of his garden. What is he to do
to-day? We are in the golden age (the æra of Commodus has been officially
declared such by a decree of the Senate) ; it is the eve of the Calends
of the Herculian month (for by another decree the calendar has been
changed, and six of the twelve months have been decorated with the names
or titles of Commodus). But even in the golden age, even in the month
Ælius, in the month Amazonius, even when one is master of the world,
ennui will intrude. Upon some thirty letters or edicts just signed, he
has been reading the formula magnificent but in the end tiresome—"The
Emperor Cæsar Lucius Ælius Aurelius Commodus Augustus Pius
(that title he took on the day when he made one of the lovers of his
mother Consul), happy Sarmaticus Maximus Germanicus Britannicus,
Pacificator of the world, unconquerable, the Roman Hercules, Pontifex
Maximus, eighteen times invested with tribunitial authority, eight times

Imperator, Father of his Country, to the Consuls, the Prætors, and the Tribunes of the people, and to the Commodian Senate (for the Senate too had taken this title, the historian says, in derision, but if it laughed you may be sure it was not out loud), to the Senate happy and Commodian, health." Yes, no doubt one is all this * * * * and yet what matter—*ennui* will intrude. * * * * Marcia comes charged to amuse her terrible husband : "What will my master be pleased to do ?" she says. "Will he have the circus prepared, and put on the habit of the green faction to win new victories ? Or will the Roman Hercules, all for his lion-skin and his club ?' Marcia had given him these fantasies about Hercules. As he must act she wanted to inspire him with a taste for acting some manly character. "My master knows that I am an Amazon, and I love the combat. Will he like me to take the helmet and cuirass to go out to the combat on the banks of the River Thermodon ? Or will he prefer to be an Amazon himself, and to fight, in a female garb, with the courage of an hero ?" "Yes,' says Commodus, "I will fight. Take off my shoes. Give me a matron's tunic shot with purple and gold. Get ready my domestic arena. Call my gladiators to come and be killed by the first gladiator in the world. What shall I kill ? Men, beasts, elephants, rhinoceros. I have killed at one single time, two elephants, five hippopotamus, some rhinoceros, beasts by the hundred—all with a single blow ! And I have pierced the horn of a gazelle with my javelin. No, I should like to spare blood to-day : I won't kill any-thing to-day, except some cripples and lame men. I am Hercules. Bring me my lion-skin and my club. These poor wretches shall be the Titans ; put some serpents [artificial, N.B.] about their limbs. I am Apollo. I will pierce them with my arrows."

Marcia, perhaps, tries to suggest some less sanguinary employment. She tells of the few amusements, comparatively innocent, by which he has signal-ised his days of special good humour. She reminds him that one day he had had two deformed dwarfs served up on a huge silver platter smothered in mustard, and, of his unheard of mercy, had been pleased not only not to eat them, but to enrich them and make them prefects ; that another day he had caused the most delicate dishes to be mixed with the dung from his stables, and had pretended to eat of them that the company at his table might be caught by them. Happy for the world when Commodus had had only these disgusting amusements. But he remembers jokes which were more enjoyable. How for one man he had dressed his beard and cut off his nose ; how he had acted as surgeon for another and cut an artery ; how he had pretended to cut the hair of another and had cut off his ear ; how he had had one enor-mously fat man embowelled that he might satisfy himself what there could be inside. He remembers how many men he had had deprived of one eye and one leg ; how many he had had killed because they were too handsome ; how many because he had met them dressed in the habits of the barbarians. For so it was that in his private life and in the retirement of his home he had his little private cruelties quite unconnected with politics.

Marcia would try to change these sanguinary instincts. She talks to Commodus of prayers and sacrifices. She hopes to excite some fear of the

gods. He replies, " I have not sacrificed to Isis for a long time. My hair
has grown again since I shaved, in order to carry the divine Anubis. Do
you remember how, as I held the image in my hand and offered it to be
kissed by the servants of Isis, I knocked it violently against their jaws ? And
when the poor wretches beat their breasts with the consecrated pine comb,
how I made them strike hard ; and the priests of Bellona, when it was
their duty to wound their arms with knives, how I made them to do it till
the blood ran well ? And how I made a serious matter of the trials which
precede the initiation to the mysteries of Mithras, trying the courage of the
postulants by the sight of blood shed in real earnest ? " Do what they may,
talk to him of his religious rites, of his orgies, of his amusements, of his
politics, it is always the man of blood that comes foremost.—(Vol. i. p. 35.)

Art. V.—LIFE AND LABOURS OF S. THOMAS OF AQUIN.

The Life and Labours of S. Thomas of Aquin. By the Very Rev. ROGER
BEDE VAUGHAN, O.S.B. In two volumes. Vol. I. London : Longmans
& Co. 1871.

THE welcome appearance of the first volume, with the
promise of a second soon to follow, of an extensive and
valuable Life of S. Thomas of Aquin, by Father Bede Vaughan,
affords the opportunity for a few general observations suggested
by such a subject. We will first of all allow the author to
speak for himself :—

The fact that no life of S. Thomas of Aquin has been written in the
English language, is a sufficient excuse, if apology be needed, for the publication of the following pages. . . . .

France, Germany, and Italy, in this respect, are better off than ourselves.
Touron, with his pious orthodoxy ; Werner, with his share of literary information ; and Fregerio, with his genuine Italian devotion—each of these
admirable men has done for his respective country that which the present
author is wishful to do for England. . . . .

The author has found it difficult to comprehend how the life of S. Thomas
of Aquin could be written, so as to content the mind of an educated man—
of one who seeks to measure the reach of principle, and the influence of
saintly genius—without embracing a considerably wider field of thought
than has been deemed necessary by those who have aimed more at composing

a book of edifying reading, than at displaying the genesis and development of truth, and the impress of a master-mind upon the age in which he lived. It has always appeared to him that one of the most telling influences exerted by the doctor-saints of God, has been that of rare intellectual power in confronting and controlling the passions and mental aberrations of epochs, as well as of blinded and swerving men. Their unaffected piety, their spotlessness of conscience, their frank simplicity, their beautiful self-distrust, their faith in the unseen, their divine unselfishness, their sovereign devotion to the Crucified ; all these form, as it were, the soil out of which their far-reaching influence springs. Keen illumination of reason, deep vision, penetrating discrimination, calm judgment, elasticity of mind, and high rectitude of will— what are these but the manifestations of a highly cultivated moral nature, and the divinely-fashioned instruments for carrying into execution some giant intellectual work ? . . . .

The object which the author of these pages has proposed to himself is this :—To unfold before the reader's mind the far-reaching and many-sided influence of heroic sanctity, when manifested by a man of massive mind, of sovereign genius, and of sagacious judgment ; and then to remind him, that as the fruit hangs from the branches, so genius of command, and steadiness of view, and unswervingness of purpose, are naturally conditioned by a certain moral habit of heart and head ; that purity, reverence, adoration, love, are the four solid corner-stones on which that Pharos reposes, which, when all about it, and far beyond it, is darkness and confusion, stands up in the midst, as the representative of order and as the minister of light, and as the token of Salvation.—(*Preface*, pp. i. ii. vii.)

For the present we shall abstain from all criticism of this important work, except so much as is implied in our heartily recommending it to every Catholic reader, especially to Catholic theologians and philosophers. On the appearance of the second volume we hope to consider it more in detail, and with a view to that just and equitable "censure" (to use the word in its etymological sense) which alone can lead to the establishing of a high standard in Catholic literature. But meanwhile every one should read it. The fruit of very great reading on the part of the author, it is put together and written in a way which no one will find dry or tedious. To enumerate the titles of the chapters would be to go over a list of subjects that can never fail in interest to the educated Catholic or the cultivated man of letters. We ourselves are disposed to prefer the pages that relate the biography of the hero himself. But many will be taken by the very original views in regard to the epoch, to the monks, the friars, and the scholastics; whilst others will be charmed by the picturesque descriptions of old Paris and its university, by the admirable account of the great theological school of S. Victor's, or by the history of Albert the Great. As a specimen of the author's style, we select the following paragraph from the chapter entitled "S. Thomas at Cologne."

At length a circumstance occurred which brought his extraordinary gifts before the notice of the schoolmaster. Albert had selected a very difficult question from the writings of Denis the Areopagite, and had given it to some of his scholars for solution. Whether in joke or in earnest, they passed on the difficulty to Thomas, and begged him to write his opinion upon it. Thomas took the paper to his cell, and, taking his pen, first stated with great lucidity all the objections that could be brought against the question, and then gave their solutions. As he was going out of his cell this paper accidentally fell near the door. One of the brothers passing picked it up and carried it at once to Master Albert. Albert was excessively astonished at the splendid talent which now for the first time by mere accident he discovered in that big, silent student. He determined to bring out, in the most public manner, abilities which had been for so long a time so modestly concealed. He desired Thomas to defend a thesis before the assembled school on the following day. The hour arrived. The hall was filled. There sat Master Albert. Doubtless the majority of those who were to witness this display imagined they were about to assist at an egregious failure. How could that heavy, silent lad, who could not speak a word in private, defend in public school, against the keenest of opponents, the difficult niceties of theology? But they were soon undeceived, for Thomas spoke with such clearness, established his thesis with such remarkable dialectical skill, saw so far into the coming difficulties, and handled the whole subject in so masterly a manner, that Albert himself was constrained to cry aloud, "Tu non videris tenere locum respondentis sed determinantis." "Master," replied Thomas, with humility, "I know not how to treat the question otherwise." Albert then thought to puzzle him and show him that he was still a disciple. So, one after another, he started objections, created a hundred labyrinths, weaving and interweaving all manner of subtle arguments, but in vain. Thomas, with his calm spirit and keen vision, saw through every complication, had the key to every fallacy, the solution for every enigma, and the art to unravel the most tangled skein, till finally Albert, no longer able to withhold the expression of his admiration, cried out to his disciples, who were almost stupefied with astonishment, "We call this young man a dumb ox, but so loud will be his bellowing in doctrine, that it will resound throughout the whole world." (p. 230.)

Great names, if they enjoy the glory, suffer also the penalty of greatness. The name of one whom men speak of but never see, whom they praise but do not care for, runs the greatest risk of passing into a bodiless abstraction. The name of Thomas of Aquin has had the fate which the Roman satirist lamented for Cæsar and Hannibal, and has headed many a chapter of declamation since the monks of Fossa Nuova closed his fragrant sepulchre, six hundred years ago. Opposite camps

have inscribed him on their standards; disciples have bound
themselves by oath to teach as he taught; Popes and Councils
have acknowledged him as their master.   In the philosophic
battle-fields of mediæval Europe, in those great universities
where robes of every hue and cowls of every shape congregated
for learning and for contest, the fortress of his name was battered
for many an eventful year by a Scotus, an Ockham, a Peter
Ramus—by Scotist, by Nominalist, and by Humanist.   When
a different battle began to rage in Europe, and the Apostasy of
the sixteenth century stilled for a time the disputes within the
camp, the reformers found time, in the midst of their ever-
widening area of combat against the Church, to devote a few
blows and a few anathemas to S. Thomas.   We hear the rude
vernacular of Luther, calling him a "phial of the wrath of
God"! and the strident war-cry of Bucer, rising more furious
as he recalls his trampled Dominican habit and his early studies
of the *Summa*, is "Get rid of Thomas, and I will smash the
Church"!   In these days, after the Kantian· earthquake
has shaken the land, and the deluge of Idealism has flooded it,
and the thick haze of a know-nothing Positivism has wrapped
it up and made it—

> A land of mist and cloud, Cimmeria !
> Where never gleam of sunlight pierces in,
> And mortals mope in darkness pitiful—

in the modern philosophic chaos, whenever a Catholic workman
begins to look about for materials to build up something that
may be called Catholic Philosophy, he makes for the great
temple that is standing yet, though its stones are storm-worn
and its threshold desolate, and he chooses what seems most
serviceable, and carries it home, not without many a look back,
partly in fear that the ghosts of old gods may be pursuing him,
partly to deprecate the noisy scorn of the passing Philistines.
And if philosophers timidly invoke the ancient name, theology
is bolder, and has never for a moment forgotten it.   Although
she may say, in the words of Lacordaire, that he is "a Pharos,
but not the end of the world," yet still she honours his lightest
word, she quotes his luminous reasoning, she apologizes for differing from him, and she is never so well contented as when
she can follow his method and adopt his very expressions.   It
is no wonder, therefore, that the name of Thomas of Aquin is
something different from most other names.   His name stands,
not for a person, but for a system, a history, a cause, a whole
cosmos of intellectual process and scientific organization.   It
stands for anything but for the actual saint.   Thomas of Aquin

once lived, as other men may live, the life of nature and of grace. His biographers have not been many, and their labours have not told as much about him as such a saint deserved. It would seem as if, even before he died or was canonized, he had passed into the region of the abstract. Yet his life, as we are permitted to know it, is full enough of beauty to challenge the devout meditation of the religious, and to claim the admiring interest of every student of mankind. Child of a region where the Italian sky stretches over frowning rock and fertile valley often vexed and spoiled by Italian storms, of a century in which the cradle of the prince's child had to be rocked in the mountain fortress, and the infant's sleep to be guarded from the shock of battle and the shouts of charging spearmen, he came down from his father's castle, and before his hand had been soiled by the hilt of the sword, sat meekly among the children of Monte Cassino. Of noble race, of a nature nobler still, so exuberant was it in intuitive genius, so calm and serene, so completely what the chronicler, in describing his contemporary, S. Louis of France, calls *"un vrai gentilhomme,"* he was never passionate but on that one occasion, when he begged to be let alone to follow the call of God and become a Dominican Friar. To the young he is one of the great patrons of chastity. To the scholar his life exhales an odour of humility that teaches what books cannot teach, and a serene ardour of union with God that plays, like the coruscations of the nocturnal sky, over the barrenness of mere intellectual discipline, and sanctifies it by the contact of a gift of the Holy Ghost. The story of his university life is the heroic page of Christian academical history, where those who, after him, are engaged upon the same body of divine truth that he delivered, may read how all natural acquisitions sink to meanness beside one touch of grace, and how all vigils and midnight labour are sterile and unproductive in comparison with a saint's prayer at the foot of his crucifix. S. Thomas of Aquin has a real personality; and in spite of the comparative meagreness of details, it is quite possible to bring it out very forcibly, as we are glad to see Father Vaughan has succeeded in doing. It would seem to be a law that the greatest works of God, in nature or in grace, have always the power of profoundly impressing the human mind. They may seem too far off or too dim to be taken in by the eye, the clouds may close and fitfully part around their summits, and the noisy prominence of smaller things may occupy the attention at this moment or at that, but let time be taken for a long and earnest look, let the shadows of night creep over the undulating foreground and darkness still the voices in hearing of the ear, and the mountain or the pyramid, seizing not so much the outward as the inward eye, fills the soul with the greatness that it truly has.   It is impossible that a reader who believes in the super-natural work of God'in this world should study, in silence and earnestness, such a life as that of the angelical doctor, without feeling what men would call deep religious emotion, but what S. Paul calls the voice of the spirit of God.

But, recommending our readers to Father Vaughan's pages for the life and spirit of S. Thomas, it is not so much our object to dwell upon them in this place, as to say a few words upon the wider subject which is suggested by so great and venerable a name.   That name has become an ideal, and if it has also made the saint somewhat of an ideal, yet that it should have become so is a fact almost as great as the existence of the saint himself.   S. Thomas of Aquin is indisputably the prince of scientific theology.   In ancient times, as in modern, it has been the custom to name sciences and arts after their inventors, or their greatest promoters.   The old world talked of Hippo-crates in medicine, of Euclid in geometry, of Socrates in philosophy, as in later days we are accustomed to speak of a Bacon, a Newton, or a Kant.   The name that has been pri-vileged to represent a science has often had but a slender right to do so.   But the name of S. Thomas of Aquin expresses a great fact.   It is not easy to describe in a few words what he has done for theology.   Recalling to mind the long list of his own written or dictated works, the still longer series of com-mentaries and expositions that so many brains have wrought at during six hundred years, and the catalogue, longest of all, of the books that have been inspired and guided by his doctrine, we do not wonder at the expressions of his panegyrists, who compare him to everything on the earth and in the heavens that is great and glorious.   One of their favourite similes is that of the sun.   When Benedict XIII., in the year 1724, said of the angelical doctor that his doctrine was "like a sun shining over the whole world, producing, in the past as in the present, most abundant fruit to the Church of Christ," the language of declamation seems to be, for once at least, identical with that of simple fact.   But, to estimate the work of S. Thomas with greater precision, let us adopt the sober descrip-tion of the great *Summa* that is given by Fleury in his " History of the Church."   " It is a work," says the French historian, " that has since been regarded in the schools as the most perfect body of theology, as well in regard to its doctrine as to its method."*   What S. Thomas has done is to construct the

---

* Hist. Eccl., 1. 85, n. 39.

most perfect body or system of theology. There is a very deep
significance in this phrase. Whether Fleury meant it or not,
the word body expresses just what S. Thomas has effected.
Other men, great and little, have written, before him and after
him, on theological questions, but he has created a theological
system. Others have even produced theological systems, but
he has given to the world the most complete and perfect of all.
The sense, however, in which it is complete and perfect must
be carefully observed, for it is there that the greatness of the
angel of the school lies concealed. "System" is of various
kinds and degrees. A writer's system may be the particular
side which he takes in a great controversy; or it may denote
the order in which he proceeds; or the point from which he
starts; or the master-truth that guides him; or it may mean
all them together. But the system of S. Thomas was something much higher than any of these. It was a synthesis of
the very highest universality and of the widest extent. He
undertook to build, and he has succeeded in building, a temple
of theology that includes within the sweep of its courts and
colonnades every science that is or can be under the sun. His
building was the court of the faith or of revelation; but physical
science was the ground on which it stood, philosophy of soul
was the ornament of its walls, ontology lent its soaring lightness
to its dome, morality had furnished the gold and the silver that
shone with such new brightness, and logic had planned and
shaped, polished and ornamented the whole. The body, or
system, or palace that S. Thomas created included all truth,
supernatural and natural, without any exception. It was the
first example (indeed, the only one, for there has never been
another) of that Catholic synthesis in which the supernatural
revelation takes its place as the queen of all earthly knowledge,
and in which she is ministered to and glorified by every faculty
and art of man, and by every physical law.

No one will understand us to mean, by what we are here
saying, that S. Thomas wrote about everything that exists or
has ever happened, or that the Catholic synthesis must include
any such omniscience as this. It is true that any one who is
acquainted with his extensive writings, or with those of his
master, Albert the Great, can hardly help having the impression
that there were few matters in the heavens or the earth or the
waters about which the men of the thirteenth century had not
something to say. But for one man to write about everything
has been impossible at least ever since the beasts came out of
the ark, and it becomes naturally more and more impossible
as observation increases and physical sciences are born and
grow up. What is meant is, that Revelation touches reason

and nature, and that the Catholic philosopher must know so much about reason and nature as to be able to show the world how this glorious contact is accomplished. The Ark of the Covenant, with the two Tables in it, must rest in a Temple made by the hands of man. Revelation supposes a human soul and its operation ; the Catholic synthesist must, therefore, know the true psychology. Revelation distinguishes the creator from the creature more clearly than reason could have done ; the Catholic philosopher must have true ideas about the infinite. Revelation informs man of the resurrection of the flesh, of the mystery of the Eucharist, of the distinct creation of each human soul ; the Catholic philosopher must try to penetrate into the secrets of body, of change, of space and of extension, of life, of sense, of the union of spirit and matter. It is not essential to revelation that she should thus be glorified. She can stand apart from all but the most rudimentary elements of human science. But it is her right that they should serve her. It is her right that her doctors should know enough of intellectual theory, of logical method and of physical law, to adorn and to illustrate her supernatural truth. If they have to stop short in ignorance when there is no supernatural mystery, or if their theories are false and their facts exploded, then the Holy Faith misses her due reverence and is dishonoured. But if they can step at will over the boundary lines that divide the supernatural truth from the truth that is in mind and nature, and can freely handle for their purpose every law and fact, every process, every analysis, every discovery, then things are right, and the beauty of order reigns.

The spirit of God, that leads the teacher of the Church into all truth, does not guarantee them any direct inerrancy in matters of philosophy or of fact.[*] It is not to be disputed that when the faith was first heard of in the world, it came without science to hold a touch to it, or to bear its train. It rather seemed to contemn the wisdom of men, and to distrust it as vain, otiose and fallacious. Such is the estimate of S. Paul ; and the spirit of his words is fully adopted by those of his successors in the doctorate who, like him, came into contact with the sophisms of philosophizing pagans or heretics ; for instance by Tertullian,[†] by S. Basil, by S. Augustine, and by S.

---

[*] Non legitur in Evangelio Dominum dixisse, Mitto vobis paracletum qui vos doceat de cursu solis et lunæ. Christianos nos facere volebat non mathematicos.—S. Augustinus, *Act. cont. Felicem*; l. i. cap. 10.

[†] Tertullian's vehemence against the philosophers is well known. In one passage of the Prescriptions (chap. vii.), after calling philosophy a breeder of strife, grinding, harsh, and disgusting, he thus winds up:—" Quid ergo Athenis

Bernard. The fact that Christianity found itself face to face with a great and firmly-rooted Pagan culture, which rapidly passed from despising the new teaching to open and deadly conflict with it, is enough to account for more hard things than we find the Catholic doctors ever used. It was natural that they should, at the very least, refuse to have any part or lot in it; both prudence and feeling dictated this much. But it could not be that the teachers of the faith should be long without recognizing, if only theoretically, that truth, wherever it might be found, belonged of right to their own camp. The Alexandrian Church, to whose history the student of the early centuries has to turn so often, as it was the first Church where scientific culture was possible, so it is the first in which we meet with a distinct statement of the relations of faith and science. The Alexandrian writers speak of human learning under the two names of "encyclical discipline," and the "philosophy of the Greeks."* Under the first was included all that was usually taught in the schools, as grammar, arithmetic, geometry, music, astronomy and rhetoric. Logic seems to have been sometimes included; but the more extended study of dialectics and of other departments of philosophy, as well as the thorough cultivation of rhetoric, naturally came after the time of childhood. The Alexandrian teachers had no doubt whatever that all learning and knowledge had God for its source, and they were prepared to impart to their scholars the whole round of science. The panegyrical oration, pronounced by S. Gregory Thaumaturgus in the presence of his master Origen (circ. A.D. 220) gives what may be called the sketch of a *Summa Theologica.* The liberal arts, logic, natural science, high philosophy, and morality, all find their place in the scheme of Origen. Clement had already stated the principles of the Alexandrian method. It was clearly understood, first of all, that the "Doctrine of Our Saviour," that is to say the revealed Truth, was "perfect in itself and in no way deficient."† If human wisdom could be added, it was an advantage; but there was no absolute necessity for it. Its use and advantages were evident. Clement, in that strange and provoking medley of "notes" which has been called the *Stromata,* has much to say about the

---

et Hierosolymis? Quid Academiæ et Ecclesiæ? Quid Hæreticis et Christianis? Nostra institutio de porticu Salomonis, qui et ipse tradiderat Dominum in simplicitate quærendum. Viderint qui Stoicum et Platonicum et Dialecticum Christianismum protulerunt." But Tertullian knew how to use philosophy when necessary; as see his proof of the immortality of the soul in the book "On the Resurrection."

* Ἡ ἐγκύκλιος παιδεία—αἱ μαθήσεις αἱ ἐγκύκλιοι. Ἡ Ἑλληνικὴ φιλοσοφία.
† *Strom.,* l. i. p. 320 (edit. Paris).

true Gnostic, or, as we should say, scientific theologian.* His
idea is, that philosophy, aud human wisdom generally, furnishes
the faith with what he calls a " setting," and thus renders it
the useful office of "demonstration," that is, exposition and
order.† It enables the expositor to be accurate and strong;
and, naturally, is therefore of great use in the " refutation "‡ of
adversaries. Learning, to be really useful, must be " referred
to the Truth; " § it must be secondary; it must make its
appéarance only where it is wanted. It may be compared to
the hedge and rampart of the vineyard. It is, perhaps, a
descent from this lofty view when Clement elsewhere pleads
that philosophy may be admitted as a recreation from more
severe pursuits, or, as he puts it, as a "sweetmeat after the
supper." But it is clear that with the Alexandrian school, the
formation of a *Summa* was only a matter of time. Human
wisdom was recognized as the " fellow-worker " with divine.
The results of their mutual labours would be sure to make their
appearance. But whether such a result was to be a Thomistic
"body of theology," to last for ages as the treasure of the
Church, would depend upon the man who was to create it. It
was attempted by one whose superior in genius has seldom been
given to the Church. But the Περὶ τῶν ἀρχῶν of Origen was
only a commencement; and even as a commencement it was
never finished. As we have it, it is almost certainly very corrupt.
A more pressing and lifelong work, the fixing of the text of the
Holy Scripture, called upon the best energies of the Adaman-
tine. If a systematic philosophy had been ready to his hand,
more, perhaps, might have been accomplished ; but Alexandria,
in the days of Origen, did not care for Aristotle, and so the
creator of an Alexandrian Summa had to choose among the
splendid fragments of Platonism, and put them together as he
could. And so the time went by. Origen died, and Arius
came, and after him the long-drawn-out troubles of Nestorianism
and Monophysism, until the Arab hosts seized Alexandria, and
her philosophy and her faith perished together in the fire that
burned the treasures of her libraries.

---

* That this is the true interpretation of Clement's ideal character, see
Petavius, *De Dogmatibus Theologicis, Prolegom.*

† Περιβολῇ πλείονι χρωμένους, ἀμηγέπη συγγυμνασίαν τινὰ πίστεως ἀπο-
δεικτικὴν ἐκπορίζεσθαι. (*Strom.,* l. i. p. 279.) Ἡ γνῶσις δὲ ἀπόδειξις τῶν διὰ
πίστεως παρειλημμένων ἰσχυρὰ καὶ βέβαιος, διὰ τῆς κυριακῆς διδασκαλίας ἐποικο-
δομουμένη τῇ πίστει. (*Strom.,* l. vii. p. 732.) The comparison of the γνῶσις to
an *edifice* may be here noted.

‡ Συναιτίοις παραγυμνάσμασι, εἰς τὴν ἀκριβῆ παράδοσιν τῆς ἀληθείας—
ἀπερίσπαστον—προφυλακὴν, κ. τ. λ. (*Strom.,* l. vi. p. 781.)

§ Τὸν πάντα ἐπὶ τὴν ἀλήθειαν ἀναφέροντα—ἀνεπιβούλευτον φυλάσσειν τὴν
πίστιν..(*Strom.,* l. i. p. 342.)

In the century of the great doctors of the Church, from
S. Hilary of Poictiers (366) to S. Leo the Great (461) no such
enterprise as a Summa was possible. Every intellect was
employed upon the definition and protection of dogma. Philosophy, without which no synthesis is possible, was not only
little cultivated, but was very generally, and not without some
reason, regarded as the root of every fantastic form of heresy.
It is true that the greatest names of that period prove themselves well read in the wisdom of the Greeks. The three
eminent doctors of Cappadocia, the two Gregories and S. Basil,
were men of too wide and large a culture themselves not
to know and admit its advantages. But if a Christain doctor
was a philosopher, it was in spite of his being a Christian. His
philosophy was a legacy from the years of his boyhood spent at
a Pagan school, or it was the half-concealed remains of the
errors and aberration of an unruly youth. Even had that
philosophy been better thought of, it would still have been of
little use in the cause of the truth. It chiefly consisted of the
half-completed analysis, the lofty dreams, the unreal speculations, that Plato's magnificent language has made so many
generations accept for philosophy. The solitary philosopher
who attempted, in that age, to give currency to the teachings
of Aristotle was unfortunately a heretic.* If ever there was an
intellect in the whole series of men who have adorned the ranks
of the teaching Church from whom a "body" of theology
might have been expected, it was S. Augustine. The acutest
and most profound of geniuses, there is hardly a philosophical
question that he has not sounded, and hardly a truth of revelation that he has not adorned. Familiar from his youth with
Greek and Roman literature of every kind, practically experienced in a leading heresy of the day—a heresy which involved
one, at least, of the most subtle difficulties that theology has
ever had to meet—he came in his manhood to know the true
faith, and received the grace so to change the whole attitude of
his mind, that when he wrote or spoke of science or of wisdom,
he could not but place the Faith in the foreground of every view.
Throughout the whole of his philosophical writings, whether he
is refuting Academicians or instructing young friends how to

---

* That is to say, Eunomius. *Neander*, Church History (Bohn's translation), vol. iii. p. 496.

It is the Aristotelianism of Eunomius that explains some of S. Basil's
strictures, which at first sight seem to bear upon philosophy generally.
"Hæc illum," says S. Basil, "ex mundi sapientiâ garrire, a quâ in præceps
abreptus hanc sermonis novitatem ingressus est, non est difficile monstrare.
Aristotelis enim sunt, &c." (*Contra Eunomium*, l. i.) S. Gregory of Nyssa
has something to the same effect.

study, encouraging his mother S. Monica to discuss the "beata vita," proving the immortality of the soul, or holding a dialogue with the young Adeodatus on subjects that remind us of the *Pædagogus* of Clement—everywhere he seems to return to one thought, "no wisdom or science without Divine Faith." To read S. Augustine in this light is to learn much about the progress of scientific theology. Hitherto philosophy had either asserted a claim to intellectual independence, as in the case of the Gnosticizing heretics, or had been obliged to stand aside, idle and mistrusted, as with many of the Christian fathers. Neither of these two states of things could be allowed to last. Philosophy must recognize a higher order of truth to which it must submit, and Faith must, on its part, cease to fear philosophy (as Clement would have said, "like children fear ghosts"), and boldly set it in its right place. It would seem as if S. Augustine's mission, as far as concerns the present subject, was to establish this relation between Faith and Philosophy. His often-repeated maxim is "Nisi credideritis, non intelligetis"*—No faith, no science. He insists upon this view so much, that it almost becomes wearisome, until the circumstances of the period are remembered, and we become conscious what a vast step towards the Catholic synthesis has been made when it has been settled that, speaking of all that body of intellectual truth which men have agreed to call "Philosophy," the first place, the place of judgment and of arbitration, not to say the place of elevation and illumination, must be given to the revealed word of God. S. Augustine did not get much further than this. His predominant view necessarily leads him often to be moral and hortatory rather than scientific. His philosophy, moreover, would most likely have broken down under the strain of having to furnish materials for a Summa. It may be doubted whether he had ever thoroughly studied Aristotle. At any rate, his predilection was for Plato.† Yet he has left one or two indications that he knew what a synthesis would be, and that he had thought over many of the points of contact between Faith and Science. It appeared to him that his favourite Plato had created a kind of Summa of philosophy. Plato had inherited

---

* Isaias vii. 9 (according to the Septuagint).

† There is a curious passage at the end of his books against "the Academicians," which seems to show he was not satisfied with his philosophical studies at the age of thirty-three. "Humanam sapientiam . . . . me video nondum percepisse . . . . quandoque adepturum . . . . quid sit verum, non credendo solum sed etiam intelligendo apprehendere ; apud Platonem quod sacris nostris non repugnet reperturum esse confido." (*Contra Acad.*, I. iii. 20.) The concluding clause is as much as to say, that if he ever had constructed a Summa, Plato would have furnished the philosophy.

the wit and acuteness of Socrates in moral matters, and all the science of things natural and things divine that the school of Pythagoras could give him. To all this he had added his own "Dialectic" to fuse the several parts into one whole, and give each one its fitting place; and so "he is said" to have formed a "perfect" science of philosophy.* And his own idea of the really "learned" man was of one who should possess, not merely Faith, but the power to contemplate, to understand, and firmly to grasp what he believes; who should be at home in deep and difficult questions, who should know what unformed matter was, what the lifeless organism, what body was, what was colour, place, time, motion, eternity, existence, and such profound and troublesome matters, and should be able to reduce all the things that so many various branches of instruction had taught him, to the one, true, and certain principle.

S. Augustine, in his old age, wrote a kind of supplement to his work, *De Correptione et Gratia,* at the instance of certain Catholics of the south-east of Gaul, represented by S. Prosper of Aquitaine.† Gallia Narbonensis was at that time one of the most learned and active seats of Ecclesiastical literature throughout the Western Church. The names of Honoratus, Salvian, John Cassian, Vincent, Prosper and Hilary, of Arausica, of Massilia and of Lerins, will recall an extensive literature of asceticism and controversy. There occurs in the celebrated work of Vincent of Lerins, the *Commonitorium,* a passage which might almost be quoted as a motto by the writer of a Theological *Summa.* In this fiery tractate, written in his solitude on the Mediterranean coast, just as the news of the conclusion of the Council of Ephesus was beginning to be well known in the further west,‡ the soldier, turned ascetic, aims at deterring men from imitating the "profane novelties" of the heretics. Yet the following extract will show what was the idea at Lerins of a possible Temple of the Faith.

O Timothy! O Priest! O Teacher! O Doctor! If by God's gift thou art fitted by talent, by practice, by learning, then be thou the Beseleel of the Spiritual Tabernacle; carve the precious jewels of God's Dogma, fit them together carefully, adorn them wisely; make the building splendid, beau-

---

* Adjiciens lepori subtilitatique Socraticæ . . . . naturalium divinarumque rerum peritiam . . . . quasi formatricem illarum partium judicemque Dialecticam . . . . perfectam dicitur composuisse philosophiæ disciplinam. (*Contra Acad.,* l. iii. 17.) But this highly coloured estimate of Plato's "synthesis" is only given as "opinion," not as certainly ascertained. Still it shows that S. Augustine knew what a *Summa* would be.

† De Prædestinatione Sanctorum et de Dono Perseverantiæ.

‡ The Commonitorium was written in 434.

tiful and attractive. What men believed already in a dark manner, let them, at thy exposition, understand more clearly. Let those that come after thee be thankful for understanding what those that went before thee venerated but did not understand. But teach nothing but what thou thyself hast learnt, that thou mayst say nothing novel when thou sayest things in a novel way.*

The school of S. Augustine, and the generation of great writers that Pelagianism had occupied, passed away. The empire of the West had fallen, and the Goth reigned at Rome and Ravenna. The great flood of the Huns had but lately devastated Italy, and the land was breathing awhile under the rule of the wise Theodoric. It was the era of Clovis, half a century after the death of S. Leo, when (in 525) the Gothic king passed sentence of death upon a man who perhaps has done more than Theodoric himself to make that prince illustrious. Standing at the point where an old civilization is dying out in trouble and confusion, and when a new barbarism has nearly completed the successive tides of its advance—only a few years before S. Benedict, at the very epoch of S. Remigius—the senator Boethius presents us with the figure of one who saves a treasure from the flood and makes many succeeding centuries his debtor. Had it nót been for the amazing energy and devotion of the man, who was the counsellor and ambassador of Popes and Princes, the Middle Ages would probably have never known even so much of the philosophy of Plato and of Aristotle as it did know. The object of the "last of the Romans," in all his lucubrations and translations, was to reconcile the philosophy of the two great Greek teachers. In him we read, for the first time in history, the metaphysical terms of Aristotle used to convey and illustrate the Christian mysteries.† He distinctly put his hand to the work which S. John Damascene was to do better, and S. Thomas of Aquin to accomplish perfectly. But, if nothing else had prevented him from leaving it complete, his busy life and premature death would have excused him. In prison, sick, without books, he could only fall back upon his genius and his vast acquired learning, and his *Summa* was the "*Consolations of Philosophy.*"

Contemporary with Boethius, a great politician like himself, and as eager a lover of learning, was his friend Cassiodorus. Here is another of the names that the monks of many a mediæval convent must have blessed, and that many a master and doctor usefully pillaged in Celtic and Teuton schools of

---

* Ut cum dicas nove, non dicas nova.—*Comm.* I.
† See, for instance, his works *De Unitate Trinitatis* and *De Persona et duabus Naturis.*

after-times. The cheerful old centenarian, who made his monks copy Aristotle and Porphyry, cultivate gardens and tend the sick in that pleasant spot of Calabria, his monastery of Vivaria, was not such a profound genius as Boethius. The troubled times not having allowed him to found a great school at Rome, as he wished, he aimed at making a compendium of all knowledge for the service of the Faith. But he had no wide plan or design. He wrote much on Holy Scripture. He wrote a complete "encyclical" course for his monks (and, though he did not know it, for many more monks than they), and he exhorted them to work hard at these "secular disciplines," calling to mind how their Fathers, such as a Cyprian, an Augustine, and a Jerome, went out from Egypt laden with plunder of many kinds, in gold and silver and vestures, and how much this sort of knowledge assisted the intelligence of Scripture, wherein it was all contained in germ. And finally, with the consolation of having pressed a multitude of able servants into what he called the "service of the Truth," he died, a few years before the elevation to the Popedom of S. Gregory the Great.*

Passing over some fifty years, we find ourselves, for the first time, seeking for science in a Teutonic race. Isidore of Seville is not absolutely the first German who has left any literary works, but he is the first who can claim to have made, in any sense, a synthesis of knowledge. The voluminous writings of the great Archbishop of Gothic Spain strike the reader as being intensely, and, above all things, practical. He collected Canons, he strung together "Sententiæ" from S. Augustine and S. Gregory the Great, he wrote introductions to Holy Scripture, he compiled history, and, finally, he has left Twenty Books of Etymologies, in which we have a little of everything, from Aristotle's Logic down to geography and clothes. This was the *Summa* of the Spanish Church in the beginning of the seventh century. Without meaning to be disrespectful to so great a saint, we may compare the Etymologies to a series of Pinnock's Catechisms. He nowhere rises beyond the point of placing natural science side by side with divine, and declaring

---

* Est enim rerum istarum [artium sc. sæcularium] procul dubio (sicut et Patribus nostris visum est) utilis et non refugienda cognitio, quando eam in litteris sacris tanquam in origine generalis perfectæque sapientiæ ubique reperis esse diffusam.— *Cassiodorus*, De Institutione Divinarum Litterarum, cap. 27.

Quod illi [sc. antiqui] ad exercendas versutias derivarunt, nos *ad veritatis obsequia* laudabili devotione revocemus ; quatenus quæ inde *furtive sublata sunt*, in obsequium rectæ intelligentiæ honestâ conditione *reddantur.—Ibid.*

that while the latter is paramount, the former is also useful.* But he often insists upon the Augustinian position, that the knowledge of God is the first thing in wisdom, and he is fond of saying (or quoting) that ignorance of "the world," or of "the elements," or of "things incorporeal and corporeal," matters little, provided there be Faith and Virtue.† And in speaking of the teachings of the philosophers, he expresses the opinion that though some things in them are "suitable to religion, others are very foreign to it indeed."‡

Venerable Bede, a hundred years later, was an English Isidore, except that he was not a bishop, and that he possessed an eloquence of which we see no traces in S. Isidore. But he, in his turn, wrote an "encyclical" course, for utility's sake, and not with any profound plan. As S. Isidore quoted the Latin fathers, so he quotes them also, and S. Isidore himself. There is no use, then, in looking to Venerable Bede for synthesis of theology and science. His indefatigable life was given to practical matters, chiefly to the Holy Scriptures. He had learnt from S. John of Beverley that it was a monk's first duty to be useful, and, as he says of himself, "either to learn, or to teach, or to write," was all life's sweetness for him.

For two hundred years after the time that Alcuin assisted Charlemagne in his great work of founding schools throughout his vast dominions, little or no advance was made towards a *Summa*. The monastic schools had plenty to occupy themselves with; such teachers as Rhaban Maur, Walfrid Strabo, and Paschasius Radbert not only kept theology alive and effective, but shed more liberal culture than superficial inquirers will admit, over the countries that were watered by the Loire, the Rhine, and the Elbe. But the light that should have shone upon them from antiquity was reduced to a very feeble ray, and it was almost as if intellectual science had to commence again from the point where Thales had left it. In time, minds would have risen up, and new creations would have appeared. Meanwhile the all-sufficing light of Faith was in the world, and there was much patristic tradition, and a few precious fragments of philosophy. S. Augustine, S. Jerome, Boethius, and Cassiodorus, S. Isidore and S. Bede, were copied out, abridged, added to, and passed from hand to hand, from school to school, from abbey to abbey; and monks and their scholars, happy in the Faith, lived peaceably and died sensibly. It is true that the erring career of John Scotus Erigena seems, for a time, to disturb the atmosphere of quiet. That Erigena was a genius seems certain, but it was certainly not his genius or his ori-

---

* *De Nat. Rer.* Præf.   † *De Sentent.* l. ii. cap. i.   ‡ *Different.* l. ii. 110.

ginality that led him into that Pantheism for which he was chiefly condemned. He was fond of Aristotle; but if he had seen better how to mistrust Plato, he might have promoted the Truth instead of damaging it.

We now approach that period which was to culminate in S. Thomas himself. Scholasticism is a word with a wide meaning. The system it expresses may be said to have been dawning when Lanfranc attacked Berengarius, in the middle of the eleventh century, with a perfection of dialectic which was never afterwards surpassed, and which was a distinct development in the relations between science and theology. When the *Monologium* and *Proslogium* of S. Anselm appeared, scholasticism was upon the world. When Roscellinus (1100) in the name of Aristotle, challenged all Platonists to prove that general ideas were anything more than empty sound, it had begun to act its mighty part in intellectual history.

Scholasticism was to result in a *Summa,* or synthesis of Catholic Faith, natural rational Truth, and natural Facts. For such a result the first thing requisite was a body or systematic summary of the Faith itself. In the twelfth century there was more than one already in existence; for instance that which appears in the "Etymologies" of S. Isidore. But in the early part of that century the work was done better by two great men. The first of these was Hugh of S. Victor, most sweet and eloquent of mediæval theologians, in his *De Sacramentis.* The latter was Peter the Lombard, in his famous *Libri Sententiarum.* The following is Father Vaughan's description of this work :—

The work of the Lombard filled a void and satisfied a craving. Men were looking for some point from which they could get a clear and sure *coup d'œil* of theologic teaching. They wished to see the truths of religion thrown into organic form. Peter satisfied them. He presented them with a work which, though not very artistic in arrangement, was essentially the expression, not so much of the notions of the individual mind, as of the objective truths of religion. It was based upon the monastic principle, and stood on S. Augustine ; it used the weightiest words of the weightiest fathers in the weightiest manner, and manifested a mind, not restlessly seeking after truth, but possessed of it ; and calmly and systematically, without swerving to the right or left, communicating it to others. (p. 262.)

This was the first of necessities. The Fathers, S. Augustine especially, had proclaimed that revelation was absolutely the judge of all other truth. The first step, therefore, towards a Summa is to state the Faith, and announce that this is to be the point of departure. And there were some reasons peculiar to the active age in which S. Thomas lived that made this

especially requisite at that time.   In the first place there were
several active heresies, or worse than heresies, living in the
atmosphere of the day.   Manichæism was so far from being a
thing of the past, that it was to the Church the greatest source
of trouble, and to the State the most difficult problem that
either had to deal with in the twelfth and thirteenth centuries.
Pantheism existed, though chiefly in the wild dreams of a few
obscure men, such as that mediæval Spinoza, David of Dinant.
Against these two foes, as well as against all the ancient
heresies, which were always liable to reappear in the mouth of
some busy dialectician, talking rapidly to enormous audiences
in Paris or Oxford, the Church had to keep her faith distinctly
formulated.   But the great necessity for asserting the principle
of revelation, of tradition, of authority, or whatever it may be
called, arose from the existence of a school which, as formerly
in S. Augustine's days, so now, insisted that Reason was the
equal of Faith, and even that Faith should be judged by the
decisions of mere human philosophy.   For an extended sketch
of the most brilliant Rationalist of that time we refer the reader
to Father Vaughan's account of Abelard.*   The very energetic
report of his doings, which S. Bernard sent to Pope Innocent II.,
is both instructive as showing us the man, and interesting as
being the very living expression of the pain which orthodox
Catholics feel in every age when any clever reasoner begins to
reason away Revelation.   It also insinuates another lesson ; the
damage, namely, which rationalists do to the cause of reason
itself, by irritating pious believers and making them exclaim
against all philosophy.   When S. Bernard cries out against
Abelard for making degrees in the Trinity, modes in the
Majesty of God, and numbers in His Eternity ; † when he
warns him that in matters of Faith there is no such thing as
" supposing," and that there must be no " disputing at
pleasure," but that he is " confined within boundaries and
fixed limits,"‡ he is asserting most important truths ; but
it is evident that men of inferior minds will only have to take
one step farther in order to reach obscurantism.   The holy
abbot of Clairvaux protests against " profane novelties," and is
indignant with the man who thus insults the " piety of Faith,"
" violently invades her sanctuary, and with irreverent hand

---

* *S. Thomas of Aquin,* vol. i. p. 151.

† Ponit in Trinitate gradus, in Majestate modos, numeros in Æternitate.
—*Tractatus de Erroribus Abelardi,* cap. i.

‡ Non licet tibi in Fide putare, vel disputare pro libitu . . .   certis
clauderis finibus, certis limitibus coarctaris.—*Ibid.,* cap. iv.

scatters her hidden treasures."* What has this man, this " second Aristotle," to offer to the world better, more profound, than the holy and wise men of the past?† What waters of stealth and bread of concealment is he going to give us? Has he forgotten the command, that we pass not beyond what our fathers have laid down? He is so rash as to say that all formulas are useless unless the hearer understand them ; and he explains mysteries by the philosophy of Plato. Let him know that our faith is not in the wisdom of words, but in the power of God; let him beware lest while he strains to prove Plato a Christian, he may only succeed in proving himself a heathen.‡ Such language, and much more of it, was due to Abelard, and was richly deserved; but it cannot be read without thinking of the use that perverse men might make of it against S. Thomas himself.§ Thus, for the work of a *Summa,* it was necessary both to form a systematic arrangement of dogma and tradition, and to insist that such a " body of doctrine " was strictly sufficient, and also to stand out boldly for the right which this supernatural body of truth possessed, of not being judged by any other whatsoever.

The next thing was an enterprise that was far more difficult. It was to find a philosophy. By " a philosophy " is meant a system of natural reason, such as could be associated with the Faith. It is evident that Revelation could accept the help of philosophy only on one condition, namely, that philosophy should be *true,* or at least should not contradict the truth that was revealed. That such a philosophy was possible no father of the Church or orthodox scholastic ever doubted. Human reason was given by God as well as Revelation, and was equally infallible in its proper sphere. But did such a philosophy exist? Was it sufficiently developed, so as to form a reasonably complete science? Would the creator of the future *Summa* have to create his philosophy first? Up to a short time before S. Thomas began to lecture on the " Sentences," it might have seemed that this last would have been the only course. As it really happened, it is well known that S. Thomas adopted the philosophy of Aristotle.

· * Irruens in arcana Fidei, thesauros absconditos pietatis tam irreverenter invadit atque discerpit.—*Ibid.,* eod. cap.

† Tot præterierit sanctos, effugerit sapientes.—*Ibid.,* cap. iii.

‡ Ubi dum multa sudat quomodo Platonem faciat Christianum, se probat ethnicum.—*ibid.,* cap. iv.

§ The reader may also compare the Brief of Gregory IX., written to the University of Paris, in 1223 (vide *Denzinger,* Enchiridion, p. 165). Among other things he tells them to be content with "the terms instituted by the fathers,"—contenti terminis a patribus institutis.

It has been already hinted, that, even if all other causes had been favourable, the predominant leaning of the Fathers and earliest scholastics to Platonic notions of metaphysics would have rendered a *connubium* between philosophy and theology impossible. In the first place, Plato, vast and imposing as his renown justly is, has not left what can by any stretch be called a "system" or "science" of philosophy. Profound, splendid, and elevating as he is at one time, trifling and tedious as he is at another, he it always fragmentary. He is a discoverer who ascends lofty heights, and, sweeping the unknown country with his far-reaching glass, writes for his friends a picturesque description, in which fact is not always kept separate from fancy. There is little that he takes the trouble to survey and map out. If his fragments were less fanciful they might have been of greater use. But real objective fact, as concerning either his own mind or the outward world, was utterly unimportant to Plato. He held that ideas were necessarily and *à priori* true, as being the real images of really existing Divine archetypes. A man's great object was to find out what he had in his own mind. Whatever was really there was sure to be an image of the good, the beautiful, and the true. It is clear that the converse proposition, that the good, the beautiful, and the true was the image of his own imaginations, was in reality the canon upon which the Platonist relied. And this leads us on to notice that Plato was not only fragmentary and fanciful, but he was also false; and false in one or two most important matters. No Christian philosopher could have explained his doctrine of ideas (without explaining it away) so as to avoid both idealism, rationalism, and pantheism. This was a vital point. The doctrine of ideas, or how we get what we know, lies at the root of Faith itself. To a Platonist, either a revelation is impossible, or it is no revelation. Whatever he knows must have been in his mind when his mind began to be. The Platonic theory of ideas was a necessary consequence of Plato's teachings concerning the union of soul and body in man. The soul was an imprisoned spirit, the body was foreign matter, and matter was the evil that was in the universe. There was no possibility of a theory of sin, or of a scientific statement of the incarnation, with such a philosophy as this. This was the philosophy which so long obstructed the building of a Temple of the Faith, though it must be allowed that many a great name in early and later ages has loved it warmly. It was loved because it seemed to harmonize so well with the Christian truths of the presence of God's light in the mind and His intimate revelation of Himself to every particular soul. It was loved because it seemed to furnish terms in which to describe that beautiful internal life, that pensive and rapt mysticism which was possible through grace; and as long as the never-failing voice of the Church was listened to (with some sacrifice of consistency) the danger was kept out, though it frequently lay very close to the door.* But Platonism obstructed scientific theology, because it held the mind too closely to the inspection of its own acts, and kept it from observing those facts and generalizations of the human and natural universe which are the fertile analogies by which, stammering, it is true (as S. Gregory says), but as well as we can, we express the lofty things of God.

If Platonism could not be the philosophical foundation of the future *Summa*, there was no other name to be thought of but Aristotle. There is nothing more curious, or shall we say more providential, than the way in which Aristotle seems to make a sudden appearance in the world of intellect at the very moment that S. Thomas was beginning to look about for him. The Stagyrite had not had the goodhap of Plato. After the destruction of the school of Cassiodorus in Southern Italy, in the sixth century, no Western student had the privilege of reading Aristotle in the original, or even in a complete translation, for a space of nearly 600 years. Up to 1230 Aristotle was only known to the scholastics by his *Organon,* or collection of logical treatises, or by the worse than useless fragments of bad translation from his other works which had come to Europe by way of the Spanish Arabs.† His name, like that of Origen, had come under the ban of the Church on account of the monstrous errors that his Jewish and Moslem interpreters had fathered upon him. In 1209, a council of Paris condemned him in company with Averroes and Avvicenna. Six years later, the legate of the Holy See, in confirming the sentence, excepted the *Organon* (which was the only work that was really Aristotle's). Later still, in 1231, Pope Gregory IX. renewed the.

---

* De Platonis philosophiâ major et antiquior est expostulatio Christianorum patrum; quòd superiores fere omnes hæreses a Platonicis inventæ excultæque sunt, aut ex eorum consutæ fabulis indidem originem repetunt. (*Petavius,* De Dogmatibus Theologicis, Proleg. II. 2.) Compare the *Anathemas* of Pope Damasus (*Denzinger,* Enchir., p. 15); the Canons of the Fifth General Council against the Origenists; the condemnation of Abelard by Innocent II. (*Ibid.,* p. 140), and of Ekkard by John XXII. (*Ibid.,* p. 179). "The Alexandrian tendency of mind," says Neander, "had it met with no opposition, and if it had been carried out without restraint of that pious spirit which tempered it in the case of a Clement and an Origen, would unquestionably have led to an idealism subvsrsive of all the historical and objective truths of Christianity."—*Church Hist.,* Bohn's Transl., vol. ii. p. 265.

† See *La Somme Théologique de S. Thomas,* par l'Abbé Drioux, *Introd.,* p. xiii.

prohibition to read the books of Aristotle until they should have been corrected. Yet after 1240 we find his name quoted in every scientific work that appears. The explanation is that the Western schools had now got possession of his original text, and were translating it correctly. By 1270, the year of the death of S. Louis, and two years after the last crusade, they were in possession of the whole of his works.

But S. Thomas had already taken him up. The master under whom he studied at Cologne (1245), the great Albert, was the first to "Christianize" Aristotle. Like some powerful giant sent on before to hew out the way and collect materials, Albert had laboured on the whole of Aristotle and the whole of Science.* When his yet greater scholar came in his turn, and while his master was yet living, to occupy the chair in the schools of Paris, he seemed to have no hesitation in declaring himself at once and thoroughly a follower of Aristotle, in all things except his manifest errors. It was by his means that a Latin translation of the whole of the philosopher's works was given to the world—a translation so accurate that its reputation is equal to that of the best MS. *codices*.† He prepared by annotating nearly the whole of his writings, for his great purpose of incorporating Aristotelianism with the doctrine of the Faith.

The time has long gone by when the name of Aristotle was a name of reproach. Yet it must be remembered, by those who are familiar with the *Summa* of S. Thomas, that Aristotle's *Metaphysics* are as good as unknown to a great part of the philosophical world even at the present day. As the mighty founder and builder-up of logic, as the author of the *Rhetoric* and the *Politics*, as the exhaustive *Ethicist*, he has been before the world ever since the times of the Humanists, when Erasmus of Rotterdam, who laughed so bitterly at his scholastic followers, printed at Basle no less than seven editions of his complete works in Greek. His Physics are now beginning to be better known than they were, thanks to such works as that of Mr. Lewes. But Aristotle's Metaphysics proper, that is to say, his Ontology and his Anthropology, including Psychology and Ideology, would even now appear, to all but real scholars, to be arbitrary in their principles, antiquated in their method, and barbarous in their terms. It is needless to say that we by no means undertake to maintain that Aristotle, or S. Thomas

---

* See the interesting chapter on "Albertus Magnus," *S. Thomas of Aquin*, l. 115.

† See Mr. Adolf Stahr's article "Aristoteles," in *Smith's Dict. of Biography and Mythology*, vol. i. p. 325.

either, is never wrong, or inadequate. But it is worth while to note briefly some of the features of that scheme which S. Thomas thought worthy to be joined in such close conjunction with God's revelation, and the employment of which the Church has so often and so emphatically approved. In drawing this out, we shall avoid all minor matters, and shall not trouble to distinguish accurately between what is Aristotle's own and the additions of S. Thomas.

There is no doubt that it was his doctrine of ideas, as contrasted with that of Plato, which induced the holy doctor to prefer Aristotle.* Broadly stated, the difference between the two was this: Plato held that all ideas are actually existent in the mind at the beginning of life, as we have already stated; Aristotle taught that for the production of every idea, or actual intellectual concept, sense and intellect must co-operate, and that all knowledge begins in sense. For man, in his view, was One; not body and soul, but Man. Whatever actuality or being or operation he had, was his One soul, which was not a mere spirit, but a spirit-in-matter. Whatever truth he possessed was obtained by a process of elaboration. His intellect had, or was, the power of performing this process: as S. Thomas said, it was the created similitude of the intellect of God. The imagination and the sense were different altogether from the intellect. Here was a system which, whatever may be said of it, could be applied to a religion which held that Revelation was one source of human knowledge; a system which could provide a preamble for faith; which made the resurrection of the flesh and the transmission of original sin,—not unmysterious, but still not absurd impossibilities; and which cut away the ground from the feet of false mysticism. We do not say it is complete. But it harmonizes so well with Revelation that it will certainly never be proved false.

Look again at the Thomistic ontology. Instead of being crabbed or arbitrary, it is founded upon the very plainest experimental processes. The sense presents an object. The first thing that the mind does is to perceive that it is. It is a being. By further experience, it perceives that it changes from time to time; that it is now of one colour, now of another, first round and then square. Two new conceptions are the result; that of accident or mode, which expresses what comes and goes, and Substance, which expresses that permanent thing in which the modes inhere. But the mind, considering further, sees that if all mode were to disappear, there would be nothing left but an

---

* See *Philosophia Christiana*, by C. Sanseverino, vol. i. Introductio, p. 78.

abstraction; and from this it obtains the idea of Individuation. Considering next the concept, just gained, of substance, it cannot help seeing that there is a difference between substance and substance; for it sees that there are some substances which are so completely *sui juris* that they do not require another substance for their existence and operation; others, on the contrary, are not their own, but are the property, so to speak, of another, of which they, in a certain sense, form part, and to which their operations are attributed. In this way Socrates, for instance, is different from his arm or his head. This discrimination furnishes the mind with the idea of a Suppositum, or Person, as distinguished from a nature or substance that has not suppositality or personality. Looking now at the substance, essence, or nature (these words are distinguishable and distinct, but not for our present purpose), the mind perceives that this can change into another substance or essence; that bread, for instance, may become flesh; one activity, or group of activities disappears, and another succeeds; with this peculiar feature, however, that those activities thus succeeding one another have this in common, that they are also passive. This analysis results in those two horns of the Peripatetics, form and matter, terms which are employed, by analogy, in many other genera besides that of substance.* But to proceed. The mind, having made out the idea, Form, looks at it by itself, irrespective of what we call matter. Even now it is limited; it is not infinite; it is made up of activity, and some kind of passivity. The mind generalizes once more. Every being is made up of Act and Power (potentiality). Especially, it is made up of what it is and its existence; for its essence does not imply actual existence. But suppose that it should? Then the mind conceives the idea of a being that is Pure Act, without any admixture of potentiality, and whose very essence is to be. This is God.

This is a rough sketch of a deep subject, but it is sufficient for our purpose. Let the reader now think of the Christian Revelation, and how many of the terms just used are employed in its statement. Let him think of person and nature in the Incarnation, of substance and accident in the Blessed Eucharist, of the definition that the soul is the form of the body,† of matter and form in the Sacraments, and of act, which itself, or in its equivalent of activity or force, is found on every page

---

* See F. Bayma's "Molecular Mechanics," p. 13. This article was written before the writer had the pleasure of reading F. Dalgairns's brilliant paper "The Theory of a Soul," in the *Contemporary Review* for December, 1870.

† Denzinger, "Enchiridion," p. 453 (Pii P. IX. Breve ad Arch. Coloniensem, de erroribus Guentheri, 15th June, 1857).

not only of theology, but of ancient and modern science,* and he will find it difficult to make up his mind that a terminology so sanctioned by the Church and by reason can be anything like utterly baseless and false.

It is difficult to see in what way it is possible for the psychology, for instance, of S. Thomas, ever to be proved wrong. Of course, we take Revelation for granted. Will man ever be proved to be a soul imprisoned in matter? Will it ever be shown that there are such things as innate ideas? Will mind and sense ever be allowed to be the same? As to his Ontology, must there not necessarily be a true objective sense in such words as nature, person, essence, generation, relation, and a thousand others that are used in the Faith? The mere fact that the Church formularies use these words, even in the many cases where no infallibility can be proved, should be quite sufficient to convince any one who values the *pietas fidei* that the philosophic system, of which they form part, will be found on examination to be very generally correct. It is quite possible that it may be yet further supplemented and developed. One matter in which it seems to us that S. Thomas, and even his best disciples, such as Joannes a S. Thomâ, have by no means said the last word, is the question as to *how* the intellect and imagination co-operate in intellection. And it is quite possible that there are others.

Any valid objection to the philosophy of S. Thomas must, it would seem, come from the side of Physics. We have insisted that the Beseleel of the Tabernacle of Revelation should be acquainted with natural science. But is it not clearer than noonday-light that S. Thomas's Physics are utterly childish? There is no such thing as substantial form, or as substance; and as for body, it is only force.

There is no such thing as substantial form, it is objected. What, then, is body? It is a congeries of atoms, or forces. We cannot, of course, discuss, in this space, the primary element of body. But, observing first that the hypothesis of atoms, though a useful one for the imagination, never has been and never can be verified, let us ask what is the mighty difference between saying that A is a system of activities with a certain bond of cohesion that makes them phenomenally one, and to say that A is simply an activity? There is a difference, certainly; but it is a difference which is of no consequence as far as theology is concerned, and of comparatively very little

---

* "The scholastic saying, *Deus est actus purus*, ridiculed as it has been by modern critics, is in truth but the expression, in technical language, of the almost unanimous voice of philosophy, both in earlier and later times."— *Mansel's Bampton Lectures*, ii. p. 33.

in regard to absolute truth.   As to body being simply force, if
Aristotle could come back he would probably say in reply, that
force is simply body; he long ago described a Nature to be
operation *in actu primo;* which we take to be force not yet
terminated.

But is not the imagination that mode inheres in substance
merely chimerical?   Unless we abandon reason (not to say
Revelation) altogether, it clearly is not.   My sense, and the
effect of an object on my sense, and the conviction that such
effect has an external cause, are three primary facts.   With one
who denies them, there is no disputing.   But what do they
involve?   First, a phenomenon; secondly, an external objective
force, or reality, which has produced the phenomenon. Aristotle
calls the first, accident; the second, substance.   If any one likes
to say that a phenomenon consists of two co-efficients, the sense
and the objective force, Aristotle would probably not mind his
objecting to the scholastic-looking term, "inheres."

But it is, perhaps, unwise to attempt such explanations as
these in the limited space at our command.   There is yet a
whole army of terms that might be justified.   And it must
be remembered that a good terminology, systematic, connected,
and complete, is the first requisite of science.   Indeed, what
scientific man ever gets much further?   We have said nothing
about the logic of S. Thomas, or his ethical writings.   We have not
even alluded to a subject that is a very sore one with anti-
Peripatetics, the Aristotelian theory of sensible cognition.   It is
certainly not because we do not think it completely defensible.

After what has been said about the splendid work that S.
Thomas has done for the Faith, it will perhaps seem a contradiction if we express the wish that another S. Thomas would arise
in this nineteenth century to write the *Summa* completely afresh.
But no one can deny that, to all appearance, there is at present
a wide divorce between current intellectual thought and scientific theology.   This is not sufficiently explained by saying that
the science of the Catholic schools is right and modern thought
all wrong.   A great many results of modern science are not
only quite true, but are widely accepted as true by theologians.
Now truth is one, and if a thing be true in science it is true
also in theology.   There is no reason whatever why terms and
analogies that have long been superseded as defective or
incorrect, and so recognized by every one, should continue to
figure in our text-books.   Such terms remind one of the
"bows and arrows" that excited the pitying horror of Captain
Dalgetty, when used by his friends the "salvages" against the
powder and lead of their enemies.   We do not wish to exaggerate, and therefore would not be understood to say that this

kind of fault is very extensive or very important in *modern Catholic philosophy*. But the important fact to notice is that a *Summa* worthy of the name is impossible unless every recognized philosophical error is excluded. It seems true to say that Catholic philosophy does not sufficiently recognize the good that is in modern thought. In matters of logic, for instance, our current text-books* seem never to have heard of the labours of the late English school. It is not too much to say that the "eight canons of Syllogism," given, for instance, in F. Liberatore's *Compendium*, are præ-scientific in presence of the anlaysis of even Sir W. Hamilton. Again, the terminology of modern biology and physics might be recognized, and not only not contradicted where it expresses truth, but shown to be in harmony with the formularies and the perpetual tradition of theology. There is no doubt that modern analysis has cleared up much in regard to the physiological side of sensation; as to nerves, for instance, brain, brain-pictures, &c. Modern thinkers, again, might be more fairly treated. Continental philosophers ought by this time to know that in England there has been much done in philosophy since Locke, Hume, Reid, and Stewart. It may be said that no current Catholic philosophical text-book bestows on Kant the attention due to him. In the present day, as in the times of Locke, or of Kant, there is a great philosophical movement going on. It is represented by such names as Bain, Mill, McCosh, Herbert Spencer, Mansel, of E. Saisset and Taine, and many others. It is true that these writers are most of them foes of the Church, and most dangerous to the young beginner in philosophy. But it is chiefly because they have possession of fragments of truth that they are dangerous, and truth, properly speaking, belongs to the Catholic camp. Scepticism, Pantheism, Rationalism, Naturalism, and all the "*deliramenta*" of the "Quanta cura," are to be found in the philosophy of the day; but there is also to be found much excellence of natural reason, and therefore of truth. Our object in thus insisting is not—very far indeed from it—to urge that Catholic philosophy—the groundwork of the future *Summa*—should conform itself to Positivism or Transcendentalism. The very point here contended for is that the terms and method of the Scholastic Theology are, as a whole, perfectly suited to the present day, because perfectly corresponding to truth and reality. Let us remember that no Catholic can doubt this—so far at least as regards its method and principles—in the presence of the thirteenth proposition con-

---

* Let us name F: Liberatore, F. Tongiorgi, and Don Sanseverino.

demned in the Syllabus.* If ever a new *Summa* is made, it must be on the lines and foundations that our fathers have laid down.

The positive and traditional statement of Dogma has made marked progress in system and completeness by the labours of Passaglia, of Schrader, and by the admirable prelections that F. Franzelin is at this moment giving to the world. F. Franzelin may be destined to be the Albert of the future S. Thomas. That such a man will be raised up in time we cannot doubt.

Meanwhile let us return to the study of S. Thomas himself. We desire to direct earnest attention to F. Vaughan's *Life*. He has given us something that is entirely new in English— we might truly say, new altogether. We commend especially his biographical chapters to the attention of those to whom S. Thomas has hitherto been little more than a great name.

Art. VI.—THE ERCKMANN-CHATRIAN NOVELS.

Romans Nationaux.	*Romans Populaires.*
L'Histoire d'un Paysan.	*Maître Daniel Rock.*
Le Conscrit de 1813.	*Contes des Bords du Rhin.*
Waterloo.	*L'Ami Fritz.*
Le Blocus.	*Un Joueur de Clarinette.*
La Guerre.	*La Maison Forestière.*
L'Homme du Peuple.	*Le Juif Polonais.*

—Paris : Hetzel.

THE series of works whose titles head this page has no fellow in literature. It stands alone, in its origin and in its kind. No instances of joint authorship supplied by the annals of poetry or prose explain the mechanism, or aid in the analysis of the inspiration of these books, in which the autobiographical form has been adopted with success unparalleled within our knowledge. That two minds have thought them out, two several hands written them, is a wonderful fact, let the proportion assigned to each author be what it may. Such is the perfection of the workmanship that the closest inspection fails to detect that proportion. But the true excellence, the height

---

* "Methodus et principia quibus antiqui doctores scholastici Theologiam excoluerunt, temporum nostrorum necessitatibus scientiarumque progressui minime congruunt." It is also a condemned proposition that the method of S. Thomas and other scholastics leads to rationalism, or is the reason why modern schools of philosophy have gone astray towards naturalism or pantheism ; and it is declared unlawful to reproach these doctors and teachers with having used their peculiar method.—See *Theses contra Traditionalismum*, set forth by the present Pontiff ; *Denzinger*, Enchir., p. 452.

of the art displayed in this joint production, is evinced in the utterance being that of a third person. What this feat signifies it takes some pains to realize, until one applies the ready test of several other famous autobiographically-constructed fictions. In this category we hold "Robinson Crusoe" to be unrivalled. Tell a child, in the full, fresh delight of the story, that it was not written by a shipwrecked man of that name, but by one Daniel Defoe, a maker of books, and he either does not believe you, or he resents the information, and tries to forget it. Could we, obliged to bend to the historic verities, conceive the possibility of Defoe's having had a partner in that work? Again, "The Vicar of Wakefield," by no means so perfect a work of art, is a production in which it is impossible to imagine the author receiving any aid. Under the careful and complete form of "Esmond," the satirist of the nineteenth century is to be traced. The imitation is admirably sustained for the most part; but one feels, while the wig and the shoe-buckles, the ruffles and the rapier are those of the Jacobite colonel, the spirit and the voice are those of Thackeray. Only the first of these three writers of fiction in the autobiographical form furnishes a parallel to the realism of the French twin authors. Goldsmith is not Primrose, Thackeray is not Esmond, and the reader cannot lose sight of either; but the authors of the "Histoire d'un Paysan" disappear utterly in Michel Bastien, they do not interfere with the conscript Joseph Bertha at Lutzen, or the veteran Joseph Bertha at Waterloo; there is not a hint of their creed or nation in the shrewd but worthy Jew, who turns the blockade of Phalsbourg to good account, or an indication of their own or any of the preceding identities, in the journeyman cabinetmaker Jean Pierre, who narrates the Revolution of 1848 in his capacity of an *homme du peuple.* What great English writers, each having only his own mind to direct steadily to the adoption of another personality, have done imperfectly at the best, these two French gentlemen have done to perfection, in a co-operation whose difficulties can hardly be over-estimated. So, as we have said, this series of novels is unique in its origin.

Neither English nor French literature supplies us with any parallel for its kind. Historical novels, illustrating certain periods of national life, are not wanting in our literature. Sir Walter Scott commented magnificently the historic scroll, from the romantic point of view, and Mr. Disraeli believes himself to have enriched the political history of England through the condescending medium of romance. The splendid pictorial imaginativeness of the first is as foreign to these novels as the flimsy theorizing of the last. Nor, beyond that constituted by

the consecutiveness of their order, is there any resemblance
between the Erckmann-Chatrian series and the most widely-
read so-called historical novels in the French language,—those
of the late M. Alexandre Dumas. In every other respect,
except indeed their power of exciting interest, which amounts
to fascination, the illustrators of the Revolution, the Republic,
the Empire, the Restoration, and the *bourgeois* Royalty which
collapsed in 1848, are absolutely different from the fantastic
and unreal, but delightfully skilful embroiderer upon the soiled
and tangled historic web of the Valois and the Bourbons.   The
novels of M. Dumas and those of MM. Erckmann-Chatrian
are absolutely opposed to each other in intention, in feeling,
and in style.   In the former, the license of the romancer is
pushed to the extreme limits consistent with adherence to a
central scrap of historic truth; in the latter, the bounds of the
probabilities of an individual's career are never exceeded, in the
illustration with minutest realism of the several phases of the
history of two-thirds of a century.   The splendour, the bad
faith, the vice, the intrigues, and the fascinations of courts and
courtiers, traditions of love and hatred, of loyalty and violence,
the "cloth of gold" side of events, presented in glowing
dramatic form, are the aspects of the one ; the serious, laborious
existence, the small aims, the narrow ambitions, the homely
pleasures, the characteristic qualities and defects, the traditional
wrongs and sufferings, the sudden awakening to and rapid progress in political life, the " cloth of frieze " side of events, presented with incomparable truth and simplicity, are the aspects of
the other. Before these works came to supply a grand exception,
the generalization which pronounced all French novels either
impure or uninteresting, was not by any means marked with
the rashness which commonly attends sweeping criticism.   The
" *roman* " was forbidden to the French " young person," and
she could hardly be seriously expected to take an interest in
the ineffable *fadeurs* of the works of imagination, whose gaudy
bindings and cheap paper and type are familiar to us, as the
rarely disturbed tenants of the domestic bookshelves of French
family life. But here is the well-known *livraison*, with the
yellow cover and the numerous illustrations, once accepted as
the outward and visible signs of an abounding superfluity of
naughtiness within, and the " young person " may, we hope
does, read them with as much profit as interest, as much
advantage to her literary taste and appreciation, as to her
understanding of the political and social history of her own
nation.
    We have long regarded MM. Erckmann-Chatrian as the
leaders of a reformation of general French literature, as well

as the inaugurators of an entirely novel special school. The widespread popularity of such works as theirs, the acceptance they have found with all classes, must tend to purify public taste, to spoil the market of the purveyors of garbage, to turn all such readers as do not love crime and license and folly for their own sakes, but are attracted by the mode of serving them up, from the monotonous ingenuity of Gaboriau's criminal puzzles, the milliner, jeweller, and upholsterer-aided licentiousness of Arsène Houssaye, and the execrable ruffian-millionaires and equally execrable French of Ponson du Terrail, that lover of socialistic democracy, who never allows it to be forgotten that he is a Vicomte. Just as fresh air, if freely admitted, will overpower foul air, so will these books, rich in every legitimate attraction of fiction, purify the realm of the "*roman.*" From an early stage of our acquaintance with them, we believed them to be an active, efficient, and deadly enemy of the now vanished Empire, an enemy which worked steadily and irresistibly by the process of instruction in realities, exposure of shams, and temperate, convincing appeal to the common sense of that large portion of the people whom imperial splendour neither warms nor dazzles, on whom military glory casts no reflected ray, and whose strength, and power to use that strength, in crises of national fate, lie in the clearness with which they perceive, and the tenacity with which they maintain their material interests. The Napoleonic Legend had no more resolute iconoclast, *la gloire* no more relentless exponent, than these gentlemen, richly endowed with poetic fancy, and full of enthusiastic patriotism, teaching the men of the present the outcome of the past, instructing the people, while the opposition and revolutionary press was merely exciting the mob, conferring with the good sense of their fellow-countrymen, while the demagogues, who are accountable for much of the fearful wreck in whose presence men's hearts fail them for fear, were recklessly appealing to their passions. This view of these works has been confirmed by a letter, written to a friend by M. Chatrian, in 1868, and published in the *Times,* 20th October, 1870, of which we translate a portion :—:

Once more I see myself a young child, between my father's knees, behind our great earthenware stove; my mother and my sisters are spinning, their spinning-wheels are buzzing; my uncle Antoine, an old soldier, is walking to and fro, his hands crossed behind his back; my brother Edward is asleep in a corner, and Jean-Baptiste, the eldest, sits at the table, by the little copper lamp, and reads to us the history of Napoleon the Great.

How I listened, how I opened my eyes, at the recital of these marches and countermarches, of these great battles, of squares broken by cavalry, of redoubts taken by assault, of colours snatched from the enemy, and of those grand dispatches, which sounded like trumpet notes of victory.

And then, when misfortunes came,—the retreat from Russia, Kulm, Danniwitz, Katzbach, Leipzig, the terrible weather, the want of ammunition and supplies, the desertion of the allies, and, finally, the invasion—how my little heart ached and sickened. I remember well how, when I heard for the first time the story of Waterloo, when my brother, with a trembling voice, cried out the fatal "Sauve qui peut!" I burst into such sobs, that my uncle Antoine told Edward to shut the book, and that my good father had great trouble in consoling me. He had to promise me that, when I became a big boy, I should go and fight the English.

These memories return to me strongly now, and make me reflect upon the influence of one's surroundings, and on the power of the first impressions of youth. I recall all that it has cost me, what energy it has needed in struggling against myself and my family, to get rid of the Napoleonic legend in which my childhood was cradled.

Thank God I have attained to that deliverance; I have even the satisfaction of feeling that I have dealt it some hard blows, and you will readily believe that I have no longer any inclination to fight the English.

He had, indeed, dealt it some hard blows. The two phases of mind referred to in this letter are wonderfully exemplified in the "Histoire d'un Paysan," the "Conscrit," and "Waterloo," books which whirl away the imagination in the track of the splendid French army, and yet hold it down to the grim truth that the meaning of it all was the desolation and the enslavement of France. In the sudden and utter ruin which has overtaken the Second Empire there is, perhaps, a more complete success than the literary companions in arms would have welcomed in anticipation, for, while it proves the instability and corruption of the edifice which was so glorious without, there is much in the manner and the results of that fall which pleads against their estimate of the grandeur, the nobility, and the morality of the Revolution of 1789. To upset an ill-wielded authority is a good thing, but to upset with it order, the principle of obedience, the aptitude for combination, the respect for discipline, reverence, and faith, this is to pull the wheat crop in eradicating the tares. That, in the sense of actively pervading principles, the great Revolution did destroy these, the history of each successive convulsion which the country has undergone proves, and the last culminating evidence is heaping itself up under the eyes of M. Chatrian, now shut up in the besieged city of Paris. That grand and worthy deeds were done in the revolutionary period, and that many good results have accrued from the widening of liberties then begun, we may freely admit, without believing the Revolution to be so grand or so worthy as these writers would fain persuade us it was. They regard those who, judging it by the horrors and cruelties which disgraced it, pronounce it accursed, as shallow and unphilosophical. Is it less shallow and unphilosophical to judge the institutions which it endeavoured to abolish, the systems it aimed at uprooting, only by the defects of the one and the abuses of the other; to acquiesce in the definition of the nobility of the period as *la mauvaise race,* and the religious orders as *les gueux,* because there were nobles in those days who abused their privileges, and monks who disgraced their vocation? The French nation was ignorant and superstitious, no doubt, before 1789, but we doubt whether it was ever so godless before the ugly episodes of *l'Etre Suprême,* and the Places of Eternal Sleep were made to indicate emancipation from monarchical rule. For the third time the free issues to which the leading free spirits of this time have been " finely touched," have a menacing resemblance to those which Michel Bastien records with exultation. It may be said that these are the sentiments of Michel Bastien, not of the writers, whose wonderful adoption of a personality is the object of our warmest admiration. But the writers are with Michel, Joseph, and Jean Pierre, otherwise they would surely have some good to tell of some one who was not a peasant, or a *bourgeois,* or an *ouvrier,* or an *assermenté* priest; and, though the political merits of the case as against the Revolution would not come within the scope of a peasant's autobiography, they would not have left them to be dimly recognised only by the coward and the buffoon of these stories.

With just so much by way of a protest, there is no more restriction to be placed on the enjoyment of these books. Among its components, the novelty of the point of view must be reckoned high. On all minds the grim and terrible fascination of the Revolution exerts a charm which in the next century may be surpassed by the series of events in this, which began with the Hohenzollern candidature, and is to end God only knows how and when, but which is yet unrivalled. But the students of that history are accustomed to see it set forth in the grand manner, -to have their attention called to the great personages, to have their fancy more or less fixed on Paris. The scarecrows of Mr. Carlyle are Paris scarecrows of the Faubourg St. Antoine, the martyrs of Beauchesne are royal martyrs, the terrible figures of the Revolution are the politicians of the Palais Royal, the Girondins, Danton and his subordinates, Robespierre and his slaves, with their true servile fear and servile vengeance—the grand and pathetic figures are the

King, the Queen, their children, Madame Elizabeth, the Princess de Lamballe, and all the other haggard phantoms which throng the Place de la Concorde, and cluster round the red shadow of the guillotine.   Among the unsolved problems of our time is, " Whether in the future Paris is to mean France."

To the students of the Great Revolution, she has always meant, and but for these works must have continued to mean, France. In vain do provincial histories and local memoirs and biographies appeal against this centralizing idea.   We are with the mob at the Tuileries, the captives at the Feuillants and the Temple, the Convention in its hall of assembly, at the Abbaye and La Force, at the Gréve and the Place Louis Quinze, at the Conciergerie, and on the steps at St. Roch with the young officer of artillery, and the cannon which belched out a message of terror and peace to maddened Paris and despairing France.   It is difficult to escape from these and similar associations in thinking of those times ; but under the guidance of the Erckmann-Chatrian novels, the reader does so effectually. He is made to see the Revolution with the eyes, to feel it with the heart, to study it with the brain, to follow it in the person of a peasant of Lorraine, to whom its local aspects are of paramount importance, who knows nothing about the shrieking scarecrows, who dismisses the prison massacres as mistaken ebullitions of popular feeling, " *contraire au bon sens*," casually mentions the execution of the Queen as an incident, like another, of no weight to engage the attention of men occupied in the serious task of reconstructing the national life ; and who regards the death of the King as the most rational termination of a difficulty.   To find these things treated in a sternly realistic sense, without the least touch of sentiment on the one hand, or of republican fanaticism on the other, is as instructive as it is novel.

The character of Michel Bastien is perhaps the most admirable and effective of these, marvellous joint achievements. The degrading penury of his childhood, the simple, ignorant, long-suffering nature of his father, the hard, embittered, prejudiced character of his mother, with her sterling love of husband and children ground down and forced out of sight on all but great occasions, by the abject toil and want of every-day, the terrible labour, but the superior comfort of his lot when Maitre Jean, blacksmith and tavern-keeper, takes him as forge-boy and servant, aid in the formation of this typical being.   He is hard, selfish, cautious, interested, honest, loyal to friends and employer, without religious reverence, self-instructed, capable of a deferential love for a woman infinitely his superior in intellect, but not comprehending that superiority so well as her strength, industry, and courage,—full of acute good sense, pitiless, reasonably brave, unenthusiastic, and with the true rural characteristics, calculation and suspicion. In his commiserating love for his father, there is the independence of the peasant who had emerged from the old bondage, and an unconscious touch of contempt for the wretched victim of a kicked-down system, unable to understand that he is no longer a serf. The realism of this work in its domestic details is surprising. We see every place, are present at every scene described, and the familias illustrations of Michel's narrative are all taken from his trade, that of a blacksmith. Only in one instance is it possible to question the strict adherence of the writers to truth and probability. This is in the keen and loving sense of the beauty of nature which is imputed to Michel Bastien. Nothing is more striking in these works than the love, the solicitous study, the intense sympathetic delight of the writers in the face of the earth; their human portraits are not more careful than the painting of the places once so remote from our knowledge or our interest, which have of late been drawn so near, made so familiar by the dreadful drama of the war. The woods, the streams, the ancient towns and their fortifications, the farmhouses, the outlying villages, the roads in their conditions at all seasons, every feature and characteristic of the beloved scenes, are set forth with equal vividness and simplicity. But we believe that this minute appreciation of natural beauty is an attribute of educated minds, very rarely, if ever, found where some notion or sentiment of art does not exist, and in which peasants and children are almost uniformly deficient. It is a sense entirely apart from the love of home and its surroundings, and from the physical pleasure imparted by fine weather and the influence of the seasons; but which combines with the latter in educated minds. The opening sentences of "La Maison Forestière," one of the best of the series of *Romans Populaires*, furnish an example of this combination, and are perfectly natural in the mouth of the speaker, a wandering artist and student. They prelude several pages of exquisite description, given with an ecstasy of enjoyment at once inspiring and affecting.

In the good time of youth (said Theodore), when the sky seems more blue, and the leaves more green, the water of the mountain rills more sonorous and impetuous, the water of the lakes calmer and more limpid, when everything our eyes rest upon is invested with a mysterious grace, when our hearts are always singing, and everything speaks to us of love, art and poetry; in that happy time I wandered all alone in the great wood of Hundsbrück. Then I did not reason upon my impressions, I accepted happiness under every form, without discussing it, for me everything had life and feeling,—the stones, the trees, the moss, and the flowers. And if when I came up to some old oak, at the turn of a path, it had suddenly spoken to me, I think I should not have been much surprised. "My lord, the oak," I should have said, "Theodore Richter, landscape painter at Dusseldorf, salutes you. He sees with pleasure that you have deigned to break your long silence in his favour. Let us talk of nature, the mother of us all. You must have good store of ideas on this matter; what do you think of the universal soul, my lord the oak?" . . . Thus from village to village, from forester's house to forester's house, I went, singing. whistling, looking about me, led only by my fancy, seeking ever a retreat still more distant, more profound, more full of trees and their delicious shade, where no noise could reach me, not even a murmur other than that of the skies and the woods."

Then comes the burst of joy of which we have spoken, and which is in prose what Shelley's Ode to a Skylark is in poetry, and this delightful appeal to sympathy.

Those who, during their youth, have had the happiness to come across such a nook in the depths of the forest, at the hour when nature, coming out of her bath of dew, wraps herself in the sun, when the light scatters itself about the foliage, or sends its golden shafts straight down into the thickets, where the mosses, the goats' herb, and the climbing plants breathe in the shade, and mingle their perfume under the brambles, where the finches flutter over the branches, pursuing the insects, and the thrushes and the blackbirds go down to the rivulet and drink there, swelling out their melodious throats, and spreading their wings over the foam of the tiny cascades, when the thieving magpies cross the sky, just over the tree-tops in flocks, screaming to each other, and directing their file-flying towards the wild cherry trees,—at the hour in short, when everything is full of life, when love and life and light hold their grand festival; those alone will comprehend my ecstasy.

Thus do these writers express the beauty of sight, the delight of sound, which in a very remarkable way pervade these works, and to all this, of which there are hundreds of examples, there can be but the response of ardent admiration and sympathy. But they do not harmonize with the character of Michel Bastien, and one feels that the more, because it is the sole touch of discord, the only instance of the *invraisemblable* in the *Histoire d'un Paysan*, which is the most perfect, as it is the most important work of the authors.

"Many people," says Michel Bastien, "have narrated the history of the Great Revolution of the people and the *bourgeois* against the nobles in 1789. But they were learned men, men of genius, who looked down upon things from a height. I am only an old peasant, and I shall speak solely of our affairs. The chief thing is to look after one's own business well. What a man has seen himself, that he knows thoroughly, and he ought to profit by it." This old peasant carries us to the Baraques, a wretched suburb of Phalsbourg, and shows us what was the existence of the poor in those days, when unbearable burdens of taxation were laid upon them; when there were no manufactures, and hardly any local industries. Touching and terrible is this narrative, quaintly and simply told, and of which the following is a grim specimen. The wretched family, already ground down by extreme penury, are harassed by a debt with usurious interest, incurred to an old miscreant named Robin, for the purpose of buying a goat. When the father cannot meet the dreaded instalment, Robin obliges him to work for him two or three days in succession, without payment, exacting the detested *corvée*, which, perhaps more than any other wrong, rankled in the hearts of the people, and remains a proverbial synonym for thankless labour and fatigue.

At length there came a little promise of better fortune. My brother Nicholas drew a white ticket at the militia ballot. The tickets were black and white, and the black were the bad numbers. What good news for us, for the idea of selling Nicholas immediately occurred to my mother. He was five feet six inches high, he could be a grenadier, and we should get more than nine crowns. All my life I shall remember the joy of the whole family. My mother held Nicholas by the arm, and said to him, "We are going to sell you. Several married men have been drawn for the militia. You can replace one."

Only married men could then be replaced, but the length of service was double, twelve years instead of six. Nicholas knew this as well as the mother, but he answered all the same:

"Just as you like. As for me, I am always content."

Our father would rather have kept him, and said that by working in the forest as a woodcutter, and fulfilling the *corvées* in the winter, he could earn a little money, and pay the debts, but our mother took him aside and spoke low to him :—

"Listen, Jean Pierre," she said, "if Nicholas stays here he will marry. I know he is running after that little Jeannette Lorisse. They will marry, and have children, and that will be worse than all for us." The father, with his eyes full of tears, asked :—

"You wish to go as a substitute, Nicholas? You would like to go away?" And he, twisting the red ribbon which hung from his old hat, cried out:

"Yes, father, I am going! I ought to be the one to pay the debt! I am the eldest, it is I who must pay!"

He was a good fellow. The mother kissed him, and clasped her arms round his neck, and told him that she knew well how he loved his parents; that she had always known it, and that he should be a grenadier, and should come back to the village with a white coat and a blue collar, and a feather.

"All right, all right," replied Nicholas. He saw through the cunning of the poor mother, who was thinking all the time of the money; but he pretended to see nothing, and besides, he liked soldiering. My father was sitting by the hearth, crying. He would have kept us all with him always; but the mother leant over his shoulder, and while the brothers and sisters were shouting to the neighbours in the doorway, she murmured in his ear: "Listen, we shall have more than nine crowns. Nicholas is five feet six—the inches pay extra—that will make twelve louis! We will buy a cow; we shall have butter, milk, cheese; we can rear a pig!" But he did not answer her, he was too sad. The next day he and Nicholas went into the town, and when they returned, my father told us Nicholas was to replace the son of Josse, the baker, but he must serve twelve years, and we should have twelve louis—one for each year of service!—that, first, we should pay off Robin; and, after that, we should see. He wished to let Nicholas keep one or two louis, but the mother cried out that he had no need of anything; he would be well clothed, and have his two good meals a day; that he would even have stockings to wear under his shoes, like all the militiamen; and that, if they let him have any money, he would only spend it at the tavern, and get himself punished.

Nicholas laughed, and said, "Very well; all right!"

Only the father could not be consoled; but you must not think the mother was glad to see Nicholas go away, no! she loved him very much, but great poverty hardens the heart; she was thinking of the little ones, Katharine and Stephen, and twelve louis was a fortune in those days.

One of the most tragical touches in this book, is the disappointment of this pitiable hope, by Nicholas's being cruelly trapped into enlisting in the line. The angry despair of the mother, the utter dejection of the father, and the conviction that *he* must rescue the family which comes to Michel, and forms the turning-point, supplies the motive of his life.

The sudden destruction of apparently stable things, the rapid succession of events which change the aspect of a nation, are much talked of among the phenomena of our time, and we are apt to think of the Great Revolution as comparatively slow in its operations, from the first indication of the coming change, given by the revelation of the deficit, the Necker affair, and the assembling of the States General. These works correct that impression more effectually than any study of dates, by the fulness of the narrative in detail, and its restriction as to space. The Calvinist *colporteur* Chauvel, who is elected one of the deputies, and sent to Paris, is a powerfully drawn character; and in his letters, addressed to his friends at Phalsbourg, written during the ever memorable session at Versailles, is contained the best history of that momentous assemblage within our knowledge. Minute, living, full of the purpose and emotion of the occasion, these terse, manly, simple accounts bring the reader into the midst of the scene; there is nothing vague, no conventional phrase, but the familiar description of a man who has been snubbed and insulted with the *Tiers Etat*, who has waited for admission in the rain, while the other *Etats* were ceremoniously conducted to their seats of honour, who has joined in the adjournment to the hall of the Jeu de Paume, who has taken part in the oath fraught with consequences at once so grand and so terrible, and taken note of that insolent announcement that he meant to play a game there, and the Tiers could not be admitted on the following day, which considerably swelled the account the people had to settle with the Count d'Artois; and who has heard Mirabeau's first manifestation of his power. To read Chauvel's letters, with the picture of the "Serment du Jeu de Paume," which is (or was) at the Louvre, clear in one's memory, is to realise this famous scene to the full. The letters of Chauvel from Paris fit easily into the narrative of revolutionary progress in the distant province of Alsace, and are as perfect as pictures of the old Paris of '89, as they are clear and striking chronicles of public events. Chauvel's character is wonderfully conceived. A stern and bitter Calvinist, hating the Catholic church and the priesthood much more than he loves anything, his life included, and intellectually much superior to his compatriots, he aids with resolute toil and watches with grim patience the development of the principles he has been for years stealthily disseminating by means of his traffic in contraband books and journals. The history of this traffic, and of its adoption by the counter-revolution, is very curious. Chauvel is an unrelenting hater of royalty and aristocracy, an exacting and sensible patriot, bent on the rights of man in the first place, and then upon revenge on those who have so long denied them. He regards the perpetrators of the excesses of the revolution with contempt, but he sees progress under the current of excess, and is grimly gratified. Yet he never loses the peasant point of view, and his letters go direct to the material interests of the peasants in every subject discussed, in every scene described in them. The impatience and misery of the provinces during the struggle of the *Veto*, the gradual upspringing of the patriotic horror of invasion, the excitement, at first general and against a system, and always retaining a notion that the king was good—the exception being the unfortunate queen, who was an object of suspicion and dislike in those provinces which had most intercourse with her own country, from the beginning—then turning to ferocious individual hatred; the first utterances which after-

wards swelled into the great cry for blood—these are brought
out with matchless power.   Here is one of many passages
descriptive of the growth of the Revolution at Phalsbourg.
The scene is the tavern of Maitre Jean, on the occasion of a
wedding, at which Chauvel is present, when Michel joins the
company.

> When I opened the door I saw an extraordinary sight.   Maître Jean's
> cousin Maurice, with his sky-blue coat, his two watches hanging down
> over his yellow breeches, his frilled shirt, his voluminous tricoloured
> cravat and his large three-cornered hat, worn crosswise, was dancing like
> a maniac or a demon; his pointed foot in the air, his knee up to his chin,
> jumping, balancing himself, making faces and gestures impossible to
> imagine.   He was singing at the same time a song called *Madame Veto*,
> full of horrible things about the queen; and all the patriots at the table,
> their noses red and their eyes round with pleasure, laughed so that they
> fell back on their chairs, with their arms hanging over the sides, and their
> mouths open from ear to ear.   The walls shook, and cousin Maurice went
> on and on, ducking his head down, and throwing his legs up in the air,
> singing—
>
> > Madame Veto a fait ceci !
> > Madame Veto a fait cela !
>
> This song began with the affair of the Cardinal and the necklace; there
> were dozens of verses in it, one worse than another.   Somehow I felt
> almost ashamed of it.   But all the others who were there, and who had
> suffered so long from the extravagance of the court, were overjoyed, and
> did not think too much could possibly be said.   By degrees they all began
> to dance, carried away by the excitement of the strange incessant move-
> ments of Maurice.   How things change in this world!   This tavern of
> the Three Pigeons, where the officers of Bonergue, of Schœnau, of
> La Fère, all the old nobility—counts, dukes, marquises, had danced
> gravely, decorously, with the ladies of the town, bending low, and entwining
> themselves like garlands of flowers, with their little violins, their delicate
> pasties carried in baskets on the back of an old soldier, and their wine
> cooling itself in the spring; this same tavern now shook to the footing of
> a new measure, the dance of the patriots.   How these nobles would have
> opened their eyes and their ears if they could have seen how they jumped
> about and distorted themselves like men possessed by devils, in a dance
> which was a mockery of all old things together, and to hear that song
> going on, on:—
>
> > Madame Veto a fait ceci!
> > Madame Veto a fait cela!
>
> Chauvel did not dance.   He sat at the end of the table, looking on with
> glistening eyes, and pale with satisfaction.   He marked the time, tapping
> the table with the handle of his knife, and encouraging them ironically.
> And now, if you would know what were that dance and that song, brought

among us for the first time by Maurice Brunet, I will tell you that it was the famous *Carmagnole*, which every one has heard of since, that dance which the Parisians danced on the Place de la Révolution, and even under the guns of the enemy. All the Revolution was in that *Carmagnole;* they added a verse each time that anything new occurred; the old verses were gradually forgotten, and the new ones made every one laugh. . . . . "I should like to hear Michel sing the *Carmagnole*," said old Raphaël, the president of our club. "Bah!" said Chauvel, who was quite grave now; "the *Carmagnole* is a jest—all very well for good patriots to sing for their amusement, after a bottle. But we want something very different, something strong and great, like the people."

The revolution retains many of its ugliest points of family resemblance. To-day, with the Prussians outside its walls, and hunger and dread within, citizens are found to buy thousands of copies of "Ratapoil Badinguet," and "La Femme Bonaparte." The exultation of the peasants over the flight of the emigrants inspires many of the cruellest passages in this book, the curious impersonal hatred, which, no doubt, inspired provincial France at that time. With many good and patriotic instincts, and especially with the good sense which saw the evil and devised the remedy with clearness which has become obscured, and readiness which does not exist in our day,—as, for instance, the grand point of difference between the Girondins and the Montagnards, whether the war was to be made on the recalcitrant French, or on the menacing foreigners and the returning emigration, — there existed a spirit of base envy of all those who had possessed the luxuries and amenities of life; which found cruel expression in derisive exultation over their fall. Michel Bastien is not quite above this, though he is an honest fellow in his way. We do not know, in all the voluminous history of the Revolution a more cruel little "bit" than this, certainly not a more perfect example of the revolutionary propagandism of the time :—

I remember that once, of a S. Nicholas' day, our club had great fun about the emigrants. Joseph Gossard, a wine vendor, from the neighbourhood of Toul, a tall thin fellow, with a red face and a curly head, a real Lorrainer, as gay as a thrush, told us about a trip he had just made to Coblenz, with samples. I think I see him now, leaning on the counter, describing to us the confusion of all those nobles, of all those monks, superiors of convents, canons and canonesses, of all those great lords and great ladies, and the crowd of servants who followed them, to wash and brush, and comb and shave them, to cut their nails, to dress and undress them like children ; and who could not live any longer at their expense, because they had not a shilling. I never heard anything so amusing. Gossard mimicked their grimaces among those poor Germans, who did not understand a word they said. He took off an old Marquise, with her flounces and her hoop, and her thick walking cane, and her grand air, in a tavern at Worms. The old woman had some money left, so she thought she could order about her, just as usual, she wanted this, she wanted that, and the servants stood looking at her, and asking, " Wass, wass ? " " Wass, wass?" cried the old woman, " I tell you to warm my bed, you blockheads." All our club were dying of laughter. And then he imitated the old nobles, who pretended to be quite jaunty, and dissipated, just as if they were still at Versailles ; the young ladies running after their lost husbands, and the astonishment of all these people when they rushed to the post, thinking they were going to receive bills on Frankfort or Amsterdam, and finding only empty letters, in which their stewards informed them that my lord's castle, forest, or lands, were under the sequestration of the nation. Gossard imitated the long faces and staring eyes of all these people, accustomed to live at the expense of their fellows, and now besieged by the waiters with their hotel bills. . . . He repeated the same performance in all the clubs along his route, he was received everywhere with cries of joy, and to tell the truth, he might have earned a great deal of money by the representation of his journey to Coblenz ; they would gladly have paid him to play this kind of comedy, but he did it all for pure patriotism, satisfied to please the patriots, and to sell them his wine.

The good sense and honesty of Michel preponderate over the coarseness and the avarice of his nature, in all that relates to his home, his family, and his duties, but the one-sidedness of an uneducated mind, which, when the desire for instruction has been awakened, seeks it from one source only, pervades the history of his life, and makes it terribly real. According to him the dispossessed have no rights, and pity is a misplaced feeling in the case of the hereditary enemies of the people. His description of the excitement among the purchasers of the " national property " (meaning the Church lands), during the King's resistance, the urgency with which they promoted the volunteer movement, is very striking. Among these is Maitre Jean, the master blacksmith ; who works like a giant-demon, with assistants gathered in from the villages, at forging the pike-heads, destined to such dreadful utility, when the furious people discovered that the arsenals were empty, and the guns rust eaten. " In two months we forged fifteen hundred pike-heads, and the forge being far too small, we worked out in the roadway. We were a sight to see, with our sleeves rolled up to our shoulders, our shirts open, our loins girt with handkerchiefs, our red caps with their cockades hanging over our ears, beating out the iron from morning to night, while one of us went and came from the fire which roared without ceasing, to the anvil, round which the travellers stood in groups all day long." Michel makes a reflection on this work, as follows :—

It has sometimes happened to me, in my mountain journeys, to find one of these old pikes, in a woodman's or sawyer's hut, put away behind the head of the old bed, or in a corner of the clock-case. These people did not know what it was! But I—I took the rusty iron in my hand, turned it round and round, and looked at it, and the good old patriotic times came back to me all at once, and I cried: "Thou hast been carried gaily through Alsace, Lorraine, and Champagne. Thou hast parried the sword-stroke of an Uhlan of Wurmser, and the drums of Brunswick have not made thee tremble in the hands that held thee."

The fury of the people when they learned that the King had vetoed the execrable decree for the deportation of the "refractory" priests,—a long step on the way of Louis' martyrdom—is quite ingenuously ascribed to their fear for their possessions, to that intense acquisitiveness and tenacity of property which, however unpleasant to contemplate in a moral point of view, are undoubtedly large elements in the national prosperity.

When Elof Collin stood up on a platform, in the middle of the market-place (says Michel), and read out to us the decree (of the 11th July, 1792), screaming like an old hawk on its nest—"Citizens, the country is in danger! Citizens, come to the aid of the country!" the enthusiasm began with the sons of the purchasers of the national property, who knew that if the *émigrés* returned, their fathers would be hanged. Therefore they all, by five and six at a time, climbed up on the platform, and inscribed themselves as volunteers. As for me, I had nothing, but I hoped to gain something, I did not wish to go on working always for other people, and besides, I shared Chauvel's ideas about liberty. And even now, in the old age which I have reached, my old blood still boils at the mere thought that any rascal should try to injure me in either my person or my goods.

So Michel becomes a volunteer, the military element enters into the story, and the patriots march away, by thousands, to the tune of that grander and stronger song, demanded by Chauvel as more like the people, "La Marseillaise."

The third part of the "Histoire d'un Paysan," begins in the "Year 1 of the Republic," far from the forge at Bois-de-Chênes, the tavern of the Three Pigeons, and the hut of old Bastien. It leads us by all the places which have seen and suffered in the present war, and shows us the prowess, the energy, the faith in their cause which then inspired French soldiers. It is not to be denied that the soldiers of the First Republic were a glorious army, and had leaders worthy of them. The interest of the details of the campaign is fascinating, and the skill of the writers marvellous, for they never lose sight of their plan, they never depart from the experience, the point of view of one man. With the Germans swarming over France, and the Imperial army in Prussian prisons, it is painful while thrilling to read, in the words of a common soldier, how the patriot soldiers took Spire, Worms, Mayence, and Frankfort; and how the Germans did nothing well but their retreating. Meantime the horrors of the Revolution commence in Paris, and Michel, in garrison at Mayence, finds it hard to understand why people should be so unreasonably interested in the trial of Louis Seize, "now called Capet." Not only the local commotion, but the furious strife in the Convention puzzles this practical peasant mind, who regards it thus:—

This King had betrayed the nation—the writings found in the iron safe made that clear—he had spent half his civil list on corrupting the deputies, and paying the *émigrés* at Coblenz ; he had summoned the Prussians and the Austrians into France, to reinstate him, his nobles, and his clergy in their former privileges, and us in our former servitude. If a poor devil had committed the quarter of those crimes, his trial would not have lasted ten minutes, but this man was a king! and to defend him, the Girondists, who called themselves Republicans, ran the risk of kindling civil war in France . . . . And all this time the dearth was increasing, the price of bread was rising from day to day ; the workmen were paid in *assignats,* not worth half their nominal value, the shopkeepers refused to take these *assignats* in payment of their merchandise ; the people had to wait for hours at the baker's shops in order to get a pound of bread ; in short the people—whose fathers, brothers, and sons were fighting in Germany and in Belgium—were dying of hunger. They cried to the Convention to save them, to fix the prices of the absolute necessaries of life ; but the Girondists did not listen to the cries of the poor miserable people, they had no pity for any one but Louis XVI.

The enthusiasm with which the army received the news of the execution of the king, their joy in this grand earnest of the equality of every one before the law, was somewhat damped when they had time to reflect that war was now *à outrance* between the Republic and all the rest of Europe, and that their precious *terres* must lie untilled until such time as they should have beaten all desire of interfering with them out of Europe. The hard work and hard times of campaigning begin in stern reality; the description of which comes home to our imagination with double force now, when the history of sieges is the story of the present. Here is a little picture, which doubtless, has many a pendant in France to-day. It is of the canteen established in the Church of S. Ignace, at Mayence, —for the Revolutionary army delighted in sacrilege then as the Garibaldians delight in it now—and presided over by Michel's sister Lisbeth and her husband, when the misery and hunger of the siege were at their height.

I frequently went to see Lisbeth (says Michel) in the church, when the roof had been all knocked to pieces by the balls, and the rain fell as if into the street. The tents and the huts of the federal soldiers filled the aisles and the chapels ; they had fitted up a theatre in the choir, and their canteen occupied the sacristy ; there the great pot was perpetually boiling, and the steam hanging about in clouds. On going into this place, which resembled a kind of fair, where the *Ca ira!* the *Carmagnole*, card-playing, and political disputes went on incessantly, one perceived a very agreeable odour of meat, for that the *sans culottes* were never without, though nobody else had any ; they caught everything—dogs, cats, and rats—with lassoes, and boxes made on purpose, and many other inventions, and they were always full of gaiety and good humour.

The evacuation of Mayence, the fate of Custine, the struggle and defeat of the Girondists, the rising in La ·Vendée, are all within the experience of Michel, who during a short visit to Phalsbourg, hears the political news from Chauvel's daughter, his betrothed, and witnesses the celebration of the 10th August, and the fury of the people at the assassination of Marat. During the march into La Vendée he says, "everywhere we found them arresting the English, in consequence of the villainy of Pitt"— another point of resemblance between that time and this, with its Prussian-spy mania. Thenceforth the chronicle is of the fighting from day to day, as Michel saw it and shared it, of the enthusiastic, fanatical zeal and desperation with which the Vendéans fought, and the terrible cruelties of both parties in this bitterest of civil wars. One masterly little touch of realism deserves especial mention in the midst of the grand action, the excitement, and the tumultuous rush of these chapters. Michel regards the Vendéans with the deepest scorn, as ignorant brutes, a prey to the lowest superstitions, worked upon by priestly rascals to fight for the reimposition of slavery, and their own degradation of body and soul; poor wretches, persuaded by "refractory" priests, under the orders of a venal hypocrite like Bernier, that they are martyr-champions of true religion, and so deceived that several among them verily believed the dead bodies of the killed should rise again on the third day, and had them watched by the women until then. He feels nothing but derision for the undrilled soldiers who go into battle, after hearing mass and receiving Holy Communion, with rosaries round their necks, and relics stitched into their shirts;—but when the full rage and terror of that awful contest, in which passions, all the fiercer because they were abstract, were let loose in a whirlwind of fury, comes upon him, his heart fails him, though he is undeniably brave, and his first impulse is to vow an offering, *ex voto*, to the humble little shrine at home, and to think how he will go there and return thanks if he be.

spared. The story of the Vendéan war has never been told as
it is told in these pages, in which the prejudices and opinions
of the speaker are not permitted to influence the facts, to
obscure the brilliant valour, or to make little of the heroically
endured sufferings of the royalists; though the hideous cruelties
which defaced the brave, hopeless struggle, and which especially
involve the Vendéan women in the reprobation and disgust
which one feels for the female fiends of Paris—are unsparingly
exposed. Nothing can exceed the terrible description of
Westermann's pursuit of the flying royalists, on the road to
Laval, after the final defeat. Did he remember that scene,
when he went his way, in a tumbril, to the guillotine, whither
a grateful republic sent so many of its defenders?

If I said that we did not massacre those who were hidden in the houses
(at le Mans), that we allowed them to escape, to shoot us afterwards, or
that many of those furious women who carried bags to put their booty in,
and knives to finish our wounded with, were spared, I should lie to you.
We, the gunners, who had to stay by our guns, and defend the position in
case of attack, had nothing to do with all that, but our comrades from
Cherbourg, who had seen their brethren shot and cut to pieces by hundreds,
took their fill of vengeance. Cries arose from all sides,—horrible cries!
Well, what would you have? War is war. It is blood, tears, agony,
fire, pillage! Woe to those who begin it against their country,—all these
horrors fall upon them. They must answer for them before the world, and
before the Supreme Being. The generals had the assembly beaten. Kléber
and Marceau, the representatives Pressis, Turreau, and Bourbotte, all tried
to stop the extermination ; speaking of law and of justice to appease the
wrath of the soldiers. Listen! We had lost more than one hundred
thousand men in this miserable Vendéan war ; we had suffered every kind
of misery for a whole year, while the Prussians, the Austrians, the Italians
the Spaniards, the English, and the Dutch, in short all Europe, was attack-
ing our country,—we were forced to refuse quarter to people who instead
of sustaining us against the foreign enemy, were shooting France in the
back! Think of all this, and let those who reproach the Republic with
cruelty be silent ; in their hearts they must acknowledge that the right
was on our side, and that we did our duty towards the country and ourselves.

And now we turn to the story of Westermann's pursuit, as
simply told, and we see, by comparing these passages, the skill of
the writers, who are true to their personation in all the inconsistency of a human being. After that self-approving protest,
we read this, the last sample we can offer of the "Histoire d'un
Paysan."

Westermann, one of our greatest cavalry generals, fearing, notwithstanding their wounds and the piercing cold of December, that the enemy

might rally before Laval, pursued them into all the villages, and his hussars massacred prodigious numbers of them. At Laval, the Breton peasants, who had seen the horrors of civil war and suffered by the insolence and the vices of the Vendéans, received them with blows from their scythes and their pitchforks, and the wives of the patriots rushed upon the fugitives and arrested them, crying for vengeance upon the slayers of their husbands and sons.

"Go and be hanged elsewhere, you vagabonds! Go and shoot Christians in the back, while you tell your beads, elsewhere, you cowardly wretches!" Such was their welcome. The marquises, the countesses, the chiefs in women's clothes, the disguised priests, begged and prayed in vain, they were thrust out of the town on the high road. And then the hussars came down upon them with dripping sabres, and cries of "There they are! There they are!" May God grant that this may serve as an example to all those who are so abandoned by Heaven as to rise against their own country; may they learn that the prosperity of criminals cannot last, and that in their adversity everything is against them. When we arrived, five days later, at Amiens, where those who remained of these poor wretches tried to cross the Loire on rafts made of planks, beams, casks, everything in short that would float, we found Westermann's hussars on the heights of La Cornuaille. They all had rings, bracelets, earrings, banners, gold crosses, some on their fingers, some hung to their sword-belts, their cartouche-boxes were full, and they were all flourishing cambric handkerchiefs, trimmed with precious lace. After that, I leave you to imagine what had become of the duchesses and the marquises! The representatives, Bourbotte and Turreau, bought a quantity of these precious things from the soldiery, and sent them to the Convention, and the officers in general presented their prizes to the Republic, for it was poor, it needed money, being attacked by the despots on all sides.

Then comes the horrible story of the raft, the flight of the royalist chiefs, the merciless march of extermination, when the soldiers of the Republic marched barefooted in the snow for eleven days, in their ardour to stamp out the last remnants of the fanatical defenders of Church and King. It is a horrid history, and the picture of the France of to-day in our minds makes it far more impressive. What have these crimes and cruelties, this great self-devotion and heroic courage, really won for France? Ninety years have not yet elapsed, and society, government, order, are all dissolved, and France lies helpless at the foot of the invader.

After the stamping out of the Vendéan insurrection, we return to the political order, and find the guillotine *en perma nence,* and the advent of the Republic of Virtue, presided over by Robespierre, confidently anticipated. Michel arrives in Paris, just in time to witness, by accident, the execution of Danton, Desmoulins, and his own general, Westermann, and returns to his village ill and exhausted. Once more we are among the quaint and homely scenes of Lorraine, and the details of Michel's marriage, and his frugal, prosperous, selfish life. The counter-revolution of *Thermidor*, the last grand insurrection of *Prairial* disturbed him much, and the *débâcle* of the patriots caused him shame and grief; but his practical caution did not forsake him. "Under such circumstances," he remarks, "the most courageous can do nothing but go home, and wait for an opportunity of asserting their rights effectually."

In the concluding portion of this work, the history of the Directory and of the Consulate, the campaigns of Napoleon, the brief glory, the terrible price paid by France for the Empire,—a price still in process of liquidation,—are all told with the same simplicity and directness, the same severe judgment. From his infamous proclamation, "Soldiers, you are ill-fed, and nearly naked; the Government owes much to you, and can do nothing for you. I am going to lead you into the most fertile plains in the world, where you will find honour, glory, and *riches.* Will you be wanting in courage?" to the disastrous end, these writers treat Napoleon as a phenomenon of evil, a brigand-chief of brigands. This is the summing-up of it all :—

Thus you know the true end to which this long story has come. You know that the people of Europe, indignant at being pillaged, fell upon us all together,—the Prussians, the Germans, the English, the Swedes, the Italians, the Spaniards, and that we had to restore all the provinces, and crowns, and pictures we had robbed them of, and to pay them an indemnity of a thousand millions of francs. These people placed their garrisons over us, they held possession of our strong places, until they had been paid the last farthing, and they also took from us the conquests of the Republic—real conquests, those. Austria and Prussia had attacked us unjustly ; we had beaten them, and all the Austrian possessions in the Low Countries, on the left bank of the Rhine, became by treaty French territory. They took the best of these away from us, *and this is just what the genius of Bonaparte was worth to us.*

The "Conscript," and the "Blockade of Phalsbourg," are stories of the Empire, and "Waterloo" concludes the valuable series. Well may M. Chatrian boast of having hit the Napoleonic Legend hard blows! But it is not only the Napoleonic Legend which he beats out of all form of beauty and attractiveness, it is war, glory, the lust of conquest, the *ignes fatui,* which have always bewildered France. In the "Conscript," together with a minute account of the campaigns of 1810, 1811, and 1812, is the history of a man's exterior and interior life. This man,—a timid quiet youth, of infirm health, and so lame that he is supposed by his friends to be secure from the cruel *sort*, apprenticed to a watchmaker, and betrothed to his cousin, a pretty country girl from the village of the Quatre Vents,—has a natural and inspired horror of war. His master, old Goulden, is one of those characters which belong as exclusively to MM. Erckmann-Chatrian, as "Père Goriot" and "La Cousine Bette" belong to Balzac—an upright old Republican, stern, honest, long-sighted, of narrow but profound sympathies, and a stickler for liberty of conscience and of action, a lover of peace, with a rooted conviction that kings and priests are the natural enemies of the human race. The history of the time is commented on by the old man as he sits in his narrow shop front at his minute work, peering through his glasses at the disturbed interiors of all the watches in the place; while regiment after regiment passes through Phalsbourg to the scene of war. One day M. Goulden addresses his apprentice—there had been a great press just then, and victory after victory has made the demand for men to fill up the ranks, imperative—

" Tell me, Joseph, how many do you think we have seen pass by since 1804 ?"

"Oh, I don't know, M. Goulden, but at least four or five hundred thousand."

" And how many have you seen return ? "

Then I understood him, and I answered :—

"Perhaps they come back by Mayence, or some other road ; otherwise——but that is not possible."

But he shook his head, and answered :—

"Those you have not seen come back are dead, as hundreds and hundreds of thousands beside them will die, if God does not take pity on us, for the Emperor loves nothing but war. He has already shed more blood, in order to put crowns on his brothers' heads, than it cost our great Revolution to gain the rights of man."

Joseph Bertha feels his horror of war culminate in 1812, when from February until May, they watch, every day, the passage of regiment after regiment, dragoons, cuirassiers, carabineers, hussars, lancers of all colours, artillery, waggons, ambulances, carriages for the staff, provisions, for ever and ever, like a flowing river of which one never sees the end. This was at the beginning of the Russian campaign, and in September came the news of the great victory of Moscow, when the grimly jesting remark was made that now it remained for the Emperor to take China. But the winter set in earlier than usual and with greater severity. The description of the cold, of the winter scenery, and the winter occupations, is most charming, full of small touches, such as one never finds in picturesque-

on-purpose books; but under all is the burthen, "Oh, our
poor soldiers, our poor soldiers." Joseph comes in from a
holiday visit to his betrothed; he has run all the way, through
the deep snow, even so the cold has almost overpowered
him; and M. Goulden arrests him solemnly with the news:—

At this moment four hundred thousand families are weeping in France;
our great army has perished in the frosts of Russia; all those vigorous
young men, who marched through our town for two long months, are lying
under the snow. The news arrived this afternoon.

One of the "hard blows" is to be found in the description
of the agony and despair of the people of Phalsbourg, when as
much of the truth as ever was made known was proclaimed in
the market-place. Nothing more touching, more simple, more
dreadfully true is in all these books, than what follows on the
reading by the sergent-de-ville, Harmentier, of the 29th
bulletin, in which the Emperor related how, every night
during the retreat, the horses perished by thousands, *but said
nothing of the men.*

The revengeful trick by which Joseph Bertha is cheated out
of his exemption from military service, is the first of a long
series of sufferings, detailed with merciless truth, as the conscript's life of fatigue, pain, danger, and heartsickness is depicted,
side by side with the ideal of war. The bleeding feet, the
aching limbs, the weariness of the unaccustomed fatigue of
marching to one whose only previous occupation had been
sedentary, the exposure, the cold, the hunger, the sense of
being only an atom in a mass of atoms, but with the power of
feeling pain and fear, in the peril of fighting for a cause not his,
and whose success can bring him no advantage; are wonderfully brought out in the story of Joseph Bertha, a man of a totally
different type from that of the "Paysan," but whose mind arrives
by quite other processes at a similar result. The "Conscript" is
not so clever, so selfish, or so narrow as the "Paysan;" there is
a strain of sentiment in him which does not exist in Michel,
and but little of the hard matter-of-fact reasoning faculty.
Like Goulden, as contrasted with Chauvel, he has a contemplative side to his character, wanting, or rather pushed aside
by the active, in the other. He has not been exposed to
grinding poverty, and some of the amenities of home life clung
about him. His frail health and feeble frame render his
bodily sufferings as a raw recruit on a forced march particularly
severe, while his superior education and the moral training
of Goulden's society, make him shrink from the occasional
coarse debauchery and the habitual savagery of the soldiers.

Here is his reasoning upon the worth of *la gloire,* which has been urged upon him by a comrade :—

"Glory is for others than we, Zebedee ;—they live well, eat well, and drink well. They have dances and merrymakings—as we see in the gazettes—and glory over and above, when we have gained it, sweating and fasting, 'and risking life and limb. Poor devils like us, whom these people force away from home, to fight their battles for them, when they come back at length, having lost, if not the hands to work with, all habits of work and skill at it, do not enjoy much of the glory. Some of their former comrades, no better or more industrious than themselves, have made money in those seven years, have opened shops, married the sweethearts of the others, and have thriving children,—they are men settled in life, municipal councillors, notables in short. And when those who return, having sought glory by killing their fellow creatures, pass them by with their stripes upon their arms, they look over their shoulders at them, and, if they chance to have red noses, from drinking bad brandy to keep themselves alive in the rain, in the snow, on the forced marches, while the others, safe at home, have been drinking good wine, they say, 'Those are drunkards !' And the conscripts, who would never have asked for anything better than to have stayed at home and worked, end by becoming beggars. That is what I think, Zebedee ; and in my opinion, it is not at all just, and I should like to see the lovers of glory go and fight themselves, and leave us quiet."

The coincidences of the story with the events of the present time are numerous. Here is one of the most remarkable. The division is at Aschaffenbourg, where Joseph has a good billet, and makes acquaintance with a " pastor," who disabuses him of the idea that France will find allies in German discontent and disunion. This man's discourse might be transferred bodily into the history of the miscalculations of Napoleon III.

Now, it is our turn to talk of Liberty and Fatherland, and that is why I believe this war will be disastrous to you. All beings who think, from simple students to professors of theology, will march against you. *You think you will have the Saxons, the Bavarians, the Badeners, and the Hessians on your side—undeceive yourselves;* the children of old Germany know well that the greatest crime and the greatest shame is to fight against one's brethren.

The first time Joseph is under fire is beautifully told. One sees and hears the battle, one follows in the pursuit of the retreating Russians, and also one's heart is full of pity for the poor boy, doing his duty, fearful, but far from cowardly, who, when it is over, and Marshal Ney has assured the troops that the Emperor shall hear of their good conduct, resumes his march with this reflection upon the fact of his having crossed the Rappach up to his waist in water. " If any one had told me all this, when I was always afraid of catching colds in my head in M. Goulden's comfortable house, and when I changed my stockings twice a week, I could not have believed it." Night comes and he sleeps beside the bivouac fire, but not until—"thinking of Catherine," he says, "I prayed to God to spare my life, and to preserve my hands to me,—so necessary, to the poor, that they may earn their bread."

The great merit of this book, apart from its accurate and close chronicle of the war, is the representation of the impressions made and the effect produced upon Joseph's mind. He is the same man, in the brief, terrible story of the Hundred Days, on the awful field of Waterloo, but he is a formed soldier then, a veteran, an *ancien*. It is the progress of this transformation that is depicted with such exquisite art,—art which omits no touch of portraiture, however trifling. The "Conscript" see things very differently from the *ancien;* he is shocked and horrified, sensitive and wretched in scenes which, though he never grows coarse or callous, though the fine strain remains always in his nature, the *ancien* regards very much as a matter of course. And then, with respect to the military manœuvres and details of the battles, the Conscript relates them with a certain laboriousness, which perfectly conveys his own difficulty in understanding them, and their unfamiliarity. By degrees this disappears, and the frightful story of the retreat from Leipsic is told with all the technical ease of an old soldier. Before that came, the Conscript had seen and suffered enough for a whole lifetime of heroism.

Joseph Bertha is severely wounded in one of the smaller battles, and loses consciousness. The scene upon which he opens his eyes is thus related. It is a sober and more impressive version of some of Mr. Lever's sketches of the Peninsular War :—

First I looked up and saw great beams, crossing one another high up in the air, and some tiles through which the light came—then I turned my head slowly, and I saw that I was in one of those great barns where the brewers in that country store their casks and their carts. All around, on mattresses and heaps of straw, were ranged a crowd of wounded men, and about the middle stood a huge kitchen table, on which lay a man, whose leg a surgeon and two assistants, with their shirt-sleeves rolled up, were cutting off, while the wounded man uttered terrible groans. Behind them was a confused heap of legs and arms. I suppose you can all imagine the ideas which passed through my mind. Five or six infantry soldiers were going round, with pitchers and mugs, giving water to the wounded. But the object which impressed me most was this surgeon, in his shirt-sleeves, who went on cutting and sawing, without hearing or seeing anything—he had hollow cheeks, and a big nose, and he was angry every minute with his assistants, because they did not give him the knives, or the pincers, or the lint, or the linen quickly enough, or because they had not caught quite all the blood in the sponge. The work did not go on badly, however for in less than a quarter of an hour, they had cut off two legs.

Outside, close to the pillars, a great cart full of straw was waiting. Just as they had laid on the table a Russian carabineer at least six feet high, with a ball in his neck under the ear, and as the surgeon was calling for knives to begin on him, a surgeon of cavalry, short, fat, and pock-marked, passed before the barn, with a portfolio under his arm, and stopped beside the cart.

"Hollo, Forel!" he called out, in a hearty, pleasant voice.

"Hollo! Duchêne, is that you?" said our surgeon, turning round. "How many wounded?"

"From seventeen to eighteen thousand."

"The deuce there are! And how are you this morning?"

"All right. I'm looking out for a tavern."

Our surgeon left the barn to shake hands with his comrade, and they stood together talking gaily while the assistants drank some wine, and the Russian lay rolling his despairing eyes around him.

"Stay. Let me see. Oh, yes! Look here, Duchêne, you have only to go down the street, by the well yonder ; you see?"

"Perfectly."

"Very well then, just opposite you will find the canteen."

"Thanks ; then I'll be off."

So he went off, and our surgeon shouted after him :—

"Good appetite, Duchêne."

Then he came back to his Russian, and began by cutting his neck open from the throat to the shoulder. He worked in an ill-humoured sort of way, and kept saying to the assistants, "Now then, gentlemen, look sharp, if you please."

You could not conceive how the Russian groaned. But he took no notice ; and at length he flung a ball on the ground, put a bandage over the wound, and said, "Take him away."

They lifted up the Russian, some soldiers laid him on a straw mattress among the others, and his successor took his place upon the table. I could never have believed that such things could come to pass in the world. But I saw many others afterwards, never to be forgotten.

Five or six mattresses beyond mine was one on which an old corporal was sitting. His leg was bandaged up, and he was winking and grinning at a wounded man beside him, whose arm had just been taken off.

"Conscript,". said he, "look into that heap. I bet you you don't pick out your own arm."

The other, who was very pale, but had shown the greatest courage, looked at the heap, and fainted.

Then the corporal began to laugh, and said :—

"He has picked it out. It is that one underneath, with the little blue flower. I never knew it to fail in knocking them over."

He admired himself for this discovery, but no one laughed with him.

M 2

"Waterloo" is the final history, the last act of this great military drama of the Empire. Joseph Bertha is living in peace, industry, and happiness, having married Catherine. We are in the midst of tranquil, nature-loving, unsophisticated life again. But a strange rumour stirs the delicious summer air, the faces of the old soldiers *en retraite* brighten. *He* is spoken of, in whispers at first, then in a burst of triumphant exultation. The emperor has landed at Cannes, he is at Grenoble, at Lyons, at Paris; adieu peace, commerce, tranquillity, family life. Joseph must shoulder his musket, and march, with *anciens* and conscripts alike, for Waterloo. The picture of the first Restoration is perfect; a worthy precedent to the sketches of the condition of Alsace and Lorraine before 1787, with which the "Histoire d'un Paysan" commences. The second portion is exclusively military, a story of marches and countermarches, to delude the enemy; of the opening of the campaign, the astonishment and joy of the Belgians at the sight of the French troops, the battle of Ligny, with its charges to the cry of "no quarter;" the terrible storm, the want of provisions, which sent the troops fasting to the field of "the battle of despair;" and the collecting of the dead, who lay three and four feet deep in the village street. The horrid fascination of this story grows from point to point, from the night passed by the troops in the corn-fields, the wet earth clogging their limbs, without fire, lest the English should discover their vicinity, to the dreadful day of Waterloo, with its crushing defeat, and the terrible pursuit of the Prussians, who cut down the flying and exhausted men. Then comes the pillage of the provision waggons, the defence of Paris, the retreat on the Loire, the desertion of the conquered conqueror of the world, and the second restoration of "that unwieldy exile," Louis XVIII. The story of this great battle has never been told so plainly, so simply, never more eloquently.

"Waterloo" is, in a certain sense, the most interesting and valuable of the series to English readers. We have many fine descriptions of the great day and its great deeds, written by Englishmen, and from their point of view, moral and local. This is the account of a French soldier of the line, looking out of his own positions at the English troops, and simply detailing every movement on the French side. It cannot fail to be interesting to those who understand military matters; while, to those who do not, it unravels that great mystery, a battle *en règle*.

The "Blocus" treats of a period included in the Conscript's story, and makes incidental mention of Joseph Bertha. As a work of art, we rate the "Blocus" very high. It is as striking an instance of the writer's power of assuming an identity as

Michel Bastien presents, and it is an assumption attendedwith greater difficulty. The narrator of the blockade of Phalsbourg is a Jew ; a small trader, an old man of pacific and avaricious instincts, but pacific in a different way from Joseph Bertha, and whose avarice takes other forms than that of Bastien. In the case of this old Moïse, the characteristics of the Hebrew character such it has become since the disgrace of the chosen people, are brought out with wonderful dexterity, and with the high art which conceals its artifice. The tone and atmosphere of the " Blocus " are completely different from those of the other *Romans Nationaux,* though it is a story of the War, and of one of its severest phases, a story of privation and disease, of bereavement and suffering—a first edition of the narrative which will probably inspire many pens presently, for, while we write, Phalsbourg has surrendered to the Prussians, and is "occupied" by the Prussian troops.* But here is no patriotic animation, no eager partizanship, no burning sense of outrage, injury, and wrong, no furious indignation at the mere thought of an invader of the sacred soil. The old Jew is a good man and an honest citizen, but he is of no country, and he feels as an individual, as a trader, not as a Frenchman and a patriot. America, whither he has judiciously sent his two sons, that they may escape the conscription, is as much his country and theirs, as France. Their commerce is to them all that country and home are to others. " If I had had children capable of wanting to be soldiers, I should have died of grief, for I should have said they are not of my race," says Moïse, and then proceeds to relate the consolation he derives from the early development of the taste and talent for traffic in Safel, his little son, the Benjamin of the family. The difference between the Jewish and the Christian morality, the divergence of the several points of view, are conveyed by innumerable fine touches, and with a delightful humour. Thus, the Jew thanks "the Eternal" for every indication of *finesse* on the part of his wife, and avowedly cherishes and carries out revenge against another Jew, for a trick played upon him. He is extraordinarily acute and avaricious in his dealings, and takes credit for those qualities without the least notion of hiding them, pointing out that they are adjuncts of that superior intelligence with which the Eternal has blessed His people. When the siege becomes imminent, old Moïse is advised by his wife, Sorlè, to lay in a provision of

---

* We have learned, since this sentence was written, that M. Erckmann, who was at Phalsbourg during the late siege, purposes to write a history of it. This projected work will be unique in another sense than that in which the whole series is unexampled.

eau-de-vie, which he does, by ordering a quantity of spirits of wine, and making preparations for admixture and adulteration on the premises. Henceforth, the state of affairs resolves itself for him into a question of whether his casks will arrive in time to be delivered before the town is shut up and the ingress of all merchandise interdicted. The whole story is exquisitely comic, and yet what tragedy underlies it. The casks are seized, close to the town, by a skirmishing party of the enemy, and the commandant, learning their contents, and aware of the probable value to his troops of such a supply, sends a party to rescue them. Full of ardour and zeal, old Moïse accompanies the party, but contrives to hide himself under a waggon while the fighting is going on and the marauders are slaughtered. The self-congratulation of the old Jew on his prudence, and the good-humoured contempt of his associates, are delightful. "It was all over in ten minutes, and then, in the darkness, I heard the sergeant call out, 'cease firing!' Presently he came up with a lantern, and, seeing me under the waggon, he cried, 'You are wounded, father Moses.' No, no,' I replied, 'but, lest a Cossack might hurt me with his lance, I took shelter here.' Then he laughed out loud, and, putting out his hand to lift me up, he said, 'Father Moses, you frightened me. Dry your back, or people might fancy you were not brave.' I laughed also, thinking, 'Let them fancy what they like, the chief thing is to live, in good health, as long as possible.' "

The speculation is exceedingly successful, and, owing to the foresight of Sorlè, the family suffer less than others from the horrors of the siege. The struggle in the old man's mind between the decent and pious sorrow he is bound to feel for the city of his sojourn, and his exultation in the immense profits he derives from its misfortune, is extremely comical, and even at the most touching portion of the story, when the beloved grandchild dies of typhus-fever,—an incident related with the simple pathos in which the writers are unrivalled— we find this charming characteristic passage :—

But I had one great satisfaction, which I shall ever recall with pride ; it is that, in the midst of our misery, when Sorlè, our daughter Ziffen, every one in short, lost our heads, forgot our business, and allowed everything to go as it would, the little Safel took upon himself the direction of our commerce. Every morning we heard him get up at six o'clock, go downstairs, open the shop, carry up the jars of *eau-de-vie* from the cellar, and serve the customers. Nobody had said a word to him about it, but Safel was the very soul of commerce. And, if anything could console a father in such misfortunes, it should be to see himself, so to speak, revived in so young a child, to recognize himself in him, and to think, " At least the good race is not quite lost ; some remain, always to preserve good sense in this world. Yes, this the only consolation a man can enjoy."

The picture of the interior of the humble Jewish household is very interesting, and the character of Sorlè as full of marked individuality and as admirably drawn as that of old Moïse. She is as interested, and even more acute, but her avarice and cunning have her husband and children for their objects, they are less narrow than the similar qualities evinced by Moïse. One Jewish peculiarity comes out strong in both, in opposition to the notions of modern Christian society. This is the stress laid upon the duty of children to aid their parents, and the exemption of parents from any reciprocal obligation. Moïse preserves his sons from the conscription by sending them to America, but he gives them none of his savings; his florins are safely hoarded, while the youths are tramping about with peltries and old iron, painfully and laboriously establishing a trade destined to flourish, and which the old father refers to complacently in conclusion (though he admits that he is very prosperous himself), as enabling them *to give him everything he wants.* The execution of *Le Blocus* is quite faultless, and there is no more forcible picture of the horrors of war, no more powerful appeal to the common sense of mankind against it, in all the series of *romans nationaux,* than the account given by the old Jew and alien, of the wounded men, fever patients laid by the roadside to die, shunned by all with terror, and the episode of " Sergeant Trubert."

" La Guerre" is the story of Souworow, " the invincible," the wonderful, ugly, *chétif* little man, who was the greatest general Russia has ever produced, told in the dramatic form. The charm of this drama is indescribable, with its noble note of war and heroism, its recital of the bravery and endurance of the troops opposed to Masséna in Souworow's retreat, and the melancholy love story which lends it a tender human charm. The remorseless cruelty of Souworow comes out in the drama, but it does not excite such disgust as it ought to excite, so dexterously and fairly are the desperate exigencies of war, the maddening excitement, the tremendous value of an opportunity, used. When the guns are driven at a gallop over the writhing bodies of his own wounded men, crushing them into the bloody mud of the narrow bridge, we shudder, but we too are made to strain our eyes forward, after the advancing troops. The devouring ambition, passion, suspicion of Souworow's nature, the faith and devotion which he inspired in the soldiers whom he sacrificed without a scruple, the iron will and courage which

carried his wretched little body through such fatigue and suffering, his pleasure in the knowledge of the hatred with which he -
had inspired the Poles, the ardent love of battle which possessed
him, the cold contemptuous cynicism with which he met his
reverses, and the vile ingratitude of the Tzar, find wonderful
expression in this powerful drama. The authors have chosen
the title well. It breathes war.

It is remarkable that the writers have only twice adopted the
dramatic form, in which they have succeeded as well as in the
autobiographical. The second instance is " Le Juif Polonais,"
than which, within our knowledge, there is no finer delineation
of a tortured conscience and the punishment it can inflict,
without aid from any human hand or the spur of detection. The
dream of the murderer at the height of his prosperity and his
respectability,—his totally unsuspected crime being the origin
of all,—is worked up with a terrible power of evolving suffering
apart from circumstances, only equalled by Victor Hugo.

In estimating the "Histoire d'un Homme du Peuple" less
highly than the preceding works, we do not lose sight of
the integral difference of the time and the events of which
it treats. A very small portion of this story is concerned
with the delightful village life and quaint peasant character
which abound in the others. This small portion has a great
deal of the familiar charm, but Jean Pierre, the "Homme du
Peuple" is only an honest workman of the comparatively modern
'48 epoch, indoctrinated by his fellows with revolutionary
notions, and led into active participation in the insurrection
which drove the Orleans family out of power.

After one has read the history of the Great Revolution, and
of the Empire, there is a decided flatness about '48. The
wrongs and the sufferings of the latter time are as much less
impressive than those which we have just been made to feel
with poignant reality, as " Mr. Smith " with his umbrella is a
less imposing and disastrous phenomenon than the Baroness
Korff and her children, in the unwieldly coach on the Route
de Varennes. MM. Erckmann-Chatrian have made the most
that could be made of their subject; there is no description of '48 to compare with this, as an actual narrative from
point to point and from hour to hour, but the elements of which
they make such unequalled use in the other epochs of the long
tragedy which we call the history of France, are wanting.

The series of " Romans Populaires " comprises a number of
short stories, and two of more important length, " L'Ami
Fritz," and " Maître Daniel Rock." The former is a charming
story of the most eccentric of good fellows, a story in which
the happy, cheery, plentiful, country life of the provinces now

lying desolate is depicted, with the minute perception and intense love of every feature of the place, and phase of the seasons, which add pathos to the tragic histories; but which is made, under this comic recital of an Alsatian bachelor turned Benedick, thoroughly delightful. "L'Ami Fritz" is full of humour, in no one *roman* is this characteristic, which they all possess, so lavishly displayed. "Maître Daniel Rock" is, on the contrary a flight of lofty, picturesque fancy, with a deep, pathetic, heart-stirring human interest underlying it, in a combination which turns the story of the enthusiasts whom it portrays into a prose poem.

In the shorter stories the two styles are intermingled. In some we find humour, so "racy of the soil" that it will not bear transplantation by quotation, so quaint and realistic that it makes one feel as though one had lived among those people with names that are half German, but hearts that are warmly and entirely French. In others, we find wild and pathetic fancy, grotesque characters, a weird legendary strain, in certain respects without parallel, but which, if we must place them in any category, we would assign to those of Hoffmann and Edgar Poe. "L'Œil Invisible" might have originated in the fancy which produced that fascinating and frightful impossibility, the automaton lover, and "Le Requiem du Corbeau," though not so repulsive, is at least as weird as "The Black Cat."

Among the various characteristics of these remarkable works, there is one feature never missing in any and paramount in all. One feature which is of surpassing importance in the historical aspect of the "Romans Nationaux," and which contributes largely to the charm of the "Romans Populaires," by its vivid and ever-present vitality. One feature which, at any time impressive, is now of absorbing and painful interest. The two series form in reality a political, social, military, and literary history of Alsace and Lorraine, during nearly a century. This history opens amidst oppression and wrong, but the condition of the provinces, as compared with their condition under German rule, is acknowledged to be far superior. What is the sentiment which animates the volunteers of Alsace and Lorraine; what is the passionate emotion which makes the peasantry and the *bourgeoisie* rise like one man? The sentiment is patriotism, the passionate emotion is hatred of the invader, indignant shame that "the stranger" should set his foot on *French* soil. *La Patrie*, an ever-sacred word when other holy things were desecrated and despised—*L'étranger*, an intolerable wrong when ground-down wretches had borne with sullen submission more unendurable material grievances—in these two words we have the key-note of this long history. It is written by men who know the provinces through and through, the people and the fields, the hearts of men, and the face of the earth, and they tell the truth. If there be a portion of France more than any other portion French at heart, it is the provinces for the seizure of which the lawless Attila of to-day desires to secure the approval of law-loving England, on the hypocritical pretence of a "restoration"! If there be a portion of France in which the individual rights of conscience are respected more than any other, it is those provinces in which Jews, Calvinists, and Catholics live together in undisturbed amity.

The attempt to engage English Protestant sympathies in the Germanization of Alsace and Lorraine is an insolent presumption on English ignorance. German Protestants have always hated French Protestants, in the true spirit of the bitter hate which has existed from the beginning of both heresies between Lutherans and Calvinists. The Protestantism of Berlin,—as distinguished from its largely preponderant rationalism and atheism,—differs from the Protestantism of Alsace and Lorraine, in kind and degree, as the Protestantism of Mr. Mackonochie differs from that of Dean Stanley, or the Protestantism of Dr. Cumming differs from that of Mr. Voysey.

If there be any one in doubt as to the magnitude of the crime and the dastardliness of the cruelty—also, as to the patience and certainty of the revenge which the brave and resolute Frenchmen of Alsace and Lorraine will aspire to, and take, when the time comes, should this cruel crime be perpetrated;—let him read MM. Erckmann-Chatrian's works. He will never learn elsewhere so well, with what intense love, and pride, these outraged provinces claim to be intimate and inseparable fibres of the great heart of France.

Art. VII.—THE DEFINITION OF PAPAL INFALLIBILITY.

Constitutio dogmatica prima de Ecclesiâ Christi.

The Vatican Council and its Definitions. By HENRY EDWARD, Archbishop of Westminster. London: Longmans.

The Council and Papal Infallibility. By the Right Rev. Bishop Ullathorne. London: Burns, Oates & Co.

Pastoral. By ROBERT, Bishop of Beverley.

The North British Review for October, 1870. London: Williams & Norgate.

THE Vatican Council naturally draws back one's thoughts to the Council of Trent its immediate predecessor, and leads one to compare the state of men's minds at the two respective periods. At both of them the civilized world was going through a revolutionary crisis of thought, of which it was impossible to foresee the end, and which threatened to overthrow a great body of truths; but in one case—it may be said perhaps with sufficient accuracy—the Church was assaulted primarily by rebellion of *will*, in the other primarily by rebellion of *intellect*. Three centuries ago men were revolting against the moral law of God, against austerity of life, against counsels of perfection; but at the present moment their chief zeal is against the dominion of any supernatural authority over their speculations and inquiries. Accordingly the Council of Trent emphatically declared the Church's doctrine on Justification, the Sacrament of Penance, Virginity, and the like; while the Vatican Council is before all things concerned with the Church's authority in teaching, and with that vast cycle of speculative truth, which is of itself within the province of reason, although more or less immediately connected with the Deposit of Faith. It is from no accidental circumstance then, but on the contrary from the very exigency of the time, that by far the most prominent thing hitherto done in the Council has been its definition of Papal Infallibility. And for the same reason we venture to prognosticate, that whenever the Council is enabled to resume its deliberations, it is still the Church's teaching authority, in one shape or other, which will supply the principal and central theme for its dogmatic decrees.

Nor are these decrees needed only as a witness to externs;

they are required also as a guide to Catholics.   Those without
the Church are in these days impatient or rather absolutely
intolerant of any authority, which claims to bridle their speculations and to throw a yoke over the freedom of their inquiries.
It is not to be expected that so subtle and pestilential a disease
shall not have in some degree infected the Church's children.
On the contrary,—as was lately observed by our contemporary the "Month" and changing our metaphor, — when
a violent storm rages in the open sea, there will always be some
considerable agitation of waves within the harbour itself.
Accordingly of late almost all error among Catholics has
principally taken the shape of depreciating, in one way or other,
the Church's teaching authority. To fix our ideas, let us confine
ourselves to what has passed before our eyes here in England.
A few years ago some Catholics were found—several of them
most loyally intentioned Catholics as we firmly believe—who
took occasion to deny in effect the infallibility of the Church's
abiding magisterium; and to imply that the purity of her
practical teaching has been impaired by the separation of
schismatics from her bosom.   Take for instance a matter so
vitally affecting the interior life as the cultus of our Blessed
Lady: such Catholics seemed to maintain that the Church
would have been more sensitive to devotional errors in that
matter, if the English and German nations had remained
integrally in her communion.   This was serious enough:
but a very short time elapsed before a more startling step
was taken; and it was expressly affirmed that Catholics are
not bound as such to accept the Church's most clear and
emphatic definitions, unless those definitions teach what was
actually delivered as revealed truth by the Apostles.   In other
words—for it comes to this—such Catholics had to maintain,
if they would be consistent, that the Council of Trent did not
impose any obligation of belief in defining the authenticity of
the Vulgate (see Archbishop Manning, p. 68) ; nor the Fifth
Œcumenical Council in anathematizing the Three Chapters;
nor the Council of Constance, approved by the Pope, in censuring
certain tenets as respectively erroneous, scandalous, and offensive
to pious ears.   Moreover (which made it the more dangerous) the
chief advocates of this error were not among those flippant, half-
hearted, rationalistic malcontents, who have been for some time
the Church's opprobrium in England; but on the contrary
were persons devoted to the Church's highest interests according
to their own conception of those interests.   Here then was a
phenomenon (to our mind) grave and disastrous in itself, and
fearful in its legitimate consequences; and yet even this was
little, in comparison with the aberrations which have been

brought to light by the proposed Vatican Definition. Since the probability of this Definition was first rumoured, various persons calling themselves Catholics have had the audacity to profess, that even the dogmatic decrees of an Œcumenical Council are not infallible, unless they are ultimately sanctioned by the sensus fidelium. " Döllinger had written in March that an article of faith required not only to be approved and accepted unanimously by the Council, but that the bishops united with the Pope are not infallible, and that the œcumenicity of their acts must be acknowledged and ratified by the whole Church."*

Now for this mass of baleful disease a remedy has been provided in the recent Definition. It is true indeed that nothing has yet been expressly laid down by the Council on the *extent* of infallibility ; or on the teaching authority of the Roman Congregations : such matters having been reserved for subsequent deliberation. Still the *last-named* of those errors which we above recited has now been so directly anathematized, that to maintain it is openly and before the world to apostatise from the Faith. And as to the other tenets which we have criticised so severely—even though (which God avert!) the further sitting of the Council should be suspended for a long period—still if they assumed so prominent a shape as to threaten the Church with any danger, the Holy Father now possesses the undisputed power of condemning them once for all by his own authority, as opposed to true " doctrine concerning faith and morals."

Never therefore, since the Council of Trent terminated its labours, has there been a doctrinal decision which can compare in fundamentality and pervasiveness with that which Catholics have now lived to see. We are not sorry however that circumstances prevented us from attempting any account of it in our last number; because at that time none of those episcopal utterances had been issued which we name at the head of our article, and we should have written therefore under circumstances of great disadvantage. Foremost among these utterances we must name the Archbishop's Pastoral; which runs to far greater length and enters into far greater detail than any of the rest. We know we are in danger of regarding in every case the Archbishop's last performance as his best; but we really do think he has never been so happy on any previous occasion, nor rendered such important service to the Church. We take for granted that all our readers will have studied the Pastoral, and we will therefore give from it only a

---

* " North British Review," p. 225.

few extended quotations; but the whole train of thought which follows has been more or less inspired by its perusal.

The Bishops of Birmingham and Beverley also have in different ways given important information, and we shall make use of their lordships' labours as we proceed. And there is another commentary on the Council, which we also name at the head of our article, viz. an article in the " North British Review " for last October. The publishers of that Review announced a year back that it is now conducted by the former Editor of the " Chronicle " ; and we suppose, as a matter of course, that we may accept the article as representing Lord Acton's views on the matters therein treated.

The natural order of our remarks will be, first of all to consider the objections which have been raised by certain soi-disant Catholics against the infallibility of the recent Definition, and then to examine the *wording* of that Definition.

On the first of these heads, a somewhat singular phenomenon meets us at the outset. There is one circumstance undoubtedly, which would have been simply fatal to the œcumenicity and authority of the Council; and it is precisely those who complain of its not being a legitimate Council, who did their best to bring this circumstance about. We refer to the interference of secular governments with conciliar freedom. It is as good as a comedy to read the " North British " article from p. 191 to p. 197 ; and to observe the exquisite simplicity with which its writer implies his wish, that statesmen *had* interfered in this purely spiritual question: while it is profoundly interesting to study, under his guidance, the means adopted by Almighty God, for protecting the Church from such unprincipled tyranny. Prince Hohenlohe, who is the first to move and who earnestly wishes to have his finger in the pie, is suspected at Vienna of complicity with Prussia, and soon afterwards, for other reasons, has to resign. In France the more thorough-going Catholics and the extreme democrats, agreeing in nought else, are able by their united action to frustrate every attempt at dictating to the Council. Germany is kept quiet by Count Bismarck's wish of standing well with Rome. The other Catholic powers have no influence at their command. Victor Emmanuel is fearful that " if the Church were molested in her freedom, excuse would be given for resisting the incorporation of Rome " (p. 191). In other words, He who " disposes all things powerfully and sweetly " had decreed that the Definition should take place, and adopted His own means to avert one particular peril which would have threatened it. " This policy of " state " intervention ignominiously failed " (p. 210). Governments did enough to show their evil disposition, yet not enough to prevent the accomplishment of God's counsels. But all this is of course far from furnishing any excuse to those traitors who, calling themselves Catholics, did all they could, that the religious rulers placed over them by God should be coerced in the exercise of their most purely spiritual duties. " It did not seem to occur " says the Archbishop

to those who invoked the interference of the Civil Powers, that they were thereby endeavouring to deprive the Council of its liberty : which, in those who were complaining, in all languages, that the Council was not free, involved a self-contradiction on which I need not comment. Neither did they seem to remember that those who invoke the secular power against the spiritual authority of the Church, whether to defeat a sentence already given or to prevent the delivery of such a sentence, are ipso facto excommunicate, and that their case is reserved to the Pope. This, which applies to any ordinary ecclesiastical judge in matters of law, surely applies in an eminent degree to an Œcumenical Council in matters of faith (pp. 19–20).

It is unconsciously admitted then by the " North British " Reviewer, and is otherwise certain, that no objection can be raised against the Œcumenicity of the Council on the ground of secular interference with its freedom ; and malcontents are driven to search for their ground of attack in quite different directions. First we may mention a vast quantity of miscellaneous dirt, which they have sedulously thrown at the Council ; the general picture they have drawn of odious contention and disorderliness ; of the clear-sighted and thoughtful few oppressed by the noisy and tyrannical majority ; of bitterness, violence, unscrupulousness, dominating every session. Full of humour is the Archbishop's account of this.

The Council was composed, at first, of 767 Fathers. We were told that their very faces were such as to compel an enlightened correspondent, at the first sight of them, to lament " that the spiritual welfare of the world should be committed to such men."

Then, by a wonderful disposition of things, for the good, no doubt, of the human race, and above all of the Church itself, the Council was divided into a majority and a minority : and, by an even more beneficent and admirable provision, it was so ordered that the theology, philosophy, science, culture, intellectual power, logical acumen, eloquence, candour, nobleness of mind, independence of spirit, courage, and elevation of character in the Council, were all to be found in the minority. The majority was naturally a Dead Sea of superstition, narrowness, shallowness, ignorance, prejudice ; without theology, philosophy, science, or eloquence ; gathered from " old Catholic countries ; " bigoted, tyrannical, deaf to reason ; with a herd of " Curial and Italian Prelates," and mere " Vicars Apostolic."

The Cardinal Presidents were men of imperious and overbearing character, who by violent ringing of bells and intemperate interruptions cut short the calm and inexorable logic of the minority.

But the conduct of the majority was still more overbearing. By violent outcries, menacing gestures, and clamorous manifestations round the tribune, they drowned the thrilling eloquence of the minority, and compelled unanswerable orators to descend.

Not satisfied with this, the majority, under the pretext that the method of conducting the discussions was imperfect, obtained from the supreme authority a new regulation, by which all liberty of discussion was finally taken from the noble few who were struggling to redeem the Council and the Church from bondage.

From that date the non-œcumenicity of the Council was no longer doubtful. Indeed, "Janus" had told the world in many tongues, long before it met, that the Council would not be free. Nevertheless, the minority persevered with heroic courage, logic which nothing could resist, and eloquence which electrified the most insensible, until a tyrannous majority, deaf to reason and incapable of argument, cut discussion short by an arbitrary exercise of power; and so silenced the only voices nobly lifted up for science, candour, and common sense.

This done, the definition of new dogmas became inevitable, and the antagonism between the ultra-romanism of a party and the progress of modern society, between independence and servility, became complete.

Such is the history of the Council written ab extra in the last nine months. I believe that every epithet I have given may be verified in the mass of extracts now before me (pp. 10–12).

The Archbishop was himself present from first to last. He gives a very different account of what took place.

Having from my earliest remembrance been a witness of public assemblies of all kinds, and especially of those among ourselves, which for gravity and dignity are supposed to exceed all others, I am able and bound to say that I have never seen such calmness, self-respect, mutual forbearance, courtesy and self-control, as in the eighty-nine sessions of the Vatican Council. In the period of nine months, the Cardinal President was compelled to recall the speakers to order perhaps twelve or fourteen times. In any other assembly they would have been inexorably recalled to the question sevenfold oftener and sooner. Nothing could exceed the consideration and respect with which this duty was discharged. Occasionally murmurs of dissent were audible; now and then a comment may have been made aloud. In a very few instances, and those happily of an exceptional kind, expressions of strong disapproval and of exhausted patience at length escaped. But the descriptions of violence, outcries, menace, denunciation, and even of personal collisions, with which certain newspapers deceived the world, I can affirm to be calumnious falsehoods, fabricated to bring the Council into odium and contempt (pp. 27–28).

Quite as strongly speaks another eye-witness, the Bishop of Birmingham.

The qualities that adorned the assemblies of the Council were order and dignity, charity and the spirit of brotherhood, kindliness and courtesy of manner, unwavering patience, and a frankness and freedom of speech which was only controlled by these virtues ; those qualities, in short, which Catholics of all nations are accustomed to contemplate in their bishops. No one could enter the Council without being struck and edified by the simple and dignified bearing of the prelates, their frank and open bearing towards each other, and that unity of brethren in the bond of charity which became the chief ministers of Christ and the dispensers of God's mysteries. Often was admiration expressed at this spectacle, which even the strongest diversity of opinion seemed never to interfere with. "And how could it be otherwise," said a bishop in my hearing, "seeing that every one here offers the Holy Sacrifice each morning, and assists at another Mass united with his brethren in this very place"? Is it necessary I should say that there were no personal altercations, except in the imagination of certain newspaper correspondents? Ardour there was in debate, but an ardour replete with gravity and with a sense of responsibility that weighed more heavily than usual upon men accustomed to bear the burden of the Church. The great freedom of speech sometimes occasioned calls to order ; but, with rare exceptions, the manifest sense of the Council anticipated the voice of the President. In no case was a discussion closed by the Presidents until either there were no more speakers who offered themselves, or until the majority of the Council plainly indicated that the subject was exhausted, and then the closing of the debate was decided by the general vote (pp. 5–6).

And the Bishop of Beverley :—

You can form no idea of the mutual charity and patience which visibly sustained the members of the Council, until you are reminded of the exceptional heat of the season, the long hours, usually five, of each sitting, the exceeding sameness and monotony of discourses lasting on an average more than half-an-hour, and some of which approached two hours' duration. It may reasonably be doubted whether, in any Council, one subject, one single point of doctrine, has ever been so long, so accurately and so thoroughly discussed, or where liberty of speech was pushed, we say it advisedly and we were present at every congregation from the commencement to the close, so far beyond all reasonable limits. Very few were ever called to order, although not unfrequently there was ample reason for doing so, while the few who met with this check were of every class of opinion (pp. 185-6).

The flippant and scurrilous insults to the Council which Catholic bishops have thus noticed and exposed, must at all events be rather considered as rhetorical appeals "ad invidiam" than as arguments. As to the latter, that on which malcontents in the first instance chiefly relied, was an allegation that the bishops were not free agents, but influenced throughout by most undue pressure from the Holy Father and the Roman authorities. Now, to begin with, nothing could be more contrary to fact than this allegation. As our contemporary the " Month " pointed out some time back, the whole movement for defining Papal infallibility originated, not with Pope, but with bishops. " It was not the Holy See," says the Bishop of Birmingham,

that brought the question into the Council. A plan of a Constitution, magnificent in its substance and incorporating the Catholic doctrine respecting the Church, was laid before the Council, and the one-half of its chapters underwent a long discussion. But although the proposed Constitution contained chapters on the Papal Supremacy, it said not a word on the Papal Infallibility. *The movement for introducing that doctrine came from the Fathers of the Council themselves.* From the beginning of its work it was evident and unmistakable that *a great number of the bishops had set their mind* on having the doctrine of the Church on this point definitively settled (p. 9).

" Some five hundred Fathers of the Council " in fact, the Archbishop tells the world

desired of the Holy See that the doctrine of the Infallibility of the Roman Pontiff should be defined. This event manifested a mind and a will so united and so decisive, as to reduce the proportions of the opposition, both numerically and morally, to very little (p. 18).

Outside the Council also, the feeling was very strong and general among loyal and devoted Catholics. Hear the Bishop of Beverley :—

The defenders of the privileges of the Holy See were neither few nor backward in so good a cause. Not only bishops and priests and even laymen, but whole religious bodies stood forward in defence of the truth ; the children of S. Basil and S. Dominic, S. Augustine and S. Bonaventure, from the east as from the west, vindicated in learned dissertations the teaching of their fathers now as in ages long gone by.

Meanwhile, the bulk of the faithful throughout the world, with the true instinct of faith which ever lives in the Church of God, gave no uncertain sound as to their belief upon this important point, and they flooded the Holy See with petitions for its definition. There could be no longer any question between satisfying the wishes of the weak, the wavering, and the disloyal, and supporting, encouraging, and confirming the loving and devoted children of the Church. Nay it was now clear that the omission of a definition would be a grave scandal, inasmuch as it would lead men to conclude that a definition was impossible, and therefore that a doctrine hitherto of all but universal belief in the Church and only not of faith, was an error.

The Fathers of the Council, therefore, in number over six hundred, petitioned for the introduction of the question in the following terms :— "The undersigned fathers humbly and earnestly beg the holy Œcumenical Council of the Vatican to define clearly, and in words that cannot be mistaken, that the authority of the Roman Pontiff is supreme, and therefore free from error, when, in matters of faith or morals, he declares and defines, what is to be believed and held, and what to be rejected and condemned by all the faithful." A petition of such importance, bearing so many names, supported by an array of virtue, of learning, of judgment and of experience such as have rarely been combined in this world, could not fail of success, and the speedy introduction of the question was formally announced to the Council by the presidents (pp. 161-62).

The " North British " Reviewer himself indeed makes the same admission

Men whose word is powerful in the centres of civilization, men who three months before were confronting martyrdom among barbarians, preachers at Notre Dame, professors from Germany, Republicans from Western America, men with every sort of training and every sort of experience, had come together *as confident and as eager as the prelates of Rome itself, to hail the Pope infallible. Resistance was improbable, for it was hopeless.* It was improbable that bishops who had refused no token of submission for twenty years would now combine to inflict dishonour on the Pope. In their address of 1867 they had confessed that he is the Father and Teacher of all Christians ; that all the things he has spoken were spoken by St. Peter through him ; that they would believe and teach all that he believed and taught. In 1854 they had allowed him to proclaim a dogma, which some of them dreaded and some opposed, but to which all submitted when he had decreed without the intervention of a Council (p. 207).

As to the German bishops in particular, who almost all, we believe, voted in the minority, the " North British " Reviewer nevertheless testifies that the words of the joint Pastoral, issued by them before the Council,

meant nothing if they did not mean that infallibility was no new dogma, and that all the bishops believed in it. Even the bishop of Orleans avoided a direct attack on the doctrine, proclaimed his own devotion to the Pope, and promised that the Council would be a scene of concord (p. 207).

"The ideas of the Coblentz address " adds the Reviewer (p. 208)—that truly disgraceful manifesto on which we commented in October, 1869 (pp. 469-74)—" had their seat in the universities "; and brought those universities "*into direct col-*

lision with the Episcopate."   In fact, according to this writer
(p. 216) "the ordinary advisers of the Pope . . . were *visibly
compelled and driven* by those who represented the majority."
So far from dreaming that the Pope was tyrannical towards the
bishops, he seems to think that the bishops were tyrannical towards the Pope.

But we do not hesitate to affirm—we say this merely to prevent misapprehension of our meaning—that had Pius IX. put
ever so urgent pressure on the Fathers of the Council, it is
no more than his duty would require him to do in any case,
where he should judge a conciliar definition of great importance,
the bishops being reluctant to put it forth.   If ever there were
councils universally recognized as œcumenical, they were those
of Ephesus and Chalcedon.   In the former of these—as the
Bishop of Birmingham reminds us (p. 33)—it was the very
profession of the assembled bishops, that they condemned
Nestorius, "*compelled*" thereto "by the sacred canons and
through the *Letter of the Most Holy Father.*"   As to Chalcedon,
one should read F. Newman's history of that Council (Essay on
Development, pp. 303-308).   He thus sums up his investigation.   "A doctrine, which *the whole East refused as a symbol,* not
once but twice, patriarch by patriarch, metropolian by metropolitan, first by the mouth of above a hundred, then of *above six
hundred* of its bishops . . . was *forced* upon the Council . . .
for its acceptance as a definition of faith under the sanction of
an anathema; forced on the Council, *by the resolution of the Pope
of the day,* acting through his legates and supported by the civil
power."   In fact, one most prominent argument urged by defenders of Papal infallibility to show the traditional prevalence
of that dogma, has always been to exhibit the absolute authority
ever conceded by councils to the Holy See in definitions of faith.
How otherwise indeed can Peter exercise the office of "confirming his brethren," except precisely by strengthening their
resolution and stimulating their action?

As time went on, the emptiness of this first objection against
the Council's œcumenicity became apparent; and a second
accordingly was raised to the place of (dis)honour.   It was
alleged that dogmatic decrees need not be infallibly true, though
enforced both by the Pope and by a large majority of the
Episcopate; that infallibility appertains only to those conciliar
definitions on which the bishops are morally unanimous.   The
thesis of these men, says their eulogizer in the "North British
Review," was that the Pope's

decrees are not free from the risk of error, unless they express *the universal
belief of the Episcopate.*   The idea that particular virtue attaches to a

certain number of bishops, or that infallibility depends on a few votes more or less, was defended by nobody. If the act of a majority of bishops in the Council, possibly not representing a majority in the Church, is infallible, it derives its infallibility from the Pope (p. 220).

Now for ourselves—even when the Pope is considered apart from the Episcopate—we never could understand how those who admit, as even Janus admits, that he is the divinely-appointed centre of unity, can doubt that he is infallible—we do not say in his minor ex cathedrâ judgments—but at all events in his definitions of *faith*.   He excludes e.g. from his communion all who deny the Immaculate Conception, and they are therefore, by God's appointment, externs to the Church. Who can believe that God excludes men from the Church for no other offence, than that of rejecting a false doctrine tyranically pressed as a revealed verity?   The notion is surely monstrous.   Yet these so-called Catholics think that the great majority of all the bishops, acting in union with the Holy See, may quite possibly be permitted by God to exclude from their communion faithful witnesses of Revelation, for no other offence except that of *being* such faithful witnesses.

But the *reason*, ordinarily given for this portentous notion, is even more fundamentally anti-Catholic than the notion itself. The assembled bishops, it is argued, cannot pronounce infallibly, except so far as they testify—each for his own diocese—that the doctrine to be defined is there universally regarded as a revealed truth handed down from the Apostles.   Now a very short consideration will show, that such reasoners deny the Church's power of either infallibly defining any one truth, or infallibly condemning any one error.   Let it even be supposed that no heretical bishop ever existed—that Nestorius, Dioscorus Sergius, are persons of romance and fable—still at successive periods Arian, Nestorian, Eutychian heretics did abound in the Church ; nor could the contemporary bishops possibly testify, each for his own diocese, that the assailed dogma was universally regarded as a revealed truth.   Then further, when any verity is defined, this can only be done by some scientific analysis, or at least by the authoritative introduction of some significant phrase : so the Nicene Fathers defined, that the Son is *Consubstantial* with the Father ; the Ephesine adopted S. Cyril's anathemas ; the Chalcedonian submitted to S. Leo's Letter, and incorporated its most characteristic expressions into their Definition.   But no one in his senses ever thought, that the word "Consubstantial," or the phraseology of S. Cyril's anathemas and S. Leo's Letter, was handed down from the Apostles ; and consequently, according to the view which we are opposing, these Councils were neither infallible in these definitions, nor in any other definitions which could possibly have been used in their place. Nor could a council have avoided the difficulty, by refraining from all scientific exposition of dogma and doing no more than condemn by name existing heresies. It is no revealed truth handed down from the Apostles, that Arius or Nestorius or Eutyches is an heresiarch : the Apostles no more knew the future existence of these men, than they knew the future existence of consols or the Great Western Railway. If infallibility is only exercised when bishops testify that some statement is universally received as Apostolical,—then it can neither be infallibly declared that the Son is Consubstantial with the Father, nor yet that Arius's teaching is heretical.

On the other hand, if a council be admitted to have the power of not *testifying* only but *judging* infallibly—of judging infallibly e.g. that " Consubstantial " is a word truly expressing the Catholic dogma, or that Arius's writings in their legitimate objective sense *contradict* that dogma—then the whole principle, on which these misbelievers base their argument, at once falls through. It is monstrously *false* to say that the assembled bishops have no infallibility, except in testifying, each for his own diocese, the received Faith of the Church.

However in the end this second line of objection also fell through : because the solemn and final judgment of the bishops *was* "morally unanimous " ; being supported by 533 out of 535. Nothing can be more intelligible than Bishop Ullathorne's account of the motives which led the minority to the course they adopted. On the other hand we have heard of no explanation possessing the slightest plausibility, which would account for their conduct on the hypothesis, that they dreamed as a body of refusing unreserved submission to any dogmatic decree, voted by the majority and confirmed by the Pope. Here is the Bishop of Birmingham's statement : the italics being our own :

It remains to say a word respecting those Fathers, who absented themselves from the Council at this session, and thus withheld their votes. The number of those who gave a negative at the previous voting was 88 : but I know more than one of that number who voted in the affirmative at the final session ; and those who had hitherto given conditional votes now gave affirmative votes. And to these 62 votes, now become affirmative, we must add 20 more, as the full increase of affirmatives over the numbers given in the previous voting. Those Fathers then, who remained absent, could scarcely have reached the number of 88, as popularly represented, even though that was the number of negatives in the previous voting.

Whatever might be its numbers when it took this step, this compact party has been called the opposition. But what did it oppose ? The popular notion is that they opposed the doctrine of the Papal Infallibility.

This is not true. *With the exception of three or four, none of them expressed opposition to the doctrine,* nay, several of them openly expressed their belief in it. They did not oppose the doctrine itself; but, in opposition to the overwhelming majority, they maintained that the definition was not expedient, or at this time opportune; and when it came to the discussion of the text, they contended, as did others, for the insertion of modifying sentences, to a greater extent than the great majority were willing to accept. So far from finally rejecting the Definition in principle, a few days before the Session this very party proposed, through its delegates, to accept the Definition, subject to the insertion of two explanatory clauses. But these clauses were not accepted; and their originators abstained from voting or being present on this policy. They still hoped that, owing to their opposition, the Sovereign Pontiff himself might be induced to alter the decree in their sense before giving his confirmation; and, out of respect for his presence, they were unwilling to give a negative vote in what so intimately concerned his prerogative: but *they likewise resolved that, in the event of the Holy Father giving his confirmation without accepting their modification, they would then give in their adhesion to the Decree.* This the most of them have already done; and I may point to the document issued from Fulda, in proof of the loyal spirit in which many of those Prelates have acted.

I am not judging, but only explaining, the policy that held this party together; and that with a view to removing the wrong impressions that prevail respecting its character. And although I had no part either in that policy or in the proceedings to which it led, I am yet able to give this much reliable information, derived from those who were themselves of the party (pp. 15, 16).

However this may be, the fact of only two "non-placets" being given, took entirely from under the feet of these objectors their plea about "moral unanimity." Then it was, that in sheer desperation—being actually at the moment under the Church's solemn anathema—those few who remained obstinate reached the very climax of their unreason. They alleged that there is no obligation of accepting the defined dogma, till the bishops shall have severally signed "definiens subscripsi" at the end of the Council. The serviceableness of this view to pertinacious rebels is obvious enough; but its impudence approaches the sublime. The Holy Ghost, it appears then, will permit Pope and bishops to combine with moral unanimity in *anathematizing* a true doctrine: but He will interfere to prevent individual bishops from *authenticating* their anathema by a "definiens subscripsi." The question turns of course upon this: When do the Pope and bishops sufficiently exhibit their intention of binding the conscience? And if the case ever existed of Pope and bishops combining, in an anathema first, and in a "definiens subscripsi" afterwards,—it is plain that the *former* act implies an obligation of assent far more emphatically than does the *latter*. It is the Catholic's most indubitable obligation to avoid the Church's anathema, so soon as that anathema is brought within his cognizance.

But it is a characteristic and grotesque circumstance, that men who pique themselves on their knowledge of ecclesiastical history should have committed themselves to such a position. We believe *there is no instance on record,* in which the members of a council held in the Pope's presence have signed "definiens subscripsi" at the end at all.* The nearest approach to an exception which we happen to know, is the Decree of Union at Florence; which was undoubtedly subscribed by the bishops, and (for that matter) by the Greek Emperor also. But they did not write "*definiens* subscripsi" : that formula being reserved for Eugenius IV. alone. If therefore the position which we are assailing could be maintained, it would thus follow that no council, which has ever sat in the Pope's presence, intended to oblige Catholics to an acceptance of its doctrinal definitions.

We leave these unhappy apostates at the lowest point of their degradation : sincerely hoping and praying, that they may have life and grace to recover from their truly ignominious position.

The Vatican Definitions then must be received by every Catholic with the very same unreserved intellectual submission, which is due to the Nicene or the Tridentine. Those which have been hitherto pronounced, have taken the shape of two Pontifical Constitutions; the "Dei Filius" and the "Pastor Æternus" : the text of which will be found in our numbers of last July and last October respectively. The fourth Chapter of the latter contains the Decree on Papal infallibility, which is our present theme; but by way of introduction, we will say a few words on the third Chapter, headed "On the power and nature of the Primacy of the Roman Pontiff." It became obvious during the past and present year (we write in 1870), that various opponents of Papal infallibility really denied, not the Pope's infallibility alone, but his supremacy. This dogma had indeed been defined as of faith before the Vatican Council; see e.g. the third con-

---

* For instance, the First Council of Lyons : " Lectâ sententiâ in Imperatorem, Dominus Papa surrexit ac incepit 'Te Deum Laudamus': quo hymno decantato, per omnia fuit Concilium dissolutum." Similarly the Second Council of Lyons.

demned proposition in the " Auctorem Fidei ": but not in such unmistakable terms as were now shown to be necessary. It is now explicitly determined, that the Pope's "power of jurisdiction over all churches," " which is truly episcopal, is *immediate ;* to which . . . . both pastors and faithful, both *individually and collectively,* are bound to submit; not only in matters which belong to faith and morals, but also those which appertain to the Church's discipline and government throughout the world": and those are anathematized who "assert that he possesses merely the principal part and not *all the fullness* of this supreme power." The Archbishop mentions (p. 56, note) that these words were added in order "to exclude all possible equivocation ; and that they were adopted after full and ample and repeated discussion."

This third Chapter is an important foundation for the fourth which follows ; because irreformableness in teaching is naturally connected with supremacy in governing. The definition of Papal infallibility in the fourth runs as follows :

" The Sacred Council approving, We teach and define that it is a dogma divinely revealed : that the Roman Pontiff, when he speaks ex cathedrâ, that is, when in discharge of the office of Pastor and Doctor of all Christians, by virtue of his supreme Apostolic authority, he defines a doctrine regarding faith or morals to be held by the Universal Church, by the divine assistance promised to him in blessed Peter, is possessed of that infallibility with which the divine Redeemer willed that His Church should be endowed for defining doctrine regarding faith or morals : and that therefore such definitions of the Roman Pontiff are irreformable of themselves, and not from the consent of the Church."

The Archbishop, from p. 57 to p. 92, sets forth with singular clearness and fulness the import and contents of this Definition. In order however to avoid a mere abridgment of what he has said, we will go over the same ground in the way of negation rather than affirmation.

1. Firstly then no such notion is countenanced by the Definition or dreamed of by any Catholic, as that the supreme Pontiff possesses, under the name of infallibility, some permanent gift or quality : such e.g. as the inspiration or infused science which was given to the Apostles. The full bearing of this remark will be more clearly understood at a later part of our comments.

2. Again, " We must never suffer ourselves to doubt " says F. Newman (The Pope and the Revolution, p. 10.) " that in the Pope's *government* of the Church *he is guided by an intelligence more than human.*" But though this is most true and is

accepted (we suppose) heartily by all loyally intentioned
Catholics, it is in no way within the scope of the Vatican
Definition.

3. Moreover, even as ruler of the Church, the Pope is infallible in one particular; viz., in matters of universal discipline.
He is infallibly prevented by the Holy Ghost from issuing any
commands to the whole Church, which cannot be obeyed without transgression of God's Law. We are not here of course
attempting to exhibit this truth accurately and precisely : we
only wish to point out, that it is external to the letter, though
most harmonious with the spirit, of the recent Definition.

4. Further, according to our own full conviction—as we
stated last January—within the local Roman Church is preserved, by special assistance of the Holy Ghost, indefectible
purity of doctrine and tradition ; in such sense, that she is the
standard and source of doctrinal purity to all other churches in
Christendom. This doctrinal purity is exhibited, under one
aspect, in her indefectible intolerance of *heresy ;* in the circumstance that, by instinct as it were or rather by guidance of the
Holy Ghost, she indefectibly refuses all communion with those,
at any given period, whose doctrine contradicts what she has
taught as of faith. But this doctrinal purity is far more widely
extended. Whatever there may be occasionally of incidental
and minor mistake, the general course of theological thought
within her bosom is ever infallibly sound; and the securest
attainable test of theological truth, on a matter not yet
expressly determined, is her judgment and testimony. All this
however is entirely beyond the scope of the " Pastor Æternus."
There is nothing in that Constitution which affirms such a
doctrine; though neither is there a syllable which ever so
distantly militates against it.

5. Then, as the Archbishop points out (p. 90), " the definition
does not decide whether the infallibility of the *Church* is derived
from " the *Pope;* though " it *does* decide that the *Pope's* infallibility is *not* derived from the *Church.*" But though this question
is not *decided,* yet we think that the words of the Preamble
tend very strongly in one particular direction. If there is any
infallibility in the Church except the Pope's, it must be pre-
eminently the infallibility of a Pontifically confirmed Œcumenical Council; and many theologians have thought, that
the infallibility of such Council is a *distinct* dogma from that
of *Papal* infallibility. But observe how this Fourth Chapter
speaks of Œcumenical Councils. We italicize a few words : —

" The Roman Pontiffs, according to the exigencies of times
and circumstances, *sometimes* assembling Œcumenical Councils ;
or asking for the mind of the Church scattered throughout the

world; *sometimes* by particular Synods; *sometimes* using *other helps* which Divine Providence supplied; defined as to be held, &c. &c. &c."

Œcumenical Councils are here spoken of, not as possessing any infallibility of their own; but exclusively as amongst the various *helps* supplied by Divine Providence, for the exercise of *Papal* infallibility. And entirely in the same direction is the form commonly used by a council held in the Pope's presence, for the purpose of promulgating its decrees. These decrees are commonly issued—as in this very case of the Vatican Council—in the Pope's name; to the Council no other office being assigned, except that of "approving" his judgment.

6. Our next negative statement lands us in a discussion, which must be carried to some little length. The assembled bishops have as yet in no way defined the *extent* of the Pope's infallibility: they have only ruled that it is co-extensive with the Church's. The question of the "object" of infallibility is so distinct from that of its "subject," that nothing but confusion could have resulted from any attempt to deal with them both in solidarity; and the latter is therefore avowedly deferred, for definition, to the *second* Constitution "on the Church of Christ." In that Constitution it will be proposed, as is known authentically from Cardinal Antonelli (see our number for last July, p. 225),—though of course no one can say how far the bishops may modify such proposal—to anathematize those who deny that infallibility extends, not only to the Deposit of Faith, but to all that is necessary for the preservation of such Deposit."* In the "Pastor Æternus" however there are but two things which have been done, towards the settlement of this further question. Firstly, the bishops have used the general term "a doctrine regarding faith or morals"; and not any more limited phrase, such as "a revealed truth," "a dogma of the Faith," or the like. And secondly they speak of such a doctrine as "to be *held* (tenendam) by the Universal Church," instead of saying "to be *believed* (credendam). Both these facts are significant, and especially the last. When revealed truths *alone* are spoken of,—such as can be immediately believed with *divine faith*,—the word "credendæ" is (we think) more commonly adopted. On the other hand, whenever truths are inclusively spoken of which can*not* be believed with divine faith,

---

* Cardinal Antonelli's letter makes it almost certain, that the report of this draft Constitution, given in the "Augsburg Gazette," however discreditably obtained, was nevertheless accurate. It is not without importance therefore to add, that it expressed an obligation as incumbent on all Catholics, of yielding assent to the Pope's teaching on his civil princedom.

the·word "tenendæ" is invariably used : as e. g. where the Syllabus enforces the obligation, incumbent on all Catholics, of "*holding* most firmly" the doctrines, defined by Pius IX. in various Allocutions and Enyclicals, on his civil princedom.

We find however with extreme surprise, that an important passage in the Preamble has been understood to signify, that Papal infallibility is limited to an exposition of those verities which are actually contained in Scripture and Tradition. It is of the utmost moment to rectify this misapprehension ; and we begin therefore with quoting at length the passage to which reference is made.

"The Roman Pontiffs [have from time to time] defined as to be held those things which with the help of God they had recognized as conformable with the Sacred Scriptures and Apostolic Tradition. For the Holy Spirit was not promised to the successors of Peter that by His revelation they might disclose new doctrine, but that by His assistance they might inviolably keep and faithfully expound the Revelation or Deposit of Faith delivered through the Apostles."

Now it is seen at starting, that the interpretation of these words which such critics suggest, "proves *too much*," as the saying is. If by the phrase "new doctrines" Papally undefinable were designated *all* doctrinal statements without exception which are not contained in Scripture and Tradition,—what would follow? On such an hypothesis it would be a "new doctrine" Papally undefinable, that Jansenius's book contains five certain propositions in its legitimate objective sense ; it would be a' "new doctrine" Papally undefinable, that this or that canonized person is a saint; it would be a "new doctrine" Papally undefinable, that the Council of Trent is Œcumenical. On the other hand, beyond all question the Vatican Council declares the Pope's infallibility to be co-extensive with the Church's. On such a view then as that which we are opposing, the Vatican Council would have quite incidentally and by the way—when not occupied at all with defining the "object" of infallibility— denied the Church's infallibility in dogmatical facts ; her infallibility in the canonization of saints; her infallibility in the authentication of Œcumenical Councils as such. This, we need not say, is too absurd a supposition to need refuting; while on the other hand those very theologians, who are most explicit in laying down the wide extent of infallibility, are no less explicit in declaring that the Church has no power of "coining new doctrines." A very little consideration however of the above quoted passage will amply suffice to show its true meaning.

We will begin with the *latter* of the two sentences comprised in the passage; and when that is understood, the meaning of the former will become obvious enough. " The Holy Spirit," says the Council, " was not promised to the successors of Peter that by His revelation they might disclose new doctrine, but that by His assistance they might inviolably keep and faithfully expound the Revelation or Deposit of Faith delivered through the Apostles." A contrast is most manifestly intended in this sentence, between the Apostles on one hand and post-Apostolic Popes on the other. First then as to the Apostles. They " disclosed new doctrine " under the Holy Ghost's " revelation."* Here two things are included : firstly the Apostles were conscious organs of revelation; and (2) in that capacity they from time to time disclosed new doctrine. At any given period ante cedent to S. John's death, one cannot be certain that some new particular was not added to the Deposit: some particular, known to the Apostle himself by his conscious acceptance of a revelation from the Holy Ghost; and believed in by Christians, because they held firmly that he was the *organ* of such revelations. Now it is easily imaginable, that successive Popes should have been invested by God with the very same power; and it is wonderful indeed how many even well-educated Protestants imagine, that this is the very Catholic doctrine of Papal infallibility. It was of great importance therefore, or rather in some sense absolutely necessary, that the Council should expressly disavow so anti-Catholic a notion.

The Council then draws two contrasts between the Apostles and S. Peter's successors in the Papacy. And first for the first of these. To the Apostles the Holy Ghost spoke as *revealing* (Eo *revelante*) : post-Apostolic Popes He only influences as *assisting* (Eo assistente). In other words, Apostles spoke as conscious instruments of the Holy Ghost; whereas post-Apostolic Popes possess no consciousness whatever of His action upon their minds. The " revelation" accorded to an Apostle entirely dispensed with any intermediate human agency; whereas the " assistance " given to a post-Apostolic Pope, as the Bishop of Beverley observes (p. 168), " not only is compatible with, but *demands* the co-operation of human means." An Apostle simply declares that which he knows God to have told him; but a post-Apostolic Pope must go through some process of reasoning, in which this or that verity, contained in Scripture and Tradition, is a conspicuous premiss. And thus we are led naturally to the *second* contrast intended by the Vatican Council between the two. The Apostles could disclose new

---

* The question of *Scriptural* inspiration is not here involved : *that* was enjoyed by S. Mark and S. Luke no less than by S. Matthew or S. John ; while many Apostles were not Scripture writers at all.,

doctrine; but S. Peter's successors in the Papacy have no other office in their infallible magisterium, except that of inviolably guarding and faithfully expounding that one Faith once given, which was finally closed and sealed up at the Apostles' death.

Now there are various verities, which are not in themselves revealed, but which nevertheless are so intimately *connected* with revealed truths, that unless they be accepted with unreserved assent, the Pope has no sufficient power for guarding and testifying the Deposit with due efficacy and impressiveness. We will not here enlarge on a theme which is familiar to the readers of our REVIEW, but will content ourselves with giving one prominent *class* of instances in the Archbishop's words,

> There are truths of mere human history, which therefore are not revealed, without which the Deposit of the Faith cannot be taught or guarded in its integrity. For instance, that St. Peter was Bishop of Rome; that the Council of Trent and the Council of the Vatican are Œcumenical, that is, legitimately celebrated and confirmed; that Pius IX. is the successor of Peter by legitimate election. These truths are not revealed. They have no place in Scripture; and except the first, they have no place in Tradition: yet they are so necessary to the order of faith, that the whole would be undermined if they were not infallibly certain. But such infallible certainty is impossible by means of human history and human evidence alone. It is created only by the infallible authority of the Church (p. 68)

Whether these truths shall be called "new doctrines," is a mere question of words: and as a matter of usage, no theologian so calls them. But either way the Vatican Definition remains entirely untouched, by our most firmly holding that they may be infallibly defined by the Pope. "The Holy Spirit," says the Council, "was not promised to the successors of Peter, that by His revelation they might disclose new doctrine." All Catholics are here in absolute accordance: no Catholic dreams that any successor of S. Peter has been, as such, recipient of a "revelation"; it is a mere Protestant misconception to suppose that any such theory exists. On the other hand, the Holy Ghost *was* promised to them, "that by His assistance they might inviolably keep and faithfully expound the Revelation or Deposit of Faith delivered through the Apostles": and moreover, as the Council evidently implies, was promised to them (as teachers) for no *other* purpose whatever. Manifestly we do not tend ever so distantly to disparage this statement, when we further say that one *means* whereby the Holy Spirit assists them in the due custody and exposition of the Deposit, is by enabling them to define infallibly certain non-revealed verities: verities which are of such a nature, that their hearty acceptance enables Catholics to apprehend revealed truth far more effectively and persuasively.

We can now easily explain the preceding sentence, which says that Roman Pontiffs have from time to time defined "those things which with the help of God they had recognised as conformable with the Sacred Scriptures and Apostolic Tradition." The Council does not say, "those things which are *contained* in Scripture and Tradition,"—but uses a far more general phrase: "those things which are *conformable*" thereto. When a Pontiff is defining one of these ministrative and subordinate doctrines of which we speak,—he is contemplating Scripture and Tradition; he is anxious for the due protection or the more effective inculcation of the dogmata therein contained; he condemns some given error as *perilous,* as *injurious* to those dogmata; or he defines some positive truth, which will give them deeper hold on the mind of Catholics. Scripture and Tradition constitute his one norm and standard : the interests of Scripture and Tradition are those which alone influence his Act. To define e.g. that Alphonsus de Liguori is a Saint, is to define a verity which is in the highest degree *conformable* to Scripture and Tradition, though certainly not *contained* therein.

We should add, that the whole run and drift of the paragraph conclusively disproves the possibility of such an interpretation as that which we are opposing. It is occupied with recounting historical facts; with approving the whole series of definitions which successive Pontiffs have issued. "Our [Pius IX.'s] predecessors ever made unwearied efforts, that the salutary doctrines of Christ might be propagated among all the nations of the earth; and with equal care watched that it might be preserved genuine and pure. Therefore the Bishops of the whole world" ever applied to the Apostolic See when danger to the Faith sprang up; "and the Roman Pontiffs "—using such "help" as "the exigencies of times and circumstances" "demanded "—"defined as to be held those things which, &c." But it is beyond the possibility of question, that (whether in confirming councils or otherwise) successive Pontiffs have defined many truths, which are not contained in Scripture and Tradition. They have defined that the Three Chapters,—and again that the "Augustinus" of Jansenius—expressed heresy; that the Vulgate is authentic; that the word "Transubstantiation" has been aptly used; and so on with a thousand other instances, which might easily be added, but of which our readers some three years ago had perhaps a surfeit.

Then lastly the well-known "monitum," which concludes the First Vatican Constitution, demonstratively establishes the true mind of the Council. When a tenet is condemned as contradictory to Scripture and Tradition, it is condemned as *heretical;* and this monitum expressly warns the faithful *against* confining their submission to those Pontifical judgments, which condemn errors as heretical. " Since it is not sufficient to shun heretical pravity, unless those errors also be diligently avoided which *more or less nearly approach it,*—we admonish all men of the further duty [i.e. in addition to accepting the Definitions of faith just recited] of observing those Constitutions and Decrees,· by which such erroneous opinions as are here not specifically enumerated have been proscribed and condemned by this Holy See." Hear the " North British" Reviewer on the effect of this monitum.

Archbishop Manning afterwards reminded them that by this vote they had implicitly accepted infallibility. They had done even more. They might conceivably contrive to bind and limit dogmatic infallibility with conditions so stringent as to evade many of the objections taken from the examples of history ; but, in requiring submission to papal decrees on matters not articles of faith, they were approving that of *which they knew the character ;* they were confirming without let or question a power *they saw in daily exercise;* they were investing with new authority the existing bulls, and giving unqualified sanction to the Inquisition and the Index, &c. &c. (pp. 223, 224).

Indubitably therefore no word used by the Council was ever intended to disparage the certain truth, that various verities have been infallibly defined by the Holy See, which are not contained in Scripture and Tradition. If it were necessary, we could cite the Archbishop and the Bishop of Beverley as witnesses to this statement; for they were present throughout, and must have known what was intended. Infallibility, says the latter (p. 173), " is never concerned with scientific questions as such, unless in so far as they *directly or indirectly* touch or affect the Deposit or *in any way imperil its safety.*" The Archbishop has treated the matter at length from p. 60 to p. 79 ; and this is indeed among the most valuable portions of his whole Pastoral. His conclusions are these two: the italics being our own.

First, the infallibility of the Church extends, as we have seen, directly to the whole matter of revealed truth, and indirectly to all truths which, though not revealed, are in such contact with revelation, that the Deposit of Faith and Morals cannot be guarded, expounded, and defended, without an infallible discernment of such unrevealed truths.

Secondly, this extension of the infallibility of the Church is, *by the unanimous teaching of all theologians, at least theologically certain ;* and, in the judgment of the majority of theologians, certain by the certainty of faith (p. 78).

He lays down his doctrine then, as "by the unanimous teaching of theologians· at least theologically certain." He had prepared his way for this judgment, by putting together in a most masterly way their various statements; and he thus sums up his citations. The sphere within which the Church is infallible, he says, is expressed by the theologians whom he has quoted "in the following and various formulas: 1. Concerning faith. 2. In things of faith and morals. 3. Things which pertain to faith. 4. Things necessary to salvation. 5. Precepts of morals binding the whole Church. 6. Things pertaining to piety. 7. Things of religion. 8. Things ·of faith, speculative and practical. 9. Things pertaining to doctrine. 10. Controversies of religion. 11. Things pertaining to the natural and Divine laws. 12. Things pertaining to the spiritual health of souls. 13. And to the salvation of the faithful. 14. To the good estate of the Church. 15. The deciding of controversies and the extermination of errors. 16. Things which regard piety and the whole Church. 17. Matters of religion." All these formulæ, he adds, "contain the same ultimate meaning; namely, that the Church has an infallible guidance in treating of all matters of faith, morals, piety, and the general good of the Church" (pp. 65, 66).

One particular point is observable in these citations. We only know of one reason which has ever been given for the allegation, that theologians have laid down a smaller extent of infallibility than that claimed by the Archbishop.* In speaking of the Pope's infallibility, they not unfrequently say that he is infallible in defining what is to be believed by all Christians with *divine faith*. Now theologians more commonly hold that nothing is to be believed with *divine faith* except what is actually revealed;† and an inference is sometimes gratuitously drawn, that these writers *confine* infallibility to things revealed. We have often replied, that theologians, when speaking on the "subject" of infallibility, for various reasons are not particular in expressing the full extent of its "object"; and that the real question therefore is, whether any one of them anywhere expressly *states* that it *is* confined to the

---

* We do not include Chrismann; who has recently been put on the Index, apparently for this very error of denying infallibility to the Church's minor censures.

† In his fifth Appendix the Archbishop states the reply given by certain theologians whom the Council consulted as to the character of those "propositions" which are "definable as de fide." One of their principles, if we rightly understand what is, said in p. 222, is that any conclusion resulting from two revealed premises should be considered as "immediately" though but "virtually" revealed.

declaration of revealed truth. Of course no one of them does expressly state this. Take Suarez as an instance. "It is a Catholic truth," he says — and the Archbishop quotes his words in p. 62,—"that the Pontiff defining ex cathedrâ is a rule of faith which cannot err, whensoever he proposes anything to be *believed of faith* to the whole Church." See, say objectors, he confines infallibility to a declaration of what is *to be believed of faith.* Yet so far is this from being a legitimate inference, that Suarez himself expresses emphatically a most opposite opinion. The Archbishop (ibid.) quotes his words. "Speaking of the Bull of Gregory XIII., 'Ascendente Domino,' by which it is declared that simple vows constitute a true religious state, he says that the truth of this definition is 'altogether infallible, so that it cannot be denied without error. The reason is, because the sentence of the Pontiff *in things which pertain to doctrine* contains infallible certainty by the institution and promise of Christ, "I have prayed for thee.'" Afterwards he adds, 'The providence of Christ our Lord over His Church would be greatly diminished, if He should permit His Vicar, *in deciding such questions ex cathedrâ* to fall into error.'"

At the same time—returning to the point from which we started—the Vatican Council has as yet *defined* nothing on the extent of infallibility, but has left the matter for the deliberation of subsequent sessions.

7. There is another particular, which of late has been much discussed, and on which the Definition is silent: viz. the test or notes whereby an ex cathedrâ Act may be discerned; or (in other words) whereby it may be known, whether in any given Act the Pontiff intends to oblige the assent of the Universal Church to some doctrinal declaration. Various theologians—not indeed speaking consistently with each other or even with themselves—have devised various purely arbitrary suggestions for this purpose. It has been said e.g. that an Act, to be ex cathedrâ, must be formally addressed to the whole Church; or must anathematize dissidents; or must expressly state the obligation of assent, which it is intended to impose. For ourselves it has always appeared to us, as we stated last January (p. 200), "that *no* universal criterion can be laid down; no cut-and-dry rule which can be applied to every instance: but that theologians are often left'to judge from the circumstances of some individual case." This was the Archbishop's view expressed in his former Pastoral; and this is certainly the inference which would naturally be derived from the Vatican Definition. The Pontiff is infallible whenever "in discharge of the office of Pastor and Doctor of all Christians, by virtue of

his supreme Apostolic authority, he defines a doctrine regarding faith or morals to be held by the Universal Church": but what are those particular instances in which he *intends* so to define, is to be decided by theologians, according to circumstances intrinsic and extrinsic, on each particular occasion. Some indeed have seemed to suppose, that one limitation has been expressed by the very word "define": that to "define" necessarily implies some accurate and scientific expression of doctrine; and that no flowing and rhetorical exposition can constitute a "Definition." But as the Archbishop points out (p. 88), "Definire is 'finem imponere' or 'finaliter judicare:'" and such final determination may be made by a flowing and rhetorical, no less than by a scientific and precise declaration. The matter is put beyond possibility of doubt by the case of the "Mirari vos." Never did a more rhetorical Act than this issue from the Holy See; and nevertheless three years afterwards, in his "Singulari nos," Gregory XVI. informed the universal Episcopate, that in that earlier Encyclical he had "*defined* the Catholic doctrine" "which alone it is lawful to follow" on the various very important "heads" which he proceeded to enumerate.

8. Nor, lastly, has the Vatican Council spoken expressly on the comparative *frequency* of ex cathedrâ Acts. At the same time we do think that one conclusion is readily deducible from its declarations; viz., that such Acts are by no means "rare,"— as a distinguished French theologian has said they are,—but on the contrary that Pius IX. alone has issued a very considerable number. We are here however referring, not to the "Pastor Æternus," but to the earlier "Dei Filius;" and therein to the following passage:—

"We therefore, following the footsteps of our predecessors, have *never ceased, by virtue of our Apostolic office,* from teaching and defending Catholic truths and condemning doctrines of error."

Now the "Pastor Æternus" declares that the Pope is infallible, whenever "in discharge of the office of Pastor and Doctor of all Christians, by virtue *of his supreme Apostolic authority,* he defines a doctrine regarding faith or morals to be held by the Universal Church." But this is the very thing which, in the "Dei Filius," the Council testifies that he "has *never ceased*" from doing. The number of his ex cathedrâ Acts then must be very considerable. The same conclusion follows from a similar expression of Pius IX. in the "Quantâ curâ;" and is also established, as we pointed out at the time, (October 1867, pp. 529-532), by the episcopal address presented to him at Rome.

At last however we admit that the number is not inconsiderable of those Pontifical Acts, in regard to which no absolute certainty is attainable, whether they are or are not ex cathedrâ. But we doubt extremely whether there is any one doctrine, taught in any one of those Acts, which is not *also* defined in others, of whose ex cathedrâ character there can be no reasonable doubt. Such indubitable ex cathedrâ utterances e. g. are the "Unam sanctam," which was republished by Leo X. as dogmatic in the Fifth Lateran Œcumenical Council; and the "Mirari vos," of which its author, three years later, testified the ex cathedrâ character to the universal Episcopate.

And now, having concluded this negative treatment of the Vatican Definition, we may sum up the positive account of its contents, as drawn out by the Archbishop from p. 58 to p. 92. According then to the teaching of this Definition, it is (not merely a theological truth but) a divinely revealed dogma, that the Roman Pontiff possesses the following privilege. When he speaks, not as a private doctor, nor as admonishing and instructing individuals, nor even as ruler and "gubernator" of the whole Church, but as pastor and doctor of all Christians in order to impose an obligation on the whole Church of accepting some religious doctrine—he is as infallible as the Church herself is infallible. This infallibility, the Council further declares, has for its efficient cause an imperceptible Divine assistance, promised on such occasions to S. Peter's successors; and such definitions are consequently irreformable, not because the Church assents to them, but antecedently to and independently of any such assent.

The Catholic's reason of course for knowing that this dogma was revealed by God, is the Definition of the Council; but the historical argument for its truth is absolutely irrefragable. The Archbishop does not enter on this theme in his present Pastoral, because he treated it so exhaustively in his preceding one. For ourselves also we shall be silent on this part of the subject; because in July 1867, while engaged with the "Eirenicon," we published an article, exhibiting (as clearly and fully as we could) the whole bearing of ecclesiastical history on the various "Papal prerogatives"; among which, that of infallibility in teaching occupies the first place.

We are of course well aware, that a large number of historical objections have quite recently been raised against the dogma, by various Catholic opponents of its definition: nor does the fact of the Definition having been issued make it less important that these arguments should be answered. Doubtless the vast majority of these writers hold now with divine faith that very verity against which they then argued; while the few remaining (if indeed there are any such) have ceased to *be* Catholics. Still an argument does not lose its force, because its author has abandoned it; and it must not therefore in controversy be ignored or neglected. For ourselves in particular, we should here mention an able pamphlet published last June on the Galileo case, chiefly in reply to our own exposition of that case. The writer has of course ceased to hold any opinion which is at variance with the recent Definition; but we must deal with the pamphlet as it stands in its integrity. The Editor's health is not yet so re-established, that we can speak of our future with anything like confidence; but we much hope that in our next number we shall be able to publish a full reply to the pamphlet in question. Meanwhile we have briefly commented on it in one of our " Notices "; and we must not omit here to thank its author sincerely for his kindly tone in regard to ourselves.

The Archbishop considers in his third chapter (p. 93) "the terminology of the doctrine of infallibility." His reason for doing so is, that so many influential opponents of the dogma have ascribed to its upholders the formula of "personal, separate, independent and absolute infallibility." After a careful and most candid examination of these various terms, the Archbishop thus sums up his argument :—

1. The privilege of infallibility is *personal,* inasmuch as it attaches to the Roman Pontiff, the successor of Peter, as a *public person,* distinct from, but inseparably united to, the Church ; but it is not personal, in that it is attached, not to the private person, but to the primacy, which he alone possesses.

2. It is also *independent,* inasmuch as it does not depend upon either the Ecclesia docens or the Ecclesia discens ; but it is not independent, in that it depends in all things upon the Divine Head of the Church, upon the institution of the primacy by Him, and upon the assistance of the Holy Ghost.

3. It is *absolute,* inasmuch as it can be circumscribed by no human or ecclesiastical law ; it is not absolute, in that it is circumscribed by the office of guarding, expounding, and defending the deposit of revelation.

4. It is *separate* in no sense, nor can be, nor can so be called, without manifold heresy, unless the word be taken to mean *distinct.* In this sense, the Roman Pontiff is distinct from the Episcopate, and is a distinct subject of infallibility ; and in the exercise of his supreme doctrinal authority, or magisterium, he does not depend for the infallibility of his definitions upon the consent or consultation of the Episcopate, but only on the Divine assistance of the Holy Ghost (pp. 112-3).

One singular fact is connected with this question of terminology. The Archbishop had said that "the Pontiff is infallible, apart from the Episcopate ;" whereupon he was accused—though

Mgr. Dupanloup explained afterwards that he had intended no such accusation—of contemplating as possible a doctrinal separation between Pope and bishops. But as the Archbishop points out in p. 107, "they who deny the Pope's infallibility do expressly assert the possibility of such a separation. And yet it is they who have imputed to the defenders of the Pontifical infallibility, that separation which on 'Ultramontane' principles is impossible; but, on the principles of those who lay the charge, such a separation is not only possible, but even of probable occurrence."

In his fourth chapter the Archbishop inflicts on the votaries of "scientific history" a castigation which they will not soon forget; nor is any other part of the Pastoral in our view comparable to this for originality and power. We shall have an early opportunity of dwelling on this very important theme, when we review the translation of "anti-Janus" which has appeared toward the end of this current quarter.

We conclude then for the present with two remarks. The first shall be made in the very words of the Archbishop.

We were told that the Definition of the Infallibility would alienate the fairest provinces of the Catholic Church, divide the Church into parties, drive the scientific and independent into separation, and set the reason of mankind against the superstitions of Rome. We were told of learned professors, theological faculties, entire universities, multitudes of laity, hundreds of clergy, the flower of the episcopate, who were prepared to protest as a body, and to secede. There was to be a secession in France, in Germany, in Austria, in Hungary. The "Old Catholics" of England would never hear of this new dogma, and with difficulty could be made to hold their peace. Day by day, these illusions have been sharply dispelled; but not a word of acknowledgment is to be heard. A professor is suspended a divinis in Germany; a score or two of lay professors, led by a handful whose names are already notorious, and a hundred or so of laymen who, before the Council met, began to protest against its acts, convoke a congress, which ends in a gathering of some twenty persons. These, with the alleged opposition of one Bishop, whose name out of respect I do not write, as the allegation has never yet been confirmed by his own word or act, these are hitherto the adverse consequences of the Definition.

On the other hand, the Bishops who, because they opposed the Definition as inopportune, were calumniously paraded as opposed to the doctrine of Infallibility, at once began to publish their submission to the acts of the Council. The greater part of the French Bishops who were once in opposition, have explicitly declared their adhesion. The German Bishops, meeting again at Fulda, issued a Pastoral Letter, so valuable in itself, that I have reprinted it in the Appendix. It was signed by seventeen, including all the chief Bishops of Germany. The others, if silent, cannot be doubted. The leading Bishops of Austria and Hungary, who may be taken as representing the Episcopates of these countries, have in like manner declared themselves. The Clergy and the faithful of these kingdoms, with the rarest exceptions of an individual here and there, are, as they have always been, of one mind in accepting the definition with joy. Ireland has spoken for itself, not only in many dioceses, and by its Bishops, but by the Triduum, or Thanksgiving of three days, held in Dublin with great solemnity and with a concourse, as I am informed by direct correspondence, such as was never seen before. Of England I need say little. The Clergy of this diocese have twice spoken for themselves; and the Clergy of England and Scotland have given unequivocal witness to their faith. As we hear so much and so often of those among us who are called "the Old Catholics," that is, the sons of our martyrs and confessors; and as their name is so lightly and officiously taken in vain by those who desire to find or to make divisions among us, you will not need, but will nevertheless be glad, to know, that both by word and by letter I have received from the chief and foremost among them, express assurance that what the Council has defined they have always believed. It is but their old faith in an explicit formula. Among the disappointments to which our adversaries, I regret so to call them, but truth must be spoken, have doomed themselves, none is greater than this. They have laboured to believe and to make others believe that the Catholic Church is internally divided; that the Council has revealed this division; and that it is nowhere more patent than in England. It is, I know, useless to contradict this illusion. It is not founded in reason, and cannot by reason be corrected. Prejudice and passion are deaf and blind. Time and facts will dispel illusions, and expose falsehoods. And to this slow but inexorable cure we must leave them. It is no evidence of division among us if here, and there a few individuals should fall away. I said before, the Council will be 'in ruinam et in resurrectionem multorum.' It is a time of spiritual danger to many; especially to those who live perpetually among adversaries, hearing diatribes all day long against the Church, the Council, and the Holy Father, reading anti-Catholic accounts and comments upon Catholic doctrines, and upon the words and acts of Catholic Bishops, and always breathing, till they are unconscious of it, an anti-Catholic atmosphere (pp. 152-155.)

In like manner speaks our contemporary "The Month."

It is quite obvious that the Vatican Council has already by the mercy of God taken its place in the minds of Catholics throughout the world by the side of that of Trent. A few littérateurs may go on writing—in Protestant papers—against it, but the appeal which any great Act of the Teaching Church makes to the loyalty of the faithful has seldom been so cordially and readily answered as on the present occasion.

We are very far from denying that circumstances may easily occur, in which even a very extensive schism is a much less evil, than that any doubt should remain on the Church's teaching in this or that momentous particular. Nor do we deny—on the contrary we ourselves venture to think—that such a schism would have been indefinitely less prejudicial to the Church's highest interest, than her continued abstinence from a dogmatic definition of Papal infallibility. Still such a schism would have been a serious evil: and it is at once a matter of deep gratitude to Almighty God, and also an indication of the loyalty and healthiness of thought prevalent on the whole among Catholics, that in the present instance there is no fear whatever of such an evil. After all, when Catholics come to see that in any given case the Ecclesia docens *claims* assent, they do not dream of refusing it.

Our other remark is this. Last April we thus expressed ourselves :

The great doctrinal evil—so it seems to us—which now afflicts the Church is this; In the normal state of things certain questions are admitted by all Catholics to be closed, and the rest are admitted by all Catholics to be open ; or, in other words, all Catholics are agreed as to what those doctrines are, which Catholics as such are certainly obliged to embrace. This is now very far from being the case. Very many—we ourselves are among the number—are confident that all Catholics are bound (materially at least) under pain of mortal sin to hold various doctrines, which other sincere and piously-disposed Catholics overtly reject (p. 494).

We cannot and do not doubt that many Catholics, otherwise very differently minded from ourselves, agree with us on the seriousness of this evil. Now it is plain that there are two different ways in which the Council might remove it : viz., on the one hand by making certain controverted questions indisputably *open,* or on the other hand by making them indisputably *close.* Several Catholics expected that something of the former kind would be done. They expected that various Pontifical Acts e. g. would be—not indeed expressly disavowed —but softened down and translated into milder and more ambiguous language; or else that their ex cathedrâ character would be implicitly denied : again, that if Papal infallibility were defined, the wording of such definition would bear the marks of transaction and compromise; would be hampered by various restrictive and qualifying clauses.

But now how stand facts ? The very first utterances of the Council set forth the intellectual evils prevalent among Catholics. Is it counted among those evils, that certain persons try to force " extreme views " on their co-religionists? that there exists some "insolent and aggressive faction," which labours to make the Church's intellectual yoke heavy and almost insupportable? There is no hint of the kind ever so distant: while on the other hand it is expressly said (Preamble of the "Dei Filius") that "many (plures) even of the children of the Catholic Church have strayed from the path of true piety;" that "by the gradual diminution of the truth they held, *the Catholic sense*" has become "*weakened* in them;" lastly, that "they are found to deprave the true sense of the doctrines which our holy Mother Church holds and teaches, and *endanger the integrity and soundness of the Faith.*" Then, instead of opening questions which some had accounted close, the Council proceeds in some sense to close what had hitherto been more open. Certainly one or two of the tenets branded in the "Dei Filius" with anathema—e.g. c. 2 can. 1; c. 3 can. 6; c. 4 can. 1—had not been previously regarded as actually *heretical:* in particular the extreme French traditionalism, anathematized in c. 2 can. 1, had never at any earlier period been so severely dealt with by the Holy Father. Again, as to the various Pontifical Acts which have condemned non-heretical errors—so far from softening them down or veiling their ex cathedrâ character—the Constitution in its concluding paragraph admonishes the faithful that they are obliged to observe them, in order to "flee from" those errors which more or less nearly approach to heresy. Proceeding to the "Pastor Æternus," we find, not only that the Pope's Supremacy is defined in far more stringent terms than had hitherto been employed; not only that his Infallibility is now for the first time defined as a dogma of the Faith; but also that its definition is accompanied by no single qualifying clause or explanation, which is not most heartily accepted by those who used to be called "the extremest Ultramontanes."

All this seems to us of grave moment, as indicating the Church's mind. It has great weight as regards the Catholic's auguries for the future; and it has great weight also (a far more practical matter) as regards his duties and his sympathies in the present.

Notices of Books.

Act of Pius IX. placing the whole Catholic Church under the Patronage of
S. Joseph.*

* We have been unable to obtain a sight of the original decree. We
borrow the following translation from our admirable contemporary the
" Tablet."

DECREE URBIS ET ORBIS.

As Almighty God appointed Joseph, son of the Patriarch Jacob, over all
the land of Egypt to save corn for the people, so when the fulness of time
was come, and He was about to send on earth His only-begotten Son the
Saviour of the World, He chose another Joseph of whom the first Joseph
had been the type, and whom He made the Lord and chief of His household and possession, and guardian of His choicest treasures. So also He
espoused to Himself the Immaculate Virgin Mary, of whom was born by
the Holy Ghost Jesus Christ Our Lord, who has before men deigned to be
reputed the Son of Joseph, and was subject unto him., And Him, whom
so many Kings and Prophets had desired to see, Joseph not only saw, but
conversed with and embraced with paternal affection, and kissed, and most
sedulously nourished, even Him whom the faithful were to receive as the
Bread that came down from Heaven, that they might obtain eternal life.
On account of this sublime dignity which God conferred on His most faithful servant, the Church has always most highly honoured and praised the
most Blessed Joseph next to his Spouse, the Virgin Mother of God, and
has besought his intercession in times of trouble. And now that in these
most troublous times the Church is beset by enemies on every side, and is
weighed down by heavy calamities, so that ungodly men imagine the gates
of hell to have at length prevailed against her, therefore, the Venerable
Prelates of the Catholic world have presented to the Sovereign Pontiff
their own petitions and those of the Faithful committed to their charge,
praying that he would vouchsafe to constitute S. Joseph Patron of the
Catholic Church. They also renewed still more earnestly this their prayer
and desire at the Sacred Œcumenical Council of the Vatican. Therefore our
most Holy Lord, Pius IX., Pope, being moved by the recent mournful
events, has been pleased to comply with the desires of the Prelates, and to
commit to Saint Joseph's most powerful patronage Himself and all the
Faithful, and has declared Saint Joseph PATRON OF THE CATHOLIC
CHURCH, and has commanded his festival, occurring on the 19th day of
March, to be celebrated for the future as a Double of the First Class, but
yet without an Octave, on account of Lent.

Finally, He has ordained that on this day, sacred to the Blessed Virgin
Mother of God and her most chaste Spouse S. Joseph, a declaration to that
effect by this present Decree of the Sacred Congregation of Rites be then
published. All things to the contrary notwithstanding.

The 8th day of December, 1870.

CONSTANTINE, Bishop of Ostia and Velletri;
Cardinal PATRIZI, Prefect of the Sacred College.

Loco ✠ Signi

D. BARTOLINI, Secretary.

The decree of the Holy Father declaring S. Joseph to be Patron of the Universal Church has come as a welcome gift from our Blessed Lady in answer to our prayers. Given to the world on the 8th day of December, the Feast of her Immaculate Conception, it is a pledge to us of her unwearied love, in thus committing during these dark wintry days of what may well be called another Egyptian Exile of the Church, both the Vicar of her Son and His whole Body Mystical to the arms of her faithful spouse, who watched over Him so lovingly during His sojourn in Egypt in the days of His flesh; while at the same time it is one more proof to us of the wonderful harmony and proportion which runs through everything connected with the Church. Not only is this harmony distinctly visible in her dogmatic definitions, and in the manner in which, part by part, the faith once delivered to the saints has been first thought out, so to speak, by the Church in her own divine mind, and then set before the minds of her children, but it is also clearly to be traced in er very devotions, and in the way in which, to each member of the Holy Family, nay, to each glorified member of Christ's Mystical Body, has been assigned its own proper place and glory in her outward worship. The history of the manner in which, for well-nigh nineteen hundred years, article after article of her majestic creed has been brought out into clearer light, although always implicitly believeved from the beginning, and in which the various relations of Christ's Mystical Body to oue another, and to their great Head, have been made apparent to the eyes of men through the devotions of the Christian people, is indeed a marvellous confirmation to every believer of the Church's divine mission to mankind. Thus the devotions of the faithful, although ever varying, are seen to be the outward manifestations of the inward breath of that *one* spirit, " Who divideth to every man according as He will," and who in His unselfish love is ever bringing back to the Church's mind sweet recollections of Jesus, and of Mary, and of Joseph, " teaching her all things, and bringing all things to her mind whatsoever Christ has said." It is not so with error; there is no harmony in false doctrine. There all is distorted; all is discord. . The fragmentary Christianity which exists outside the unity of God's Catholic Church has no beauty of proportion, no slow and sure growth or deveiopment, no variety of devotions springing out of and interlacing one another, yet always exactly corresponding with the wants of every age. It is but a succession of distorted and unconnected doctrines, abortive efforts and stunted growths.

How clearly is all this brought out in the last honour which the Holy Father has decreed to S. Joseph. It was meet and fitting that the full prerogatives of Jesus and of Mary should first of all be realized, before those of holy Joseph should be fully recognized. Most meet and fitting was it that the Real Body of Christ should be enthroned in all its majesty in the worship of the Church, which is His Mystical Body, and that Mary, from whose virginal blood that Real Body was taken, and who is also the true mother of His Mystical Body, should sit at His Right Hand " in a vesture of gold, girt about with variety," before the Foster-Father of Jesus, and the spouse and guardian of Mary, should be proclaimed before angels and men the protector and patron in heaven of Christ's Mystical Body upon earth. No doubt, as indeed is implied in the Apostolic Decree, devotion to S. Joseph has existed in all ages of the Church, even from the first; but, for the most part, it may be said to have been in the Church's deep heart, silent and unexpressed, until, through the intercession of Our Blessed Lady, God the Holy Ghost breathed upon her own peacefu retreats of Carmel, and raised up S. Teresa to be its apostle and teacher. Since then the Christian people have caught hold of it, as it were, and meditated lovingly upon it, and carried it out into practice, and have grown zealous in its behalf, until this very year the sound of the prayers of many nations, and tribes, and tongues and peoples, like that the patronage of S. Joseph over the Universal Church might be solemnly recognized and affirmed, like the sound of many waters, has risen up before the Apostolic throne, at a moment, too, when it was surrounded by all the princes of the Church; and now at last it has seemed good to the Vicar of Christ to declare that the guardian of the Holy Family is also the Patron of God's great family upon earth.

And how sweetly and gently it has been brought about! As it has ever been since Mary spoke the first of the new Creation, so is it now. All graces, all good things, even the fruits of the devotions of the Church, come to us through her. The very sense of the faithful is her gift. Our Lady of Carmel speaks to God the Holy Ghost, and He whispers to His Church, and teaches her how to pray. He Himself becomes her Intercessor, and " asketh for the Saints according to God," and then in His good time He crowns His own prayer, and its blessed fruit is some new gift of strength for the Mystical Body of Mary's Son.

And so too, how happily has the time been chosen for this new honour to S. Joseph, just when some new gift of strength was most required! Only a year ago, we stated in the pages of this Review, that with the *one* exception of the temporal government of the Holy Father, all the governments of Christendom had apostatized from Christ. Since then even that last witness to Christ's Sovereignty over the world has been taken away, at least for a time, and the foundation-stone of the Christian Commonwealth has been removed out of its place. Christ in His Mystical Body is once again in Egypt. It is at such a time as this that God has been pleased to wrap His Church in the mantle of S. Joseph, even as He wrapped His only-begotten Son in the hour of His helpless exile. We need not fear. Darker days may still be in store for us; nation may rise against nation, and kingdom against kingdom, but the end is not yet. The idols of the world, like those of Egypt, will be broken into pieces, and S. Joseph will lead God's family back again through the desert with Jesus and Mary, to witness the final triumph of the Kingdom of the Prince of Peace.

We have one last wish to express, one last prayer to utter. The definition of Our Lady's Immaculate Conception has led to a great increase in devotion to S. Joseph. The holy Pontiff who pronounced Mary Immaculate, has also been chosen to declare S. Joseph to be the Patron of the Universal Church. May we not hope, that in his turn S. Joseph will bring about from the same holy lips the dogmatic definition of Our Lady's

Assumption into heaven. Thus S. Joseph's hands, which guarded so lovingly her virginal body upon earth, will help to place the last crown on her glorified head in heaven, as well as upon the Pontificate of her own Pontiff-King.* '

---

* F. Herbert Vaughan projects a Church, in connection with S. Joseph's College for Foreign Missions, in commemoration of Pius IX.'s act. The following is his statement :—

" It is for many reasons highly desirable that we should complete the work and build the Church without delay. The *economical* reason is that by continuing the works under our Dutch contractor and his men we shall effect a saving of nearly £1,000. The *educational* reason is, that the performance of the solemn services of the Church is an essential part of Ecclesiastical Education : and it is impossible to carry them out when half of a community-room is all the space that can be set apart for a Chapel. The *parochial and public* reason has also its weight. Zeal for the glory of God's worship, where it can be solemnly performed as it can in a Seminary of Ecclesiastical Students, and the religious influence this is calculated to have upon the neighbourhood, besides the accommodation of the people, absolutely require a Church rather than the confined limits of a private room.

" A Church then having become necessary, I propose not only to appeal for it in honour of S. Joseph, who has built our College, but to make it a MONUMENT commemorative of the happy event whereby the Holy Father has been inspired to place Himself and all the Pastors and Faithful of the Church by a Solemn Decree (Dec. 8, 1870) under the Special patronage of this Great Saint. May it become a standing memorial of the devotion to S. Joseph of the 150,000 Catholics of this Kingdom who petitioned that he might be declared PATRON OF THE CATHOLIC CHURCH! Their prayer has been heard. Let us then build at once a Church in his Name to commemorate the event. Let us publish our gratitude to the whole world. Let us proclaim his praises.

" The site proposed for this Act of Devotion is not inappropriate.

" The Church, surmounted by a statue of the ' PATRON OF THE CATHOLIC CHURCH,' will stand upon a hill, visible for miles over the surrounding country, as well as from two of the principal approaches to the metropolis, the Midland and North-Western Railways.

" It will be attached to, and served by, what may be called a National Institution, the first Foreign Missionary College to the Heathen in this vast empire. S. Joseph was fitly chosen for its special Patron, as having himself been the first Foreign Missionary of the Church, since it was he who carried Jesus and Mary into the heathen land, which, in consequence, became converted for centuries afterwards into a Garden of Saints.

" It is proposed that the names of all contributors towards this first solemn Act of Devotion towards the PATRON OF THE CATHOLIC CHURCH shall be enclosed in a Heart, to be inserted in the Commemorative Statue of the Patriarch which will crown the edifice."

Rome, the Capital of Christendom; a Sermon by HENRY EDWARD, Archbishop of Westminster. London : Longmans.

The Christian Kingdom; a Sermon by the Rev. H. J. COLERIDGE, S.J. London : Burns, Oates, & Co.

The Kingly Office of the Church; a Sermon by W. G. TODD, D.D. London: Longmans.

THESE three admirable sermons are occupied, in one shape or other, with the Holy Father's temporary loss of his dominions, and with Victor Emmanuel's shameless aggression. We deal with this subject from our own point of view in the first article of our present number ; and here we are to supplement our remarks by such further thoughts as these publications suggest.

In treating of the Holy Father's civil princedom, there is, of course, a broad line to be drawn, between those truths on the subject which have been infallibly determined by the Holy See, and the further speculations of individuals. As to the former, Pius IX. has declared in the Syllabus that all Catholics are bound (debeut) to hold most firmly that " doctrine " on the matter which is " clearly laid down " in six Pontifical Acts there mentioned. In those Acts he teaches that his civil princedom was ordered by Divine Providence, that the Pope might have that liberty which is " required " for his spiritual office (" Quibus quantisque "); which is so " *necessary* for the flock's salvation " (" Si semper "); that this princedom " has a spiritual character from its relation to the Church's good " (" Cum Catholica "); that the aggressive acts of its assailants are " plainly null and void " (" Novos et ante ") ; that Victor Emmanuel's former " spoliation " of the Roman territory was " nefarious and sacrilegious " (" Jamdudum cernimus ").*

In accordance with these definitions, the Archbishop teaches that Victor Emmanuel's recent act is " a manifold injustice even against the laws of nature"; " a sin " and " a sacrilege" (pp. 10–12). F. Coleridge denounces it (p. 23) as an " outrage against public justice and Christian conscience ; " " a measure of persecution against the whole Catholic Church throughout

---

* Dr. Pusey charges Pius IX. with having by these declarations invented a " new matter of faith." But where does Pius IX. call his doctrine a matter of faith ? or, when has any Catholic designated it by such a name? There cannot be a more authentic exposition on this head, than the letter written by Cardinal Caterini, at Pius IX.'s command; of which the "Month" published a translation in February, 1869, reprinted by ourselves in the following July. The Cardinal urges, no doubt, that the doctrine in question "had been taught by the whole Catholic Church," and that to reject it is to incur " the dread sentence pronounced on those who refuse to 'hear the Church.'" But he explains himself by adding, that "besides the articles *strictly of faith,* there are others *closely connected therewith.*"

the world " (*ib.*), because it confines her ruler's due liberty in teaching and governing her. And Dr. Todd enforces the truth (p. 18) that the Church is thereby placed, so far as human power can place her, "in fetters and bondage and subjection."

But there is a further verity, which has not been (so far as we know) infallibly declared by the Church, but on which nevertheless there is a consensus of all loyal and thoughtful Catholics. "The Church," says the Archbishop (p.15), "has a twofold mission : the one, to convert individuals one by one to Faith, and to bind them into a spiritual society ; the other, to civilize and to elevate the political order of mankind. It was this latter office of the Church which, when nations were converted to the Faith, united them under public Christian laws, and bound them together by international compacts under one supreme judge of all. Of the former part of its mission, nothing under God can deprive the Church. Of the second it may easily be discharged. If the political order of the world separates itself from the unity of faith and from the authority of the Church, then the Church can no longer fulfil its mission as the guide of the civil society of men." And the Pope's civil princedom, as he implies throughout, is at once the symbol, and also one principal means, of her *exercising* this guidance. This truth is F. Coleridge's principal theme, and his exposition of it leaves nothing to be desired.

Concerning one point there seems, on the surface, some difference of view between the Archbishop and F. Coleridge ; but on more careful examination this supposed difference will be found to disappear. The Archbishop says (p. 16) that the "last union of public law and Christianity " is now "dissolved " ; whereas F. Coleridge holds (p. 18) that "the Christian principles do obtain and influence governments elsewhere than at Rome." But the Archbishop means only that the union of Christianity with politics is dissolved in *principle,* and F. Coleridge means only that this total dissolution has not yet resulted in *fact.* The following statement of his impresses us as singularly fair and well-balanced :—

"It must be confessed," he says (p. 19), "that we can find no place where Christian principles are fully and exclusively maintained, but in the dominions of the Holy See. Elsewhere the assault against them has been successful, in one respect here, in another respect there. In one place the legitimate rights of the sovereign have been broken down, in another the lawful rights of the subjects of the sovereign. Here it has been the State which has taken on itself to lay down laws as to what shall and what shall not be marriage ; there it has been a similar encroachment on the parental right of education, or, again, an abdication of that duty of witnessing to the true Faith to which our Lord's words point. Everywhere something has been attacked successfully ; and now the attempt is made to sweep away the one State in Europe which is still thoroughly Christian, still the home and refuge of all those regenerating and elevating principles of social order which have been undermined in detail elsewhere."

And this is exactly the Archbishop's view. We italicise a few words to show this :—

"Wheresoever the plague of revolution enters, its effects are anti-Christian and anti-social. Two things surely follow in its train : the dissolution of Christian marriage by divorce, and the abolition of Christian education. Where these things are, society is smitten at its root, and the offspring of society grow up without faith, and therefore without God. Woe to the people among whom the young are rising to manhood without Christianity! And how shall they be Christian, if Christianity be expelled from education? And what dissolves States, dissolves also homes, and in the end the canker eats into men and their very nature. The intellect, developed without faith, is the prey of all error and perversion. The will, grown strong without Christian law, is the source of all rebellion. And to such a state of nature the public apostasy of nations from Christianity *is reconducting* society, homes, and man. All this may seem far-fetched. But so is the early calculation by which the shoals and reefs and sands *are foreknown and avoided.*" (p. 17.)

The Archbishop travels over much wider ground than F. Coleridge. After setting forth the true history of what has taken place, he proceeds to inquire what are its results. As regards the Church, it will not of course interfere with her spiritual powers (p. 13), though indefinitely impeding their free exercise. "The Church is wounded," as Dr. Todd declares (p. 17), in accidentals, she cannot receive a wound in essentials. Nay, one happy result, the Archbishop thinks, may ensue from these miseries. "When the world persecutes, persecution purifies" (p. 13). "We shall have among us fewer bad Catholics, worldly Catholics, lax Catholics, and *liberal Catholics.*" "Nominal Catholics are our weakness and vexation, our scandal and our shame, *sometimes our greatest danger.*"

As regards the effects of this sacrilege on society, we have already exhibited the Archbishop's view. He cites Lord Shaftesbury (p. 18)—mentioning his name with great respect—as a witness to the condition of Protestant London.

At last however, as he says, "the Roman question (p. 19) which men say is now ended, is only now beginning"; and the principles on which Victor Emmanuel has acted are simply fatal to every existing government (pp. 22–35).

We will conclude with drawing attention to Dr. Todd's excellent exposure of journalistic hypocrisy (pp. 14–17). So long as the Pope's dominion was left him, the newspapers maintained that the true interests of Catholicity demanded its abandonment. When the blow was struck, they loudly proclaimed that "the fall of the temporal is only a prelude to the fall of the spiritual power."

Anti-Janus. By Dr. HERGENROTHER. Translated by J. B. ROBERTSON, Esq. Dublin: Kelly.

IT is most easy to show that Janus has no positive standing whatever; that his arguments and citations, if they have any force at all, tell not against what men used to call "Ultramontanism," but against the very idea of an infallible Church; nay, against the divine origin of Christianity.

But these arguments and citations none the less, as is evident, are among those which require to be dealt with by the Catholic controversialist. Now this can be done in two different ways. On the one hand such a controversialist might enter at length into every point raised by Janus, and show that the allegations of that book are either false or irrelevant: but then this would manifestly require a work of many volumes. Undoubtedly therefore Dr. Hergenrother has taken the wisest course, in referring extensively to Catholic works, in which Janus's reasoning had been answered by anticipation. Never was there a less original production than that of Janus; and it would have wasted time, had our author devised new answers to old objections, when the old answers were amply sufficient. The chief Catholic work, though by no means the only one, to which he refers, is that of Bennetti's ; which is perhaps less generally known by English Catholics than it deserves to be.

So far as we have yet had leisure to compare in detail Janus with his opponent, Dr. Hergenrother seems to have done his work with singular completeness, and to have left no single blow of Janus unparried. In our next number we purpose to review this volume, in connection with Janus himself, and in connection also with the memorable and truly admirable remarks on "scientific history" to be found in Archbishop Manning's Pastoral on the Vatican Definitions. For the present we will content ourselves with citing one or two instances, culled almost at random, of the extraordinary and (we must say) unscrupulous inaccuracy which is Janus's characteristic.

Janus declares (p. 18) that Archbishop Ketteler, of Mayence, in a recently published work, "insists that the Church so thoroughly respects freedom of conscience, as to repudiate all outward coercion of those beyond her pale as immoral and utterly unlawful ; that nothing is further from her mind than to employ any physical force against those who, as being baptized, are her members; &c. &c." What Mgr. Ketteler did say (Anti-Janus, p. 34) is: "There is no established maxim in the Church that should *prevent* a Catholic from holding that, *under certain given relations*, the State *would do best* to grant full religious freedom, &c. &c."

Janus says, and Dr. Döllinger has also said, that Pope S. Agatho was the first who applied to S. Peter's successors the well-known "confirma fratres" of Luke xxii. 32. But (Anti-Janus, p. 60) this interpretation had already been given by Popes Gelasius, Pelagius II., and Gregory the Great; and before them all by the great Leo I.

Janus says (p. 159) that "to the end of the twelfth century" Popes "had called themselves Vicars of Peter, but since Innocent III. this title was superseded by Vicar of Christ." But (Anti-Janus, p. 102) the latter epithet is found applied to Popes as early as the fifth century ; and if not so frequently as later, the obvious reason is that "the ancients" commonly "used the word 'Vicar' as synonymous with '*successor*.'"

Janus says (p. 192) that when the bishops wished to return home from the Fourth Lateran Council, "the Pope forbade them until they had paid him large sums of money." But he omits to add (Anti-Janus, p. 194) that the funds were for a crusade, to which the Pope alone contributed

£30,000 ; and to which both Pope and cardinals were for three years to devote one-tenth of their income.

We have to thank Professor Robertson heartily for taking the pains to translate so invaluable a work. We have also to thank him for the very interesting introduction which he has prefixed, on the rise and fall of Gallicanism in France. He points out that the Four Articles gave great protection to Jansenism (p. xi) and directly caused the schism called Blanchardism (p. xiii) : while Napoleon I. made them one chief instrument of his tyranny (pp. xiv–xx). Passing for a moment beyond France, he shows their intimate connection with the detestable heresy of Febronianism. Still more important are the Professor's remarks on the gradual rise of sounder doctrine in France from the period of the Restoration (pp. xxx–xxxix). He commemorates the great services of Lamennais before his fall, and of the great Joseph de Maistre ; and he adds that Gregory XVI.'s condemnation of the " Avenir" added a great impulse to the fall of Gallicanism.

We only hope no one will infer from this Introduction that Janus's is a "Gallican" volume ; for it is no more Gallican than it is " Ultramontane." Even before the Vatican Definition, its doctrine was simply heretical ; while its tendency, as we have already said, is to promote total unbelief.

Hear the Church. By R. A. COFFIN, Provincial of the Congregation of the Most Holy Redeemer. London : Burns, Oates, & Co.

THIS is a simple, practical instruction, enforcing with much earnestness and plain speaking the obligation of accepting the Vatican definitions. We extract the following :—

" And should you, my dear brethren, hear it objected that, before the decrees were solemnly published by the Holy Father, some bishops were opposed to the defining of the doctrines contained in them, because they considered such definitions inopportune, you must remember that up to the present moment not one single bishop has *publicly* refused his assent to the doctrines ; and, supposing that one or another bishop should, either now or later, refuse his assent, such a bishop would be also simply a heretic. Such an event would not be without precedent, for, to cite one instance, at the second General Council, A.D. 381, there were present 150 Catholic bishops, assembled to condemn the errors of Macedonius, Bishop of Constantinople, who denied the divinity of the Holy Ghost. There were also present thirty-six bishops of the Macedonian sect who were unwilling to make the Nicene profession of faith, and therefore left the Council before its close. (p. 15.)

We will but add one qualification of this, from which we do not think F. Coffin would dissent. One or two bishops have long dearly cherished a tenet now condemned by the Vatican Council, and have regarded it as resting on irrefragable historical grounds which they have mastered. It was but reasonable, we think, that before finally giving in their submission, they should take time thoroughly to examine the new position of things, and consider what precisely has been done. They have now made a noble intellectual sacrifice, for which God will reward them.

The Pontifical Decrees against the motion of the Earth considered in their bearings on the theory of advanced Ultramontanism. London : Longmans.

WE have said a few words on this pamphlet towards the end of our article on the Definition of Papal Infallibility ; and have expressed our hope that in April we shall be able to publish a full reply. At present we have only to make two observations.

All ordinary readers, we think, on reading its title and perusing its contents, will understand the author as criticising the Abbé Bouix and ourselves on the ground of our "advanced Ultramontanism." Further, as regards *ourselves,* such readers will understand our "advanced Ultramontanism" to consist, according to the writer, in our having confidently maintained as an important thesis, that all doctrinal decrees of a Pontifical congregation, which purport to be published by the Pope's command, or which otherwise express his assent, are to be accounted his ex cathedrâ Acts. Now we are far from having thus spoken. The theory in question, we said (Dr. Ward's "Doctrinal Decisions," p. 131) "is at least *very plausible ;*" "we *strongly incline*" to it (p. 129) ; but the question "at last is of no very great practical moment" (p. 131). Our argument in fact had comparatively little concern with ex cathedrâ Acts *at all ;* and so far as it did deal with them, our thesis was—not that congregational decrees are infallible if confirmed by the Pope—but that they are most certainly *not* infallible if *not* confirmed by him.

The writer before us, however, pursues another course of reasoning, which is in every way immeasurably more important than his criticism of Dr. Ward. He maintains that, according to *the principles laid down by Popes themselves,* the Pontifical condemnations of Galileo were ex cathedrâ. In our future article it will be our principal business to encounter this course of reasoning. Secondly and subordinately, we shall defend all which was done with Papal sanction in the matter of Galileo ; and we shall speak in particular on the intellectual submission due to those doctrinal decisions of the supreme ecclesiastical authority, which are not strictly infallible.

endschreiben an einen Deutschen Bischof des Vaticanischen Concils. Von
Lord ACTON. September, 1870. Nördlingen.

THE world has lately seen renewed a spectacle often witnessed before
in the history of the Church. A doctrinal discussion has been
closed. A certain number of bishops have maintained their opinion up to
the moment of its condemnation. They defended it with perseverance, with
ingenuity, with warmth ; but no sooner has the question been unmistake-
ably decided, than they accept the Church's teaching *ex animo.* On the
other hand, in the history of most doctrinal controversies we meet with
men who, though they have argued before the Church's synods as if they
acknowledged their competency, have no sooner found the decision against
themselves than they have repudiated it, and appealed to some other
tribunal—Cæsar, or a future council, or private judgment, or violence.
Small indeed, happily, is the number of those who have revolted against
the teaching of the Vatican Council ; but it is painful for English Catholics
to find prominent in that small number a name once honourable amongst
themselves. Lord Acton's " Letter to a German Bishop " is unhappily an
open and decisive revolt against the Church. Its direct object is to reproach
the bishops who, during the discussions in the Council were opposed to the
definition of Papal Infallibility, with inconsistency in discontinuing their
opposition after its promulgation. The author devotes the greater part of
his letter to justifying this reproach by a reference to the words used by
the bishops during the discussions ; and he declares that many have felt
their faith in the bishops' sincerity shaken by their subsequent conduct in
"publishing the decree without a word of warning that it contains
erroneous doctrine and is issued by an incompetent authority ! "

Lord Acton has received his reward. His letter has been greeted with
the usual chorus of applause, which the Protestant and infidel press of
England never fails to award to acts of disloyalty and revolt against the
Church. The " Times " and the " Saturday Review," like Pilate and Herod,
have been able for once to agree, and this short letter of sixteen pages has
been thought worthy of a review of a column and a half in the leading
journal.

It is scarcely necessary to point out to our readers that the bishops of
whom Lord Acton complains have been guilty of no inconsistency. At
the very time when they argued against the definition they were equally
certain of two things ; first, that their individual opinion was not infallible,
and second, that the decision of the Pope and Council, when finally pronounced *would* be infallible. As soon, therefore, as the decree was promulgated they were aware that their fallible opinion had been in fact
mistaken, and they abandoned it on their previously held principles.
The completeness of this explanation, obvious enough to ordinary
Catholics, is evident even to the Protestant but candid " Spectator." In a
striking article headed " Sudden Changes of Belief," in the number for

December 3rd, 1870, the "Spectator" defends the bishops of the minority against the unreasonable attack of Lord Acton. "It is legerdemain," says the writer, "to change beliefs at a given word of command, if we do not really trust the authority of the person who gives the command ; but if we trust it far more than we trusted our own previous reasons for disbelief, it is no legerdemain, but simple rationality. Now, as far as we know, this is precisely what good Roman Catholics have always maintained about Œcumenical Councils. What they have held is . . . . that the Œcumenical Council is much *more* sure to be right in a decree on any theological matter, than a council of surgeons on a surgical matter, or a council of politicians on a matter of official politics. The former are believed to have the authority of God's word for infallibility, while the latter have only the evidence of their own trained senses and minds."

With this single remark Lord Acton's letter is answered, so far as its avowed purport is concerned. There remains, however, the effect which its author probably calculated on producing by the quotations from the speeches or written observations of the bishops, which form its principal contents. On this subject we feel compelled to make a few remarks.

1. As the Archbishop of Mayence has pointed out, in the severe and dignified rebuke which he has addressed to Lord Acton in reply to his letter,* the observations of the bishops "have only reached publicity by a violation of the secrecy imposed upon the proceedings. No Catholic, therefore, can appeal to them without violating his loyalty to the Church." We may add that no one can appeal to them without injustice to the bishops themselves. They spoke in the assurance that their utterances were protected from publication by the wise precaution of the Pontifical secret. They had reason to believe that their words would fall under the eyes only of theologians able to attach to them their accurate and often technical value, with a full knowledge of the precise point in the discussion to which they were meant to apply ; and it would have grievously hampered their freedom, could they have foreseen that their observations would be used as Lord Acton has used them ;—thrown broadcast before an undiscriminating public, who will necessarily judge them in the loosest and most misleading manner.

2. The passages as they are quoted are misleading on other grounds. Many were directed only against the first draft of the decree, many against the opportuneness of a definition. They are separated from their contexts, and many of them put forward difficulties, not as insoluble objections, but simply *as* difficulties requiring a thorough sifting.

3. We regret to have to charge Lord Acton with unfaithfulness in his quotations. "Lord Acton is careful," says the "Times," "to quote their [the bishops'] *ipsissima verba*—a service for which we do not expect them to feel particularly grateful to him." We have already suggested a reason

---

* The Minority at the Council ; Answer to 'Lord Acton's 'Letter to a German Bishop of the Vatican Council,' by William Emmanuel von Ketteler, Archbishop of Mayence." An English translation of this letter is published as a supplement to the "Tablet" of November 12th, 1870,

why the bishops should indeed feel little gratitude for this service, but they will certainly feel less still by reason of the distortion in many cases of their words, whilst it is pretended that they are given accurately. It is true Lord Acton has given in footnotes the passages to which he appeals, in the original Latin; but the German text, sure to be read by many who will not compare it with the notes, and by many more unacquainted with Latin, is not a faithful translation. Thus, to take the very first quotation, a bishop, speaking of the proposed decree whilst it was under discussion, declared that, "foreseeing the lamentable loss of souls which was to be feared, he would rather die than support the proposed synodal decree" (*quam decreti synodalis argumento patrocinari*). This Lord Acton has worded in the text "so that one bishop . . . preferred to die rather than to receive the decree" (*als das Decret annehmen*). Observe, the bishop was not speaking of accepting the decree in case of its being passed, but of supporting it while still under discussion. Now, apart from all context, "*das Decret annehmen*" might perhaps have meant "to agree to the passing of the decree;" but how does the case stand? Lord Acton has just charged the bishops with inconsistency in now submitting: his argument therefore requires him to show that their language previous to the Definition went the length of declaring that they would not submit to it if passed; and therefore we maintain that to translate the Latin words under these circumstances by an expression whose first and most natural meaning would be that which is needed by the exigencies of his argument, is an equivocation amounting to an untruth.

But the very next page furnishes an instance where there is no ambiguity. The Archbishop of St. Louis is made in the text to say that "Catholicism, changed by this addition, would no longer be defensible against the unanswerable witness of history, save by ridiculous evasions; for the lives and teachings of the Popes are sufficient to show that they were incapable of being the possessors of infallibility." It is certainly curious to refer to the footnote and find nothing like this sentence. The archbishop really says that it is a mistake to suppose that the waves will be stilled by the Definition. He thinks the contrary the more probable result. Catholics who submit to the Definition will find themselves surrounded with difficulties. Governments will hold them in suspicion. "The enemies of the Church will not fear to harass them, now objecting against them the errors which Popes are said to have either taught or approved by their conduct; whilst they will receive with derision the sole answer that can be given, that the Pontiffs sanctioned these errors, not as Popes, but as private Roman bishops. They will also bring forward" the scandals related of some of the Popes "as arguments of a want of consistency in the Catholic faith, not distinguishing between infallibility and impeccability, from the fact that they seem to depend one on the other, and to be inseparably connected." It is, to say the least, not honest to profess to give the very words of the archbishop, and then to put into his mouth as his own sentiments the objections, more or less plausible, which he thinks it probable that "the enemies of the Church" will make. Thus, again, the Bishop of Orleans is stated to have called the doctrine "an unheard of absurdity," whilst his own words in the footnote only say that *" 7he mode of expression of the draft decree* supposes a double infallibility in the Church ; namely, that of the Church and that of the Roman Pontiff, *which* is absurd and unheard of." Whatever may have been the opinion of the Bishop of Orleans about the doctrine of Papal infallibility, he certainly would not have said that it was "unheard of." We should imagine Lord Acton himself would hardly have the courage to make that statement.

In the same way Cardinal Rauscher is represented as speaking of the doctrine as one which can be defended *" only* by unworthy and transparent sophisms." We look down at the footnote to which Lord Acton appeals, and once more we find no justification for the statement in the text. The Cardinal's words are :—" By subterfuges such as *not a few theologians* have used in defence of Honorius, I should expose myself to derision. The use of sophisms appears to me unworthy both of the episcopal office and of the subject under discussion, which ought to be handled in the fear of the Lord, &c."

4. Lord Acton has presented " a picture of the Vatican Council and its work, given," he says, " by such men as Schwarzenburg, Rauscher, Dupanloup, Haynald, Ketteler, Clifford, Purcell, Connolly, Darboy, Héféle, Strossmayer, and Kenrick. The Council is thus judged by the lips of its most able members. They depict it as a conspiracy against divine truth and right. They declare that the new dogmas were neither taught by the Apostles, nor believed by the Fathers ; that they are soul-destroying errors, opposed to the true teaching of the Church, founded on imposture, a dishonour to Catholics." On this shameful passage Mgr. Ketteler observes in the letter to which we have already referred : " As my name is here cited among those of the bishops who are stated to have painted the Council ' as a conspiracy against divine truth and right,' who are said to have maintained that ' the new dogmas were neither taught by the Apostles nor believed by the Fathers ; that they are 'soul-destroying errors, opposed to the true teaching of the Church, founded on imposture, a dishonour to Catholics,' I declare, in the first place, that Lord Acton has departed, in an unexampled manner, from the truth, by putting such statements into my mouth. And further I declare that I never heard any such statements from other members of the so-called minority, and that I would never have belonged to any assembly in which such statements could have been made unrebuked." We need add no comments to the archbishop's words.

There is a certain number of writers upon whom their own pretensions and the well-merited irony of Catholics have combined to fasten the title of " scientific historians." Ever ready to bring against Catholic writers unjustifiable charges of fraud, suppression, forgery, and tampering with history ; judging with a lofty tone of severity the literary morality of past ages, and often condemning as moral delinquencies what were but the involuntary results of the existing state of criticism, these writers are themselves gross and frequent offenders against literary honesty—witness the wholesale and shameless untruthfulness of ' Janus,' and the garbling and unretracted misstatements of Dr. Döllinger, e. g., on the question of

Honorius in his Papstfabeln,[*] and on the subject of the Florentine Decree of Union.[†] No one can reasonably deny Lord Acton's right to be classed amongst the "scientific historians."

What is the meaning of the late Definition? an Inquiry by WILLIAM MASKELL, A.M. London : Toovey.

IF we were to judge of Mr. Maskell's intentions by their result,—we should suppose that he has wished to show, how much more can be said for a conclusion which he knows to be false, than for one which he maintains to be true. He frankly admits (p. 4) that "if we do not give to" the "doctrine" of Papal Infallibility as defined in the Vatican Council "the same interior, complete and absolute assent as we give to all the articles of the Apostles' Creed, we . . . wilfully cast ourselves out of the Church"; and yet he devotes eight pages out of his twelve to giving reasons *against* there being any obligation of such assent. We cannot guess what he aims at in this part of his pamphlet, and we leave it therefore without comment.

Mr. Maskell's scope in his remaining pages is to minimize the amount of instruction conveyed in the said Definition. He regards e.g. (p. 10) the Definition as consistent with an opinion,—which he considers indeed to be held by "one of the most learned of the French bishops,"—that "no Pope hitherto, so far as we can possibly learn, has spoken ex cathedrâ," and that accordingly "it is not probable that any ever will hereafter." Now this is just one of those grandly-sounding sentences, which at first sight appear of momentous significance, but which when examined are seen to be simply unmeaning. Take an illustration. Physicists have proved by the methods of their science, that "all diamonds are combustible." Suppose some eccentric person were to say, that this proposition is of no practical value whatever, because it does not declare that there *are* such things as diamonds. Men of common sense would reply, as soon as their astonishment permitted them, that they know *aliunde* the existence of diamonds; and that the proposition therefore conveys to them an important truth. So in the present case. The Vatican Council has explained, that the Pope speaks ex cathedrâ, whenever "in discharge of the office of Pastor and Doctor of all Christians, by virtue of his supreme Apostolic authority, he defines a doctrine regarding faith or morals to be held by the Universal Church." But Catholics know *aliunde* that he has very frequently so spoken. In consequence therefore of the Vatican Definition they believe with divine faith that all such utterances have been and will be infallible.

---

[*] *See* F. Schneemann's "Studien über die Honorius-Frage," p. 30.
[†] *See* DUBLIN REVIEW for April, 1870, pp. 513–520.

What means have Catholics for knowing that Popes have thus spoken ? The most obvious of all is when a Pope has himself *testified* the fact. Thus Gregory XVI. announced to all the bishops of the Church, that, in the "Mirari vos," "in virtue of his office (pro nostri officii munere)," "according to the authority given him (pro auctoritate humilitati nostræ tradita)" he had "declared to the whole Catholic world," and "defined" "the Catholic doctrine" "which alone it is lawful to follow" on the various "heads" which he then proceeded to enumerate. At all events then, as regards that particular utterance the "Mirari vos," it is absolutely undeniable that its promulgator "by virtue of his supreme Apostolic authority" was "defining a doctrine regarding faith or morals to be held by the Universal Church" : or, in other words, was speaking ex cathedrâ. Again a Pope may *equivalently* declare that he is speaking ex cathedrâ : as e.g. when he pronounces an anathema on those who do not submit to his teaching, as in the "Ineffabilis" ; or when, in some "Constitutio perpetuo valitura", as in the "Unigenitus" and the "Auctorem Fidei", he commands all Catholics to accept his declarations with interior assent ; or in various other ways which might easily be specified. The Vatican Council has pronounced it to be de fide Catholicâ, that in all such cases he speaks infallibly.

In page 10 Mr. Maskell recites various interpretations, which he accounts permissible, of the recent Definition. "Some hold," he says (p. 10), "that as yet the Vatican Council has merely given the sanction of its authority to what was already the well-known and universally acknowledged teaching of the Church ; and that with respect to the personal infallibility of the Pope as it has been taught in theological schools, the Definition, so far as it settles anything, limits and in that sense lowers the supposed prerogative." This is substantially our own opinion ; subject to two explanations. We consider that the doctrine now defined was, even before its Definition, morally speaking, "the universally acknowledged teaching of the Church" ; i. e., that Gallicans were so few and so discredited, as to be reasonably kept out of account in the numeration. Moreover we fully admit that the recent Definition does not express the *whole* doctrine of Papal infallibility as "taught in theological schools" ; because it is avowedly silent on the "*extent* of infallibility," which is to be defined in a future session.

"Others," adds Mr. Maskell, who accept the Definition, nevertheless "believe that the Pope speaks ex cathedrâ" only "when he speaks in Œcumenical Council." But even if the Definition were silent on this head, it is impossible to doubt (as we have already explained) that the Pope speaks as "Pastor and Doctor of all Christians," whenever he expressly or equivalently *declares* himself so to speak : and this he has very often done externally to any Œcumenical Council. It is quite a mistake however to allege that the Definition *is* silent on this particular. The Bishop of Birmingham, in his Pastoral on "the Council and Papal Infallibility," gives expression to the common-sense view, that the Preamble is the one authentic exposition of the Definition ; or in other words that all are bound to accept the Definition in that precise sense, which is indicated by the Preamble. And this is indeed Mr. Maskell's own opinion ; for he says (pp. 9, 10) that "if a doubt exists as to the meaning of the Definition, the only authority which can remove it is that which left the Definition as it stands." Now the Preamble lays down, that the "assembling" of "Œcumenical Councils" is but one out of the various "helps which Divine Providence" has "supplied" to Pontiffs, for defining infallibly : that these latter have often defined infallibly after consulting only "the Church dispersed" ; or "particular Synods" ; or otherwise "according to the exigencies of times and circumstances."

Mr. Maskell proceeds. "Others hold that nothing has been passed to prohibit the concurrent opinion, that if a Pope contradicted any clear article of faith, he would, instead of being infallible in so doing, ipso facto cease to be Pope." Most true. When the sky falls, you will be able to catch larks ; and whenever some Pope shall officially * contradict "a clear article of faith"—i. e., some dogma which has hitherto been unquestionably taught by Pope and bishops as an obligatory dogma of the Faith —Catholics will have to face the question raised by Mr. Maskell. For ourselves we follow the enormous majority of theologians, in holding that, by sure Divine promise, no such phenomenon will ever be permitted.

If we have considered Mr. Maskell's remarks at some length, it has not been from fear that they will exercise permanent influence. Malcontents may at the moment make use of them, as some mitigation of their annoyance in having to accept the Definition ; but the common sense and common integrity of mankind—of Catholics and non-Catholics alike—will in the long run repudiate what we are obliged to call such paltry evasions. We are as far as possible from questioning the uprightness of Mr. Maskell's intentions : we are but criticizing what we consider the legitimate objective drift and tendency of his words.

He appends a most gratuitous and unfounded attack on the Archbishop. Thus he censures his Grace (p. 12) for introducing such terms as "the personal, separate independent and absolute infallibility of the Pope " ; of which terms, adds Mr. Maskell, "not a trace is to be found in the Definition." Why it was the Archbishop's very *point* to mention that, whereas no such terms occur in the Definition, so neither had they been used by himself, but had been falsely ascribed to him. See the Archbishop's Pastoral, pp. 93, 94.

Then again the passage, quoted by Mr. Maskell, (p. 11) from p. 89 of the same Pastoral, must of course be interpreted by what his Grace had already said in p. 78. "The definition of the *extent* of infallibility . . . *has not been treated as yet*, but is left for the second part of the schema 'de Ecclesiâ.' " Yet Mr. Maskell alleges that the Archbishop represents that doctrine, concerning the extent of infallibillity, which he has derived from a consensus of theologians, as enforced by that Definition which has *already* been given.

---

* We use the word "officially" here, to mean "with every external appearance of an ex cathedrâ Act."

Mr. Maskell concludes (pp. 11, 12) with some amazing remarks, main. taining the Church's fallibility in her canonization of Saints. It is impossible here even to enter on so large and important a theme ; and we will content ourselves therefore with one quotation, from the standard work on canonization written by Lambertini, afterwards Benedict XIV. " It is *the common opinion,*" says that great theologian, " of theologians and canonists (juris Pontificii periorum) that the Supreme Pontiff cannot err in his canonization of Saints : but there is still disputation among them, whether this truth be [strictly] *de fide.*"

We must conclude with a hearty protest against Mr. Maskell's intro. ductory attack on our excellent contemporary " The Tablet." It is impossible however to *answer* his criticisms of that journal, as they consist in the vaguest and most indefinite generalities.

Mixed Education in Ireland : The Confessions of a Queen's Collegian. By F. HUGH O'DONNELL, M.A., &c. In two volumes. Vol. I. *The Faculty of Arts.* London : Longmans. 1870.

IN the reply of Sir George Grey, then Secretary of State, to the Memorial of the Catholic Prelates of Ireland in 1866, he stated that Her Majesty's Government were " unable to concur in the belief expressed in the Memorial," that the Queen's Colleges " have been a signal failure." Mr. O'Donnell addresses himself in the work before us to all the matters necessary for forming a candid opinion on the issue thus raised between the Irish bishops and the official heads of the great Liberal party. It is impossible for any one to examine the proofs he gives in support of his position, without coming to the conclusion at which he arrives. As an instrument of higher education, the Queen's Colleges in Ireland are not only a failure, but the most expensive and ridiculous failure of which any notion can be conceived. Mr. Lowe claims to be considered a very economical manager of the public money. Yet Mr. Lowe has always been one of the most strenuous champions not only of mixed education in the abstract, but especially of mixed education in that concrete form which it has taken in the Irish godless colleges. His mind is subtle enough to reconcile to itself and to recommend by ingenuous argument to others, the strangest paradoxes ; but we shall certainly be curious to hear how he will account to the House of Commons for his maintenance of so flagrant an imposition as the Irish College system, on principles consistent with his duty as a faithful guardian of the Imperial exchequer.

It will be said, perhaps, that Mr. O'Donnell is a disappointed man. He begins his work by laying great stress upon that fact himself. But what he has been disappointed with is the hollow and unsubstantial nature of the so-called education offered to him in one of those institutions, where he went to obtain a high class of knowledge. He asked for bread, and he received a stone. In no other sense is it possible for any one but the most egregious of dunces to be at all disappointed with the provision which the bounty of Parliament and the two Sir Robert Peels has made for him in these pleasant places. Before a boy has learned his grammar at school, a Queen's College will not only fold him to her matriculating bosom but will, if he be a boy of any promise, reward him with an exhibition or a scholarship for having done her the favour of taking refuge there. "No less than 1,938 junior scholarships, amounting to the total sum of £47,286, have been disbursed in direct payment of undergraduates during the twenty years that the colleges have been opened." When the ingenious youth aspires to his B.A. degree, two examinations test his proficiency ; the first of which is very much easier than that which must be gone through for *matriculation* in the University of London, and in this he may be even an honourman if he gets the modest proportion of fifteen marks out of 124. The second stage was made a little more difficult, and remained so till 1858, when the astute heads of the colleges perceived that it had the unfortunate effect of diminishing the number of graduates to a point which could not but attract and arrest public attention. A change was therefore made, and the result is now that any one may become a B.A. of the Queen's University in Ireland with the same amount and range of knowledge as is possessed by any fairly intelligent boy of thirteen who has had the advantage of being taught at any good school or by any good tutor. We speak of a fact which we know when we state that a youth of very fair abilities, much above the average, who had taken several scholarships in one of the Queen's Colleges, and had got his B.A. degree with honours, failed totally in his examination for a sizarship at the University of Dublin. The mere circumstance of a person presenting himself to begin his studies at a real university, after he had obtained a degree at an institution which tried to pass for one, is of itself a sufficient proof that the latter was a hollow sham.

"Why," exclaims Mr. O'Donnell, "to enter the lower class of Greek and Latin at Maynooth, in the junior house, at the commencement of the whole course, what is known to professors as Humanities, to students, I believe, disdainfully as *chubbery*, candidates are liable to examination 'in two Greek and two Latin books, one prose and one poetry in each language.' So far as classical authors are concerned, students who enter into 'Chubbery' at Maynooth in order to pursue during two years Latin and Greek, without any logic, physics, or theology until later, are already fully entitled to the B.A. degree of the Queen's University ! And yet Dr. Maguire, the Galway Queen's College Professor of Latin, in his 'Maynooth Resolutions Considered,' has the audacity to declare that, 'as a body the clergy of all creeds are inferior to the members of the other professions in general intelligence and cultivation. Their course of professional study is narrow and technical !' And Dr. Ball, the recent convert to Mixed Education, could cite this ridiculous Galway Professor in the House of Commons as 'one of the most distinguished Roman Catholics !' And the House of Commons were gulled into imagining that this Galway Professor was really an enlightened friend of education, and really a representative of the Catholic laity protesting against an ignorant priesthood ! "

Notwithstanding the enormity of the bribes offered and the less than mediocrity of the merit required, notwithstanding each progressive raising of the bounty and lowering of the standard, what (can our readers imagine) are the results obtained ? In twenty years, the graduates of the Queen's University in Ireland have with difficulty reached the number of 700 ! The mountains of expenditure which have been in travail to produce this truly *ridiculus mus* are these :—

Junior Scholarships.	£47,286
Senior Scholarships	14,280
Collegiate Prizes	6,000
University Prizes	5,100
Peel Exhibitions	3,480
Payment Professors	180,000
Total . . .	£256,146

So that every graduate of the Queen's University in Ireland—that is to say, every mock graduate of a sham university—has cost the imperial exchequer the sum of £365 18*s*. The British empire is certainly very rich, and we do not know what to do with all our money, but never in the annals of administrative wastefulness has there been anything even remotely comparable to this incredible extravagance. If we had spent the money in trying to grow mangoes on the coast of Clare, or to cover the Giant's Causeway with date-trees, it would not have been a more preposterous monument of folly and absurdity. Not the least serious evil of it is this, that, when there is question of the Imperial administration of Irish revenues, our Liberal legislators always point to such figures as these to show how fairly Irish revenue is balanced by Irish expenditure. Does any one suppose that an Irish Parliament, even if all its members were as silly as Mr. O'Sullivan of Cork, would make ducks and drakes of the people's money in such an outrageous fashion as this ? Another misfortune is, as Mr. O'Donnell points out, that these miserable abortions of colleges have not only failed to educate the sons of the Irish middle-classes themselves, but have destroyed, by a lavishness of bribery which defied competition, the schools previously existing. " When a master of the Galway Grammar School of Erasmus Smith was asked by the Endowed Schools Commissioners if he could give ' the reason for the decline of the school,' he had to say the reason was, that the Queen's College took away his pupils ' *before they knew their grammar at school.* ' "

There is no getting over Mr. O'Donnell's facts and figures ; for his facts are given in the words of the heads and teachers of the colleges themselves, and his figures are official. All public men who wish to understand the question will find ample materials provided for them by him. We may reasonably hope, that, with the information here brought ready to their hand, Irish members will not let the coming Session pass without turning the bull's-eye full upon an iniquity which public opinion will not tolerate when once it is brought into public view. We hear, indeed, that the Galway College is already doomed ; that the *reductio ad absurdum* is there too glaring to be any longer disguised. But the objections to the Cork College are the same in kind ; they differ only in degree. The Belfast College succeeds, it is true ; but as a sectarian institution. Whatever the Queen's Colleges have done towards solving the problem of education in Ireland has been in proving that Mixed Education is impossible. But, as Mr. O'Donnell says, " on grounds of secular education alone, the first step towards any educational reform, the first step towards any settlement of the Irish Education question, must be preceded by their unreserved and radical abolition."

We are happy to see that Mr. O'Donnell is pursuing his task of fighting against the godless system in a journal called the *Catholic Critic,* published every month in Galway, of which he is the Editor. In No. 2 (for November) there is a short article on " Catholic Education in Prussia," in which the recent intervention of the Prussian Government at Bonn is thus referred to :—

" Two professors in the Theological Faculty—there is a Faculty of Theology in this Mixed University of a Protestant State—had presumed, according to the tenets of that heretical school, of which Lord Acton is so deplorable a representative in England, to call in question the dogma of Infallibility. For this they were to be deprived of their chairs by the Archbishop of Cologne, who very naturally thinks that professors are for something else than leading their students astray. What we have especially to refer to is, that the Prussian Government have recognised the right of the Archbishop to inter-fere with authority in such a case. . . . . British statesmen have of late been very ready to admit that Prussia can afford to teach them a lesson in armaments and organization. We may be excused for believing that the lesson might advantageously extend to the most elementary guiding principles of public instruction also. In Protestant and rationalistic Prussia, mixed education is not carried to the extremes with which Irishmen are familiar, and that contempt for Catholic feeling is not to be found among the com-patriots of Luther, which is an established axiom of state in the government of Catholic Ireland."

The other articles, especially one on " Goethe and Chaucer," are interest-ing and well written. Mr. O'Donnell is doing a good and necessary work, and is doing it well.

An Essay on the Spiritual Life of Mediæval England. By J. DALGAIRNS. Prefixed to HILTON's *Scale of Perfection.* London : John Philp.

WE do not quite understand why another edition of F. Hilton's work should appear ; and one certainly inferior in type to F. Guy's, which we reviewed more than a year ago. But we cannot be sorry for what has occasioned F. Dalgairns' admirable Essay.

Its purpose is to point out, that in two different ways the contrast between mediæval and modern Catholicity has been egregiously exaggerated. The Church of the middle ages was very far indeed from being, either on the one hand so powerful over society, or on the other hand so deficient in ascetical literature and in special popular devotion, as it is the fashion to suppose.

Firstly then, F. Dalgairns' seems to hold an opinion, which we ourselves have more than once expressed ; viz., that so far from the mediæval Popes having possessed undue influence over society, politics, and kings,—they were only able to exercise a comparatively small portion of the authority divinely given them. Let any one carefully study the magnificent doctrine infallibly laid down in the " Unam Sanctam ; " and he will see how much greater power is vested by God in the Holy See, than even Innocent III. and Boniface VIII. were able to wield. " There were continual fluctuations of victory and defeat " (p. xxii.) in the conflict between them and the world, and even their greatest victories were but imperfect. In one particular indeed, Popes are more powerful in the 19th than they were in the 13th century. Since the first session of the Vatican Council it is of faith that the Pope's episcopal power is immediate over all Christians throughout the world ; but certainly local churches have been much less practically prone to *recognize* this power in the earlier than in the later period.

But, secondly—and this is, of course, F. Dalgairns' principal point – recent investigations have conclusively established, " that there was much more of what we should now call spirituality everywhere in the middle ages than even Catholics were disposed to think " (p. viii.) In England e.g. hermits and anchorets abounded—the latter the more austere and solitary of the two (p. x.)—living a life of prayer ; and there was a whole class of literature addressed to their special vocation. In fact, " there is undoubtedly a kind of tender pathetic love " towards Jesus Christ " which is to be found in old English writers, and which is peculiarly their own. If I were asked to select the grace which is prominent in their writings, I should say it was piety in the sense in which the word is applied to a gift of the Holy Ghost." " The anchoress had no peculiar habit, and her office was, as has been said, not that of the choir, but that of the lay brothers. She is encouraged to say English prayers. At midday she made a meditation on the crucifix. Holy meditations are especially recommended to her. Though, according to the practice of the Church of the time, she made only fifteen communions a-year, yet there is a marked devotion to the Blessed Sacrament throughout the treatise. Its perpetual presence in the Church is held out as a refuge against temptation, and it is plain that from the window which looked into the church, the anchoress often knelt in prayer, with her eyes fixed upon the altar where Jesus lay in the sacrament of his love." (pp. xv. xvi.)

Then, as regards the people at large, " we have only got to look at Mone's collection of mediæval hymns, and to observe the frequent notices of translations, not only into German, but into French and Italian, to be convinced that *the songs of the Church were accessible to the poor, and even in common use amongst them in their own language.* Jacopone de Todi's beautiful hymns are a proof of the popularity of *spiritual songs other than the liturgical hymns of the Breviary.* There are extant also hymns sung and *prayers said in various languages*—French, Provençal, German, and English—*to be used at the Elevation, the Holy Communion, and on various feasts.* Didactic books of devotion *in the vernacular tongue*, such as Tauler's Nachfolge, l'Internelle Consolation, and in English the Ayenbite of Inwit or Remorse of Conscience prove that spiritual reading was practised. It is plain, then, that our mediæval ancestors were by no means so chained to the letter, so unspiritual as some have supposed."

F. Dalgairns, however, concludes by pointing out that there was one marked contrast between earlier times and those commencing with the close of the feudal period, which exercised a very important effect on devotional literature. The result of the political changes which gradually took place has been "the total disruption of all necessary connection between property and occupation, the creation of a very large class of men and women who can live, if they please, without doing anything at all. I do not mean to say that any man breathing is born without duties ; but I mean that there is a very large class of beings who can eat, drink, and perform all the functions of life, whether they do their duties or not.

"It is evident that this state of things requires something peculiar to meet it. What is to be done with all this superfluity of unemployed life ? What is a man thus set free from obligation to do with his time ? In the middle ages life itself imposed an unvarying rule of living. Is man now to live without a rule ? A thousand moral and religious questions start up and cry out for an answer. Things have become possible now which were not possible before. Men and women can spend their lives in an unvarying round of amusements and excitements, even without supposing them to seek vicious pleasures. Theatres, operas, balls, novels—things unknown to their ancestors —may make up their life. Is this right ? Is it safe ? A most momentous question this, which requires an answer. Here is a new thing upon earth, or at least a state of things which has not existed since the Teutonic nations were converted—the upper classes of society able to live in a constant round of amusement, and *thinking themselves satisfactorily sure of salvation, because of the hypothetical absence of great sin.* Are unlimited balls and unlimited sacraments compatible ? Or *is a worldly life a perilous one for those who live it ?* Or rather ought not Christians to spend more time in prayer, in devotion, in voluntary almsgiving, and works of charity, in proportion as they are set free from many duties? Is not life more dangerous and salvation more insecure because of this terrible invasion of the world, with audacious requirements, and unblushing exigencies ? Considering the cool impudence with which the world insists on its own innocence, nay, has even the impertinence to look upon its general mode of life as a duty to society, it does seem as if this new attitude of the world called for new rules and a greater strictness to counteract its dangers.

"Now, the 'Scale of Perfection' is valuable because it is an English book containing an answer to this question. If not written for, it was at least adopted by an English princess, a king's mother, living at court in the reign of Henry VII. In fact, it contains the old English Catholic view before Protestantism existed. The answer to the above question is unequivocal, and is contained in the following words : ' When men and women who are free from worldly businesses if they will, and may have their needful sustenance without much solicitude about it, especially religious men and women—and other men also in secular estate, that have good abilities and understanding, and may, if they will dispose themselves, come to much grace ; these men are more to blame than those who are so busyed with worldly things which are needful to be done. Verily it is *perilous* for a soul not to seek to make any further progress.' · The only safe thing is to 'set his heart fully to come to more grace and give himself heartily to prayer, meditating and other good wishes.'

" Such was the old Catholic life, before we were corrupted by the society of Protestants. The moral of the book is that a supernatural life is common to all Christians, and that there is no such infinite distinction between Christians in the world and religious. Both, in different degrees and modes, are not safe unless they aim at ' profiting in grace.'" (pp. xxxviii–xl.)

We cannot better conclude our notice of F. Dalgairns' Essay than with these inestimably valuable hints.

Contemporary Review for December 1870. Article II. *Theory of the Human Soul.* By Rev. FATHER DALGAIRNS.

WE have no intention of here considering F. Dalgairns's admirable exposition of Catholic doctrine on the human soul. Such an attempt would find its place in the series of philosophical articles, which we still hope we may be able to publish in due course. But the following remarks of the author's are upon ground common to all philosophical questions ; and they are of such vital importance in these days, that we wish to place them before Catholics who may not see the " Contemporary Review." Meanwhile we must cordially thank the Editor of that very able miscellany, for giving Catholics their full opportunity of being heard by thoughtful Protestants.

" We must begin by understanding our opponents. If we are to make any impression on the nineteenth century, we must boldly look difficulties full in the face, and frankly acknowledge them. We must cheerfully accept all facts, however they at first sight tell against us. We must pierce down to the very core of things.

" Furthermore, we must make ourselves understood, and for this purpose we must use modern terms. If I may venture to speak of myself, after having done my best to believe in modern philosophy, I have returned to the Aristotle which, thank heaven, I learned many years ago at Oxford, when Newman was king. I believe that, on the whole, truth is to be found in the system of the old heathen, into the form of whose terms the Church has, to a great extent, cast her theology ; though its most strenuous supporters 'have no intention to deny that the old philosophy may be perfected by some of the labours of the new.' Nevertheless, holding its truth as I do, I am perfectly convinced that you may as well address the House of Commons in Chaldee as attempt to reach the intellect of the world with scholastic philosophy. If you would aim at Christianizing English science, you must speak, not bad Latin, but plain English. *Materia prima,* whether true or false, will never convert the world. You may define your terms if you will, but your definitions will fall cold upon the hearts of men whose minds have been cast in another mould, and to whose whole mode of thought the very ideas are grotesquely strange. For fighting purposes the schoolmen are as wooden ships to ironclads. You will never get within range, and your arguments will never penetrate the iron-bound hide of your adversary. Our very first condition of obtaining a hearing is being intelligible." (p. 21.)

Two Essays on Scripture Miracles and on Ecclesiastical. By JOHN HENRY NEWMAN. Second Edition. Pickering, London: 1870.

IN reprinting, or allowing to be reprinted, the works which he wrote as an Anglican, Dr. Newman could not omit the Essays on Miracles. Yet if there is a line of his writings that we could afford to allow to go out of print, we could make up our minds to want the first of these two essays. Dr. Newman has said many "strong things" against the Catholic Church, chiefly in reviews and fugitive pieces, which he is not likely to allow to be brought out afresh. The direct and unpleasant way in which this Essay on Scripture Miracles scoffs at the Church, and puts down with contempt the miraculous history of her saints, makes us almost wish that he had allowed it to remain no better known than it has hitherto been in the pages of the *Encyclopædia Metropolitana,* or in the pamphlet that curious readers have seen. Every one knows that its author hates and detests, now, every word he has uttered, though without fault of his, against the Church he has suffered so much for; and the newly-added notes in the reprint before us briefly remind the reader of this. Still it appears to us, though we say it with diffidence, that the intrinsic value of the argument does not make up for the disadvantage just mentioned. It was written when the author was somewhere about twenty-four, that is to say, forty-five years ago. To many readers it will prove interesting as a study of Dr. Newman's early style. No one will be surprised that such a writer should write well, even in his earliest public essays, and many a one has left a fair reputation who never wrote better than the young author who is here seen almost commencing his career. Serious, clear, terse, and well-expressed, the essay has some of the best qualities of two admirable models of English—of Locke and of Paley. But it does not escape some of Locke's slovenliness and rudeness of sentence, and it is not free from the didactic primness with which Paley at one time presents his good sense, at another adorns his insular narrowness. The exquisite finish of the "Sermons," the robust and rhythmical emphasis, as of strong tunes chimed on bells, of the "Lectures," do not exist as yet. There are few traces of the epigrammatic flashes, of the wealth of illustration and the magisterial power that appear in his treatment of the most abstract of the subjects which he has handled in his riper years. But the singular absence of all appearance of juvenility is calculated to surprise those who are accustomed to expect that the dawn of a genius will be accompanied by redness and clouds, by a certain disorderly extravagance which is at once a proof of power and a sign of immaturity. Dr. Newman's style has ever been of the nature of white light, destined, indeed, to grow more luminous and more intense, but never obscured by smoke or defiled by garish colour.

Up to the time when this first essay was written, the chief antagonist of miracles, or at least the most difficult to answer satisfactorily, had been Hume; Voltaire and the French school of profane scoffers had little weight in England. Middleton had made a vigorous onslaught, but by admitting that a miracle was possible, he had reduced the question to an historical debate. But Hume had cut at the root of all possibility of discerning or admitting a miracle; his view was that it was "more probable that the testimony of a miracle should be false than that the miracle should be true." It is this kind of objection that one would have wished to see answered in an "Essay on Scripture Miracles;" but the writer states that "it has been so ably met by various writers that . . . it need not be considered here."

"It derives its force from the assumption that a miracle is strictly a causeless phenomenon, a self-originating violation of nature; and is solved by referring the event to divine agency, a principle which (it cannot be denied) has originated works indicative of power at least as great as any miracle requires. An adequate cause being thus found for the production of a miracle, the objection vanishes, as far as the mere question of power is concerned, and it remains to be considered whether the anomalous fact be of such a character as to admit of being referred to the Supreme Being. For if it cannot with propriety be referred to Him, it remains as improbable as if no such agent were known to exist. At this point, then, I propose taking up the argument; and by examining what miracles are, in their nature and circumstances, referable to divine agency, I shall be providing a reply to the former of the three objections just noticed, in which the alleged similarity of all miraculous narratives one to another is made a reason for a common rejection of all." (p. 15.)

In this paragraph it is evident that Hume's argument is "solved" a little too much off-hand, considering Hume's views about cause and effect; but we have in it a sort of summary of the essay. The writer's main object is to decide what miracles are referable to God. He finds the answer to this problem, first in the fact that the moral law (as well as the physical) is part of the "system" intended by God; and, secondly, in a number of canons, some of them arbitrary enough, as to what kind of a miracle is or is not in harmony with the (supposed) designs or attributes

of God. As the "designs" of God are calculated from a strongly Protestant point of view, and as His "attributes" are estimated in the scales
of one who had imbibed a portion of the spirit of Middleton, it is not surprising that room is found for very few miracles indeed. Still, as far as it
goes, the essay is cogent, clear, and conclusive. But its fragmentary character and narrow stand-point, declining as it does to meet the rationalistic
argument, and stopping short in the barest Protestantism, make it unsatis-
factory, and perhaps even dangerous to shallow minds.

The second essay, on the "Miracles of early Ecclesiastical History," is
of a very different stamp. It was written in 1842-43, as a preface to a
translation of a portion of Fleury's "Ecclesiastical History." Changes
manifold and deep had passed over the mind of the man whom the Light
was gradually leading to know itself, since the days when he was guided
by Newton, Milner, and Romaine. In the first place, he had been shaping
out for himself that theory of certitude and probability which he has but
lately placed before the world in the "Grammar of Assent." It was from
Keble, as he tells us in the "Apologia," that he gained the notion that the
firmness of assent which we owe to religious doctrine is to be ascribed, "not
to the probabilities which introduce it, but to the living power of faith and
love which accept it." (*Apologia*, p. 79.) This principle, which has gained
its author "many hard names," he supplemented by an elaborate theory,
which he brings forward in No. 8 of "Tracts for the Times," which he sum-
marizes in pp. 80 and 81 of the "Apologia," and which he has drawn out
in detail in the latest of his works. It was chiefly owing to its influence
that the second essay differs so much from the first. "The main difference," he says (*Apologia*, p. 82) "between my Essay on Miracles in 1826,
and my Essay in 1842 is this—that in 1826 I considered that miracles
were sharply divided into two classes,—those which were to be received, and
those which were to be rejected; whereas, in 1842, I saw that they were
to be regarded according to their greater or less probability, which was in
some cases sufficient to create certitude about them, in other cases only
belief or opinion." This "classification" of miracles (in 1826) into
"those that were to be received and those that were to be rejected," in
other words, into miracles and impositions or no-miracles, would seem to
be one which might have been safely admitted even in 1842. But the
force of the distinction lies in the word "sharply." In 1826 it seemed to
him that miracles could be thus divided "sharply," that is, on clear and
evident principles; in 1842 he saw that these principles of discernment
were not clear and evident; no "sharp" division was possible. The view
which he had abandoned he thus describes, speaking of Protestant apologists for miracles.

"They tacitly grant that the antecedent improbability of miracles is at
least so great that it can only be overcome by the strongest and most overpowering evidence; that second-best evidence does not even tend to prove
them; that they are absolutely incredible up to the very moment that all
doubt is decisively set at rest; that there can be no degrees of proof, no
incipient and accumulating arguments to recommend them; that no re-
lenting of mind or suspense of judgment is justifiable, as various fainter

evidences are found to conspire in their favour ; that they may be scorned as fictions, if they are not to be venerated as truths." (*Ecclesiastical Miracles,* p. 177.)

But it would be doing injustice to this masterly essay to suppose that its chief excellence is the disposition to accept "second-best" evidence, and to beg a place for the Miracles of the Saints somewhere in the region of the probable. On the contrary, it contains the development of a new element in the *antecedent* credibility of miracles. It is clear that it is of no use presenting a Protestant with any amount of evidence (not even excepting ocular demonstration) if he already harbours a prejudice that makes him peremptorily reject it as a snare. Douglas, Leslie, and others, whilst expostulating with Hume for his unreasonableness in rejecting all miracles *à priori*, are quite as unreasonable, in their turn, when they reject *à priori* all miracles except those for which they have made out an *à priori* canon and asserted it as exclusive of all others. In refutation of this illogical view (which, it is needless to say, still flourishes among Protestants proper) Dr. Newman dwells upon the various motives which lend antecedent probability to the hypothesis of ecclesiastical miracles. The argument from analogy—so fruitful on all religious themes since the master-work of Butler, a hundred and forty years ago—had already led him to reconsider his views on evidence ; it now furnishes him with the keynote of one of those richly-varied and elaborately-wrought intellectual symphonies, for so many of which we have to thank him in all the higher regions of thought ; and the *motivo*, in this case, is that " while the physical system bears such an analogy to the supernatural, viewed in its Biblical and ecclesiastical portions together, as forms a strong argument in defence of the supernatural, it is, on the other hand, so far unlike the Biblical portion of that supernatural, when that portion is taken by itself, as to protect the portion not Biblical from objections drawn from any differences observable between it and the portion which is Biblical." The reader will find this drawn out from page 147 to page 154. In the same connection we may also direct attention to the splendid generalization involved in the comparison of the Mosaic period in its relations to the Prophetical, with the period of Gospel history in its relation to the Ecclesiastical (p. 166 *et seq.*) ; but perhaps the most important part of the essay is that in which he actually developes the new antecedent motive of credibility, which, as our readers will be aware, is no other than the belief of the supernatural character and life of the Church in all ages. The Church is divine. She is different from all other societies of men, being possessed of supernatural powers, missionary and sacramental ; it is not unnatural, therefore, when we hear of a miracle, to remember such truths as these, and, on their account, to incline rather to believe a respectably established miracle than to reject it. A controversialist who refuses to credit a given miracle is frequently only expressing his own disbelief in the grace committed to the Church. On the other hand, one who realizes that the bodies of the saints were in their lifetime " the temple of the Holiest," and that they are to rise hereafter, will have little difficulty in believing they can work miracles. To sum up in the writer's own words :—

"If the miracles alleged are in harmony with the course of Divine Providence in the world, and with the analogy of faith as contained in
Scripture, if it is possible to account for them, if they are referable to a
known course or system, and especially if it can be shown that they are
recognized, promised, or predicted in Scripture, *very little positive evidence*
is necessary to induce us to listen to them, or even accept them, if not one
by one, at least viewed as a collective body." (p. 190.)

Nothing can be better than this; but we are conscious how much it
loses by being transplanted from the luxuriant pages where it stands. If
we had space we should like, moreover, to quote the whole of the commentary on our Lord's charge to His disciples at the end of S. Mark's
Gospel. It embodies one of those wonderful intuitions which mark the
difference between the genius and the common mind. It is not quite
correct, perhaps, to refer to the illative sense in connection with the
clearest demonstration ; that useful faculty works where daylight fails,
and dares, like the Homeric chief—

"Ire per excubias et se committere nocti."

But it may be permitted to suggest that the very force and farsightedness
of the mental eye may make its possessor a little impatient, and not quite
safe when he tries to explain to mortals of average vision that they do see,
when they feel conscious that they do not see. Winged creatures may fly
from point to point without touching the ground that lies between, but to
recommend that process to beings that are only blessed with legs would
be merely to invite a catastrophe.

At the end of the second essay the author examines with particular care
eight or nine miracles or miraculous narratives that occur in the history
of the early Church. His object in this critical examination is to show
that even believers in miracles are not disposed to accept indiscriminately
every alleged miracle, and also to give himself the opportunity of making
some general remarks for which he had hitherto found no place. In truth,
these appended dissertations are so many valuable lessons in historical
method. Let the reader note the completeness of each "case" in point of
materials, the resoluteness with which everything is got at first-hand and
from original sources, the skilful condensation, the analysis of the various
authorities as to weight and credibility, the patient statement of objections
and the judicial calmness of each conclusion as it irresistibly stands out in
the interests of truth and right.

Since the latter of these two essays was written, the controversy about
miracles has not stood still. Spinozism has been revived—as it will continue to be revived periodically, until the time when Antichrist shall begin
to deceive, by his lying wonders (if it were possible) even the elect ; for
Spinozism is, in plain language, at its first stage the ignoring of God
in His own universe, at its last the utter negation that there is a God. The
most brilliant writers of the age have done their best to teach the world
that science has no other meaning except unvarying sequence. English
positivism, represented by the " Westminster Review," and assisted by the
ablest of the smaller periodicals, analyzes everything into stark and bare
fact or " event," and is pitilessly severe on the weak superstition that looks

upwards for light, backwards for instruction, or forwards for consolation and hope. Mr. Lecky, if he writes as ably as Gibbon, and with a warmth that Gibbon neither possessed nor coveted, has the dangerous talent for building a theory out of too scanty a supply of facts, and insists, in argument that is chiefly reiteration, that men are ceasing to believe in miracles in proportion as the world advances in civilization.* Protestants are still trying to stand steady on their narrow plank, between the Church on the one hand and the encroaching tide of rationalism on the other. Mr. Babbage advances to their aid with his calculating machine, and thinks the machine of nature may have been so made, when it was started on its long day's work, that an odd miracle-wheel was provided here and there, to amaze the world and put out the philosophers. Mr. Mozley preaches Bampton Lectures, and hardly alludes to Dr. Newman, much less faces the canon of *à priori* probability that we quoted above. Bishop Fitzgerald, in the " Bible Dictionary," speaks at Dr. Newman, but mentions him by name only in a note. And both the Protestant champions display the old familiarity with Almighty God's " designs " and " purposes," which entitles them to pronounce with confidence as to what must be His action in the world. For our part we wish Dr. Newman would write a third essay on miracles, and still further develop the fertile canon in which he has grounded the antecedent probability of the miraculous on the continued existence of the unseen supernatural. The Catholic Church may claim to know as much about the " designs " of Providence as her opponents, and she maintains, not only that miracles happened in the early Church, but that they are happening every day. The antecedent probability of the miraculous in the lives of the saints would furnish a theme that Catholic genius might treat so as to display before men no small portion of the heavenly beauty of that divine faith which they so often despise. It is not strange, it is, rather, both fitting and beautiful, that those who have so far overcome the flesh, and brought back in their own persons the state of Paradise, should enjoy some of the privileges of Paradise, and have dominion over matter. A saint is more to God than the laws of nature, and the souls of the " little ones," who see His wonders and love Him the more, have not yet ceased to be the special objects of His Providence. We should never be afraid of the miraculous in the lives of the saints. Far from being troubled at the number of the wonders that are related in them, we ought rather to expect them, to long for them, to welcome them, and to glory in them. Far from trying captiously or timidly to explain them away, or to excuse them, we should calmly and reasonably, but gladly, uphold them, and profess our conviction, not only of their possibility, but also of their probability. We do not believe that " the world " is growing to disregard miracles ; it is only that Mr. Lecky's " world " is growing to be more and more like a certain old world of which it is written, that to it Christ crucified was foolishness. But Catholic men of science and the faithful of every degree should do their best to prove that they still believe.

---

* Rationalism in Europe, vol. i. chap. ii.

The Ammergau Passion Play (reprinted by permission from the " Times "),
   *with some introductory remarks on the Origin and Development of
   Miracle Plays, and some Practical Hints for the use of intending
   Visitors.* By the Rev. MALCOLM MACCOLL, M.A., Chaplain to the
   Right Honourable Lord Napier, K.T. Rivingtons, 1870. Second
   Edition.

Art in the Mountains ; the Story of the Passion Play. By HENRY BLACK-
   BURN. Sampson Low, Son, and Marston. 1870.

THE least praise we can give to these two books is, that they are very
   pleasant reading on a more than ordinarily interesting subject.
But they deserve a somewhat fuller notice. The interest awakened throughout England by the Ober-Ammergau Passion Play during the course of last
summer was a sign of the times. The accounts published in the daily press
and periodicals were no less so. That the interest was no passing curiosity
may be inferred from the subsequent publication of two such volumes as
those we are noticing.

   The Passion Play which forms their subject is no novelty. It has been
renewed at intervals of ten years for more than two centuries ; it had been
visited by tourists ; it is to be found mentioned in the appropriate corner of
Murray. But could any good thing come out of Nazareth ? It is only
recently that we have emerged in part from the atmosphere of that dense
prejudice which was assured beforehand, that any distinctive custom of a
Catholic population must be corrupt, superstitious, and the direct fruit of
ignorance. It is but lately that any large portion of educated Protestant
Englishmen has been prepared to feel and to own its admiration for an
essentially and exceptionally Catholic people, on the score of " their honesty,
their intelligence, and their religious earnestness," qualities of which the
Rev. Mr. MacColl speaks as characteristic of the people of Ober-Ammergau,
and to which he even appeals as tests of the fruits of the play (p. 82). It
needed a spirit hitherto uncommon amongst our countrymen to describe the
performance of a Mystery play, as Mr. Henry Blackburn does, as an instance
of " a whole population, from old men to children, agreed to do a noble act in
a noble way " (Art in the Mountains, p. 62). Even Mr. Blackburn's book,
indeed, contains one passage, which we must consider somewhat of a blemish,
savouring of the old state of mind. Instancing recent religious plays in
Spain and Belgium, " sanctioned by priestly patrons and (like the ceremonials
of their church) made a vehicle for tinsel and display," he passes a sweeping
judgment both on " such experiences and the early history of religious plays
both in our own country and in Germany " (pp. 21-22). Mr. MacColl has
studied the question more conscientiously. In an introductory chapter he
traces the religious drama from the earliest Christian times to our own day.
He notices first, that " a considerable dramatic element enters into the composition of all the early Christian liturgies, and still more into the circum-

stances attending the celebration of the principal festivals of the Church ;"
but "as soon as Christianity emerged from the catacombs and found itself in
the enjoyment of freedom, it made a bolder and more direct attempt to
enlist the sympathies of its converts by means of dramatic representation.
We find Greek tragedies on sacred subjects almost coeval with the establishment of Christianity, and there is direct evidence of their representation at
Constantinople. One of these is the "Dying Christ" of St John Chrysostom,
which was acted in church, partly in *tableaux vivants*, and partly in dialogue"
(pp. 8–9). Of the English mystery plays he does not speak highly. They
soon "degenerated into buffoonery, and were frequently placed under the
ban of the Church, as tending to bring sacred things into contempt" (p. 11);
but of the religious drama in Germany he gives a very different account. Of
a specimen from the 14th century, of which he gives a detailed description,
he speaks thus: —

"It is impossible to read the 'Tragedy of the Ten Virgins' without being
struck with the healthy and elevated morality which runs through it. It
may be assumed, I suppose, that the drama of a period is a fair index of its
moral and religious condition. If this be granted, we may argue that the
state of society which is depicted in the 'Tragedy of the Ten Virgins' could
not have been so hopelessly bad as some declamations on the vice and
ignorance of the 'Dark Ages' would lead us to believe. When we reflect,
too, that the 'Tragedy' is the composition of a Dominican preacher, we may
infer that mediæval divines were not so incapable of preaching the pure
Gospel as they are sometimes represented."

With regard to the Ammergau Play, both authors have given interesting
accounts of the routes to the picturesque Ammerthal, of the village itself,
(though neither seems to us to appreciate sufficiently its extreme beauty,
cleanliness, or look of piety, with its cross-crowned gables, and sacred
frescoes on the house fronts), and of the exciting day before the performance,
with the perpetual inflowing crowd of vehicles of every kind, and picturesque
pilgrims on foot. Then follow detailed descriptions of the Passion Play itself,
with its various scenes, and the types represented before each in *tableaux
vivants*. Most of our readers will have read either Mr. MacColl's description,
which appeared originally in the *Times*, or some other of the many accounts
by newspaper correspondents which appeared during last summer, amongst
which may be especially particularized the acutely observant and gracefully
written letters communicated to the *Spectator* by a lady. There is but
one voice of astonishment and admiration. "Those *tableaux* are quite
wonderful for their vivid realism and artistic grace," writes Mr. MacColl
(p. 53). "Here (in the *tableau* of the giving of the manna), as in some other
tableaux, there were nearly 300 figures in every variety of posture, yet the
most minute inspection failed to discover a single ungainly attitude or
ungraceful *pose*, and they were all—even mites of children three years old—
as motionless as statues" (p. 60). Of the acting of the indignities offered to
our Lord before Caiphas, he says, "The Gospel narrative is strictly adhered
to in all its details, and the whole scene is acted with great power, but with
an entire absence of anything approaching to irreverence. The conduct
of the soldiers and other persecutors is, of course, irreverent enough, but the

object of their indignities preserves such a majestic calm, and such dignified bearing through it all, that pity, mingled with indignation and awe, absorbs the feelings of the audiencè " (p. 66). So with Mr. Blackburn. Of the entrance into Jerusalem, he says, "The effect was different from anything to be witnessed on the modern stage. Every eye was turned to the grand figure of Joseph Mair (the Christus), as he slowly dismounted from the ass and came into the midst of the crowd. · It was as if the finest picture of the Saviour that had ever been painted by the early Italian masters was moving before us" (p. 72). "The number of persons on the stage must have been nearly 300, amongst whom were many little children ; but there was not one of that number who reminded the audience that they were witnessing a mimic scene" (p. 80). "Two of the principal Munich actors, who had come to see the play for the first time, confessed that they had never seen such excellent acting" (p. 84). Another scene he declares to have been "absolutely sublime" (p. 109).

Of the whole effect of the Passion Play Mr. MacColl gives the following judgment, and Mr. Blackburn expressly endorses it:—

"I went to see it with very mixed feelings. From what I had heard and read, I was prepared for a striking exhibition, but also half prepared for some rude shocks to one's natural sense of religious propriety. So impossible did it seem to represent on a public stage and in a worthy manner the sublime story of Gethsemane and Golgotha. Well, I have seen it, and I shall go home with the conviction that the thing is not impossible where a vivid faith and an intense devotion are combined in the representation. I have never seen so affecting a spectacle or one more calculated to draw out the best and purest feelings of the heart." (p. 80.)

Of its teaching power, he says, with a candour which does him infinite honour:—

"I am not ashamed to confess, for my own part, that I have realized here, with a vividness I never felt before, the marvellous unity which binds together the Old Testament and the New, so that a series of compositions, separated from each other by every circumstance of time and place and authorship, are instinctively felt to be one Book, teaching one high morality, telling the same tale of sorrowful hope, and pointing to one central mysterious Figure, in whom type and psalm and sacrifice find their meet accomplishment." (p. 82.)

We must add to what we have said of Mr. Blackburn's "Art in the Mountains" that it is quite an artist's book, printed with beautiful paper and type, and illustrated with the prettiest sketches. Of the portraits of the different characters which he gives, we are able to give personal evidence that they are excellent likenesses.

Ecclesia. Church Problems considered in a Series of Essays. Edited by
HENRY ROBERT REYNOLDS, D.D., President of Cheshunt College; Fellow
of University College, London. London: Hodden & Stoughton. 1870.

THIS volume is a remarkable sign of the times. It is a collection of
Essays on church subjects, written by nine Protestant Nonconformists,
and edited by the principal of a Nonconformist college. It is evidently
written on the plan of the volumes which have appeared of late years, and
of which the well-known "Essays and Reviews," the exponent of the
extreme Broad or Rationalistic school, was the first, and, indeed, set the
fashion. It has now been followed, we believe, by every school of theological
opinion in England of any appreciable size. The Ritualists have for several
years brought out an annual volume entitled "The Church and the World."
The old High Church party, of whom Dr. Hook, the Dean of Chichester,
may be taken as the representative, have lately followed suit. There has
been, if we remember right, a volume representing the "Low Church," or
Evangelical school. And here is a similar manifesto from the Protestant
dissenters.

Of this last we are bound to say, that not only is it fully equal to the
others, both in external appearance, type, paper, &c., and in the more refined
proofs of mental culture, learning, scholarship, thought, refinement of mind,
&c.; but, what is much more remarkable, that some of the writers at least
incline much more strongly to what may be called the sacramental or ecclesiastical view of Christianity than the mass of Church of England men will go
with them.

This, as we have already said, is a sign of the times. Some forty years
ago, when the Oxford Tracts first made their appearance, the assertions that
it is mainly through the sacraments that the grace of God is vouchsafed and
assured to Christians, and that valid ordination is essential to the effectual
administration of the sacraments, appeared to Church of England men in
general so "extreme" and paradoxical, that at first they were hardly inclined
to consider them. Already these views are admitted, more or less consistently,
by the great majority of Church of England clergy, and by a large number
of the laity. This volume proves that the subject is already arresting serious
attention among the Protestant dissenters, who, beyond all question, forty
years ago would have been inclined to laugh at the very mention of it.
We cannot but regard this as a proof that truth has só far come into
direct collision with falsehood among our countrymen, and that the result
is that truth has already, in a great measure, commended itself. Should the
progress in the next thirty years be as great as it has been in the last forty,
how different will the state of religious opinion in England be in the year
1900 from what it was in 1800.

We value this volume, among other reasons, as a refutation of the claim,
so preposterous in itself, and so boldly advanced by the Ritualist party in
the Established Church, that they, together with the Greek schismatics, are

branches of the Catholic Church. Their custom has been to take for granted that no other Protestant body except the Anglican can make any claim, on their principles, to the Catholic name. They say, We claim to have valid ordination, and we hold what we maintain to be the primitive doctrine; therefore we are Catholics. Well, the writers of these essays say exactly the same. They also claim valid ordination, and maintain that, in the Primitive Church, the ordinations were the same as theirs, and they also profess to prove that they hold the primitive doctrine, as well as that they retain the primitive mode of ordination. We really do not see anything to make a substantial distinction between the two cases.

Lastly, the volume will of course be useful to English Catholics, thrown, as they necessarily are, into dealings with Protestants of the Nonconformist sects, even more frequently than with Anglicans. For the large towns, in which of necessity Catholic churches are now almost exclusively placed, are exactly the places in which the Nonconformists are more numerous than the Anglicans. We need hardly say that a Catholic who knows the ground taken by educated Dissenters, and the arguments by which they think it is to be defended, has a great advantage in a conference with them. Nothing so much destroys our influence with any thoughtful man as that he should discover, when we come to converse with him, that we do not know what he holds. It is this which makes it really difficult to a Catholic, in any real sense of the word, to reason with an ordinary Protestant. The man is so absolutely in the dark as to what the Catholic believes and practises, that before the subject can really be discussed before him, he must be informed as to the facts, and this usually is found impossible, because most Protestants assume that they know better than any Catholic what the Catholic Church does teach and practise. Into this error we are hardly likely to fall. But the effect would be in some measure the same if, in discussing, for instance, with the writers of these essays, we were to take for granted that their first principle is, that each man must make a system for himself out of Scripture, and Scripture alone, which unquestionably has been the common system of Protestants, and especially of Nonconformists, in times past.

The two first of these essays are entitled respectively " Primitive Ecclesia," and " The Idea of the Church historically developed." They both assume that a Christian Church ought to be ordered and administered as were the churches founded by the Apostles, and existing in their times. They then turn to Scripture and to the earliest Christian remains to show what, in their opinion, was the actual constitution of these proto-primitive churches, and their inference of course is, that the Church in each city was a separate distinct organization, with no necessary connection with any other ; with a constitution, on the whole, highly democratic, and with officers chosen by the people and ordained by the ministers. This is, we need hardly say, the idea of a modern Protestant Congregational society. The fundamental difference between them and a Catholic in their mode of conceiving of a primitive society, is that the Catholic begins from the top and goes down, these gentlemen begin from beneath and go up. That is, the Catholic takes for granted the powers and commission given by our Lord himself to S.

Peter and the College of the Apostles, and in the exercise of which they were guided and directed by the Holy Spirit. These writers assume, of course, that the Apostles were aided by Divine direction in constituting the Church, but assume also that, when constituted, they left it to itself, not during their own lives (they would admit that, as long as the Apostle lived, by whom any particular church was founded, he would continue to exercise some control over it), but as soon as they died.

. Thus the difference really is much the same as that which exists between men who imagine that God created, indeed, the world, but then left it to be governed without His interference, and those who know that He is ever its governor as truly as He was its creator. So the essayists admit that the Primitive churches were founded by apostolic authority. We know that all churches have ever since been governed by it. But the truly strange thing is that the essayists take for granted that the apostolic authority and office were to die with the original Apostles, without thinking it necessary in any way to attempt to prove it. It seems to us, therefore, that in discussion with them, and those who think with them, our principal business is to insist on the necessity of the perpetual continuance of the authority and office originally given to the Apostles.

Of course the answer to this will be, that the first Apostles had miraculous gifts, which have not been given to all their successors—a poor answer, but the best of which the case admits.

With regard to the authority of the successors of S. Peter, these writers seem to take much the same view as the mass of Anglican writers have done.

The essay on "The Religious Life and Christian Society" contains a number of most interesting remarks on the monastic life. We wish we had room to extract them. The writer does full justice to the great motive of the monastic life, the intense contemplation of the Lord Jesus, overmastering love to Him as the reigning principle of life, and the desire to imitate Him. (See, in particular, pages 166 to 177.) He admits "To live as He lived, poor, homeless, wayfaring, and apart from domestic bonds and joys, was the ideal of Christian life, which the first ages cherished, and it would be easy to show from the writings and sermons of the great monks through the whole monastic period how this remained the supreme inspiration—nay, it is vivid in many a great heart among "the religious" to this day."

So wonderful is the power of prejudice that the writer believes there is a higher life than this. He means, if we do not mistake his meaning, which we have very sincerely tried not to do, such a life as is led by the mass of the Protestant clergy and religious people among the laity in our own day. Not that he is satisfied with that, for he says " we judge these men as if the pure form of the truth were ours at last. We shall live to be as [much] ashamed of the impurities we have mixed with it as . . . . We have not yet reached the point which might justify us in judging the monastic life by our standard, if we compare it with the standard of Christ, let us place ourselves beside the monks as we judge them, and own for them and for ourselves a double shame." He holds (we conceive) that the monastic age lasted to the Reformation, then began what he calls the doctrinal æra, better than it, but not perfect— lastly, " the age is coming, nay, is already come, which will be as startled at the image of Christ which we have been presenting during the doctrinal æra which is closing, as we are at the image which was presented in a monastic life," &c. He believes that a new form of Christianity is now to be exhibited to the world as much superior to evangelical Protestantism as that again was superior to the Christianity of S. Augustine and S. Bernard. Strange as this is, there is an evident earnestness in the writer's tone, which makes it impossible to doubt that he really thinks what he says.

The Editor supplies a thoughtful and very learned article on the " Forgiveness and Absolution of Sins." He begins by pointing out the degree to which ideas have been confused by ambiguous language, and then says that " the forgiveness of sins " is an instance, being sometimes taken for " a principle and action of the Divine will—a law of the Divine operation," and sometimes for " an human experience." He lays down that " in this matter the free Churches of England (with few exceptions) hold fundamentally the great revelation which is expressed alike in the writings of the early fathers, in the decrees of the Council of Trent, in the thirty-nine articles, and in the Westminster and Augsburg Confessions." Any one who knows the common language of Protestant writers on this subject, may well be amazed to find an English Nonconformist minister laying it down that upon the forgiveness of sins all these are substantially agreed. Many Protestants hold not only that the Catholic Church denies the remission of sins through Christ, but that the bringing in of that doctrine was the fundamental gain effected by the Reformation. We heartily wish we had space to enter into the parts of this able essay which differ from, and still more the parts which agree with, the teaching of the Catholic Church. Of course the author denies the power of absolution by the priests of the Catholic Church, and he goes on to show unanswerably that even if that were admitted, it would be absurd to suppose that the Anglican clergy are priests in the same sense as the Catholic priests. But we have filled our space, and to do justice to the essay would require not a short notice, but an article of full length.

The only other essay on which we shall speak is that on " The Doctrine or the Real Presence and of the Lord's Supper." It is indeed a very remarkable one. The author has studied the subject. He has evidently thought over it. The prejudices of his education have, as yet, been too strong to allow him to come to the truth. But it is to be remembered he approaches it, not as it is our blessed privilege to do, led by the hand of the Church whose teaching we know cannot err, but groping his way in the dark. He says, what is no doubt true, that the mass of his sect are " Zwinglians of the purest type." They hold that in the Eucharist Christians receive bread and wine merely in memory of the body and blood of their Lord. This view he opposes, as he does also the teaching of the Catholic Church. He "passionately resents " the notion that he and those who think with him deny the doctrine of the " Real Presence." What he holds is, so far as we can understand it, the Anglican doctrine, namely, that Christ is present not in the elements but in the rite—that He is " really, and indeed received by the faithful in the supper," but that there is no change in the elements, and therefore that after consecration they are not to be worshipped. He shows that this was the opinion of the founders, and early members of the Independent and other Protestant sects, although as always happens in such sects, the present members of them have fallen off into mere denial of the Real Presence, forgetting the theory which they substituted for it.

Here we must end, not because we have said all we wish, but because we have no space for more, and we can promise our readers that in this volume, although they will find much which unhappily differs from the one Truth, they will also find much that shows that the authors are feeling after it, and much to inspire thought and interest in a Catholic reader.

The Men and Women of the English Reformation, from the days of Wolsey to the death of Cranmer; Papal and Anti-Papal notables. By the Author of " The Monastic Houses of England, their Accusers and Defenders." London : Washbourne. 1870. Part I. pp. 64.

THE author takes as his motto " Time unveils all Truth," and his work, so far as it is yet published, verifies it. We, in these days, can hardly imagine to ourselves the astonishment and indignation with which many of his statements would have been received, say a century ago ; when the Life of Cardinal Pole (merely because less unjust to him than people were wont to be), excited such violent indignation that a dignitary of the Established Church, not content with writing what he deemed an answer to it, actually called on the government of the day to take legal measures against the Catholic author. The author says :—

" In writing biographies and incidents of certain periods, authors have seldom escaped the accusation of prejudice. The interweaving of individual feeling in a web so complicated as that in which simple truth is too often confined, has hitherto presented many difficulties in unravelling the *real* in place of its opposite. Hitherto writers of history have mostly dealt in eulogy or depreciation of the by-gone, as well as of the various notables of the period.

" To the end of time the past of man must teach the future—to respect, practise, reverence, or avoid. Long before the Mosaic dispensation the wise men of Egypt instituted a laudable and beneficial custom in their country. It became a law and afterwards a *cultus* in reference to deceased celebrities. The kings and chief nobles were subjected to a *post-mortem* examination of character, in which the reputation of the dead should be submitted to investigation, and the fiat of desert or unworthiness pronounced by chosen censors, without fear and without favour. Whether the idea was ever carried out in its integrity, the mausolea of the Pyramids have never disclosed, nor has Champollion succeeded in elucidating it by the papyri found amidst the mummies, which date from the days of Sesostris to the time when the hair of an Egyptian queen was set by a Latin poet in the assembly of the stars. It was a grand idea nevertheless—rather a noble ordinance, standing not only as mediator between the past and the present, but furnishing securities for the future. No station amongst ' our Fathers by the Nile,' freed the dead from the ordeal which must have been, in unsophisticated times, a potent incentive to virtue, as well as a powerful menace to crime. Imbued with the spirit of a law like this, the historian now-a-days should journey. The milestones of truth are at hand in our national records, the stepping-off places from the continental archives are almost as facilely present. Peculiar sources of information have been made use of in this work, under the most kindly and favourable auspices.

"Placed in such circumstances, an unprejudiced historian, entering on a field not hitherto impartially trodden, may give himself for his task fairly to record the evil as well as the good qualities, the failings as well as the virtues of the ancestors of our race, with the noble hope of giving an unswayed book to enlighten their descendants."

We have made rather a long extract that our readers may judge for them selves of the author's style. The impression produced upon ourselves by a page of fine writing like this, is, we confess, like that of walking in one of the mists of which we have just now many more than we wish. The general meaning of the writer, like the general direction of the road, is clear. The passage we have quoted means, evidently enough, that the author is resolved to write, fairly and impartially, the truth with regard to the men and women of the English Reformation, without fear and without favour, and after examining with all diligence the original authorities. But what the separate sentences and clauses mean we are not so ambitious as to aim at understanding. We presume the author knew exactly what "the milestones of truth," and "the stepping-off places from the continental archives" may mean. The meaning however is too deep for simple men like us.

We regret this, because, so far as the specimen of this work now before us enables us to judge, we think that the author really has done what he has promised. These few pages really contain a great amount of curious and useful information, gathered together with evident care, and we think with great fairness. Happily also, as it seems to us, in the body of his work the author has, as a general rule, been too much intent upon giving us facts to allow himself to indulge in fine writing, so that what he says is really not too finely written to be understood. For ourselves we expect to read the future numbers of this work with real pleasure and profit. The writer has evidently examined the authorities on which the history of these times must depend with the most laudable diligence. He gives us much valuable information, and a good deal which, to ourselves at least, is new. The matter is arranged under the following heads:—1. Henry VIII. His Love Correspondence with Anna Boleyn. The letters given under this head from the originals in the Vatican library are very interesting. So far as we have read them they would reflect honour upon the writer and his love, but for the one damning fact that they were written by a married man. 2. The Divorce Question. 3. Arrival of Campeggio. Public Procession. 4. The Trial of Katharine. 5. The Regular Clergy and the People. 6. The Sweating Sickness. 7. Wolsey and his Contemporaries. We doubt whether there is one of these heads upon which almost every reader will not find in these few pages many facts unknown to him, and well worth knowing. The book is not a continued narrative; it would have been more correctly described as " A Collection of Facts Elucidating the Times of the Reformation," or " Commonplace Book of the Reformation," for in truth it very much reminds us of such a collection of facts as might be made by a careful student reading the original records, and comparing them with modern history.

Take one example :—

" Burnet represents Campeggio as an 'immoral man even in his old age, bringing his bastard son with him to the English court.' It did not suit Burnet's policy to make any particular inquiry as to Campeggio's public or private life. Campeggio was an Italian gentleman of ancient family. He had been married in early life ; and, on the death of his wife, in 1509, he resolved to take holy orders. In private life he was known as a virtuous, good man, a distinguished scholar, a theologian, and a statesman. He not alone attracted the attention of the Pontiffs, but of several neighbouring sovereigns. He discharged some important diplomatic missions to the entire satisfaction of a discriminating master, Leo X. He enjoyed the apparent friendship of Henry VIII. and Wolsey. In 1517 he was created a cardinal, and then entered zealously into the service of the Papacy. On his arrival in England he was accompanied by his second son, Rodolfo, on whom Henry conferred the honour of knighthood. Rodolfo was a poet and a musician, and consequently an acceptable guest to King Henry. So much for Burnet's relation of the ' cardinal and his bastard.' " (p. 43.)

Nothing could be more characteristic of Burnet than at once to jump to the conclusion that a cardinal who was accompanied by a son must, of necessity, be " an immoral man," and his son a " bastard." It was his rule to take for granted as facts, any conjectures he made discreditable to persons whom he hated, and then to assert them as if he had ascertained their truth. We do not suppose he meant to publish falsehoods. Rather he never thought any proof necessary, if the statement was to the discredit of those whom, for their political and religious principles, he hated.

One omission we would earnestly beg the author to supply in future " Parts " of his book. A work so full of facts must derive its value solely from that of the authorities on which they are given. Otherwise each statement really comes to be nothing more than the opinion of an anonymous writer, whose manner gives the reader an impression that he is speaking accurately from book. How is it possible to quote a fact upon such authority ? Now we do not see so much as one reference in support of all the multitude of interesting and important facts here stated. It is an omission which the evident learning of the writer will enable him easily to supply, and which, till supplied, really destroys the value of his work. With this hint we wish him farewell, hoping to meet again before long.

Anglican Friends in Council ; a Conversation on Papal Infallibility.
London : Burns & Oates.

A LITTLE pamphlet of twenty pages, well worth careful considera-tion, it seems to us, by all who hold the theory of the Unionists,— that the Roman and Anglican Churches are branches of the one Catholic

Church. It is a conversation between three Anglican clergymen holding that view, and the more advanced urges that the late definition and the anathema against those who deny it are facts quite inconsistent with the theory. In passing, the theory of Mr. Cobb (the author of "The Kiss of Peace") is discussed, although none of the three are disposed to accept it. This is "that the Church of Rome is really and truly the one Catholic Church, but yet that we, who are out of communion with her, are not in schism, but only in a state of justifiable separation." Mr. Cobb has lately written a letter arguing that the infallibility of the Pope is not a matter capable of being defined, because it is "a question of fact, not of faith;" that it is "a purely rational question, and by reason only can it be determined." What he appears to mean is that historical difficulties may be raised, by showing, or pretending to show, that Popes actually have contradicted each other on matters of faith, and that such difficulties (real or apparent) must preclude the Church from judging in this matter in the same way that she judges in matters which altogether transcend our reason (such as the doctrine of the Blessed Trinity, Transubstantiation, and others). The answer to this is crushing—one of the friends says, "He must surely have forgotten that there are some matters of faith which are quite open to attack on historical grounds (not of course that there is any real doubt about them). Such, for instance, as that our Lord was crucified by order of Pontius Pilate; this is a fact of history, but it is contained in the Apostles' Creed, and is most strictly a part of the Catholic Faith."

The conversation ends with some remarks which cleverly illustrate the real nature of the obstacles which tend to prevent Anglicans from fairly judging of the Catholic Church. First, C., the married country rector, is obliged to go. He says :—

" I think I see my wife coming to call me. I promised her I would come and help to prepare the school-room for the festival the children are going to have this evening; and I have got to see the parish doctor, and learn what he thinks of two of my people who are ill; and I have undertaken to get a set of vestments made for a friend of mine who is just going to introduce them into his church, and they are being made here under my own eye, and I must go and see they are doing it all rightly; and there are one or two poor people I ought to see, and I must manage to call on the squire of my parish, and try to conciliate him a little. He is a very prejudiced man, and would not come to church this morning; and then I have other things to do before evening service. And, indeed, I have had enough of controversy for one day; if I did not relieve myself by attending to parochial duties, I should almost go distracted by thinking about controversy " (p. 16).

This is no exaggeration. Most of us must have known good and earnest men who, so far from concealing from themselves, avow to others, that when doubts as to their position force themselves on their minds they overcome them by active work. We have known instances of friends blaming clergymen who have become converts for not doing so. And yet what is this but making work a dissipation? How does it differ in principle from the conduct of those who avoid serious thought by plunging in a whirl of amusements? In both cases people are putting away the question—"What will

God have me to do"? In the Catholic Church the first recommendation given to a man who seriously doubts what the will of God is, would be, to go into a retreat for the purpose of making up his mind. Among many Anglicans the advice given in such cases is, throw yourself so much into work as to have no time to consider it. We hardly know a fact which more deserves to be seriously weighed by religious Anglicans. When Saul of Tarsus asked, "Lord, what wilt Thou have me to do?" he was sent into the city, and there, without sight, and neither eating nor drinking, was three days alone with God. There are those who would have blamed him for not plunging into such oceans of work as to prevent his question pressing on his mind. Another of the three friends determines to read a classical English author, "I don't like light reading, but I really appreciate some of these authors; I find nothing so completely restores the balance of one's mind as literary pursuits." The third tells how he has been perplexed by a remark dropped by a Roman Catholic gentleman, who said, quite abruptly as if thinking aloud, "If the loaves and fishes belonged to us instead of the Anglican Church, I wonder how many of these objectors to the Pope's infallibility would remain"? He is sure he is not consciously influenced by his position, but fears he may be influenced unconsciously, and resolves to go home and think over this. " I was going to add that it is impossible not to fear that worldly motives may act unconsciously, when they are so strong as they undoubtedly are in my case."

History of the Foundation of the Order of the Visitation; and the Lives of Mademoiselle de la Fayette, and several other members of the Order. Baltimore: Kelly. 1870. (pp. xiv.—271.)

THIS very valuable anonymous volume is evidently the result of a meritorious zeal for the glory of God and for the honour of a religious order which, as the author says, has " shared, for almost three-quarters of a century, the burden of Catholic female education in the United States, whose pupils are spread over the length and breadth of the land, and whose slow but steady increase promises it a still wider field for future cultivation." It contains, first, the " History of the Foundation of the Order of the Visitation," extracted from the French Life of S. Francis de Sales, by the Curé of S. Sulpice, the Abbé Hamon. This occupies ninety-seven pages. Then follows the Life of Mademoiselle de la Fayette, in religion Mother Louise Angélique. This is published, for the first time, " from the Annals of the Order," to which additions have been made from a letter to herself, written by the Jesuit Father Caussin, who had been confessor to Louis XIII., when Mademoiselle de la Fayette was maid of honour to his queen, Anne of Austria; and who relates the circumstances which led to her taking the veil. Some things also are taken from the Memoirs of Madame de Motteville, her intimate friend, and from the History of

R 2

Louis XIII., by P. Griffet. We have read this life with peculiar interest. Apart from its strictly religious value as a work of spiritual reading, the glimpse it affords of the interior of the court of Louis XIII. under the administration of Richelieu, gives it considerable historical value ; and the author, so far as we can judge, has used the materials with laudable diligence and judgment. The next life is that of Dona Theresa de Bourke, in religion Mother Mary Anne Theresa. This is taken from the Annals of the Convent of the Visitation at Rome. Her family was one of that noble band of Irish emigrants who, in the seventeenth and eighteenth centuries, made the name of Ireland illustrious in all the Catholic countries of Europe, at the very time when the Catholic Irishman was trodden under foot as a Pariah in the land of his fathers. Her father held high office in the Spanish court. There is a curious account of her adventures when only ten years old. She was taken prisoner by Algerine corsairs on her voyage from the South of France to Spain. The vessel of their captors was wrecked on the coast of Africa, and she was enslaved by a Moor : the details of her sufferings and rescue are very curious. She entered the Order of the Visitation in Rome when twenty-six years of age, and died on the Friday in Passion week, 1792, aged 83. Then follows the Life of Alexandra Mackinnon, in religion Sister Mary Frances Joseph, a Protestant lady of high Scotch family, from the Annals of the Convent of the Visitation at Westbury. She was a member of the family of her brother, the chief of the clan MacLeod, at Dunvegan Castle, when it was visited by Dr. Johnson on his " Visit to the Hebrides." The Doctor records that " Lady MacLeod, who had lived many years in England, was newly come hither with her son and four daughters, who knew all the arts of southern elegance and all the modes of English economy. Here, therefore, we settled, and did not spoil the present hour with the thoughts of departure." Modern facilities of travelling have made the Western Highlands as easily accessible to English travellers as any part of England. It is not easy for us to imagine the widely different state of things in those days. Johnson's journey really was what he evidently felt it— an act of strange daring and endurance. He says, " The hospitality of this remote region is like that of the golden age ; we have found ourselves treated at every house, as if we came to confer a benefit." " At Dunvegan I had tasted lotus, and was in danger of forgetting that I was ever to part, till Mr. Boswell sagely reproved me for my sluggishness and softness. I had no very forcible defence to make, and we agreed to pursue our journey." Alexandra used, in after-life, to tell how he one day found her reading, and asked, " What are you reading, Miss ? " " Burnett's History of England," she replied. " It is a book filled with falsehoods and calumnies against the Catholic religion," said Dr. Johnson, adding with emphasis, by way of a play on the name, " Burn it." In 1773 she married MacKinnon, a distant relative. After some years of marriage and the birth of two children, she refused to live with him—the author says, " We will not enter into the details," and leaving her children, returned to her mother, accompanied her to France, and there, although a Protestant, for the sake of retirement, became boarder in a convent. There is a curious account of her gradual conversion to the Catholic Faith. She remained there till driven home by the Revolution. There is an amusing account of her acquaintance with a young Protestant lawyer in London, in after-days Dr. Griffith, the Vicar-Apostolic. She ultimately became a religious in the Convent at Shepton Mallet, afterwards removed to Westbury, where she died in 1841. There is a very curious account of the conversion and death of her son. Next follows the Life of Mary Theresa Weld, sister to the Cardinal, in religion Sister Mary de Sales, from the Annals of the Convent at Westbury. She died as lately as January, 1866, wanting only five days of ninety-two years. Two of her nephews are now Catholic bishops in England. The last is the life of a lay-sister, Mary Raymondina Jullian, from the Annals of the Convent at Chambery. She died in 1713, aged 70.

We have said enough to prove that this is no ordinary volume. Apart from its religious interest, it contains a very considerable amount of very curious biographical and historical information; but it is also full of valuable spiritual reading. It seems to us very decidedly above the average standard of literary merit, both in the translation of the large part taken from the French, and in the original part. We do not mean that it would not be easy to point out many blemishes in both, and in particular the style has less of simplicity than we quite like. But in these respects it is a decided improvement on most books of the same class. The type might be better than it is. It does not equal that of some of the works we have lately received from New York. But these blemishes are forgotten in the great interest of the volume, and the originality of most of its contents. In pages 97 to 100 we have an account to delight any Catholic heart, of the progress and success of the Order in the United States, where it has now sixteen convents, the first founded in 1817, the last in 1868. Esto perpetua.

A Plain Account of the English Bible; from the earliest Times of its Translation to the present Day. By JOHN HENRY BLUNT, M.A., F.S.A., &c. Rivingtons. 1870.

THE "Protestant tradition" (to borrow a phrase which Dr. Newman has made almost a household word) is that, until the change of religion under Henry VIII. and Elizabeth, the Bible did not exist in England. Happily, the more studious class of Anglicans have risen above this thick layer of mist, and the little book before us will help to disabuse others. Its author was formerly Professor of Divinity at Cambridge. He is ludicrously anti-Catholic, has published a history of the Reformation, and is as bitterly Protestant as any one could wish to see. Neither is he in any degree connected with the Unionist party. What he says, therefore, will gain a hearing even with Protestants.

His little book was occasioned by the steps lately taken about the revision of the Protestant translation. His own tone is shown by one little outbreak of insolence. He says, " The venerable Pusey—our greatest Hebrew scholar and theologian—together with Dr. Newman and some other Dissenters, declined to accept the invitation thus sent to them, but the remainder began their work of revision on June 22nd, 1870." This impertinence is unworthy of a man who, from his situation at least, ought to be a gentleman. Nothing has done more to alienate the mass of the English people from the Establishment than the fact that many of its clergy, in times past, have considered that their position, as the clergy " by law established," entitled them to treat everybody else with rudeness. It is hardly prudent, one would say, to go on with that in the present state of society and feeling. However, that is a matter for their own consideration. A similar tone of gratuitous insolence runs through this little book, whenever the writer finds or makes occasion to refer in any way to the Catholic Church. For instance, he allows his spleen so far to get the better of his common sense as to say (p. 98), " an English Bible was provided for that sect by the Divines of the Flemish College of Douay."

This childish petulance makes the testimony of Mr. Blunt against the common Protestant tradition even more valuable. Thus he says (p. 31), " It is sad to be obliged to warn the reader that there are gross exaggerations in much that has been written about the translation of the Bible. Spalatinus, the authority who is responsible for Tyndale's linguistic accomplishments, immediately after adds, that the English were so eager for the Gospel as to affirm that they would buy a New Testament even if they had to give 100,000 pieces of money for it. So when Cranmer wrote to Cromwell that his sanction of a translation gave him more pleasure than £1,000, Grafton immediately reported it as £10,000 " (the reference for this is *Brit. Mus. MSS. Clop.* E. v. fol. 358, 349). The fact is, these stories about the enormous cost of Bibles before the change of religion have been quite a favourite subject of invention and exaggeration with Protestant writers. Not a few of them are amusingly exposed in a volume published by a very Protestant clergyman near forty years ago, " Maitland's Dark Ages." But we must not lengthen this article by indulging ourselves in any quotation from that well-known, very learned, and amusing work.

Then our author quotes Sir Thomas More, to prove not only that there were English Bibles before the time of Wickliffe (who is commonly supposed to have made the first of them), but that they were still to be had in his own time, and were allowed to be held by all men. The words are—

" The whole Bible was, long before Wickliffe's days, by virtuous and well-learned men, translated into the English tongue, and by good and godly people, with devotion and soberness, well and reverendly read."

And then, speaking of the canon passed in Convocation under Archbishop Arundel, which forbids Wickliffe's translation, he says :—

" This order neither forbade the translations to be read that were done of old, before Wickliffe's days, nor condemned his because it was new, but because it was naught " [*i.e.* bad].

On another occasion the same learned and well-informed writer says :—

" I have showed you that the clergy keep no Bible from the laity that can no more than their mother tongue, but such translations as be either not approved for good, or such as be already reproved for naught, as Wickliffe's was. For as for old ones that were before Wickliffe's days, they remain lawful, and be in some folks hands. Myself have seen and can show you Bibles, fair and old, which have been known and seen by the Bishop of the Diocese, and left in laymen's hands and women's, to such as he knew for good and Catholic folk that used it with soberness and devotion."

Then Mr. Blunt explains why few of these older Bibles now exist. He says that both Sir Thomas More, Cranmer, and Foxe (who also speaks of them)—

" Were acute men, not likely to be deceived into mistaking Bibles of a recent for those of an ancient date. More, in particular, who doubtless thought Wickliffe's Bible 'naught,' was a critic of much literary experience, while Cranmer speaks of early English Bibles, in 1540, being in old abbeys in just the same way, as a writer of the fourteenth century, quoted at page 2, had said in 1398, that they were there. That they have not come down to us, is doubtless owing to the fact that in Edward VI.'s day all old libraries were ruthlessly destroyed. The University Library of Oxford, the library of Merton College, that of the Guildhall, London, and those of the dissolved monasteries, were packed off as waste paper to any one who would buy them, and the very shelves and benches of the first named library were sold for fire-wood. The earlier the English in which old books were written, the less intelligible and the more pernicious they would seem to the silly vandals who wrought such destruction." (The reference is to *Macray's Annals of the Bodleian Library*, p. 12.)

As to the reference to Cranmer, Mr. Blunt says :—

" When Cranmer specified, 'not much above an hundred years,' as the limit of the anti-vernacular epoch, he was probably thinking of a canon which was passed at a Convocation held at Oxford, under Archbishop Arundel, in the year 1408. This canon, after stating, on the authority of S. Jerome, the risk which was incurred in translating the Bible, lest the sense of the inspired writers should not really be given, goes on as follows :—' We therefore decree and ordain, that from henceforth no unauthorized person shall translate any portion of Holy Scripture into English or any other language under any form of book or treatise. Neither shall any such book or treatise or version, made either in Wickliffe's time or since, be read either in whole or in part, publicly or privately, under the penalty of the greater excommunication, till the said translation shall be approved, either by the Bishop of the Diocese, or, if necessary, by a provincial council."

Our author remarks that not only does this canon forbid no translation made before Wickliffe's time (for which he quotes also Bishop Lynwood, who wrote about 1430, and whose words, as those of " a learned divine and cautious lawyer," clearly prove the existence, in his day, of vernacular Bibles, earlier than that of Wickliffe), but also that " the clause itself seems to show that an authorized version was then contemplated, as ' a provincial council ' would not be called upon to look through, and to sanction or condemn particular copies of the Bible, while the supervision of a new translation was exactly within its range of duties."

Thus far we have given Mr. Blunt's refutation of the falsehood that, before the change of religion, the English people were ravenous for Holy Scripture, and were debarred from it by "the priests." But the more valuable part of his work is what may be called the genealogy of the present Protestant translation. This is commonly supposed to have been the work of the Reformers ; and many persons, whose literary taste leads them to admire its language, have a natural and laudable feeling of disgust towards it, in consequence of believing it to be the work of evil men and heretics. Mr. Blunt declares, from close examination, that it is founded, not upon the earlier Protestant versions, but upon those which had been in use among English Catholics from times almost strictly contemporary with S. Augustine of Canterbury, although revised and improved in each succeeding generation. Thus he says of Tyndale, the first of the so-called Reformers who published a translation—"His manner of writing about sacred subjects is often inexpressibly shocking," and he adds, in contradiction of the opinion of Canon Westcott, that "if a comparison is made it will be seen that the language of our authorized version is so much in agreement with that of the fourteenth century Bible, as to make it certain that the latter and not Tyndale's version is the true nucleus of our existing English Bible." Tyndale's professed to be taken from Luther's translation, and it was declared on its title-page to be "out of Dutch and Latin." Mr. Blunt gives instances of direct dishonesty in the rendering, as, for instance, in the very first page Tyndale substitutes "married" instead of "espoused" in speaking of our Blessed Lady, and in S. Peter's first Epistle he wholly omits one clause, because it enjoined "obedience to the King." Mr. Blunt amusingly adds, "such tricks as these were simply heresy and treason to churchmen and statesmen of that day, and unless they were intended as such by Tyndale, it is difficult to say how or why they should have been perpetrated." This wretched man was an Apostate Franciscan.

In the first section Mr. Blunt gives us an account of those ancient versions which have survived the wholesale destruction coeval with the unhappy change of religion. They are but a remnant, but they throw singular light, not only on the gradual formation and perfecting of the English Bible, but also upon the growth and ripening of the English language itself. He mentions especially translations by S. Adhelm, bishop of Sherborne, born about fifty years after the death of S. Augustine (still existing in the Imperial Library at Paris), S. Aidan, S. Bede, King Alfred, Archbishop Ælfric, Schorhan, vicar of Chart Sutton in Kent, and Rolle, a chantry priest, near Dorchester. These still exist, wholly or in part, and Mr. Blunt gives some valuable extracts from several of them, to illustrate the gradual change of our native tongue, and to prove that the later translations were not new, but merely revisions of a version which came down, substantially the same, from the earliest times. At last, about the fifteenth century, the language had become fixed, and when this was the case, revised versions were much less frequently needed. Mr. Blunt's violent prejudices lead him to adopt the vulgar notion that the reason why new versions were less frequently made in the last century before the change of religion, was because "the clergy" at that one period "discouraged English Bibles." The extreme absurdity of this notion is that, if we are to infer that the Scriptures were not allowed to be read in any particular century because new versions were not put out in that century then, assuredly, there has been no time in English history at which they have been so little allowed to be read, as in the last three centuries, for we have now been without a new revision for near 300 years, the last having been put out after the accession of James I., in 1603.

The result of Mr. Blunt's investigations is, that the existing English version was not the·work of any one man or any one age, but grew up, like the great works of nature, by a slow process continued through centuries ; and that the so-called reformers did no more than revise it, correcting it by comparison with the Greek and Hebrew, and thus caused it to represent both those languages and "the great ecclesiastical tongue of western Christendom." "Modern translators," he says, "would perhaps have reversed the process, going at once to the Divine originals, using the Septuagint and the Vulgate only by way of auxiliary criticism, and making the English that of their own time. But it may be questioned whether the result would have been better. 'Change the language as little as possible' has been the principle upon which all our translators have done their work." If our author's theory be true, and we think it cannot be doubted, the subject obviously deserves much more attention than it has as yet received, especially from Catholics.

It disposes, at once and for ever, of all the boasts so often repeated by Protestants as to the literary beauty of the Protestant Bible. It no doubt has great literary beauty, just as York or Lincoln Minster has wonderful architectural beauty ; but, if Mr. Blunt is right, the Protestant reformers and their followers have just as much claim to one of these beauties as to the other. The literary beauties of King James's Bible, he assures us, were the result of a long period of ages, during which it was gradually formed and ripened, those ages being, without any exception, purely and exclusively Catholic. All that Protestant labourers have done since is, in his judgment, to revise and correct that ancient Catholic version by the aid of modern learning and criticism. In this process they could not fail to make some improvements ; but we much wish that some Catholic sufficiently versed in the old English should carefully examine the old translations, in order to show what the changes introduced by the reformers actually were. All the world knows that there are passages in which the original is wrongly translated, with the effect, if not with the object, of favouring the heresies of Calvin and his followers.* It would be worth while to ascertain whether, after all, the modern Bible is not indebted to the Catholic translators for all that is beautiful, and to the Protestant revisers only or chiefly for rendering it more or less heretical. We trust this subject will be carefully examined.

The bearing of Mr. Blunt's theory upon the Douay version we need hardly point out. He is pleased, of course, to speak scornfully of it, as if the ac-

---

* *E.g.*—" Such as should be saved," in Acts ii. 47. " Whereunto also they were appointed," in 1 Peter ii. 8. " Whosoever shall eat this bread and drink this cup of the Lord unworthily," 1 Corinthians xi. 27.

knowledged literary beauty of that which he has himself just proved to be the old Catholic version, were a boast for Protestantism. We would suggest to him a parallel. We read that no man was listened to in the Council of Nice with greater reverence than Paphnutius, who, as the Apostle expresses it, bore on his body the marks of the Lord Jesus, being a cripple in consequence of having been mutilated in the Dioclesian persecution.* It is very probable that his manner of walking may have been far less elegant than that of many young men who had grown up under the favour of the Christian court of Constantine. Still it may be questioned whether Christians of that day would have thought it very religious and becoming to mock and jeer at his halting gait, and to boast themselves on their own superiority. What else is Mr. Blunt doing? It was for the sake of the same Lord and the same Faith that the Douay translators had abandoned father and mother, house and home, their beloved country and the sweet sound of their mother tongue, and had lived for years as exiles in a foreign land. Their want of vernacular English was but the lameness of Paphnutius, the badge of their long martyrdom, the note of their highest glory. Of course, this is no reason why men who have not had the glory of martyrdom, but who have had the advantage of speaking English familiarly ever since they learned to speak at all, should fancy themselves better Catholics because they imitate the Latin, French, or Flemish words and idioms into which those glorious confessors unavoidably fell. This is, in fact, only for a sound and healthy man to pride himself upon imitating the limping gait of Paphnutius.

Perhaps the most perfect and most absolutely Catholic version of Scripture that could be made would be one adapted, by such corrections as the change of the language has made indispensable, from the old Catholic versions in use before the time of Tyndale, all of which, be it remembered, Mr. Blunt expressly shows to have been made from the Vulgate, and which Sir T. More says were allowed by Catholic authorities in his day. If desired, these could be "diligently compared with the Hebrew, Greek, &c." (to adopt the expressions of the Title-page of our modern Catholic Bibles), for of course these texts have been made more critically exact and elucidated by modern criticism. Such a version would no doubt, in many respects, closely resemble that which Protestants unjustly claim as their own, because they have stolen it, as they have our old cathedrals; so much the better—because it will prove to all men whence came the literary merits which they now so unjustly claim as their own. There is no reason why we should surrender to them the ancient versions, any more than the mediæval architecture, both of which are, by inheritance, equally ours.

---

* Tillemont, vol. vi., Histoire du Concile de Nicée, art. v.

Joannis Bapt. Franzelin e Societate Jesu in Collegio Romano S. Theologiæ Professoris Tractatus de Deo Uno secundum Naturam. Romæ, Typis S. C. de Propag. Fide. 1870.

WE have already had various opportunities of expressing our high appreciation of the dogmatical works of this celebrated Jesuit Professor of the Roman College, when noticing his treatise on the Sacraments, on the Blessed Trinity, and on the Incarnation. We need hardly therefore, say how thankful we are that he has now published another volume, thereby giving to theological students at large the privilege which before was restricted to those who had the good fortune to hear him in the Gregorian University at Rome. We cordially join in the wish expressed some little time ago by M. Bouix in his " Revue des Sciences Ecclésiastiques," as to F. Franzelin, " Puisse le cours complet du savant Père, qui unit la profondeur allemande à la clarté française, être bientôt dans toutes les mains, et retremper l'enseignement théologique de nos séminaires ! " Without entering into any discussion as to whether his depth be altogether German, or his clearness only French, we heartily hope that a course of theology, so superior in depth and clearness to any modern one that we have met with, may speedily find its way into all our theological schools.

The treatise before us is divided into five sections :—De Cognitione existentiæ Dei ; De modo nostræ Cognitionis quid Deus sit ; De essentiâ Dei et proprietatibus absolutis ; De Scientiâ divinâ ; and De Voluntate Dei salvificâ. We would refer to the first section as being especially interesting in illustration of the doctrine defined in the first Constitution of the Vatican Council. In the first two chapters of the section the doctrine of Scripture and Tradition, respecting our knowledge of God by the natural light of human reason, is set forth with great fulness and completeness.

In the second section the doctrine of the Fathers against the Eunomians, as to the immediate intuition of God, is set forth with such force as completely to overthrow the pretentions of the ontologistic school.

In the fourth section F. Franzelin supports the doctrine of the " Scientia Media," and points out that it is as unjust to accuse Fonseca and Molina of having pretended that they were the inventors of this opinion, as to say that they were really its originators. From their own words he shows that they, in common with all defenders of the " Scientia Media," boasted that they had derived their doctrine from the Holy Scriptures and from the Fathers.

In the last section he defends the doctrine of predestination to glory, " post prævisa merita." The hermeneutical theses on S. Augustine's and S. Thomas's teaching on this point, as well as that on the meaning of the ninth chapter of S. Paul to the Romans, are especially worthy of notice.

We will conclude by hoping that F. Franzelin may be enabled to complete the publication of the works which he has so successfully begun; that the Roman College may long possess him as its professor; and that the persecution to which that great college is now subjected may soon be brought to an end.

Hortus Animæ ; or, Garden of the Soul. London : John Philp, 7, Orchard Street, Portman Square.

THIS book is so beautifully got up, and eminently comprehensive, that it cannot fail to meet with the appreciation it deserves. While adhering rigidly to the wording of the old "Garden of the Soul" (except for a very few obvious improvements) in all that it contains in common with that useful prayer-book, the "Hortus Animæ" possesses so many additions suited to modern devotion, that the elegant and compact size of the volume becomes in itself a marvel. We observe that a differently worded translation is given of the Psalms to that used in the ordinary "Garden of the Soul," or the 'Golden Manual" ; but we have not had leisure to compare the merits of the two.

Among the innumerable additions contained in this new "Garden of the Soul," we particularly observe the Little Office of the B. Virgin ; the Common of Vespers for Apostles, Martyrs, Confessors, &c. &c., with their hymns and Antiphons ; also the Proper of Vespers for Chief Festivals, including not only days of obligation, but so many feasts of any note, that the "Vesper-book" will be almost superseded by this comprehensive prayer-book. The Epistles and Gospels for Sundays and festivals, as also the Passion in Latin and English at the end, cause the "Hortus Animæ" to partake little less of the Missal than the Vesper-book.

We have left to the last the tribute we must pay to the beauty of the numerous engravings with which the book is so richly decorated. Their style is in imitation of the ancient illuminations, of which they naturally lack the gorgeous colouring ; but their design is so varied, and they are scattered over the pages in such profusion, that they cannot fail to please all classes. The type is exceedingly ornamental, but will, perhaps, be found rather trying to any but good and clear eyesight.

THE

DUBLIN REVIEW.

APRIL, 1871.

Art. I.—CERTITUDE IN RELIGIOUS ASSENT.

An Essay in Aid of a Grammar of Assent. By JOHN HENRY NEWMAN, D.D.,
of the Oratory. London : Burns, Oates, & Co.

F. NEWMAN deserves the warm gratitude of his co-
religionists, were it only as being the first to fix Catholic
attention on what is certainly the one chief stronghold of philosophical objectors against the Church ; and he deserves still
more gratitude, for the singular power of argument and felicity
of illustration which he has brought to his task. There are
undoubtedly various incidental statements in his volume, with
which we are far from agreeing ; but it is not our intention to
say much of them on the present occasion. The series of
able articles from the pen of F. Harper, now appearing in the
" Month," will doubtless in due course be collected into a
separate publication ; and their appearance in that state will
give us the opportunity of expressing our own humble opinion
on the points at issue. But we are at all events thoroughly
in accordance with what we regard as F. Newman's central
position ; and to this part of his work we shall confine ourselves in what we are now going to say.

What then is that " chief stronghold of philosophical objectors against the Church," on which F. Newman has been the
first to fix Catholic attention ? This : that since the strength of
assent, given to any proposition, should invariably be proportioned to the amount of evidence on which that proposition
rests, — no man loves truth for its own sake, who does
not labour, in every single matter of thought, to effect this
equation between his strength of proof and his firmness of
conviction. See e.g. F. Newman, pp. 155-6 ; p. 167 ; p. 169,
&c., &c. Let us begin then with pointing out the powerful
argument which an anti-Catholic could at once build up, if
this foundation were conceded him.

" Catholics are taught to regard it as a sacred duty that

" they shall hold, most firmly and without a shadow of doubt,
" the truth of certain marvels, which are alleged to have taken
" place some nineteen centuries ago. As to examining the
" *evidence* for those truths, the great mass of Catholics are of
" course philosophically uncultured and simply incompetent to
" such a task. But even were they competent thereto, they
" are prevented from attempting it. Except a select few of
" them, they are all forbidden to read or knowingly to hear one
" syllable of argument on the other side. Under such circum-
" stances, *proof* for their creed they can have none ; any more
" than a *judge* can have proof, who has only heard witnesses
" on one side, and them not cross-examined. So far from
" proportioning their assent to the evidence on which their
" doctrine rests, the assent claimed from them is the very
" highest, while the evidence afforded them is less than the
" least.

" But take even any one of the select few, who are permitted
" to study both sides of the question. He will tell you quite
" frankly, that his belief was as firm before his examination
" began, as it is now ; nay, and that he regards it as a sin,
" which unrepented would involve him in eternal misery, if he
" allowed himself so much as one deliberate doubt on the
" truth of Catholicity. I place before him some serious dif-
" ficulty, which tells against the most central facts of his reli-
" gion : he had never heard of the difficulty before, and he is
" now not at all sure that he will be able to answer it. I
" should have expected (were it not for my knowledge of
" Catholics) that the confidence of his conviction would be
" *diminished* by this circumstance ; for plainly an unanswered
" difficulty is no slight abatement from the body of proof
" on which his creed reposes. But he says unblushingly, that
" if he were to study ten years without seeing how to meet
" the point I have suggested, — his belief in his Church,
" whose claim of authority he recognizes as divinely autho-
" rized, would be in no respect or degree affected by the
" circumstance.

" Nor is it for themselves alone, but for all mankind, that
" Catholics prescribe this rebellion against reason. They
" maintain that every human being, to whom their Gospel is
" preached, is under an obligation of accepting with firmest
" faith the whole mass of Catholic facts ; the miraculous Con-
" ception, Resurrection, Ascension, &c., &c : while it is simply
" undeniable, that 999 out of every 1,000 are absolutely inca-
" pable of appreciating ever so distantly the evidence on
" which these facts are alleged to repose.

" Nor, to do them justice, do they show the slightest dis-

"position to conceal or veil their maxims. The Vatican
" Council itself has openly anathematized all those who shall
" allege, that Catholics may lawfully suspend their judgment
" on the truth of Catholicity, until they have obtained for
" themselves scientific proof of its truth.*

" I have no general prejudice against Catholics; on the
" contrary, I think many of them possess some first-rate
" qualities. But while their avowed intellectual maxims are
" those above recited, I must regard them as external to the
" pale of intellectual civilization. I have no more ground on
" which I can argue with a Catholic, than I have ground on
" which I can argue with a savage."

We shall have repeatedly, in our present article, to comment on the principle, set forth and applied in this objection;
and it will be much more convenient therefore at once to give
it a name. Perhaps we may be permitted to call it the principle
of " equationism"; the principle which alleges, that there is
an obligation on every one who loves truth, of setting himself expressly to the task of effecting an " equation" between
the strength of his convictions and the amount of proof on
which they respectively rest. And as to those Catholics who
regard with suspicion the general tendency of F. Newman's
volume, we would entreat them to consider how the objection
of equationists, as above stated, can be otherwise met, than
by the substantial adoption of his doctrine. However we have
no kind of right to constitute ourselves his interpreters. Our
purpose in the present article is only to solve the above objection in our own way, making abundant use for that purpose
of the invaluable materials which he has supplied. And we
shall understand the doctrine of these equationists, not as one
of their number might explain it when cross-questioned, but
in the sense it must bear if it is to warrant the anti-Catholic
objections just now recited.

We cannot proceed however one step in our task, till
we have made some explanation of our terminology. F.
Newman uses the word " certitude" in a sense different
from that usually given by Catholic philosophers. They
divide certitude into two elements: as signifying, firstly,
the reasonable absence of all doubt; and, secondly, a
certain *degree* of positive adhesion to the truth embraced.

---

* Si quis dixerit parem esse conditionem fidelium, &c., &c., ita ut Catho-
lici justam causam habere possint fidem, quam sub Ecclesiæ magisterio jam
susceperunt, assensu suspenso in dubium vocandi donec demonstrationem
scientificam credibilitatis et veritatis fidei suæ absolverint, anathema sit."
" Dei Filius," c. 3, canon 6.

F. Newman includes in the term only the *former* of the two elements; and in saying therefore that certitude has no *degrees* as regards the absence of doubt, he entirely concurs with them in their doctrine.* We shall ourselves, so far, use the word "certitude" in F. Newman's sense. In p. 204 however he draws a distinction between what he calls "material" and "formal" certitude; which we do not find useful for our own purpose, and which we shall therefore not adopt.† We shall speak of "certitude" existing in my mind as to any truth, whenever I undoubtingly assent to that truth on grounds which legitimately generate such undoubtingness;— ou grounds, we mean, which *conclusively establish* the truth in question.   Undoubting assent itself we shall call "absolute assent"; whether it do or do not rest on fully adequate grounds.   By "absolute assent" (in other words) we understand an assent, which is not only *unaccompanied* by doubt, but which is so firm as to *expel* doubt; to be *incompatible* with the presence of doubt.   And we shall say that an absolute assent, resting on *in*adequate grounds, possesses "*putative* certitude" only.

Here however, before going further, we must interpose an explanation; which has no bearing indeed on our argument, but which is necessary for the prevention of possible misunderstanding.   No "certitude," in the sense we have given the word, can be *greater* than another; but it may be very much more *irresistible* than another.   Wherever grounds for certitude exist, doubt is *unreasonable*; but in one case, very far more than in another, it is *possible*.   Suppose I have gone through Euclid I., prop. 47, and satisfied myself that the whole argument is cogent.   I am as *certain* of that proposition, as I am of the axiom that things equal to the same are equal to each other; but plainly it is far more *possible*, though not more *reasonable*, to doubt the former than the latter verity.

This then being laid down, we give two answers to the equationist doctrine: our answers, we believe, being substan-

---

* Take Liberatore for instance. "Quòd una [certitudo] alteri præstet, facile suadetur : si non attendas ad partem negativam, nimirum *exclusionem dubii*, quæ indivisibilis omnino est et *gradus non habet ;* sed attendas ad partem positivam, nimirum intensitatem adhæsionis, &c."—Logica, n. 11. Dmowski, again.   "Omnis naturalis certitudo formaliter spectata est æqualis." Vol. i. p. 32.

† There is one part of F. Newman's view, on which he himself lays very great stress, but which we have not yet been able to apprehend.   It is his speaking of "assent" as in its nature "unconditional," and independent of the inferential act which may have led to it.

tially the same with F. Newman's. Firstly, there are no *degrees* of certitude; and consequently, when complete certitude is once obtained, additional *proofs* can add nothing to the certitude itself as regards all absence of doubt. For instance. To speak quite within bounds, by the time I was twenty-five years old, I possessed abundantly sufficient ground for complete certitude that there are such cities in the world as Paris and Vienna. Since that date, my *proofs* for this conclusion have much more than doubled; but it is simply ludicrous to say, that I should now be more than twice as certain of the fact as I was then. I was completely certain of it then; and I cannot be *more* than completely certain of it now.

Take another case. My father is a man of singularly spotless integrity; and I have lived continually with him, from my infancy down to the prime of life in which I now am. It is very long since I acquired a complete certitude of such being his character. Five years ago, a heavy charge was brought against his morals; and he frankly told me that he was wholly unable for the moment to explain those suspicions which pressed against him so heavily. Indubitably there was at that time one argument of weight on the adverse side; and equationists must in consistency maintain, that my only reasonable course was to diminish pro tanto my confidence in his character. But though they are bound *in consistency* to maintain it, we do not dream that they *will* maintain it. On the contrary, the common voice of mankind declares that, had I so acted, I should have done what is no less intellectually unreasonable than morally detestable. It is intellectually unreasonable; because if I possess certitude of any truth, I thereby *also* possess certitude that apparent objections against it are worthless.

This latter illustration leads us to a second remark, which is of vital moment in the present discussion. It is in the highest degree noteworthy, how many of men's strongest, most important, and most reasonable convictions rest on *implicit* premisses. Nay, many truly momentous conclusions depend on premisses, which are not only implicit, but in their present shape are no more than confused memories of the past. My conviction that Paris and Vienna exist—my conviction that my father is a man of spotless integrity—are both cases in point. To insist that in either of these cases I shall expressly labour to equate the strength of my conviction with the degree of its evidence, would be to take the surest means of rendering it utterly *dis*proportioned thereto. In either case premiss has for years succeeded premiss, each

leaving its legitimate impression on my mind and then forgotten. How is it possible that I can labour to equate my
conviction with its evidence, when that evidence, in its original
and adequate shape, is wholly inaccessible, having left behind
it but a vague record on my memory? In like manner every
acute and intelligent person, who has lived an active life among
men, possesses, stored within him, all sorts of miscellaneous
convictions on the fit way of dealing with mankind, the result
of his past experience. These are indeed among his most valuable possessions, so far as this world is concerned; and yet it
would be the merest child's play if he professed to remember
the individual experiences which have gradually built them
up. It is rather a hopeless task certainly for the thinker to
aim at proportioning his conviction to its premises; when
these premises, in their original and adequate shape, are no
longer present to his mind.*

Equationists however may hope to meet the *first* of our
two objections, by asking leave to amend their plea. ˙ They
will no longer perhaps speak of proportioning the *degree* of
conviction to the *degree* of evidence; but will urge that
every one should sedulously take heed that he hold no proposition with absolute assent, for which he does not possess
evidence abundantly sufficient. And their doctrine certainly
deserves much more respectful·consideration in its new shape,
than it deserved in its old.

We concede then that (putting aside one or two exceptional
instances on which there is no need to insist) it would cæteris
paribus be *a great advantage,* if no one yielded more
unreserved assent to any proposition, than is warranted
by the evidence he possesses.† But this is a most different
proposition from saying, that all men should expressly *aim* at
obtaining for themselves this advantage. Take an obvious
illustration. It would be a great advantage cæteris paribus
(putting aside one or two exceptional instances) if all men
enjoyed excellent bodily health; but it does not at all follow
from this, that men would act wisely in *pursuing* this object
through every detail of their life. Such a course would lead

---

* We cannot however concur with F. Newman, if we rightly understand
him (p. 160), that such a conviction is now "self-sustained in our minds."
On the contrary we would submit, that those confused memories of the past,
which now exist, are its reasonable and amply sufficient basis.

† If our readers are surprised that we should admit *any* "exceptional
instances", we will mention (as one of their number) the assent given by a
child of ten years old to his parent's trustworthiness. Would it really be
universally an advantage, that this assent should not be more unreserved
than his premises warrant?

to two evils: for, firstly, this minute care would so occupy their attention, as indefinitely to weaken their energy in more important directions; and, secondly, the constant *endeavour* for bodily health would be injurious to bodily health. Now let us apply this illustration: and we will begin with far the less important reason of the two.

Firstly then, we say, if all men were thus to busy themselves with pruning down their putative certitudes, they would disastrously diminish their energy in other more important directions. Let us take one case out of a thousand. No one will deny that *philanthropists* have done great service to mankind: yet how far stronger are their beliefs than their premisses warrant! Each one holds implicitly an undoubting conviction, that his own particular hobby is the one most important element of human happiness. Now we ask which of the two following alternatives is more for the welfare of mankind? On the one hand, that he should proceed steadily in his admirable and disinterested efforts for benefiting his fellow men? Or on the other hand, that he should largely divert his energy from this noble course, to the far less congenial employment, of lowering down his view on the importance of what he is about to the exact level warranted by evidence? Again, take a much graver case. I am fifteen years old; and I have a father—not of comparatively spotless excellence as in a former illustration—but of mixed character; by no means predominantly wicked, yet with serious faults. And for one reason or another it is very important for me to have a true implicit *impression* of that character. Would it on that account be desirable, that I should apply myself directly to the study? labour to obtain all requisite candour? contend laboriously against my tendency, prompted by affection, to undervalue his defects?

But now, secondly and much more importantly, however desirable it may be that putative certitudes should be pruned down, it continually happens that the worst possible means of *effecting* this object will be for the thinker himself to aim directly at its accomplishment. In the immense majority of cases men are absolutely incapable of any such effort. Take the whole class of labourers, farmers, tradesmen; or take a large number of hunting country gentlemen. They hold with absolute assent a large number of convictions; many resting on fully sufficient grounds, many on grounds more or less inadequate, many on no grounds at all. Various influences may be brought to bear on these men by a more cultured mind, with the result of considerably diminishing this intellectual evil; but it is more like a bad joke than a grave suggestion, to advise that they shall be summoned to pass under review their various beliefs, and reject those which are insufficiently supported. The grave philosopher, who should urge this, could not get them to understand so much as what he means. And even if he could, they would be no more competent to the task, than the said philosopher would himself be competent to the task of riding across country after the hounds. Each man has his speciality.

Then even as regards one of the most cultivated mind. Is it true that he has always the power of confronting his conclusion with the grounds on which it rests, in order to estimate its reasonableness ? Why in many cases, as we have already pointed out, those grounds are no longer accessible in their original shape ; having left behind them but a vague record on the memory. But further, even when his premisses are actually before him, they very often defy his power of analysis. F. Newman has illustrated this with exquisite felicity.

As by the use of our eyesight we recognize two brothers, yet without being able to express what it is by which we distinguish them ; as at first sight we perhaps confuse them together, but on better knowledge, we see no likeness between them at all ; as it requires an artist's eye to determine what lines and shades make a countenance look young or old, amiable, thoughtful, angry or conceited, the principle of discrimination being in each case real, but implicit ;—so is the mind unequal to a complete analysis of the motives which carry it on to a particular conclusion, and is swayed and determined by a body of proof, *which it recognizes only as a body, and not in its constituent parts* (p. 285).

Take as one instance the case of medicine, to which F. Newman refers at p. 325. A third-rate practitioner is one, who forms his conclusions *theoretically :* who derives universal propositions from his acquaintance with treatises; and deals no otherwise with each particular case, than by classing it under one or other of these universal propositions. The physician of *genius*, while availing himself to the utmost of past experience as recorded in treatises, at the same time studies each several case on its own merits; and forms a conclusion based on the whole phenomena before him. Is that conclusion to be accounted *unreasonable*, until he is able to produce those phenomena one by one before his conscious observation? Then all the most important cures have been wrought by unreasonable men; and the patient, if a " lover of truth," would rather have been left to die " secundum artem." Turn indeed where you will externally to the region of pure mathematics, the same fact will meet your observation. The careful student of history e.g. will pronounce with absolute confidence, that such or such a nation would be so or so affected by such or such a circumstance; that such or such a change has been wrought in that nation's character since such or such a period. Is he able to exhibit in detail, for his own satisfaction, the precise premisses which have led him to these conclusions? No one will think so. F. Newman again points to a different field of illustration. He gives extracts (p. 321) from a work, with which we are not otherwise acquainted, on "the authorship of a certain anonymous publication as suggested mainly by internal evidence." We preserve F. Newman's italics. "Rumour," says this author,—

Speaks uniformly and clearly enough in attributing it to the pen of a particular individual. Nor, although a cursory reader might well skim the book without finding in it any thing to suggest, &c., . . . will it appear improbable to the more attentive student of its internal evidence ; and the improbability will decrease more and more, in proportion as the *reader is capable* of judging and appreciating the *delicate, and at first invisible touches,* which limit, to *those who understand them,* the individuals who can have written it to a very small number indeed. The utmost scepticism as to its authorship (*which we do not feel ourselves*) cannot remove it farther from him than to that of some one among his most intimate friends ; so that, leaving others to discuss antecedent probabilities, &c. (p. 321).

On this passage F. Newman thus comments :—

Here is a writer who professes to have no doubt at all about the authorship of a book,—which at the same time he cannot prove by mere argumentation set down in words. The reasons of his conviction are too delicate, too intricate ; nay, they are in part invisible, except to those who from circumstances have an intellectual perception of what does not appear to the many. They are personal to the individual. This again is an instance, distinctly set before us, of the particular mode in which the mind progresses in concrete matter, viz. from merely probable antecedents to the sufficient proof of a fact or a truth, and, after the proof, to an act of certitude about it. (Ib.)

Criticism of this kind affords a large field for illustrating the proposition with which we are engaged. There are many passages e.g. of which a good scholar would pronounce with most absolute certitude, that they were not written by Cicero or by Tacitus as the case may be. Yet how hopeless his attempt of exhibiting, for his own inspection, the various premisses which make this conclusion legitimate ! *

Now we do not for a moment deny, that even the most philosophically cultured men often enough yield absolute

---

* On this part of our theme, see an article on "Explicit and Implicit Thought," in our number for October, 1869.

assent to some propositions on insufficient evidence; nor again do we deny, that they may with great advantage put themselves through some course of intellectual discipline, with the view of diminishing this evil. Some of their conclusions doubtless—though we believe that these are with most men comparatively few—have been entirely arrived at by *explicit* reasoning; i.e. by *argument*: and, it will certainly be very useful to confront these from time to time with the arguments on which they rest. Then as to those far more numerous assents which rest mainly or partly on implicit premisses,—it is often very important that a philosophically cultured lover of truth shall impartially examine every *argument*, whether favourable or adverse to them, with which he can become acquainted. And there is another remedy against prejudice which is also available to such minds : viz., that they labour to analyse their various opinions; compare them with each other ; and compare them also with all cognisable phenomena. But after allowing all this, it still remains true, with the highly-educated man no less than with the most uncultured, that the number of convictions is very considerable, for which he has no evidence capable of being placed distinctly before his mind. And it is also true, that there are not a few among the number which he intimately feels to rest on evidence super-superabundantly sufficient, nay in some cases simply irresistible; and which he could not eradicate, without rending his whole moral and intellectual nature.

Let so much have been said on the philosophical principle of equationism, whether in its original or its amended shape. We will now proceed to consider those two fundamental theses, on which the devout Catholic rests his whole hope for this life and the next: the truth of Theism, and the truth of Catholicity. We affirm that any ordinary Catholic, however uneducated, has access to superabundantly conclusive evidence for these truths. As regards Theism, we placed before our readers in Oct. 1869 a long and most striking passage to this effect from F. Kleutgen (pp. 422-425), which we hope they will read again in the present context. Nor can we do better here than supplement it with another, from a later portion of his great work, in which (as will be seen) he incidentally applies the same principle to the evidence of *Catholicity*. As in the former case, we italicise a few sentences to which we invite special attention ; and we here and there add a word or two within brackets, to make clear what we conceive to be the author's meaning.

Our reasonable nature is so constituted that, with but little reflection, we are excited and constrained, not only by a spontaneous inclination of heart but by a necessitated power of mind (esprit), to acknowledge the Existence of a Supreme and Absolute Being, Cause and Sovereign Master of all things. And this necessity especially makes itself felt, when we vividly represent to ourselves our imperfection and dependence. Why ? Partly no doubt because God at the same time *makes Himself felt within us by His moral law as an August Power to which we are subject ;* but partly also because it is conformable to the laws of our intelligence, thus to conclude from things relative and dependent to the Absolute and Sovereign Being Who is their Cause. This is the explanation given long ago by the Fathers of the Church, as to the origin of that knowledge of God which is natural to us. Nevertheless it may easily happen that the human understanding, in virtue of a law inherent in its nature, is led on from one truth to the knowledge of another, without [explicitly] going through those reasonings which (according to that very law) are the steps from premiss to conclusion ; nay, even without reflecting on the fact that it *has* passed from premiss to conclusion *at all.**

Now to require that in the *scientific examination* of those convictions which rise up within us (it may be said) without our own agency [qui naissent en nous, on dirait, sans nous] no mention should be made of those intermediate considerations [which are the implicit stepping-stones from the first premiss to the last conclusion], and that attention should only be given to what is found in the spontaneous and (as it were) instinctive deductions of reason, this would be entirely to misunderstand the office of science. *How many truths are there, concerning moral duty, concerning nature and art, which a man of good judgment* [bon sens] *knows with perfect accuracy, without being distinctly cognisant how he passes in his successive judgments from one truth to another.* Now this distinct knowledge, which he does not possess and often cannot obtain, is precisely what we expect to derive from science ; which, exhibiting the connection between divers cognitions, strengthens those spontaneous convictions ; and not only defines their object more distinctly, but makes the knowledge of them clearer. Why then should not science take as the object of its researches *that knowledge of God which we instinctively possess,* in order to make clear on what principle we can legitimately reason, from the dependence of our own being, to the Existence—not of some generally conceived first cause—but of the Absolute and Independent Being [whom we call God] : in order thus to strengthen our convictions on His Existence and to arrive at a more intimate knowledge of His Nature ? Do we not proceed in the same way when we desire to satisfy ourselves *on the foundations of the Christian Faith ?* All that we have heard from infancy on the foundation and stability of our holy religion, suffices abundantly to convince us without much reasoning that God only can be its author. *It is true that in order to form this judgment we are assisted by the light of grace ; but neither is that* [instinctive] *knowledge of*

---

* As we have translated this last clause rather freely, we subjoin the words of the authorized French translation :— "Sans qu'elle fasse les raisonnements qui, d'après cette loi même, nous font passer de l'une à l'autre, et même sans que nous ayons conscience de cette transition."

God on which we have spoken obtained without Divine aids of the natural order. Now theology develops those reasons which we have for believing in the divinity of the Christian religion. . . . . In the same way philosophy is able and is bound to show that that method of reasoning from the world's existence to God's, to *which our intellect is spontaneously impelled,* is conformable to the clearly known laws of our thought " (Phil. Scol., n. 929).

If our readers will peruse, in connection with this striking passage, the extracts which we gave in October 1869, they will find that F. Kleutgen's doctrine is such as the following; and it is the doctrine which we ourselves cordially embrace. All men have access to super-superabundant evidence for the truth of Theism ; and all Catholics have access to super-superabundant evidence for the truth of Catholicity. Moreover God in His tender love deals with men one by one ; presses such premisses efficaciously on their attention ; and strengthens their mind that they may draw the legitimate conclusion. Such assistance, in bringing home to men's mind the truth of Catholicity, is the work of supernatural grace ; while such assistance in bringing home to men's mind the truth of Theism, appertains (says F. Kleutgen) not to supernatural grace, but to divine aid of the natural order. We need not ourselves here consider in any way this distinction between natural and supernatural auxilia; which would lead us entirely beyond the bounds of philosophical disquisition : otherwise (as we have said) we are prepared heartily to defend F. Kleutgen's doctrine.

The criticism of this doctrine, put forth by anti-Catholic philosophers on first hearing it, will probably be, not merely that it is *untrue,* but that it is *manifestly* and *on the surface* untrue ; that it is obviously and undeniably inconsistent with phenomena. Our first task must be to meet this allegation ; and to argue that the theory before us may be firmly held, without in any way contradicting obvious and ascertainable facts. For this purpose we would submit to our opponents the following considerations :—

(1.) We have already pointed out that certitude (in the sense we give that term) admits of no degrees; and consequently, that when premisses sufficient for certitude have once been accumulated, *additional* premisses cannot increase the undoubtingness of one who acts faultlessly on the principles of sound reason. We would now add however, what must not be forgotten, that such additional premisses are often of invaluable service. A has a mind indefinitely more acute and profound than B; and may draw the legitimate conclusion at the first moment (so to speak) when it *becomes* legitimate. But B with the best intentions remains unconvinced; and it is only through the multitude of reasons which keep thronging in, that the fort of his reason (made as it is of somewhat impenetrable material) can at length be stormed. The super-superabundance therefore of evidence, on which (as we consider) Theism and Catholicity respectively rest, is a circumstance of great force towards the conviction of ordinary minds.

(2.) There is no more remarkable fact in psychology, than the extraordinary number of operations which may be elicited by the human mind without its own consciousness. As regards the case of cultured persons, one illustration will suffice. We suppose such an experience as the following will be common to many of our readers. I am intensely interested in some author—say Gerdil—some of whose treatises are in Latin and some in French; two languages which I can read with about equal facility. Immediately on finishing one of these treatises, I ask myself whether it was in Latin or in French; and I find myself entirely unable to answer. Now how many operations have thus unconsciously passed through my mind! Firstly the letters have been read, each one separately, and all together; (2) the letters formed into words; (3) the words translated from a foreign language into English; (4) the construction of the sentences mastered so that the words shall group themselves in proper order; (5) the ideas expressed by the sentences conveyed to my understanding. Every single part of this long and complicated chain must by necessity have traversed my thoughts; for there is literally no connection between the letters which I read and the ideas which I receive, except by means of it: and yet it has left absolutely no trace on the memory.

But now this phenomenon is by no means confined to philosophically cultured intellects. Consider the extraordinary quickness with which some uneducated mariner will prognosticate, on some fine evening, that there will be a storm before next morn. He fixes his attention on a certain assemblage of phenomena; accurately distinguishes them from others with which they have a greater or less resemblance; brings to bear on them the confused memory of innumerable former occasions, on which he has observed appearances precisely similar; and draws the one conclusion legitimately resulting from his premisses. In fact he has gone correctly through the various processes described in Mill's Logic, with no more suspicion of the fact than if he had been all along fast asleep. Or take the rustic's firm conviction that such or such of his companions is honest and trustworthy and friendly to himself. How large a number of premisses must be intimately known, and how lengthy a chain of reasoning gone through, to warrant the conclusion ! Yet again and again the rustic will arrive at such a conclusion with faultless certitude, and without the faintest suspicion that his mind has been engaged in any special exercise. To the same effect is an illustration which we gave in October 1869 (pp. 427-8), and which is fully within the most uneducated man's compass. "I am intimately acquainted with a certain relative: and some fine morning I have not been with him more than five minutes, before I am perfectly convinced, and on most conclusive grounds, that (for whatever reason) he is out of sorts with me. It is little to say that I could not so analyze my grounds of conviction as to make *another* see the force of my reasoning ; I could not so analyze them, as that their exhibition shall be in the slightest degree satisfactory to *myself*. Especially in proportion as I am less philosophical and less clever in psychological analysis, all attempts at exhibiting my premisses in due form hopelessly break down. Yet none the less it remains true, both that my premisses are known to me with certainty, and that my conclusion follows from them irresistibly. There is an enormous number of past instances, in which these symptoms *have* co-existed with ill-humour; there is no single known case in which they have existed *without* it ; they all admit of being referred to ill-humour as effects to their cause ; they are so heterogeneous, that any other cause except ill-humour which shall account for them all is quite incredible, while it is no less incredible that they co-exist fortuitously ; &c. &c. &c. Why, in all probability the very Newtonian theory of gravitation does not rest on firmer and more irrefragable grounds." Yet it is not only true that I cannot *analyze* my process of conviction; I should naturally never dream of thinking that I have *gone through* any such process. The whole has as simply escaped my notice, as though it had never been.

(3.) Nothing is more easily imaginable, than that the illative faculty (if we may borrow F. Newman's adjective) should be indefinitely strengthened by God for a special purpose. Another faculty, that of memory, will supply a ready illustration. Of course it would be simply unmeaning to say that God so strengthens my memory, as to give me knowledge of things which I never experienced; but it would be most intelligible that he should so stimulate it, as to give me certain knowledge of every past thought, word, and act of mine, however transitory. In like manner it would be simply unmeaning to say that God so assists my illative faculty, as to enable me to draw confident conclusions from premisses which do not warrant certitude; and · such a notion we entirely put aside. But it is most intelligible that He so elevates it in some particular process, as to enable me to discern the legitimacy of certain inferences, which *are* legitimate, but which I should never by my natural strength of mind have *discerned* so to be. Or putting the thing more generally. It is a most intelligible statement that God, for the sake of obtaining my assent to some momentous verity, (1) specially presses on my attention this that and the other premiss; and (2) so strengthens my illative faculty, as to make me see (what otherwise I should *not* have seen) the full sufficiency of those premisses as. establishing the verity in question.

We will next then apply what has been said to those cardinal doctrines, the truth of Theism and the truth of Catholicity. We begin with the former.

All mankind have access to premisses, the cumulative force of which is super-superabundantly sufficient for the proof of God's Existence. We reserve to a future article a consideration of what those premisses precisely are, and what their ratiocinative force. We will here but briefly enumerate one or two of their number. First and foremost we must mention those deducible from the testimony of the Moral Faculty.* So importunate and at the same time so authoritative are the utterances of man's moral voice, that no adult, except for his own grave fault, can be ignorant of their essential teaching. No one, we say, except for his own grave fault, can be ignorant of the truth that, as F. Kleutgen expresses it, there exists "an absolute good and a sovereign rule over our wills and actions"; "an august and sacred power which is [in authority] over us." But this truth is only part of what may be called man's natural stock of Theistic premisses ;† of those premisses with which every one is familiar, as he advances towards maturity. Thus the manifold and most unmistakable marks of order and design, visible in creation, sink deeply into his

---

* Pius IX. speaks of "præcepta [legis naturalis] *in omnium cordibus à Deo insculpta*" (Encycl. "Quanto conficiamur.")

† F. Newman seems to speak here and there (see e.g. p. 101) as though men had no conclusive proof of God's Existence, except that derived from the moral voice within them. If he intends this, we much regret the statement ; but if he intends no more than to give this particular argument the chief and most prominent place, he entirely agrees with F. Kleutgen. According to that great champion of scholasticism, as we have seen, all men are so created as to receive spontaneously, from the first dawn of reason, a certitude of God's Existence: and the very principal means by which He produces this result, is the "making Himself *felt within us* by His moral law as an August Power to which we are subject."

mind and make their due impression. Other premisses again are supplied by the great principle of causation;* which is as inevitably and as constantly (however unconsciously) recognised by the most uncultured rustic, as by the profoundest philosopher. And these at last are but specimens and samples, though principal ones, of a class.

Such are the premisses which, as we maintain after F. Kleutgen, are pressed by God on the implicit attention of all adults; and which legitimately issue in a most firm and most reasonable conviction of His Existence. F. Kleutgen further points out (see our number for Oct. 1869, p. 422) a very significant fact. "When the Fathers of the Church," he says, "declare unanimously that knowledge of God is really found and established among all men, the importance of their testimony is better understood by remembering that they lived in the midst of heathen populations." This theme,—the prevalence of implicit Theism among the most inveterate polytheists,—is worthy of far more attention than we can here give it.

But it must never be forgotten how indefinitely higher and happier is the state of those, who have been educated in explicit Theism, and who have practised the lessons of their education. Reverting to a former distinction—if in all men doubt of God's Existence is *unreasonable,* to these men it is (in some sense) *impossible.* Take that premiss on which F. Kleutgen lays by far his most prominent stress; the truth that there exists "an absolute good and a sovereign rule over our actions," "an august power which is over us." It is only in proportion as men act consistently and energetically on the dictates of their moral faculty, that this truth impresses itself on their minds with an evidence, which is not luminous only but simply irresistible; and none but Theists *can* act thus consistently and energetically.† And this leads us to another most cogent and persuasive proof, which is the special property of what we may call practising Theists; for they have

---

* We deeply deplore F. Newman's language in pp. 63-4, concerning the axiom of causation. It would appear indeed that he has here expressed himself somewhat hastily ; for within six lines he represents the doctrine that " everything must have a cause," as identical with the doctrine that " nothing *happens* without a cause." But the first-named expression, as he himself points out, would include *God* as caused ; whereas the other expression excludes Him. As F. Harper explains (" Month," December, 1870, p. 682), the axiom of causation which " grave authors seem to enunciate as an intuitive truth," is that every *new* existence or *changed* existence has a cause.

‡ † This is one of the several momentous propositions, which we are obliged in our present article to assume, for want of space to argue them.

experience of the singular assistance derived from *prayer* towards fulfilment of the moral law. Such evidences as we have just now recounted, we say, are accessible to every man, —not in proportion as he is philosophically cultured,—but in proportion as he has been zealous in obeying and serving that God, Whom from the first dawn of reason he has instinctively known.

So much on the truth of Theism. We now proceed to similar considerations on the truth of Catholicity. In doing so however, we will invert our previous course; and *begin* with considering what evidences are available to those—however destitute they may be of mental culture—who have been trained from childhood in the Catholic religion. We must content ourselves, in this as in other parts of our article, with the merest skeleton outline of what we would say.

(1.) Firstly, there is no fact more profoundly impressed on the Catholic at every turn, than that the Church claims emphatically to be God's one accredited messenger; infallible in teaching and intolerant of rivals. All her allegations are in harmony with this claim. She professes that Apostles established their divine commission by miracles and by the fulfilment of prophecy; that they regarded one of their number as placed by God over the rest; that that one has had a successor unintermittently through intervening centuries; that the society which he governs is one in faith and communion, holy, Catholic, and (of course) Apostolic.* The humblest Catholic knows, that all his educated coreligionists are firmly convinced of these facts, as of undoubted historical truths.

(2.) On the other hand there is no writing, nor any *other* society whatever, which makes a parallel claim; which alleges itself to be God's one accredited messenger to mankind. Most certainly Scripture does not put forth any such claim in *its own* behalf.

(3.) Moreover to put forth such a claim without foundation, is nothing less than insolent blasphemy. The Catholic Church

---

* "Till these last centuries," says F. Newman (p. 372), "the Visible Church was, at least to her children, the light of the world, as conspicuous as the sun in the heavens ; and the Creed was written on her forehead, and proclaimed through her voice, by a teaching as precise as it was emphatical ; in accordance with the text, ' Who is she that looketh forth at the dawn, fair as the moon, bright as the sun, terrible as an army set in array ? ' It was not, strictly speaking, a miracle, doubtless ; but in its effect, nay, in its circumstances, it was little less. Of course I would not allow that the Church fails in this manifestation of the truth now, any more than in former times, though the clouds have come over the sun ; for what she has lost in her appeal to the imagination, she has gained in philosophical cogency, by the evidence of her persistent vitality."

is necessarily either Vice-God or Anti-God;* and this fact wonderfully simplifies the issue.

(4.) There is a certain type of morality, impressed on all Catholics in their various devotional books, their hagiologies, their catechisms, their religious practices; a type, which those who disapprove it commonly call the "ascetical." Reason rightly directed, we affirm, peremptorily declares, that this is the one type conformable with eternal truth; and the most uneducated Catholic, in proportion as he is devout, has had his reason thus rightly directed.

(5.) The various revealed dogmata, which in themselves are wholly inaccessible to reason, are nevertheless found by a believer to be in deep and mysterious harmony on many points with this true type of morality. To meditate on them and bring them in every possible way to bear on practical action, has a singular effect in elevating his mind towards the true moral standard. "The Catholic religion is true," says F. Newman (p. 205), among other reasons, "because it has about it an odour of truth and sanctity sui generis, as perceptible to my moral nature as flowers to my sense, such as can only come from heaven."

(6.) Then all who really hold the Catholic Faith, are more or less keenly impressed with a sense of *sin*. If they labour to serve God, in proportion as they do so they feel profoundly their numberless faults; because clearness of moral perception grows far more quickly than consistency of moral action. On the other hand, if they retain the Faith *without* labouring to serve God, they see by the light of reason (no less than by the light of faith) that such omission is most sinful. All Catholics then, really such, are impressed with a reasonable conviction, that there can be no surer note of a divinely-sent religion, than its prominent recognition of human sinfulness. To our mind there is no greater excellence in F. Newman's volume, than his repeated inculcation of this truth. But this note is a special characteristic of Catholicity in many different respects. Consider e.g. the dogma of the Atonement: how marvellously it appeals to man's sense of sin!

(7.) Emphatically also to be considered is the *experienced effect* of Catholicity, as assisting a believer in all increase of virtue and piety. As one instance out of many, consider that power of resisting the foulest and most importunate temptations, which is obtained by Catholic prayer, by frequentation of the Sacraments, by the constant and tender worship of Mary Most Holy.

---

* This is taken from a phrase of F. Newman's; who says that the Church, from her claims, must be either Vice-Christ or Anti-Christ.

Now all the reasons'which we have mentioned are accessible to the most unintellectual Catholics; and they are reasons moreover, which admit of being pressed home to the mind with special impressiveness by divine agency. In their legitimate effect, they are super-superabundantly sufficient to produce certitude; and our affirmation is, that the Holy Ghost uses these and similar reasons for that very purpose in the soul of Catholics. From first to last undoubtedly the Catholic is perfectly free to *reject* that which he has such abundant reason for accepting; but in proportion as he surrenders the whole current of his life to the influences of his Faith, in that proportion the divine origin of that Faith is more vividly and efficaciously evidenced to his mind.

As to the reasons available for the conversion of uncultured non-Catholics, we cannot even enter into that amount of detail which we gave to the last case; but we heartily concur with the whole of F. Newman's magnificent sermon—" Dispositions for Faith "—which stands fifth in the " Occasional " volume. For ourselves we can only make two, and those most general, observations. Firstly, in proportion as externs are brought more closely into contact with the Church, they are enabled more clearly to discern such *notes* of the Church as we have already mentioned. Secondly we are most strongly disposed to concur with what F. Newman has consistently advocated (we may say) through his whole theological life; viz. that by far the most hopeful course for an extern (speaking generally and allowing for exceptions) is to act energetically, under the guidance of his moral faculty, on what is placed before him as moral truth by his parents and teachers.* These are his words in the volume before us :—

> Of the two, I would rather have to maintain that we ought to begin with believing everything that is offered to our acceptance, than that it is our duty to doubt of everything. This, indeed, seems the true way of learning. In that case, we soon discover and discard what is contradictory ; and error having always some portion of truth in it, and the truth having a reality which error has not, we may expect, that when there is an honest purpose and fair talents, we shall somehow make our way forward, the error falling off from the mind, and the truth developing and occupying it. Thus it is that the Catholic religion is reached, as we see, by inquirers from all points of the compass ; as if it mattered not where a man began, so that he had an eye and a heart for the truth (pp. 371, 372).

Now the purpose of our article is, as our readers will

---

* If this be admitted, here will be a second exception to the general truth, that it is in itself a great advantage for men to hold no conclusion more strongly than is warranted by its evidence.

remember, to consider a certain " chief stronghold of philosophical objections against the Church," which we set forth at
starting. And we suppose we may assume without express
argument that, if Catholics have really such super-superabundant ground for their belief as we have affirmed, a thoroughly
satisfactory answer is furnished by such a fact to the philosophical objection. The whole question therefore turns on the
issue, whether the account we have given of Catholic evidence
is substantially true.

Hitherto we have been merely arguing, that at all events it
cannot be *disproved;* that it contains nothing inconsistent
with phenomena. No such inconsistency, so far as we see,
can be even alleged, except by assuming that such processes
as we suppose to have traversed a Catholic's mind, must (if
they really did so) have left behind them some record on the
memory. But the illustrations we have given amply refute
any such attempted argument. Indeed there is perhaps no
one point in which psychologians of the present day have so
outstripped their predecessors, as in their very strong doctrine
on the multitude and importance of implicit mental processes.*

We have proved then, we trust, to philosophical non-
Catholics, that our theory is not inconsistent with phenomena;
but can we further prove to them that it is *true ?* Even if we
could not prove this to *them,* this theory might nevertheless be
cognisable by *Catholics* as true, and might therefore be obligatory on their action. Let us revert to our familiar illustration.
I have the firmest conviction of my father's integrity. I may
be utterly unable to make my friends *sharers* in this conviction : but I am none the less bound to act on it *myself,* and
should be greatly culpable if I did otherwise. The application
is obvious. Catholics are responsible for their conduct to
their Creator, and not to their non-Catholic fellow-creatures.

But we say much more than this. We say that the only
question really at issue is, whether the historical and philosophical arguments, adduced by educated Catholics for the
truth of their religion, be really conclusive. *This* of course is
a question entirely external to the present article, and we are
obliged to *assume* the affirmative answer.† But what we wish

---

* We should add however, that the doctrine itself cannot possibly be
stated with greater clearness, than it was by Lugo two centuries back.
" Hæc est virtus intellectûs et voluntatis, ut uno actu brevissimo et sub-
tilissimo attingant compendiosè totam illam seriem motivorum," &c. de
Fide, d. i, n. 98. See also n. 87 and n. 91.

† F. Newman does not hesitate to say ("Lectures on the Present Position
of Catholics in England," Preface, p. viii.) that " the proof" of Catholicity
" is irresistible, so as even to master and carry away the intellect directly it

here to say is this. Whatever arguments suffice to convince an educated man that the Catholic religion is *true,* should suffice *also* to convince him that uneducated Catholics have full *evidence* of its truth. There are two reasons for this, either sufficient.

(1.) Suppose an educated man to become convinced that Catholicity is true. He thereby becomes convinced that, wherever the Gospel is duly preached, all men are under an obligation of accepting what the Church teaches; and that her Gospel is more especially directed to the uneducated and poor. If then it is their *duty* to accept what the Church teaches, they must have sufficient evidence to make such acceptance *reasonable.*

(2.) Then again. Suppose an educated man becomes convinced that Catholicity is true, he thereby becomes convinced that the Church is infallible in faith and morals. But no one ever questioned, that she prescribes to her children that very course of conduct, set forth in the philosophical objection against which our whole argument has been directed. If an educated man then becomes convinced that Catholicity is true, he thereby becomes convinced that this very course of conduct is conformable to right reason. But it is *not* conformable to right reason, unless an uneducated Catholic has access to such implicit evidence as we have alleged. The inference is obvious.

In saying however what we have said, we have had no thought of doubting, that an educated Catholic will often find it of great importance to enter on an explicit investigation * of Catholic evidences in this or that direction. Here again we are brought to a very important theme, which it is impossible to handle in our brief remaining space; and we can but state most briefly the opinions which we should humbly advocate. On the one hand we cannot but think, that the implicit grounds of belief, possessed by educated and uneducated alike and pressed on the attention of all by divine grace, will ever remain the strongest and most satisfying basis of conviction.† On the other hand an educated

---

is stated." We rather fancy him however here to assume as *granted,* that Christianity in one shape or another is of divine origin, and that the facts narrated in the New Testament are substantially true. So understood, we thoroughly concur with his statement.

 * F. Newman (p. 184) draws a very important distinction between "investigation" and "inquiry."

 † So F. Newman. "The grounds, on which we hold the divine origin of the Church, and the previous truths which are taught us by nature—the being of a God, and the immortality of the soul—are felt by most men to be *recondite and impalpable, in proportion to their depth and reality.* As we

Catholic will often be tempted to doubt, however unreasonably, the conclusiveness of these grounds, unless he has learned to see how strongly reinforced they are by *explicit* reasoning, derived from every branch of human thought and study. Moreover, as we need hardly add, it is of vital moment, that a sufficient number of able Catholic thinkers shall be, for controversial purposes, thoroughly acquainted with the vast variety of arguments adducible for the truth of Catholicity.

In the article which we here conclude, we have not unfrequently verged on the confines of various delicate philosophical questions, which we have thought it better to avoid. It seems to us abundantly plain, that the view we have put forth is substantially true, so far as it goes; while it is nevertheless constantly ignored by anti-Catholic disputants. If we can obtain the concurrence of such persons to the truth of what has here been said, we shall be in a far more favourable position for treating the more anxious and difficult questions which remain behind.

As to F. Newman's volume, which has been the occasion of our remarks though hardly their principal theme, it is so conspicuous for genius and power, and treats so many questions which are of extreme moment in the present crisis of European thought, that we shall be brought across it again and again in the articles we hope to publish from time to time on the relations between religion and philosophy.

---

cannot see ourselves, so we cannot well see intellectual motives which are so intimately ours, and which spring up from the very constitution of our minds" (pp. 328, 329). And he thus concludes the fifth of his "Occasional Sermons," to which we have already referred. "This is a day in which much stress is laid upon the *arguments* producible for believing Religion, Natural and Revealed ; and books are written to prove that we ought to believe, and why. These books are called Natural Theology and Evidences of Christianity ; and it is often said by our enemies, that Catholics do not know why they believe. Now I have no intention whatever of denying the beauty and the cogency of the arguments which these books contain ; but I question much, whether in matter of fact they make or keep men Christians. I have no such doubt about the argument which I have been here recommending to you. Be sure, my Brethren, that the best argument, better than all the books in the world, better than all that astronomy, and geology, and physiology, and all other sciences, can supply,—an argument intelligible to those who cannot read as well as to those who can,—an argument which is ' within us,'—an argument intellectually conclusive, and practically persuasive, whether for proving the Being of a God, or for laying the ground for Christianity,—is that which arises out of a careful attention to the teachings of our heart, and a comparison between the claims of conscience and the announcements of the Gospel" (pp. 98, 99).

Art. II.—PIUS VII. AND NAPOLEON I.

L'Église Romaine et le Premier Empire, 1800–1814. Par M. Le Comte
D'Haussonville. Lévy : Paris. Vol. iii.

THE history of the relations between Pius VII. and Napoleon I. naturally divides itself into two periods. The
first embraces the years in which Pius was a Sovereign in
possession of his dominions, and communicated with Napoleon
as one monarch with another. The second includes those in
which Pius VII. was a prisoner, in the power of the French
Emperor. This may be considered to have commenced on
February 2, 1808, the day on which the French took military
possession of Rome, because on that day the temporal government of the Pope really came to an end; although the States
of the Church were not formally annexed to the French
Empire until May 17, 1809. We have already called attention to the portion of M. D'Haussonville's work in which
he relates the events of the first period: we now propose to
examine his account of the other, which extends from Feb. 2,
1808, to the restoration of Pius VII. to the Vatican, May 24,
1814. In many respects this last is by far the most valuable
part of his work. As long as Pius VII. was in fact, as well
as right, an independent sovereign, and recognized as such
by Napoleon himself, all communications between the two
governments were in their nature to a considerable degree
public, and even those which were at the moment secret were
in the possession of both parties : it was therefore comparatively
difficult to the French Government to give to the world a
wholly false account of them. From the day on which the
Pope was a prisoner things were in this respect very different.
Absolute secresy as to everything which it did not suit the
despot to make public was the universal system of the French
Empire. The penalties by which it was enforced were so
tremendous that the attempt to preserve this secresy actually
succeeded to a degree which, to men who, like ourselves, have
lived all our lives under a system of which entire publicity is the
principal characteristic, seems almost inconceivable. And this
secresy was maintained in order to keep the field open for the
free action of a system of lying so enormous as to be truly
portentous. To what extent this system was carried was, we
believe, never known or even imagined even by the French

themselves before the publication of the result of M. D'Haussonville's researches. For although secresy and lying were
the characteristics of all Napoleon's dealings, both with the
people of the French Empire and with the world around it,
there was one department in which he felt it specially necessary to employ them. This was in all that regarded religion. Upon this he expressly wrote to his ministers,—"I
do not wish people to talk at all about ecclesiastical affairs;"
and by a system of terror, unscrupulously carried out, he succeeded in making it during almost fourteen years quite impossible for private friends, priests, bishops, and cardinals so
much as to speak of them, except with all the secresy and
restraint which marks the councils of men plotting against
a strong and unscrupulous government. The consequence
. was that what really happened with regard to the Pope, while
he was a prisoner in the power of Napoleon, was unknown at
the time; in a great measure, even to Napoleon's own ministers,
and absolutely to the French clergy and laity, and (it need not
be said) to the world at large. It might have been expected
that as soon as the First Empire had fallen all would be made
public. Many things no doubt were. Private journals, written
by men who had taken part in the ecclesiastical events of that
Empire, have years ago been published, and have thrown
light upon many of them. The Memoirs of Cardinal Pacca,
for instance, made known a vast number of most valuable and
interesting facts. But there was very much of which no record
existed, except in the secret correspondence of Napoleon himself with his ministers, and in that which went on between
them and their agents, especially those who from time to time
were entrusted with the charge of the Pope's person, or who
though he regarded them as his friends were in reality placed
as spies about him; or, again, who were commissioned to negotiate with him on the part of the Emperor. All these invaluable
documents have been carefully preserved, and many of them
have already been published in the vast collection of the
" Correspondence of Napoleon I.," which was published at
the expense of the French Government during the Second
Empire. That collection is a mine of invaluable historical
materials, and it professes to supply the means of writing a
true and correct history of the ecclesiastical relations of Napoleon I., and especially of his conduct towards Pius VII., no less
than of his military and political acts. In fact, very many of his
letters, instructions, memoranda, and other documents bearing
on these subjects are actually given. Everything has been
done which could possibly suggest to a diligent student of
that huge collection, that it is a full and fair account of all

that happened while Pius VII. was a prisoner, so far as it was known at the time to the French Government itself. That it is so, has, we believe, always been taken for granted. As a matter of fact, however, the impression given is as false as it could be made by the *suppressio veri.* This has been M. D'Haussonville's great discovery. He has, most carefully and successfully, sought out the letters, reports, and other documents which the commissioners, appointed by Napoleon III. to publish the correspondence of his uncle, have suppressed without giving the least notice of their existence. These suppressed documents supply the materials of the whole of his narrative during several successive years.

It appeared at a fortunate moment, when the extreme severity with which the press was silenced during the earlier years of the Second Empire had been relaxed, but before the overthrow of that Empire. At an earlier period the work would at once have been suppressed, for the picture it presents of Napoleon personally, as well as of his system of government, is most disgraceful—nay, contemptible. Especially it exposes the gross, wilful, and deliberate falsehood of the whole of that portion of the memoirs dictated to his friends by the dethroned tyrant at St. Helena, which refers to the ecclesiastical events of his reign, whether relating to Pius VII. himself, or to the bishops and clergy of the Empire. That this was felt to be the case by the Government of Napoleon III. is proved by the manner in which they dealt with it. A few years earlier it is certain that the serial work in which M. D'Haussonville's labours were first published, the *Revue des Deux Mondes* would not have dared to publish it, and that any periodical which had ventured to do so would have been suppressed. When the laws against free publication were relaxed, the Government showed its dislike to the book as well as it could, by giving orders that M. D'Haussonville should be exceptionally refused access to the documents in the " Archives," which were open to the public in general. The book may have lost something by this exclusion, but it has gained more, for it proves that the attention of the Emperor and his Government had been turned to it, and that, if they could, they would have denied the authenticity of the very numerous letters and documents of Napoleon I. which the author gives, but which had been suppressed by the commissioners appointed to publish his writings. Again, had the work first appeared after the fall of the Second Empire, some doubt might have been thrown upon it, as it actually has upon the papers of Napoleon III. published under the " Government of Defence." All this is now prevented, and M. D'Haussonville's volumes, in which he carefully puts together both all that has before been published, and also all that has hitherto been suppressed, will henceforth be the main authority for historians who undertake to treat of the conduct of Napoleon, either towards the Pope or towards the Church in his Empire.

Neither must it be supposed that it is, like the " Correspondence" itself, so unwieldy as to be without value to any except historians and deep students. The work extends to five volumes. But it is luxuriously printed (nearly three pages would make only a page of the DUBLIN REVIEW), and a very large proportion of each volume consists of " Pièces Justificatives," consisting of Napoleon's suppressed letters and other documents, which, though invaluable as authorities for what is stated in the text, need not be read by any ordinary student who will be satisfied with the account given of them by the author. In the fifth volume, for instance, these documents occupy two hundred and fifteen pages out of five hundred and sixty-seven. The narrative, moreover, is so interesting as to carry the reader on, whether he intends it or not; and it is much easier to take up the book than to lay it down.

The early part of the third volume gives an account of the state of things in Rome during the seventeen months which elapsed between the occupation of the city by Napoleon's troops, and the violent carrying away of the Holy Father into France. It is impossible not to be struck with the parallel between the situation of Pius VII. during these months and that of Pius IX. at the present moment. Thus we find that the French took possession of the printing-offices and the post-offices in obedience to positive commands from Napoleon himself, who wrote to his representative at Rome (vol. iii. p. 9) to " prevent the publication of any printed papers or acts, of whatever kind, opposed to France, which might be put out by the Roman Government, and to make the police and the booksellers of Rome responsible for them." The Holy Father, however, had already drawn up a protest against the occupation, which must have been printed before the entrance of the French troops, as it was posted at all the usual places on the day they came in. It is said to have been " clandestinely printed during the night, and to have made its unexpected appearance on the walls of Rome." It declared—

His Holiness Pius VII., being unable to fulfil all the demands made upon him on the part of the French Government, because he is forbidden to do so by the voice of conscience and by his sacred duties, feels himself bound to submit to all the disastrous consequences with which he has been threatened in case of refusal, and even to the military occupation of his capital.

Resigned in humility of heart to the impenetrable judgments of Heaven, he puts his cause into the hands of God, but he will not fail in the essential obligation of maintaining his Sovereign rights, and has therefore commanded us to protest, and he does hereby formally protest, in his own name and in that of his successors, against all usurpation of his dominions: it being his will that the rights of the Holy See should ever be and remain intact (iii. p. 5).

A protest, in the main similar, was also presented to all the ambassadors of foreign powers in Rome. After this the Holy Father (like Pius IX. at this moment) remained passive.

Satisfied that he had saved his honour by the protest affixed to the walls of his capital, having made up his mind in spite of the importunities of the *corps diplomatique* not to stir out of the enclosure of the Quirinal, so as to mark the more strongly that he considered himself a prisoner ; Pius VII. had laid in a stock of patience. He did not dislike, in his capacity of Sovereign, to shut himself up as long as possible in a resistance purely passive, and there was no saying to what point his resignation would go (iii. p. 28).

Thus, as the author says, the only embarrassment caused by the occupation of Rome was that felt by the usurper.

What was to be the next move ? Napoleon had already resolved to annex the States of the Church; but he always liked to make some excuse for every outrage, and the modern custom of *plébiscites*, though a " Napoleonic idea," had not yet been applied to such cases. He would have thought himself degraded by such a device as that employed the other day by Victor Emmanuel. Not that he would have felt that there was anything degrading in its falsehood. That was a notion which evidently never presented itself to his imagination. So far he would have been the last man to have any scruple in professing to have received in a day twice as many votes as could physically have been taken in the time by the method of voting adopted; but he would have felt it unworthy of his dignity to profess that he held Rome merely by the election of a Roman mob. What he did resolve upon was to drive the Holy Father to resistance by further injuries, and he chose them with his usual skill. The Pope had shown that he was ready to submit to any outrage upon his temporal sovereignty, although he would neither do nor omit anything by which he might make himself responsible for it. Napoleon therefore resolved to interfere with his spiritual administration. This could not be carried on without the assistance of a body of ecclesiastics. The Emperor therefore determined, that all the dignitaries of the Church, cardinals, bishops, priests, &c., " including those who discharged about the Pope's person

purely spiritual functions, relating only to the cure of souls,"
should be driven or forcibly carried away from Rome. The
only exception was to be in the case of natives of the States
of the Church. The Pope gave positive commands to each
cardinal not to leave Rome, and, should he be carried away
by force, not to continue his journey any farther than he was
so taken. The Emperor began with the cardinals, and then
went on to the bishops and other prelates, born in the kingdom of Naples, many of whom occupied the most important
positions in the Pope's spiritual administration. The Neapo-
litan cardinals were carried away by force, the prelates received orders to follow them. The Pope (against the advice
of those around him) recalled his legate from Paris, and
having no other means of publicly expressing his feelings,
(for the printing-presses had been seized,) he collected the
cardinals remaining in Rome and addressed to them in an
allocution the strongest protest, ending,—

" We exhort, nay we entreat,-we conjure the Emperor and King Napoleon
to change his resolution, and to return to the sentiments which he manifested
at the beginning of his reign. Let him remember that the Lord God is a
King far above all kings, far above himself, all-powerful as he may be ; that
He accepts no man's person, and respects no grandeur, be it what it may ; and
that those who command others will themselves be one day most severely
judged by Him. We understand that we have now a great persecution to
endure, but we are fully prepared for it, being fortified by those words of
the Divine Master, ' Blessed are they who suffer persecution for the sake of
righteousness.' "

There was no possibility of delusion ; and at Rome especially none was
entertained. The recal of the cardinal legate and the allocution pronounced
by the Holy Father in the Consistory of March 16th, were acts which could
not fail to excite to the extremest point the fury of the Emperor. For
several weeks the members of the Sacred College and all the functionaries of
the Pontifical Government were in trembling expectation of seeing ruthless
orders arrive from France which would bring the fatal dispute to a crisis
(iii. p. 40).

Yet the expected thunderbolt was delayed, and the reason
of the delay was characteristic. It was a rule with Napoleon
never to run the slightest risk of having on his hands two difficult matters at the same time. Daring and unscrupulous as
he ever was, never until he had become intoxicated by the
long continuance of success and prosperity such as never fell
to the lot of any other man of whom history speaks, did he,
in a single instance, forget the restraint which this rule
imposed. He was at this moment starting to Bayonne,
whither he had lured the King of Spain. His whole mind

was engrossed with plans, all perfidious and shameless, but each weighed with the calmest and most calculating prudence, as to the future fate of the monarch who had been so unhappy as to trust to his honour, and of the kingdom of which he resolved to deprive him; and no provocation would have moved him to get into any difficulty about the Pope so long as there was any possibility that the Spanish affair might yet give him any trouble. Neither was it his way to threaten when he had made up his mind to strike. As he wrote at this very crisis to his brother Louis, offering him, before it was taken from the head of Ferdinand, the crown of which he intended to dispose (iii. p. 41), " A thing should be completed before it is known that we have even thought of it." As yet therefore he took no decisive measure, but left it to his ministers to keep the Holy Father in a state of perpetual torment by one act of aggression after another. Thus the Marches and Umbria were formally annexed to his " Kingdom of Italy," and formed into three departments. All cardinals, prelates, officers, and other functionaries born in that kingdom were ordered immediately to return to it, on pain of the confiscation of all their property. The French troops (by a disgraceful stratagem) forced their way into the Quirinal and disarmed the Pope's guards. Pius VII. then wrote to the Bishops of Umbria and the Marches to forbid both clergy and laity to take any oath of fidelity to the intrusive Government, or accept any employment under it. The bishops and clergy were not to sing *Te Deum* on its establishment, but an oath of passive obedience, submission, and non-resistance might be taken. Individuals should never disturb the public peace by plots and factions, because this commonly results in still more grave disasters and scandals (p. 52). The French general at Rome replied to this by seizing, in the Quirinal, and carrying off to Sinigaglia (of which he was bishop) the Pope's Secretary of State, Cardinal Gabrielli, successor to Cardinal Doria, who being a Genoese by birth, had already been ordered to return home, Genoa having been annexed to France. When the news of these events reached Napoleon, who was still at Bayonne, his repeated charge to his agents in Italy was to keep things quiet, to take care that nothing got into print, and that no noise was made.

Cardinal Pacca was now made the Pope's minister. The French general gave him notice that the Emperor had given him orders to hang or shoot any person in the States of the Church who should oppose his sovereign will. " General," replied the Cardinal, " you ought by this time to have discovered that the ministers of His Holiness do not allow themselves to be intimidated by threats. As far as I am personally concerned, I shall faithfully execute the orders of my sovereign come what may." There the matter rested for the moment. On September 6th, 1808, two French officers arrested Pacca in his apartment in the Quirinal, and told him they were to conduct him to Benevento, his native place. He obtained leave to send word to the Pope, and in a few minutes the door was thrown open and Pius VII. entered. He forbad the Cardinal to submit, took him by the hand, and led him to his own apartments, where he kept him. Of this scene we have a most curious description. And thus things went on for several months. Rome was in a strange state.

The Holy Father was still morally obeyed and reverenced by the immense majority of his subjects as if still in possession of his temporal power. The French general on his side allied, by the necessity of his position, against his own will, to the faction of disorder, maintained discipline not only in the ranks of his own army, which was exemplary in its conduct, but also among his compromising allies." (iii. p. 81).

But it became more and more clear that this state of things could not last much longer. Napoleon, though so anxious to keep everything quiet, was not too busy to think of petty annoyances which he thought it possible to offer to the Holy Father, or to write to his agents from the heart of Spain to prescribe them. When the spring of 1809 came he had left Spain and had for a second time made himself master of Vienna, the Austrian empire having renewed the war : and from Schönbrunn he sent orders for the annexation of Rome to his empire.

On the 10th of June, at two o'clock p.m., the Pontifical flag was pulled down from the castle of S. Angelo and the tricolour hoisted. It was saluted by a discharge of artillery, while the French troops proclaimed through the city, with the sound of trumpets, the Imperial decree, dated from Vienna.

The minister of the Pope shall tell his own tale. " I rushed," writes Cardinal Pacca, " into the apartment of the Holy Father, and as we met, each pronounced the words of our Saviour, *Consummatum est.* It is difficult to describe my feelings, but the sight of the Holy Father, who preserved an unalterable tranquillity, both greatly edified me and restored my courage. A few minutes later my nephew brought me a copy of the Imperial decree. The Pope rose and followed me to the window to hear me read it. I tried to overcome the first pain of the moment, and to read with attention this important document, by which the measures we had to take were to be regulated, but my just and deep indignation at the sacrilege that hour consummated, the presence close to me, before my face, of my unfortunate Sovereign the Vicar of Jesus Christ, waiting to hear from my mouth his sentence of dethronement, the calumnies which at the first glance of my eye I saw in this impious decree, the continual roar of the cannon which announced with insulting triumph the most iniquitous sacrilege,—all this so deeply moved me, and so much affected my sight, that I was unable to read, without frequent interruption and a half-choked voice, the principal articles of the decree. Then, attentively watching the Pope, I saw his countenance affected at the first words, and remarked the signs, not of fear or dejection, but of an indignation only too natural. By degrees he recovered himself, and listened to what I read with great calmness and resignation. When it was finished the Holy Father went to the table, and, without saying a word, signed the copies of a protest in Italian which was stuck up in Rome the night following (iii. p. 98).

Two forms of a Bull of Excommunication had already been drawn up by Cardinal Pietro, one to be signed if Napoleon should seize the person of the Pope at the same time that he took possession of Rome; the other if he should (as actually happened) leave him for the moment at liberty. This last was signed the same day and posted at S. Peter's, S. Mary Major, S. John Lateran, and the Market Place. Although posted in the broad day, none of the persons who did it were arrested or even discovered. It is stated by well-informed persons at Rome (but not mentioned by our author) that this was managed by a man who carried on his back a large barrel like those in which wine is carried at Rome. He leaned his burden against the wall, as if to relieve himself of its weight; while he thus stood a boy who was concealed in the barrel opened a small door which had been prepared in it, and pasted the paper on the wall. When the man moved on it was left behind, and yet he had not so much as turned his eyes towards the wall. The publication of this Bull was immediately followed by the seizing of the Pope's person.

Napoleon always declared, he wrote in his memoirs, he repeated several times over to M. de Las Casas in his conversations at St. Helena, that he never gave orders for the arrest of the Pope. When he made this prodigious assertion, Napoleon I. did not suspect that his correspondence would at a later period be officially published by Napoleon III. . . . . The letter written to his brother-in-law, the King of Naples, leaves no room for evasion. " If the Pope, contrary to the spirit of his order and of the Gospel, preaches revolt, and tries to make use of the immunity of his house to cause circulars to be printed, *he must be arrested* " (iii. p. 102).

It is remarkable, observes our author, that " we already possess four accounts of the carrying away of the Holy Father, all written by eye-witnesses, or, to speak more exactly, by actors in the drama." The Pope ordered the doors to be locked, and no person whatever to be admitted after dark. Sentinels stood where they could see any one who approached the palace, and the populace continually watched all the movements of the troops, and gave notice of everything to Cardinal Pacca. General Radet wrote to the French minister for war: "The horizon gets darker. The Pope governs more effectually by lifting his finger than we do with our bayonets." It was essential that the violence about to be done to his person should be concealed from the people till it was completed; and this was skilfully managed. The general found that the Pope's sentinel left his post at daybreak. Some French soldiers who had waited till then got in at an upstairs window into an unoccupied room, and opened the door. The general did not know the way to the apartment of the Vicar of Christ; but, that the resemblance to his Lord might be more complete, those who came to seize him were guided by a traitor, a servant, who had been a thief, and who had accepted hire for his treason. It was at daybreak on the 6th of July, 1809; yet, early as it was, Pius VII. was found quietly seated on the sofa opposite the door of his apartment, with the two Cardinals, Pacca and Despuig, sitting on either side; for he had given the most positive orders that he should immediately be awakened in case of any alarm, and, on hurrying to his room, they had found him dressing. "Now," he had said, " I am with my true friends." Cardinal Despuig had then proposed that he should retire to the private chapel, and there await the soldiers; but the Pope thought there would not be time, and that if he were overtaken going to the chapel, it would look as if he were flying. The French soldiers came on, breaking open the doors of the antechambers:—

To avoid disorder, he gave orders that the door of the room should be opened. Then Radet came in, not yet knowing either where or in whose presence he was; but he soon discovered it by the manner of the men who followed him, some of whom (not to mention him who acted as guide) were Romans, to whom the person of the Holy Father was known. Finding that he was in the Presence, Radet took off his hat, and sending back most of his band caused to enter one by one the greater part of the officers of his suite and some non-commissioned officers of gendarmerie, who, silently gliding in at the half-opened door and along the wall of the apartment, ranged themselves in order, with drawn swords and arms grounded, on his right and left. Thus the room was occupied by two groups drawn up facing each other. At the head of the one General Radet, his hat in his hand, booted and spurred, his sword at his side, in the attitude of a military man who has just been taking a place by assault, but perfectly respectful, and at his side a dozen Frenchmen, officers commissioned and non-commissioned, with whom were mixed two or three officers of the Roman civic guard, who were followed by some of the dregs of the people. Opposite to him the Pope, in an ecclesiastical habit as simple as possible, wearing on his finger (says our Italian authority) the Pontifical ring which Pius VI. had worn during his captivity in France, the two Cardinals seated by him, and behind him a group made up of the principal servants of his household. Each party looked at the other, and silence lasted for more than five minutes. It was evident that General Radet was much disconcerted. He could not without difficulty recover his self-control ; it seemed that he'wished to speak, but the words would not come. At last he came forward a few steps, bowed low, and said to his Holiness that he had to perform a painful mission—a mission imposed on him by his oath and by the sacred duties of his position. At these words the Pope stood up, and looking at him with dignity, said, " What do you want with me? and why have you come at such an hour to disturb my rest and my house ? " " Most Holy Father," replied General Radet, "I come in the' name of my Government, to repeat to your Holiness the proposal of giving up your temporal power. If your Holiness consents to this, I have no doubt matters can be arranged, and the Emperor will treat your Holiness with the greatest respect." Pius VII. replied, " If you have felt yourself bound to execute such orders of your Emperor because of your oath of fidelity aud obedience, consider the duty imposed on us—on us, We say,—to maintain the rights of the Holy See, to which we are bound by oaths so numerous. We have no power either to yield or abandon what is not our own. The Temporalities belong to the Church, and we are merely the administrator. The Emperor may have power to tear us in pieces, but that he will not obtain from us. After all that we have done for him, could we look for treatment such as this ? " Radet was more and more discon- certed. " I know, Holy Father, that the Emperor is under great obligations to you." " Yes ; and more than you are aware of. But, to cut this short, what are your orders ? " " Most Holy Father, I regret the commission im- posed upon me ; but since such is the resolution of your Holiness, I am com- pelled to say that my orders are to conduct you with me." At these words the Holy Father, who till then had maintained the most dignified tone, suddenly addressed himself to Radet and said, with an air of tenderness and compas- sion, " Indeed, my son, that commission is not one to bring down on you the Divine Blessing." Then, lifting his eyes to heaven, " This, then, is the return made to me for all that I have done for your Emperor. This is the reward for my great concessions towards himself and towards the Church of France. But perhaps God has seen that I have committed a fault in them. It is His will to punish me, and I submit with all humility." (iii. p. 120.)

As Radet was`leading him to his bedroom, he suggested to the Pope to commit any valuable property to safe hands. He replied, " A man who does not care for life cares less for worldly property."

He then took only his Breviary, and the Crucifix which he usually carried hanging at his breast. Then, leaning on Radet's arm and followed by Car- dinal Pacca, he went down the great staircase of the Quirinal. On reaching the great doors, Pius VII. stood still, and gave his blessing to Rome. The French troops were drawn up in order of battle on the Great Place of Monte- Cavallo. None of the population of Rome were either there or at the win- dows. It was four in the morning, and profound silence reigned everywhere.

General Radet says that the soldiers received with a sacred reverence the Blessing of the Pope. He then caused the Pope and Cardinal Pacca to get into a carriage, the blinds of which had been carefully nailed, and the doors of which were then locked by a *gendarme*, took his place on the box with a quartermaster, and gave orders to the postillions to go out of the city by the Porta Pia and go round, outside the wall, to the Porta del Popolo. The carriage was escorted by a detachment of *gendarmerie*." (iii. p. 123.)

It was nearly five A.M. when the carriage, with fresh post-horses, started at full speed for Florence. The Pope asked the Cardinal whether he had any money. They found that the Cardinal had about sevenpence halfpenny, the Pope tenpence. "We are travelling in apostolic fashion," said Pacca. Pius VII. added with a smile, "This is all that remains to me of my dominions." The Cardinal had a secret feeling of uneasiness, because it had been by himself that the publication of the Bull of Excommunication had been advised. He was relieved when the Pope added with an air of satisfaction, "It is well that we published the Bull of June 10th, for how could we have done it now?"

Pius VII. was aged, and afflicted with a painful disease, which was aggravated by travelling, and he suffered much on his journey. He reached Florence on the 8th, near midnight. It was governed by Napoleon's sister, Eliza. At three A.M. a colonel arrived with orders that the Pope should instantly go farther. He particularly wished to stay to say mass, especially as it was Sunday, but she would hear of no delay. This was not from cruelty, but from absolute terror. Three days brought him in a very suffering state to the immediate neighbourhood of Genoa. This was then called part of France. But the fear of the authorities was as great as it had been in Tuscany. The mountains came so near to the sea, that there was no possibility of sending the august prisoner by land in any way which would avoid the city. But he was hurried by night to the shore, and carried by sea across the Gulf of Genoa. Thus he reached Alessandria on his way towards Turin. But the Prince Borghese, who governed Turin, was far too much alarmed to let him come there, and he was hurried on by Mondovri and Rivoli to Grenoble.

Whence all this fear? It cannot be doubted that each of Napoleon's satraps had at heart a real terror, like that which induced the Philistines to send away the Ark of God—a sincere dread of the Divine judgments upon any one who should take any part in keeping as a prisoner the Vicar of Christ. But mixed with this was a horrible dread of the tyrant whose instruments they were. They had received no commands from the Emperor. How was the Pope to be received? If he were treated either with too great or too little severity, who could say into what disgrace they might fall? There he was, an old and ailing man; what if he should die in their hands? The matter was made ten times worse by the enthusiasm of the people. The Holy Father had been hurried from Rome unknown to the inhabitants. But the tidings of his having been carried off soon spread, not by newspapers, for none were allowed to publish anything without the special permission of the authorities, but from mouth to mouth. The farther he went, the longer the news had been spreading, and, therefore, the greater the enthusiasm of the people, and the crowds who assembled by the road-side in the country and in the market-places of the towns to kneel for his blessing. "The journey," says our author, "which at its beginning had been that of a martyr, soon became a procession of triumph." The farther he went the more decidedly was this the case, and the greater was the fear of the subordinate authorities. The people, naturally enough, could not believe that their religious Emperor could be otherwise than pleased by their expressions of loyalty to the Pope, whom they had so lately greeted with the same enthusiasm as he went to Paris for the coronation.

When news of these things reached Napoleon he was far from pleased. To deny that he had ever authorized the arrest of the Pope was naturally his first instinct, for no lie was too mean for that mighty monarch, that vast genius. As things were, he ordered that he should be sent to Savona on the Riviera, and that Cardinal Pacca should be separated from him, and shut up in the State Prison of Fenestrella. It is a curious instance of the absolute suppression of all news in France under his tyranny, that no journal was allowed to allude to the fact that the Pope had ever come into France. At Grenoble, at the moment when the town was thronged with multitudes from all the country round to kneel for his blessing, the local official journal made no allusion to his' having ever been there. Throughout France and in Paris nothing was known about it. Strange to say, there appeared in the *Moniteur* a letter dated from Grenoble on the very day on which the Pope was hurried away by orders given by Fouché in obedience to those of Napoleon. Those who had heard reports that he had been there, and knew not what to believe, turned eagerly, says our author, expecting some official news on the matter. The letter said: " All men's minds here are occupied by the passage through the commune of Bornin (which the Pope passed through on approaching Grenoble)' of an unknown animal. The marks it left seem to show that it must have been a reptile of extraordinary size." Then followed half a page of details about this reptile, which, it was added, after having wholly engrossed public attention, disappeared in a torrent. What induced Fouché to publish this one can hardly imagine. Was it an attempt to laugh at the Pope? Napoleon, at least, evidently felt the whole thing to be no laughing matter. Nothing could exceed the precautions taken to keep the Pope's journey from Grenoble to Savona out of public observation. He was not allowed to pass through any town when it could be avoided, and so strictly was he watched, that when the uncle of the Emperor, Cardinal Fesch, who was Archbishop of Lyons, sent his Grand Vicars to pay homage to the Holy Father and present him with some money, they were not allowed access to him. For a long time France was not let to know that the Pope had ever left Rome. At last, when it became necessary to admit that he was at Savona, the only version of the matter which Napoleon allowed to be published was that he had gone thither of his own accord. As late as 1811, when he had been in the most strict imprisonment for nearly two years, the Emperor declared in his official message to the clergy of France assembled by his command in what he called a National Council, "The Pope had so acted that his presence at Rome became useless; and some of his partisans might, against his own will, make it dangerous. On the 6th of July he left Rome without the knowledge of the Emperor, and came to Savona, where his Majesty caused him to be received, entertained, and established with all the respect due to misfortune." (iii. p. 141.)

Pius VII. reached Savona on the 21st of August, 1809. All that passed there until he was carried, still as a prisoner, to Fontainebleau on the 9th of June, 1812, was kept at the time absolutely secret; and our author says (vol. v. p. 140) that at least the whole of the negotiations carried on with him on the part of Napoleon have been till now wholly unknown, "no historian, either ecclesiastical or lay, having made any mention of them." His own account of them, in general very minute, is taken exclusively from the official documents, and although there are expressions here and there which a Catholic could not have used, we cannot but express our astonishment, on the whole, at the tone of fairness maintained by our author, who, it is to be specially observed, is a French Protestant. We must in justice confess that we doubt whether any English Protestant, even if he belonged to the school which most louldly claims to call itself Catholic, would have written in a tone of so much candour and even reverence towards the Pope. But this we believe to be the natural result of the different position of Protestantism in the two countries. In England Protestantism, as a religion, is in its death-struggle. In France it has long ago been dead and buried; and a French Protestant, even if, like M. Guizot, he presents the strange inconsistency of being still a really religious man, is, in truth, only a "Christian unattached." There are, no doubt, plenty of the same class in England, but they are not our religious men, still less are they to be found in the school which cares most about religious questions. Such persons would have written, and we fear will read, the deeply interesting history before us with their minds occupied with the idea of proving that communion with the Pope is not essential to a Catholic position, and such other figments, which to an impartial looker-on like M. D'Haussonville would seem very pitiful nonsense. That he never felt any wish to be a Catholic is only too probable. But that he would feel it childish and absurd to pretend to be a Catholic without being in communion with Pius IX. is most certain and evident. Such nonsense is a growth indigenous in our happy island, and peculiar to it.

When the Pope arrived at Savona, after residing four days in the family of Count Egidio Santone, where he was received with all due reverence, he was moved to the Episcopal Palace, where his apartments were fitted up, by order of the Emperor, in a manner suited to "a sovereign prince of the first dignity" (iii. p. 395). He was surrounded with servants to whom high salaries were offered in the name of the Emperor. He was using "a poor copper lamp and a very ordinary desk"; but this was no sooner seen than "a superb silver lustre and an escritoire magnificently inlaid with gold" were substituted for them. "Equipages, horses, &c., were supplied, and an income of four thousand pounds monthly promised him." All this was declined "with great gentleness and many thanks," and those around him were requested to receive nothing except actual necessaries. General Cæsar Berthier (brother to the Prince of Wagram) was sent to preside over his household, with orders to keep up a good establishment, and invite habitually the friends of the Holy Father, to whom all possible reverence was to be shown. At the same time the strictest *surveillance* was to be maintained. The general was never to be absent from the Pope's *levées*, or, if absent, was to be represented there by an officer of *gendarmerie*. At the same time there must be nothing which could suggest the idea of captivity. The difficulty of reconciling these orders, says our author, was increased because the Pope would not in any degree lend himself to lessen it. He found pleasure in returning to the simple life he had led as a monk before he rose in the Church. He refused to attend the Cathedral pontifically, and would only say mass in his private chapel. "There he was often found in tears, praying not only for the oppressed Church, but also for the prince who, after having so decidedly protected it, had suddenly become its most vehement persecutor. His only relaxation was to walk in the walled garden of the Episcopal Palace, where his walk was only about fifty paces backward and forward." It was difficult for Napoleon to deal with a man of habits like these. Where wealth and splendour were considered no gain, it was hard to discover what would be felt as a loss. Hitherto the Emperor had found that if he began with violence and intimidation his victims were only too glad to accept a reconciliation upon any terms he might be so gracious as to concede. He had calculated without a misgiving that such must be the case with Pius VII. But he found himself wholly mistaken. Unluckily, he could not go on as if nothing had happened, for do what he would, he could not help negotiating with his prisoner. Cardinal Pacca might be left at Fenestrella till he died, and things in France would go on quietly; but without Bulls from the Holy Father no Bishop could take possession of his See, and he could not leave the Sees vacant. Almost from the first, therefore, he discovered that by violence against the Pope instead of smoothing the course of affairs, he had thrown them into a state of embarrassment out of which he himself, all-powerful as he was, was utterly unable to extricate them, and that, however unwillingly, he must negotiate with his unresisting prisoner. This was a position wholly new and eminently distasteful to him.

His first step was to suggest to' his uncle, Cardinal Fesch, to the Cardinals Caprara and Maury, on whom he could reckon, and to several of the French bishops, to write, as if of their own will, to the Holy Father, and explain how much the Church was suffering by the want of canonical bishops. The letters would have been delivered to the Pope before he reached Savona, if they had not been intercepted by the zeal of Fouché. When they arrived, there was a remarkable difference between them. "The letter of Cardinal Fesch was full of expressions of reverence and of a sincere sympathy for the recent sufferings of the Holy Father. That of Cardinal Maury made evident and becoming allusion to them." Cardinal Caprara, who had been the Legate of Pius VII. at Paris, and M. de Barral, Archbishop of Tours, made no allusion to the subject. The

Archbishop seemed to suppose that the refusal of the Pope to institute " proceeded from some childish caprice, and that he had no motive to assign for it." The cardinal did not seem even to have heard, either of the departure of the Pope from Rome or of the seizure of his dominions. The Pope's answer would have made him aware of these facts if he had really been ignorant. It ended by declaring his wish to fill up the Sees, but that he could not do so, consistently with his duty, till he had about him his natural councillors, the members of the sacred college. When Napoleon saw this answer, says our author, he seems for the first time in his life to have felt a doubt as to the wisdom of his own manner of proceeding. He resolved that while the Pope should have no ecclesiastical advisers, he would have some for himself, and he constituted an " ecclesiastical committee " composed of a few whom he believed he could trust. This committee at least saved him from one inconceivable absurdity which he had so far contemplated, as, according to his custom, to make his minister write him a report as to the details of the plan. This was that of calling a general council by his own authority, and presiding in it himself. The committee seem to have convinced him that this would not do, and he took up another idea (which Cardinal Maury says he suggested to him), that the bishops nominated might be sent to administer their Dioceses, receiving from the Chapters faculties as Vicars Capitular, a plan from which the unfortunate ecclesiastics shrank with the strongest repulsion.

The fact is that the contest of Napoleon against the Church was in truth a necessary part of his system, and must have come on sooner or later, even if the questions connected with the temporal power of the Pope and the difficulties about the institution of the bishops springing out of it, had never been raised. The real cause of the quarrel was, that he was resolved to be an absolute despot, with control and without limitation. Now the Church is the kingdom of Heaven, and it was even more impossible that a man, who had made up his mind to be absolute master of the civilized world, could be content that the souls of his own subjects and their spiritual relations should be exempted from his dominion, than that he should be content that the neighbouring kingdoms should enjoy a real independence. His attack upon the Pope was as certain to come on as his wars with Austria, Prussia, or Russia. Upon this point M. Thiers and M. D'Haussonville are of one mind.* M. Thiers says what he wanted from the Pope

---

* Thiers, t. xiii. 35, quoted by D'Haussonville, iii. 412.

was, "the suppression of the temporal power of the Holy See —the annexation of Rome to the territory of the Empire— the establishment of a Papacy dependent upon the new Emperor of the West, residing at Paris or Avignon, enjoying splendid palaces, a salary of eighty thousand pounds, and many other advantages, but placed under the authority of the Emperor of the French, as the Russian Church is under the authority of the Czars, and Islamism under the authority of the Sultans." M. D'Haussonville himself says—

Let us repeat; for upon this point delusion is impossible, the two monstrous chimeras of domination over all Catholic consciences and of the resurrection of a new Empire of the West, entertained at the same time and caressed with the same love by this strange genius, had now become to his disordered imagination substantial realities. In order to put his hand officially to the work, Napoleon, as we shall soon see, was waiting only till he had won a decisive victory over his last adversary on the Continent—the Emperor Alexander. On the morrow of some triumphant treaty, signed at the gates of St. Petersburg or Moscow, a decree like that which, after Wagram pronounced the deposition of the Pope from his temporal dominion—a decree all the particulars of which were already long since matured in his own mind— was all of a sudden to proclaim the Pope's subordination in spirituals to the will of the chief of the French Empire. The final catastrophe of the Russian expedition was necessary in order that Europe might be spared the spectacle, not less strange than lamentable, of the two despots reconciled and dividing between themselves the nations like a miserable flock, and each making himself in his own dominion the absolute master not only of the political destinies, but of the religious faith, of his wretched subjects. How would Napoleon have set about the realization of his universal supremacy with regard to the Catholic faith? By what means would the terrible despot have set himself to overcome the obstacles, moral and material, which would certainly have been opposed to him by the branches of the Roman Church, which, spread over the European Continent, were not subject to his Empire, and those (more numerous still) in England, the United States, South America, the East, and over the whole surface of the globe, which were out of his reach? No man knows, and the world will never know ; for the Emperor did not think fit to explain to us in his Memoirs, how he intended to set about a task so extraordinary. He preferred to carry with him to the grave this incomprehensible secret (iii. p. 314).

But, though his Memoirs do not explain how he imagined it possible to set about the undertaking, they leave no doubt that he really intended it, and it need hardly be said that the mere forming of such a design implied the deliberate intention of engaging in a life-and-death struggle with the Catholic Church. And as it was his marriage with an Austrian archduchess which brought to the highest point the intoxication of his ambition, it was from that moment that he seems to

have made up his mind to begin his attack upon the spiritual
powers of the Pope. On the second Sunday after his marriage, April 15, 1810, he directed his *ministre des cultes* to
draw up a paper upon religious affairs, in which he was
not only to lay down principles, but to give in detail all the
measures which it would be expedient to adopt. It is explained,
that this paper is "not exactly a decree, because it will not
be put into execution or published, but is to remain in the
hands of the minister," and that as circumstances arose which
made it expedient that one or another part of the arrangements detailed in it should be carried into execution, a decree
was to be published embodying them. Thus, writes Napoleon, "the trouble of successive reports will be saved, and
every time there is a measure to be taken the minister will
recite both how much of the plan has been carried out and
how much remains to be carried out." "These general
arrangements," he adds, "must be divided according to the different territories and according to the order of matters." This
paper therefore, if we had it, which unfortunately is not the
case, would show Napoleon's ideal of Church affairs, which he
intended to carry out ultimately and by degrees. The order
to the minister shows what that ideal was; for he says, "things
are to be laid down as they ought to be, and in an absolute
manner, *as if no Pope existed.*" Nothing could more clearly
show that he had, at this period, deliberately made up his
mind, ultimately to take upon himself the whole power of the
Pope throughout the world. In the meantime, however, he
must begin by dealing with Pius VII., and how to do that
was a matter of difficulty—a difficulty which he had himself
created by his own violence and tyranny. By carrying the
Pope away as a prisoner he had hoped to compel him to begin
negotiations, and to approach Napoleon as a petitioner. That
hope had been completely frustrated. It now appeared that
he might wait as long as the Pope lived, and that things
would remain exactly as they were. This was quite inconsistent with the Emperor's plans, and therefore he found
himself compelled, in some way or other, to open negotiations
with his prisoner. In order to sound him, he began by
allowing an Austrian minister, who had been well known to
Pius VII. at Rome, to have an interview with him, ostensibly
merely upon some affairs in Austria, but with secret instructions to introduce the subject of the Pope's relations with
Napoleon, and to report what was the state of his mind
with regard to them. This unauthorized agent reported, that
"he had found the Pope a little aged, but in good health;
calm, serene, as usual, saying not one word of the least bitter-

nêss, even when entering on subjects upon which he could
not but feel most keenly." He had asked the Holy Father
whether he could do nothing to prevent the dangers to the
Church which the present state of things implied, and had
been struck to observe the tone of affectionate feeling towards
Napoleon with which he spoke, decidedly more so than towards
his own master, the Austrian Emperor. But he had said—

For ourselves we ask nothing of the Emperor. We have nothing more to
lose. We have sacrificed all to our duty. We are old and without wants.
What personal consideration could turn us aside from the line which our
conscience prescribes ! There is absolutely nothing that we desire. We
wish for no income, we wish for no honours. The alms of the faithful will
be enough for us. There have been Popes poorer than we, and we form no
wishes beyond the narrow enclosure in which you see us. But we do
ardently long that we may be restored to free communications with the
bishops and with the faithful (iii. p. 419).

Still there was evidently no disposition to give way, for he
added—

When opinions are founded on the voice of conscience and on sentiments
of duty, they are unchangeable, and be sure that there is in the world no
physical force which can long contend with a moral force of this nature.
The judgment we have pronounced as to the unhappy events which have
taken place in our Apostolic See has been dictated by such sentiments, and
therefore cannot vary so long as our duty obliges us to pronounce anything
upon them (iii. p. 421).

It was plain enough, from this report, that the time was
not come for making overtures to the Holy Father. Napoleon next sent two Cardinals, upon whom he felt that he could
depend to act as his creatures, still without any acknowledged
mission, but with secret instructions. The Pope, divining
why they were come, received them with civility, but still remained purely passive, only saying, in answer to their suggestions, that he would not go to Paris except as a prisoner, nor
negotiate with the Emperor, unless he had two cardinals of
his own choice for advisers.

The unfavourable report of these new commissioners decided
Napoleon to change his policy, and show that he could manage
the ecclesiastical affairs of France without the Pope's action.
He at once ordered the persons whom he had already nominated to the Sees of Asti, Liége, Poitiers, and St. Flour, but
who were waiting for canonical institution, to go to their
respective dioceses ; his minister had already explained to
him their extreme reluctance to do this, and it had hitherto
been indulged. At the same time he determined to fill up,

without waiting for canonical institution, the See of Paris. It had been vacant for two years, and Napoleon had nominated to it his uncle, Cardinal Fesch, whom the Chapter had at once made Vicar Capitular, glad to have the uncle of the Emperor as their medium of communication with the Government. He was already Archbishop of Lyons, and the excellent Abbé Emery, who was his confessor, had warned him not to assume at the same time the administration of the two most onerous Sees in France. Fesch, however, had the confidence in his own powers which marked the Bonaparte family, and had now for two years acted both as Archbishop of Lyons and Archbishop nominate of Paris. He was now required to act, without the Pope's authority, as Archbishop in full right. He refused. Napoleon insisted. His uncle replied, " Sire, *potius mori.*" " Ah ! ah !" replied the Emperor, "*potius mori;* rather Maury. Well,—be it so. Maury it shall be ;" and Cardinal Maury was nominated. He was a man of talent, and especially of eloquence, who had become distinguished under the old *régime,* and had resisted with great eloquence the attacks on the Church in the Constituent Assembly. He had been driven from France, and had been made a cardinal by Pius VI.; had returned to France after the *concordat,* and unhappily tarnished a great reputation by becoming a mere tool of Napoleon. He now submitted to the terms which Fesch had refused, and acted as Archbishop of Paris. It happened that there was in the Chapter of Paris a certain Abbé d'Astros. "He was," says our Protestant author, " anything but a fanatical priest. He was not only prudent and moderate, but a man penetrated with respect for the public authorities, and naturally inclined to conciliation. His tendencies were moderately Gallican. He had been one of the most decided in the Chapter in favour of conferring upon Cardinal Fesch the provisional administration of his diocese." He was, however, conscientious, and he had since discovered that, in doing this, he had made a mistake, and acted in opposition to the manifest intentions of the Holy Father. He had therefore voted against giving the same authority to Cardinal Maury, although as President of the Chapter he had spoken in the name of the commission which announced the vote to him. On that occasion the cardinal had declared that " he would never take his seat on the episcopal throne of Paris except the Pope should take him by the hand to conduct him to it." The cardinal showed no intention of keeping this engagement, but the Abbé d'Astros watched him closely. One day in society the cardinal introduced him and his colleagues as " my Grand Vicars." " Your Eminence is mistaken," said the Abbé,

" not the Grand Vicars of your Eminence, but of the Chapter." Another day the cardinal, in grand state, was administering ordination, and proceeded to require from a newly-ordained priest the usual oath of obedience to himself as his bishop. " Monseigneur," interrupted the Abbé, out loud, "permit me to observe, for the information of this young priest, that your Eminence has no right to demand from him this promise." On days of ceremony he had also forbidden the crossbearer to carry before the cardinal the Cross which is the emblem of Episcopal authority, and had bade him take it back to the sanctuary. This brave man wrote to the Pope at Savona to ask of him directions as to his conduct. Before he received an answer, he obtained privately a copy of a brief, addressed to the cardinal, forbidding him to exercise any jurisdiction in the Arch-diocese of Paris. Of this he could make no public use, but he privately consulted his own first cousin, M. Portalis, a member of Napoleon's Council and " Director of Publications," who advised him to keep it secret " in the interest of religion," adding that, if it were published, it would be his own official duty to suppress it as " unauthenticated and dangerous." A few days later, a brief addressed to the Abbé d'Astros himself, fell into the hands of the Police in which Pius VII. declared that : " To remove all doubt and for greater security he took away from Cardinal Maury all power and jurisdiction, declaring null and void everything done in opposition hereto, whether knowingly or ignorantly." This brief the Abbé had not received, it having been intercepted. Napoleon's wrath was gathering.

On New Year's Day it was the custom that all the authorities in Church and State attended the Emperor's reception, and on that day Napoleon I. delighted to make a scene by breaking out into violence against some man who had given him offence. This he did, as we all know, in March, 1803, in the case of the English Ambassador, Lord Whitworth, and was imitated by Napoleon III. in 1859 when he wished to quarrel with Austria. In 1811 the humble Abbé d'Astros was selected as the victim of such an explosion. The Emperor passed by the Senate, the generals, and officers with an angry air, and requiring Cardinal Maury to present his Grand Vicars, made one of his usual speeches to the poor Abbé about Bossuet, Gregory VII., the Gallican liberties, and the like, and that a man should be a Frenchman first, and that that was the way to be a good Christian, ending—

" I know that you are opposed to the measures which my policy prescribes. In all my empire you are the most suspected man. But I have the sword at my side (putting his hand on the hilt, an action familiar with Napoleon but rather out of place under the circumstances); take care of yourself." M. d'Astros says, "Nothing could be more pitiable than these last words and this menace of a sovereign who dominated over all Europe, against a poor priest in rochet and mozetta, armed only with his square cap. I said nothing, but contented myself with looking unaffectedly at the Emperor" (iii. p. 486).

When the reception was over the Cardinal asked M. d'Astros to go with him to the Minister of Police, the Duke of Rovigo, who after questioning and threatening him, and saying that if he did not confess he would never again see his family, "perhaps never the light," told him that his cousin M. Portalis had confessed that M. d'Astros had shown him the brief addressed to the Cardinal. This was simply false, but the Abbé fell into the trap and admitted it. Napoleon at once declared that he should be shot. One of his followers remonstrated that this would be a stain on his own glory, and he gave way, saying "Let him be thrown into prison for the rest of his life." He actually was sent the same day to the dungeon of Vincennes, where he was kept utterly without news of anything in the outer world till the fall of the Empire.* M. Portalis was publicly rated by the Emperor on the Council of State, deprived of all his offices, and sent into banishment. With regard to the Archbishopric of Florence much the same thing happened, except that the Emperor induced the man whom he had nominated, to undertake the office by personally assuring him that the whole question with the Pope would be arranged in a very few days, and that his Bulls would arrive before he could reach Florence. When he said this, he must have known not only that what he said was false, but that its falsehood would in a few days be evident to the man he was deceiving. It does not appear that the idea of there being something undignified in deliberate falsehood ever struck the mind of Napoleon.

We have in general confined ourselves to the history of the Holy Father, not having space to show in detail the monstrous tyranny of the Emperor toward the French clergy; we have made an exception in the case of the Abbé d'Astros because it did very materially affect the treatment of the Pope. He had hitherto been allowed to correspond with the clergy of the Empire through the instrumentality of the Bishop of Savona. Napoleon had not been unwilling that he should grant marriage dispensations and the like. But that he should direct the conscience of bishops, and that against the will of the

---

* He was Archbishop of Toulouse and Cardinal under the restoration.

Emperor, he considered a monstrous crime. The letters he wrote on this occasion are among those suppressed by the official editors of his correspondence. He at once wrote ordering the Pope's household to be cut down, his carriages and horses (which he had refused to accept) to be taken away, that he should be deprived of books, pen and ink, should not be allowed to communicate with any one, and that spies should be posted in all the inns at Savona to see that none obtained access to him. He even gave orders that his ring, the *an-nulus Piscatoris*, should be taken from him and sent to Paris. Pius VII. gave it up, but took care first to break it.

It is painful to read these orders, written with his own hand, by the man who when himself a prisoner at St. Helena complained so bitterly of the sufferings of captivity ; and reproached his jailor for treatment, the rudeness of which never approached to that which he cruelly practised towards the prisoner of Savona. The object of the Emperor was to give himself the pleasure of inflicting personal suffering upon the Pope, nor did he attempt to conceal it. He wrote " You will make the Prefect and Prince Borghese understand, that it is my intention that the Pope should himself intimately feel my displeasure at his conduct." His agent, M. de Chabrol, reports " that in conformity with his instructions he had markedly treated the Pope as one ignorant of what is due to sovereigns " (iii. 479).

The Emperor also gave orders that the director of his archives should publish an historical book against the Popes : and was even thinking of deposing him by his own authority, for he directed his librarian to examine and report, " whether there were any examples of Emperors who had deposed or suspended Popes.

The extreme violence of Napoleon's conduct at this period has been supposed to have been caused by passion, and he himself gave this account of the matter at St. Helena. Our author is convinced that it was deliberately adopted, that he believed he had almost completed his military victories, and was resolved to make himself absolute master at home. In civil matters this was already done; the only difficulty foreseen by his " marvellous sagacity as a despot " was in the Catholic Church; and here he resolved to put down opposition to his absolute will by sheer terror. The evidence that this was the deliberate reason of his demonstrations of passion was, that he took pains to make them known. Thus he wrote a special letter to the Viceroy of Italy to tell him of his disgraceful outbreak of rage against M. Portalis. Just at the same time, by way of increasing the terror, he seized and committed to dungeons, avowedly for life, three cardinals and a very large number of ecclesiastics, accused of no offence except that they were sus-

pected of feeling sympathy with his victims. Two great ladies
were seized, detained for a while, and threatened with the
same fate. He even thought of imitating Henry VIII. by
regulating all the affairs of the Church by a decree of his
legislative body, and was dissuaded from this madness only
by Cambacérès and other members of his council, who, though
themselves unbelievers, saw its extreme wildness. They, no
doubt saw, what his own immense penetration would have
made plain to him, if he had not now been intoxicated by his
wonderful prosperity, that the same thing cannot be done in
states of society widely unlike ; and that the period in which
an Anglican Church could be created by Act of Parliament
was gone by for ever. But though he gave up this, he did
not give up the hope of making himself as absolute in spiritual
matters as he already was in temporal. He resolved that no
one should even talk of ecclesiastical affairs ; and, carrying
out this resolution, made an address to his " Legislative
Body," in which, while professing to go over all that had happened since its last session, he passed over without a word the
carrying away of the Pope from Rome and his imprisonment
at Savona. The Minister for Worship had to make a report
to the " ecclesiastical commission," and though it consisted of
his own creatures on whom he could safely depend, Napoleon
would not allow the facts to be stated even to them. " The
habit of invariable lying was too strong for him," adds our
author, and he returned to the minister his proposed address
requiring him to leave out of it what he had said about the
Holy Father.

It seemed curious that while so anxious to prevent all mention of the Pope, and of what he had done and what he was
actually suffering, he allowed the *Moniteur* day after day for
months together to publish addresses from different ecclesiastical bodies which professed the most absolute devotion to
his policy, and especially supported his claims, as opposed to
those of the Holy Father, as to the vacant bishoprics. The
first of these addresses purported to be from the Chapter of
Notre Dame at Paris. Our author gives a curious and interesting history in detail of the drawing up of this address,
which was dictated by Napoleon himself, received in silence
by the mass of the Chapter when read to them, objected to
by the saintly Abbé Emery, altered owing to his objection,
and then published by Napoleon, not as the Chapter had
agreed to it, but as he had drawn it up. It appeared in the
Moniteur, and then for months were published addresses echo-
ing it from all the chapters and ecclesiastical bodies, in the
empire and in the kingdom of Italy. The space in the official

journal formerly occupied by war was now devoted to these declarations of the clergy against the Holy Father. No doubt, what the author says is true, that the servility which he found among them inspired Napoleon with contempt for the clergy in general. He was wont to say that Emery was the only man who inspired him with fear, yet with all this he revered him, and said in his better moments that he should die more happy if he could feel that he left the education of the next generation in hands like his. Yet it was evidently nothing but his opportune death which saved Emery himself from persecution, and his community was actually broken up. It must be remembered, moreover, that although Napoleon found much servility, he did not find that alone. How many hundreds of priests died in his dungeons will never be known till they and he stand together before the judgment-seat of Christ. And as for these addresses, we only know the details of one case, and in that one we know that the canons refused to vote the address which Napoleon dictated, and that he published it declaring they had voted it. How many more of the addresses may have been forgeries we know not.

But what was Napoleon's object in departing from his ordinary policy of entirely suppressing all expression of opinion on religious matters, by publishing in the *Moniteur* these addresses and a discussion in the Council of State to which our author calls attention, when it professed to make null and void the decree of the Holy Father about the archbishopric of Florence? There can, we think, be no doubt that our author gives the true answer to this question. Pius VII. was now a close prisoner. No friend, no intelligence from the outer world could reach him except by the connivance of his jailor, M. de Chabrol, Prefect of Montenotte. Care was taken that every cardinal and bishop who was admitted to see him repeated to him, however respectfully in manner, that the Church was in a desperate state, and that the only cause of all its miseries was that he himself refused to make arrangements which might be made without any sacrifice of principle, which were absolutely necessary in the changed state of society, and which the whole Church agreed in desiring. Then as to reading, M. de Chabrol took care to supply him with the *Moniteur*, and he never saw anything else. No letters, except such as were written in exactly the same spirit, were allowed to penetrate to him. And in the *Moniteur* he saw addresses from all the ecclesiastical bodies of the Empire and of the Kingdom of Italy, all re-echoing the same statements. There are well-known stories of men who have been convinced of facts opposed to the positive evidence of their own senses by what seemed to them the independent testimony of a number of witnesses all agreeing together.* Never was this device tried upon any man so unscrupulously, so ably, so consistently, and for so long a period together as it was upon Pius VII. To add that it was not wholly without success is really to say little more than that he was a man. This great conspiracy was not set in motion with any intention of changing the doctrines which he believed and taught, and of which he would at once have said, " Though we or an angel from heaven preach any other doctrine, let him be anathema." All that was desired was to convince him that the good of the Church required that he should agree to certain practical measures, not in themselves desirable, but which had become absolutely necessary in the existing state of the political world. Many of his predecessors had made concessions, more or less important upon similar subjects. Nay, he himself had done the same in the concordat which he had made with Napoleon in 1801. He might very naturally be persuaded, that he was mistaken in refusing to make new concessions of the same class, if he found that all Catholics, cardinals, bishops, chapters, priests, theologians, laymen, all the wisest and all the most learned, all the most devoted men, were of one mind in declaring that he was wrong, and that his error was entailing upon the Church the most fatal consequences. This was the plan which Napoleon determined to carry out, and in which he was unscrupulously seconded by many able French ecclesiastics. They persuaded themselves no doubt that the object was good. But it is difficult to believe that they did not know that multitudes of the ablest, wisest, and best men in the Church believed that the concessions demanded by Napoleon were such as Pius VII. could not make with a safe conscience, or without grievous injury to the Church: and therefore if they had allowed themselves to think fairly on the subject, they would surely have seen, that however good they might consider the end proposed, the means by which it was to be obtained implied or required that they should practise a very gross deception upon the Holy Father.

How this deception was carried on, and the degree of success it obtained, are related by our author with extraordinary research and great skill in his fourth and fifth volumes. The result, thank God, all who take up the history know beforehand. On the part of the Holy Father, there was great bodily weakness, all the infirmities of age, and a

---

* Our readers will find an instance of this very amusingly described by Macaulay, in his "Critical and Historical Essays,—Mr. Robert Montgomery."

habitual distrust in his own judgment, which made it seem almost impossible that he should stand firm under a trial like that to which he was subjected. But there was a single eye, a fixed resolution to adhere to his duty as far as he could see what it was; and, above all, he had on his side the power of God, and when, humanly speaking, all seemed most certain to go against him, it turned out that the moment was come, the moment of man's extremity and of God's opportunity, in which, with His own right hand and His holy arm, He interfered to get to Himself the victory over every enemy.

Art. III.—THE PRIEST ON THE MISSION.

The Priest on the Mission. A Course of Lectures on Missionary and Parochial Duties, by FREDERICK CANON OAKELEY, M.A. Longmans, 1871.

IT is with no ordinary pleasure that we welcome the appearance of Canon Oakeley's " Priest on the Mission," or " Course of Lectures on Missionary and Parochial Duties." These Lectures suggest to the mind many encouraging thoughts. They point to a steady advance in England towards a more and more perfect ecclesiastical spirit; and are tokens of a great work which is being initiated by the unostentatious perseverance of devoted men in the promising Seminary of the arch-diocese. When we see in this country a house of studies wholly set apart for the training of ecclesiastics, separated from the inevitable drawbacks and inconveniences of secular college life, with a firm yet gentle discipline, with learned and experienced professors, with every element, in germ at all events, that tends in the direction of true progress,—we cannot help hoping in a future of which we have at present so many prophetic tokens of success. If the ground be well prepared, and the seed be well sown, a fruitful harvest may fairly be expected.

That Canon Oakeley has proved himself to be a skilful and successful husbandman, the Lectures before us amply testify. He has worked the ground with care, he has selected seed most adapted to the soil, and has sown it with a hand which appears accustomed to the task.

It is our purpose in the present article to convey to the reader a general conception of the work achieved by Canon

Oakeley. We hold his book to be of great practical utility. It is written in an animated and flowing style. It is withal a work which contains deep principles, which cannot be realized without considerable study; and offers experiences to the reader which could not have been acquired without a long practical knowledge of the life of a missionary priest in England. A man may pick up a certain class of principles from his philosophy, but there are certain other elements of valuable knowledge which can only be acquired through the frictions and intercourses of daily life. Canon Oakeley happily combines the deep thought of a Christian philosopher with the practical common sense, with the delicacy and grace of an educated man of the world.

The subject-matter of the " Priest on the Mission " is made up of three lectures on " Preaching," one on " Writing and Speaking English," another on " the Priest in his Relations with the Young "; " the Confessional," " Occasional Advice," " Reception and Treatment of Converts," " the Visitation of the Sick and of Prisoners "; then " The Priest in his Church, in his Presbytery, and in his Social and Collateral Relations ";— three separate lectures which complete the twelve.

The first question which suggests itself in regard to any manual of knowledge is,—What is it worth? What is the use of it? We may reply without hesitation, in regard to this one, that it is worthy of deep and attentive study; and that to the young divine, who would secure a shrewd and practical guide into a dangerous and unknown country, it will assuredly render inestimable service. In it he will learn beforehand what are the perils with which he will be surrounded in a future day; in it he will discover the securest way of meeting them, and find himself fore-armed by being thoroughly fore-warned. The book contains information for which many a man would have paid a high price, had he known how much it would have saved him.

He alone who has been nearly lost in the pathless wood, or has all but slipped into the morass, knows how to be really grateful to the kindly hand which offers to guide him on the way, or can be adequately thankful to him who presents those in whom he feels an interest with a valuable guide-book, which will teach them how to avoid the danger of falling into kindred perils.

The value of such a book would, no doubt, greatly depend upon the accuracy with which it describes the dangers of the priest's path, and the skill with which it suggests methods by which he may avoid them.

To achieve such a task as this the writer must possess

priestly wisdom, a practical and sound judgment, and a somewhat wide experience. That Canon Oakeley possesses these
qualifications, and that in an unusual degree, cannot be questioned for a moment.

To begin with the qualification of a wide experience. Here
the author can speak for himself:—

> When I was called to the duties of the mission, rather more than twenty-
> two years ago, I felt sensibly the want of some treatise embodying and
> applying the practical experience of priests who had spent many years
> in the holy service to which I was about to devote myself. . . . Yet,
> if the need in question came powerfully home to one who was called to
> these duties in middle age, and after no inconsiderable experience of some,
> at least, of their number in another communion, with far greater force must
> it be apt to press on the more thoughtful of those who are suddenly trans-
> ferred from college to missionary life. . . . Hence I formed a sort of resolu-
> tion that, if God should give me health and strength to pass any considerable
> portion of my life in the discharge of missionary or parochial duties, I would
> place my experience on record for the benefit, if so be, of those who might
> come after me. (Preface, p. xi.)

Then with that modesty which accompanies genuine worth,
and that grace which is the first-born child of culture, the
writer continues :—

> I had for a long time no thought of giving publicity to this experience
> during my life, and for the plain reason that I might thereby seem to set
> myself up as a teacher of my brethren, at the feet of many among whom I
> ought rather to sit as a learner. (Preface, pp. xi.-xii.)

However, the difficulty was fortunately removed by his
Grace the Archbishop, who invited our author to give a course
of lectures to the students of the Theological Seminary, and
who, after they had been delivered, " expressed a hope that
the lecturer would give them a chance of circulation beyond
the limits of the Seminary." (Preface, p. xii.)

Here then we have the record of the experience of over
twenty-two years of active missionary life, and that not in the
country, but in the busy midst of London. And not this only,
but more than this. The author had his eye upon a work
containing, at all events, the substance of the present one,
before many of those to whom he delivered his lectures had
come to the use of reason. There is a vast difference in value
between a book thrown off in heat and a work which embodies
the carefully matured experiences of a long active missionary
career. There is one more point worthy of remark in Canon
Oakeley's preface. He says :—

It may be said that instruction given to ecclesiastical students on the practical duties of the office for which they are preparing should be confined within the walls of a college, instead of being exposed to the view of a critical, not to say hostile, public. I have carefully considered this objection, and have come to the deliberate conclusion that it ought not to prevail with me. I am convinced that the more generally our methods of dealing with those committed to our charge are known, the more will their value be appreciated by the wise and good of every class in this country. (Preface, p. xiii.)

Then, giving his own experience, which, no doubt, represents the feeling of many educated Anglicans at the present day, he says :—

With regard especially to Catholic colleges, I used to believe that their processes were as dark and mysterious as those of a Masonic lodge ; and ignorance, as I need hardly say, is the feeder of imagination. (Preface, p. xiv.)

The " Preliminary Address " is written with graceful ease, and contains passages of rare beauty. But what is far beyond style is the deep principle which it impresses ; viz., that the young ecclesiastic would do well to master the solemn meaning of the Church in the liturgy of Ordination. And, indeed, who can read those mystic words, and ponder on the sweet, powerful action of the Church over those who have been called to serve *in atriis Domini*, without being deeply moved ? Both those who look forward, and those who cast a glance back, to their ordination day, can feed upon the rich promises described in such touching words by Canon Oakeley, in the inspiring Hymn with which he closes his introductory discourse :—

> The kingdom of thy Lord is all thine own,
>   His boundless wealth the treasure of thy reign ;
> The Church thy court, the altar-step thy throne,
>   The field of heavenly love thy rich domain.

Having thus recalled to the young ecclesiastic's attention the high commission of the priesthood, our author proceeds to deliver his lectures—lectures which touch upon the most important, and some of the most delicate, duties of a missionary priest.

Here is manifested, in our humble opinion, that clear practical judgment which is the second qualification necessary for giving value to a work such as that before us.

The three first lectures, occupying about fifty pages, and dealing with preaching, its modes, and its kinds, are full of useful information, and meet, to our mind, more completely than any others, the main question regarding the conditions of successful preaching, and the most effective method of " getting up " a sermon. Most treatises with which we are

acquainted bear about them an impress of the studio, and seem
to sacrifice, more than is advisable, the practical realities of
the pulpit to the theories of the student, or the dreams of the
philosopher. The reverse of this lends to the Lectures before
us their peculiar charm, and gives to them a more than
ordinary value. We perceive, at once, that, though we are
addressed by a polished scholar, we are not in the hands of a
mere literary craftsman. Canon Oakeley's teachings on how
men should be preached to, are founded on his experience
of society, of nature, and of the operations of grace on the
human heart. He has carefully studied, and has as carefully
retained, the accumulated experience of many years' laborious
work; and now he affords us the benefit of his valuable
opinions upon questions of the highest importance, and especially to priests in England. And the results he has
arrived at, we cannot help feeling, will, in the main at least,
approve themselves to the mind of any man who has had
experience in the pulpit. They illustrate that sound and
practical judgment which is so valuable a gift to one who
undertakes to guide others in perilous walks. Who is the
best preacher according to Canon Oakeley?

> The best of all preachers surely is he who, while deeply feeling the
> momentous nature of his office, and distinctly realizing the truth of the
> announcement he is making, so expresses and so delivers himself as best to
> make his auditory share his own convictions in all their force and fulness.
> (p. 14.)
> The first condition of good preaching is that the preacher should be
> powerfully and habitually impressed with the importance of his office, and
> the greatness of his responsibility. (*Ibid.*)

Thus the preacher should be thoroughly earnest, thoroughly
direct, and perfectly simple. And here the lecturer touches
with great force and felicity upon a requisite for successful
preaching, which we do not remember to have seen brought
out with such vividness before. He strongly insists upon
reality in preaching. This consists in "a certain just proportion between our utterances and our convictions" (p. 17).
Or, he expresses himself thus :—

> When I say that the preacher should mean what he says, I intend that
> he should be especially careful to avoid exaggeration. I suppose we ought
> never to enforce upon our people what we are not ourselves prepared at least
> to attempt. This rule will make us cautious of indulging in an over-wrought
> and high-flown strain of exhortation, and will also guard us against the
> reproach of saying from the pulpit what our practice habitually contradicts.
> (*Ibid.*)

Again,—

Sincerity is sure to make itself felt, while hearers are very quick in finding out when we are not in earnest. (p. 16.)

Here it appears to us Canon Oakeley has got at the root of the matter. Let a man be thoroughly in earnest,—let him feel in his inmost soul that his one object in coming in contact with his people is to help them on to God,—to make them love Him more, and sin less; and he will, as earnest men do in other walks of life, find the straight road to their hearts. He will know what he is at; and they will quickly become sensible of his power. They will be stirred and roused by him; they will rise from sleep at his command; and he will pour, out of the fulness of his own heart, life, and zeal, and sacrifice into theirs. He will have no temptation to indulge in self-display,—to let off *bouquets* of variegated metaphor, which may amuse the worldly, but which make serious men feel sad. Artifice of all kinds, pretentiousness in any shape, unreality, which proceeds from lethargy of spirit, self-conceit, or a lukewarmness in saving souls, will find no place in such a character as this. He has one earnest aim— to get at souls, and to teach them how to get at heaven. He will speak with the direct simplicity of truth; he will convince his hearers with the arguments that act most powerfully on himself; and, however ignorant they may appear to be, he will reach their hearts, and carry them along with him through the very energy of that earnestness which animates his soul and gives an unmistakable evidence of sincerity to his career. It is because the simple majesty of truth is too beautiful to require either enamel or paint, that anything which looks like trick is so revolting in the pulpit. " Nothing," says our author, " spoils the effect of a sermon so much as the look of artifice, whether it be artifice in the structure, or artifice in the composition " (p. 20). Canon Oakeley seems never to weary in repeating,—and never can it be reiterated too often,—that " reality " or " subjective truthfulness " is the great secret of persuasion :—

It seems to me that the best of all sermons will be that which forms the most faithful transcript of an habitually religious mind. That reality, or as I may call it, subjective truthfulness, is the secret of persuasion, is no more than was said by the masters of rhetoric in the days of classical antiquity. " He," says one of them, " who would have me weep must himself be the first to grieve." And a greater authority has ruled that the best condition of rhetorical persuasiveness is what he calls the ethical proof,—that is, the impression of personal character stamped on the speech itself. (p. 25.)

Truly, a worldly priest, preaching the high doctrine of the Cross from the pulpit; a man, in a word, who preaches one thing and practises another, exhibits one of the most painful pictures of religious inconsistency which can be presented before the human imagination. Whereas, a thoroughly devoted missioner,—one who is known to spend himself, and to be spent in the great office of saving souls, when he opens his mouth, though he be not gifted with eloquence or grace,— will exert a power, which, springing straight out of the energy of the heart, surpasses all the attractions of courtly manner, and all the charms of rhetorical display.

With regard to the "different modes of preaching," there are some most useful instructions in the second lecture. We can, without any misgiving, recommend Canon Oakeley's solution of the question, "Which is the best mode?" to the attention of our readers, as being the only true one. He gives four modes of constructing a sermon :—

First, there is the purely *extempore* method . . . I need hardly say that I mention this mode of preaching, without even mental preparation, only in order to warn you against it (p. 28). I come, in the second place, to sermons delivered from manuscript. . . . A person who has his eye on his manuscript cannot fix it on those he is addressing without the danger of going astray from the words before him (p. 30). I shall now say a few words on the practice of learning sermons by heart, which is a sort of middle course between those of which I have just spoken. . . . But I am not sure, that like most middle courses, it does not unite the properties of the two systems between which it mediates, at some considerable cost of the characteristic benefits of each (p. 32).

I come, in the last place, to that mode which, as it seems to me, is on the whole preferable to any other—I mean that of carefully preparing sermons, in skeleton, as we may say, beforehand, and trusting to our natural powers of expression, improved by habits of training, for filling them out in delivery. This plan, unlike both the preceding, seems really to unite the advantages of the two opposite methods of using a manuscript on the one hand, and preaching without book on the other. It obviates the danger of shallowness and empty wordiness, which besets unprepared or ill-prepared preaching without book, while it secures the advantages of an off-hand delivery, without the embarrassment of writing with a view to it. The materials which we prepare to our hand may be reduced to order with any amount of care and completeness we may like to bestow on them, provided always that they are not reproduced in public by a mere effort of memory. I have heard that Father Faber was in the habit of writing out the greater part of his sermons before he preached them, and then of preaching them with such variety of expression as was suggested to him at the moment (pp. 33–34).

We are quite at one with Canon Oakeley in the view expressed so lucidly in this quotation. And, in point of fact, a missionary priest, who has the care of a large flock (we may not say "congregation," see p. 75), cannot find the leisure for writing out his whole discourse, or for learning it by heart. Still, the practice of writing out fully, and learning too, is not, it appears to us, an unhealthy exercise for young divines who are being taught how to pen fair English, and to use their mother tongue with accuracy and ease. To *begin* simply with "notes," when exercising in the Seminary, might easily lead to a slovenly manner, and to that diffuseness which is the rock on which all *extempore* speakers are liable to split. When the student has for a few years been exercised in writing carefully, and in learning his sermon off, then he may be advanced to practise "preaching" upon a well-digested subject, and to emulate those efforts which are gracefully achieved by men who have had the advantage of practice and experience. Birds learn to fly, and children learn to walk, after many efforts, and by slow degrees.

Speaking of the best "mode," Canon Oakeley continues:—

It is of the greatest importance, as I have before observed, to start with the foresight of a definite plan and orderly arrangement. Any neglect of this rule will be sure to result in a confused and ineffective discourse, which, whatever good instruction it may incidentally contain, will leave no lasting impression on the mind of the hearer. I think also that it is useful to commit to memory not any large portion of a sermon, but such parts of it as are especially important, since, although we may not give what we have prepared in the same words, we shall perhaps give it in words only varied from the original in a slight degree, and that generally for the better rather than for the worse. (p. 39.)

Of course to practise this successfully, it is implied that the preacher possesses considerable command of language. The portion learnt by heart must be brought into the running discourse, so as not to interfere with its general texture. And there is danger, too, of the mind becoming confused, if the preacher has not got his prepared sentences *quite* off, the judgment having to determine, with the quickness of a flash, whether a paraphrase is to be attempted, or whether the tongue is to try to repeat *verbatim* the portion which has been prepared. To our mind, a man who could successfully make the body of his discourse flow naturally into a peroration learnt off by heart, would possess a greater power over his mother tongue than falls to the lot of the great majority of young divines. But we do not forget that Canon Oakeley is not merely teaching the students of the Theological College what they should do now, but also what they should aim at later on. And this being borne in mind, we entirely agree with the instruction delivered on the point by our accomplished author.

The third lecture, " On Different Kinds of Preaching," contains much valuable instruction. We heartily concur in the following :—

> I have said in a former lecture that a sermon in the course of the High Mass should consist, as a general rule, of a short explanatory and practical application of the Epistle or Gospel of the day, and especially of the latter. There is no rule without an exception ; but I think that long sermons on topics which have no immediate connection with the subject of the day are out of place in the middle of Mass. Besides protracting the Mass to an inconvenient length, they tend to interrupt its continuity. This objection applies especially to long sermons, and still more to irrelevant sermons on the greater festivals, as, for example, on Easter-day, when the spirit of the Church is expressed by brief and brilliant scintillations of a joy too deep to be eloquent. For, as it has been somewhere said :—
>
> " Joy, like grief, is simple-spoken ;
> Each its cherish'd secret hoards ;
> Hearts when full, and hearts when broken,
> Veil their thoughts and stint their words."
>
> On the other hand, nothing can be more appropriate, as a general rule, than a short affective and effective commentary on that portion of the Mass which is designed for instruction, and which is really the only portion of it that seems to call for the aid of the vernacular. The Gospels especially, containing, as they do, the words and actions of our blessed Lord, are full of suggestive matter for the preacher, and furnish him with the readiest and easiest, as well as most suitable subject of his Sunday morning's instruction. (pp. 42-43.)

We would direct earnest attention to Canon Oakeley's remarks on " Controversial Discourses." He says, with great truth, that, " Good controversial preaching and writing are as rare as they are valuable. Bad or defective controversy is unhappily anything but rare, and not only valueless, but highly damaging to truth " (p. 50). Our author has done good service in bringing out that fact with such distinctness. Perhaps Englishmen, the great majority of them, are militant by nature. This natural tendency is liable, there is no doubt, unless men be on their guard, to manifest itself even in the pulpit. The temptation is all the greater from the fact that the preacher for the time being has it all his own way. He has no fear of being checked, contradicted, brought to his bearings, proved mistaken or exaggerated; he has the full swing, all to himself, of mind and imagination; and is contending with an enemy sometimes, possibly, in part, of his own creation ; one from whom he has no idea of receiving a reply. All this is a temptation to talk somewhat at random, and not to be over nice in thoroughly understanding an opponent, and dealing with him with that fairness which in ordinary life one man shows towards another. And yet those come to listen who are keen enough to perceive when their position has not been understood; and are quite impatient enough to extinguish every doubt when they are conscious that the exponent of the creed which they had been led to imagine might be the true one, has not the grace to state their difficulties with fairness, or the will or talent to look at them fully in the face. Many conversions have doubtless been made by controversial sermons; how many men have been detained in darkness through them, it is impossible to say.

But we must pass on to other portions of these Lectures, and try to show how great a store of priestly wisdom is contained in many of the instructions given in them. And here we cannot help feeling that Canon Oakeley is specially in his vocation. If there is one thing more than another which shines brightly in the work before us, it is that spirit of charity and gentleness, fear of giving pain and giving offence, which should characterize the loving heart of a genuine priest. The priest's sympathy, based on the supernatural love of God, is as widespread as his responsibility; and to him every sinful child of Adam is an object of deep tenderness, and we may say, of almost divine compassion. He it is who draws souls out of perdition, and sets them in the narrow way, and binds them with the cords of Adam to the cross. This beautiful charity and priestly tenderness is met, like some sweet *aroma*, all through these Lectures; lending a grace and dignity to the most trivial incident, and giving the key to much that is incidentally advanced. Priestly wisdom seems to consist in being " all to all," and yet so that the sacredness of the sacerdotal character never becomes less awful, and the respect felt for the priest grows in the heart in proportion as he takes possession of it.

The Seventh Lecture, on " Occasional Advice," manifests the wisdom which we speak of with great transparency.

Referring to the temptations which beset priests to be " cold-hearted," resulting from education, selfishness, and familiarity with suffering, our author says, as truly as beautifully—

I do not think that any corrective of this tendency is so efficacious as meditation on the life and actions of our blessed Lord, in whose character this quality of tender compassion for the sufferings of others was so conspicuous. Instances of it are to be found in almost every page of the Gospel history, and the argument which they suggest to us is of this kind, that if our Divine Master, who came from heaven to die for the sins of the world, could yet be moved to tears at the grave of Lazarus, or work a miracle to relieve the hunger of those whose wants He anticipated before they were expressed, we, His servants, must never allow ourselves to underrate the claims of temporal suffering or necessity because of the incomparably higher importance of those spiritual ailments or needs which address themselves in the first instance to our sympathy. (pp. 115-116.)

How beautiful is the following !—

But the contemplation of the crucifix is, after all, the best and truest remedy for human sorrow. In it every form of distress finds its expression, and, together with its expression, its relief. Is it bodily pain ? Here it is realized in its greatest intensity. Is it bereavement, or the desertion of friends ? All the apostles, save one, have forsaken Him and fled. Is it the sting of calumny ? In the Crucifixion, the malignity of enemies had at once its triumph and its cure. Is it the sight of sorrow which we cannot alleviate ? Our Lady is at the foot of the Cross. Is it that most terrible of all the power of our Enemy, the sense of desolation and desertion by God ? The words " Eloi, Eloi !" are on the lips of our dying Redeemer. Is it, lastly, the weariness of spirit that comes with sorrow, and makes us feel as though it had no end ? The fifth word from the Cross is soon to be followed by a sixth, " It is consummated ;" and the seventh, "Into Thy hands I commend my spirit." (pp. 119-120.)

These are pattern words of priestly wisdom : no thoughts could sink deeper than these : no comfort can soothe the crushed heart, if Christ cannot do it as He looks down from the bleeding cross.

Here are some wholesome pieces of advice, and some wise sayings :—

As a rule, it is very desirable that priests should not mix themselves up with family matters (p. 121). Let me urge upon you, never, if you can avoid it, to have anything to do with making a will, unless, indeed, it be your own (p. 123). We live in the midst of temptations to priestly pusillanimity, as well as to priestly avarice (*ibid.*). Even a Catholic priest, in this our England, who remains long enough at his post, loves his work, keeps peace with his neighbours, and pays his bills (the last condition of influence being by no means the least important), may reckon on outgrowing the bitterest hostility (p. 125).

The Eighth Lecture, on " The Reception and Treatment of Converts," has a value special to itself. Canon Oakeley is himself a convert—of very old standing indeed, yet still a convert. He alone who has had practical experience of the Anglican, or Protestant mind, is able adequately to realize the position of one who is searching about for light. Of course, according to a man's natural sagacity, and to his *gratiæ status*, he is able to comprehend, help, enlighten, and console those who have been, or still are, struggling in darkness amidst the *umbra mortis.* But it would seem almost presumption for one who has never been in the position himself, to lay down the law, or to give directions regarding those who are advancing in the direction of the Church. As our Catholic world is wholly different from the Anglican, so the Anglican (it is a truism to say so) is wholly different from ours. We know how little Protestants can understand us with their best endeavour; do we as keenly perceive that we are liable to find a difficulty in understanding them? And, humanly speaking, unless a man be understood, he cannot easily be dealt with. We remember how, a few years since, a pious and enthusiastic Italian priest came to England with the design of converting the country. And we remember well how bitterly disappointed he was, how utterly amazed, that the good people he met in travelling by rail did not instantly beseech him to receive them, after he had explained to them what an immense treasure of grace and of salvation would at once be poured into their souls on the reception of the Sacraments. Doubtless we know far better than this; yet it still is very possible that we flatter ourselves that we are acquainted with many things regarding the spirit of the Anglican mind of which we possess in reality a very slender store of information. Canon Oakeley's lecture is therefore of very great value, as it records the twofold experience of a Protestant and of a priest; and that in a manner which at once commands attention and respect. He shows that even after converts have been received into the Church, they " have certain tendencies which make them the fit subjects of special direction " (p. 144). After speaking of conceit and eccentricity, he continues:—

No spirit is more dangerous than the spirit of the reformer. Closely allied to this temper is that of a sensitive fastidiousness about persons and things. Thus converts are disposed to overlook the great and consistent moral and spiritual excellence of some hereditary Catholic or other, because he does not come up to their standard of refinement. They make too little account of unavoidable differences in education and social antecedents between themselves and those with whom they are suddenly thrown in a later age. (p. 146.)

Such converts as these should also remember, we may add, in the words of Dr. Newman, that " it is wonderful, that, with all their advantages, so many Protestants leave the University, with so little real liberality and refinement of mind, in consequence of the discipline to which they have been subjected.

Much allowance must be made here for original nature; much for the detestable narrowness and (I cannot find a better word) the priggishness of their religion. Catholics, on the other hand, are, compared with them, almost born gentlemen." *

It is evident that the knife cuts both ways, and that there is cockle amongst the wheat, whether it come from a Protestant University or from Catholic Colleges and Schools. There is much sensitiveness and touchiness on the one side, and much boldness and bluffness on the other; prigs are found here as well as there, as poppies grow in many fields; and in every society there must be a "give and take." Converts gain much by intercourse with hereditary Catholics; hereditary Catholics are large gainers by the convert element, which acts as a leaven amongst them. The "fastidiousness" and "hobbies" and "crotchets" and "eccentricities" and "conceits" which Canon Oakeley speaks of in some converts, are not the result of *being* converts, but proceed simply, it appears to us, from the peculiar cast of the individual mind. A man of large intellect and wide sympathies, who looks upon the world and the Church with the eye of an exalted Faith, would be as free from littleness as he would be full of gratitude to that Providence which had brought him into the saving Ark. The fact of a small mind receiving the grace of faith, or of a large mind losing that grace, does not change a man's calibre: it changes his religious and logical position, and saves his soul in the one case, and damns it in the other.

But we are forgetting the work before us. We would fain quote largely from each lecture, and give the reader a specimen of the priestly wisdom which comes out in the prudent and kindly words of our gifted author. His remarks on the priest's relations with the young, on the Confessional, on Visitation of the Sick, on the Priest in his Church, in his Presbytery, and in his social and collateral relations, are, as we have said, the ripe fruit of wide experience, and offer much food for priestly meditation. We find it difficult to restrain our pen, but our limits forbid us. And we have already, it may be hoped, done enough to call the attention of our readers to the merits of the work, and to convince them—we are anxious to do so for their own sakes—that much profitable information may be acquired in its pages. Many an ecclesiastic who may sit down to read it will, we venture to say, rise up after the reading "a wiser and a better man."

We cannot better conclude this brief review than by quoting

---

* "Discourses on University Education," Preface, p. xx.

a singularly graceful example of our author's style,—a style which is pure, simple, and pellucid, and with just that living spark in it (like the fire in a precious stone) which lends it warmth and colour. Speaking of the preacher's office, he says :—

> We have the noblest subjects, the most ample spheres, the most docile audience. We are provided with a complete armoury of weapons, and are masters of the situation. We have the angels for our spectators, and the saints for our advocates, the terrors of hell to barb our warnings, and the joys of heaven to gild our encouragements. We have the Catholic Church for our pillar and guide, with its strong guarantees of infallible authority, steadfastness, and indefectibility. We have her far-reaching history to confirm our precedents, and her boundless literature to supply our illustrations. We have hearers who hang on our lips, and imbibe our teaching with attentive ears, into tender hearts. What, then, are we, my brethren ? and what ought we to be ? ("Preaching," p. 24.)

Art. IV.—TWO ENGLISH NOVELISTS: DICKENS AND THACKERAY.

The Works of Charles Dickens (Charles Dickens Edition). London : Chapman & Hall.

The Works of William Makepeace Thackeray. London : Smith, Elder, & Co.

WHILE Mr. Thackeray and Mr. Dickens were both living, and each was pursuing a successful literary career, they were frequently made the subject of elaborate comparison. After Mr. Thackeray's death, when the summing up which always ensues upon the decease of a man of eminence took place, and which in his case was quite free from the familiar and yet overstrained sentimentality which has been lavished upon the memory of his brother novelist, frequent allusion was made to Mr. Dickens, and to the relative position of the two in the ranks of writers of fiction. The world accepted the necessity of comparison between them, and analytical criticism was bound to keep the fact before it, in its operations. It appears to us that this was a mistaken and delusive view, and that it led to some injustice—in the sense of applying certain identical tests of criticism to writers than whom we cannot call to mind any two, whose labours are to be ranged under the technical head of fiction, more integrally different. They were contemporaries, for a brief period, and they were both very remarkable members of a class which has increased immensely in numbers, and altered considerably in general characteristics within the period covered by the two literary careers. But even this parallel is not complete. Mr. Dickens made his mark, while he was yet a very young man, long before Mr. Thackeray was known; he outlived him several years, still working vigorously, though he did nothing like the quantity of work executed by the older man within the same time;—there is thus a period of nearly double the extent to be considered when the achievements of Mr. Dickens are enumerated. The one writer gave us the fruits of his mature, full-statured intellect, in profusion, and almost all he produced bore the marks of high and careful cultivation. The other burst upon the world in the mingled romance and gleefulness of youth, and ever after it seemed as if he had no time to mature, to correct or trim down exuberance, or indeed to acquire a knowledge of facts; for the faults of his earliest writings are but exaggerated in his latest, and their merits and beauties are meritorious and beautiful in the self-same way. The one had a contemplative comprehension of youth, and a sad sort of sympathy with it, counterbalanced by the keenest sense of its unreasonableness and absurdity; the other never lost the buoyancy, and the exaggeration, the ignorance of proportion in human affairs, the one-sidedness, the pomposity, and the sentimentality of youth itself. Mr. Thackeray always wrote (never more emphatically than in his first and greatest novel, " Vanity Fair ") like a man who had " waited and come to forty years," with the predicted results before he began to write; while it is plain that Mr. Dickens quite genuinely admired Miss Rosa Bud until, literally, the day of his death; and while he could depict the " hot and restless " stages of existence as vigorously as ever, had no more notion of realizing the " tired and slow," than when he drew his pretty preposterous picture of Master Humphrey as a typical old man.

Both were more than novelists, and humorists; both were preachers, in the sense in which every great writer of fiction must be, whether intentionally or not. To him a system is as indispensable as it is to the prosecution and the defence in a French criminal trial. Such writers do not propose to themselves merely to amuse the world, and are not to be confounded with the numerous delineators of modern manners, who, like Lydia Languish, " place the ' Innocent Adultery '

in the 'Whole Duty of Man,' " and fit up modern life with
impossible scenery and decorations; writers who are less
pernicious than the most immoral French novelists only because they are less skilful and more vulgar. Mr. Dickens
wrote with a purpose in which he believed. His earlier novels
may be classed with Eugène Sue's " Sept Péchés Capitaux,"
for directness of illustration. " Nicholas Nickleby" is a novel
in which avarice is exposed and denounced. " Martin Chuzzlewit " is concerned with selfishness and hypocrisy ; " Oliver
Twist" with the vice of thieving and the oppression of the poor.
" David Copperfield " illustrates one popular form of the sin
of impurity ; and " Bleak House" illustrates another, in addition
to the exposure of the " glorious uncertainty," and tediousness
of the law, and the terrible example of the old Krook, which is
a counterblast to the more than tolerant treatment the sin of
drunkenness had previously received at Mr. Dickens's hands.
" Dombey and Son " is a story of pride and arrogance under
their most odious forms.   " Little Dorritt " deals with dishonesty on the great and small scale. " Hard Times " is a
tremendous indictment of society in general by the poor man.
These are the broad outlines of his works, from Merdle the
wholesale swindler to Dorritt the pitiful pretender ; but he fills
them up with innumerable touches of complaint, censure, and
ridicule, which include almost every class of grievance known
to our present social condition. Mr. Dickens had immense faith
in his own judgment, and in his style of treating the subjects
on which he brought his judgment to bear, and he accepted
in all sincerity the praise which was lavished upon him for
elevating the public tone, and combining the qualities of the
humorist and the moralist.   Therefore, we . have a right to
take him at that valuation, and to judge his works accordingly. How sincerely he believed in himself,—with what good
faith he accepted the " mission " with which it became the
fashion to accredit him,—is plainly to be seen in the prefaces
to the " Charles Dickens edition " of his works, whose simple
and transparent egotism is astonishing. A great deal of nonsense was talked about him during his lifetime, which, if one
will but consider how intoxicating nonsense in laudation of
one's self is, he may be excused for having taken, as he
evidently did, for sound sense and absolute truth. A man
who has been flattered to such an extent that he actually
listens gravely and complacently to (otherwise) rational men
talking about his going to the United States on a commercial
literary speculation, as an international event, fraught with
vast consequences to the human race, is to be forgiven for
treating his own works as epochs in the history of literature,

and landmarks in the development of morals.   Mr. Thackeray
was the opposite of Mr. Dickens in this respect.   He, too,
wrote with a purpose, and was a preacher, but he had no
overweening opinion of his own sense and judgment; he constantly took pains to assure his readers that he was as
ignorant and as shallow as themselves, and while he de-
lineated the evils of society with his unsparing touch, expressed himself with reticent misgiving as to their reduction
in his or any body else's time.   Catholic readers of the works
of Mr. Dickens, who had a jovial "system," and of Mr.
Thackeray, who had only a dim, hinting hope that things
will be better for every body in the next world, know that
each was wrong in his handling of the grievous wound of
humanity, and far astray in his notions of the cure, in his
prescriptions for the relief of the sufferers.

In proportion to a writer's popularity, his influence is
harmful or beneficial.   Mr. Dickens has been praised for
the unexceptionable morality of his works, and as scrupulous
an adherence to the respect due to "the young person" as
his own absurd Podsnap could prescribe.   He was certainly
a moral writer, and he did laud the household virtues; but
there is a higher aspect of morality, one in which Catholic
readers are bound to regard every book which professes to
deal with the condition of men, and, so regarded, Mr. Dickens's
works are as false as any of those of the undisguisedly mate-
rialistic writers of the day.   He cried "Peace, peace, where
there is no peace;" he vaunted the quack nostrums of good
fellowship and sentimental tenderness, of human institutions,
and the natural virtues, as remedies for sin, sorrow, and the
weariness of life.   There are not many conversions among his
personages more gravely and reasonably set forth than that
of Ebenezer Scrooge,—whose conversion is mischievously
false in principle, because it has no compunction in it; it is
repentance towards man, but not towards God.   All comes
right in the end, through the intermediary of a number of
amiable and gifted people who correct abuses, and turn evil
into good,—as if evil were a mere external accident, having no
root in the heart of man,—without a trace of spiritual action
or any evidence of belief in its existence.   Were ever means
more inadequate to the end than these?   In none of them is
there any recognition of the place and condition of man
as a creature, or of the place and condition of God as the
Creator.   Mr. Dickens writes well and often about duty, its
elevating influence and its pleasant and profitable results;
about the general prosperity and jollity to which its performance leads; but, of the inexorable, inevitable responsibility of

the soul to its Redeemer, of the body to its Maker,—a responsibility infinitely above all others, which excludes every other motive as a primary cause of action, which is the first great *law*, never to be broken without the incurrence of doom,—there is not a trace in these books. They preach quite another gospel,—and it is against "any other" that S. Paul warns us;—an easier, a pleasanter, a more speedily remunerative gospel—one that finds acceptance with critics of a school largely given to cant (which they forcibly deprecate in every other school),—a genial, human, undifficult gospel, by which the middle and lower orders are to be converted to a generally prosperous, amiable, and charming condition, which shall include a good deal of play-going, and of Christmas-keeping in the material and sentimental sense. His love of nature, to which Mr. Thackeray seems to have been indifferent, almost insensible, did not lift his mind to nature's God. The associations which it evokes in him are all material or sentimental, and exclusive of any spiritual influence. Man, according to Mr. Dickens, is as sufficient to himself for his amelioration, as, according to the teaching of Our Lord and His apostles, he is insufficient. Can any writer, however amiable, moral, wise, or witty, be quite harmless, who departs so utterly from the truth—who leads the mind of his readers so far from the "fountain opened for sin and uncleanness," and from every source of supernatural enlightenment?

If we consider the whole series of Mr. Dickens's works, we shall find that the only persons introduced who are actuated by any spiritual motives, are represented as gloomy fanatics. For instance, Mrs. Clennam, Esther Summerson's godmother, and Mr. Haredale. We do not now refer at all to the patent hypocrites whom Mr. Dickens makes so amusing, to Stiggins, Uriah Heap, or Pecksniff, but to those persons to whom he imputes real spirituality, living faith in any form of religion, and notably, in the latter instance, faith in the Catholic Church. "Barnaby Rudge" is a fine work. The murder which blights Mr. Haredale's life for the second time (it is remarkable that authors like Mr. Dickens believe that none but blighted lives are ever dedicated to God) is finely described; the sacking of the old Maypole is full of grandeur, and the Gordon Riots are narrated in a masterly manner. There is no religious tone at all in the narrative, and the preface to the "Charles Dickens edition" expressly disclaims any sympathy with the Church. We do not complain of this; we do not expect sympathy; it is not indeed compatible with ignorance of the Catholic Verity, and the Divine Commission of the Church;—our point is, the unreligiousness of Mr. Dickens's works, in their absence of recognition of Grace; and their harmfulness in the substitution of what is false for what is true. The remedies which he prescribes are good things in themselves, and in their proper places, but, as substitutes for those prescribed by the Great Physician, Who has appended them inseparably to the promise that He will make us whole, they are worse than useless. The last state of the man who applies them to himself, the last state of the society which seeks its salvation in them, is worse than the first. "Take *my* yoke upon you," is the counsel, the command of Him who had imposed it as God, and who carried it as Man, and we have no assurance that any other yoke will be easy. "Come unto *me*, and *I* will give you rest:" we have no reason to believe that any where else there is repose. All systems other and outside this are "earthen vessels which hold no water." How they have been believed in! How they have been talked about, from the soliloquies of Little Nell, prettiest of utterances of the "religion of the blue sky," to the Enthu- siasm of Humanity, which substitutes itself for the love of God, and His Church, and for charity towards mankind for the sake and in the strength of that love! How empty, how useless, how vain they all are, how invariably detected, and renounced, sadly and wearily by the serious, contemptuously by the cynical; and still the City of God stands upon a hill, stead- fast, and satisfying the eyes of all who look towards her, in the perplexity of repeated failure!

Mr. Thackeray is also a preacher, and he preaches that which is not true. We do not now refer to his cynicism, to what Mr. Hutton describes as that "flavour of sarcastic innuendo in which he delighted;" that "tone in which he justified to his readers the severity of his criticisms, by trying to show that they were all of them open to criticisms at least as severe;" * but to the practice which the same critic, most equitable and most acute of the many who have discussed his writings, describes thus: "It was of the essence of his genius to lay bare unrealities, and leave the sound life almost un- touched. It was rather a relief than otherwise to see him playing with his dissecting-knife after one of his keenest probing feats; you understand better how limited his purpose is,—that he has been in search of organic disease,—and you are not surprised, therefore, to find that he has found little that was healthy." He preached on one text, as if there were no other; and whereas Mr. Dickens eliminated the grace of God from his system, and proposed a universal rectification of

---

* Essays Theological and Literary, vol. ii., p. 308.

error and making of things comfortable, by means of confidence in that same human nature which had brought them to their present condition, Mr. Thackeray declined to see any way out of the mire whatever, and has no more encouraging epithet than "good, simple souls," admiringly but incredulously applied, for those who do believe in the supernatural governance of the world. The vague awe, the distant and constrained respect with which he mentions Almighty God, the atmosphere of mystery—not in the sense of wonderful, all merciful, sacramental mystery, but of hopeless, dreary, ineffable obscurity—are all manifestations of an erroneous attitude of the soul in relation to the purpose with which the soul is created. Where is the hope of the Christian to be found in Mr. Thackeray's works? He writes about prayer, and pardon; about the account to be rendered hereafter, of the pure in heart, and a number of generalities, to which his massive manner on such occasions seems to give a meaning; but when one examines them they are no more than the vague assent of a mind too philosophical and too well cultivated to reject belief in its own immortality, and unable, by itself, to discover the truth concerning itself, to the formulas in which modern speech embodies the idea of a future life and an unknown God. We borrow from Mr. Hutton's essay on "George Eliot" a passage which seems to us a perfect definition of Mr. Thackeray's habit of mind in spiritual things :—

The drawing-room school of novelists do not and cannot often go down into a stratum of life deep enough to come upon the springs of faith. Miss Austen never touches upon them. Thackeray turns dizzy with the very mobility of his own sympathies, and finding a distinct type of faith in every man's mind, not only proclaims the inscrutability of all divine topics, but refuses to assign any strong motive power to religious emotions at all in his delineations of human life . . . . he held that the stronger class of intellects meddle least with the subject,—at all events, intellectually.

Such comprehensiveness of sympathy is only intelligible on the supposition that Mr. Thackeray did not believe that absolute, entire truth exists in the order of spiritual things, and that he drew no distinction between "the faith in every man's mind," and the object of that faith. What else do all his books come to? Are we unfair in thus summing them up? "My friends, we are all very wicked and very silly—especially very silly; we do not believe what we say, and we do not know what we do believe, or what there is which, really, on the whole, ought to be believed. Life is short, and not merry; there is not much in it worth having, and when we have got that not much, it is, nine times out of ten, a sham. Life is very hollow, and on the whole a humbug; it will never be more sound or less humbugging, but we shall be wiser, or at least get credit for greater wisdom, if we do not believe in any one or any thing. As for the future life, we know nothing, we can know nothing; but it is wholesome and pleasant to entertain a faith in it, which for this life is folly." There is not much to choose, for the human race, between being left alone, to the vague desultory better look-out for the future, into which the dreary "sympathies" of Mr. Thackeray resolve themselves, and the gospel of geniality as inculcated by Mr. Dickens. The real Gospel is so precise, so definite, and so distinctly ungenial; and of that true Gospel the two great novelists were profoundly—we hope invincibly—ignorant.

Which is the greater of the two, is a question which each of their readers will, for some time to come, answer according to his individual taste, and the majority of voices will be for Mr. Dickens; because in this use of it "great" is an undefined quantity, a loose expression, yet inevitable, for there is something invidious in Mr. Froude's nicely-calculated phrase "a considerable man," as applied to either of them. Mr. Thackeray's works are unknown to thousands to whom Mr. Dickens's creations are household words; and we believe that the future will prove these last to be incomparably more popular, and considerably sooner obsolete, than the finished and scholarly productions of the novelist who quizzes sentiment, ignores low life, has no taste for rurality, avoids local colouring with such skill and success that it never occurs to his readers to think where the people are in whose life-drama he is absorbed—they are as perfectly content with the generality "a club," or "London," or "Spa," as Shakspeare's audience with his first and second murderers—and who makes every woman in his picture gallery distinct before their eyes, though he has only one method, and that a commonplace one, of describing a pretty girl. Rosy cheeks, bright eyes, a round figure, and a becoming trick of blushing are the main points in all his portraits. But Amelia Osborne is totally unlike Laura Bell; Laura leaves no impression upon the memory which it is possible to confound with that produced by Ethel Newcome, the Lambert girls, or Charlotte Baynes. We do not mean that Mr. Thackeray's young ladies are among his strong points; on the contrary. But they are as much better in point of both art and nature, as Mr. Dickens's young ladies, as Little Nell and Mary Graham, Dora Spenlow, Agnes Wickfield, and Kate Nickleby are more admired, more liked, more realized than they. In the time to come, when the classes who are now ill-educated, and who do read Mr. Dickens but do not read Mr. Thackeray, shall be well educated, they will read both, and reverse the popular verdict. The author of "Vanity Fair" and "The Newcomes" will not be popular, to the full extent of the word, until it shall have ceased to require an intellectual effort to understand him. The simplest test in the world applied to the two will explain the difference, which, while it leaves to each his individual wholly distinct eminence, renders comparison between them unjust in any other sense than that of strong and interesting contrast. We have only to ask ourselves, what books must any person who proposes to enjoy the perusal of Mr. Dickens's works have previously read? What amount and manner of acquaintance with the world of men, cities, or letters, with politics, art, or philosophy, must he possess? Surely little or none. As far as the greater number of his works are concerned, they might be the only books in existence, and be just as intelligible and delightful; and in the case of those which form the exceptions to this rule, "Hard Times" and "A Tale of Two Cities," we do not think the political and social views of the former, or the historical appreciation of the latter, sufficiently sound or profound to merit the attention of educated minds, though they are striking and picturesque enough to interest the uneducated.

The charm of association is entirely wanting in Mr. Dickens's works, but it would be thrown away upon many of his most cordial admirers, while the educated readers—who most appreciate the subtle and delicate infusion of art, learning, and *savoir vivre* which flavours the whole of Mr. Thackeray's novels—are quite content to do without it; satisfied with the racy originality, the exuberant animal spirits, and not repelled by the undeniable vulgarity, always healthy when it is not sentimental, of those of Mr. Dickens. When the caricaturist shall have died out of men's memory, the satirist will live. We need a key for the comprehension of Churchill; the last speaker of the English tongue will discern the spirit of Pope. Gilray is consigned to museums, but they who run may read Hogarth. Mr. Dickens was not, correctly speaking, a satirist; he drew exaggerated pictures of persons and things and then pierced the canvas with many darts. His feats of battle were always more or less like his own fantastic conception of Quilp hammering the countenance of the ship's figurehead, under the delusive notion that it was Kit's "image, his very self!" And thus, though delightfully amusing, he is not seriously impressive. His readers are always inwardly conscious that they laugh a good deal at, as well as with, him.

There is no analogy between the kind of pleasure afforded

by the works of the one writer and that which we derive
from the works of the other; and therein we find a reason
why they ought not to be compared in any sense of rivalry.
A greater number of persons, at various stages of life, read
and enjoy Mr. Dickens's novels, but there are chords in the
human heart touched, mysterious recesses of the human spirit
sounded by Mr. Thackeray, which the other never sought to
reach, of whose very existence he does not seem to have been
aware. In one respect only they produce a similar effect.
Each is an author from whose works one selects bits, to read
over and over again, and to be recalled by the slightest effort
of memory. We fancy these bits are always taken from the
drollest passages in Mr. Dickens's works, and from the most
serious or the most cynical in Mr. Thackeray's; they are
grotesquely funny sayings or descriptions in the one case;
they are passages of stately pathos or gems of pure clear wit,
provoking an almost solemn admiration, but no laughter,
because of their keen merciless truth, in the other. Mrs.
Skewton, in her lodgings at Leamington, being taken to pieces
by her maid, carrying on a grisly flirtation with Joey B., or
performing the part of Cleopatra in her galley, with the
assistance of a Bath chair, moves us to uncompunctious
laughter; but we do not believe any one ever laughed over
the terrible brilliant description of the Duchesse d'Ivry, with
her mimicry of Mary Stuart, her Rizzio, her Châstelar, her
Lochleven, and her implacable foe.

In the early days of Mr. Dickens's fame his style of sentiment had many hearty admirers among his young readers.
They were enraptured with Little Nell; they copied whole
pages about her and her death into their albums; and Smike
was also a great favourite. Nothing more opposed to truth
was ever written than the apostrophe to that " dread disease,"
consumption, in " Nicholas Nickleby," but, twenty-five years
ago young ladies learned it by heart, and inscribed it on
those many-coloured pages which were innocent and pretty
enough records of their passing tastes and fancies. We suspect there are very few young people of the present day so
" exceedingly young," as Mr. Littimer would say, as to be
attracted by Mr. Dickens's pathos. We do not affirm this as
an improvement, but only as a fact. It is sufficient for his
fame that he has made one generation cry in his and their
time. He will make a few generations to come laugh. Not
as the great and terrible wits make the men and women of
the ages which come after them laugh,—by the sparkling
result of their deep proficiency in the "noblest study,"
whose subject, "man," is ever the same;—but because his

humour is so rich, so thorough, so varied, and so original that
it must always appeal to the liking for oddities and eccentricities inherent in human nature, which increases with the
pace of life, and is felt more and more as a relief to its growing
weariness. There is humour which does not exactly amuse,
though it receive the utmost recognition. There is humour
which simply amuses, which is merely quite delightful. Mr.
Dickens had extraordinary humour of the latter sort. He
may have intended sometimes to be savagely satirical, but
could not keep from caricature, and with exaggeration savage-
ness, even severity, is done away. He was infinitely droll and
various in his mirthful moods, and the animal spirits which
overflow through all his earlier writings abounded up to the
latest of them.

That the sentimental creations of Mr. Dickens, the impossible children, the preposterous mechanics, the jovial landladies, the charming youths of the David Copperfield and
Edwin Drood school, will be entirely repudiated by future
generations (they are barely tolerated now) we make no
doubt, but we believe that the delightful absurdities, of whom
the chief are Dick Swiveller and Mark Tapley, Miggs and Mrs.
Gamp (who has been flattered by imitation more extensively
than any personage in the history of fiction) will be delightful
to reading humanity for a long time to come.

Mr. Thackeray was a humorist in the other category. There
is profound intellectual satisfaction in our helpless involuntary
recognition of the truth of his delineations of the smallnesses,
the weaknesses, the follies, and the absurdities of ourselves
and our fellows,—but especially ourselves. His insight is only
equalled by the dexterity with which he exposes his discoveries.
But it does so much more than amuse that it does less. It
occupies so entirely; it is so suggestive; it comes so thoroughly
home to the reader; it is so sad, with all its good humour; so
depressing, with all its sparkle and finish; so savagely satirical,
with its contemptuous admission that no one is much less of
a fool, or a snob, or a swindler, pretender, ass, or coquette,
of a hero, saint, exemplary person, bore, or Philistine than
his neighbour; it has, for all its power and extent, such a
monotonous *refrain*, that it does not rest or refresh. It taxes
the mind, and while we recognize the great gift, and its cultivated and lavish use, it no more cheers one's spirits or turns
one's thoughts out of a work-a-day groove than a comedy of
Molière does. By general consent all novels are classed as
" light reading." Mr. Thackeray's ought to be excepted.
They are amazingly clever, and in parts incomparably entertaining, but they are serious reading, and make treacherous

divergences into generalities from which we all shrink with
the shame of self-detection. Mr. Thackeray, in his humorous
moods, is like a snowballer of whose good faith one is not
sure. That brilliant soft-seeming missile coming after its
bright snowy brethren may have a very hard stone in it,
and the aim is unerring. Mr. Thackeray has no invariably
comic . characters. Many of Mr. Dickens's personages are
brought upon the scene to make one laugh with as single a
purpose as a clown is ushered on the stage with a tumble
after a transformation scene, and others are never intended to
provoke a smile through twelve green Numbers.

Mr. Thackeray's power was at its highest, at its most intense, when he had to deal with the kind of situation which
Mr. Dickens made bombastic, unreal, and—to tell the truth,
which is hard because of its surroundings and the tenderness
they inspire—ridiculous. Let us detach from "Dombey and
Son" the final interview between the pompous, vulgar, preposterous Dombey, and the absurd anomaly who is bullied
into marrying him by her wretched old mother, otherwise her
abject flatterer and slave, and who, having bullied him successfully to all appearance, ruins herself for ever in order to
convince him of her contempt. Let us detach from "Vanity
Fair" the terrible, simple, marvellous picture of the final
interview between the unprincipled, uneducated Guardsman,
convinced of the perfidy of the woman who has thoroughly
enslaved him for years, and with the forlorn remnant of the
gentleman's instinct aroused within him, and the defeated
adventuress, in whom taste and talent are so strong that
even in that minute, and fearfully as they tell against herself,
she feels irrepressible admiration for the strength, the daring,
and the manly rage which transforms the lout on whose
loutishness she has calculated a little too far. The more we
study that scene between Rawdon Crawley and Becky the
more we recognize its grandeur and finish, the more we see
its nature and its art. The admirable use of accessories so
slight, so telling, furnishes one strong feature in the contrast
we are pointing out. Edith Dombey, in the midst of a violent
and threatening altercation with her husband, at the supreme
crisis of her life, is not oblivious of the diamonds in her hair,
but drags them out, "straining her rich black locks with heed-
less cruelty," and thereupon we have an apostrophe to the
diamonds, in which we are told fine things about their turning—supposing they had known all about it, had not been
diamonds in fact—"dull as tarnished honour." If Mr. Dickens
had adopted the tone of a cynic or a satirist, if he had been
the kind of writer who would relate how a woman going to the

scaffold would consult her looking-glass as to the state of her complexion, or a woman going to faint would dispose the folds of her dress after the best models in drapery, the episode of the diamonds might be esteemed consistent—not with truth, not with the fierce yet stern passion of a woman who had made a desperate position for herself—but wtih the author's tone and style. But Mr. Dickens assumes no such attitude; he is telling a story which he takes to be tragical, after a fashion which he holds to be dramatic. Becky Sharpe too is decked in diamonds when the crisis of her life comes upon her. She has lost or sold herself for these diamonds mainly, but when her husband has torn the badges of her shame and his dishonour from her neck and ordered her to take them off her arms and fingers, she obeys him. When he bids her throw them down upon the floor she does so, and when he goes away and leaves her *she forgets the diamonds*, and the deserting lady's maid steals them. Edith Dombey despises her possessions, but plays a part of her rôle out with her jewels. Becky, who is as greedy and covetous as she is in every other way wicked, forgets the price of her iniquity in the crash of her detection. Where the one writer is strong the other is weak; and this is true in the converse cases also. Where there is youth, merriment, hope, and anything of festivity to be depicted, Mr. Dickens is in, and Mr. Thackeray is out of his element. The latter has the air of an observant spectator, kindly and good-humoured, but not deluded by appearances, who knows it will not last; while Mr. Dickens writes like a partaker and actor in all the bustle and pleasure of the scene, believing in it, enjoying it, undepressed . by philosophical reflection. Mr. Dickens appeals to his readers' feelings so successfully that they do not critically examine the grounds of the appeal, and are frequently imposed upon, as may be seen if we examine the persons and the circumstances set forth to secure our sympathy. Mr. Thackeray addresses the intellect of his readers directly and continuously, rarely touching the emotional chords, but on these infrequent occasions touching them with a master's hand. He never asks us for sympathy which the coolest reasoning ought to lead us to refuse, and he produces his most powerful effects by simple and direct means.

The motives of the two famous novelists are as distinct as the mechanism which they employed.

The "Shaksperian" quality which has been claimed for Mr. Dickens as a humorist we do not quite understand. The word has so much general and so little particular meaning that it is impossible to define the thought of the critics who employ it; but the thing which we take it to signify is decidedly wanting in Mr. Thackeray. If it means that Mr. Dickens took a very wide range of subjects, and made them forcible, dramatic, and so entirely individual by his treatment that any one and every one must see and understand them; that he took possession of them first, and then of the reader, introducing him to them as to living people, whose faces and ways would henceforth be familiar and real to him; if this be " Shaksperian," and it is, at least, a bit of Shaksperianism, then Mr. Thackeray is assuredly not Shaksperian. His works never can be universally popular; the enjoyment of them will always be restricted to certain classes; and the more artificial society grows, the more the shams he detected and ridiculed become prevalent, the more the struggles he respected and mildly quizzed become necessary, the more his works will be appreciated.

Remarkable evenness of manner characterizes Mr. Thackeray's works, and also a certain sameness of flavour. Not one of them is entirely free from tediousness, though, if we analyze the portions which weary us, we shall generally find them full of point, and composed of minute, marvellous touches of extreme skill. A collection might be made merely of his digressions, which would be an ample exhibition of all his greatest qualities and best effects; but, as digressions, we are disposed to quarrel with them; we are sometimes vexed by the persistence with which he exhibits the reverse of every medal. As monotonous and ceaseless as the everlasting voice of the sea is his " Vanitas Vanitatum ! " and though we know he is right, we do not like to be kept so vigilantly mindful of the skeleton in the cupboard at home, the death's head at the board where we sit as guests, the snake in the green grass of the fields of fancy into which we turn for a stroll. There is something in Mr. Thackeray's works which would be wholesome mortification, and a salutary lesson to every one of us, if with rebuke were administered precept,—if with the diagnosis of disease came the prescription of remedy. It might be a good thing to be taught to regard our race with the sorrowful contempt due to its ignominy, if the lesson went further; if, after having been made to look into, we were encouraged to look out of, ourselves. Is it not because there is no such corrective in these books, that their wit and their wisdom, marvellous and admirable as they are, are somewhat dreary and distasteful ?

There was no decline in Mr. Thackeray's powers from the first to the last. The fragment of the work upon which he was engaged (the notes show us with what thoroughness, industry, and research), when the sudden summons came to him, which, a few years later, was to come as suddenly to his famous contemporary, is equal, in all points, to any of its predecessors, and has a touch of novelty in the style and subject which would have made it welcome to his admirers. The vigour of the descriptions in the fragment of " Denis Duval " which we possess is an earnest of what we might have looked for, the breaking of new ground, and the evolution of new sympathies.

We are taken out of town, away from drawing-rooms, ateliers, clubs, the great world which he has shown to be so little, and the small world, smaller for its efforts to seem great, from pretence, selfishness, and scheming in " society," to scenes of terrible emotion, hard life, adventure, and the unending human drama of love, fear, error, and death. The writer never did finer, more earnest, or more laborious work than that which was cut short by his sudden death. This was not so in the case of Mr. Dickens. " Great Expectations " and " Our Mutual Friend " are inferior to any of their predecessors, except " Little Dorritt ; " although the former has some striking merits. The characters of Joe Gargery and his wife are among his finest traits of humour, while Pumblechook and the Pocket household—a feeble repetition of the Jellybys, with Traddles revived in Herbert,—are among his worst failures. The description of the convict, Magwitch, is his best achievement after Dennis the hangman. The fragment of the work on which he was engaged when his death occurred, which we naturally regard with the tenderness and interest inspired by the circumstances, and due to one to whom we are indebted for a great deal of pleasure, and a number of friends hardly to be called fictitious, is not comparable with any of the books written in his prime. Affectations and eccentricities encumber the style, and there is an intricate laboriousness about the portions meant to be funny, which effectually frustrate that intention. " The Mystery of Edwin Drood " is, in some respects, a singular repetition of its immediate predecessor. In " Our Mutual Friend," and in " Edwin Drood," we have a young lady and a young gentleman betrothed to one another by other people, and very doubtful of the wisdom of the arrangement. In both, the young gentleman disappears, the young lady believes him to be dead, and is affectionately guarded by his confidential friend (in each case an amiable eccentric) who is the only person in possession of the secret. Julius Handford and Edwin Drood, Bella Wilfer and Rosa Bud, Mr. Boffin and Mr. Grewgious, play analogous parts in these stories, and the old woman who tramps down to Rochester, mumbles and begs in the street, and talks oracularly to Edwin Drood, is a repetition of the good Mrs. Brown, who sold the Grinder's harshly exacted confidence to Mr. Dombey. There are passages of good description, which remind us of Mr. Dickens at his happiest time ; that one, in particular, in which Jasper falls insensible at the feet of Mr. Grewgious, when that odd person's communication makes him aware that the irrevocable crime he has committed was wholly unnecessary ; that the scene he had taken to mean a renewal of love's vows was really their relinquishment. But, on the whole, we do not think, if "The Mystery of Edwin Drood" had been completed, it would have added to the author's fame.

The two novelists looked at life and their fellow-men from different points of view. The mind of Mr. Dickens was not philosophical, but his fancy was vivid and impressionable, and his sympathies were wide and keen. Mr. Thackeray's mind was philosophical, and his sympathies were narrow, but intense. The benevolence of the former was real and eager, though unpractical, and injured by his habit of regarding all established systems as mingled cant and harshness ; but Mr. Thackeray seems to have thought that there really is not much good to be done in and for the world, and, if one only gives away as much money as one can spare, one need not meddle further with a rather hopeless state of affairs. We are excessively amused by the fussy and interested philanthropy of Pitt Crawley, but nowhere does the author of " Vanity Fair " depict a really great and useful public career. He did not use his novels, as Mr. Dickens used some of his, as Mr. Wilkie Collins has used "No Name," and " Man and Wife," to ventilate public grievances, and the wrongs of certain classes ; he accepted these things, and mused upon them gravely and humorously, but he did not propose to himself to ameliorate society. " Oh, my friends, ere we be old, let us learn to love and pray !" his apostrophe to his readers, when he tells them the grim, terrible, pathetic, droll, and hateful story of old Miss Crawley, is repeated, in various forms, in his works ; but he does not seem to put much trust in the efficacy of love, or to realize what might actually be done for the world by prayer.

He has depicted old men and old women more variously than any other English writer, and with exquisite skill, irony, satire, pathos, and sadness. He has drawn several pictures of the death of old people. How beautiful some of those pictures are ! Not only that of Colonel Newcome, which has been written and talked of more than the most brilliant, keen, and elaborate passages of his writings, but others. The death of Mrs. Sedley, in her fallen fortunes, when quite defeated · by her cares, and worn out, she is forced to leave the " poor old man ; " the death of old Sedley, after all his maundering and tediousness, and Amelia's gentle, dutiful ministrations; the death of Helen Pendennis, on which occasion only Arthur ceases to be a conceited bore, and commands all our sympathy ; and the few lines in which Colonel Esmond's story is finished, which tell that " there has been some bankruptcy of the heart which his spirit never recovered ; he submitted to life rather than enjoyed it, and was never in better spirits than in his last hours, when he was going to lay it down." If he makes death so solemn and pathetic, he makes it grim, awful, ghastly too. Sir Pitt Crawley, and old Matilda, the neglected Lady Crawley, dying in her solitary room ; Isabel Castlewood, foreshadowing in her life and death the beautiful Beatrix, both daughters of a house which inherited, from generation to generation, the doom of a splendid shame ; Beatrix herself, one of the most powerful and terrible creations in all·the achievements of fiction. Can anything be more profoundly painful than the picture of her death ? There are two pictures, by a Spanish artist, in the Kensington Museum, called respectively by the commonplace titles, " Youth " and " Age." They are like the description, first, of Beatrix Esmond as she comes down the stair at Castlewood, in all the bloom and fragrance of her exquisite beauty and grace ; secondly, of the Baroness Bernstein, when the end is coming.

Mr. Dickens handled the solemn topics of age and death in a totally different manner. He touches us, or amuses us, as he intends to do, by his old people, but he wields no terrible power like that put forth in the story of Beatrix ; no keen, forcible, ruthless, and yet amusing realism like that which depicts the vain, coarse, selfish, proud, kindly, generous, insolent, shrewd " old heathen," Miss Crawley. The death of Nell's grandfather is prettily told ; and the closing scene, in which Mrs. Skewton makes a pitiful appeal to her daughter, who is unnatural in every sense, are the best specimens ; but he is unreal in his treatment of such subjects. Old age is not pleasant, or jovial ; it may be dignified, serene, and happy, if only you have the grace of God to make it so : and Death is the king of terrors, a king triumphant too, unless he be vanquished by Him who is finally to tread him under His foot. Pretty sentiment, and vague generalities of speculative religion, the sort of thing which has been aptly called " the religion of the blue sky," are all ·that Mr. Dickens opposes to the awful inexorable despotism of death; and, as even those who do not know what it is that ought to be opposed to that despotism, feel the insufficiency of these, he is never effective in his treatment. The merely *pretty* pictures of death in his works we do not propose to discuss at length. They are about as much like reality as the decease of a stage heroine, who expires to slow music. The old women, full of worldliness, shrewdness, sarcasm, and sound sense, who play so prominent a part in "The Newcomes" and "The Virginians," whose characters are so skilfully varied, but whose influence over the lives of all connected with them is not to be evaded, are almost entirely unrepresented in Mr. Dickens's novels. The Old Soldier is a very clumsy, and comparatively harmless schemer, in comparison with the Campaigner, the odious mother of Clive Newcome's silly wife. Mrs. Skewton is a futile fool when placed beside the wonderful Lady Kew, one of Mr. Thackeray's master-pieces. Was there ever such vulgar insolence, such unblushing covetousness and tyranny as the Campaigner's? Was there ever such high-bred, dignified ferocity, and such vile and candid worldliness as Lady Kew's? The old peeress is perfectly abhorrent; the poison of asps is indeed under her tongue, but her breeding is perfect, and her gallantry in the combat with Madame d'Ivry is wonderful. *Bon sang ne peut mentir*, when it comes to fighting, but it can, and does, lie to any extent when pursuing aims which are of a world-wide and levelling vulgarity.

Mr. Dickens gives us, for his part, such amusing and harmless old ladies as Mrs. Nickleby and Miss La Creevy, as Miss Tox and Mrs. Blimber, as Mrs. Todgers and Miss Trotwood. They are not like life, but they are very amusing; every one of them has become a reality to us, and we like them.

All Mr. Thackeray's works bear countless indications of extensive and various reading. His style, elaborately simple, with that simplicity which is the final attainment of high art, tells of great cultivation; and his works are full of illustration, association, and suggestion drawn from art, philosophy, science, politics, history, and literature. Two of his works, "Esmond" and "The Virginians," are notably products of close and laborious study. "Esmond" is indeed the most perfect work of its kind in existence, and "The Virginians" amply sustains the merit and continues the characteristics of "Esmond." To write these books, the author required to have a thorough acquaintance with the history of the time to which they are supposed to belong; of the modes, the manners, the literature, the terms of speech, the slang, the small talk, the court scandals and truths, the popular amusements, the social phases, the male and female celebrities, the public resorts, the atmosphere of society,—in short, the actual daily life of the period. His latest work is of the same order, and required as much study. We cannot judge whether "Denis Duval" would have been a less painful story than "Esmond," whether it would have commanded a more pleasant kind of sympathy than "The Virginians," whether the wit and the wisdom which pervade both would have been manifested as fully in it; we only know that it was rich in promise, and that Mr. Thackeray rarely failed in fulfilment.

The memoir of Barry Lyndon is much less known than "Esmond" and "The Virginians;" like them, it exhibits the writer's knowledge of social epochs, in detail, and his painfully keen insight into the evil and the meanness of human nature. It is a work of extraordinary talent, but we heartily wish Mr. Thackeray had not written it. It is an evil book, though the vileness which it portrays is sternly reprobated and severely punished, and though there is nothing finer or more pathetic in all the author's writings than the wretched Lady Lyndon's hesitation at the last moment, when she has outwitted the monster of wickedness, guilty of every crime towards her, but is once more softened by her silly, unworthy love of him. We do the genius of the book ample justice; we recognize it as superior to that which animates "Vanity Fair," and as amazingly subtle and unerring. The episode of Mr. Barry's Prussian experiences, the description of the detestable perfection of the spy system—a legacy of the odious little Carlyle-worshipped despot to his descendants, which they have duly appreciated,—is an admirable piece of historical writing. The wit of the book is admirable, its satire is scathing, and its plot skilful. Nevertheless, it is bad and hateful; and it is painful to contemplate such a mind as the writer's concentrated for the time which its composition must have occupied, upon an unrelieved picture of hideous dishonesty and ruffianly brutality. It can hardly have been written for the mere gratification of Mr. Thackeray's prejudices with respect to Ireland, for no man knew better than he that a caricature does no harm; that it is only truth which hurts; and he was as well aware as his readers that "Barry Lyndon" is the grossest of caricatures. Captain Costigan, the Mulligans, Shandon, Sir Michael O'Dowd, the incomparable Peggy, and Glorvina, are types which we can accept, and which amuse Irish ladies and gentlemen, we suspect, far more than they amuse English ladies and gentlemen. We do not think any one unfamiliar with Dublin,—or, indeed, not familiar to the point of extreme intimacy,—can thoroughly appreciate Peggy O'Dowd. But the detestable, base, sickening wretch on whose vile life Mr. Thackeray expended as much labour as Colonel Newcome cost him, is not true to the worst side of his supposed nationality, and is simply a monster, a hideous excrescence on any class in any country. It is assuredly not good to read such a book—as savage and as mean as anything written by Swift; indeed, since Jonathan Wild no author has ever taken such a base and perverted wretch for a hero ; and it cannot have been good to write it. There is nothing to modify the revolting picture of Barry Lyndon. In the author's other works he draws men and women as they are. If he shows to us a Rawdon Crawley, a Lord Steyne, a Barnes Newcome, a Will Esmond, a Sir Francis Clavering, he shows us also Dobbin, Clive, and his father, Henry Esmond, Sir George Warrington, and, guiding us through many back slums of villany, vulgarity, pretence, vanity, greed, and sensuality, does not deny us the broad and open way of virtue, honour, honesty, refinement, purity, and good sense. But in " Barry Lyndon " there is no relief. The atmosphere is always odious; the way is always miry ; we sink deeper and deeper in ill-smelling mud. Every man in the book is a brute, a bully, a swindler, a stupid knave, a vicious fool, or a nonentity. Every woman is vulgar, ignorant, violent, vicious, or incredibly silly, false, affected, or stupid ; and some of them combine most of these qualities. We do not know a woman in fiction more offensive to womankind than Lady Lyndon,—more coarse, vulgar, and base than Mrs. Barry ; and we feel tolerably convinced that the English peeress is not less unlike any reality of any time than the well-born Irishwoman in reduced circumstances, who is almost as great a monster as her son. " Barry Lyndon " is an offensive book in every way, and in one especially in which Mr. Thackeray rarely transgresses the laws of good taste. The incomparable ruffian who relates his life and crimes gives the following account of the religious opinions of his parents :—

My mother was the most beautiful woman of her day in Dublin, and universally called the Dasher there. Seeing her at the assembly, my father became passionately attached to her ; but her soul was above marrying a Papist or an attorney's clerk ; and so for the love of her, the good old laws being then in force, my dear father slipped into my uncle Cornelius's shoes, and took the family estate. Besides the force of my mother's bright eyes, several persons, and of the genteelest society too, contributed to this happy change ; and I have often heard my mother laughingly tell the story of my father's recantation, which was solemnly pronounced at the tavern in the company of Sir Dick Ringwood, Lord Bagwig, Captain Punter, and two or three other young sparks. Roaring Barry won three hundred pieces that night at faro, and laid the necessary information the next morning against his brother.

This can hardly be an agreeable passage to Protestant readers, while to Catholics it is extremely painful. Is it in any sense a necessary portion of Mr. Barry Lyndon's biography? Would it have injured the wit, or the completeness of the book, to omit the introduction of a shocking act of apostasy and impiety into the pages of a novel? If Mr. Thackeray's Catholic readers have cause to complain of this passage, he gives his Protestant readers as much cause of offence afterwards. When Mr. Barry begins to scheme for the hand of the unhappy Lady Lyndon, he first corrupts her son's tutor, who is her private chaplain, one Mr. Runt, "who was," he says, "fond of pleasure, of a glass of Rhenish in the garden-houses in the summer evenings, and of a sly throw of the dice when occasion offered; and I took care to make friends with this person, who, being a college-tutor and an Englishman, was ready to go on his knees to any one who resembled a man of fashion." Nothing can exceed the coarseness of Barry's contempt for this Protestant clergyman, whom he approaches in the following manner:—

I never shall forget the poor wretch's astonishment when I asked him to dine, with two counts, off gold plate, at the little room in the casino; he was made happy by being allowed to win a few pieces of us, became exceedingly tipsy, sang Cambridge songs, and recreated the company by telling us, in his horrid Yorkshire French, stories about all the lords that had ever been in his college. I encouraged him to come and see me oftener, and bring with him his little viscount, for whom, though the boy always detested me, I took care to have a good stock of sweetmeats, toys, and picture-books when he came. I then began to enter into a controversy with Mr. Runt, and confided to him some doubts I had, and a very, very earnest leaning towards the Church of Rome. I made a certain abbé whom I knew write me letters upon transubstantiation, &c., which the honest tutor was rather puzzled to answer, and I knew they would be communicated to his lady, as they were; for, asking leave to attend the English service which was celebrated in her apartments, and frequented by the best English then in Spa, on the second Sunday she condescended to look at me, on the third she replied to my profound bow by a curtsey; the next day I followed up the acquaintance by another obeisance in the public walk, and, to make a long story short, her ladyship and I were in full correspondence on transubstantiation before six weeks were over.

From our point of view this is horribly profane; from the Protestant point of view we conceive it is indecent and insulting. Both meet on the ground of its extreme bad taste, and its unnecessary coarseness. For the rest, there is in all

Mr. Thackeray's books no more painful and pitiful creation than Lady Lyndon,—" Calista," as the vain, weak creature calls herself, in the brief time of her pride and folly; but pity is swamped by the contempt she inspires.

There is also among Mr. Dickens's works one which it would be well for his future fame if he had not written. It is to be supposed that the world, which is to be so much better educated immediately, will not henceforth tolerate books made up of flimsy, intolerant, and ignorant remarks upon a number of subjects of which the writers know nothing; and therefore we anticipate that " Pictures from Italy " will modify the estimate of the next generation of its author's powers and place in literature. The complacency of his ignorance, when he treats of subjects which need information for their correct appreciation, is provoking to educated people. His mind was distinctly objective, and his descriptions, when he kept clear of his characteristic affectations, were reliable and delightfully fresh. Not so his observations and deductions. His writings give us reason to believe that he had very little knowledge of art, literature, and politics, no reverence for them, and scant sympathy with the minds to which they are interesting, important, and precious. The social questions which he illustrates are treated with more zeal than knowledge; and though his good faith and good feeling are evident, he is much too vehement, and deals too largely in the picturesque to be regarded as a public instructor on all or any of his topics. " Hard Times " is amusing and clever, but while he exaggerates out of all practical utility as an example the Gradgrind system, we regard that which Mr. Dickens would have substituted for it with little more favour. We do not think he had any of the elements of a social reformer in him, except that of a keen perception of evil, and a happy facility for pooh-poohing difficulties which he was not called upon to combat or expected to overcome. Only the cheerfulness of an uneducated mind could inspire the complacent self-glorification of his tone when he ridicules and reproves the institutions of his own country, institutions which grave, educated, and gifted men are content to pass their lives in the effort to improve, day by day, here a little and there a little—those among them who are God-fearing and God-loving, with an awful sense of insufficiency and responsibility. This is still more remarkable, and is reinforced by an exuberant sense of the absurdity naturally and inevitably inherent in anything which he does not admire or like when his subject is a foreign country and a foreign race. It does not readily occur to uneducated people, unless they have the grace of humility, that more exists in what they are looking at than they can see, and that things which puzzle them may possibly be above their comprehension, instead of being beneath their notice. That old story in the Gospel repeats itself every day. *We* do not understand what you say, and *therefore* you are talking nonsense; or *nobody* can believe that kind of thing, *therefore* you are mad, or have a devil, to keep on talking such fables.* To minds of this order, history, tradition, faith, fancy are all absurd, all stupid. They respect their own fancies, they believe in their own notions, but they cannot perceive that the very minority they are in, the written, built, painted, graven, sung testimony of the ages and their multitudes, attest the meaning of that which they jeer at as folly, and the vitality of that which they mock as exploded by common consent of that wise portion of mankind of which the individual critic is the very wisest. Mr. Dickens wrote two works of travel. One is "American Notes," the other is "Pictures from Italy." There was every reason why he should do the former well, and every reason why he should do the latter badly. The United States are a young country, with a newspaper history, animated wholly by modern motives, with purposes sanctioned and approved by the spirit of the age, without old associations without a past laborious to learn, and difficult to judge impartially—a country which imports its art and its literature, and buys both bran new. A great country ; a big, patent, portentous fact, full of actual prosperity, and unincumbered with traditions; ready to hand, so to speak, — the most congenial field possible for a popular writer with an objective mind, a pleasant style, and unhesitating confidence in his own judgment. He acquitted himself of the task very well. His "American Notes" are amusing; they give the reader a clear idea of a great number of places, objects, and institutions; they do not bore him with deep reflections, and they keep him, if he be an Englishman, in very good humour with his own country all the time.

Italy was the exact opposite of America. Without taking into account the present wretched condition of the country,

—— a cui feó la sorte
Dona infelice di tanta bellezzá,

and the still more fatal gift of the most shamelessly immoral race of politicians the Western world has ever seen, its history had for a long period offered a contrast to the prosperity and the development of America. When Mr. Dickens visited

---

* St. John's Gospel, ch. 8.

Italy, it had all the faults, but it also retained the beauties, the venerableness, and the time-honoured graces of an old country. These things were quite out of his line. The complicated, splendid, changeful, terrible, in many respects shameful, in some respects glorious history of the States which were then included in the "geographical expression," Italy was, apparently, unknown to him. There is not a trace of historical reading in the flippant, flimsy, Cockney volume called "Pictures from Italy,"—an unlucky title, by the way, for nothing in it is more evident than the author's ignorance of art. No writer has said more about width and toleration,—this book is a curious instance of narrowness and intolerance. Mr. Dickens visits, and believes that he describes, the most Catholic country in Europe; one would think that the fact of Catholicism, as obtrusive and as omnipresent as the sky and the language, would have made him regard some slight acquaintance with the nature of Catholic doctrine and the discipline of the Catholic Church as a desirable preparation for the understanding of that which he was about to see and describe. People who visit Deseret, and sojourn in the City of the Saints, find out as much as they possibly can about Mormonism, and take care to get their information from Brigham Young and Elder Kimball. But Mr. Dickens was only going to Italy, and a few scraps of ordinary abusive cant, filched from the exuberance of the McNeiles and Murphys of the day, sufficed to this inquiring mind as a guide for his study at its head-quarters of the system which had lived nearly nineteen hundred years. Mr. Dickens shows himself totally ignorant of the most ordinary doctrines and practices of the Catholic Church, which he makes the subject of some of his feeblest and most strained jokes. Whole pages of "Pictures from Italy" might be classed with the prologue to "A Tale of Two Cities," the Chuzzlewit pedigree, the episode of Mrs. Nickleby's mad neighbour, the Brick Lane Branch scene in "Pickwick," Twemlow and the Veneerings, the introductory chapter about the Pickwick Club, and the series of pictures of the Wilfer household which make "Our Mutual Friend" intolerably tiresome,—as samples of the execrably bad fun to which a really great humorist sometimes descends when he is accustomed to a public as ready to laugh when he gives them a sign as Mr. Hardcastle's servants at "grouse in the gunroom." But it is not only of the Church which he shows himself ignorant; not only the religious faith, hope, and practices of the people which he treats with flippant scorn; though, happily for Italy in the past, and, we trust, hopefully for her in the future, when she shall be "clothed and in her right

mind," and sitting at the feet of the Saviour in the person of
His Vicar, the Catholic faith has so pervaded her intellectual
and artistic history that the distinction is difficult to draw,—
it is of all those things which persons of more education and
less vanity consider it necessary to know. He was evidently
unacquainted with the history of Italy, of its polity, its commerce, or its art; and he never attempted to acquire that
intellectual attitude of sympathy with the life, the motives,
and the characteristics of the people which only renders travel
useful to the traveller, and its record profitable to the public.
What would be thought of a writer who visited China and
wrote of the porcelain tower at Pekin as "a pile of plates,"
or who visited Hindoostan and looked upon the Taj Mahal
without an inquiry into its origin, without an idea of seeking
the motive of that wondrous love-song in marble? Is a
popular English author less impertinent or less ignorant who
briefly summarises Genoa, that city of a splendid history and
most poetic and romantic fame, as "a city of pink jails"?
In Mr. Dickens's eyes the past was always wrong and generally ridiculous, and he was wanting in reverence as a principle, though he wrote prettily about it as a sentiment. In
this respect Mr. Thackeray was his exact opposite. His cultivated mind had a distinctly reverential tone, and his utterances, in the face of the great facts, men, and monuments of
the past, were few, solemn, and simple, because he conceived
it not only possible, but likely, that those things around which
the tradition of respect had grown and clung for ages, were
deserving of honour.

Mr. Dickens's works possess one prominent and charming characteristic entirely wanting in those of Mr. Thackeray.
It is the familiar love of nature. We have alluded to Mr.
Thackeray's disdain of local colouring, and we believe it
was a great proof of the extent of his ability, as well as a
chief characteristic of its kind, that he could afford to dis-
pense with it. Mr. Dickens's works abound in local colouring,
and we welcome and delight in it. All his life he was in
the habit of walking a great deal, and his descriptions of
scenery by day and by night are such as could only be given
by an observer at such close quarters. There is no exaggeration, no staginess, no sickliness, no inflation in them. He
sometimes peoples the places he tells of with absurdities, but
the places are real and beautiful. Such effects as he never
approached by any machinery of human emotion or passion,
he accomplishes by his descriptions of the face of the earth
and the sky, by his suggestions of the scents and sounds and
hues of Nature, and man's susceptibility to them, through his

nerves, his feelings, and his conscience. When Mr. Dickens
turns aside from the action of his story to draw the portrait of
a country road for us, or to describe the route of a journey, we
do not count it a digression, we do not resent it, we linger over
it in delight. The journey of Little Nell and her grandfather,
Tom Pinch's drive from Salisbury to London, Bill Sykes's
wandering after he has murdered Nance, the night journey
of Jonas Chuzzlewit, the description of the wood " down,
down, down, into" which the doomed man goes, several
sketches of the river Thames, the Cathedral of Cloisterham and
its surroundings, David Copperfield's dreary tramp from London to his aunt's cottage, Yarmouth and the Essex flats, with
the old boat-house on the sands, the marshes where Pip and
Magwitch met, the windings of the river by which Bradley
Headstone went in pursuit of his victim, the " black country"
where Stephen Blackpool and Rachel dragged out their weary,
parted lives,—these are some of the instances which occur to
the memory. But there are two which no doubt stand apart
from all the others in the minds of Mr. Dickens's readers.
These are the wonderful description of Carker's flight through
France, and the yet more wonderful description of the storm
in which Steerforth was shipwrecked and drowned. There is
nothing to equal these in the author's writings; they will bear
to be read over and over again, and never lose their freshness,
their vividness, their awe ; just as we may read Mr. Thackeray's
story of the agonized wretches at Brussels ever so often, and
yet feel the shock of the death of George Osborne at Waterloo
—just as we can never grow into the familiarity which blunts
emotion with that most beautiful scene in which Colonel Newcome answers " *adsum !* " They are masterly in the way in
which the material landscape is transfused with the human
emotion, and both are forced upon us. The haste and the
exhaustion, the terror, the effort of a hunted, despairing creature, whose physical weariness is as pitiable as his dazed sense
of defeat, combine in our sensations as we read, with the characteristics of the French roads, trees, woods, châteaux, towns,
and churches, as we flit by them with Carker, in that jingling,
scrambling gallop, amid the bewilderment of " bells, and
wheels, and horses' feet and no rest." As the storm begins
to gather in the clouds when David Copperfield is going down
to the ruined. home of Little Em'ly, it begins to stir our
nerves, to fill us with a vague anxiety, to roll ever on and
on, with a strange monotony underlying the increasing and
various and unspeakable tumult, so that one's voice is hurried,
and one's breath comes short and quick, and the strife and
power, the resistless might of the tempest, grows and grows,

until the horrible beating and rolling of the ship, close in
shore comes upon us with a real shock, and we know what
was the frantic and imploring agony with which David
besought the fishermen, in the storm which blew his words
away like dust, and would have rushed on destruction himself
in the maddening horror of the hour. The rage and strife of
the elements, and the helplessness of the men, make up a
picture far finer than any other by the same hand. Next to
it, and furnishing an interesting contrast—because in this instance men are the masters and an element their servant—comes
the account of the burning of Newgate by the mob in the
Gordon riots. The whole of Mr. Dickens's description of that
disgraceful episode in the history of ignorance, bigotry, and
folly, is masterly. It forms a portion of the best plot he ever
constructed, and of the only book written by him which is not
disfigured by affectations.

Neither Mr. Thackeray nor Mr. Dickens excelled in the
construction of plots; such excellence is indeed a literary
growth of a later day than theirs. Mr. Wilkie Collins was the
first novelist whose scientific building set criticism on the
alert in this direction; but their readers are indifferent to
their deficiencies, for dissimilar reasons. We do not care
about Mr. Thackeray's plots,—indeed, we almost forget the
incidents; because the interest excited by his characters is so
great and varied, that we are absorbed in them, and events
merely develop them. The persons are everything, the com-
binations are nothing. We know that George Osborne could
not have gone off with Becky, under the (military) circumstances, if she had said "Yes," in reply to the note which
Becky afterwards produces with such complete à *propos*, in
the interests of Dobbin; and we are conscious that "Vanity
Fair" winds up clumsily with a hazy mist about the cha-
rade and its interpretation,—but who cares? Major Pendennis, Costigan, Shandon, Foker, and Warrington are sufficient to atone for the old, old trick of the double bigamy
in "Pendennis"; and the accessory wit and wisdom reconcile us to the futility, selfishness, and priggishness of
Arthur Pendennis, whom, indeed, we are confident Mr. Thackeray never genuinely liked, but knew and intended to be a
snob. "Esmond" is his best plot, but it is, after "Barry
Lyndon," his most painful story, and objectionable in point of
morality. Master as he was in the study of human nature, it
is to be regretted that he should have left the track of natural
human emotions, passions, joys, and sorrows, for the crooked
ways of fantastic sin and morbid suffering. The history of
Lady Castlewood's passion for a man who is, first, her boy

page, then her intended son-in-law, and who finally becomes
her husband, without ceasing to cherish a disappointed love
for her daughter, whom she never loved, and of whom she is
always jealous; is a terrible one;—impossible to read without
pain, without the revolt of conscience and feeling against it.
The extraordinary power and beauty of the book are only additional elements in the regret with which we are forced to regard
such an aberration from right as the investiture of a passion
like this with dignity and pathos, and the description of the
woman who cherishes it as saintly, indeed angelic. "The Newcomes" has hardly any plot, and is so voluminous, intricate, and
digressive, that we do not keep in mind what there is, but are
carried on by the people, as we should be by watching actual
lives, without regard to future contingencies. We know the
author will bring it right somehow, by means of a judicious
apportioning of death and marriage, it does not matter how.
"The Virginians," a more elaborately-constructed plot, produces
a similar effect. It is a less interesting book; but the writer's
minute knowledge is delightfully brought out, and its humour
is captivating. The supposed death of the elder brother,
and his turning up when the younger has dissipated his
fortune, is not a novel incident; but it is used with such
success, with such genuine and healthy pathos, that we forget
it has served the purpose of other novelists; and even of Mr.
Thackeray, who allows it to be supposed that Lord Bulling-
don is killed, and puts Mr. Barry Lindon's little son in his step-
brother's place. But the resemblance is the merest coincidence; while the difference in treatment is as wide as it can be.

Mr. Dickens's plots are all better than Mr. Thackeray's;
but two among their number are very superior to the rest.
They are "Barnaby Rudge" (one of his two romances); and
"A Tale of Two Cities." We call "Barnaby Rudge" and
"The Old Curiosity Shop" romances, as distinguished from his
other works, which are novels, though some of his best realistic
passages are to be found in the two former; and the latter
abound in improbabilities. It is unnecessary to allude to his
miscellaneous writings. Among his short stories, "The
Christmas Carol" is the only remarkable production. "The
Uncommercial Traveller" has not much merit beyond a
few happy touches of description. In the two stories under
the silly general title, "Master Humphrey's Clock," the
writer gave vent to the exuberance of his fancy, and displayed
the vigour of his inventive powers. In them he revels in
fun, he is utterly fantastic and delightful, and he overflows
with sentiment of a kind which he was never able to improve
or strengthen, but which he did somewhat restrain in his

subsequent works; sentiment which one sees through and pardons, when youth, in which we liked it, is past. "Barnaby Rudge" is a fine conception, finely sustained. It has all the dramatic, and many of the poetic requisites for a great plot, and its extravagance, grander in kind, is not greater in degree than that of the "Old Curiosity Shop." There never was an idiot so bountifully endowed with practical wisdom and heroic courage, with such fine feelings and such fidelity as "Barnaby;" but then, one does not judge him by ordinary rules. We believe in Grip on Mr. Dickens's authority, but we are in no wise required to believe in Grip's master. It is interesting to contrast with the realistic criminals whom Mr. Dickens depicted in later times, the criminal of the romance, the melo-dramatic Rudge, for ever haunted by his imagination, precisely as we are told by persons familiar with them, murderers are *not* haunted, leading a self-tortured life for years, and then impelled to revisit the scene of his crime,—at which ideal of a ruffian who had escaped detection by a very clever ruse, modern experience would smile. But we do not smile; the story is too much for us; it is too powerful to be resisted, though it is utterly untrue; therefore, we regard it as one of the finest romances ever written. Mr. Dickens's earlier and later murderers are of a different type. Bill Sykes is probably as near to the truth as the author dared to make him. He is as revolting a ruffian as could be borne; and is not injured in the effect of his ruffianism by the foil provided in the person of Nance. Few people could read the scene of the murder in "Oliver Twist" unmoved, and yet we suppose no one ever read it without being conscious of the utter absurdity of the girl's appeal to Sykes, not only in its manner, though nothing short of an inspiration could possibly have made her aware that such words existed, but in its matter. To paint a picture of honest expiatory industry, in the most refined and touching language, as an inducement to spare her, to a villain who is going to murder her because he foresees, through her means, a sudden check to his life of brutality and crime, is an absurdity which tests the author's power over his readers. But, in the midst of all this unreality, the girl's description of her own position, and the contrast it offers to Rose Maylie's, is as true as it is touching. Mr. Thackeray, in his memorable essay upon "Going to see a Man hanged," made some just remarks upon Nance, in which there is, we think, a clue to his own remarkable abstention from a certain class of topics. "Boz, who knows life well," he says, "knows that his Miss Nancy is the most unreal, fantastical personage possible—no more like a thief's mistress than one of Gessner's

shepherdesses resembles a real country wench.   He dares not
tell the truth concerning such young ladies.   They have, no
doubt, virtues like other human creatures; nay, their position
engenders virtues that are not called into exercise among
other women.   But on these an honest painter of human
nature has no right to dwell.   Not being able to paint the whole
portrait, he has no right to present one or two favourable
points as characterising the whole, and therefore, in fact, had
better leave the picture alone altogether."

Mr. Thackeray kept within a narrow range in his studies of
human nature.   The bad men and bad women who are also
genteel, the sinners of and in society, were his themes, and
no doubt he thus stayed his hand because he desired to be a
thoroughly honest painter of human nature, and because he
knew that if he went for his models into such company as
frequented Fagin's academy, his canvases would not be fit for
exhibition.   He was, so far as intention went, an honest
painter of human nature in a hard style.   A faithful painter—
we think no one who has not the Catholic verity to guide
him in his observation and aid him in his appreciation, can
be.   We remember to have heard that the story of Bill
Sykes and Nancy had a great effect in stirring up the zeal of
ladies in England, and that numerous associations and plans
were formed for the reformation of the wretched class to
which Nancy is made to belong.   We cannot criticize too
strictly the novel which set English ladies to imitate a work
which thousands of devoted women in the Catholic Church had
been doing for ages ; but we do feel a little curious to know
what was the result when they found out that there were no
Nancies.

Jonas Chuzzlewit and Mademoiselle Hortense are murderers
of distinct types; the former much superior to the latter.
But for Mr. Bucket we could not be interested or horrified
by the inconsequent French woman, who walks through the
wet grass without her shoes, apparently for the purpose of
spiting Lady Dedlock, who is not on the spot, and knows
nothing about the performance.   Mr. Bucket's forefinger is a
nuisance, like Mrs. Merdle's bosom, and M. Blandois' nose
and moustache, with their perpetual motion, which seems
to be intended to supply him with meaning otherwise
wanting.   But not his own forefinger, or, worse still, the
numerous imitations of the original detective officer, which
have been inflicted upon the novel-reading world, can prevent
our pleasure in contemplating Mr. Bucket, and our gratitude to
him for relieving the dulness of " Bleak House."   The plot
of " Martin Chuzzlewit " is a strange mixture of clumsiness

and dexterity, and the least interesting persons in it are those who are officially the leading personages. Martin Chuzzlewit is an odious young man, and no less odious after his sudden conversion than before; and Mary Graham is hardly excelled in want of interest and probability by Madeline Bray herself, a young lady who, viewed in the light of a heroine, is ludicrous. The story of the Chuzzlewit family relations is a jumble of incongruities, but the book, for all that, is a fine book. We are inclined to think it is its author's best. . Mrs. Gamp, Bailey Junior and Mark Tapley, the latter one of the writer's happiest absurdities, are gems of humour which he has not equalled elsewhere. We doubt whether any personage in fiction has ever afforded the world so much amusement as Mrs. Gamp. Mr. Pecksniff, his daughters, his family arrangements, Tom Pinch and Mrs. Todgers, are caricatures, very amusing, and admirably drawn—but still caricatures. The humility of Uriah Heep and the hypocrisy of Mr. Pecksniff are of the same order, so elaborately manifest as to fail of their effect. If Mr. Dickens had portrayed in Mr. Pecksniff a person who could possibly have imposed upon any body, old Anthony's explanation, " Don't be a hypocrite ! " would have more point; but Pecksniff's reply, " Charity, my dear, when I take my chamber candlestick to-night, remind me to be more than usually particular in praying for Mr. Anthony Chuzzlewit, who has done me an injustice," could hardly be more comic. The American scenes, though liberally overdrawn, are delightfully entertaining, and the vivacity of the whole book is charming. In " Martin Chuzzlewit " we have the realistic contrasted with the romantic murderer very ably, and yet there is one point of resemblance. Jonas Chuzzlewit is as unlike Sykes as he is unlike Rudge, but the conscience-nerves in the three are touched in the same way. The burglar is haunted by the eyes of the woman he has killed; the highwayman is haunted by the sound of the bell rung by his victim; the swindler, parricide, and murderer is haunted by the method of the blow he struck in the wood.

" Oliver Twist " is the most unequal of the author's works in construction. The plot is good in some respects, and absurdly feeble in others. Bumble and Mrs. Corney are among the best of his humorous creations; Monks, Rose Maylie, the tiresome old philanthropist, and Mr. Grimwig, are failures; Oliver is a feeble sketch, but Fagin ranks with Dennis the hangman, and the Artful Dodger stands alone. " Nicholas Nickleby " is also defective in plot. Modern novelists are subjected to rules unknown in Mr. Dickens's early days; their machinery is more complicated, and not one of them would venture upon the episode of Madeline Bray, or the employment of so clumsy a *Deus ex machinâ* as Brooker and the story of Smike's parentage. But the reader is not influenced by these considerations; he is charmed with the vitality and *verve* of Nicholas, accepts his sudden development into a successful actor with good humour, if not with faith, and heartily enjoys the wit of the book. In the characters of Ralph Nickleby and Arthur Gride, Mr. Dickens drew a finer distinction than was his wont. They are both actuated by an identical passion, —the love of money. But Ralph Nickleby is more than a miser. He is a man who loves the power which money gives, and who expends money in securing the gratification alike of avarice and revenge. Arthur Gride is a mere sordid miser, a wretched hoarder of coins, a starveling fool, who has not sense to feed his watchdog. Peg Sliderskew's explanation of her theft to Squeers is one of the best achievements of the author. That much-abused prototype Mrs. Nickleby, Miss La Creevy, the Kenwigses, Newman Noggs, John Brodie, Fanny Squeers, 'Tilda, for how much keen pleasure are we indebted to their drollery, their squabbles, their intense vulgarity? The book has some gross absurdities; for instance, the Wittitterlys and Pyke and Pluck (think of Wenham and Wagg in comparison with them!) while the registry office episodes, and indeed Frank Cheeryble himself, are mere excrescences. These earlier novels have a charm, even in their eccentricities, which the later ones want. For instance, Smike is as improbable a creature as Jenny Wren, but how much more credible, how much more touching! Maypole Hugh is as complete and unredeemed a ruffian as Rogue Riderhood, and is a wildly romantic freak of fancy besides; but the author means us to have a strange, unreasonable liking for Maypole Hugh, and forces us to feel it, whereas the scoundrel who talks to the walking gentleman of "Our Mutual Friend" about "t'other governor," and "t'otherest governor," as not the clumsiest-tongued hind ever talked, is not only abhorrent, but dull and tiresome. Who can resist the creeping aversion which Dennis the hangman inspires? Is there any reader who has not succumbed to the fascination of that incomparable little monster, Quilp? who has not taken delight in the Marchioness? and who does not love Dick Swiveller? Does any one look upon Miggs as merely a fancy sketch, or feel that a real Tom Pinch would be a blundering nuisance? or regard with gratitude the critic who makes it clear that Mr. Peggotty is not the least like a Yarmouth boatman, and that the very worst method he could have adopted for finding Em'ly (presumably taken abroad by her base lover) as speedily as possible, was that of setting off *to walk* to the coast? No writer gets such a hold of our feelings at the expense of our common sense, or fails more completely to secure sympathy where he claims it most eagerly and ostentatiously. Who cares about his young lady heroines? Though Sydney Carton,—one of the finest of Mr. Dickens's creations,—died for her, Lucie Manette is not really interesting, in spite of the use made of her expressive forehead and her golden hair. Emma Haredale is the most noble and attractive of the series of girl heroines, but we see little of her, and she is always in an exceptional position. Dolly Varden is charming, chiefly because she is *not* a young lady, and her coquetries and affectations are of an original sort. Mary Graham is the most shadowy of heroines. Ada, the "darling" of Miss Esther Summerson, is rather more sly and deceitful than is quite consonant with our idea of an "angel girl." Estella is an impossibility, happily of a kind which not the most impressionable of Mr. Dickens's young readers will try to imitate. Little Dorritt is the dreariest of heroines, a Mrs. Gummidge without the drollery of that doleful relict of the "old 'un." Florence Dombey, whose grim and exclusive bringing up leads to such incongruous consequences, is the most interesting, though not the least improbable in the long list. Rosa Bud, the last of the young lady heroines, is a *resumé* of the silliness of all her predecessors, with the addition of a special silliness peculiar to herself.

Mr. Thackeray's young ladies have been much derided and decried, and, with the exception of Ethel Newcome, we have nothing to say for them; but we suspect Amelia Sedley or Charlotte Laynes would be a more endurable companion for a rational man through life than Dora or Rosa, and Miss Laura Bell or Theo Leigh, though they are both, in their several ways, wearisome, are incomparably less so than those dreadful specimens of the "household angel" class, Ruth Pinch and Esther Summerson. In the first place, they are ladies, while Miss Pinch and Miss Summerson are as fussy and vulgar as they are vapid and tiresome. Esther Summerson is a striking example of the false sentiment which pervades Mr. Dickens's writings. She is by way of being a model of humility, usefulness, modesty, and good sense—she is, in reality, an affected, self-seeking, self-conscious egotist, recording every compliment paid her with the air of an *ingénue*, but not hiding the smirk of self-satisfaction, and perpetually jingling her household virtues about our ears with those everlasting keys, of which we grow as tired as of Mr. Wemmick's "post-office" mouth, or Canon Crisparkle's "China shepherdess" mother.

Kate Nickleby is Mr. Dickens's most pleasing girl-heroine, but she is out of sight for two-thirds of the story, and those the most amusing. Little Em'ly is an impossible, or at least a phenomenal being, considering her surroundings, and the interest which she undeniably excites is not a wholesome sentiment; nor is her return to her uncle actuated by high motive or sound repentance. But she is a touching, pitiable creature; and the weak credulity of David Copperfield, the facility with which he permits himself to be made a catspaw by his unprincipled friend, throws her feebleness of character into the shade. It did not occur to David, or to Mr. Dickens, apparently, that Steerforth was merely an overbearing bully. Miss Dartle and Miss Wade are two of the most glaring absurdities ever produced by any writer of fiction, and utterly unredeemed by any trait of humour or picturesque accessories. They are superfluous to the stories in which they respectively appear, and without excuse in themselves. If we turn from his girl portraits, and from the daring eccentricities which his vanity led him to produce, and for which his popularity secured his pardon, to the memorable list of his genuinely humorous female characters, we feel how great his genius was, we feel the width of its scope and its versatility. We can see every one of them. Mrs. Jiniwin, Sally Brass, the Marchioness, and Mrs. Jarley; Mrs. Varden and Miggs—that incomparable pair—Mrs. Nickleby, Miss La Creevy, Madame Mantalini, Mrs. Chick, Susan Nipper, Cornelia Blimber and her absurd mother, Polly Toodles and Mrs. MacStinger—(Mr. Dickens is strong on the subject of landladies)—Miss Trotwood, Peggotty, Mrs. Micawber, Miss Moucher, Mrs. Crupp, the Old Soldier; Charity Pecksniff, Mrs. Todgers, Mrs. Gamp, and Mrs. Hominy; Mrs. Jellyby, Mrs. Pardiggle, Miss Pross, and Joe Gargery's exasperating wife. "Little Dorritt" and "Our Mutual Friend" are the only two books which leave no impression of humour upon the reader's mind, which present him with nothing but caricatures. We do not want to remember them, or any of the people in them.

Two female figures occupy a distinct place in the long gallery of portraits drawn by Mr. Dickens. They are those of Edith Dombey and Lady Dedlock. They are both instances of his extraordinary power of throwing an irresistible interest around inconsistent characters and incongruous situations. Edith Dombey's story, told by any other writer, would have been received with mingled ridicule and reprobation. Lady Dedlock's story is equally inconsistent with reason and with itself. These two women, whose pride is insisted on with as much iteration as their beauty, are guilty of the worst kinds of meanness. Both sell themselves for money. Edith Dombey resents so bitterly the bargain she has made, towards the man with whom she has made it, and whose motives were pure in comparison with hers, that she can find no indemnification but one which thrusts her out from the society of honest women for ever,—surely the most eccentric development of pride ever imagined. Lady Dedlock systematically deceives her husband, and finally breaks his heart and humbles him to the dust, by anticipating the consequences of detection —after having deserted her child and lived a lie for years, in order to provide against such a possibility. And yet, if there is any conclusion to be drawn from the description of Sir Leicester Dedlock's conduct to his wife, and of his really fine and noble character—which we may presume so remarkably clever a woman as Lady Dedlock was capable of understanding, and which it was undoubtedly her interest to study —it is that she might have told him the truth, and trusted to his indulgence with perfect safety. In that case Mr. Dickens must have changed his story, it is true, but as he tells it he contradicts himself, and takes the meaning out of one of his best delineations, that of the kind and prejudiced baronet, with a tender heart and " a head seven hundred years thick."

In this enumeration of Mr. Dickens's works, we have hitherto purposely omitted that one which inaugurated his fame, and which is generally regarded as the representative specimen, *par excellence*, of his humour; not because we do not recognize to the full the genuine fun of the incidents, and the exuberant comicality of the characters in the " Pickwick Papers." In certain respects this is Mr. Dickens's best, and it will probably be long regarded as his typical work. But we have a serious quarrel with it. Never was there a more earthy book. Not only is it thoroughly vulgar—that is, in its plan and of its essence, and pardonable—but it is grovelling. It would be relieved by some of the sentimentality with which we are impatient in Mr. Dickens's other works; anything would be welcome which should temper its pothouse flavour. Sam Weller's best sayings would be much better if they were not always an accompaniment to pipes and beer; his father could have been made as amusing without being perpetually represented ordering, consuming, and dispensing liquor; and the journeys of Mr. Pickwick and his friends would be less monotonous if the eating and drinking at every stage of them did not occupy so prominent and continuous a place in the narrative. Mr. Pickwick is an amiable person, no doubt, but no mental quality of his is so forcibly depicted as his faculty for drinking brandy and water, and he is never described with so much relish and humour as when he returns to Dingley Dell in a state of intoxication, and again when he is driven off to the Pound dead drunk. Every man in the book is perpetually drinking; kindness, compassion, charity exhibit themselves in orders for drink, all the entertainments are drinking bouts, and the subject which is made most elaborately ridiculous— the subject of a long, laboured, and execrably bad joke—is a Temperance Society. Such powers of humour as Mr. Dickens displayed in this book, in which the coarsest material pleasures occupy an inordinate space, are indeed lamentably employed in surrounding such worthless and degrading lives with an irresistible attraction of whimsicality and laughter. We hold it to be a public misfortune that a book, in which a habit admitted by public opinion to be vile and demoralizing, and which is likewise a deadly sin, is treated jocularly, as good fun, and without a hint of its danger and disgrace, should be so widely popular as the " Pickwick Papers."

There is nothing of this kind in Mr. Thackeray's works. The scorn with which he treats vice, evil habits, and degrading self-indulgence, is not the best form of protest against them; but it is better than the jovial, cheery good-fellowship with which Mr. Dickens records the feats of eating and drinking performed by Mr. Pickwick and his friends, and the habitual intemperance of Dick Swiveller, whom he endows with many fine qualities, and makes irresistibly droll and attractive.

No writers of fiction since Sir Walter Scott have given so much pleasure to the world as these two English novelists— pleasure distinct in the case of each in kind and degree. Each is also held in a different sort of remembrance by his countrymen. The publicity, the familiarity with his readers— otherwise than through his works—which Mr. Dickens sought of late years, would have been distasteful to Mr. Thackeray, who was not the centre of any system or clique. Mr. Dickens inaugurated a school of writing. Men talked of him as " the chief " and " the master," and deliberately, though it must be acknowledged unsuccessfully, imitated him. Mr. Thackeray found few imitators; such as he had were among the class of novelists who are at once bold and feeble; and he has no successor.

Art. V.—COPERNICANISM AND POPE PAUL V.

The Pontifical Decrees against the Motion of the Earth considered in their bearing on Advanced Ultramontanism. London : Longmans.

THIS temperately-written pamphlet is directed to the establishment of two principal conclusions: firstly that Paul V. condemned heliocentricism ex cathedrâ; and secondly that, even were the case otherwise, the Roman Congregations so acted in the matter of Galileo, as to show themselves utterly unworthy of that intellectual submission, which has been claimed as due to them by Pius IX. speaking ex cathedrâ. We differ widely from our author on both these conclusions ; but the *former* fills us with simple amazement. It is this former conclusion, of course, which forms the principal count of the author's indictment; and our present article shall be exclusively devoted to its treatment. We have every hope of placing before our readers in July a full reply to the rest of the pamphlet.

We regard then our author's first conclusion as not less than extravagantly untenable. But as some of our readers may possibly not consider our reasoning so conclusive as it appears to ourselves, we must not omit to point out at starting that the onus probandi rests entirely on the writer. His opponents hold most firmly — since the Vatican Definition they hold with divine faith—that the Pope is infallible when speaking ex cathedrâ; and they have repeatedly adduced a large body of historical proof in support of that dogma. Suppose for a moment that the facts of the Galileo case were *indecisive* : this circumstance would leave untouched—just where it was—the vast mass of evidence for Papal infallibility. Our critic does nothing whatever to advance his cause, unless he shows that the facts he adduces are *conclusive* in his favour. And this indeed is the very thing which he professes to do.

Now we have repeatedly pointed out in this Review, that there are two different classes of ex cathedrâ judgments, widely differing from each other in significance and importance : there are firstly definitions of *faith,* and there are secondly *minor* ex cathedrâ pronouncements. By the former of these the Pontiff brands dissentients with the special note of *heresy ;*

and, in accordance with this sentence, utterly cuts them off
from his communion and from the Visible Church: whereas no
such result is involved in his minor judgments.   The practical
difference is most wide between the two.   Suppose I disbelieve (e.g.) the dogma of Transubstantiation, though I well
know that it is taught as of faith by the Church in communion
with Rome.   However invincible may be my ignorance of that
Church's authority—and however convinced a priest may be of
such invincibleness—he cannot nevertheless give me the sacraments, because I am external to the Visible Church.*   But
suppose that, through invincible ignorance, I disbelieve some
doctrine, which is infallibly taught by the Holy See, yet not as
strictly *of faith ;* say e.g. the doctrine of the necessity of the
Pope's civil princedom for the Church's well-being: the priest
then, who accounts my ignorance invincible, is *not* bound to
refuse me absolution.   And from this broad and momentous
difference between the two classes of ex cathedrâ judgments,
it has resulted that definitions *of faith* are commonly pronounced with special emphasis and solemnity.

It is essential then to the present inquiry, that all our
readers should understand *how much* is implied in the allegations of this pamphlet.   Any one who reads the facts therein
so usefully brought together, will see that the charge against
heliocentricism was nothing less than a charge of *heresy*.   It
was considered by the Pope and the ecclesiastical authorities,
that this theory is "opposed to Scripture" (p. 5); "contrary
to Scripture" (p. 20); "repugnant to Scripture" (p. 21); a
"heresy" (p. 21).   Supposing therefore that Paul V. had really
pronounced this judgment ex cathedrâ, his declaration would
have been nothing less than a *definition of faith :* for every
Pontifical definition ex cathedrâ, which ascribes *heresy* or *repug-
nancy against Scripture* to dissentients, must be a definition *of
faith*.   In other words, according to our opponent, Paul V.
defined it to be a. dogma of the Faith that the sun moves
round the earth, precisely as Pius IX. long afterwards
defined it to be a dogma of the Faith that Mary was imma-
culately conceived.   Pius IX. pronounced in effect, on December 8, 1854, that thenceforward to the end of the world no
one could be a member of the Visible Church, who should
deny the Immaculate Conception; and in like manner, according to our opponent, Paul V. pronounced in effect, on March 5,
1616, that thenceforward to the end of the world no one could

---

* We are not here of course referring to exceptional cases ; such as when
a dying Catholic labours under some misapprehension which there is no time
for removing ; but to the *principle* of the thing.

be a member of the Visible Church, who should deny the geocentric theory.

Considering the number of Copernicans even at that time, it is difficult to exaggerate the importance which Paul V. himself must have ascribed to such a pronouncement; and our readers will be anxious to see at once the form which he adopted for its utterance. Unspeakable will be their astonishment at our opponent's answer. We translate the document on which he relies, as it stands in pp. 4, 5, of his pamphlet :—

" DECREE OF THE HOLY CONGREGATION OF MOST ILLUSTRIOUS CARDINALS SPECIALLY DEPUTED BY THE HOLY FATHER PAUL V. AND THE APOSTOLIC SEE FOR [DRAWING UP] THE INDEX OF [PROHIBITED] BOOKS, AND FOR THE PERMISSION, PROHIBITION, EXPURGATION, AND PRINTING OF BOOKS IN THE WHOLE CHRISTIAN WORLD, TO BE PUBLISHED EVERYWHERE.

" Whereas some little time since, among other books, there have appeared some containing various heresies and errors—therefore the Sacred Congregation of most illustrious Cardinals deputed [to be] over the Index, lest from the reading of these books evils every day heavier should arise in the whole Christian world, hath willed that they be entirely condemned and prohibited; as by the present Decree it doth altogether condemn and prohibit them, wherever and in whatever language they have been or may be printed. Commanding that no man henceforth, of whatever grade and condition—under the penalties contained in the sacred Council of Trent, and in the Index of prohibited books—shall dare to print them, or have them printed, or in any way whatever keep them in his possession or read them. And under the same penalties, let all men who now or who may hereafter possess them, be bound, immediately after the present Decree comes to their knowledge, to give them up to the Ordinaries of their respective abodes or to the Inquisitors. The books are those underwritten, namely :—

" ' Theologiæ Calvinistarum Libri tres, auctore Courado Schlusserburgio.

" ' Scotanus Redivivus, sive Comentarius Erotematicus in tres priores libros Codicis, &c.

" ' Gravissimæ Quæstionis de Christianarum Ecclesiarum, in occidentis præsertim partibus, ab Apostolicis temporibus ad nostram usque ætatem continua successione et statu, historica explicatio. Auctore Jacobo Usserio, S. Theologiæ in Dubliniensi Academia apud Hybernos Professore.

" ' Frederici Achillis Ducis Wirtemberg. Consultatio de

Principatu inter Provincias Europæ, habita Tubingæ in Illustri Collegio, anno Christi 1612.

" 'Donnelli Enucleati sive Comentariorum Hugonis Donelli de Jure Civili in compendium ita redactorum,' &c.

"And whereas it has also come to the knowledge of the above-named Holy Congregation that that false Pythagorean doctrine, altogether opposed to the divine Scripture, on the mobility of the earth and the immobility of the sun,—which Nicolas Copernicus in his work 'De Revolutionibus Orbium Cœlestium,' and Didacus a Stunica in his commentary on Job, teach,—is being promulgated and accepted by many, as may be seen from a printed letter of a certain Carmelite father, entitled 'Lettera del R. Padre Maestro Paolo Antonio Foscarini sopra l' opinione de' Pittagorici, e del Copernico della mobilità della Terra e stabilità del Sole, &c.,' wherein the said father has endeavoured to show that the doctrine of the immobility of the sun in the centre of the universe, and the mobility of the earth, is consonant to truth and is not opposed to Holy Scripture ; therefore, lest an opinion of this kind insinuate itself further to the destruction of Catholic truth, this Congregation has decreed that the said books—'Nicolas Copernicus De Revolutionibus' and 'Didacus a Stunica on Job'—be suspended till they are corrected; but that the book of Father Paul Antony Foscarini the Carmelite be altogether prohibited and condemned, and all other books that teach the same thing ; as the present decree respectively prohibits, condemns, and suspends all. In witness whereof this decree was signed and sealed with the hand and seal of the most illustrious and Reverend Lord Cardinal of Saint Cæcilia, Bishop of Albano, on the 5th day of March, 1616."

According to our opponent, the *first* part of this Decree is indeed nothing more nor less than the disciplinary enactment of a Roman Congregation ; but the *second* part is a Definition of faith issued by Pope Paul V. The Pope's name, it will bo observed, is not so much as alluded to from first to last, except as having appointed to their office the Cardinals who issued the Decree. And to *what* office had he appointed them? To the office of issuing definitions of faith? of excluding persons from the communion of the Church? By no manner of means ; but to the office of permitting and prohibiting *books* throughout Christendom. In fulfilling the office assigned to them, these Cardinals, on March 6, 1616, issued two prohibitions : they prohibited the further publication and possession (1) of certain specified theological works ; and (2) of all books advocating the heliocentric theory. For both these prohibitions they express their reasons. The

reason they give for the first is, that such books produce
daily heavier evils throughout the Church ; and the reason
they give for the second is, that many Catholics are beginning to accept, not as a mere hypothesis but as a truth,
"that false Pythagorean doctrine altogether opposed to the
Divine Scripture," which was originated by Copernicus. A
controversialist must be extraordinarily pressed for an argument against Papal infallibility, when he attempts to make
capital out of such a Decree as this. By such methods anything
may mean anything. A Pontifical Congregation prohibits
Copernican books: this is equivalently, we are told, and
indeed is but another way of expressing, that the Pontiff
smites all Copernicans with an anathema. If it be evident
from history—as it is abundantly evident—that Paul V.
heartily approved the Congregational Decree, this is a still
further argument against our opponent: for what possible
reason, in that case, can be given for the absence of the
Pontiff's name, except his desire that the Decree should
not possibly be accounted a Pontifical utterance? He might
or might not have intended to *follow up* the Decree by more
stringent measures, and even by a definition of faith ; but
surely it is the ne plus ultra of unreason to regard this *Decree*
as such a definition.

However, let us grant for argument's sake—which certainly we cannot otherwise grant—that the Pope might possibly have issued a definition of faith, in the form of a Congregational Decree which does not so much as mention his name.
In that event, he must have intended to make manifest by
extrinsic circumstances, what the Decree's *intrinsic* character
rendered so violently improbable. But so far is this from
being the case, that extrinsic circumstances *taken by themselves* are absolutely decisive against our critic's extraordinary
theory. In our former articles we mentioned such facts as
the following. "If one theologian," we said, "were more
prominent than another in his opposition to Galileo, it was
Bellarmine : yet his words are recorded by F. Grassi, also an
opponent of Galileo, to the following effect : ' When a demonstration shall be found to establish the earth's motion, it will
be proper to interpret the Holy Scriptures otherwise than they
have hitherto been, in those passages where mention is made
of the movement of the heavens and the stability of the
earth.'"* This was in 1624. Just imagine F. Perrone
saying in the year 1862 that some unexpected light may
possibly hereafter be obtained, which will make it proper

---

* " Doctrinal Decisions, &c.," p. 160.

to interpret Scripture and Tradition as opposed to the Immaculate ʻConception! Yet Bellarmine's statement would be precisely equivalent to this, if Copernicanism had really been condemned ex cathedrâ. And our opponent neither denies the truth nor the relevancy of our statement about Bellarmine, but simply leaves it alone.

Fromond of Louvain, we proceeded,* argues that the Congregational Decree could not be a definition ex cathedrâ, because Popes "always issue such decrees in their own, and not in other persons' names." Our opponent (p. 16, note) refers to this testimony; but his remarks only strengthen the evidence for its cogency. We never *doubted* that the Decree "had been examined and ratified by the Pope"; but we did strenuously deny that the Pope spoke, in that Decree, as the Church's Universal Teacher. Fromond says precisely this. Moreover, we added, † Riccioli and many other contemporaries of Galileo had been permitted by the Roman censorship to say, after the Decree of 1616, " that no anti-Copernican definition had issued from the Supreme Pontiff." Now let any one imagine, that in the year 1860 the Roman censorship had permitted various writers to declare that the Immaculate Conception is not of faith! Yet on our opponent's view the cases would be precisely parallel; and what makes the case stronger is, that these were all zealous anti-Copernicans, who would be induced by every motive to brand heliocentricism with the severest censure which truth would permit. Our opponent, in reply, adduces (p. 55, note) two anti-Copernicans, who thought that heliocentricism *had* been condemned ex cathedrâ.‡ But such facts do not affect our reasoning in the slightest degree. Let us suppose that, in the year 1860, two writers indeed had declared the Immaculate Conception to be of faith, but that many others had been permitted by the Roman censorship to express an opposite opinion. Such a fact would make it absolutely certain, that the reigning Pontiff did not consider the Definition of 1854 to have been ex cathedrâ.

" The question, when does the Pope act as Pope ? " says our opponent (p. 24)—and by parity of reason, the question, when does he speak as Universal Teacher?—" must be determined not by what theologians in a difficulty choose to assert, but by

---

* " Doctrinal Decisions, &c.," p. 16].

† Ib., pp. 161-2.

‡ A third writer whom he cites, Cazræus, does not differ from our own view, except that (by a manifest historical mistake) he calls the *Congregational* a *Pontifical* Decree. He regards that Decree as purely disciplinary: "ne in posterum verbo aut scripto *doceretur*, sanctissimè prohibuerit."

the language and practice of the Pope himself." We most heartily concur with this; indeed, amidst all the subtleties introduced on this head by theologians, it is the one common-sense principle which alone is satisfactory. In the case before us, "the language and the practice of the Pope" are absolutely conclusive *against* our opponent. In *language*, no Pope has ever *claimed* to have condemned Copernicanism ex cathedrâ; and in *practice*, no Pope has *acted* as though it had been so condemned.

On the other hand, we contended in our former articles, (1) that the Decree of 1616 was imperatively called for, in order to preserve the Church against a grave theological scandal; (2) that the doctrine, on which it avowedly rested, was that which legitimately followed from all the data cognizable in 1616; and (3) that a certain real interior assent was due to that doctrine, from Galileo and from all contemporary Catholics. We do not here speak of an absolute, unreserved, and (so to speak) *irreformable* assent; for such assent can be due only to an *infallible* pronouncement: but of an assent similar in kind to that due, e.g., from a youth of fourteen, to his father's instruction in the facts and principles of history. We shall not here attempt to reason for these three opinions; because they are, in fact, the very questions which we reserve for treatment in our next number. But we are obliged to state our view, in order to make intelligible the general course of our criticism. Moreover, we quite admit that many plausible arguments may be adduced against us on *this* ground; though, after the best consideration we can give the matter, we think, even more strongly than we thought before, that they are *only* plausible and not solid. But, with great respect for our opponent, we must nevertheless stoutly maintain, that his notion of the Congregational Decree having been an ex cathedrâ Pontifical Act, is a "monstrum nullâ virtute redemptum"; a simple prodigy of unreason. And it is against *this* notion that we are arguing in our present article.

Our next business then, will be to examine what positive grounds he adduces for his conclusion: and we shall find that they are for the most part as singular as that conclusion itself. Firstly and chiefly he argues (p. 6) that such a Congregational Decree, if it stated on its surface the Pope's approval and confirmation, must necessarily be admitted by every "Ultramontanist" as "infallibly true" in doctrine. But then—so he proceeds—the practice of stating the Pope's approval by a special clausula did not originate till long after the time of Galileo (p. 7). Consequently, he infers, "Ultramontanists" must in consistency admit that in Galileo's time

Congregational Decrees, even *without* the clausula, were universally intended to be ex cathedrâ, if they included any doctrinal statements as their avowed basis.   Such an inference is very curious; but we must first say a few words on its fundamental premiss.

"The Ultramontanist," he says (p. 6), "does and must admit that if" the Decree of 1616 had contained the clausula, "its declaration ought, on his theory, to be infallibly true." We are quite at a loss to understand this statement.   The great majority of those who defend Papal infallibility, hold no such opinion as he alleges : indeed it is surely this very opinion, which he designates in his title as "*advanced* Ultramontanism"; and of which he says, in his very last sentence (p. 67), that he accounts it to be "at variance with the sense of the majority of educated Catholics."   Moreover, we believe all Catholics would deny — certainly for ourselves we should strenuously deny—that the Pope has ever issued a *definition of faith* by means of a Congregational decree, whether or no that decree contained the clausula.

Certainly we are ourselves disposed to think, that *minor* ex cathedrâ judgments are occasionally uttered by the Pontiff, in the form of Congregational decrees expressing the Pontifical confirmation.   We speak here with great diffidence, and with great deference to those excellent Catholics who think otherwise.   Nor certainly do we hold this opinion as demonstrable *from the nature of the case :* for on the contrary we should rather more naturally understand the Pope, when he confirms Congregational decrees, to act in no other capacity than that of the Church's Supreme *Ruler.*   "The Pope," as we said in our former article, " exercises two different functions, not to speak of more : (1) that of the Church's Infallible Teacher; and (2) that of her Supreme Governor.   The former he can in no sense delegate; but of .the latter he may delegate a greater or less portion, as to him may seem good.   Moreover, in either of these characters he may put forth a doctrinal decree; but with a somewhat different bearing.   If he put it forth as Universal Teacher, he says, in effect, ' I teach the whole Church such a doctrine : ' and the doctrine is of course known thereby to be infallibly true.   But if he put forth a doctrinal decree as Supreme Governor, he says, in effect, ' I shall govern the Church on the principle that this doctrine is true; ' " and in doing this, of course, he by no means puts forth an infallible definition.   We should add that such doctrinal decrees are almost universally issued in the shape of disciplinary commands : as is evidenced in the very case before us.   What the Congregation did *directly,* was to prohibit certain books: the *doctrinal* declaration is introduced *indirectly*, and as a *reason* for this disciplinary command.*

But it does seem to us—speaking entirely under correction —that on two different occasions Pius IX. has implied a doctrine, not contradictory to this, but supplementary thereof. We think he has implied, that whenever a Congregational decree proceeds avowedly on doctrinal grounds, and also expresses the Pontifical confirmation, the Pope intends thereby to speak, not merely as Ruler, but also as Universal Teacher. One of those occasions is that mentioned by our opponent from p. 13 to p. 15. The other is perhaps a still more significant case. We refer to the condemnation of four Louvain professors, and to the documents connected therewith, which we published in January, 1868, from p. 279 to p. 288. We gave a general recapitulation of what is involved in these documents, from p. 237 to p. 240 of the same number. The upshot of the matter is, that certain doctrinal decrees, issued by a Roman Congregation and expressing the Pope's confirmation, were described by Pius IX.'s authority as "decisions of the Holy See,"—not "disciplinary," but "doctrinal"; to which the professors were required to "submit themselves fully, perfectly, and absolutely." †

Now our opponent argues (pp. 7, 11) that to deny the infallibility of the anti-Copernican Decree, is to abandon the only ground, on which we can defend the ex cathedrâ character of decrees *containing* the clausula. In all our experience of controversy, we never met with a more simply gratuitous assertion. We incline to hold the ex cathedrâ character of decrees containing the clausula, because on two occasions Pius IX. seems so to have declared. Where has Pius IX. or any other Pope intimated ever so distantly, that the Pope speaks ex cathedrâ in those Congregational decrees, which do not so much as mention his *name?* " Such a decree," we said in our former article, "in no sense comes to the Church immediately from the Pope, but only from the Congregation as his delegate. Now in which capacity of his is the Congregation his delegate? Exclusively in his capacity of

---

* Our opponent is unquestionably right in saying (p. 41) that no other decree was issued in 1616 concerning heliocentricism, except the disciplinary one ; and that we were quite mistaken in supposing otherwise. Indeed, F. Ryder, in his " Idealism," had suggested the same correction. We need hardly point out that, as regards the argument of our present article, this circumstance makes our case all the stronger.

† We would submit with much confidence, as resulting from this history, that either such decrees are ex cathedrâ, *or* that very large intellectual submission can be justly claimed for a fallible judgment.

Supreme Governor." Our opponent's idea is a pure theological invention, for which he has not even *professed* to adduce one single authority.

Instead of doing so, he indulges in what we must call mere random talk. Thus he cites (pp. 15, 16) a previous Bull, issued by Sixtus V., which commands that the Congregations, and especially that of the Index, should act under Papal guidance. "Let graver matters" in the case of all the Congregations "be referred to us or our successors; that we may by God's grace maturely resolve on what is *expedient*." Why the question in so many words is one of *expediency;* and the Pope therefore is consulted, not as the Church's *Teacher*, but her *Ruler* and *Gubernator*. And the same remark is applicable in all its force to what the same Pope says about the Congregation of the Index. We heartily agree with our critic (p. 16) that "as soon as the Decree" of 1616 "appeared, Catholics ought to have presumed from Sixtus V.'s Bull that it expressed the judgment of the Pope, and that his Holiness had directly sanctioned its issue." But who ever *doubted* that the Decree expressed Paul V.'s judgment, and that his Holiness had directly sanctioned its issue? The one *relevant* question is the one on which he is *silent;* viz., whether Paul V., in sanctioning that Decree—a Decree which did not even mention his name—was intending to define geocentricism as a dogma of the Faith, and to brand Copernicans with an anathema.

Then again our opponent prints at the end of his pamphlet, as highly important, the Bull " Speculatores " issued by Alexander VII. in 1664. But it is evident to the most cursory reader, that this Bull is disciplinary from first to last. Alexander VII. "confirms and approves" the general Index now published by his order, "with all and singular the things therein contained ": one of which " things contained " is the Decree " Cùm ab aliquo tempore." We have no doubt whatever that Alexander VII. was as zealous against Copernicanism, as had been Paul V. and Urban VIII.; and as resolved to prevent Catholics, if he could, from writing or reading Copernican treatises, or embracing the Copernican theory. All honour to him for his pious zeal! The only *relevant* question is again the only one on which our opponent is *dumb*: did Alexander VII. intend by his Bull to recognize geocentricism as an infallibly defined dogma of the Faith, such as is the Trinity or the Incarnation? Merely to suggest such a question is to answer it.

We are astonished our critic does not see, that the more he dwells on the anti-Copernican zeal of successive Pontiffs, the more impressively he sets forth the providentialness of their never having pronounced on the matter ex cathedrâ.*

Since writing the previous paragraphs, it has occurred to us that possibly our opponent does not allege these considerations as having weight *in themselves,* but only as arguments *ad hominem* against M. Bouix. But if he meant only this, he should have expressly said so; for he himself states (p. 12) that we are by no means entirely at one with M. Bouix on every particular connected with the question.† It is no business of ours to defend M. Bouix, but we cannot think that this pamphlet at all succeeds in answering his remarks.

So much for the first argument attempted by our critic. His second is undoubtedly more plausible on the surface; being derived from the use of the word " *define,*" on the part of ecclesiastical authority, in reference to Galileo's condemnation. Thus the Holy Office in 1633 says that heliocentricism has been " declared and *defined* as contrary to the Sacred Scriptures." Again, it is one of the gravamina against Galileo in 1632 (see our opponent, pp. 27, 41), that he " treats the matter as not decided; and as though its *definition* were still waited for, instead of being *presupposed.*"

But this objection becomes actually an argument in our favour, when the context of the Inquisitional Decree is taken into account. The word " define" is in itself ambiguous. It *may* mean undoubtedly to " decide infallibly ": but it *need* not mean more than to " decide in the last resort"; to " put forth a decision from which there is no appeal." So this very Decree of 1633 says : " by this our *definitive* sentence . . . . we say, judge, and declare," &c. &c.; and yet our opponent does not himself allege that *this* Decree was accounted infallible. In like manner a Decision emanating from the Congregation of the Index and ratified by the Pope—even though it contained no mention of the Pope's name—was indubitably a " decision in the last resort "; a " decision from which there was no appeal ": though, no *less* indubitably, it was altogether different from a Pontifical definition *ex cathedrâ.* Now it may be conclusively established, that in the present case the word " define" was *not* used in the sense of " infallibly deciding."

---

* We argue in a later part of our article, that Paul V. had no *motive* for pronouncing ex cathedrâ : but this by no means applies to his successors.

† " Dr. Ward," he says (p. 12), " does not choose to see" what M. Bouix really maintains. What right has he thus to speak ? We nowhere professed agreement with M. Bouix on the thesis criticised by our opponent; and we are well aware that there are differences of some little moment between M. Bouix and ourselves. Undoubtedly, in pp. 118-19, we expressed agreement with M. Bouix on a *different* question.

No one alleges that any ecclesiastical authority can define infallibly, except the Pope or a Council confirmed by the Pope. Had the Holy Office therefore intended to say that heliocentricism had been *infallibly* declared contrary to Scripture, they would have taken care to say that it had been so defined by *Pontifical authority*. Moreover they were dwelling in their sentence on all the various reasons which aggravated Galileo's offence; yet not one hint do they give of a far more grievous offence than any which they do mention, viz., his rebellion against an infallible judgment. According to the Inquisitional Decree of 1633, it was by *the Congregation of the Index*, and *not* by the Pope, that heliocentricism had been declared in 1616 to be false and contrary to Scripture. * In speaking of a Definition put forth by *the Congregation of the Index*, the Holy Office could not possibly have intended to speak of an *infallible* definition.† We repeat then, that this objection of our opponent's is really converted into an argument for our own view.

There is another argument, here and there implied in the pamphlet before us, though nowhere distinctly stated. See, e. g., p. 25, note. Paul V. and Urban VIII. enjoined Galileo, so it is alleged, to make an act of *divine faith* in the geocentric doctrine; and thereby claimed infallibility for the Decree of 1616.

We reply in the first place, that even if they had enjoined this, such injunction would have involved no claim of infallibility; as is evident from a very obvious illustration. I have an intelligent son, who is in the habit of reading the Gospels, and making an act of divine faith (as he proceeds) in every fact therein declared. He comes to Matt. xxvii. 45; and being unacquainted with the Hebrew computation of time, he makes an act, phenomenally indistinguishable from one of divine faith,‡ in the supposed fact of darkness having covered the land from six till nine o'clock p.m. I explain to him what is

---

* The Latin runs thus : "Emanavit Decretum a Sacrâ Congregatione Indicis, quo fuerunt prohibiti libri qui tractant de hujusmodi doctrinâ ; et ea declarata fuit falsa et omnino contraria sacræ ac divinæ Scripturæ." We are not a little surprised by the author's remark (p. 42) on our translation of this. We maintain confidently that the " quo [decreto]" is governed, not merely by " fuerunt prohibiti," but no less by " declarata fuit."

† We have all along fully admitted that, not the Holy Office only, but the Pope considered a certain real interior assent as due to this Definition from contemporary Catholics. It is one of the principal points we are to treat in our next number.

‡ Such acts are recognized in all theological courses : as, e.g., when a rustic misunderstands what his parochus has placed before him as a dogma of the Faith.

universally admitted to be the passage's true meaning; and enjoin him to make a true act of faith in S. Matthew's inspired and infallible declaration. Certainly no one would dream of saying, that I hereby have claimed for myself infallibility in the interpretation of Scripture.

But this illustration far more than covers the case of Galileo. The authorities did not enjoin him to embrace the geocentric theory with divine faith; but only to reject the Copernican,* which is a very different thing. Let us suppose that his mind were in such a state as this. He considers that there are weighty scientific presumptions for Copernicanism, though of course very far from conclusive. On the other hand he sees that that theory contradicts the one obvious and the one traditional sense of certain Scriptural texts. In the interpretation of Scripture he absolutely distrusts his own judgment: on such matters he is desirous of regulating his assent by that authority which, even when not speaking infallibly, is his divinely-appointed guide,† and is immeasurably better instructed than himself in things theological. He holds with *divine faith* that these various declarations of Scripture are true, whatever be their real meaning; and (in deference to Pope and Congregations) he holds strongly the *opinion*, that Copernicanism is opposed to those declarations and is for that reason heretical. Let this have been Galileo's state of mind, and he could with perfect ease have given the Congregations every assurance which they desired at his hands.

Lastly, our opponent cites against us (p. 37) former statements of our own, on the characteristics of an ex cathedrâ Act. Such citations at the utmost could only be available *ad hominem*; but in fact not one of them in any way countenances the thesis, for which they are now adduced. We will take them one by one.

(1) " In a thousand different ways the Pope may sufficiently indicate his intention of teaching the Church ": i. e. of pronouncing as Universal Teacher. " But whenever and however he may do so, the Holy Ghost interposes to preserve his instructions from every the slightest intermixture of error." We have only to add that, in cases like the present, where he has unmistakably expressed his intention of *not* speaking as Universal Teacher, he enjoys *no* such immunity from error.

(2) "In the Christian Church there is no ' acceptation of

---

* " Ut omnino desisteres à dicta falsâ opinione," says the Holy Office in 1633 ; " Ut omnino desererem falsam opinionem," says Galileo in his Abjuration.

† Just as a father is his youthful son's " divinely-appointed guide."

persons '; no doctrinal favouritism : whatever doctrine is infallibly revealed *at all*, is infallibly revealed *for the whole Church*. The Apostle may have originally addressed it to a local church, or even to an individual; but he none the less delivered it in his capacity of Universal Teacher. Still, then, we have come to no point of difference between the Apostolic Rule of Faith as understood by all Christians, and the modern Roman Catholic Rule as understood by Roman Catholics ; except, indeed, that in the former there were twelve Universal Teachers, and in the latter there is no more than one." We have not a dream, what syllable of this passage is considered relevant to the Copernican question.

(3) " The question is not about addressing himself, but about commanding interior assent. But the Pope never exacts absolute and unreserved assent to any doctrine from individual Catholics, except where he exacts such assent from the whole body of Christians : otherwise he would himself destroy that unity of faith which it is his office to maintain." Well, but no one ever thought of exacting from Galileo " absolute and unreserved* assent " to the " doctrine " of geocentricism. On the other hand, neither Paul V. nor Urban VIII. made any distinction between Galileo and others : they accounted it the duty of *all* contemporary Catholics, and not merely of Galileo, to renounce all interior acceptance of Copernicanism after the Decree of 1616. Indeed only two pages before (p. 34, note) our author had himself pointed this out.

(4) " An ex cathedrâ Act is an Act in which some Pope purports to teach the whole Church obligatory doctrine " : *therefore*, so reasons our opponent, we are bound to regard the Decree of 1616 as an ex cathedrâ Act. He must have been labouring under some temporary obscuration of intellect, when he broached this extraordinary argument. Why in the Decree of 1616 *the Pope* did not " purport " to do anything at all ; and the *Congregation* only " purported " to forbid certain books on certain doctrinal grounds.

We have now answered all the arguments without exception, which our critic has adduced for his thesis, that the Decree of 1616 was a Pontifical ex cathedrâ Act. But at last the completest reply will perhaps be found, in a simple narration of the facts which attended that Decree. In our former article we endeavoured to make the best case we could for

---

* We have quite invariably on former occasions used the words " absolute and unreserved," to express the *irreformable* assent due to an *infallible* definition : in order to distinguish it from that less absolute assent due (as we have always maintained) to certain fallible ecclesiastical judgments.

Galileo's personal character; but our opponent (p. 35, note says that certain of his letters overthrow our attempts at apology. We have no wish to take the trouble of reading his letters ; and we will willingly, if our opponent desires it, concede that Galileo was as dastardly a liar and poltroon as he thinks. As to the Decree of 1616, the facts of the case, as we understand them, are such as these.

Copernicus never advocated heliocentricism except as an hypothesis ;* and for many years after his volume was published, the question excited little interest. But Galileo's scientific ability and energy gave the theory far greater vogue and currency; and a school was rapidly forming, which advocated heliocentricism, not as an useful hypothesis but as a truth. Probably enough, among the opponents of that school were several narrow-minded and prejudiced men ; for such men are commonly to be found on the right side as well as on the wrong in theological controversies. But all Catholics, in proportion as they were pious and enlightened, must have been shocked beyond measure at Galileo's course. Doubtless no irreverence is displayed towards Scripture in giving its words even a very unobvious sense, when such sense is affixed in deference to some definite objective tangible rule, the reasonableness of which is sufficiently established. Accordingly at this day, when Copernicanism is scientifically proved, Catholics interpret Holy Writ in accordance with its view. But what was the scientific aspect of Copernicanism, when Galileo advocated it as true ? The one argument in its favour on which he laid immeasurably his greatest stress—the argument from flux and reflux of tides—was generally opposed by scientific men of the greatest eminence, and is now universally admitted to have been absolutely worthless. Yet on the strength of his random scientific conjecture, he assailed the one obvious and the one traditional sense of God's Inspired Word. And after what fashion did he proceed with this task ? By declaring that " Scripture should not be appealed to in matters which do not concern the Faith "; that in physical discussions " Scripture holds the last place "; that " certain expressions of Scripture are inaccurate." †

It was not to be expected under any circumstances, that a Pontiff so zealous for the Faith as Paul V. should have permitted the continuance of such a scandal,in the Church. But in fact Galileo was delated to the Congregation of the Index by one of his opponents ; and that Congregation was accord-

---

* " Doctrinal Decisions," p. 153.
+ " Revue des Questions Historiques," livraison v. p. 89.

ingly obliged to pronounce on the whole matter. Our readers have seen its decision; and acting on that decision, the Holy Office (with the full sanction of Paul V.) commissioned Cardinal Bellarmine to take practical action. The Cardinal accordingly summoned Galileo; communicated to him the Decree of the Index, then immediately about to appear; enjoined him accordingly to abandon all interior acceptance of the heliocentric theory; and prohibited him from teaching it or treating it in any way thereafter even as an hypothesis. Galileo faithfully promised obedience to this command, and was forthwith dismissed. In fact, if we accept (as probably we should) our opponent's view of Galileo's real mind, the astronomer obtained his liberation, by giving to the Vicar of Christ a solemn promise, which at that very moment he intended to violate, thereafter to the end of his life, as often as he conveniently could.

Now looking at the matter from its divine side, of course all Catholics firmly hold that the Holy Ghost would never have permitted Paul V. to condemn Copernicanism ex cathedrâ. But what we wish our readers to observe is, that looking at the matter from its *human* side there was no *motive* for his doing so. When the existing ecclesiastical tribunals are insufficient for putting down some heresy or dangerous error, *then* arises the motive for an ex cathedrâ definition. But Galileo from the very first assured the authorities of his full interior submission to whatever *the established tribunals* might decree. Our opponent is convinced, and probably with justice, that this profession was a piece of sacrilegious mendacity : but how was *the Pope* to suspect Galileo of such baseness? How was he to dream that he was dealing with an offender, who was restrained by no sense of truth, of loyalty, or of honour? He was naturally persuaded that, by setting in motion the existing Congregations, he had done enough to save the Church from those evils which threatened her : he had no reason then for proceeding further, and dismissed the whole matter from his thoughts.

For ourselves we can thoroughly understand the view of those, who think that Paul V. and Urban VIII. had no right of claiming interior assent for a fallible Decree ; or again who consider great evils to have accrued from the fact, that a long series of Popes, in their governance of the Church, assumed the anti-Scripturalness of Copernicanism. We cannot *agree* with either of these views, and we shall argue against them in our next number; but we can quite *understand* them. What we are *unable* to understand is, how any man of ordinary education and ability—with the facts of the case before him—

can suppose that geocentricism was defined ex cathedrâ by Paul V. as a dogma of the Faith. This, and this alone, is the allegation against which we have contended in our present article. And if any one can still hold such a notion after the arguments we have already detailed, we have one final remark to make, which must convince, one would think, the most determined objector.

Suppose that in the year 1860 some one had been delated to the ecclesiastical tribunals, on suspicion of heresy : that heresy being a denial of the Immaculate Conception. It is most obvious, that the *heretical* character of this opinion would have been laid down as consisting in its opposition to the ex cathedrâ Act of 1854. It is indefinitely more certain that deniers of the Immaculate Conception contradict the Definition of 1854, than it is certain—apart from the evidence afforded by that Definition—that they contradict any truth contained in Scripture and Tradition. Now if the Decree of 1616 had been ex cathedrâ, the case of heliocentricism would have been precisely similar. It was indefinitely more certain that Copernicans contradicted the doctrine of that Decree, than it was certain— apart from any evidence afforded by an ex cathedrâ Act—that they contradicted any statement of Scripture. Now by the Inquisitional Decree of 1633 Galileo was condemned, precisely for having incurred suspicion of heresy : that heresy being the heliocentric doctrine. Nothing in the whole world can be more certain on one hand, than that if the Decree of 1616 had been accounted a definition of faith, the heresy of heliocentricism would have been laid down as consisting in its opposition to that Decree. And nothing in the whole world can be more certain on the other hand, than that the Holy Office in 1633 did not give the very faintest hint of the kind. The later Decree *recounts* indeed the earlier, as one among the various antecedents which bear on Galileo's conduct; but heliocentricism is described as a *heresy* on no other ground whatever, than that of its opposition to the plain words of *Scripture.* " You have rendered yourself to this Holy Office vehemently suspected of *heresy,* that is that you hold that doctrine which is false and *contrary to the sacred Scriptures.*"

Our opponent has spoken of us throughout in language of courtesy and kindliness; and we trust we have not erred against these virtues in the tone of our reply. If we are rightly informed as to his personality, he is one for whose self-denying zeal and disinterested labours we entertain profound respect. But he has spoken (as was quite legitimate) with considerable plainness and confidence, on what he considers the emptiness and confusedness of our reasoning ; and we have hinted in reply, that we think such emptiness and confusedness should rather be ascribed to *his.* It is only one part however of his pamphlet, which we criticise thus severely : we think he has written with great ability on the matters which we are to treat in our next number, though he has entirely failed to affect our convictions. .But as regards his allegation that the Decree of 1616 was a Pontifical ex cathedrâ Act, we must plainly express our amazement, that a writer of his calibre can have thought such a position to be even (what lawyers call) *arguable :* to have the faintest plausibility or colour of truth. The task of the Catholic controversialist would indeed be marvellously lightened, if no more substantial argument could be adduced against the infallibility of Papal ex cathedrâ definitions, than any derivable from the relations between Copernicanism and Pope Paul V.

We should have added in its proper place, that Polaccus, one of the two writers cited by our opponent who regarded Copernicanism as having been infallibly condemned, based his ' opinion, not on the Decree of 1616, but on the abjuration exacted from Galileo.

Art. VI.—THE SEE OF ROME IN THE MIDDLE AGES.

The See of Rome in the Middle Ages. By the Rev. Oswald J. Reichel, B.C.L. and M.A., Vicar of Sparsholt, Vice-Principal of Cuddesden College, and sometime Scholar of the Queen's College, Oxford. London : Longmans. 1870.

THE See of Rome has been before the eyes of men for more than eighteen hundred years, and yet there are people at this day who understand it as little as did Nero or Seneca when it was heard of for the first time. Some excuse might be made for pagans, but it is not so easy to explain modern ignorance or mistakes, after so much disputing, and the alleged possession of so much culture grafted on the gift of criticism fostered by science, which is so brilliant in itself. As the world would not know the Master, it cannot understand the servant, and the outraged Vicar is, to every generation in its turn, what He was Himself, one without a place where He could rest His Head. It is a fact, not to be laid aside, perhaps it should be called a portent, that educated men, men who certainly claim to have received the highest education possible, are profoundly ignorant of the nature of the Church. There is only one institution in the world, the claims of which on men's attention are stronger than all other claims whatever, and yet that very institution is the one of which men of leisure and of learning know absolutely nothing as it ought to be known. Then, again, on the other hand, there is hardly a man able to read or write who has not made up his mind, not only that the Church has no claims on him, but that the claims she makes on any body are simply absurd. Everybody can settle the Roman controversy, and everybody does settle it, in a way that only Satan himself can approve of, for he alone gains by it.

Here we have before us a history of the See of Rome in the Middle Ages, written apparently without the least intention of being unjust, and professedly in what is called an impartial spirit. More than that, the writer disclaims "the charge of being indifferent," and that is certainly in his favour, because it shows that he would prefer truth to falsehood, and is a sign that he means to be earnest and serious in his work. We have no reason to doubt Mr. Reichel's seriousness, and we are therefore driven to another way of accounting for the strange history of the See of Rome which he has given us.

The Sovereign Pontificate, according to Mr. Reichel—but he does not pretend to be the inventor of the theory—is an institution which has grown apparently out of nothing; it is no part of the Church, and may be "regarded as a result of natural growth, produced by natural causes" (Pref. viii.). In the opening of the book he writes thus :—

> Whatever variety of opinion may prevail as to the precise period at which the history of what are called the Middle Ages begins, it is at least clear that under the episcopate of Gregory the Great the power of the See of Rome in the West commences. (p. 1.)

He does not, of course, say that the great S. Gregory was the first Pope, but only that he was the first bishop of Rome who exercised his authority in the West, and so he thinks the Middle Ages commenced with S. Gregory, at the close of the sixth century, and ended with Leo X., who died on the first of December, 1521.

We have no objection to make to such an arrangement of time, so far as the Middle Ages are concerned; if it is convenient for Mr. Reichel, it is not inconvenient for us. But he goes on to say that the Church was changed during the Middle Ages :—

> During these centuries a new and hitherto unexplored field was opened out for the Church. Christianity changed its ground, and with that change

the character and constitutions [? constitution] of the Church changed as well. (p. 1.)

" Christianity changed its ground." That may mean that the Christian religion changed the objects it originally aimed at, or that it changed its method of aiming at them, or that it was itself substantially changed; probably the latter alternative was meant, because he says that the character of the Church changed as well. In short, mediæval Christianity was not primitive Christianity, and of course it is not the Teutonic Christianity, of which Mr. Reichel is one of the preachers, and of which we hear so much in the book before us.

According to our author the Teutons were unfairly dealt with by the missioners of Holy Church, and their simplicity shamelessly abused. The savage dwellers in the forests were not equally matched when they were met by S. Boniface and others; these latter were too cunning, and the "noble savage" was simply cheated. Well, he has had his revenge. This is Mr. Reichel's account:—

> The Germanic nations received Christianity and the Roman supremacy together, and have constantly confounded the two. Years elapsed before they became conscious of the confusion ; a still longer period before this consciousness found expression ; and nine centuries had gone by before they dared to rise in rebellion against a primary usurpation, and rid themselves of an error which they had imbibed from their first teachers. (p. 3.)

Something, surely, may be said for the Teutons who were thus deluded, and held in their delusion for nine hundred years. If they accepted "Christianity and the Roman supremacy together," it may be they had no choice; they were like other nations who believed the heavenly message. Mr. Reichel cannot surely find out that there were either missioners or books, which severed Christianity from the Roman supremacy, when the first Teuton bowed his head under the regenerating waters. If the ancient Teutons were less polished than the modern, they were certainly more learned, for they never conceived a religion which is not a law, nor a law without a judge to decide the questions that might arise. The old Teutons were a sober and an honest race, and they did not wander into the mazes of error till they listened to the ravings of a drunken friar, and saw the blessedness of taking property which was not their own.

The Teutons, nevertheless, continued in their delusion, according to Mr. Reichel, for nine centuries; it was a long time to find out one mistake. Nine hundred years of error before the Teuton shook himself free. We might suspect the

Teutonic intelligence; but he did so at last, and is now hopelessly wandering.

> The long-slumbering, long-suppressed self-consciousness of the Teutonic
> mind awoke. The sway of Latin Christianity in the West was at an end.
> A new spirit began to reform the Church. (p. 549.)

Mr. Reichel may rejoice over the fall of what he calls
"Latin Christianity," but is he quite sure that he has got anything in its place? The self-consciousness of the Teutonic
mind has done strange things, and we should be doing injustice
to Mr. Reichel, we are sure, if we did not take for granted that
these strange things are not altogether what he likes, though
he does think that they will be changed in the Church of
the future. The Church, in the conception of Mr. Reichel,
is not a supernatural institution, and that is one reason why he
speaks of it as he does. He never takes into account that the
Church is not a human system, which men may modify or
improve, and so he discovers the "germs of 'the Papacy'" in
the fifth century, "becoming permanent towards the beginning
of the seventh" (p. 13). So far is he from suspecting her
divine origin, that he quietly says in the same place, and in a
way as if it was an undoubted fact, that those "germs" which
he discovered "culminated in the twelfth century in an ecclesiastical monarchy, claiming to be the ecclesiastical counterpart
of the Roman Empire."

Certainly no man has yet shown that the Church ever made
any claim of the kind; but there are people who complain of
her for setting up the empire in the West. We presume that
Mr. Reichel does not mean to say that the Church claimed to
be the counterpart of the pagan empire. Now the Church,
certainly, has claimed to be nothing more than what our Lord
made her, and it will be a difficult feat, even for the self-conscious Teuton, to show that the Empire was the model of the
divine kingdom which our Redeemer established and maintains.

If men will shut their eyes to the succession of the Popes
from S. Peter, and ignore the authority and power given him,
and to his successors for ever, they must fall—for they cannot
help it—into most grievous errors. Thus Mr. Reichel, utterly
unconscious of the meaning of our Lord's words, and ignorant,
we must suppose, of the history of some five centuries during
which people lived as Christians, tells the world quite gravely
that the Pope, S. Gregory the Great, took advantage of his
position, and made himself a great ruler of men on the model
of the emperor. These are the words:—

> To a great extent Gregory's general policy in ecclesiastical matters was the

result of the view he entertained of his position, as within the Church corresponding to that of the emperor within the State : recognizing himself as
subject to the emperor no doubt in temporal concerns, but in ecclesiastical
matters as wholly independent. The Empire was the one great institution
raised above natural peculiarities by ignoring them, embracing all excluding
none. It was the one political power to which all others were, or were believed
to be, subject ; and since the extinction of the Western Empire by the barbarians, and the reconquest of Italy, it was reunited under one head in the
Eastern Emperor. Such an institution too was the Church, an outward
visible society, knowing no distinction of Jew or Greek, of barbarian or
Scythian. Ought not this society likewise to have one supreme head in the
person of S. Peter's successor. Such may have been the thought as it presented itself to the mind of Gregory. (p. 21.)

It is plain from this that, according to Mr. Reichel, the
Church was neither one body nor one government under one
head before S. Gregory the Great's time ; but what her state
was he does not tell us, it being easier to destroy than to build,
unless it be that he regarded her as a sort of federation of
independent princes. Something of that kind is clearly hinted
at, if not expressed, for we have from him the following portentous statement. That an " observant eye "

Might have observed how the centralizing influence of the feudal system was
simultaneously consolidating both Church and State : wresting the power out
of the hands of the people to place it in the hands of the emperor, out of the
hands of the clergy to place it in the hands of the Popes. The Church had
become an aristocratic, not a democratic, institution. She was soon to become
imperial. The local bishops of the three first centuries, with their parliaments
of presbyters, had disappeared ; metropolitan bishops with absolute powers
had succeeded them : they were about to be displaced by one more powerful
than they. (p. 183.)

Mr. Reichel has clearly not yet learned what is meant by the
" Church," and is as ignorant of her constitution and her history
as the most contemptuous pagan who sent her children to the
lions or the mines. According to him there was no such thing
as the Church in the world before the pontificate of S. Gregory
the Great, and then it was nothing else but a human institution
founded on fraud and maintained by oppression. The priests
had been robbed of their rights by the bishops, the bishops
in their turn by the metropolitans, and those with great justice
by the Pope, who was dethroned again in his turn " when the
Teutonic laity threw off their allegiance to the Pope for ever."
(p. 199).

The learned men who refuse to see what is visible on the surface before them, have never shown much skill in the invention
of theories to account for what they do not like. Mr. Reichel

has but taken the old account, turned upside down, for his predecessors generally say that the Church grew out of the desires
of priests to be ruled by bishops, out of the desires of bishops
to be ruled by metropolitans, and out of the desires of the latter
to be ruled by patriarchs, who had the same desire to find
themselves under a Pope. Mr. Reichel does not admit this
longing for unity, for his notion is that the stronger defeated
the weaker, and that by a "natural selection" the strongest of
all, the Bishop of Rome, made himself master of all.

A history of the See of Rome is therefore beyond the powers
of Mr. Reichel, because he does not know what the See of Rome
is. It is impossible he can understand its relations or its influences, because he does not know its origin or its power. To
him the Church is a human system like a republic or a constitutional monarchy, and the Divine authority of the Supreme
Pontiff is a secret he has never discovered. Thus in the very
beginning of his book he gives us a list of the "Bishops of
Rome," of whom the first, according to him, were "Peter and
Paul," not successively, but simultaneously, and as the Blessed
Apostles were martyred on the same day, it is an inevitable conclusion, from Mr. Reichel's history, that he does not believe
S. Peter ever was the sole Pope, or Bishop of Rome.

Of the same nature is the assertion that clergy and laity
were undistinguishable in primitive times.

> In all these regulations the Council [of Constance] did but go back to the
> example of the earliest ages, in which that sharp distinction between bishops
> and other clergy, between clergy and laity, which circumstances, the super-
> stition and the ignorance of the Middle Ages had drawn, was as yet
> unknown. (p. 479.)

The "Middle Ages" is a very convenient phrase, and is held
to account for many things of which the men and women who
lived in those ages were innocent. Certainly the distinction
between bishop and priest, between clergy and laity, was not an
invention of the Middle Ages, nor was that distinction made
more sharp in the Middle Ages than it was before those ages
began. Mr. Reichel can find no age or country in which
people did not know the difference between a layman and a
clerk in holy orders. Even the heretics testify against him and
refute an opinion which sounds strangely in the mouth of a man
who is a member of the national establishment. At the same
time we must not forget that the spirit now ruling in that
establishment has made a change. Anglican orders are now,
by Act of Parliament, deprived of their former characteristics,
for men who have had the misfortune to accept them may lay

them aside, when they are tired of them, and we believe may resume them again, without reordination or penance, whenever they wish to return to their former state. Mr. Reichel would probably be glad to think that in primitive times holy orders were thought as little of as his friends think of them now.

If the Papacy grew and became strong, so Mr. Reichel holds, the conclusion from such premises is that the Papacy became old and weak, for, according to him, the Papacy is but a human, and not a divine institution. He tells us with great confidence, that in the begining of the fourteenth century, "the glories of the Papacy were over" (p. 409). That is, the Sovereign Pontiffs were successful and prosperous men to the time when Boniface VIII. lost, as it is supposed, the supremacy which he and his predecessors wielded. Mr. Reichel is not the only one who thinks that the Sovereign Pontificate lost much of its power when Boniface VIII. was, in the eyes of the world, defeated by Philip le Bel. Men have very gravely theorized in that sense, and, by the profundity of their learning, have terrified many into the belief that the authority of the Holy See received a grievous blow when the Frenchmen of the fourteenth century showed themselves in the ranks as soldiers of Herod and struck the Vicar of God in the face.

Mr. Reichel seems to have no misgivings on this point for he thus writes :—

In this emergency, Clement V., unwilling to see his patron [Boniface VIII.] impeached, but unable to refuse the demands of the French king, resorted to an expedient which had been twice suggested in the time of Boniface, and which was then taken to be indicative of decay in the Papal power. (p. 415.)

It is here taken for granted that the men then living did actually think that the Papal power was wasting and had wasted away, and that the authority of the Pontiffs had suffered loss in the struggle between Boniface VIII. and the King of the Franks.

Such a notion as this proceeds from a confusion of mind. It may be said, fairly enough, that a king loses power when he loses territory or subjects, for the power of a king is, no doubt, external to himself. He may even lose rights, and thereby also become less powerful than he was before. But it is unreasonable to speak thus of the Popes. Their authority is not human, and does not depend on the number of their subjects. The power of the Pope is not lessened when he is imprisoned, not even if he have but one subject, or none, left to own his rule. His power and authority come directly from God, and are not dependent on the number of his subjects. The power of S. Peter was complete before he had converted a single person, and was never increased after conversions. He was not more powerful in Rome than he had been in Antioch, not more powerful there than he had been in Jerusalem. Boniface VIII. was for three days in prison, unable to communicate with the world without, except with the permission of the rude men who were sent by Philip le Bel to seize him, but he was still the Supreme Pontiff, and his power was not in the slightest degree impaired.

Rebellion against the Holy See is not as rebellion against a secular prince; the latter may be driven out of his dominions, and his subjects may set up another in his place, and then all his power is gone. It is otherwise with the Pope. No rebellion can succeed; his subjects can never depose him, and no rival can ever occupy his throne. Anti-popes have been set up from time to time, and whole nations have submitted to them, but there was no loss of power in the Pope consequent on the revolt, and on the recognition of the Anti-pope. The Anti-pope was the Anti-pope for ever, and never had any authority in the Catholic Church, never any jurisdiction over the souls of men.

But even admitting the interpretation which Mr. Reichel gives us of the great struggle in which he thinks Boniface VIII. was defeated and shorn of power, we can lay it aside as inapplicable to that struggle in any sense in which it is not applicable to all others. Alexander III. had to contend with the powers of this world, and with an Anti-pope at the same time, and was unable to save S. Thomas of Canterbury from the rage of Henry II. It might be said as truly of him, as of Boniface VIII. at a later age, that the power of the Pontiff decayed in his hands, but it is not true to say so of either. Innocent III. came after Alexander III., who had himself seen the Emperor of Germany at his feet, and Eugenius IV. came after Boniface VIII. The majesty and power of the Pontiffs never decay, because the jurisdiction they wield does not depend on men, but comes directly from God, and is to continue in its original strength to the end of time.

Mr. Reichel sets out on his journey upon an erroneous notion, and his misfortunes occasion no surprise. He does not see that the Church is a divine institution, and accordingly he speaks of her as he would of a secular principality, and apparently with less veneration than he speaks of the Teutons who have rebelled against the Divine lawgiver. He is, nevertheless, troubled by one thing; he cannot find out that the Popes ever acknowledged the fact which he has discovered. He says that the Sovereign Pontiffs, the immediate successors of Boniface VIII., who, unable to live in Rome, because of the wretchedness of their subjects, resided in Avignon, were dependent on the King of

France, who had, upon his theory, brought low the power of the Pope. He sees clearly this dependence, and builds a story on it, but for all that this is the confession he is forced to make :—

Nothing daunted by their own actual condition of dependence, the Popes at Avignon were not behind their predecessors in advancing their claims to power ; nor had their claims grown less as time advanced. They seem, in fact, to have increased in proportion as the real power of the Popes diminished. (p. 418.)

It might strike some people that there must be some mistake here; for on the whole the Popes are not regarded as men without common sense ; they are too often credited with a skill and cunning which are not thought desirable. Mr. Reichel admits that, notwithstanding the loss of power, they continued to claim what their predecessors possessed, and that the claims they made did not grow less with that loss. If he had not been under the dominion of a theory which is unconnected with facts, he might have suspected the true reason, namely, that the Popes, who must know better than Mr. Reichel, had not lost any power, and were therefore only ignorant of what had never taken place.

Now, we are not able to see in Mr. Reichel's book any attempt at proving the statement, that the Popes in Avignon were in a "condition of dependence." But as Mr. Reichel is not the first to say so, and probably not the last, we shall ourselves make another statement, which we believe to be better founded and more in accordance with theory and fact. We need not discuss the story of Villani that Philip le Bel made a pact with Bertrand de Got, and that Bertrand de Got became Pope Clement V. in consequence of that pact. Bertrand was, before his election, Archbishop of Bordeaux, and Bordeaux at that time was not subject to Philip, but to the King of England. Then, from the time of his election he never placed himself in the power of Philip; went to Lyons for his coronation, and at that day Lyons did not belong to the King of the Franks. In 1307 Philip petitioned the Pope then in Poitou, but the Pope with the cardinals refused to listen to him,* and in the following year when he prayed the Pope to absolve William de Nogaret, he refused, and spoke of such a prayer with disgust ; the wretched man being still impenitent. It may be admitted that Philip le Bel pressed heavily on Clement V., but there is no proof that the Pope was either afraid of him or dependent on him. He was a wise and prudent Pope, and also patient. He bore long

---

* Ptolem., Lucens, in vitâ Clement V.

with the king and the king's agents; but he suffered no loss of dignity, certainly none of power; and the attempt of Philip to brand the memory of Boniface VIII. tried the Pope to the utmost, but the attempt failed. The unflagging patience of the Pontiff baffled the wiles of some of the most cunning lawyers ever employed in a bad cause : in the end Philip withdrew, and paid a heavy sum into the Papal treasury, to indemnify the Pontiff for the costs and charges so wantonly thrown upon his court.

Mr. Reichel says that Clement V. "referred the inquiry into his predecessor's conduct from his own tribunal to that of a general council" (p. 426); but he does not say on whose authority he makes that assertion. We are obliged to call it in question, for it is not so accurate as it might be. Clement V. put an end to the "inquiry," and that with something more than the consent of Philip, in April, 1311, for the Bull which is the record of that fact, is dated April 27 of that year. The Council of Vienne under Clement V. had nothing to do with that inquiry, and could have nothing to do with it, for the first session thereof was held only in October of that year, nearly six months, certainly more than five months subsequent to the date of the Bull, which put an end to the impious prosecution of the Pope, then gone to his eternal rest.

It was only in the later years of Clement V. that the Papal residence became settled in Avignon, and he must be a bold man who maintains—but there are those who have done so—that Clement's successor, John XXII., was ever dependent on the King of France or any other king; certainly, in Avignon the Pope was out of the king's reach, for Avignon did not belong to France, and the city and country were afterwards purchased by Clement VI., so that there could be henceforth no pretext for saying that the Pope was subject to any secular prince, even when in exile from Rome. Avignon became the property of the Holy See before the middle of the fourteenth century, and continued to be so till Louis XV. disgracefully seized it; but whether France has gained by the robbery let others judge; certain it is that the robbery has brought no blessing with it, and that the sacrilege was followed by the revolution and the multiplied disasters that have ever since been the heritage of France. Avignon belongs by right to the Holy See to this day, for the robbery has never been condoned, the sacrilege has never been expiated, and the excommunication has never been removed.

Mr. Reichel weighs the Church in his own balance, and discusses her strength on principles which are not hers. I. the Church were a human system, or what is called "a school of thought," he might perhaps be in the right; but he is not in the right because the Church is altogether divine, governed by divine laws, the sanctions of which are divine also. If we catch occasionally a glimpse of those dread penalties which men earn by breaking her laws, we catch after all only a glimpse; sight does not come near to faith, and faith tells a story which men without it cannot hear with patience: but then it is none the less true, and the retribution none the less certain.

Mr. Reichel is good enough to trace for us the many steps by which the Supreme Pontificate tended to decay. When he comes down with his story to the middle of the fifteenth century, he there discovers another great failure, or rather a change; the progress of the great Teutons by this time being a visible and palpable fact. Thus he begins the sixteenth chapter of his book—

> The old mediæval Papacy, holding a position of acknowledged supremacy as the head of Western Christendom, to which homage was universally paid, was now fast passing away, and making room for the modern Papacy, an institution historically, indeed, connected with its predecessor, but yet of a very different character, being a headship of only one portion of Christendom, and depending for its authority on a voluntary recognition of its claims. (p. 514.)

If we were not accustomed to the confusion which reigns over " Teutonic" minds, we should have expressed our surprise at such writing as this, and we should have maintained it to have been the outpourings of a man whose education had been neglected, and whose instruction was incomplete, or one whose powers of reasoning were somehow or other feeble or enfeebled. The " mediæval" papacy differs from the "modern," according to Mr. Reichel, because its subjects are fewer, and because it depends "for its authority on a voluntary recognition of its claims." We believe that to be the meaning of the passage we have extracted; and it it be not, we retract what we have said, and shall be sorry also for what we are about to add.

Now it is as clear as the sun at noon on a summer's day that the Supreme Pontificate, being a divine institution, cannot be in the least degree affected as to its character by the fewness or the multitude of those who obey. S. Peter was as much Pope before the day of Pentecost as he was the day after. He had not more power in Rome than he had in Antioch. He had more subjects on the day of his crucifixion than he had on the day when he was made Pope, but he had no greater power, and that power never depended on its being recognised, whether that recognition be voluntary or not. The recognition had nothing in the world to do with it.

Mr. Reichel's notions of the Catholic Church being thus imperfect and obscure, we need not be surprised at the rest of his book. The Church grows, is strong, and then wastes away. Mr. Reichel certainly does regret the mediæval splendours, but he is satisfied with the "Teutonic ideas" as good for their day, and perhaps is, on the whole, proud of them. Yet the Teuton himself is not to live for ever. Mr. Reichel sees into the future, and before his opened eyes there arises a new something or other, in the presence of which the Catholic Church must give way, and that new something will do a feat that nobody yet ever did, it is a thing that "can look beyond its own narrow horizon" (p. 630), but he does not tell us how the power of vision is to be raised above itself and be itself at the same time. This new religion is to see round corners and beyond the limits of its vision, and then the Teutonic ideas will have done their work.

Mr. Reichel is a man of progress even in religion, and is by no means sure that he will not change every opinion he holds. He has traced the rise and growth and decay of the Papacy, the rise and growth of its antagonist, the "Teutonic ideas," and is now most prudently prepared for the decay of those ideas in their turn. To him there is nothing certain, and even God himself must change according to this modern notion, which men have invented in order to escape from the recognition of the truth.

Then, on the other hand, it is a marvel how an educated man, conversant with books, could write what Mr. Reichel has done. The fact is unquestionable, that ignorance and learning cannot be distinguished, one from the other, when the Catholic Church is talked about. Mr. Reichel is without a shadow of misgiving over his mind when he says that the Papacy has fallen, that the Church of Rome has become a national Church, taking "her place as one among many other churches, as co-ordinate, not as supreme" (p. 570). Again,

National churches were everywhere established; the Papacy itself was reduced to the rank of a national institution, and became henceforth ultramontane.] (p. 629.)

The clearness of vision and acuteness of understanding which makes Ultramontanism an effect of nationalizing the Papacy are, we believe, unsurpassed in all the range of modern learning.

Mr. Reichel deprives us of this last comfort of possessing a Papacy as a national institution; for having done his work as an historian, he sits down on the three-legged stool of Pythia, so that the sulphurous vapours shall fill his brain, and asks these two terrible questions, in the interests certainly of Paganism. "For what after all are national churches but things of the day, passing forms in the development of Christianity? What are their exclusive pretensions to infallibility but tinkling brass and a sounding cymbal?" (p. 631.)

With the awful threat involved in the form in which he puts his questions, Mr. Reichel dismisses the wearied reader in the mist, and leaves him without hope. If Christianity is to be developed out of its passing forms, a prudent sceptic might think it wise to wait till he knows what he may be required to believe or do. We are not told what and where those national churches are which put forth "exclusive pretensions to infallibility," and we know of none. Perhaps Mr. Reichel meant nothing more than a parting kick to the Papacy which he says is worn out. It is very likely nothing more than what we call "claptrap;" for Mr. Reichel is mortal, and, like public speakers, falls into the snare spread before all who are for the moment more anxious to please than to tell the whole truth, even if they knew it.

We must now look at the other side of Mr. Reichel's work: a man who sits in judgment and who delivers his decision with so much confidence, may expect, not unreasonably, to meet with persons who dispute his competency. Certainly we have been surprised at the confidence of the writer, and, at the same time, at his mistakes. But the explanation is to be found no doubt in the preface (p. ix).

> It would not have been difficult to advance pretensions to learning by giving references, quoted at second hand, to works which few are likely to consult. The writer has in this case preferred to follow another course, and has made a point of giving (as far as possible) references to well known books, so that they may be easily verified. The works which are most constantly appealed to as authorities are the following.

Before we furnish the previous catalogue of his authorities, we must call the reader's attention to something else. If Mr. Reichel had given us "references," surely they need not have been "at second-hand." A man who discoursed as he did, before a learned audience, on the history of the Church, is generally supposed to have read something more than modern compilations. Mr. Reichel seems to think otherwise, and one interpretation of his words is—we do not say it is the correct one—that he could have given references to authorities copied from the modern books he followed, but did not. Anyhow the passage in the preface is obscure, and makes us suspicious, and there is reason to fear that Mr. Reichel trusted implicitly to his authorities. The authorities were the councils: that is as it should be; but a collection of councils, to be understood, needs much reading of contemporary documents. After the councils come Neander, Gieseler, Milman and Hallam, that is all. It is a puzzle to us how any man who knows anything of history could for a moment produce Neander and Milman as trustworthy authorities. It is done no doubt by too many, for there are men who think that Milman and Hallam may be safely trusted in matters of the Christian religion. But then we do not expect this in a man like Mr. Reichel, who has passed through modern Oxford, where men learn history, and wher3 there are grave critics who can resolve the Pentateuch itself into its constituent elements, and assign every verse therein to its proper author. How came such an one to put his faith in Neander and Milman? How came he to think that men will accept Hallam without suspicion? He may speak of the decay of the Papacy, but no decay has yet brought it to accept "authorities" of this kind.

Mr. Reichel, either trusting to those " authorities " or carri3d away by his own learning, has made mistakes which we really think are not very much to his credit. Thus he writes :—

To make sure of the allegiance of all the officers in the ecclesiastical army the Popes had, as early as 1080 A.D., begun to confirm episcopal elections. (p. 298.)

Here Mr. Reichel refers us to a Council held in Rome in the year he mentions, but the Council says nothing of the kind ; nor, indeed, did it make any change whatever in the law and practice of the Church. The Pope confirmed the patriarchs, and in the West, the metropolitans, and had always done so, and the Council to which Mr. Reichel refers us expressly maintains the rights which the Holy See had conferred on the archbishops, and respects them as much as the rights of the Pope.* He continues as follows :—

From confirming an election it was an easy transition to nominating a bishop ; and in the year 1093, for the first time, there occurs a case of nomination : the Bishop of Amatus in his will, styling himself bishop by "the grace of God and the favour of the Apostolic See." (*Ibid.*)

We need not travel out of England for the refutation of this statement so confidently made. The hierarchy of England was

---

* Can. VI. Electionis vero potestas omnis in deliberatione sedis Apostolicæ sive metropolitani sui consistat.

created by S. Gregory the Great, and S. Augustin was appointed the first bishop therein by the Pope. If Mr. Reichel objects, and says that this is no answer, because S. Augustin was sent to convert the country, and that before that day there could be no settled rule, we refer him to the nomination of the seventh in succession from S. Augustin—to Theodore of Tarsus, whom Pope Vitalian nominated and consecrated Archbishop of Canterbury in 668. Does Mr. Reichel doubt that Theodore has a right to the place he holds in the line of the Archbishops of Canterbury?

The " Bishop of Amatus," though repeated in the Index, is no doubt, a mistake, so we shall not insist on it, though we do not know how it was made. Mr. Reichel meant to refer to Amatus, bishop of Nusco, in the province of Salerno, and we are afraid that in this instance he has " quoted at second hand." The bishop's formula is *Apostolicæ sedis gratia*, neither more nor less ; " by the grace of the Apostolic See."

The Council of Pisa, as it is called, set up an Anti-pope in the year 1409, known as Alexander V., who, thinking himself Pope, issued a Bull in favour of the Mendicants, against which Gerson preached an elaborate sermon, though he was in the schism of the Anti-pope. The contents of that Bull are of no value, but still Mr. Reichel might have been, at least, accurate in his account of them. This is the way he speaks ; and it is not to be forgotten that he thinks the Bull was authoritative, and Alexander V. a true Pope.

> The language of the Bull was subversive of the higher claims of the Popes, since it rescinded and nullified seven propositions advanced by the preceding Popes. Of one proposition it even averred that it was propounded by John XXI. when under condemnation for heresy. (p. 472.)

If all this were true it would be of no moment, for Alexander V. was not the Pope, but it is completely inexact. Alexander V. maintained the doctrine of preceding Popes, and condemned what they had comdemned, notwithstanding his sad position. It is a hallucination of Mr. Reichel, and the statement that John XXI. " propounded" anything " when under condemnation for heresy," is due to an erratic imagination, and to a too rapid reading of documents by persons not familiar with them. In the document, called by excessive courtesy a Bull of Alexander V., are recited certain propositions which are condemned. One of them is—

> The constitution of John XXII. *Vas electionis,* is null and void, because he was a heretic when he made it, &c.

It is a proposition condemned by Alexander V., and he is so far from " averring " it, that he pronounces it false and erroneous, rejects and condemns it, and even adds that anybody who should maintain certain propositions, of which this is one, is to be regarded as a heretic. Mr. Reichel might almost as well argue that the Syllabus of Condemned Propositions attached to the Encyclical of 1864 contains a correct exposition of modern Roman doctrine.

Perhaps Mr. Reichel is not altogether responsible for this. He has probably been led into the ditch by trusting his guide, for the authority cited in a note is Milman. And we have no reason to doubt the correctness of that note. It would have been better if he had read the Bull itself.

But there is no excuse for Mr. Reichel when he blunders about a fact in English history,—and that a fact in the story of the conflicts between S. Thomas of Canterbury and Henry II.

> The struggle took place more particularly on a question of criminal jurisdiction. The punishment which the ecclesiastical courts had imposed on Philip de Brois, canon of Bedford, when convicted of manslaughter, seemed altogether inadequate to the greatness of his offence. (p. 370.)

A man who writes a history of the See of Rome ought to be at least careful of his facts, and Mr. Reichel was bound to be cautious, because he wrote in an unfriendly spirit. Now, Philip de Brois is indifferent at this moment to Mr. Reichel's censure, but Philip de Brois was an ecclesiastic and a canon, who claimed immunities, and in whose immunities the honour of the Holy See is concerned.

Philip de Brois was a canon of Lincoln, but he happened at one time of his life to be living in Bedford. It is true that he was accused of manslaughter, perhaps of murder,. and also true that he was tried. He was tried in the bishop's court, as the law and custom required; but the prosecution failed to prove its case, and Philip asserted his innocence on oath to the satisfaction not only of the judge, but of the relatives of the dead man, who themselves proclaimed him guiltless, *liber a parentibus clamatus est.* He never was convicted of manslaughter, nor is it suggested that he was guilty, and Mr. Reichel does not tell us on what authority he made so grievous a charge against a man of whom nothing worse is known than that he lost his temper—what any canon might have done—when the king's justice, who had no jurisdiction whatever in the matter, made an attempt to try him again after his acquittal, and that in the civil court, to further the political ends of Henry II., who then

2 c 2

was planning how to reduce the clergy into subjection to himself.

There are many things in the book before us which ought not to be passed over without observation, but as they would almost always lead to long discussions and tedious examinations we shall be content with pointing out instances, from which the rest may be inferred. Mr. Reichel, as a Protestant, cannot understand one-half of what he has been writing about, and his explanations of most of the facts being the notions of the Teutonic mind, must be necessarily incomplete. Thus, in writing of S. Gregory VII., he says of him—

> He ventured to do what he dared not attempt towards the haughty William the Conqueror, guilty of the same offence. (p. 205.)

And in the Index the Pope is described as " cringing to William the Conqueror."

What the " offence " was we cannot quite see. In some passages it seems to be simony, in others, the lay investiture. We do not deny that the Conqueror was guilty of the latter, but we do deny that he was guilty of simony. It was the absence of simony, then so prevalent, that moved S. Gregory to be so gentle with the king. The Pope in one of his letters, lib. ix. ep. 5, regrets that the Conqueror was not such as the Pope wished him to be; but he confesses that he was distinguished among kings for his justice, and that he kept his hands pure, and neither sold churches nor wasted their goods. It seems to us very hard to charge the Pontiff with "cringing," or even to say that he was more afraid of William the Conqueror than he was of the Emperor of Germany, who certainly was the stronger of the two.

The other instance is this—

> A proof of his avarice was given in his shortening the time yet to intervene before the year of jubilee after the lapse of thirty-three years ; a jubilee however, the benefits of which it fell to the lot of his successor to reap. (p. 443.)

This charge is brought against Urban VI., and is one of those about which men may dispute for ever: because we cannot know the secret thoughts which moved the Pope to do in his turn what Clement VI. had done before him. Boniface VIII. instituted or restored the jubilee, and ordained it to be kept once in a hundred years. Clement VI., in consideration of the shortness of human life, reduced the interval to fifty years, and then Urban VI. reduced it to thirty-three years. But he says that his reason was his desire to honour the three-

and-thirty years which our Lord lived on the earth. Mr. Reichel probably thinks the Pope told a deliberate untruth, and that so far from wishing to honour our Lord's life in the flesh, he had no thoughts of that, but of making money by the concourse of pilgrims. We ought to add that the authority for the statement, which nothing can justify, is Neander. If people will write books about the Popes, it would certainly be for the interests of truth if they were thoroughly Protestant, and accepted no authorities whatever. They might then think, occasionally at least, that they cannot be quite sure about the interior dispositions of men they have never seen, and about whom their knowledge must be necessarily scanty. Even their very guesses must be useless, for they can know nothing of the mind of Catholics, still less of the Pope's. They are moreover disqualified by their hatred of the Pontiffs, for hatred brings darkness over the understanding, and throws the inner consciousness, even of a Teuton, into confusion. Facts may be accumulated, and references may be exact, but if the living spirit be wanting the story will be dull. It will be but a book of dry bones, and the sole benefit derivable from it is the amusement of the reader as he goes on from one blunder to another.

Art. VII.—THE BREHON LAW OF IRELAND.

Ancient Laws of Ireland. Senchus Mor. Parts I. and II. Published under the direction of the Commissioners for publishing the Ancient Laws and Institutes of Ireland. Dublin : A. Thom. London: Longmans.

THE year of grace 1602 was in Ireland remarkable for two critical events,—the surrender of Kinsale, and the fall of the Castle of Dunboy. The last was fatal to the hopes of any further aid from Spain for the native Irish, and from the first may be dated the commencement of that great change in their habits and social government consequent on the abolition of the power of their chieftains. It is true that it was not until some years afterwards that the flight of the northern Earls from the shores of Lough Swilly and the death of Sir Cahir O'Doherty, the young chieftain of Innisowen, sealed its final extinction. Nor was it until 1612, the ninth year of the reign of James I., that the custom of tanistry and division of land by gavelkind were declared illegal, and the common law of

England became throughout Ireland the jurisprudence of the country. In that year the judges first proceeded on circuit, and held assize in districts where for ages before the Brehon law had alone been promulgated.

Long before this date, indeed so far back as the year 1593, an Act had been passed in the reign of Elizabeth, after the murder of Shane Dymas O'Neill by the Clannaboy Scots, declaring it to be high treason to assume the dreaded title of the O'Neill, and abolishing the old system of chieftaincy or captainship among the Irishrie. Yet outside the Pale this legal prohibition was laughed to scorn, and even by the English Government was practically set aside on their acknowledging Tirlogh Lynogh as the O'Neill, in succession to the turbulent Shane. But with the surrender of Kinsale and the destruction of Dunboy, the axe was laid to the root of the clanship of the Irish, and soon afterwards this great primeval oak of the Celtic forest fell with all its spreading branches a mighty ruin to the earth.

Dating from a period covered with the mists of traditional antiquity, and stretching far beyond the horizon of established history, when their Scythic ancestors crossed in tribes the plains or poured through the passes of Northern Germany, this system of government had certainly existed in Ireland for upwards of 1,600 years. Guided by laws simple in principle but complex in detail, patriarchal in authority yet absolute in practice, mild in regulation yet sternly opposed to progress and antagonistic to individual liberty, the system had a wonderful vitality on Irish soil. Within six centuries England had thrice changed her language and her laws and twice her religion. But no corresponding changes in that period had occurred in Ireland. There the people spoke in the same tongue and worshipped at the same altars that their forefathers had spoken in and knelt at for ages back. Outside the Pale the Brehon in Ireland was as implicitly obeyed in the fifteenth as he had been in the fifth century. The war-cry of the Celt against the pikemen and musqueteers of Elizabeth's troops was the same with which his ancestors had met the lances of the knights of the second Henry. The practice of tanistry, or the election of a successor to a chieftain during his lifetime, might be traced to that distant period when the nomadic Celts fought their way through a hostile country, with their leaders battling in the front ranks, exposed to sudden death at any moment by an arrow-head or chance thrust of a spear, thus leaving the tribe in a position of confusion and peril. But the practice remained for long centuries after those tribes had found a settled abiding place and had become a consolidated nation.

Co-existing with it was their wonderful Brehon law. From the prominent position the Brehon occupies in the foreground of Irish history, without a practical knowledge of the laws of which he was the exponent, those readers of the annals of Ireland who learn them through the medium of the English language (and after all in the present day they are the most influential and numerous class) would still be unable to form a correct idea of the social and political status of the native Irish. The publication of the *Senchus Mor* has met this requirement, and throwing a clear light on the pages of the Brehon laws, hitherto those of a sealed book, makes them accessible and legible to every English inquirer and scholar.

That those laws were constructed with the utmost care, and adapted to the needs of a civilized people apparently satisfied with the conditions of their social state, no one can, we think, deny. Of course a primitive and insular people who lived 1,400 years ago, in a densely-wooded country, a people whose wealth was herds, whose trade was barter, and whose currency was cows, could have but little in common with other nations; and while it is true that there is sufficient proof to show that, from the days of Himilco the Carthaginian to those of Tacitus, the Irish ports were well known to the merchants trading from the Spanish shore of the Mediterranean and from the coasts of Africa; that from the sixth century the fame of the Irish schools stood high in Europe; and that from the earliest Christian era in the west, the Irish missionaries spread far and wide, teaching the truths of the Gospel—yet it is equally true that those circumstances had no disturbing influence on the internal condition of the country. Dense forests, broad rivers, and long tracts of moor and bog prevented frequent communication with the interior of the island; and on a soil which the foot of a Roman soldier had never trod we must look in vain for any trace of the civilization of the mistress of the world.

If, however, we have to regret the absence of classic rampart and fallen temple in the country to assist us in our historical inquiries, we at the same time must congratulate ourselves that our annals are unsullied by the fables and traditions of ancient Rome. No fictitious accounts of the destruction of Troy and flight to Ireland of any of the Homeric heroes sully the genealogies of the Gael. While our seannachies and bards delight to trace our origin back to the dispersion of nations on the plains of Shinar and the followers of the great Shepherd Kings, they altogether ignore any attempt to claim a common descent with the helmeted warriors of the Tiber. If our traditions are rude they are original, if romantic they are still our own, and free from the taint of a classic literature, unlike, in this respect, the ancient Britons, who by the lengthened occupation of their country for four hundred years by the Romans, became so lost to self-respect as to delight, in the words of the learned Lappenberg, in wearing " the faded tinsel of their conquerors." No travesty like the landing of Brute, the great grandson of Æneas, on the shores of Britain is to be found in our ancient chronicles. From any attempt to assimilate their early traditions with the fables of Italian.poets the ancient Irish are free. In fact, their national proclivities were not towards Pagan Rome, but towards her rival, Carthage. The visits of the Phœnician traders to the Irish ports, and the conquest of the seaboard by a horde of African pirates (*Formories*), were favourite themes with their bards. To this intercourse with the great Sea Queen has been attributed, and justly, we think, the introduction of the worship of Baal among the Pagan Irish, and while by some antiquarians a Phœnician origin has been given to the *Bearla Fine*, or ancient dialect of the country, others have collated in a remarkable manner the Punic of Plautus with the vernacular of the Gael. But as all traces of the Carthaginian language have been lost, and all records of her literature and laws destroyed by the barbarous policy of her triumphant rival, we must look in vain towards a city whose past history is a blank and over whose foundations the sands are heaped, for any assistance in the matter. Any advance, therefore, the ancient Irish had made in the social conditions of life, in intellectual improvement and administrative government, must be measured by a standard of their own, and that standard is now happily supplied by the publication of their Brehon laws.

Long before the fifth century, when Christianity was first preached in Ireland, the Brehon law purports to have been in force. Previous to that date those laws partook of the compensatory character of the Jewish code, "an eye for an eye, a tooth for a tooth" being the principle on which they were founded; but with the spread of the great truths of Christianity in the land, and the preaching of its divine precepts inculcating mercy and forgiveness of injuries, a modification of the ancient laws became a necessity. Well and wisely, and with a thorough perception of the Irish character, was this change effected. Nine of the chief men of the land, three of them being bishops, including the great apostle of the Irish, three more being kings, including Laery, the *Ard Righ* or Sovran himself, and the three remaining Brehons, one of whom was especially skilled in the *Bearla Fine* or ancient dialect of the country, were appointed to consult and legislate on the matter. The labours of these eminent men extended to a period of nine years. Before them all the previous Brehon laws and decisions were unrolled and discussed. Rejecting those they considered obsolete, pertaining to Pagan rites, or unsuited to the altered conditions of the people, the remainder were embodied in the *Cain Patriac,* and were finally embodied by those three spiritual, three temporal, and three judicial authorities into the *Senchus Mor,* or Great Book of Irish Law, which bishop, king, or Brehon never attempted afterwards to alter. For it is a remarkable fact that, no matter what battles were fought, no matter what kings were deposed or elected, the Brehon laws, like those of the Medes and Persians, remained unaltered, and thus, after a lapse of one thousand years, were in Ireland in their integrity the same in the fifteenth as they had been in the fifth century.

This rough outline will explain the great assistance that the publishing the two volumes of the *Senchus Mor,* or Code of Brehon laws, gives to the inquirer who wishes to arrive at a fair estimate of the condition of the Irish Gael. With this antique guide in our hands we cross the borders of the English Pale, with its belt of watch-towers garrisoned by warders who day and night scrutinize the woods spread before them ready to flash a warning of the approach of the Irish enemy. Into those woods we enter, as it were, and pass from them into the clearings where the dwellings of the chiefs are placed. And as we journey along, in place of the savage neglect we expected to find, we observe a certain order and regularity. The roads and pathways are kept clean and free from brambles and brushwood, the streams are spanned with rustic bridges, and here and there the sound of a mill is heard. The land, too, is tilled, and where the countless cattle are browsing we hear the sound of bells tinkling from the necks of the foremost leaders of the herds, and observe that the grass-fields are irrigated. We pass by an enclosed space or pound, where trespassing cattle are imprisoned, and onwards through an orchard resonant with the humming of bee-hives, and stand before the circular rath or dwelling-place of the chieftain and his tribe.

Now this is no ideal sketch. There is not a single feature of the landscape we have thus brought before us for which law and authority cannot be quoted from the *Senchus Mor :* the roads freed from brambles, the watercourses, the mill, its wheels, hopper, and grinding-stones, the rustic bridge, the tilled lands, the irrigated grass-fields, the enclosed pound, the tinkling cattle-bells, and the orchard and its bee-hives are all mentioned in its pages. Not only so, but distinct provisions are laid down for their protection and recovery of their estimated value.

Nor is it alone of the external characteristics of ancient

Irish life that we acquire a knowledge in this wonderful book. With it in our hands we enter the habitation of the chieftain, we sit beneath his roof-tree and listen to the laws of his household, the items of its expenditure, its domestic economy, and the sources from which it derives its supplies. The disputes of the tribe, the distribution of its lands, and the distinction of rank and grades of position among the chieftain's followers are brought before us. Nor is this information limited to an individual household. On the contrary, the pages of the *Senchus Mor* contain the laws of the entire kingdom. To its enactments every one, from the Ard Righ on his throne to the woodkerne in the forest, from the mitred bishop to the solitary hermit, must submit. The *Senchus Mor* is the common law of the land, and all therein, cleric as well as laic, are bound to obey it.

The variety of the cases on which there are (in legal parlance) rulings in the *Senchus Mor* is marvellous. We think this may be accounted for by an inquiry into the executive system of the Brehon law; and in order to make this inquiry we must first glance at the administrative government of the ancient Irish. From the fifth century, when the *Senchus Mor* was compiled, and how many centuries before that epoch, to the usurpation of that master-spirit Brian Boromhe in the tenth, Ireland was governed at least nominally by a Pentarchy. This Pentarchy consisted of four provincial and one sovran king, the latter, or Ard Righ, in reality, having less power and a smaller territory than his subordinates. His kingdom was little more than a royal demesne. It was situated exactly in the centre of Ireland, and was composed of the present counties of Meath, Westmeath, parts of Dublin and Kildare, and King's County, and a portion of Louth and Cavan. In it, however, stood the royal palace of Tara, the hill of Uisniach, to which a peculiar veneration attached, from its being the termination of the four provinces, and the plain of Teltain, " of the royal games," on which the great annual fair of the kingdom was held. In the territory of the Ard Righ, also, the triennial gathering, or Feis, of the kings, bishops, Brehons and bards, took place. But those advantages were more imposing than solid, and, in reality, the power of the Ard Righ, like his territory, was circumscribed within narrow limits, and jealously watched by the surrounding kings, who nominally acknowledged him as their supreme head.

This Ard Righ, or sovran king, had attached to his court a council of chief Brehons, or judges, assisted by Poets, or Files (*Fileadhs*), and Ollaves, or lawyers (*Ollamhs*), of the highest rank, who settled all matters within the central province, and decided on the mutual obligations of the four provincial kings to each other, and also their obligations to the Ard Righ. Not the least singular circumstance connected with the Brehon system, is the intimate connection of Files, or poets, with its execution. Apparently the Bards performed the same office of reference on legal points and quotation of precedents to the Brehons that the well-selected law library does for the judges of our present day. Passing beyond the boundary of the Ard Righ's demesne, we find that every provincial king had also his circle of Brehons and assistants, but of lower rank than those of Ard Righ, to decide on all matters connected with the internal administration of their respective territories; and, finally, every chief in the kingdom had one or more Brehons, or lawyers, attached to his household, to decide on the lawsuits and quarrels of his tribe. It will be thus seen that the executive Brehon system was composed of concentric circles, of which the Brehons, Files, and Ollamhs of the Ard Righ formed the head-centre, and that a complicated network of law was spread over the entire Pentarchy. In addition to this we find that the judgments of the Brehons were generally given in the open air, and on elevated mounds or heights.

Bearing in mind that all the Brehons, from the highest at Tara to the simple adviser of a chieftain on the hill-side, devoted their whole lives to the study of the law, and that they were now summoned from all parts of the island to submit the decisions given by them and their predecessors for a lengthened period in their respective localities to the committee of nine, composed, as we have observed, of eight natives and one stranger, it will be at once seen that an infinite number o judgments, on almost every conceivable subject and question of political and domestic economy in Ireland, would be brought to light; and that consequently—when by the patient labours of this committee for nine years all those judgments, after having been sifted, canvassed, and approved, were finally enrolled in one great code of Celtic law—every part of the Pentarchy, from Arran to Carnsore, from Rathlin to Tralee, would have its interests represented, requirements recognized, and its individual contingencies legislated on.

The great book of Irish law opens with the following simple preface :—:

In the *Senchus Mor* were established laws for king and vassal, queen and subject, chief and dependent, wealthy and poor, prosperous and unprosperous.

In it were established the *Dire fine* of each one according to his dignity; for the world was at an equality until the *Senchus Mor* was established.

In the *Senchus Mor* was established equal *Dire fine* for a king and a bishop, and the head of the written law and the chief poet, who composed extemporaneously and for the Brewey, who is paid *Dire fine* for his hundreds, and who has the ever full Caldron and his lawful wealth.

In the *Senchus Mor* it was provided that good should not be assigned to bad, nor bad to good.

In the *Senchus Mor* were promulgated four laws. The law of fosterage, the law relating to free tenants, and the law relating to tax tenants, the law of social relationship : *also the binding of all by verbal contract, for the world would be in a state of confusion if verbal contracts were not binding.*

But equally as the *Senchus Mor* could enunciate great principles of national ethics such as the foregoing, it could descend to notice the most minute circumstances of domestic Irish life. Out of many instances we shall quote one. Apparently 1,400 years ago children played and gambolled pretty much as they do at the present day, and as we trust they always will do. They had toys in those days, moreover; and it is amusing to find what little change there is in their description from those used by the rising generation. Over those toys the *Senchus Mor* actually gravely throws the protection of its laws, and imposes a *Dire fine* on their value, and grave commentators in the following glosses explain it thus :—" For the toys of children, i.e. they must be restored in one day, i.e., those goodly things which remove dulness from little boys, viz., hurlets, balls, and hoops, except little dogs and cats, for it is in three days the cats are to be restored." Evidently the Celts loved cats. The patriarchal simplicity of a primitive state of society is plainly visible in many similar enactments.

The glosses, or interlined remarks, of numerous commentators at different periods are exceedingly curious, and were of incalculable value in the translation of the original text. In fact, they are to the *Senchus Mor* what the Rosetta stone has been to the study of the Egyptian hieroglyphics. Some of them are lucid, and all interesting. But others are so elaborate in their minute explanations as to be utterly perplexing, and, like the chorus of a Greek tragedy, make the subject much more puzzling than it was before. We feel as it were dazzled with the excess of light thrown on the grand obscure text of the *Senchus Mor*, and so bewildered by the earnest instructions of half a dozen grave ollaves, that we are unable to understand them or it. Still in every way they deserve a careful study.

The minute classification of the enactments of the *Senchus Mor* may, we think, be accounted for by the same reason that exists for the almost infinite variety of subjects of which it takes cognizance, noticing, as it does, every possible transaction of ancient Irish life, from the *Eric* of a king to the diet of an insolvent debtor, which it sternly limits to half a cake and as much milk " *as will fill twelve hen egg-shells* " per diem. From the salvage of a whale cast on the sea-shore (whose bones, we are informed by the commentators, are required for the bottoms of corn sieves and the backs of saddles), to the honour price of the chieftain's chess-board, or that of the griddle on which the bread of his household is baked, there is mention in the pages of this great book of Irish law, and ample directions given for the recovery of the assigned value of each article. It will be thus seen that the executive Brehon system of the Irish was essentially and practically different from that of their English neighbours, although some slight similarity may be traced between their triennial Feis, or national assembly, and the Wittenagemot of the Anglo-Saxon, and the Parliaments of the Norman race. It is only in the early history of the Jews that we find a close parallel for the Brehon system.

The fact of every tribe having its own judge or lawyer has somewhat a resemblance to the distribution of the Levites among the tents of the children of Israel. So long, therefore, as every rath in the Pentarchy had its own especial Brehon, before whom all the disputes of the clan were brought, and whose decision thereon was final, an infinite number of cases and judgments, varying according to the localities where the raths were situated, would be sure to occur. Thus, while a chieftain who dwelt by the sea-side would have the law relating to everything connected with nets, boats, and wrecks, and other marine matters plainly laid down, the Brehon of another chieftain who dwelt inland among rich pastures, would have constantly to decide on disputes concerning cattle and herds and the irrigation of grass-fields. The specialty of a third would be tillage, the repairs of fences, the sowing of seeds, the reaping and stacking of grain, its grinding into flour at the chieftain's mill, and the rights of watercourses and other similar matters. A fourth would be well up in the growth of flax and its weaving into cloth; a fifth in the law-suits of a game-abounding country; a sixth in the questions and rights connected with the digging of metals and protection of miners' tools and property, and so on, until there would be thus enrolled in the *Senchus Mor* a Brehon decision on almost every question which could possibly arise in any part of the five provinces.

It remains for us to examine briefly the proceedings detailed in this great book of Irish law, to inquire into the authenticity of the documents from which it has been condensed into its present shape, and finally to endeavour to trace its influence, whether for good or for evil, on the peculiar people for whom its enactments were made.

For the first, we cannot do better than extract the following

summary from Dr. Neilson Hancock's lucid preface to the first
volume of the *Senchus Mor* : —

The subject-matter of the portions of the *Senchus Mor* in the present volume is the law of distress.   So far as it is contained in the
Harleian manuscript, it appears to have been the universal remedy by
which rights were vindicated and wrongs redressed.   The following
account will give an idea of the general steps of the process, and will help
towards the understanding of the several rules of law as given in detail in
the book itself.

The plaintiff or creditor having first given the proper notice, proceeded, in the case of a defendant or a debtor *not of chieftain grade*, to dis-
train.   If the plaintiff did not within a certain time receive satisfaction
for his claim, or a pledge therefor, he forthwith (accompanied by a law
agent, witness, and others) seized his distress.   The distress, when seized,
was in certain cases liable to a stay (*anadh*), which was a period, varying
according to fixed rules, during which the debtor received back the distress, and retained it in his possession, the creditor having still a lien upon
it.   Such a distress is (*athgabhail ar fut*) a distress with time ; but under
certain circumstances, and in particular cases, an immediate distress (*tul
athgabhail*) was made, the peculiarity of which was that, during the fixed
period of the stay, the distress was not allowed to remain in the debtor's
possession, but in that of the creditor, or in one of the recognized greens
or pounds.

If the debt was not paid at the end of the stay, the creditor took away
the distress, and put it in a pound.   He then served notice of the distress
on the debtor whom he had distrained, letting him know where what was
distrained was impounded.

The distress remained in the pound a certain period, fixed according
to its nature (*dithim*, translated " delay in pound "), and the expense of
feeding and tending ran against the distress (we may remark that in those
primitive times the distress was invariably levied on cattle), and was pay-
able out of it for the period.   At the end of the delay in pound, the *for-
feiting time* (*lobadh*) began to run, during which the distress became forfeited, at the rate of three "*seds*" a-day, until entirely forfeited.   If the
entire value of the distress thus forfeited was exactly equal to the original
debt and the subsequent expenses, the debt was liquidated ; if it was less,
a second distress was taken for the difference, and if more, the surplus was
returned.   All these proceedings were managed by the party himself, or
his law agent, with the several witnesses of the various steps, and other
necessary parties.   -

But if, instead of allowing his cattle to go to pound, the debtor gave a
sufficient pledge (*gill*), i.e. his son, or some article of value, to the creditor that he would within a certain time try the right to the distress by
law, the creditor was bound to receive such pledge.   If he did not go to
law as he so undertook, the pledge became forfeited for the original debt.
At any time up to the end of the *dithim* the debtor could recover his cattle
by paying the debt and. such expenses as had been incurred ; but if he

neglected to redeem them until the *dithim* had expired, then he could only redeem such of them as were still unforfeited.

Such is a general outline of the ordinary process of distress, but the distinctions in the different cases in which the distress had a stay of one, two, three, five, or ten days, and all other details, can only be ascertained by reference to the work itself.

It will be thus seen that the principle of the ancient Brehon law of distress does not essentially differ from that of the modern one. The proceedings detailed are remarkable, strange to say, for their deliberate character, and the fairness with which at every stage they afford an opportunity to the defendant or debtor to appeal to the Brehon for judgment, or to redeem the seizure by payment of original lien and costs incurred. But it must be borne in mind that the legal process we have quoted refers only to cases where the defendant or debtor *was not of chieftain grade.* In cases where one of chieftain rank was the defendant or debtor, an additional preliminary step of a peculiar and oriental character was to be taken by the plaintiff. In such cases the plaintiff, in addition to giving the customary notice on the defendant, was obliged " *to fast upon him.*" This fasting upon him (*dherna*) consisted in going to the chief's residence and waiting there a certain time without food.

That many of the customs of the ancient Irish were of oriental origin has long been admitted. The hereditary transmission in individual families among them of certain professions, such as medicine and law, the privileges and prohibitions attached to certain ranks so analogous to the system of caste in India, the names of the promontories and hills identified with the worship of fire, the existence of that potent and incomprehensible *geasca,* and other singular practices and traditions, all prove not only that one of the many races that colonized Ireland in the early ages came from the East, but that moreover this mysterious people was a dominant and a law-giving one. If any additional evidence was required to substantiate this opinion, the pages of the *Senchus Mor* supply it. A direct parallel to the Brehon practice of fasting upon a debtor among the ancient Irish existed, and probably still exists, in India, under the name of sitting *dherna* at the door of a debtor, and abstaining from food, until by fear of the creditor dying at his door, compliance on the part of the " debtor is exacted " —an alarming species of importunity, as Dr. Hancock remarks, and expressly prohibited in the Bengal provinces by one of the regulations of the Indian Government. Although the Irish fasting upon a debtor does not appear to have been so stringent as the Indian, yet we have no doubt that the spectacle of a hungry and clamorous creditor (the law, while it enjoined him to shut his mouth, did not require him to hold his tongue) sitting at the gateway of a chieftain and proclaiming his wrongs to the passers-by would be a disgrace that neither the proud Celtic potentate himself nor any of his tribe would brook to endure for a moment, if by any means they could avoid it.

Another prominent feature in the Brehon law is the system of *Eric* or *life price*, and *Dire fine* or *honour price* enjoined by it. This custom, based on the principle that everything in the world has an equivalent or assigned value, dates from the earliest ages of antiquity. It was not peculiar to the ancient Irish. Homer, in his description of the shield of Achilles, assigns one compartment of its disc to a group disputing in the market-place about a *death fine*. The *Weregild* of the Germans, and the *Kinbot* of the Swedes, are identical with it. It is recognized in the Salic and Ripuarian laws of the Franks. When, therefore, continues Dr. Hancock, we find the principle of compensation for murder prevailing among Greeks, Germans, Franks, and Anglo-Saxons, noticed with approval by the Roman historian Tacitus, and leaving traces, according to Sir William Blackstone, in English law also, there is no foundation for the assertion that this principle of *Eric*, however objectionable, is repugnant to all civil law, or that it is peculiar to the ancient code of Ireland.

The statements, therefore, of Spenser (on all Irish matters an unfair critic) and of Sir John Davies on this point, are scarcely worthy of notice, and prove only their ignorance of the laws of their own country, as well as their prejudice against those they were writing about. In fact, a modification of *Eric* and *Dire fine* exists in our laws to the present time, for, when a widow sues for damages against a railway company for the loss of her husband's life, when an outraged father or deserted husband appeals to his countrymen for redress for their social wrongs and compensation for loss of service of daughter or of wife, in what material point does the amount sought for and awarded differ from the *Eric* or *life price* and the *Dire fine* or *honour price* of the Brehon laws? Call the result *Eric* or *Dire fine*, compensation or damages, the principle is still the same. And as to the abolition of the Jewish code of a life for a life on the introduction of Christianity into Ireland, and the substitution of *Eric* and other penalties in place thereof being proof of a savage state of society, it may be doubted whether the spectacle so common in London at the latter end of the eighteenth century, of twenty to twenty-five persons hanging in the sunshine on a summer's morning from the gallows of Newgate, many of them for stealing a horse, some for clipping the edges of the king's coin, and others for highway robbery, is a sufficient proof of the superiority of the English code of the eighteenth century over the much-abused Brehon one of the eighth; and it may be further doubted whether the pressings to death, the disembowellings, and boilings in hot tar of the dead bodies of the miserable criminals, the spiking of skulls and hanging in chains of skeletons on every heath and highway in the kingdom will satisfactorily establish the advance made by the great Anglo-Saxon race of that period in social condition, domestic government, or moral feeling, over the well-abused Celtic race of former ages, more especially as the former had the advantage of a thousand years of civilization to elevate and improve their natures and their laws.

Let us turn to the second part of our subject. Whether the Irish had an alphabet and a literature of their own before the arrival of S. Patrick in the fifth century was, for a long time, a contested question. It is now, however, generally admitted that there is every reason to believe they had both. Dr. Todd, a writer exceedingly cautious in making any assertions, or advancing any opinions without being prepared to corroborate them by sufficient proof, has endorsed this view in very explicit terms. It is also highly probable that the alphabet of the Pagan Irish was derived from the Eastern, and not the Western world. Taking into consideration the coincidence of the ancient Irish characters (sixteen) with the old Cadmean number, admittedly derived from the Phœnicians by the Greeks, the frequent visits of the former to the Irish shores as merchants or colonists (it may be as both) it is almost a certainty that, along with their religion and Baal worship, they introduced their language and their literature. But, while we claim this remote date for the use of letters by the Irish, we may admit with Moore and Todd that their knowledge was confined to the Druidical and Bardic classes, and formed a portion of those mysteries which gave so peculiar an authority to the ministers of religion in the earlier ages of the world.

But, in making this statement, we must not be supposed to claim the same remote antiquity for the present characters of the Irish alphabet. Both General Vallancey and Dr. Todd have declared that they are not older than the fifth century, and to such authority we may bow. But, while pointing out this fact, Dr. Todd also states that there is every reason to believe that the Irish had an alphabet before the coming of S. Patrick, and that this ancient alphabet was superseded by the present Roman characters introduced by him. Now we submit that our great and wise Apostle, acting on his well-known policy in winning over the Pagan Irish to Christianity, while he taught his converts to use the Roman characters, retained their Druidical tree names, thus identifying the new alphabet with the familiar sound of the old, with which many of his disciples, especially those who had been Druids, were previously acquainted. Hence we have the characters of an alphabet in Ireland of the fifth century called by the names of a literature centuries older than that date.

To gradually supersede this alphabet, while he retained the peculiar tree names of its characters, S. Patrick sedulously introduced the Roman one. It was the alphabet with which he taught his disciples and converts to write copies of the Holy Scriptures, missals, and other sacred books required for the use of the Church. Hence the art of writing after his coming was no longer an occult piece of learning confined to a particular class. It became known to the early Christian converts of the saint in Ireland, and soon the alphabet which had been before peculiar to the Druids and the initiated became extinct. It will be thus seen that the art of writing became in the fifth century in Ireland with the disciples of S. Patrick an attribute of their new religion.

"The age of the Church 438, the tenth year of Laoghaire, the *Senchus* and *Feenachus* were purified and written." This purification evidently alludes to the selection made by the committee of nine of the laws and precedents to remain in force in the New Code, and their rejection of previous Pagan and obsolete enactments. The word " written," we submit, means copying the manuscripts into one volume.

That, accordingly, many copies of this great book of Irish law were made by the disciples and converts of S. Patrick in the fifth century, and subsequently transcribed in after times, we have no reason to doubt. It was the law of the land, and identified with the great Apostle himself and the religion which he preached, and it protected, moreover, in a remarkable manner, the interests of the order to which he belonged. "There are three things," says the *Senchus Mor*, " which are paid—viz., *Tythes* and *first fruits* and *alms,* which prevent the period of a plague and the suspension of amity between a king and the country, and which also prevent the occurrence of a general war." Such an authority would be carefully preserved in cell and cloister, and frequently referred to in a country that knew no other code of laws for more than 1,000 years. That many of those copies remained in ecclesiastical custody is also probable, but equally, so we regret to add, that many were destroyed during the merciless onslaughts of the Danes and northern pirates on the Irish coast from the latter end of the eighth to the beginning of the eleventh century. The peculiar ferocity with which the savage followers of Odin burned and destroyed the religious buildings, schools, and abbeys of the early Irish Church, is matter of history. In their flames perished not only their blameless occupants, martyrs to the faith, but also the manuscripts entrusted to their care. But as the ravages of the Danes seldom penetrated further than the sea-coast, many copies were still preserved, especially such as were in the custody of the Brehons themselves. That office was hereditary in certain families, and with the office were transmitted from father to son the manuscript copies of the laws. And to this undoubted fact the existence in the present day of three precious manuscripts of the *Senchus Mor* in the library of Trinity College, or, more correctly, one comparatively full copy and two large fragments, and an extensive fragment among the Harleian manuscripts in the British Museum, must be attributed. One of the fragments in the Trinity College manuscripts (H. 3. 18) is undoubtedly upwards of 500 years old.

Their preservation must be mainly attributed to the earnest labours and the learned antiquarian research of an Englishman, Lieutenant-Colonel, afterwards Major-General Vallancey, of the Royal Engineers. About the year 1788, Colonel Vallancey, who had previously spent many years in India, was sent by Government to superintend the erection of certain fortifications in and about the Cove of Cork. He was a distinguished Oriental scholar, a doctor of laws, and a member of several learned societies. A man of impulsive and enthusiastic temperament, of kind heart and warm feelings, he appears at once to have taken an interest in the down-trodden Celts. He has himself told us how his attention was first directed to the study of Irish antiquities by overhearing, on a summer's evening at the Cove, a peasant point out the constellation Orion by the identical name by which it is known in Hindustan, namely, the "Helmeted Head or Warrior." His curiosity thus singularly aroused led him to devote himself to the study of the Irish language, in which he soon became a proficient, and in which he tells us he was greatly assisted by his previous knowledge of the Oriental tongues. As he advanced in his researches into Irish antiquities, he became more enthusiastic. Bringing to bear on the etymology of the language of the Gael his great knowledge of Oriental dialects, and the wonderful amount of out-of-the-way learning stored in his retentive mind, he traced its presence through the Persian, the Syrian, and the Hebrew, and, like a lapidary who holds up a precious jewel to every ray of light, and discovers new beauties by each change of position, he collated the Irish language with

2 D 2

the Arabic and Phœnician of Plautus, he compared it word for word with the Chinese, the Japanese, and the Maltese, and in each saw, or fancied he saw, the presence of the great Celtic mother tongue. In his opinion the Irish language furnished the key to all others, and explained the myths and mysteries that had puzzled wise and learned men for ages. Devoting himself with that enthusiasm and assiduity which kindly Englishmen some-times exhibit in Irish matters, Colonel Vallancey became *Hibernissimus Hibernorum, the* Irish antiquarian of the day. Nor were the benefits he conferred merely speculative and visionary. He established, or if he did not establish, he brought into notice, the Society of Hibernian Antiquaries in Dublin. Under the name of " Collectanea de Rebus Hibernicis," he edited four volumes, containing the papers and essays contributed by the members. In England and on the Continent these volumes attracted considerable attention, and, while they contain much that is preposterous, much that is worthless, and much that is fanciful, they also contain far more that is valuable, original, and learned. The fact of the addition of a man of Vallancey's position and literary standing to the ranks of the advocates for the early civilization of a race that for many years it had been the pleasant pastime of the literary fops and witlings of the London coffee-houses to ridicule, was in itself startling, nor was the surprise lessened by his publication of the " Collectanea de Rebus Hibernicis." The essays were freely commented on, and found some upholders and many keen opponents, among whom Dr. Campbell, a Scotchman by birth or blood, was a prominent disputant. But no papers were more vigorously attacked than those contributed by Vallancey himself, especially those purporting to be translations from the ancient manuscripts of the *Senchus Mor,* and his essays on the Brehon laws of Ireland. The history of those manuscripts is curious.

About seventy years previously Edward Lhwyd, the great Cymric scholar and learned editor of the laws of *Howell Dha,* had made a tour throughout Ireland, and had picked up some old manuscripts, which in a letter to the Royal Society (*Philos. Trans.,* 336) he thus describes :—" I have procured in divers parts of Ireland about twenty or thirty MSS. on parchment, and although I consulted O'Flaherty, author of the ' Ogygia,' one of the chief Irish critics and others, they could scarcely interpret one page. What is most valuable among them is their *old laws,* which might give some light on their national customs." Subsequently those manu-scripts formed a portion of the Chandos collection, and from thence came into the hands of Sir John Seabright. About the year 1782, the Earl of Charlemont obtained permission for

Vallancey to inspect and copy them. He did so, and published in the Collectanea a translation of some portions. As might be expected, from the difficulty of the task, these translations were imperfect and erroneous, but still a really wonderful achievement, taking into consideration the short time he was acquainted with the Irish language. Deeply impressed with the value of the MSS., Lieutenant-Colonel Vallancey wrote to Edmund Burke pointing out their national importance and soliciting his influence with Sir John Seabright for their restoration to Irish custody.

The calm and far-seeing judgment of our great countryman is evident in his reply, dated 15th August, 1783, to the enthusiastic Englishman. After a polite acknowledgment of his letter and expression of regret, at being unable to read the MSS., Burke goes on to detail the conditions on which he had prevailed on Sir John Seabright to place the manuscripts in the library of Trinity College, Dublin, the most important being the requirement, " that the original text at some future day should be published with a literal translation in Latin or English, so that it might become the proper subject for criticism and comparison. It was in the hope," he adds, " that some such thing would be done, that I originally prevailed on my friend Sir John Seabright, to let me have his manuscripts, and that I sent them by Dr. Leland to Dublin."

Thus, paradoxical as it may appear, it is literally true that to the antiquarian industry of a Welshman, the zealous enthusiasm of an Englishman, the generous liberality of a Scotchman, and the wise foresight of an Irishman, we owe not only the original preservation of the manuscripts of the *Senchus Mor*, their safe custody in the sanctuary of our venerable university, but eventually their present translation and publication.

In the library of Trinity College they remained undisturbed for seventy years. O'Reilly, who probably was the only man at that time capable of understanding them, saw them there in 1824. In his prize Essay he gives extracts, a catalogue and list of contents. After that year, beyond a passing reference by some of our antiquarians, they remained unnoticed and almost forgotten. Many causes led to this result. By some the Brehon manuscripts were held to be of a comparatively modern date, the production of some monk of the twelfth century or the rhapsodies of bards of a century or two earlier. Others, while admitting their authenticity, declared that they could not be translated by any modern Irish scholar. We must recollect that the original text of the *Senchus Mor*, the *Bearla fine* has been obsolete, if not extinct, for upwards of

a thousand years, and that it was only by collating the interlined glosses of successive commentators, gradually reaching to
comparatively recent times, that any clue to the original could
be obtained, and that in many cases both the gloss and text
were alike obsolete. Add to this the complicated contractions
of words in which our ancient scribes so freely indulged, partly
from fanciful vagaries and partly to economize the parchment
on which the manuscript was written; add to these also such
contrivances as are called Ceꞃꞃꞃꞃ ejce, " the head of the
Ridge," and Coꞃ ꞃꞃ cꞃꞃꞃꞃ " The Reapers' path," which abound
in the original manuscripts of the *Senchus Mor,* as well as in
all our old writings, and, above all, that extraordinary handi-
craft of calligraphic cunning the *Ceanfhochras* (Ceáꞃꞃꞃoꞃꞃaꞃ)
or placing of wrong initial letters to words in order to
baffle an ordinary reader, and conceal the meaning of the
sentence from every one but the initiated, who were furnished
with a key for the purpose; the dilapidation caused to the
original document by neglect, damp, and fire, and the fading of
the ink through time—group all these together, and some idea,
and that far short of the reality, may be formed of the amount
and varied character of the difficulties that beset any attempt
to translate the Seabright manuscripts of the *Senchus Mor.*
But enough of the old race remained in the land, and still
remains in it, to meet and overcome the obstacles, and
O'Donovan and O'Curry lived to accomplish that task which
O'Flaherty had declined, O'Connor had despaired of, and
Ledwich pronounced to be impossible.

Nor less gratifying is it to record the fact that the Government of the country, wise by experience, so far from ignoring
the claims of Ireland to a past history and an early civilization,
has frankly aided and generously assisted the labours of her
scholars and antiquarians in the matter; nor must it be forgotten that it is to the liberality of the Parliament of the United
Kingdom, that we owe the present publication of the first
volumes of the *Senchus Mor.* Let us hope that the good work,
so happily begun, may be suitably finished, and that successive volumes will complete the publication of the Brehon laws,
for which ample materials are in the possession of commissioners appointed for the purpose.

In 1852 the Rev. Dr. Todd and the Very Rev. Dr. Graves,
Fellows of Trinity College, submitted to the Irish Government
a proposal for the transcribing, translation, and publication of
the ancient laws and institutes of Ireland from the manuscripts
deposited in Trinity College, Dublin, the Bodleian library,
Oxford, and the British Museum, London. Warmly assisted
by the then Lord-Lieutenant, the Earl of Carlisle, the applica-

tion found favour in the eyes of the imperial Government, and the request was granted.

On the 11th November, 1852, a commission was issued to Lord Chancellor Blackburn, the Earl of Rosse, the Earl of Dunraven, Lord Talbot de Malahide, Chief Baron Pigot, Mr. Joseph Napier, then Attorney-General, the Rev. Thomas Romney Robinson, D.D., the Rev. James Henthorn Todd, D.D., the Rev. Charles Graves, D.D., George Petrie, LL.D., and Major Thomas Askew Larcom, appointing them commissioners to direct, superintend, and carry into effect the transcription and translation of the ancient laws of Ireland.

In pursuance of this authority the commissioners employed Dr. O'Donovan and Professor O'Curry in transcribing various law tracts in the Irish language in the libraries of Trinity College, Dublin, of the Royal Irish Academy, of the British Museum, and in the Bodleian Library at Oxford.

The transcripts made by Dr. O'Donovan (we quote from the preface of the *Senchus Mor*) comprising 2,491 pages, extend to nine volumes, and the transcripts made by O'Curry are contained in eight volumes, extending to 2,906 pages. After the translation of such of the law tracts as the commissioners deemed it well to publish, a preliminary translation of almost all the transcripts was made by either Dr. O'Donovan or Professor O'Curry, and some few portions were translated by both. They did not however live to revise and complete their translations. When the translation had so far progressed, the commissioners employed Dr. Neilson Hancock to prepare the first part of the *Senchus Mor*. The steps taken by Dr. Hancock, in carrying out the directions of the commissioners, first with Dr. O'Donovan, and after his death with the assistance of the Rev. Thaddeus O'Mahoney, Professor of Irish in the University of Dublin, are fully detailed in the preface to the *Senchus Mor*, and will well repay perusal.

A melancholy interest thus attaches to the translation of the *Senchus Mor*, from the fact that in rapid succession both O'Donovan and O'Curry died while engaged on it. Foremost among Irish scholars were those two great men, and so long as the Irish language lasts will the result of their united labours remain identified with it. A few days before his death O'Donovan corrected himself some pages of the first and second proofs of the translation. We cannot imagine a more fitting subject for a painting for an Irish National Gallery, than the great Irish scholar on his death-bed, surrounded by his comrades and fellow-labourers in the translation of the *Senchus Mor*, returning to them with failing sight and feeble hand the proof sheets of what to him was a work of love, the object of a life.

We shall now briefly deal with the question whether the Brehon laws were beneficial to the national or individual character of the race for whom they were compiled, and with strong leanings the other way, we must admit they were not. They had two great radical defects,—first, their immutability, and secondly, their antagonism to individual liberty. They were essentially made for the benefit of the aristocratic orders. In a state of society where the individual was nothing and the clan everything, there was no room for the formation of that great element of a nation, a self-supporting, self-depending middle class. So long as the horizon of the Irish Gael was bounded by the narrow limits of his tribe, so long would he be deficient in self-reliance, and his mode of thought, manner of action, and expression of feeling be regulated by those of the chieftain of his tribe, while those of the chieftains and ruling classes were equally on certain points restricted by the unchangeable code. Especially was this system injurious to a right national feeling : under it, the native was less an Irishman than a clansman. His tribe became his country, his chief the immediate object of his reverence and his loyalty. As M. Jules de Lasteyrie, in his able article on the *Senchus Mor* in the "Revue des Deux Mondes" remarks :—"The principle of the system was the solidarity of the members of the tribe, and the isolation of the clan in the midst of the nation." Under such a rule patriotism would be feeble, and a sound nationality unknown. But those evils were not peculiar to ancient Ireland, nor solely originating with the Brehon laws. They were just as rampant among the ancient Britons in the time of Cæsar. "The land in Britain," says Dr. Lappenberg, "was divided among many tribes, and their kings, who, slightly bound to each other, lived independently near each other, cherishing their love of strife, and training up their youths in civil quarrels, without manifesting at a later period, in the days of the destruction of the common liberty, the judgment and energy necessary for a general resistance."

Hence was also the great difficulty in Ireland to keep together, for any length of time, the tribes and clans for any common purpose, irrespective of individual advantage to their respective interests; and hence also, in time of war, success in military matters became a necessity. A powerful mind like Mahomet, it is true, might, by the agency of religious fanaticism, have enrolled all those tribes under the banner of a new faith, but happily no such character appeared in Irish history. Taking therefore into consideration the many evils springing from this system, the fruitful seeds of strife and dissension sown in every tribe by the laws which regulated the succession of their chiefs and division of their lands, it is almost impossible to account for its wonderful vitality on Irish soil. Nor was it alone over its own defects and internal elements of decay that chieftancy was in Ireland triumphant. It actually opposed, and eventually absorbed, in a remarkable manner, a portion of the feudal military system of Europe brought in contact with it. Many of the descendants of the Anglo-Norman barons and knights, who landed as invaders on our shores in the reign of the second Henry, became, in less than two centuries, Irish chieftains, wearing the Irish garb, speaking the Irish tongue, and following the Irish usages of gossipred and fosterage as strictly as their neighbours of pure Celtic blood, until, finally, the Earls of the great houses of Desmond, Kildare, and De Burgo, and the representatives of the chivalrous Raymond Le Gros, De Barry, and other Norman knights, were better known beyond the Pale as the heads of the Clan Gerald, the Mac-William, the Grace and the Barry Mor, than by their ancestral titles, and, in fact, became more Irish than the Irish themselves in devotion to the land of their birth, and adoption of its Celtic institutions.

The other great defect of the Brehon laws, namely, their immutability is as evident as it is singular. To suppose that society would remain in the same condition for more than one thousand years, and that the laws which regulated it at the commencement of that period would remain in force at its close, was a monstrous absurdity. Yet this is actually the result the Brehon law effected, and it is only in the laws of the Medes and Persians in the olden times, and in those of the Chinese of the present day, we can find any parallel. We acquit the wise and good and learned men who compiled the Brehon laws into the Cain Patrick from any intention of doing this, or having such an object in view. The fault lay in after times, in the blind veneration and devotion paid to those laws by the natives themselves. They built in the early ages, as it were, a bulwark around themselves against which the waves of progress and improvement for a long period beat in vain. Hence was it, as the able French reviewer remarks, that every stranger was an object of suspicion to the ancient Irish, and was treated as an alien in the clan. Any one not being a member of the clan who had property on its territory, received only a part of the produce of his land, and could not go to law unless a member of the tribe joined as co-plaintiff. Any person not a member of the clan and having no property in its territory, and yet found in it, was immediately conducted to the frontiers. But *inside* the clan, though the law made a vast distinction between the proprietor, tenant, and servile or inferior class, kindness and humanity found a large scope. Every year a part of the land of the clan was put at the disposal of the chief, to be distributed among the poor. The aged, the infirm, the sick, and the mentally afflicted were tenderly cared for. The *Senchus Mor* says of the three objects of the law—namely, government, honour, and the soul—government belongs to the chiefs, honour and soul belong to all. This reservation of power to a class is significant.

It will be readily seen that the Brehon code of the Celtic race was in many things diametrically opposed to the judicial system of the Teutonic nations. Thus among the Anglo-Saxons the decision of important matters was never intrusted to single individuals, as in such cases the *Ealderman* decided only with the assent of the *Witan* of the shire. Nay, the monarch himself was, in all cases affecting his people, dependent on the legislative assembly of his kingdom, composed of ecclesiastics and laymen from all parts under his rule, and forming the great wittenagemot of the realm. But with the Irish Gael the decision of a single judge was final. Neither king nor bishop, neither judge nor assembly, could alter the unchangeable Brehon law. It towered above them all, immutable and omnipresent, and all classes and all ranks bowed in submission before it. No monarch, king, or chief could at his pleasure, or by the vote of any body of men, levy or impose any tax other than was imposed by the Brehon laws regulating the tributes to be paid to the chieftains of clans, and the provincial or sovran kings. In only one instance, that of the *Boroimhe Laeghean* (Leinster tribute), was this fundamental law of the Irish constitution ever broken through, and this breach was the frequent and enduring cause of sanguinary wars between the people of Leinster and the Ard Righ of Ireland for generations afterwards.

The chief historical value of the *Senchus Mor*, as has been remarked, is due to the purity of its origin. The Salic and Ripuarian laws do, it is true, refer to ancient usages, but these semi-barbarous and semi-Christian laws were composed *after* the Conquest, when primitive society had been modified by contact with Roman civilization. In Ireland, on the contrary, in the fifth century everything was primitive. Ireland was unconquered; no foreign element had at that period mingled with the old national traditions; for while S. Patrick introduced Christianity he left the national institutions unimpaired. He improved, but not eradicated. "It is this," observes the able writer in the "Revue des Deux Mondes," "which makes the publication of the *Senchus Mor* a great literary fact, enabling the reader to appreciate the true nature of a nationality and the institutions of a society which resembled neither Germanic, feudal, Roman, nor modern society—a nationality and a society which are intrinsically and *per se* Irish." In addition to this, M. de Lasteyrie might have added that the publication of the *Senchus Mor* silences for ever those libellers on the national character who, from Giraldus Cambrensis to Spenser, and from Spenser to Pinkerton, and from Pinkerton downwards to writers in our own days, have persistently slandered the institutions of a people of whose very language they were totally ignorant.

But, as we have already said, we are bound to admit that the Brehon code was on the whole injurious to the national as well as the individual character of the Irish; it fostered no public spirit, and was antagonistic to private enterprise. In fact those laws were made for the advantage of the ruling classes, and carefully excluded the popular elements. Under their shadow there was no growth of free character or independent action. Thus no one of the people—unless by the adoption of the unpleasant fasting process, or through the agency or under the banner of a rival chieftain—could prosecute at law a member of the governing class; and although this to a certain extent was remedied by what in mechanism is called a compensating balance—namely, that any individual who had even one under-tenant or follower ranked as a chief in the eye of the Brehon law, and was entitled to the privileges of his order, yet it is evident that this restriction cut off from the great bulk of the community redress for grievances inflicted by the aristocracy. That principle, which a great American writer remarks is most characteristic of the Teutonic race, namely, a tendency to individuality, was jealously repressed in the Celtic code. The individual and the country were nowhere, the clan and the chief everywhere and everything. Outside of the law, moreover, and debarred of its privileges, was a large servile class. It is but just to point out that the cup of slavery which the ancient Irish gave to their serfs was, in after times, returned to their own lips. There is every reason to believe that there were both foreign and domestic slaves among the ancient Irish in Pagan times, and even in the earlier ages of Christianity. Our great Apostle, it is asserted, was sold as a slave, and served as such under a harsh task-master.

That the Irish, with " that indignant swelling after libertie," which even a bitter enemy remarked they possessed in a remarkable degree, could have submitted for so many centuries to such a code, is positively marvellous. It is one of the many anomalies which so frequently startle and bewilder the student of their annals. Yet, bearing in mind that the history of

those remote ages comes to us through the agency of writers
identified with the ruling classes, there is good reason to believe
that any event or transaction injurious to the interests of the
governing orders would be suppressed or slightingly alluded
to. But one remarkable event is chronicled, which throws an
unexpected light on the question. Every student of Irish
history is aware that for 590 years the sovran king or Ard Righ
belonged to either the northern or southern branch of one great
house. "The northern and southern race of O'Nialls," writes
Sir Bernard Burke, "exclusively occupied the throne of Ireland
from the fourth to the eleventh century, a period of time which
no reigning dynasty can boast of, the sovereign of Rome alone
excepted." Long before this first century a strange people,
called the *Attacotti*, appeared in Ireland, and became possessed
of the government of the kingdom, and placed one of their
chieftains, *Cairbre* by name, on the throne. He reigned for
some years, and then voluntarily abdicated in favour of the
legitimate dynastic king. But coupled with this relinquishment of sovereignty was the remarkable fact that the son of
the outgoing king, known as Moran the Just, became the
supreme judge of the kingdom.

Now this singular episode has been a stumbling-block to our
early historians. The whole of the circumstances connected
with it appear to be attended with a certain air of mystery and
reserve. For a long period of time the *Attacotti* were considered to have been a race of foreign invaders, who had conquered the country (one of the many human waves that rose
from the sea and surged over the land in remote antiquity). Moreover, those *Attacotti* were in bad repute, and had left behind
them an indifferent character. They bewildered S. Jerome, perplexed the Venerable Bede, and mystified Richard of Cirencester.
By the first they were called cannibals, by the second a wicked
people, and by the third the terror of neighbouring nations.
In fact, were we to believe our early monkish and bardic
historians, the *Attacotti* were a dangerous and an abominable
race. Various conjectures were, from time to time, hazarded
as to their original native country, and many wild theories propounded as to its position, and the cause of their emigration from
it. But the most learned, as well as the most extraordinary of
all those theories, has been given by Vallancey. *Attacotti!*—the
sound was singular, the name was suggestive, and accordingly
the general indulges in the wildest speculations on the subject.
We copy the entire passage as illustrative of the learned and
discursive manner in which he is too apt to discuss Irish
subjects. "*Coth, Corrach, Croich*," thus he writes, "in Irish
signify also a hide or boat, hence the *Magogians* or original

Scythi, and inventors of that kind of boat, called themselves, or were called, *Aittach Cothi,* i. e., old navigators or shipmen, a name corrupted by the Latins into *Attacotti.* Hence the original סיכותא. *M'Cathæ, Navis, Ægypt. Katoa* : Sic Kitii populi Scythiæ circa mare Caspianum apud Strabonem, nec aliunde nomen hoc, quam a *Kithiis* hodie *Cataino* (Boxbornius) ; hence *Cathi* or *Gethi. Getæ* were synonymous names of the children of *Gomer* and *Magog,* confused in succeeding ages by a mixture of the *Scuthi,* whence *Syncellus,* Σκύθαι καὶ Κοῦθοι λεγόμενοι ἐπιχωρίαις, Scythæ qui etiam *Gothi* sua lingua et Trebellius Pollio Scythæ, *i. e.* pars, Gothorum Asiam vastabant. The Greeks and Latins know not how to make the distinction, which caused Salmasius to observe." But here we must pause to breathe after all those names of learned length and mystic sound, and refer our readers to the fourth vol. Collect. Hiber., page xxix. to xlvii., for any further information they may require on the subject. Now patient investigation and comparison of authorities in modern times has elicited the truth concerning the mysterious *Attacotti.* They were neither cannibals nor Caspians, neither murderers nor mariners,' neither Scuthi nor sailors, and had as little to do with Magog as they had with Moses. The true etymology of the words *Aiteach, Coiteach, vile or common rabble, ignobile vulgus,* furnishes the clue to the riddle. The *Attacotti* were merely the oppressed and down-trodden serfs and slaves, many of them descendants of a gallant though conquered race, who rose up in arms, about the middle of the first century in Ireland, against their tyrants, attacked them unawares at their general assembly on the plains of Meath, slew many of their oppressors, defeated the remainder, and finally placed triumphantly one of their chiefs on the sovran throne of Ireland, and, on his abdication, secured justice for their grade, and vindicated the rights of the common people by the appointment of his son, Moran the Just, to the high office of supreme judge and Brehon in the kingdom. The rising of the *Attacotti* was, in fact, a Celtic jacquerie against the domineering insolence of the chieftain class. But as the historians of those days were all identified with the aristocratic class, while compelled to record in their chronicles the disagreeable event we have mentioned, they revenged themselves by slandering the characters of the actors in it, even to attaching an ignominious name, " *Ceann. Cait,* or *Cat Head,"* to the *parvenu* sovran, who was thus forcibly placed on the throne of their legitimate king. There is therefore reason to believe that, as in the progress of time the ancient Irish became, from a cluster of families and tribes, a numerous people, they were sensible of the deficiencies of their primitive system of legislation to meet the developments of a large community, and that, even before the landing of Strongbow, many of them were anxious for a change and improvement in their code of laws.

The obstinate fidelity with which, for six hundred years, they afterwards clung to the Brehon laws, cannot be adduced in argument against this assertion. They obeyed their Brehon laws, and repudiated those of the stranger, for the simple fact that they found no protection for life or property in the legislation of the Anglo-Norman. No mere Irishman could, for centuries, plead in an English court in Ireland. To rob an Irishman was no theft, to slay him was no crime, no matter how foully or cruelly the deed was done. If accused, the murderer had only to plead that the victim was a mere Irishman, *merus Hibernicus*, and that plea in English law was sufficient to acquit him of the capital charge. It is true, he was liable to a fine for slaying the king's Irishman, pretty much as he would be for killing the king's hawk, and far less than for hunting the king's deer.

If any other proof were required to establish the statement that an acute and intelligent race, when brought in contact with the English law as administered for Englishmen, soon perceived its superiority, in securing individual liberty and promoting progress, over their own primitive code, it can be readily supplied by the facts of recorded history. O'Reilly, in his treatise on the Brehon laws, quotes two remarkable instances of this feeling. He remarks that several of the Irish princes, wearied of the perpetual warfare between themselves and the English colonists, so far back as the reign of Edward III., were desirous of becoming subjects to the crown of England, and being governed by English laws. In the second year of the reign of that monarch a petition was presented by the natives, praying that an act might pass in Ireland, whereby all the Irishrie might be enabled to use and enjoy the laws of England. This most reasonable request was refused ; and not only refused, but an act was afterwards passed in the same reign, enacting that for any one of English blood to intermarry with the Irish, to foster any of their children, or even to stand sponsor for them at the font in baptism, would be *high treason!* To use an Irish name, to speak in the Irish tongue, or wear an Irish garb, was an offence punishable by imprisonment. To permit Irish cattle to graze on lands within the English Pale was a penal offence, while to present an Irish priest to a benefice, or give a night's shelter to an Irish minstrel, was positive felony !

That this anxiety to be admitted within the benefit of the English law was not confined to any particular locality in

Ireland, but was a wide-spread feeling throughout the entire country, is proved by another petition presented by O'Donnell, chieftain of Donegal in the north, in the twenty-third year of Henry VIII., and by O'Byrne, chieftain of Imayle in the south-east of Ireland, to the same effect, both praying to be granted the protection of the English laws; but such was the execrable policy of the period that those moderate requests were not only refused, but actually in the same reign, all the odious decrees against the native Irish were re-enacted and renewed.

Whereby it is manifest (writes Sir John Davies, attorney-general to James I.) that such as had the government under the Crown of England did intend to make a perpetual separation and animosity between the English and the Irish. Intending, no doubt, that the English should, in the end, root out the Irish, which the English, not being able to do, caused a perpetual warfare between the two nations, *which lasted for four hundred years, and would have lasted to the world's end*, if, in the reign of Queen Elizabeth, the Irish had not been broken and conquered by the sword, and since, in the beginning of his majesty's reign, had not been protected and governed by the law. . . . This, then, I note as a great defect in the civil policy of the kingdom, in that, for the space of 350 years at least after the Conquest, the English laws were not communicated to the Irish, nor the benefit and protection thereof allowed unto them, *although they earnestly desired and sought the same.* For, so long as they were out of the protection of the law, so every Englishman might oppresse, spoyle, and kill them without contentment, how was it possible they should bee other than outlawes and enemies to the crown of England?

In closing the pages of this great book of Irish law, we may be permitted to express an earnest hope that the wise and learned men who have so far superintended and secured its publication will not relax in their efforts, and that other volumes may speedily follow the *Senchus Mor,* until the whole series is finished—a priceless gift to the literature of Ireland and of all Europe. Let them feel assured that as the records of a grateful people have preserved through fourteen centuries the names of the first compilers of that law, equally so in future generations will the names of those true patriots be cherished who have removed a foul aspersion from the fair fame of their country, and restored her to so high a place among the law-giving nations of the earth.

ART. VIII.—DEVOTION TO S. JOSEPH.

Act of Pius IX. placing the whole Catholic Church under the Patronage of S. Joseph.

Acta Sanctorum. Ad diem 19 Martii.

A Manual of Practical Devotion to the Glorious Patriarch S. Joseph. Translated from the Italian of Father Patrignani, S.J. Dublin : Duffy.

Life of S. Joseph. By Father JOSEPH IGNATIUS VALLEJO, S.J. Dublin : Duffy.

The Blessed Sacrament. By F. FABER. Book II., Sect V.—" The Foster-Father and the Child."

IN noticing in our last number the Act of the Holy Father which declared S. Joseph to be Patron of the Universal Church, we spoke not only of its appropriateness at the present time, but of its being a striking instance of the harmony and beauty of proportion which God the Holy Ghost has stamped upon everything connected with the Church. We pointed out that this seal, so to speak, of the spirit of God, is to be found not merely in the doctrinal developments of " the faith once delivered to the Saints," by which article after article of the Church's creed has been first thought out in her own deep mind, and then placed in clearer and sharper outline before the minds of her children through her dogmatic definitions, but even in the very devotions of the Christian people, which, though varying from age to age, are all channels of the " one spirit," whereby in His unselfish love, according to our Lord's promise, " He takes not of His own," but " of what is Christ's, and shows it unto us." Thus He " brings back to our remembrance whatsoever Christ has said," and realizes outwardly in the history of the Church Militant the several mysteries of God's Human Life upon earth. Thus too the life and office of each member of the Holy Family, of Jesus, Mary, and Joseph, are shadowed forth and renewed in the historical development of the Church's leading devotions ; while by the kindred and concurrent operation of the *Cultus* of the Saints, the relationship of the various members of Christ's Mystical Body to one another and to their Great Head is made manifest to the eyes of angels and of men, " until we all meet into the unity of faith, and of the knowledge of the Son of God, unto a perfect man, unto the measure of the age of the fulness of Christ." Nay further, the harmony of the Church's devotions springs from and is dependent upon the higher harmony of her doctrine, which in its turn is interpenetrated and influenced by the former; for just as dogmatic definitions are the expressions of the Church's mind, so devotions are the expression of the Church's heart, and although the heart is guided and ruled by the mind, yet the mind is ever influenced by the heart. This is why, to use the words of F. Faber, the " devotions of one age become the dogmas of another, as in the case of the Immaculate Conception; and the dogmas of one age become devotions in others, as it was with the mysteries of the Sacred Humanity and the Maternity of Mary. Thus time goes on, commuting dogma into devotion, and devotion into dogma by a double process continually. There is no safety in devotion, if it be separated from dogma, though it may sometimes go before, and sometimes follow after."*

We also pointed out that this mutual harmony of doctrine and of devotion, which may very well be said to correspond with what S. Paul calls the " unity of the faith, and of the knowledge of the Son of God," is the exclusive prerogative of the Catholic Church, and therefore a marvellous confirmation to every believer of her divine mission to mankind; for no mere human system could ever have succeeded in weaving together so many countless threads into one harmonious design, as are to be found in the perfect unity of the elaborate lacework of the Church's definitions and devotions—we might even add, of her Ritual and Office. " There is no harmony," we said, " in false doctrine. There all is distorted, all is discord. The fragmentary Christianity which exists outside the unity of God's Catholic Church has no beauty of proportion, no slow and sure growth or development, no variety of devotions springing out of and interlacing one another, yet always exactly corresponding with the wants of every age. It is but an orderless succession of distorted and unconnected doctrines, abortive efforts, and stunted growths."†

It is our purpose in the present article to develop these thoughts in connection with devotion to S. Joseph, upon which the Holy Father may be said to have just placed the crown by his recent Act, at somewhat greater length than we were able to do in our last number.

Looking back, then, at the historical development of this

---

* "Blessed Sacrament," p. 382.
† Dublin Review, January, 1871, p. 203.

devotion, we shall find that both the position held by the great Foster-Father of our Lord and Spouse of our Lady in the outward worship of the Church, and as his relation to the Mystical Body of Christ, correspond in an admirable manner with the position which he once held in the Holy Family upon earth, and with his relation to the Real Body of our Lord; 2ndly. That devotion to S. Joseph takes possession, so to speak, of the minds and hearts of the faithful just in those ages of the Church for which it is best adapted; and, 3rdly. That the manner of its growth is in exact harmony with the hidden character of S. Joseph himself, just as his recent exaltation as Patron of the Universal Church is the just reward of the Saint of the Hidden Life. These are, indeed, but the leading harmonies, lying, so to speak, on the surface of the devotion; and there are many others that might easily be pointed out, but these would carry us far beyond the limits allotted to our present article.

I. The first thing which strikes us in looking back on the history of this devotion is the silence of the Church with regard to S. Joseph for many centuries, a silence which, at first sight, might appear almost unnecessarily prolonged. Are we, then, to conclude that there was no devotion to S. Joseph in the early ages; that the Church had, as it were, forgotten him? This would indeed be a wrong and hasty conclusion, as well as contrary to the Apostolic Decree, which states that "the Church has *always* most highly honoured and praised the most blessed Joseph, *next to His Spouse, the Virgin Mother of God*, and has besought his intercession in times of trouble." We might as well say that a young mother has forgotten her love and devotion to her husband, because, in the first transports of her joy, all her love, and anxiety, and interest are concentrated upon her new-born child. Outwardly, indeed, she has no eyes, no care but for her little one, yet we know that all the while that other love, although unexpressed, is lying treasured up in the deep places of her heart, and that, in due time, it will break forth again in even greater strength, and join itself with his love, so as to form the steadfast support of her after-life, when her child has grown up "to the measure of the perfect man." So too was it with the Church and her devotion to S. Joseph, for, ever since God became man, the type of the mother and the child is that which best explains the apparent difficulties of "the mystery of godliness manifest in the flesh." In order, then, the better to understand the Church's long silence about S. Joseph, let us dwell a little upon this comparison of the mother and the child. As we shall shortly see, it is pregnant with an even deeper meaning. In the early ages the Church was wholly busied with the " Man-Child," which the old dragon was seeking to devour. She herself had to flee away into the wilderness, " into a place prepared by God, and to be fed by Him for a thousand two hundred and sixty days." She had to see that her " child was taken up to God and seated on His Throne;" she had to teach mankind that her little one was " God of God, Light of light, very God of very God;" God and man, yet one Christ; one, " not by the conversion of the Godhead into flesh, but by the taking of the manhood into God." To bring this out before the eyes of men,—to lay for ever in their hearts the sure foundations of Revealed Truth, she had to concentrate all her love, all her devotion, all her interest, all her care, upon the great central figure of the Holy Family, the child of Mary, the foster-child of Joseph, and to proclaim the relation in which He, the God-Man, stood both to God and men. It was meet then and fitting that there should fall first of all from her lips the clear enunciation of the great fundamental doctrines of the Trinity and Unity, and of the Unity in Trinity, of the Perfect Manhood of Jesus, of His Eternal Godhead, of His One Person, of the unconfusedness of His Natures, of the duality of His Wills, of his Rights and Prerogatives, and " all those magnificent truths about His Soul, and the method of the Hypostatic Union, which were to be left to the faithful as so many prolific fountains of glorious theology."* Then, as time went on, she had to teach the true doctrine of the everlasting years,—how matter was not eternal, but the creation of God, who in time had Himself become a creature; how evil had entered into the world and sin, and death by sin; and how both death and sin had been swallowed up in victory by the Death and Resurrection of the Human Body of her God. And, last of all, in the middle ages of her life she set the Crown, as it were, upon the whole of her grand system con-·cerning His Real Body, by proclaiming the great central truth of the reality of its Presence in her midst in the Sacrament of the Holy Eucharist, and by enthroning it high above her altars, as the source of all her life and strength. The " Man-Child had been taken up to God, and set upon His Throne," and lo! He was no longer a child; He had grown in her system of doctrine " unto the measure of the Perfect Man!"

And yet another harmony! All the while that the Church had been gazing upon the face of the Holy Child Jesus, she

---

* " Blessed Sacrament," p. 197.

2 E 2

had felt that she herself was but the type of another, even His Real Mother. All the while she had felt that her own glorious prerogatives and privileges belonged not to herself alone, but to the Mother of God as well, and that everything in God's Word which had been spoken of herself, as of His kingdom of grace or glory, had been no less truly spoken of the Blessed Mary, as its highest living type, and most perfect living representative. Thus the Church had recognized in herself the image and likeness of Mary, and, with the instinct of a true mother's heart, had found no better way of securing the adoration of the Son, than by fencing it round about with the worship of the Mother. And so it came to pass that, without ever lifting her eyes from the Holy Child, the Church began to gaze more earnestly upon the face of the Mother of God, and to drink in ever more and more the majesty and beauty of her spotless purity, which lay even as " a sea of glass like unto crystal in the sight of His Throne." Then gradually she unfolded to her children the royal dignity of God's Mother, her high prerogatives, her glorious privileges, her freedom from actual sin, her marvellous grace; the dogma of her Divine Maternity in relation both to God and men assuming, as time went on, the same central position in the doctrinal system of the Mother, as that which was occupied by the dogma of the Real Presence of the Body and Blood of God Incarnate which He had drawn from her own virginal Blood, in the doctrinal system of the Son. Each doctrine became the centre of its own system, in which all other doctrines met, and thus clearly and distinctly was realized in the Church's mind the true position of the Mother as well as of the Son, of Mary as well as of Jesus.

But this was not all. Throughout the whole of this process of development, (and here we have harmony within harmony,) the devotions of the Church had corresponded, and gone hand in hand with her doctrine. " As the noise and dust of all the conflicts with heresy settled down," says F. Faber, "clear to the eyes of all, as it was to S. John in the island of Patmos, rose the gorgeous vision of the Mother of the Man-Child, with twelve stars around her head, and the moon beneath her feet. Thus the adoration of Jesus and the devotion to Mary had taken their places immovably *in the sense of the faithful,* and *in the practical system* of the Church, one shedding light upon the other, and both instructing, illuminating, nourishing, and sanctifying the people." It would be interesting to point this out in detail, in reference both to the Son and the Mother, and to contrast the devotional aspect of the Early and Mediæval Church with that of the Modern, as illustrative of the distinctive doctrinal aspect of each period; but such a task would require an article to itself. We must hurry on, merely touching upon the subject when we come to speak on the devotion to S. Joseph.

Our readers will have perceived that in the course of our rapid sketch of the Church's doctrinal development we paused at the solemn enthronement of the Real Body of Christ in the outward worship of the members of His Mystical Body. We did so advisedly, for we believe that in very truth this was the centre and turning point of the Church's mystical life. From that moment the current of her thought and love passed into another channel; but it was only the channel that was changed, the deep waters of her doctrine and devotion were still the same as when they first gushed forth from the open side of the Second Adam during His Death-sleep on Calvary. The cycle of the doctrines relating to Christ's Real Body having been completed, these in their turn began to give place to those which related to His Mystical Body. And so the Church unfolded before the eyes of men its constitution, its authority, its sacraments, and its rites ; ever bringing out into clearer light the mutual relationship of its members, whether militant, suffering, or glorified, as well as the royal dignity, prerogatives, and privileges of its earthly head, the Holy Roman Pontiff, until that long-looked-for Midsummer day came at last when, not yet a year ago, she crowned her doctrine about Christ's Mystical Body with the solemn definition of the Infallibility of His Vicar upon earth. And so too, by a parallel development, the grand doctrine of the Divine Maternity of Mary, who is the Mother of Christ's Mystical Body, because she is the true Mother of His Real Body, gradually unfolded all the riches of its treasures, until the happy morning dawned, which many kings and prophets have desired to see, and have not seen, but which *we* have seen, when the Mother of the Man-Child appeared seated upon her throne, high above this poor fallen world of ours, not only with twelve stars around her head, and the moon beneath her feet, but clothed with the stainless rays of the Sun of justice. And yet again, to this further development of doctrine the development of devotion had exactly corresponded. Hence all that striking multiplication of special devotions to the Sacred Humanity of Jesus, which harmonize so beautifully with the later developments of doctrine, and with the necessities of the later times, and which may be said to date or at least to spring from the solemn enthronement of the Blessed Sacrament in the outward worship of the Church, devotions to our Lord's Passion, to His Head crowned with thorns, to His wounded hands and feet, to His open bleeding side, to His pierced Heart, to His red precious Blood. Hence, too, the multiplication of feasts and devotions of almost infinite variety in honour of the Mother of God, by which both the Head and the members of the Mystical Body are knit ever closer together in the embrace of her maternal love. And these too spring from increase of devotion to the Blessed Sacrament, these too may be said to date from Its solemn enthronement in the outward worship of the Church. "Who can doubt," says F. Faber in that same suggestive book from which we have already quoted, "that there is a close and invariable connection between devotion to our dear Mother and devotion to the Blessed Sacrament? The force of terms would be enough to prove it. The lives of the Saints and the teaching of spiritual books are both full of it. But we do not need them for proofs; for the experience of every one of us proves it decisively, to ourselves at least. We have felt and known that in proportion as we loved our Blessed Lady our devotion to the Blessed Sacrament grew more tender and more reverent, and the more we were with the Blessed Sacrament, even without seeming to think of Mary, the more an intense devotion to her took possession of the very depths of our heart. This is a phenomenon which is universal throughout the life of the Church, and which needs no further commentary than the remembrance that one is the Mother, and one the Son."

We have dwelt somewhat at length upon the position held by the Son and the Mother in the doctrinal and devotional development of the Church's mystical life, because it not only helps us to understand the silence of the early and even the mediæval Church about S. Joseph, (not however to the entire exclusion of other reasons for this silence,) but it also enables us to point out the fitness both of time and manner in which devotion to the Foster-Father of our Lord first began to join itself on to the earlier devotions of which we have been speaking, in order with them to complete the full and perfect mystical development which they had begun. To make use for a moment of another comparison, borrowed from that glorious architecture which sprang from the inspiration of the Mediæval Church, we may compare the development of doctrines relating to Christ's Real Body to the costly sanctuary of some vast cathedral, with the dogma of the Real Presence as its high altar and tabernacle. This is first built. Then after this comes the long nave, or central aisle, built out of the hewn stones of the doctrines which relate to our Lord's Mystical Body. Then side by side with the great central aisle there springs up on the right hand another aisle of delicate and smaller proportions, terminating in the Lady Chapel of the worship of God's Mother. Then, last of all, in the fulness of time, in order to complete the three-aisled temple of the Triune God, the third aisle is raised under the patronage of the third person of the earthly Trinity, who is himself the shadow of the Eternal Father, the Foster-Father of Jesus and the Spouse of Mary. Nor should we forget, if we would complete the comparison, the chapels of the Saints, which cluster round the sanctuary and gird the aisles, thus forming, as it were, an outer circle of worship around Mary, Jesus, and Joseph.

It now remains for us to trace, so far as we may be able, the origin of devotion to S. Joseph. We have said that it was of later growth, but in speaking of the Mother and her Child we have implied all along that in germ it had existed from the first. How indeed could it be otherwise, if, as we have seen, the Church is a type of Mary, just as Mary is of the Church. Could Mary have forgotten Joseph her Spouse, the Foster-Father of her Child? If not, then must the Church have learnt from her lips the true dignity and position of S. Joseph, and gathered from her heart deep feelings of love and devotion to him. Surely we can have no doubt of this, since Mary was left by her Son to be the teacher even of the Apostles and of the infant Church. Still, as we have pointed out at considerable length, the very duties of the Church towards the Child required, not indeed the exclusion, but the temporary suppression of all other feelings. Nor can we argue from the early establishment of Mary's true position in the Church's doctrinal and devotional system that a like privilege was extended to S. Joseph; for we saw that the doctrine of the Divine Maternity was the safeguard of the Godhead of her Son, whereas until belief in His Godhead had been firmly rooted into the sense of the faithful, devotion to an earthly father, foster-father though he might be, might have overshadowed the true Paternity of His Father who was in heaven.* And yet we meet with anticipations, as it were, of this devotion scattered here and there in the early Church, and distinct and numerous enough to convince us that although unexpressed by the general voice of the Church, it lay ever pent up in the silence of her heart. And it is no doubt to these anticipations of her later practice that the Apostolic Decree alludes in the words already quoted, although, if we mistake not, the Holy Father intends to refer to the Church's implicit

---

* S. Bernardine of Sienna, Serm. de S. Josepho.

rather than explicit recognition of S. Joseph's position in the heavenly Hierarchy.

In looking for any early indications of the Church's devotion to the Foster-Father of our Lord, our eyes naturally turn first of all to the East, and especially to those countries in which recollections of the Sacred Infancy and of the Holy Family may be supposed to have been more vividly preserved. Nor are we altogether disappointed, for it seems not improbable, according to Papebroeck, that the traditional recollection of S. Joseph's stay in Egypt had led to his veneration and the celebration of his festival amongst the Copts, even before S. Athanasius sent missionaries in the fourth century to instruct the Abyssinian nation in the rites of the Church of Alexandria.* So, too, among the Christians of Syria, as there is nothing to fix the antiquity of the *cultus* of S. Joseph, we may not unfairly conclude that it has existed from time immemorial. In the Greek Church also it is undoubtedly of great antiquity, as may be gathered from its menologies and hymns, and from the ancient custom of taking the name of Joseph, to which the Bollandists allude, and of which we find traces even in the West at an early period. But it was upon the mysterious mountain of Carmel, with its grand old traditions stretching back through well-nigh nine centuries of the Written Law,—upon Carmel, where the schools of the prophets had anticipated the ascetic life of the New Law,—upon Carmel where Elias the Prophet had seen the little cloud rise out of the sea, no bigger than the " foot of a man," which first spread over the whole heavens, and then fell down in a great rain upon the thirsty earth, fit type of her who is herself the " decor Carmeli," and the Mercy-Cloud of God,—upon Carmel, to which the Christians of the infant Church seem to have fled for refuge, and where, in the firm rock of the memory of Elias, they laid the first living stones of the temple of Mary's worship,—it was even there, upon beautiful " Carmel by the Sea," that the flame of devotion to S. Joseph was chiefly, although secretly, nourished and maintained, until the moment came, in God's good Providence, that it should be carried forth from the East to the West, in order to warm the whole world into greater love to Jesus and to Mary. And when was it that that moment came ? When was it that the flame of devotion to S. Joseph was no longer to be confined to the top of Carmel, or to send forth fitful sparks in the far distant East, but to shine forth bright and clear as a beacon

---

* Acta Bollandiana Vindicata, art. 10, sect. 5, quoted by Vallejo.

to all mankind? When was it that the Third Person of the " Earthly Trinity " was to be manifested to the eyes of men? When was it that the third aisle of the great Mystical Temple of the Living God was to rise up from its foundations under the patronage of the Foster-Father of the Son of Mary? It was just at the time, (oh, the marvellous harmony of the Spirit's workings!) it was just at the time when the Church had, as it were, completed the long series of her doctrines concerning the Real Body of her Lord, and was about to turn to those which related to His Mystical Body; it was just at the time when she was about to erect the High Altar of her Sanctuary, of which we have spoken above; it was even then that S. Joseph passed from the East to the West, from Carmel into Europe, bearing the Holy Child Jesus in his arms, with our Lady of Mount Carmel adoring at His side. It was in the Pontificate of the third Honorius, when outwardly, perhaps, even to the eyes of men the Church might have seemed falling into ruin; nay, as it had actually appeared to be falling to his predecessor Innocent III., as we learn from the vision in which he saw its roof mysteriously supported by S. Francis and S. Dominic; it was then that devotion to S. Joseph began to be spread slowly in the West by the Brethren of our Lady of Mount Carmel, whom she herself in vision had commanded the Supreme Pontiff solemnly to recognize and approve.* It was Mary's doing, for all graces flow through her blessed hands, but now she had brought Joseph with her; and lo! before half a century had passed away, the solemn feast and office of the Blessed Sacrament had been established in the Church, and yet a little while, and the devotion to S. Joseph had passed from the Order of Mount Carmel to the children of S. Francis and S. Dominic. " It is to the ancient Carmelites," says Pope Benedict XIV., " that, according to the *common* opinion of learned writers, we ought to ascribe the rapid spread from East to West of the laudable custom of honouring S. Joseph with peculiar devotion."† So, too, the Bollandists, whom Tillemont cites approvingly, seem to favour the opinion that the Carmelites introduced the " cultus " and the Feast of the

---

* Rom. Brev. Lessons of Second Nocturn, Feast of Our Lady of Mount Carmel (July xvi.). The Fourth Council of Lateran, which declared that in the Holy Eucharist " the bread is *transubstantiated* into the Body of Christ, and the wine into His Blood, by divine power," was held in 1215. A year after this (1216) Honorius III. ascended the Pontifical Throne, and only seven years before (1208) B. Juliana of Mont-Cornillon had been favoured with her mysterious vision, which afterwards moved Urban IV. to establish the Feast of the B. Sacrament in 1264.

† De Beatif. et Canoniz., lib. iv. part ii. chap. xx. n. 17.

Holy Patriarch from the East; and that from the Carmelites it passed to the Franciscans, and so to all the Churches of the West.* We are aware that F. Faber seems to speak of the devotion to S. Joseph as having sprung up directly in the West, rather than as having been borrowed from the East; yet we think the opinion which we have followed the truer and the weightier one, favoured as it is by the high authority of Benedict XIV. and the Bollandists. However, whichever opinion we may adopt, the main point in our argument as to the object for which the "cultus" of S. Joseph first joined itself in a prominent manner to the adoration of the Son and devotion to the Mother, and as to its intimate connection with the increase of outward worship to the Blessed Sacrament, will not be to any great extent affected.† Its remarkable connection with the Order of Mount Carmel, at a later period, is of course admitted by all. The passage in which F. Faber speaks of the rise of the "cultus" of S. Joseph in the West, is of such singular beauty that, although well known, we cannot refrain from placing it before our readers:—

Beautiful Provence ! it rose up in the west from your delightful land, like the cloud of delicate almond blossom that seems to float and shine between heaven and earth over your fields in spring. It rose from a confraternity in the white city of Avignon, and was cradled by the swift Rhone, that river of martyr memories that runs by Lyons, Orange, Vienna, and Arles, and flows into the same sea that laves the shores of Palestine. The land which the contemplative Magdalen had consecrated by her hermit life, and where the songs of Martha's school of virgins had been heard praising God, and where Lazarus had worn a mitre instead of a grave-cloth ; it was there that he, who was so marvellously Mary and Martha combined, first received the glory of his devotion. Then it spread over the Church.‡

But S. Joseph had another mission still. He had come, at Mary's bidding, not only to enthrone the Holy Child in His Own Sweet Sacrament of Love, by obtaining for It the more solemn outward worship of the Church, but also to throw the protection of his mantle over the Mystical Body of Mary's

---

* Ad Diem 19 Martii. Tillemont, i. 79.

† Even if we accept F. Faber's view, the first outward manifestation of devotion to S. Joseph in the West will still be connected with the wants of the Mystical Body during the residence of the Popes at Avignon, and as a safeguard against the schism of the West, and the dangers of modern times, of which we are about to speak. But as we have said, the *communis eruditorum sententia*, to which Bened. XIV. alludes, is in favour of the opposite view.

‡ "Blessed Sacrament," book ii. sect. v. In a note to this passage F. Faber alludes to the opinion which we have ourselves followed.

Son, in its hour of danger. He had come, as F. Faber tells us, " when times were dark, and calamities were rife." In 1264 the Feast of the Blessed Sacrament had been established, in 1378 the great schism of the West began, and between these two dates there had been the captivity of Avignon. Then came rough, evil days, when men strove to rend the seamless garment of Christ, and to tear asunder the members of His Mystical Body from their earthly Head, by setting up false Popes in the chair of S. Peter, but although men saw it not, the mantle of S. Joseph was over all. Even long before the storm broke out, devotion to him, as we have seen, had been slowly but surely growing. Albert the Great, the teacher of S. Thomas, the doctor of the Blessed Sacrament, had himself, it is said, composed an office in his honour; and before his time, Brother Bartholomew, of Trent, another Dominican, had written his biography. Then God raised up Gerson, the Chancellor of the University of Paris, to be the doctor and champion of the devotion, and in season and out of season, through good report and evil report, to spread it ever more and more. From him we learn that the schism itself had but added to its growth. Then in 1399, the general chapter of the Franciscan Order established a feast in honour of the Holy Patriarch, and in 1414 the Council of Constance was held, in one of the sessions of which (1416) Gerson proposed special devotion to S. Joseph as a beacon-light to the Church and to the world, and as a most efficacious means of bringing about a total reformation of the morals of mankind. Before the legates of the Holy See, more than twenty cardinals, two hundred bishops, and many doctors and theologians, he argued that this great saint, having been the guardian and instructor of Jesus Christ, acts in the same capacity to His whole Mystical Body, and that the only way to give back the Church to one husband, to one true supreme Pontiff, the Vicegerent of Christ, was to have recourse to the merits of Mary, and the intercession of Joseph, who, when he pleads with his Foster-Son, commands rather than entreats.* His words were listened to; the devotion spread wider and wider; and yet another year and peace was restored to the Church, although the full manifestation of the Patronage of S. Joseph was not to take place at Constance. Time went on ; heresy took the place of schism, with its still more deadly weapons of destruction, and then God raised up for the devotion

---

* Ita Mariæ meritis et intercessione tanti tamque potentis imperiosi Josephi, et si fas est dicere, quodam jure jubentis, Ecclesia reddatur unico viro, et certo Summo Pontifici, Sponso suo vice Christi.

a new saint and champion in S. Teresa, a new missionary in S. Francis de Sales. The hearts of the children were turned to their fathers, and the old spirit of devotion to S. Joseph lived again with a new life in the peaceful retreats of Carmel. It was caught up by every order in the Church, while at the same time it began to leaven the popular devotions of the faithful. Whole nations were torn away from the Church's bosom; but S. Joseph took up the Holy Child in his arms, and, with Mary by his side, went away into far distant heathen lands, into other Egypts, into a newly-discovered world, and, as of old, the idols fell upon their faces, and new kingdoms were won to Christ. India, China, and Japan, Mexico and Peru, Canada, North America, and the islands of the sea, all alike have been evangelised by the Foster-Father of Mary's Child. S. Joseph becomes the great missionary and apostle of modern times.*

" The contemplative," says F. Faber, " took up the devotion and fed upon it : the active laid hold of it, and nursed the sick and fed the hungry in its name. The working people fastened on it ; for both the Saint and the devotion were of them. The young were drawn to it, and it made them pure ; the aged rested on it, for it made them peaceful. S. Sulpice took it up, and it became the spirit of the secular clergy : and when the great Society of Jesus had taken refuge in the S. Heart, and the Fathers of the S. Heart were keeping their lamps burning ready for the resurrection of the Society, devotion to S. Joseph was their stay and consolation, and they cast the seeds of a new devotion to the Heart of Joseph, which will some day flourish and abound. So it gathered into itself orders and congregations, high and low, young and old, ecclesiastical and lay, schools and confraternities, hospitals, orphanages, and penitentiaries, everywhere holding up Jesus, everywhere hand in hand with Mary, everywhere the refreshing shadow of the Eternal Father. Then when it had filled Europe with its odour, it went over the Atlantic, plunged into the damp umbrage of the backwoods, embraced all Canada, became a mighty missionary power, and tens of thousands of savages filled the forests and the rolling prairies at sundown with hymns to S. Joseph, the praises of the Foster-Father of our Lord." †

And all the while, as the devotion grew, the Church herself had blessed its growth with indulgences and other spiritual favours, and by establishing new festivals in honour of S. Joseph. Thus to the Feast on which his memory is celebrated, she added that of his Espousals, the origin of which

---

* Most appropriately therefore has S. Joseph been chosen as the Patron of our new Missionary College, which we trust will not only one day become a mighty instrument in his hands for the conversion of the heathen, but will also draw down countless blessings upon England.

† " Blessed Sacrament," book ii. sec. v.

is also bound up with the labours of his faithful Gerson, and
to these again in later times the Festival of his Patronage.
And now in our own days it has fallen to the lot of Mary's
chosen Pontiff to crown the desire of centuries, as well as the
wishes of all the faithful, scattered through all the nations of
the world, by solemnly recognizing and proclaiming the Spouse
of Mary and Foster-Father of Jesus to be the protector of His
whole Body Mystical, the Patron of the Universal Church.
Thus the true position of the Third Person of the earthly
Trinity stands clearly marked out before the eyes of men.
The fair proportions of the third aisle of God's Mystical Temple
are distinctly seen.   From the solemn approval of the order
of our Lady of Mount Carmel to our own days, from the
Council of Constance to the Council of the Vatican, what a
marvellous interweaving and blending together of doctrine
and devotion, of devotion and doctrine !   What a variety in
unity !   What a unity in ever-varying change !   What a marvellous reproduction in the history of the Church of the life
of S. Joseph in the Holy Family upon earth !   Were we not
then right in saying, that both the position held by the Foster-
Father of our Lord in the outward worship of the Church,
and his relation to the Mystical Body of Christ correspond
with the position which he once held in the Holy Family as
well as with his relation to Christ's Real Body, in the days of
His infancy?   In the early ages of the Church S. Joseph
guards the great doctrines of the Incarnation and of the Divine
Maternity, by keeping in the background, until the Godhead
of the Holy Child and the virginity of His Blessed Mother had
been fully acknowledged and worshipped by mankind.   But
when no injury can be done to the Child or His Mother by
his own more prominent manifestation, and when Christ's
Mystical Body is in danger and has to be carried, so to speak,
into Egypt again and again ; then it is that S. Joseph, as the
true Foster-Father of Jesus and Guardian of Mary, presses forward, and throws his mantle over the Church, which is alike
the Body of Christ and the type of His Virgin Mother.   Well
indeed may the Church herself sing,—

Cœlitum Joseph decus, atque *nostræ*
Certa spes vitæ, columenque mundi,
Quas tibi læti canimus, benignus
Suscipe laudes.

Te Sator rerum statuit pudicæ
Virginis Sponsum, voluitque Verbi
Te patrem dici, dedit et ministrum
Esse salutis.

II. Again, even from the very imperfect sketch which we have given of the rise and growth of devotion to S. Joseph, it is evident that it took possession of the hearts of the faithful just in those ages, for which it is best adapted. Still we may dwell upon this second harmony for a few moments longer, looking at it from a somewhat different point of view. What has been the spirit uppermost in the minds of men during the later ages of the Church? Whence have the persecutions of the Church arisen? Surely the spirit with which she has had to struggle from the thirteenth century, and even earlier, down to our own times has been resistance to her own spiritual authority, as the Mystical Body of Christ. Surely the persecutions from which she has had to suffer have come, not from heathen tyrants, but from the corruption and apostacy of Christendom. Thus we find this evil spirit manifesting itself first of all in schism, in the West as well as in the East; then in heresies such as Protestantism and Jansenism; and last of all in the revolution of these latter days, which, if such a spirit could be embodied at all, may be called the embodiment of the spirit of lawlessness and antichrist. Now how admirably opposed to all this is the spirit of S. Joseph, the great pattern of humility, the Saint of the Holy Family, and of the hidden life! How beautifully is each advance of this evil spirit met, by an advance of devotion to S. Joseph! It was in the schism of the West, as Gerson tells us, that this devotion gathered strength; it grew stronger still in time of heresy, as we know from the lives of S. Teresa, and S. Francis de Sales; it is strongest of all now at this very moment, when the revolution has seized the Holy City, and is holding the Vicar of Christ a prisoner in the Vatican. Let the recent Decree of our most Holy Father be our witness. And so too what better means could God the Holy Ghost have chosen to heal the wounds of Christendom? What better safeguard could He have given the Church against the persecution of excommunicated monarchs and apostate nations, than by knitting together the members of the Church into closer communion with their Supreme Head and Father upon earth, under the patronage of the Foster-Father of our Lord? Yet has not this been the great work of the Spirit of God in these latter ages? And has not the definition of the Infallibility of the Roman Pontiff been followed almost immediately by the proclamation of the Patronage of S. Joseph? And so too devotion to S. Joseph has brought with it a closer contemplation of the sacred Humanity of Jesus, and of the Hidden Life of the Holy Family, which the spirit of lawlessness and antichrist is ever seeking to dissolve. Hence to the "Cultus" of S. Joseph as well as to greater outward devotion to the B. Sacrament is to be ascribed the great increase of every kind of devotion in later times to each member of Christ's glorified Human Body, and to the Holy Family itself; hence also the multiplication of confraternities.of the Holy Family in the large cities and towns of Christendom.

III. Lastly, we may notice, although very briefly, how the growth of this devotion to S. Joseph has been in harmony with the hidden character of the Saint himself. For centuries it was a hidden devotion, yet even since the time of its manifestation how hidden has been its growth! We may illustrate this by the one example of his Patronage.* When Gerson proposed it to the Universal Church at Constance, who would have thought that more than four centuries must pass away before the Church would openly and solemnly proclaim S. Joseph to be her patron? All the while she has kept the knowledge of his sure patronage hidden in her heart, suffering indeed her children freely to rejoice in it; but it is only now in our own day that she has proclaimed it openly to the world in immediate connection with herself. Yet although the growth of devotion to S. Joseph has been hidden, how magnificent is the openness of its reward! After centuries of waiting, there arises at last from all nations and kindreds and peoples, and tribes and tongues, the prayer of the Universal Church to the Supreme Pontiff, the universal Father, the representative of S. Joseph upon earth, for this new honour for the Foster-Father of our Lord, and the prayer is heard. " He who humbleth himself shall be exalted." *Qui custos est Domini sui glorificabitur.*

And what shall the end of these things be? "What is it that hath been? the same that shall be, for behold it hath already gone before in the ages that have been before us." As at Constance, so now once again at Rome, peace will be given to the Church, and the common Father of the faithful will rule over the evening of her life on earth under the more manifest patronage of S. Joseph, who is himself the shadow of the Eternal Father, "of whom all fatherhood in heaven and on earth is named."

---

* For further illustration of this thought we may refer our readers to the "Month of S. Joseph" (Philp, London), recently edited by F. Mackey, O.P., with an Introductory Letter by his Lordship the Bishop of Birmingham, which we regret we had not an opportunity of seeing before this article was sent to the press.

Art. IX.—PARIS AND FRANCE.

Le Père Duchêne. 10 Germinal, an 79. Imprimerie Sornet, Rue du
Croissart, 16 : Paris.

WE live in a world of which good part appears to have
taken leave of its senses, and the area of anarchy tends
to extend. By a phrase quite natural and ordinary, in the circumstances of the case, and therefore possibly destined to be
one of the terrible proverbs of history, a correspondent of the
Times described the state of Paris three weeks ago. " Paris,"
he said, with an unaffected and sublime simplicity, " resembles
a vast madhouse." Yet the madmen were then hardly at large,
and had not begun to act on their hallucinations. They have
since, wherever their power extends, restricted, previously to
abolishing, the worship of God, and they are exhibiting a degree
of courage, skill, and energy in killing their neighbours of which
they gave no sign against the public enemy. Again and again,
during the seven months that have elapsed since the capitulation of Sedan, has the state of France appeared to reach its
lowest depth, but in the lowest depth a lower deep still opened
wide, and threatens yet to yawn down to the gates of hell.
For, as Mr. Carlyle wrote of "the Improvised Commune"
of 1792—"The dead cerements are rent into cobwebs; and
she fronts you in that terrible strength of Nature, which
no man has measured, which goes down to madness and
Tophet: see now how you will deal with her." It is not
certainly easy to see how Paris will be dealt with now. In
1792, the Germans were beyond the Vosges, and the aristo-
crats were far away from Versailles. But in 1871 as we
contemplate M. Thiers besieging the Parisians in Paris with
the guns of all his own forts except one turned against him or
in Prussian occupation—as we conceive the late Fenian
Generalissimo Cluseret directing from the ministry of war
where Carnot organized victory, whence Clarke went to be
Governor-General of Prussia, in which Niel compounded the
brittle army of the Second Empire ; as we conceive this Adju-
tant-General of Mr. James Stephens and hero of Mr. Disraeli
directing a not ineffectual resistance on the part of the army of
Paris to the army of Versailles, commanded by the valiant and
respectable Marshal MacMahon—when we hear that Mont

Valérien, whose principal feat during the first siege was the destruction of the exquisite Palace of St. Cloud, has now, in the course of the second, incidentally shelled the Arc de Triomphe—finally, when we figure the German enemy serenely surveying from St. Denis the gathering of all the elements of this mysterious and tremendous storm of doom—we are tempted to think that there never was such a complete exemplification of the action of the Devil in history. The elaborate and complex irony of the situation ; the tragedy that at its most awful pitch bursts into farce of a preternatural and callous grotesqueness ; the furibund levity of this accomplished population, which, between two fires, sings and dances, revels and blasphemes, spoils the altar of its chalice and flings it down to dance the can-can, wheels like an old crow at the sight of a Prussian gun, and rushes like a tiger at a battery, if only there be Frenchmen behind it—when we contemplate all this, and the unsteadiness of all that is, and the uncertainty of all that is to be, so that one supposes we must have at last arrived at a pass in which the wisest are outwitted, in which neither M. Thiers nor Prince Bismarck sees a yard farther than the rest of the world, in which God alone knows His own will and His own way—our emotions are manifold ; but, after all, we feel that we have not learned the Catholic Catechism in vain, and that the Vicar of Christ has not condemned and anathematized the spirit possessing the modern world, of which Paris has long been the chosen see, in extravagant or indefinite terms.

As yet, only one volcano flames ; but those who have skilled ears may note the subterranean rumblings of the grand international solidarity. The Secret Societies are at work throughout Europe ; and we can hardly suppose that many days will elapse before we hear of another revolution attempted, if not accomplished. Garibaldi will not go to Paris, for he has higher work in hand ; but he names Dombrowski, whose military talents he holds in much esteem. Cluseret, whose authority is now spoken of as *L'Empire Cluseret,* holds the key to every Secret Society on the globe, from the Marianne to the Phœnix. The gravity of the crisis is very curiously intimated in the fact lately announced, that the *fons et mater* of all the Secret Societies, even Freemasonry, has at last cast aside its mask—that of being merely an association of jolly good fellows, altogether given to charity and conviviality, with just a fantastic perfume of mystery and a little legerdemain—and has actually offered to make peace between the Commune and M. Thiers. But the peace that is to come will, we fear, only come through war beyond the walls of Paris, beyond the walls and moats of France itself. *Ca ira* is again the anthem of the hour, and

who shall tell how far, indeed, it will go, when mountain
answers mountain? For Paris is only the head-quarters of the
Revolution, whose energies have long been employed in corrod-
ing the great supports and sanctions of civil and religious
society throughout Central and Southern Europe. Belgium,
or at least Brussels, will, it is supposed by those who ought to
know, promptly follow suit; and Signor Mazzini three months
ago bade farewell to his friends in England, and betook himself
to Rome, there to consummate the grand ambition of his life
—to destroy at once the Italian monarchy and the Papacy,
and to found on the Capitol the new religion, "which is
destined to give life to the world in the future."* The
Italian Kingdom will not indeed long survive the French Empire,
though it is hardly from Signor Mazzini that it will receive
its death-blow—but the days of the Papacy are destined to
be numbered not by men but by angels. Our sad days however swarm with events, and the events become more and more
portentous; but the issue exquisitely and terribly definite. It
will take a great deal of prayer and fasting, and also a good
deal of blood and iron, to reduce to order the enemies of God
and man, who are now openly devastating or secretly under-
mining Christendom. But as the struggle comes closer, and
becomes more desperate, there is a certain satisfaction in
the sense that it also becomes more open. The time when the
apostles and heroes of the Revolution only ventured to strike
terror by the occasional use of the "sacred dagger," or by
flinging an Orsini bomb into a harmless crowd on the chance
of killing some one of their enemies, is, at all events, past.
They begin to feel strong enough to act in the light of day.
The hour has even come when they must disclose their designs,
and take the risk of realizing them, or die the death due to men
who know not how to obey Divine or human laws. The crisis
too has come when good men must combine to give them their
deserts. The day of half-knowledge, maudlin sympathy, and
pusillanimous patience is past. The Revolution cannot now
pretend that it is conspiring merely against the personal rule of
Napoleon, or the pressure of Austria on Italy, or the misgovern-
ment of this or that Bourbon prince, or even the Pope's civil
sovereignty. It is on the Church of God and civil society that
it wages open war, with the aid of the most criminal and
ignorant classes of the populace; and it is provoking a contest
so close, so desperate, and so thorough, that we cannot but

---

* *See* Mazzini's Address to the Roman People, of Dec., 1866 quoted in
the DUBLIN REVIEW, Jan. 1867, p. 210 ; and his Letter in the *Fortnightly
Review* of last January.

doubt the result will be a long period of peace upon earth among men of good will.

Evidently much, though by no means all, depends upon the result of the contest which appears to be immediately imminent between the army of Marshal MacMahon and the National Guard of Paris. M. Thiers has been, in this country, almost universally censured for the want of vigour in his policy, which has allowed the Reds to gain such vantage ground in Paris. It may be that he has shrunk as long as possible from risking his popularity by making himself responsible for a massacre far exceeding the *coup d'état*, or even the days of June 1848 in its exigencies of bloodshed. It may be that his councils have no definite object, no moral inspiration, and that they lag behind instead of forecasting events. His words certainly grow of more and more uncertain sound. Much allowance is nevertheless due to a man of his age called upon to cope with such a catastrophe, and who is, after all, the only man in France qualified by his capacity, experience, and general influence to assume the head of the Executive Power at this moment. To the character of his statesmanship during the reign of King Louis Philippe, and towards many of his peculiar views of French policy, we feel an antipathy; but it is impossible not to honour the wonderful, unceasing, unwearied energy, devotion, and resource which he has exhibited in the service of his country during the last six months, in the special mission which he undertook to the Courts of Florence, Vienna, St. Petersburg, and St. James's; in his subsequent management of the negotiations for peace; and in his conduct of affairs in so far as he has had power, especially in the character of his appointments, ever since. In the very serious question whether he should have attacked the Commune sooner than he has done, we hold that he is absolutely absolved by the supreme consideration of military prudence.

When Paris first revolted against his government, he did not know whether he had an army on which he could rely to fight. The majority of the soldiers of the line actually in Paris as yet had chosen to fraternize instead; and as to the temper of the troops at Versailles, M. Thiers was obliged to learn what it was from their officers, and to wait, under whatever misconception, until they felt they had got their men well in hand again. Nor were officers, however personally brave, who were aware that two generals had been publicly killed in Paris, and that in the very ranks soldiers had fired on their captains in the name of the Commune, likely in a few days to feel quite sure of their control of that very volatile though energetic essence, *esprit de corps.* But even when it was found that the army of Versailles

2 F 2

would really fire upon and stand fire from the army of Paris,
and even now, when a decisive movement is apparently about
to be attempted, it is extremely doubtful whether the Government has an adequate force for the task which it is obliged to
undertake. There is no operation in the whole art of war
which a wise general so little likes as the taking of a town
defended from street to street by a fighting population. The
Germans showed their usual wisdom in reducing Paris by
hunger; and if it were possible for Marshal MacMahon to
follow their example in this particular, it is the course no doubt
which his military judgment would approve. But in Paris now-
a-days, the Commune would be sure to initiate a process of
starvation by selection, beginning with the priests they hold in
prison. In 1848, General Cavaignac, after three days' hard
fighting, crushed the first great revolt of the Red Republicans,
He had 50,000 troops of the line, admirably commanded and
absolutely stanch. The National Guard of Paris, a very different force from what it is now, was, with scant exceptions,
on his side. The National Guard of the surrounding departments marched in aid. The Reds had no artillery, no Chasse-
pôts; had not been skilfully and continuously drilled for six
months before as their two hundred battalions have now been,
but rushed from their workshops in their blouses, robbed
a gunsmith's shop, or surprised a guard-house to get weapons;
they had possession of none of the grand points of vantage,
but on a sudden built in a scramble barricades how and where
they could. Their barricades were battered with artillery, to
which they had no means of replying; the houses which they
occupied were mined and blown up. But these Red Republicans, then comparatively a very small section of the population of Paris, were only beaten inch by inch, and with frightful
losses on the part of the army; for it is easy to fancy that
soldiers fighting in a street, with a barricade before, and houses
on each side, occupied by screened marksmen, are rather
damaged than served by the instinct of discipline, which especially in a street leads them to hold together. When it was
all over, General Cavaignac, who was a soldier skilled in his
art, and proud of his vocation, assumed no tone of triumph,
but, on the contrary, as if he feared that his conduct might be
drawn into a precedent, and so mislead another general placed
in similar circumstances, expressly excused himself for not
having retired from Paris, and cut the communications of the
insurgents, on the score that he had a very great preponderance
of military force, and that he could completely rely upon it.
But it was only when the very ground was mined under their
feet, and when the troops had burned upwards of two million

of cartridges, that the insurgents surrendered. The task which awaits the Duc de Magenta appears to be at least ten times more formidable than that which Cavaignac, Bedeau, and Lamoricière with such difficulty achieved. The Commune has absolute control of Paris. It holds several of the forts. It holds the entire inner line of defence prepared against the Prussians. It has erected a system of barricades around the peculiar precinct of its power, solid works of military engineering, capable of carrying artillery, and tunnelled so as to allow of a fire sweeping the level of the street. It has artillery and artillerymen, and it commands that half of the garrison of Paris which knows Paris as its home, its country, its religion, almost its heaven. The siege was a long spell of time for such a master of drill as Trochu to have at his command ; and the army of the Commune has all the drill that could be given to it in that time by eager and skilful officers. No soldier at least will venture to say that the task of Marshal MacMahon is a light one. It may be made easy by the sudden prostration of manly spirit which has sometimes given the Prussians snatch victories. But if the Reds of 1871 fight as the Reds of 1848 fought, Paris may be laid in ashes slaked by blood before they shall be subdued.

It is almost a habit of thought in this country at the present time to seek the causes of the paralysed and ruined condition of France in the system of government pursued by the Emperor during the twenty years in which he held sway. It was not our wont, when he stood at the pinnacle of his power, to speak of his authority or policy with any very exuberant respect. His name was to us, ever since he went into Italy in 1859, a hissing and a reproach, crowned with a certain and inevitable curse. If he were to be judged only by what he destroyed and by what he created, or suffered to come into being in that most miserable country, sinister indeed would be the aspect of his figure in history. After all, he is—he can never escape from the shame nor they from the scandal—the true Liberator of Italy. Italy did *not* make itself. *He* made Italy—fought Austria for it, gave it Lombardy, helped it to take the Duchies and the Legations, allowed it to seize the Two Sicilies, counselled it how to get 'the Marches, held Venice in trust for it, and slipped the keys of Rome into its hand. He ruined himself and his country through entangling his policy with its cause, and he holds the place that is his due in the memory of that grateful nation. He made Italy; and (it was a necessary corollary to the making of Italy, the ruin of Austria being a common factor to the two operations) he made Germany, which had also been a geographical expression previously to his reign. But it is at least due to

fallen—perhaps we should borrow Mr. Grattan's crafty phrase
regarding the Bourbons, and "rather say to interrupted
greatness," to suggest that, after all, Napoleon III. did not
make Paris or the populace of Paris. On the contrary, it was,
until lately, admitted by many who sincerely opposed his
internal method of administration, or the general line of his
foreign policy, that his rule, at least, gave great guarantees
against a Red Revolution; that his rebuilding of Paris had
rendered the barricade as obsolete as the portcullis; and that
there was at least this virtue in the name of Napoleon, that it
exercised such a spell over the French soldier's mind, as checked
the weak-kneed tendency to fraternise with rabble in arms
against public order. But the populace of Paris is to-day what
it was when Voltaire characterized it as half-tiger, half-monkey;
and as when he invoked, with all his powers of verse and prose,
the Prussian sword and the Prussian rod to reduce it to good
behaviour. Surely there is not another populace on the face
of the earth so brilliantly and inconsequently idiotic as this,
whose last act on the eve of the Prussian siege was to inaugurate
a statue to Voltaire with enthusiasm and effusion! But that
populace is what it was in June, 1848, and in September, 1792,
loving blood, choosing as its own the colour of blood, calling
its reign Terror, and fraternal after the fashion of Cain. May
it prove to be as amenable to that dose of grape-shot which
Marshal de Broglie declared was the true medicine for its mala-
dies in 1789, and which at last got administered with such a happy
effect on one of the two days which alone remain in the memory
of men of the calendar to which they belonged, the 13th
Vendémiaire and the 18th Brumaire! Napoleon III. no
more produced the constituents of the Commune of 1871
than Louis XVI. improvised the elements of the Commune of
1792.

Whether the system of the Imperial government based
itself broadly enough, irrespectively of party, on the talents,
virtues, and merits of Frenchmen in general, is a question the
discussion of which will perhaps much more perplex the
historian, when he proceeds hereafter to account for the
collapse of the Empire. But their contemporaries are bound
to acknowledge the fact that government *à l'Anglaise* and
especially opposition *à l'Anglaise* are not as yet, if they ever
shall be, according to the genius of the French. It may be not
unfairly said of this great nation, that no opposition is regarded by them as real, unless it goes to the very bottom
of things and then overflows with inextinguishable, but far
from inexpressible indignation at what it finds there. Was,
—may we dare to ask in sad and simple earnest,—M.

Thiers or M. Berryer, M. de Montalembert or M. Favre, a person for whom the Emperor could have sent at any period of his reign with the same unhesitating trust as Queen Victoria would send for Mr. Disraeli or Lord Carnarvon, if Mr. Gladstone experienced any difficulty in conducting her government? These eminent persons had all taken the oath of allegiance to the Emperor, but with mental reservations, which did not prevent them from being at heart irreconcilable to the Empire, and from always hoping that it would come to a sudden end in favour of—no matter what. The Orleanist did not hope for the coming of the Comte de Paris, or the Legitimist for the reign of King Henry, or even the Republican for the Republic, with half the longing that they all felt when they hoped for the fall of the Empire. If Ireland were to elect thirty or forty Fenians, and if many of them happened to be persons of eminent talents, great skill in public affairs, unspotted integrity, and wide-spread influence,—that they differed among themselves as to whether Ireland ought to be a Pentarchy, or a Monarchy, or a Republic, or a State of the American Union, but were all agreed on not having British connexion in any form or at any price,—we might be able to realize some conception of the true basis of a French opposition. It is impossible for France, for Frenchmen at large, to evade their responsibility for the government they have had during the last twenty years. All M. Hugo's passion torn to tatters, and the ignoble virulence of Mr. Kinglake's hysterical history will not persuade posterity that Louis Napoleon seized France by the throat like a footpad, and made her his slave in spite of herself. He had, before 1848, twice tried to attain to supreme power in France by surprise, with sufficiently disastrous results. Why, knowing his name, his tradition, his ideas, his avowed ambition, did millions upon millions of Frenchmen vote for him in 1848 that he might be President of the Republic rather that General Cavaignac? Why, but because they knew than General Cavaignac was as true a Republican as Washington, and because it was not in human nature to expect that a Bonaparte, but especially that the author of the *Idées Napoléoniennes* and the prisoner of Ham, should be a true Republican! Why, but because, France then, as now, wanted to get rid of the Republic which had been imposed upon her by Paris as speedily, as decently, and as effectually as she could; and therefore chose, as the readiest way of effecting her purpose without civil war, the Prince who was heir of an Empire as her President! What would the world have understood the American people to mean if, in 1812, they had elected the then Prince of Wales, or Duke of York, instead of General Jackson, as their President? What

would a British prince have understood the essential meaning of
the *vox populi* to be in such a case? What would the world,
the French nation, and the Elect of millions himself, understand if the Comte de Paris, or the Duc d'Aumale were now
by plebiscitum appointed at M. Thiers' instance first President of the Third Republic? Do we, then, justify the *coup
d'état?* It is hardly a justification of it to say that we believe it was implicitly conditioned in the election of the Prince
as President; and that it concurred with the expectation and
ambition of the French people was soon and abundantly proved
by the increasing support which his not very hurried assumption of the purple elicited. We remember well M. de Montalembert's opinion at the moment. He was not a Bonapartist.
He loved liberty, honour, and order. But the circumstances
of the time were such, the danger of a Red Revolution was so
imminent, the continuance of the President's authority so seemed
to be the sole mainstay of peaceable government in France,
that he declared, " He who does not support the President is a
bad Frenchman and a worse Catholic." We do not justify the
coup d'état ; but in treating of the affairs of a country where
the *coup d'état* is as much a recognized political process as a
dissolution of Parliament is in England, or a military *pro-
nunciamento* in Spain, and where every party has either effected
or is waiting for its opportunity to achieve a *coup d'état* on its
own account, we cannot affect to feel any too superfluous
horror at this particular one, or pretend to believe that
history will regard the *coup d'état* of December 2nd, 1851,
as of any very different degree of criminality from that, for
example, of September 4th, 1870. But, it may be said, the
President had, in the first case, sworn allegiance to the Constitution. It is true, and it is also true that M. Gambetta
took from time to time one or more oaths of allegiance to the
Emperor which no one in France believed he had the slightest
intention of observing, if he saw a favourable opportunity of
destroying the Empire and the Emperor with it. So did
M. Thiers, M. Berryer, M. Favre, M. Rochefort. Alas, who in
France is unforsworn? Contemplate even the case of the mild
and melancholy Breton, who gave his plan for the deliverance
of Paris and his last will and testament to his attorney together,
and who formed that grand Government of all the talents, all
the virtues, all the idiots and all the rascals—the Government
of the National Defence, the list of whose names reads more
like the list of the Board of a Limited Liability Company got
together in the very last stages of the financial fever of
1866, than like any other list of the names of men that
ever sat round a table together! General Trochu was, as

soldier, as deputy, as Governor of Paris, bound by a triple oath
—and he as a work of supererogation also swore, we have
heard and believe, on the eve of his assumption of the supreme
government, that the Revolution should only reach the Empress-
Regent over his dead body. But when the Revolution punctu-
ally arrived, General Trochu was particularly engaged elsewhere. He did not even take the least precaution for the
protection from outrage of that august and valiant woman,
whose bearing throughout those crashing vicissitudes has
shown that, though not born in the purple, she has the spirit
of a queen as well as the resolute faith of a Catholic and the
innate dignity of a Spaniard.

The capitulation of Sedan is no retribution for the *coup
d'état.* But a great Empire never falls without just and
adequate cause. The Emperor, during the last ten years of his
reign, abandoned first Italy, then the Papacy, then France
itself, to the Revolution. He declared war against Prussia in
the name of "les idées civilisatrices de notre grande Révolution." Thus his foreign policy had become a falsification
of the principles upon which he was raised to supreme power
by the people of France; and yet it did not win to him the
loyalty of the populace of Paris. During this same period,
liberty of the press did not exactly exist in France; but
license of the press did. Blasphemy and obscenity cir-
culated uncontrolled. So long as men of letters contented
themselves with assailing the Divinity of our Lord or decrying
the authority of His Church, with polluting the public mind by
romances and comedies from which Ariosto would have recoiled
with shame, and which Byron would have flung in the fire, they
wrote with their hands quite free. Mr. Burke rather lightly
spoke of the vice of the old French court as a "vice which lost
half its evil in losing all its grossness." But the vice of modern
French society had become a vice prurient, semi-simious and
sodden, the vice of a race which had wasted down to the lees of
life, a vice which lost some of its danger through the disgust it
inspired, and which had not even the vigour to be gross. *Cor-
ruptio optimi pessima!* The "most Christian nation" had all but
ceased to fulfil the Divine command to "increase and multiply."
In its letters, in its art, in the very aspect of its chief city, it
had fallen into a condition which angels and devils might contrast with the state of Rome in the time of Tiberius, but which
certainly did not exist elsewhere among men. It is proof
enough of this to contrast the moral character of the fashionable
novel of the day or the most successful play of the day in Paris
and in London at any time during the last twenty years; and
yet London is no example to the universe. Meantime the

Emperor looked on and made no sign. Herein his policy was
in absolute opposition to that of his uncle. It is a suggestive
fact that the works of Voltaire and Rousseau were not reprinted
in France during the whole course of the reign of Napoleon I.
He knew by profound experience what Mr. Burke had foreseen, that it was " their licentious philosophy which had helped
to bring on their ruin." He once said that Rousseau was the
real author of the Revolution, and he said it with a deep scorn
of both Rousseau and the Revolution. When a romance not
more vile, we venture to assume, than hundreds that have
been published in Paris of late years, got itself into print under
the First Empire, Napoleon sent for the book, read it, became
persuaded or pretended to believe that the man who wrote anything so impure must be insane, and had him straightway shut
up in a lunatic asylum, *pour encourager les autres.* We
remember, on the other hand, to have read of a lady of rank
appearing in the attire of Salambo at a fancy ball in the
Tuileries, under the Second Empire. As the crapulous obscenity
of Rousseau thus once more spread itself through one considerable region of popular literature, so the cold sarcastic scepticism, the utter dereliction of Faith, the almost demonic hatred
of God and the things of God, which belonged to the mind of
Voltaire, seemed to have arisen again, and entered, and imbued,
and possessed the mind of another generation. It remains for
Red Paris to erect as its own monument a statue to Rousseau
beside that of Voltaire. They have very effectually brought
her to what she is. Under the Second Empire, it is not too
much to say, that blasphemy and obscenity enjoyed free trade,
and were even the fashion. On the other hand, the publicists,
whom the Imperial censors regarded with the most severe
suspicion, were the apologists and champions of the Catholic
Church. We cannot recall to memory the name of any French
journal that was absolutely suppressed after the proclamation of
the Empire except the *Univers;* nor the name of any French
journalist who was interdicted from writing in any French
journal, except M. Veuillot. Yet it would be impossible, we
venture to say, to produce a line from M. Veuillot's writings
calculated to excite sedition, or lead to a breach of the law.
The Comte de Montalembert was prosecuted when occasion
offered, with a peculiar and relentless animosity. Even after
Republican opinions began to get uttered again with impunity,
Catholic opinions, whether Ultramontane or Liberal, were
restrained by the strictest surveillance of the police. The
Emperor did not even shrink from the fatuity of allowing his
ministers to interdict throughout the Empire the publication of
the great Encyclical of 8th December, 1864. Who could then

have foreseen what an exegetic commentary on the Syllabus
the history of the fall of the Empire was fated so soon to
afford !

But the Empire has fallen, and what follows the Empire?
The authority of M. Thiers is of course exceptional, provisional,
transitional. There is certainly no man in France to whom the
immediate circumstances under which he exercises supreme
authority could be so fraught with the anguish which baulks
clear and constant resolution. The forts of Paris were, he had
fondly hoped, the grand monument of his fame. No foreign
army or group of foreign armies should, he might well have
supposed, while they stood sentry, ever again occupy Paris as
the Russians, and Austrians, and English, and Prussians did in
1814 and 1815. Sedan capitulated ; Metz fell ; still Paris held
the cunning barbarian at bay. But the day came when the new
tricolor of blood and iron, the flag of black and white and red,
flaunted over Valérien's domineering range, while, under the
shelter of its guns, the Uhlans cantered into the fallen city.
M. Thiers, however, had at least succeeded in limiting the occupation to one quarter of the town, and the time to a few days.
He could not save Paris from dishonour ; but he had saved her
from utter humiliation. How often he, of all men, must now
bewail that the German terms were not a great deal harder !
If they had only insisted on disarming and occupying the
whole city, and on blowing up the fortifications ! M. Thiers's
engineers occupy the works just evacuated by the Prussians,
hoping to take his own forts so as to turn their fire upon Paris,
while the guns of the one that he holds take the range of their
shells by that Arc de Triomphe which is the history of the
Consulate and Empire written in stone. Is there an atheist in
the world so stupid as not to see evidence of the most delicate
and distinct design in the great judgment which has befallen
France? But what human heart is there which, contemplating
his position, can fail to feel a profound and terrible pity for the
present ruler of France? Is he in his seventy-fourth year to
be called upon to crush Paris with cannon balls, or to " stew "
her and starve her into submission ? Napoleon was called on
to cure the ills of the Commune in 1795 ; and he unhesitatingly
administered grape-shot with a happy and lasting effect.
Henry IV. besieged Paris, and at last famished it into surrender. Napoleon and Henry of Navarre nevertheless lived to
be the peculiar idols of Paris. But what can M. Thiers hope
except after a few months to lay down his gray hairs in the
grave, after having subjugated and in good part destroyed the
city whose defence had been the chief work of his life.

Nor can we imagine that the Germans will see their advantage in shedding a single further drop of German blood in this quarrel. When Count Bismarck signed the Peace, he did not hide his belief that France would rapidly rally her energies and accumulate and form her force for another desperate duel. It was not without some grave misgiving that he contemplated the difficulties of governing Alsace and Lorraine in the interval. Now, without an effort of his, he finds himself occupying that peculiar attitude of a " benevolent neutral," of which history had hitherto failed to furnish an effective illustration. The Germans are on excellent terms with the Government of Versailles, and on excellent terms with the Commune. The inhabitants of the German zone of occupation know that under the ægis of the *pickelhaub,* Frenchmen may, at all events, sow and sell and build in safety. Thus the animosity engendered by the war evaporates. With what feelings do the people of the ceded provinces now look back and look forward? It is not easy to tell; but certain it is that every month of Civil War in France is as a year of peace gained to Germany. It is true, the payment of the indemnity may be delayed; but Prince Bismarck knows that he holds excellent security for the money, and may possibly see that it is not bad policy to prolong the period for its payment. That eminent person has an excellent knowledge of the history of his country, and he will perhaps recollect that when Prussia had to pay an indemnity of 150 millions of francs to France in 1807, Napoleon was induced by the Czar not merely to extend the time, but to remit some of the amount. It is true, Napoleon doubted if the King of Prussia would be so moderate were he making peace at Paris.

This was the time when Napoleon addressed his Corps Législatif as follows :—" If the House of Brandenbourg, which first conspired against our independence, still reigns, it owes it to the sincere friendship with which the powerful Emperor of the North has inspired me."[*] Prince Bismarck, if he be not belied, has often regretted since Sedan, and may often have cause to regret again, that the House of Brandenbourg, even with the aid of the Czar, could not maintain, and cannot restore, the House of Bonaparte to the throne of France. The conquest of Prussia by Napoleon I. and the overthrow of France by William I. will often, no doubt, be contrasted by future historians; and always, we suspect, to the advantage of France. Prussia was more easily, more rapidly, more completely, and more thoroughly defeated by France in 1806 than France was by Prussia in the late war. Prussia was, in fact, conquered, and accepted the fact that it was conquered, and was governed

---

[*] Correspondance de Napoléon I., tom. xv. p. 498.

as a conquered country without much trouble for a year by an Irish General. If Napoleon had at that time chosen to place his brother Joseph on the throne of Prussia instead of the throne of Spain, it can hardly be doubted he would have found comparatively little difficulty in doing so. But the friendship of the Czar then, as now, was the *præsidium et dulce decus* of the Hohenzollerns. Then, as now, the close accord of policy at the really critical moments of European history has seemed to justify Mr. Urquhart's bizarre, but not the less profound, saying, that after all at bottom Prussia is only Russia plus the P. Such a contrast between Prussia in 1806-7 and France in 1870-1 will, however, at once turn to the disadvantage of France at the moment of the conclusion of Peace. Prussia at once applied herself to the restoration and reorganization of her power. Prussia had no knowledge then, and has hardly any even now, of immortal, civilizing, revolutionary principles, —had not, and has perhaps not even yet, developed the elements capable of sustaining a considerable civil war in her constitution. But France still carries her miserable malady about with her, loudly insisting that it is the one universal cure, and urgent to inoculate all other nations with the *Morbus Gallicus* of '89.

Were even the civil war now raging well ended by the absolute submission of Paris, either on terms or through major force, the reconstitution of solid government in the country is one of the most difficult problems—is perhaps, on the whole, the most difficult that has ever presented itself to the legislative authorities of a civilized nation. There are the conventional three courses open to France, of course—the Constitutional Monarchy, the Empire, and the Republic. But she has tried each of them, and discarded all three, not once merely, but twice over within a period of three generations. The Second Empire has just fallen ; and it is the Third Republic which, at the foot of their official documents, the constituted authorities at present humbly solicit to be so good as to live. But is there life in it, and is it such life as may be the light of men ? Talk of the *coup d'état !* Of all the scandalous and incapable tyrannies that ever was imposed upon France, assuredly the one most disgraceful to her was the Republic which sprung from the scuffle of the 4th of September, and which ultimately resolved itself into the autocracy of M. Gambetta. What, then, did M. Gambetta do ? Any man, great or small, who gets hold of the highly organized administrative machinery of France can do, or at least appear to do, vast works. He has only to issue an order, and it electrifies a great nation. Men spring from the ground ; money floats through the air ; opinion takes its cue ; if he deign to ask them, even

priests pray at ten thousand altars that he may be wisely inspired and have the help of God. Everything is centralized,
all movement is centripetal, and he is at the centre. Frenchmen who hated and despised M. Gambetta obeyed him as they
had obeyed M. de Persigny before him, and as they may have
to obey M. Pyat hereafter, perhaps. Levies and further levies
were summoned by a stroke of his pen, and they came and
were converted into armies. Then the real question arose,
what M. Gambetta could or would do with the power which
France had put into his hands. We believe the answer which
history will give is, that he wasted it and ruined it; that he so
interfered with the strategy of the army before Orleans as to
paralyze its action at a most critical moment; that he so meddled
with Chanzy's plans as to utterly confuse his campaign; and
that he sent Bourbaki towards Belfort without any adequate
consideration of the supplies necessary for his army, when his
success in the enterprise he was ordered to undertake was out
of the question, and when the detachment of his corps deprived
the army of the Loire of its last chance. When the secret papers
of that Government are published, for which purpose we are not
sorry to see the Commune has just appointed a commission, we
believe the documents of the Empire, which, with little sense
of dignity, or, indeed, decency, General Trochu permitted to be
printed while the Prussians were at the gates of Paris, will not
suffer by comparison. Whatever remorse Marshal Lebœuf has
carried with him into his present obscurity can hardly be greater
than that which ought to haunt M. Gambetta. But it may
certainly be pleaded in mitigation of the not very different
judgment which history will pass upon both, that they were, in
some sense, victims of Paris. In each stage of the war, before
the capitulation of Sedan as well as before the Treaty of Versailles, the authorities for the time being committed themselves
to a line of policy, and undertook a course of military operations, not because they were even sound in themselves, not to
say the wisest that could be conceived in the interest of the
French people at large, but because it was absolutely necessary
to propitiate the populace of Paris. Whether Prussia or France
were really the more guilty of devising, plotting, and preci-
pitating the war, is a question not so easily resolved now when
the diplomatic evidence has almost all transpired,* as it was
decided off-hand by English opinion at the commencement of

---

* The lucid and carefully authenticated argument of Scrutator, "Who
is Responsible for the War?" (Rivingtons) has, to our mind, completely
destroyed the theory of the attitude of Prussia almost universally accepted
in England last autumn.

the war. But whenever the Emperor wavered the voice of Paris was for war. Of all the Left only one member, M. Glais Bizoin, voted against it. The alternative to the undertaking of Marshal MacMahon's ill-inspired and fatal march to Sedan, was, in the judgment of the Government of the Empress. Regent, a Paris revolution, and there is no reason, knowing what we do know of the populace of Paris, to doubt that the judgment of that Government was correct. But Marshal Mac-Mahon should have retired rather than undertaken such a movement. It failed. There was a Paris revolution forthwith. Had that march not been attempted, it is possible that there need have been no siege of Paris, whether by Count Moltke or by Marshal MacMahon. But when the movements of the armies of a great nation are dictated, as their ultimate reason, by the consideration of what may be acceptable to the mind of a mob which holds the executive of the country in a sort of chronic custody, what becomes of the State?

The late General Prim, when he was urged to found a Republic in Spain, with great good sense, said, " But you cannot have a Republic in a country where there are no Repub-licans." He did not speak with absolute accuracy, for there are Republicans in Spain—but in Spain, and still more especially in France, they are a minority, violent, not very reputable, amazingly ignorant, and utterly intolerant in the use of power. An individual Republican may generally be singled out from a group of other Frenchmen by his long unkempt hair and beard, his evident scorn of soap, a certain wild look in the eyes which is the outward expression of a chronic explosiveness of character, and an irrepressible tendency to blasphemy. If you inquire into his antecedents, you will discover that they are not very regular; if you sound his knowledge, you will find it is built on news-papers; into his private habits you had better not inquire. The Republicans of France have three times had possession of supreme power. Did a more infamous tyranny ever exist among men than that which Danton, Robespierre, and Marat founded in 1792, that tyranny which extinguished the worship and denied the very existence of God; the symbol of whose authority was the guillotine; under which to be suspected was to be sentenced to death, until at last all true patriots began to suspect and execute each other? What claim on the respect of Frenchmen did the theatrical folly, called a Republic, over which M. de Lamartine presided in 1848, establish—a theatrical folly which, however, did not come to its end without a bloody massacre, of which the object was to establish the right of one party of Republicans to extinguish another? Has the Republic, which M. Gambetta founded in September last, not yet organized disaster enough to satiate the worst enemy of France, if such there be now outside her own frontier? If the French people, the people who really bear the burdens, sustain the honour, and are the state of France—that ancient, once pious, and valiant race, through whom even in these days the *Gesta Dei per Francos* are in some degree continued—if they are to be permitted to have a voice in the form of their future government, can we doubt that they will take the first opportunity that offers of discarding the Republic? If the French people were called upon to vote to-morrow by universal suffrage on the simple issue Monarchy or Republic, can there be a doubt as to what their answer would be? At Paris, even at Versailles, a mere minority is for the time imposing its will on the preponderant majority of the nation; and it succeeds for the time, because the question is not merely Monarchy or Republic, but what Monarchy, and also what Republic?

The name of Napoleon has long had such a hold on the French imagination that we can well conceive those who have the conduct of affairs hesitating to allow the name of the next sovereign of France to be settled by plebiscitum. The policy of all advanced politicians in that country, at present, indeed, appears to be, in the interest of liberty, to prevent as far as possible the people from enjoying self-government. Some exceedingly enlightened Liberals even declare that both the peasantry who are ignorant and the townspeople who are violent, should be interdicted from having any influence in the conduct of public business. If the Emperor were still in adequate vigour of mind and body, and if he so chose, the mere nickname of the "man of Sedan" would hardly have power to prevent his return. But he is in his sixty-fourth year, his health is gravely impaired, his strength of mind had visibly relaxed long before the commencement of the German war. His ignoble abandonment of the Pope, the terrible fate of the Emperor Maximilian, his policy towards Denmark and Poland, the way he was outwitted by M. Bismarck before and after Sadowa, had all contributed to loosen the hold that the Second Empire had had on the loyalty of the French people during the first nine or ten years of its existence. He has lost within a very few years the advisers upon whose counsels he most relied—De Morny, Fould, Walewski, Billault, Thouvenel, Troplong, Niel. The inspired air, the fine form, the masterly will which characterized his public documents have of late somehow faded away. Never did a sovereign speak to a nation as this man once knew how to speak. But of late years only the form was there, and the words had an uncertain sound. The Emperor has repeated his uncle's acts more than once, not without impressing upon the performance a character marked and distinct of his own. But we venture to predict that he will not attempt to repeat the return from Elba. It might not, it probably could not succeed, and then it would only be confounded with the adventures of Strasburg and Boulogne, which history will excuse, because of the faith afterwards justified which they showed, and also because of the early days in which they occurred.

To restore the monarchy of King Louis Philippe in the person of the Comte de Paris, is a project which doubtless many persons of intelligence at present discuss with interest, but which no serious politician has yet ventured to propose. The two great veteran statesmen of the Revolution of 1830 are now in frequent communication with public opinion,—M. Guizot by a letter to the editor of the *Times* once a month on the average, M. Thiers by almost daily speeches and circulars to prefects. M. Guizot does not even advert to the possibility of the existence of such a personage as a King Louis Philippe the Second. M. Thiers declares solemnly, specifically, on every possible opportunity, that it is his mission to maintain the Republic one and indivisible. It is to the credit of his countenance, and also, let us trust, of his character, that he makes these declarations before an assembly that contains a larger proportion of dukes and marquises than any perhaps that has sat in France since the States-General, and who may fairly enough ask themselves what business dukes and marquises have in a country in which there is no king. The imagination fails to conceive a Duke of Brooklyn or a Marquis of Manhattan, or even a Count Chicago. If the American citizen should happen to meet with a crowd of such personages in Congress, he would calculate, with the natural shrewdness of his race, that the reign of Ulysses I. was nigh at hand. The founders of the Western Republic so strongly felt that the idea of title, except in connection with public office, was incompatible with that equality which is the basis of democratic right, that they refused to found an American Legion of Honour, the order of Cincinnatus. The Red Flag may not rule France, but the Red Riband, we venture to say, will have a good deal to do with its Government for a very long time to come.

An Orleanist restoration would merely be the reproduction of a throne of lath and plaster, sure to fall before the first gale. It would combine the weaknesses of a Republic with those of a Monarchy, and would possess the strength of neither. A monarchy must rest either on hereditary right or on the will of the people. The title of the Orleans family is in itself a violation of hereditary right, while, if the will of the people is sufficient to create a valid title, then it is the Bonaparte family, and not the family of Louis Philippe, who are qualified to claim that they are the dynasty to which the nation has given its sanction. If a popular vote were to be taken on the question, should the Comte de Paris be crowned King of the French, where would the strength of his party lie? The bourgeoisie were the true constituency of the citizen king; but the bourgeoisie no longer govern France, and there is even a new generation of bourgeois, which does not know its own mind over clearly perhaps, but which it would be a very wild generalization to describe as Orleanist in sentiment. His Royal Highness would hardly claim to be considered the candidate of the peasants or of the priests; and might not even find it quite safe to trust the defence of his constitutional throne to the army which was formed by the Empire or the army which was formed by the Republic. The populace of Paris is reputed to be so intensely hostile to his claims that, even were he elected, he might find it necessary to make Orleans or Bourges his capital for a time. His most ardent supporters are, we strongly suspect, men of letters—especially that class of men of letters who wish for a government under which they may have full liberty to pit speculation against revelation, and in which a newspaper office may again be regarded as the natural apprenticeship of a statesman. But if there be anything certain as to the future of France, it is that it is not a country to be governed by Mandarins; also that speculation has been pushed so far as to corrode to a considerable extent in the mind of its people, faith, hope, and charity, from which flow courage, energy, and patience, and manly spirit and civic virtue. Even M. de Laveleye admits that its press must somehow or other be reformed. Infidel and licentious ideas can no more be scattered broadcast with impunity than the scurf of small-pox or the offal of cholera. In France, perhaps elsewhere, the true remedy would be to raise journalism to the rank of a regular profession, and to require those who form and direct public opinion to be educated and to graduate, as men do before they practice law or medicine. Parties would not probably be fewer or less decidedly divided. But an effectual dam would be gradually built up against the flood of ignorant and inflammatory balderdash, which now periodically produces a flood of blood. A throne based upon the circulation of the *Journal des Débats*—such perhaps would be the most exact description of the monarchy of Louis Philippe II. We trust, however, that France, if there is to be an Orleans restoration, will not resort to the expedient of setting up the temporary presidency of the Duc d'Aumale, in the hope of finding the Republic again converted into a Monarchy in the course of a night by the process of a *coup-d'état*. Such a proceeding would in these days as little consist with the honour of the Orleans family as with that of France, and would only inaugurate a new period of insecurity and conspiracy.

The true policy of the French nation, if indeed it be, as we assume, determined to discard the Republic, is to restore that Prince who by birth is King of France, but who, by the will of his people, has been so long an exile, to the throne of his ancestors. Leading an obscure and studious life, seldom speaking on French affairs, but on such rare occasions speaking in language of touching dignity, of vivid force, subtle insight, and fine skill of expression, few even of his adherents know the rare and kingly qualities which belong to the character of the Comte de Chambord. In all the illustrious line to which he belongs, there has not been a Prince less unworthy to wear the crown of St. Louis. He is not the less worthy that he has never deigned to intrigue or to conspire, but has always declared that he would never return to France save as king by the grace of God and the will of the people. Is it not time that the French should try to get a king whom they could at least call the Good, and who if, with the help of God, he should close the era of revolution as he might well hope to do, would deserve to be named the Great? He is the last of his line. Should he die without issue, a new right, we venture to think, would arise in the younger branch of the Bourbons, which it is not their true policy to anticipate, or to disparage by cabals and conspiracies. Their true policy is to atone for the repeated acts of family treason, which for now nearly two centuries have made the family of Orleans fatal to the peace of the state of France. In England, where they have lived so long, and where they are so sincerely respected, they know that in the conduct of great affairs men are proud of saying that the path of duty is the path of glory. It is especially, essentially so for Princes. For twenty-three years they have lived in exile within sight of a sovereignty based as well on the right of succession, as on the loyalty of the nation. They are in exile because the late king attempted to establish a sovereignty which seemed, and only seemed to have the latter sanction, but which was a flagrant violation of the former. To the French nation, and to the House of Bourbon, they owe an act of abdication and atonement, which, if done in the spirit of faith and duty, might communicate its inspiration to the whole future of France. That country is perishing for lack of loyalty, self-abnegation, civil courage, common trust, and Christian charity. Let its princes show its people an example.

APPENDIX TO THE ARTICLE ON GRIGNON DE MONTFORT.

IN the second article of our last number we said, in effect, that the biographer of Mother Margaret had gone out of her way to charge S. Alphonsus and Grignon de Montfort with " exaggerated and preposterous expressions." Dr. Northcote however has written to the Catholic newspapers, testifying from his own knowledge that the excellent writer intended no such charge. It is our bounden duty of course, under such circumstances, to make this disavowal as public as was the original allegation; and to express our sincere regret, for having most unintentionally wronged her through our misapprehension of her meaning.

But Dr. Northcote assumes the aggressive. He " cannot sufficiently express his amazement at the charge " thus "*falsely*" made ; which he characterizes indeed as a " calumnious misstatement," and as no less " unfounded " than " offensive." It is necessary therefore to defend ourselves against this assault. And indeed, though we much regret to find ourselves in controversy with one so universally and justly respected as Dr. Northcote,—we are, for more than one reason, not sorry for an opportunity of speaking on the matter more at length.

The passage from Mother Margaret's Life ran as follows in the first edition :—

" When, as [F. Newman's Letter to Dr. Pusey] was read aloud to her, the reader came to that page in which he enumerates, in order to condemn, certain exaggerated and preposterous expressions culled by a Protestant controversialist out of various foreign writers (some of them on the Index; she stopped her ears, and desired that they might be passed over in silence."

In July, 1869, we published a notice of the biography, which spoke in the warmest praise of the volume itself, and with profound veneration of its saintly subject ;* but which protested against the above sentence. These were our words :—

" This passage misrepresents not only Mother Margaret, but Father New-

---

* It is better perhaps to explain distinctly, that this notice was not by the present writer, but by an old and intimate friend of Mother Margaret's.

man. That she stopped her ears we have no doubt ; as who would not on hearing that 'in a literal and absolute sense ;' 'simply' and 'unconditionally' 'the Blessed Virgin is superior to God'? Of course Mother Margaret, with Father Newman and every man who had not taken leave of his senses, 'would rather believe that there is no God at all, than that Mary is greater than God.' But that is a very different thing from saying that these were 'exaggerated and preposterous expressions culled out of foreign writers.' This is implying that these expressions, as used by foreign writers, were exaggerated and preposterous ; and siding with the 'Protestant controversialist' who took them in their literal sense. This is what Father Newman expressly denies. He says that he is looking at them, not 'as spoken by the tongues of angels, but according to that literal sense which they bear in the mouths of English men and English women.' Mother Margaret would have been the last person in the world to use the term 'foreign' as a term of reproach to Catholic writers, least of all would she have thus applied the epithet to S. Alfonso Liguori. We trust that, in a second edition, these words, which were not in Mother Margaret's mouth or mind when she stopped her ears, may be omitted."

No change however was made in the second edition, except to substitute the phrase "*one* of them on the Index" for the less accurate "*some* of them." Accordingly in our last number we returned to the subject, being naturally led to do so by the recently published translation of "Montfort's Life and Remains." These were our words :—

"Not seculars alone have assailed his works, but an excellent religious has gone out of her way, to accuse him of 'exaggerated and preposterous expressions' in regard to our Blessed Lady. The biography, to which we refer as written by that religious, is so singularly beautiful, and its subject is so noble and saintly a person, that we feel ourselves more especially bound to protest against a statement, which will come before a large number of readers as invested with such persuasive authority."

To this we appended a note :—

"It is not only the Venerable Grignon de Montfort, but a canonized Saint —S. Alphonsus—who is charged in the same passage with 'exaggerated and preposterous expressions.'

" We do not for a moment deny—in a few pages later we expressly affirm— that it is most possible for a saintly writer to *express* inaccurately thoughts which *in themselves* are orthodox ; and we should rejoice to think that no more than this is intended in the passage which we criticise : but such certainly is not its obvious sense.

"As for F. Newman, to whom the said passage refers, the case is most simple. Until he read the Eirenicon, he had never even heard of Montfort's name ; and he expressed himself as certain that Dr. Pusey misunderstood that holy writer."

It is on this text and note that Dr. Northcote comments in his letter.   After quoting them, he proceeds as follows :—

"It is impossible to mistake the biography which is here alluded to ; it can only be 'The Life of Mother Margaret Mary Hallahan,' by her religious children, with a preface by the Bishop of Birmingham (Longmans).   And I cannot sufficiently express my amazement at the charge which is thus plainly, but falsely, brought against it.   I have read the book from cover to cover some half-dozen times or more, and am continually taking it in hand again with renewed pleasure and edification ; and I knew that there was absolutely no foundation for so calumnious a misstatement.   I wrote therefore to the Editor of the DUBLIN for a distinct specification of the passage or passages on which it was supposed to rest.   In reply, I am referred to the following passage in p. 327 of the 3rd edition.   ' She intensely admired Dr. Newman's ' Letter' (to Dr. Pusey, on his ' Eirenicon '), and was only deterred by timidity from writing him her thanks ; but when, as it was read aloud to her, the reader came to that page in which he enumerates, in order to condemn, certain exaggerated and preposterous expressions culled by a Protestant controversialist out of various foreign writers (one of them on the Index), she stopped her ears, and desired that they might be passed over in silence.' Now, sir, I must not overload your columns by quoting the page of Dr. Newman's ' Letter' here referred to ; nor is it necessary.   I find an analysis of it ready made to my hands in the pages of the DUBLIN REVIEW itself (July, 1866).   It is there described as containing twenty-two propositions, which are severally enumerated and commented upon.   Of these, four or five are attributed to S. Alphonsus ; one to S. Bernardine of Siena ; one to Bernardine de Bustis ; two to M. Olier ; four to Salazar ; six to Grignon de Montfort ; and three, says the writer, ' are taken from a young ecclesiastic named Oswald, whose work was placed on the Index.'   Your readers will observe that this last is the *only* writer *personally* indicated by the author of Mother Margaret's Life.   By what right then does the critic in the DUBLIN REVIEW select two other names out of the remaining half-dozen, and say that ' the excellent Religious has accused *these* of exaggerated and preposterous expressions in regard to Our Blessed Lady ' ?   To the best of my belief, no reader of the Life could gather from its pages that either of the two holy personages whom the DUBLIN has been pleased to individualize ever had an historic existence at all.   It has spoken in the vaguest terms of *certain* expressions of *various* writers ; and we have seen from the DUBLIN itself that the number of these writers is seven, and that one of them at least was blameworthy, for his work was put on the Index.   If it can be shown, then, that the expressions used by any of the remaining half-dozen were equally open to censure, the justice of the statement in the Life is at once established. The DUBLIN itself shall be once more our witness.   In the article from which I have already quoted, it says of the two expressions used by M. Olier that, ' if he intended them dogmatically, he undoubtedly uttered two heresies, and must have written them under some temporary absence or obscuration of mind.   But,' the writer continues, ' we cannot help regarding it as far more probable that he did not intend them dogmatically at all, but merely as a practical exhortation to sinners that they should approach Mary as their special advocate and mediatrix when they have offended her Son.' A strange apology, by the way, for uttering two heresies. But this is not to the present purpose. What I want to ask is, how the DUBLIN Reviewer imagines himself to know that the author of Margaret Hallahan's Life had not this very passage of M. Olier specially in her eye when she spoke of 'exaggerated and preposterous expressions' (adding parenthetically that *I* happen to know that this is precisely what she *was* thinking of) ; and, secondly, why an 'excellent Religious' may not condemn as 'exaggerated and preposterous expressions' passages in which the critic of the DUBLIN detects 'two undoubted heresies' ?

"Again, we should like to ask why, whilst Dr. Newman is exonerated from all blame for writing the passage in his Letter, the biographer, who has but alluded to that passage, and that for historic and not for controversial purposes, is made to feel all the weight of the Reviewer's displeasure ? 'The case of Dr. N.,' he says, 'is very simple.' He only did so and so. To my mind, the case of the writer of Mother Margaret's Life is simpler still ; she does but record a fact, and, as I hope presently to show, a highly interesting and important fact, necessary to the integrity of her work.

"But first, one word more on the Reviewer. The writer of the Life speaks of 'certain exaggerated and preposterous *expressions ;*' and the Reviewer acknowledges and maintains that 'even a saintly writer may *express* inaccurately thoughts which *in themselves* are orthodox;' but he says 'this is not the obvious sense' of the passage in the Life. Again, I ask, how does he know that this is not what she means ? Anyhow, it is absolutely and precisely what she has *said.* She has implied a condemnation of certain *expressions,* and I have to blush for my own obtuseness if any obvious sense lies in this word 'expressions' beyond 'what is expressed.'

"I think I have said enough, sir, to show that it is not the author of Mother Margaret's Life, but the DUBLIN Reviewer, who has 'gone out of his way' to make a charge as unfounded as it is offensive. Unhappily, this is by no means the only occasion on which our Quarterly Review has shown itself thus lynx-eyed to detect hidden heterodoxy in a writer whose sympathies it knows, or imagines, are not in all points identical with its own ; but in the present instance this seems to me the more reprehensible, because the person attacked is precluded by her position from the usual means of self-defence.

"However, it is not altogether for the purpose of defending the author of Mother Margaret's Life that I write this letter ; it is rather the fact which that lady has recorded, and which (I suspect) constitutes her *real* offence in the eyes of the DUBLIN, which to my mind seems of sufficient importance to deserve insisting upon ; and the more so, as her Reviewer accuses her of having 'gone out of her way to record what he so much dislikes. The biographer had been giving examples of that singular devotion which Mother Margaret ever bore to the blessed Mother of God ; and she takes occasion to point out the instructive fact, that one whose devotion to Our Lady could hardly be surpassed in degree, and which moreover was avowedly of that tender and familiar kind which Protestants are wont to identify with a phraseology shocking to their prejudices, was so far from advocating the use of such language that it was opposed to her taste, and that her own glowing and impassioned feelings ever found their truest expression in the sublime but chastened language of the Catholic Ritual. Nay, more than this, when certain phrases met her ears, which sought to translate the style and sentiment—I am not speaking of the doctrine—of foreign countries into the language of our own, an experiment rarely felicitous in all its results, it jarred those delicate instincts which in her took the place of scientific analysis, and she felt a discordant thrill, as on the occasion cited. The fact is important, as a real feature in Mother Margaret's character, whether readers like it or not ; and her biographer would hardly have been justified in withholding it, if she wished to set before us a real, and not a fancy portrait of her dear and venerated Mother. But there was also a duty of charity in recording it, since, as far as it goes, it is calculated to remove difficulties out of the way of those who are disposed to think that every good Catholic is bound, as such, not only to accept, but to use, and even to relish, the writings of every approved author. That it has actually removed, or at any rate lessened, such difficulties in one important instance, has been acknowledged by no less an authority than Dr. Pusey himself ; and if I had been the author of the Life, I should have felt that this circumstance outweighs the censure of an anonymous Reviewer.—I remain, Sir, yours truly,

"Oscott, Jan. 24th, 1871."   " J. Spencer Northcote. ʼ

We must begin our comment on this letter, by reminding our readers of what they will not have failed to observe ; viz. the general *tone* of the remarks in our last number. We expressed ourselves in terms of entire respect for the biographer, of hearty admiration for her work, and of unaffected reverence for the " noble and saintly person " of whom it treated. We venture to think, that it would have been better if Dr. Northcote had expressed some recognition of this ; and we venture still more confidently to think, that the tone of his own reply is not what might have been expected. He has not even taken the trouble to say, what of course he intended to admit, that the misrepresentation which he ascribes to us was not intentional: and he speaks of " the charge so *falsely* brought" by us ; a phrase more commonly applied, we think, to *deliberate* misrepresentation. But the very last thing we wish is to promote any kind of ill-feeling between Dr. Northcote and ourselves. In times like these, when the Church is exposed to such serious perils, not only from avowed Protestants and infidels but still more from unsound and from nominal Catholics, we cannot be provoked into saying one word which shall even savour of disrespect, to so excellent a Catholic and one who is doing such good work in the Church. We flatter ourselves indeed that the general course of our remarks will lead him to see that, on Marian devotion at least, there is no such difference of view between him and ourselves as he seems to think.

The immediate question at issue turns on a very simple point. The biographer speaks of "that page" in which F. Newman "enumerates, in order to condemn, certain exaggerated and preposterous expressions culled by a Protestant controversialist out of various foreign writers." We maintain that, according to the universal use of language, the epithets "exaggerated and preposterous" are here applied to *all* those "expressions, culled by" Dr. Pusey "out of various foreign writers," which F. Newman "enumerates in order to condemn." We now know from Dr. Northcote's testimony that the excellent authoress did not intend this; but of course when we wrote we had nothing to guide us, except the legitimate objective sense of her words. Now the decision in a case of this kind—on the legitimate objective sense of certain English words—rests with the common judgment of educated Englishmen; and in order fairly to elicit this judgment, we will remove the matter from the domain of theology to that of literature. Let us suppose we are dealing with some critic, who denies Miss Austen's claims to be considered a correct writer. "In behalf of his proposition," we say, "he enumerates, in order to condemn, certain faultily expressed sentences culled by a previous writer from her various novels." Our readers, without exception, would certainly understand us to admit, that *all* the sentences which the critic "enumerates in order to condemn" are in truth "faultily expressed." We are confident that Dr. Northcote himself would never even imagine any different interpretation of our remark. Had we thought that only *some* of the enumerated sentences were faultily expressed, we should have said, "*as being* faultily expressed," or used some other turn of language. The present case is entirely similar. We assure Dr. Northcote, it never even occurred to us to *doubt* that her meaning was as we have above set forth. Even when we received Dr. Northcote's private letter, we racked our brains in vain to imagine what the authoress could possibly have intended, different from what (to our mind) she had so distinctly said.

We should add that our contributor of 1869 had understood the sentence just as we did; and had protested especially against S. Alphonsus being included among those "foreign writers" who,—as the biographer had seemed to imply, —were uncongenial to Mother Margaret's taste. Nor indeed can we quite understand why Dr. Northcote did not *then* object to what he must have considered so grave a misconception of the authoress's meaning.

Now of the "expressions" which F. Newman "enumerated in order to condemn," Dr. Northcote himself states that four or five were taken from S. Alphonsus, and six from Grignon de Montfort. We must really contend therefore, that we did but understand the authoress's words in their obvious and legitimate sense, when we said that she charged those two holy writers with the use of "exaggerated and preposterous expressions." We are now aware that she did *not* intend so to charge them, and we entirely retract our affirmation to the contrary. But, so far from pleading guilty to the charge of "calumnious misstatement," we unhesitatingly allege that we understood her words just as every educated Englishman, who did not otherwise know her personal intention, must necessarily have understood them.

· But Dr. Northcote asks, "Why is F. Newman exonerated from all blame for writing the passage in his Letter?" The reply is most easy. We have never indeed expressed or implied—very far from it—any kind of sympathy with the particular method which F. Newman adopted, for meeting Dr. Pusey's citations ; but it is a simple fact, that he has carefully avoided passing any kind of censure, either on S. Alphonsus, or on Montfort, or on any "foreign writer" whomsoever adduced by Dr. Pusey.* His words are express to this effect; and this very contrast indeed, between him and Mother Margaret's biographer, was drawn in our original notice of the biography. " The writers," he says, " doubtless did not use " those phrases " as any Protestant would naturally take them ;" " I do not speak of the statements as they are found in their authors; " " I cannot believe that they mean what you [Dr. Pusey] say ; " " I am looking at them, not as spoken *by the tongues of angels*, but according to that literal sense which they bear in the mouths of English men and English women ; " " as spoken by man to man in England in the nineteenth century.' (Letter to Dr. Pusey, pp. 118—121.) The utterances then of those " foreign writers " are ascribed by F. Newman to "the tongues of angels ; " and their most reverential admirer can wish for no stronger phrase.

· We were very unwilling from the first to believe, that the biographer of Mother Margaret really intended what her sentence seemed to convey. Having however no clue to her meaning, we suggested in her behalf a possible interpretation of her words, which would greatly lessen the ground of objection. " It is most possible," we said, " for a saintly writer " such

---

* So far as F. Newman's blame falls on any one, it falls on those who have in the present century translated such works into English. We need not say how far we are ourselves from thinking that they deserve aught but gratitude.

as S. Alphonsus or Montfort " to *express* inaccurately thoughts which *in themselves* are orthodox ; and we should rejoice to think that no more is meant in the passage which we criticise : but such certainly is not its obvious sense." This remark of ours has led Dr. Northcote to execute (what, with great respect for him, we must be allowed to call) one of the most singular argumentative evolutions we ever encountered. We had represented the authoress throughout, as ascribing " exaggerated and preposterous expressions " to S. Alphonsus and to Montfort ; and this representation has been called by Dr. Northcote " a calumnious misstatement " " as unfounded as it is offensive." But our statement, even if mistaken, could not be " calumnious " and " offensive," unless it were *injurious ;* and Dr. Northcote therefore, by such language as the above, implies most emphatically that the authoress would have said something *gravely objectionable,* had she really spoken as we supposed. Yet, in his last paragraph but two, he turns right round ; and declares that if she had said just what we understood her to say, she would have been perfectly justified in so doing. Does he or does he not think that it was an " offensive calumny " to allege what we alleged ? We cannot make out for the life of us. He calls our statement " calumnious " in an earlier paragraph, and " offensive " in a later ; while in the paragraph before us he affirms, that at last we have ascribed to the authoress nothing against which just exception can be taken.

For our own part we cannot but think, that had the authoress really intended to say what we understood her to say, but what (we now know) was never in her mind—such language would have been most regrettable. Firstly, to have used such a phrase concerning holy men, would surely not have been to treat them with due reverence. But secondly and more importantly, the phrase " exaggerated and preposterous expressions "—if used without addition or qualification —would be understood according to universal usage as including, not the *expressions* only, but the thoughts *expressed.* It was for this reason we said that the interpretation, which we suggested as possible, was not the sentence's " obvious sense."

Dr. Northcote proceeds to declare that " this is by no means the only occasion on which " we " have shown ourselves thus lynx-eyed to detect hidden heterodoxy in a writer whose sympathies, we know or imagine, are not in all points identical with our own." We may fairly call on our critic to name the instances which he has in his mind. We should account it detestable and anti-Christian to sow divisions between Catholic

and Catholic, merely because the " sympathies " of one differ—
as is of course inevitable—from the " sympathies" of another.
We have never done so designedly; we entirely disbelieve that
we have ever done so at all.

But " in the present instance," it is added, our conduct is
" the more reprehensible, because the person attacked is precluded by her position from the usual means of self-defence."
Yet to publish a book, is ipso facto to invite public criticism ; and criticism, bound down to be exclusively favourable,
is in fact no criticism at all. Nor will Dr. Northcote himself
say that our language has been deficient, in expressing either
respect for the authoress's high personal character or reverence for her noble vocation. Moreover ·he should remember,
that we had every reason for understanding her to charge S.
Alphonsus and Montfort with " exaggerated and preposterous
expressions." Surely a layman is warranted in defending a
Saint even against a good religious.

In Dr. Northcote's opinion, there are some " who are disposed to think that every good Catholic is bound, as such, not
only to accept, but to use and even to relish, the writings of
every approved author." We never heard of such persons ;
and at all events we wish Dr. Northcote had distinctly explained, how very far *we* are from being among the number.
In the article itself which has provoked his comment (p. 42)
we expressed our hearty agreement with the translator of Montfort, that " any one who finds " that holy man's " writings out
of harmony with his mind or unsuited to his devotion, has
the most perfect liberty not to use them." But Dr. Northcote has also been looking at an earlier article of ours, published in July 1866. Now in this article we said, among other
things, that every Catholic who is discomposed by such writings
should " banish them from his mind " (p. 178); and that
" many practices, most beneficial to one man, may be injurious
to another " (p. 199). In fact we have nowhere said or implied anything whatever about any obligation concerning
them, except what Dr. Northcote says as strongly as we ; viz.
that no Catholic is at liberty to censure them as unsound and
abnormal.

We cannot concur however with Dr. Northcote in thinking
that important light is thrown on Mother Margaret's character,
by the fact of her having been excessively shocked at the
expressions cited by F. Newman. Dr. Northcote thinks that
this shows her aversion to a certain "*phraseology,*" in regard
to certain *doctrines* which she held in common with all
Catholics. Yet he had mentioned, as a fact within his own
knowledge, that what the authoress " was precisely think-

ing of" was a passage which, if understood dogmatically, contained two heresies. How can the fact that Mother Margaret was shocked at two *heresies*, throw any light on her sentiments in regard to a particular way of expressing *sound doctrine?*

But look at F. Newman's whole page. He does not take his quotations from any "foreign writer" whomsoever; but from Dr. Pusey's *citation* of foreign writers. Now Dr. Pusey invariably divorced his citations from the context; sometimes mutilated them; sometimes mistranslated them. Moreover in one or two instances F. Newman does not do justice to them, even as they stand in Dr. Pusey's pages.* Here then are a number of statements, some heretical, others unsound, the rest needing careful explanation from their context, tossed (as it were) roughly together into one heterogeneous mass. That Mother Margaret shut her ears in horror at such apparent blasphemy, does not (we must really contend) furnish even the faintest presumption, that she would have read otherwise than with keen delight and edification the "Glories of Mary" or the "True Devotion."

As to the "difficulties" of those external to the Church, we think they might be met far more effectively, than by publishing a fact concerning Mother Margaret which has no bearing on them whatever.

We believe it is true that many a Catholic, both in England and in other countries, is repelled rather than attracted by various expressions, constantly found in the most saintly writers. And the obvious course for such a Catholic to pursue, is to avoid such expressions himself, while he forbears nevertheless to criticise what the Church permits and in some sense approves. On the other hand we are equally convinced, that there are very many Catholics, English as well as foreign, in whom these fervent words elicit a responsive fervour of heart and affection, which is a help simply invaluable towards solid

---

* Thus Salazar, as quoted by Dr. Pusey, says that His Mother's wish would have sufficed as a motive to our Blessed Lord for undergoing death : but F. Newman understands him as saying, "that it would have sufficed for *the salvation of men* if our Lord had died only to comply with His Mother's wish." Then one of F. Newman's citations is — "Mary alone can obtain a Protestant's conversion :" for which Dr. Pusey gives him no warrant, except by saying that he had been far oftener asked by Catholics to pray for his conversion to our Lady than to her Son. And lastly comes the expression, to which we referred in July 1869, and which has no vestige of foundation in any of Dr. Pusey's citations, even as they stand in the Eirenicon : viz., "that *unconditionally* it is safer to seek her than her Son," and "that He is *simply* subject to her command." F. Newman places the words "unconditionally" and "simply" in brackets : but this would not appear in *reading aloud.*

piety and the love of God.   It is cruel tyranny (in our humble
view), however piously intended, to put obstacles in the way
of such men; or to say a word tending to close against them
one of those devotional paths, which the Church has permitted to their free choice.

In conclusion we must again express the hope, which we
expressed in July 1869, that in future editions this passage
may be altered.   By such alteration the authoress would
remove its only serious blot, from what is certainly among
the most edifying and charming works of its kind whichever
were published.

Roman Documents.

THE RESTORATION OF FRANCE.

(From the Civiltà Cattolica.)

THE unparalleled misfortunes to which France has been subjected during the last few months of war have prevented her sincerest friends from expressing almost any other feelings than those of pity for her immense calamities. But that pity has not prevented Christian thinkers and students of the true philosophy of history from descrying in her cruel sufferings, the fulfilment of those providential laws which rule the moral and the physical world alike, and from the effects of which no people can escape. Even amongst the French themselves, many really intellectual men were the first to recognize the hand of Providence in their national misfortune, and to acknowledge, in speech and in writing, that France was perishing under the chastening hand of heaven, on account of her eighty years' worship of the Revolution.

Amongst the most memorable are the words uttered in Paris by Louis Veuillot, on the very day Paris capitulated, and which have been greatly approved throughout France :—" We succumb," says the Catholic publicist in the *Univers*, " by an unexpected concourse of the most unfortunate circumstances, but principally through want of one thing, which is not in us, and which we must regain. We shall fail in everything until we have done so. A victory would not have restored it to us, nor a hundred victories. We succumb through want of faith, want of loyalty, want of justice within us, and around us. We have not been slain by the Republic of 1870, nor by the Empire, nor even by the preceding régime ; all these shapes and systems are but different forms of the same disease, derived from the same vitiated blood. We are dying of the Revolution, and yet all of us, some more and some less, would fain keep the poison in our veins. If the formidable remedy we are undergoing leave it there, it is useless to strive with the evil, vain to attempt to stifle it ; nothing will remain but to rot. What *may* be done, the last possible cure, the miracle that we still may hope to obtain, since we still have power to implore and to deserve it, is that we may be rid of the Revolution. But this will be a miracle identical with that of springing out of the arms of death."

France, therefore, as the *Moniteur* of Bordeaux repeated soon after, France " is dying through the Revolution ; " nor can she hope for a vital restoration unless she returns to what she was of old, the most Christian of nations, the arm of God throughout Christendom. " France desires to live," continues this journal ; " she is right to resuscitate the race of the Franks, the *gens inclyta Francorum,* the progeny of Clovis, of S. Louis, of Henry IV., the descendants of the Crusaders ; for it seems as if she still had to accomplish in the world a few of those feats which an historian named *Gesta Dei per Francos.*

Such, then, is the conclusion offered to this noble country, and forced, by their present misfortunes, upon the minds of many of the warmest partisans of the boasted conquests of liberty and civilization, as derived from the principles of 1789. They are now recognized to be fatal victories ; and Providence, by suffering the corollaries of these principles, like seeds of death, to be evolved to the uttermost in their own history, has endeavoured to bring France to a sense of its error, which has lasted little less than a century. The terrible experiences of 1793, 1814, and 1848, did not suffice to convince France. That of 1870 was necessary, and she must be brought to feel herself breathing her last between two enemies at the same time, —the exterminating sword of the Germans, and the blows of her domestic barbarians,—without being able to pronounce which of the two will inflict on her the most deadly wound.

We may briefly illustrate this conclusion, which is an abridgment of the past curse of France, and shows her sole chance of salvation in the future, by quoting S. Remy's answer to Clovis, when he questioned him as to how he might transform himself into the first Christian king of the Franks ; *Adora quod incendisti, et incende quod adorasti.*

II.

The vital nature of *Revolution,* whose ordinary system lies in the so-called principles of liberty, which prevailed in France at the end of the last century, and afterwards pushed their way into the Catholic nations of the south of Europe, is *social apostasy* from God, His Christ, and His Church. The Revolution, offspring of the *modern spirit,* or of Satan, as he manifests himself in our age, is not entirely political as it strives to appear, but it is intrinsically religious. The object of its being and of its works is the total separation of society from God, its reconstitution without the influence of a supernatural religion ; and the establishment of the throne, the community, the family, the individual, and even the laws and education altogether without God. In virtue of this system Jesus Christ and His Church remain outside society, and the divine faith is called free *opinion,* no more and no less than the theogony of the Greeks, and the mythology of the Indians. This is the actual essence of the Revolution. The rest is accessory. The forms of government and the constitutions of States matter little, provided they carry out the intention of *secularizing,* or, better still, of *unchristianizing* society. Political organizations are its means ; the destruction of Christianity is its end. Freemasonry is the supreme director and executor of this satanic enterprise, according to the different ranks, and the various sects into which it is divided.

For about a century, France, through her Governments, and as far as regards her civil aspect, has been thrown into the arms of this apostate spirit ; and too truly has she acquired, at home and abroad, the name of an essentially revolutionary nation. After having perverted Christian order at home, she has sent forth throughout Europe, first by the power of her arms, and then by that of her ideas, the same perversity and the same confusion as that which devastated her own soil. From 1789 to 1870 it has been the passionate desire of the greater number of French politicians and statesmen to efface every sign of the social reign of Christ all over Christendom, under pretext of civilizing it; and to induce the neighbouring and sister countries to stamp themselves with the image of *revolutionary* France. Italy, Spain, Portugal, Mexico, and even Austria and Belgium, know this through sad experience. The nation which was formerly Most Christian has become the apostle, no longer of the Christ of the *illustrious Franks*, her ancestors, but of the Satan of the Druids, under the pretext of advancing civilization.

The late war with Germany, by which France brought upon herself one of the heaviest punishments that ever befel a vast empire, was it not fore-shadowed in the songs and carousals that rendered the crimes of her *Great Revolution* of the last century so famous? And did not Napoleon III. dare to announce to the world, that he was carrying forth a banner inscribed with the principles of 1789 against the Germans, which banner was changed, on the heights of Sedan, into the funeral pall of his throne.

Nay, in the beginning of this war, was not God put aside to such an extent that in no public act was He invoked or was He even named? And yet the object was to lead a Christian Catholic Nation against a Protestant Power. It was for the Protestant Potentate to teach the Christian Catholic Nation that the holy name of God is to be invoked. "While the French philosophers and legislators," remarks one of the most illustrious thinkers of Italy, "were ashamed to name God on the approach of great events, King William assumes the language of religion. He says :—' *From my youth have I learnt to consider all things as depending on the benign help of God.*' And he orders prayers and public penance at Berlin and throughout his realm. What folly, what a scandal, for the Catholic rulers! Then, unsheathing his sword, he goes forth in the name of Providence. Such events are scourges, no doubt, but they seem to be scourges incurred by our faults. After all, what difference can one see between Attila, spurred on by the impetuous fury of his ferocious Huns, exclaiming,—'*I go against those people by whom God is despised ;*' and this new relative of his, King William, who, relating the battle of Sedan to Queen Augusta, writes, '*God alone designed me, my army, and my allies as instruments of His will*'? The ancestor and the descendant alike try to conquer the dullard with the scourge. The North teaches God and His Providence to the degenerate remains of Latin civilization."

But this impious apostasy carries the punishment of its madness with it to individuals as well as to nations. *Non est pax impiis*, says the

Word of God, *impii quasi mare fervens quod quiescere non potest.* And truly, France, having banished Christ from her social life, cannot rest, but has become a stormy sea whose waves are in continual agitation, which has done away with all stability, and fall back, almost periodically, into disorderly divisions which bring her to the verge of destruction. So the most *revolutionary* nation has become the most *convulsive* of our time. Four times in eighty years has she changed her dynasty ; twelve times has she remade her own constitution ; and to-day, after changing and re-changing, making and re-making, she finds herself without any dynasty, without any constitut ; nor does she know what Government she may have to-morrow.

We do not mean to assert that the Christian spirit is extinct in France, and that the mass of her population has apostatised from the Church. Nothing could be more false. Individually, and in private society, the Church possesses in France a numerous army of faithful children, ruled by the most edifying episcopacy and clergy who ever existed. France is the cradle of the wonderful work of the *Propagation of the Faith ;* she sends numbers of apostles of the Gospel to Catholic missions spread all over the globe ; she founded the incomparable society of S. Vincent of Paul ; she was the first to give to the Holy See the immortal Pontifical Zouaves. The merits of the French Catholics in the sight of the Church and of the Roman Pontiff are more dazzling than the sun. But they are the merits of Frenchmen and not of France. Those pure, generous, and heroic souls, remarks the Archbishop of Malines, lament the fact of living in an unfaithful land—not in an unfaithful land where God is unknown, but in an unfaithful land where God is forgotten. As the political order which influences her social dependencies so strongly, has always maintained itself in a revolutionary state,—that is to say, in an atheistic state, adverse to the Catholic Church and parted from Christianity,—therefore, nationally, in everything that relates to her Government, to her legal and public institutions, France for more than eighty years has apostatised from God and from His Christ. She has likewise denied the knowledge of Christianity to the Arabs of Algeria, whom she has conquered, in a military sense, but whom in the religious order she has abandoned to Mahomet.

Napoleon I. might easily have repaired this great evil, immediately after the atrocious revolts against the Empire to which it gave rise, considering that the French nation, universally, had remained Catholic, in spite of the internal foes who were destroying her ; but instead, he consolidated it. By founding upon it his own power, his laws, and his dynasty, he already, as his nephew Napoleon III. asserted, looked upon himself as the testamentary executor of the Revolution, from which he had inherited his sceptre. He refused to receive the crown from the hands of Christ represented by those of His Vicar ; and shortly after he chained up those hands, as though he should reign more freely that Christ was prevented from concurring in his dominion. After him came the Bourbons, to whom it would not have been difficult to purify France from revolutionary poison, if it had not been their misfortune as Joseph de Maistre wisely remarked, to ascend the throne,—not of their fathers,—but of Bonaparte. And so, trafficking, more or less, with the Revolution, they opened under their own feet the pit which swallowed them up, and made room for the Orleans, who carried still further the degradation of France, and educated a generation more worthy to serve Napoleon III., whose supremely revolutionary reign has perhaps been more corrupt and more conducive to corruption than any which the French annals record.

During the twenty years' duration of the Empire, social atheism took possession to a certain extent of the whole country, and spread itself widely outside of it. As soon as public authority had succeeded in applying it to all branches of civil administration, to diplomacy, and to the army, fashion infused it into the habits, the ideas, the languages, and the customs of the people. Books, journals, theatres, clubs, schools, colleges, universities, on a large scale, were changed into laboratories from whence the immoral atheistic and anti-Christian principles of the Revolution were propagated among all classes of the people, under the high dominion of Freemasonry, which exercised an absolute control over the Emperor. The monster of *Socialism* was nursed in France by the arts of the State ; the so-called *Liberalism*, true essence of the apostate principles of 1789, corrupted the mass of the national blood, and infected a crowd of even good Catholics. Did we not see them infatuated to the extent of opposing the Vatican Council through the fear of its prescribing remedies too efficacious against the *revolutionary* plague of these days?

Such was, in his interior government of France, the policy of Napoleon III., who formed the France of 1870 : the France which displayed to the scandalized world its Fescennine corruption and Punic perfidy ; families without union, young people devoid of modesty, matrimony without fecundity, diplomatists without faith, governors without conscience, people without restraint ; the triumph of voluptuousness, the apotheosis of profligacy, the exaltation of blasphemy, the follies of luxury ; and which has at last produced upon the battle-field an army without discipline, led by commanders nearly all without intellect. A man who was elevated to empire by the suffrage of the people, that he might save them from anarchy, has lost himself in disgrace and France in an abyss, through his twenty years' revolutionary policy. He has spent twenty years in scooping out, with his principles of 1789, a grave for his own dynasty and ruin for the nation at large, in the centre of the State. And outside of the State, what has been the success of the policy of this unfortunate ruler, so skilled in all the wisdom of the Revolution? To overthrow Austria, *and to overthrow her Catholicism*, as Prince Napoleon declared in his speech, June 23, 1860, and to create a strong kingdom of Italy that might put down the Pope, and help the Bonapartes to dispossess Germany of the Rhenish Provinces was his design. Instead of which, by over-throwing Austria, he has only managed to set up a sort of plaster cast of Italy, and has created a powerful German Empire, which has wrenched the sceptre from him, and has torn from France Alsace and Metz.

The old Prince Theodore Metternich, at the end of 1849, predicted that

the simple President of the French Republic would succeed in becoming
Emperor, and that he would be ruined as a *Revolutionary Emperor* by
Italy. Donoso Cortes, Marquess of Valdegamas, predicted, soon after,
that Bonaparte, once made an emperor, would accomplish much work, but
that the fruit of his labour should be gathered by some other whom he
was unable to indicate. Both these clear-sighted statesmen knew Louis
Napoleon, the secret links that bound him to factions, and the revolutionary clouds that were darkening his intellect. And both have hit the
blot ; since Napoleon III. has really made it his business, during the whole
course of his reign, to play the *Revolutionary Emperor* in Italy ; and
with all his superfine policy has only worked for the King of Prussia,
who, thanks to this Italian polciy, enjoys the Empire of Germany,
erected over the ruins of his throne and the fragments of the army of
France.

Added to these misfortunes, brought upon the French nation by the
man who boasted that he personified the principles of the Revolution, is
the infamy he has inflicted upon that nation by using her as an instrument to torment, to denude, and then to betray the Roman Pontiff.
Vying with the First Napoleon, he turned the French power in the nineteenth century to levelling the edifice which the Franks of the eighth
century had so gloriously established in Italy and in Rome. Then, like
his uncle, he coveted the titles of Charlemagne. The Julian of the Papacy
aspired to be proclaimed its Constantine ; he who deserved to be defined
by the words by which Pius VII. in the Bull of Excommunication of
the 10th of June, 1810, described his hypocritical uncle : *One who had
called himself a friend of the Church, but had joined the impious with the
sole view of annihilating her and of betraying her more easily ; one who
had pretended to protect her, so as to oppress her more securely.*

It is well known that the destruction of the Lombard power in Italy,
and the spoliation of the Holy See, took place against the general national
will of the French. These were Napoleonic enterprises, acts of his conspiring despotism. But it is also certain that France allowed herself to
be led into these acts, so opposed to French honour, and to second them
with her blood, her gold, her name, her weaknesses ; and that the decline
of the Pope's Sovereignty worked itself out under the patronage, and was
consummated by the treacherous disappearance, of the French banner.
Therefore as the justice of God seems to have put down the fall of Rome
to the account of France, history also will impute it to her. It is as the
last ignominious mark made on her story by the man who for twenty
years poisoned her with Revolution.

The penalty has followed close upon the fault. In two days after the
French garrison abandoned the Vicar of Christ, the eagles of Napoleon were
defeated in three battles, Weissenbourg, Wörth, and Spickeren ; and at the
end of that war, which had been made a pretext for withdrawing from
Civita Vecchia the five thousand soldiers that were there to defend the
Pope, France, defeated in twenty-three great battles, finds herself
essened by five hundred thousand men, made prisoners by the German
conqueror. A hundred thousand exactly for every thousand men taken
from the Pontiff !

is therefore manifest that France, after eighty years of *revolutionary* poisoning, at last feels herself dying, and dying of the Revolution. The great victim of her principles of 1789, she is judged by Heaven for her scandalous apostasy ; a tremendous example perhaps of the anger of the Lord against Christian nations which separate socially from Christ ; a formidable warning to those Catholics who tread carelessly in her steps ; and the clearest proof of the divine truth that the greatest of all sins, apostasy, especially when social, is the greatest of all national miseries— *miseros facit populos peccatum.* May the lamentable sight of this judgment of God enlighten Italy, Spain, Portugal, and Austria. From the heap of ashes, of ruins, of wounds, and of sorrow to which she that was the great nation is to-day reduced, there is a voice rising which cries out to each of them—*Hodie mihi, cras tibi !*

If France would return to the right path and become once more the *gens inclyta Francorum* of Clovis, of Charlemagne, of Saint Louis, she must burn the idol of the Revolution, which, until now, she has adored.

III.

But, this fatal Moloch consumed, France must again adore God's Christ, whom, until now, she has as a nation burned. This is the sole remedy for her, for it alone can reinstate her at the post assigned to her by God, as a Christian nation, out of which, as such, there is no reason for her existence.

" Every nation," wrote Joseph de Maistre in his 'day, " has received from God an office which she ought to fulfil. France exercises over the world a true primacy, which cannot be denied, and of which she took an unworthy advantage. She headed the religious movement ; whence her king was, with a good right, called *Most Christian.* Bossuet did not exaggerate this truth. But now, as France has availed herself of her authority to contradict her own vocation and to spoil the world, we must not wonder that she should be led back by frightful warnings."

These wise sentences, which seem as if written to-day, throw full light on the only mode of restoration for France. If she is to be restored and wills it, she must absolutely return to the post where God placed her, and resume the fulfilment of the *mission* for which God elected her, when he drew her socially into the pale of His Church.

" The mission of a people," remarks the loyal Almonda," begins with the formation of that people, and is born with them. It is a star that shines over the cradle of nations. And so it happened with regard to France. From the day of their baptism, Clovis and his soldiers raised the sublime cry—*Vivat Christus ! Amat Francos.* They spoke the truth ; for God chose France to fulfil the great deeds of His love, the great works of His glory. He made her the first-born child of the Church. With what prayers, with what promises, was the fine nation of the Franks founded ! "

The kingdom of France, which, as says Annibal Caro, *lies, like a large shell, between two seas and two famous mountains, Alps and Pyrenees,* the kingdom which Ugo Grozio defined as *the finest after the Kingdom of Heaven*, which an historian says is made by bishops as honey is made by bçes, was the object of Christ's predilection, *Christus amat Francos*, in order that France might return Him that love, and display it by devoting to Him her strength. That was the *exhibitio operis* required from the *probatio dilectionis*. Wherefore Pope Gregory IX. wrote to the king Saint Louis: *It is manifest that this kingdom, blessed by God, was chosen by our Redeemer to be the special executor of His Divine Will.* Thence the motto by which France is constituted! the soldier of Christ and of His Church throughout the world, *Gesta Dei per Francos*, and which sums up the whole Christian mission of the kingdom.

So long as she remained faithful to her mission, history shows us that France grew in happiness, greatness, and power. Her corruptors, deforming her, by changing her into a soldier of the Revolution, inspired her with a mad hatred for the Middle Ages, from Clovis to Saint Louis, her own golden age, with a mad passion for the new era of 1789, which marks her sudden fall. But what has been the result, even in a material point of view, of the noisy feats accomplished by France in this new era, as a soldier of the Revolution?

Nothing, after all, but defeats, invasions, and territorial dismemberments. Defeats, invasions, and dismemberments, through the war in 1814; defeats, invasions, and dismemberments through that of 1815; and worse defeats, invasions, and dismemberments by that which is now closing in 1871. In little more than fifty years, foreign armies have encamped three times in her proud Paris. When did the France of the most Christian kings undergo losses and humiliations comparable to the losses and humiliations entailed by the downfall of her two revolutionary emperors?

It is necessary, then, if France would revive, full of a strong social life, from the depth of her present miseries, that she should extend her hand to the Church that made her, and alone can re-make her, and allow herself to be led, like the prodigal son, by that Church, to the feet of Christ her King, so madly forsaken. That she should offer herself to be socially re-baptized in His name, and reinstated in that glorious place destined for her by the Eternal King; and above all, that she should root out of her constitution the principles of 1789, and replace them by the historical formula of the illustrious Franks:—REGNANTE DOMINO NOSTRO. JESU CHRISTO IN PERPETUUM. If she do all this she will feel how true it is, even in our century, that *Christus amat Francos*—and that He' is keeping in store for her an *épopée* of salutary enterprises in our world which has returned to barbarism; that again *Gesta Dei per Francos* will crown her amongst nations—not with that ephemeral and bloody diadem' with which the two Bonapartes shamed her brow, but with the bright and glorious crown, won for her by Charlemagne and her kings of the Crusaqes.

She cannot, indeed, return to the olden time in its order, its laws, its abuses. No; this is impossible, after so many changes have been introduced into civilization, and so many alterations have taken place in public institutions and in the habits of people; besides, then what principle ot restoration would she find in the pagan forms of government presented to her by the Cæsarism of the seventeenth century, or in the cowardices of Gallicanism, which prepared the way for the abject depravity of Voltaire's century?

In the reconstitution of States fallen into dissolution, as France so nearly is, the varying and the contingent must be severed from the unchanging and the necessary : the one will apportion itself to the times which change ; the other will remain, because it belongs to all times. One refers to the accidental ; the other to the foundations of the order to be reconstructed.

The most substantial foundation on which a socially Christian order can be reconstructed, is the acknowledgment, in theory and in practice, of the supreme dominion of God and His inviolable sovereignty over nations ; of God, not only as the Creator of Nature, but as the revealed of Faith, author of the supernatural, and redeemer of men, who continues the work of salvation by means of the Church instituted by Him, and whose head is His vicar, the Roman Pontiff. This is the corner-stone upon which France of old erected the social edifice of the kingdom and maintained it for centuries, but which the demented France of 1789 rejected of her own accord, to substitute for it a permanent rebellion against God and the legal apostasy of Christ. Wherefore, the edifices of her four or five democratic republics, of her three constitutional kingdoms, and of her two despotic empires, came to ruin all at once, in mud, or blood. They had all been planted on the sand, they had no foundation. The God who creates and saves nations had had no part in their structure ; nay, they had been raised against Him like so many towers of Babel. What wonder if they fell of themselves, for it is written in heaven and in earth that *Nisi Dominus ædificaverit domum, in vanum laboraverant qui ædificant eam.*

The restorative principle of France, as a nation, can be no other than this if she aspires to a life that shall not be worse than death. Let her return to the post that God designed for her amongst the nations; let God return to the place that He has a right to hold above the nations. Let her become Christian in her laws, in her institutions, and in the habits of her civilization. Let her be socially reconciled with the Church of Christ, which was, and still is a mother to her, and not an enemy, and which still regards her in the light of a first-born child. Let her reinstate herself to the Roman Pontiff, and in the sacred duties that have bound her to him since the reign of Pepin the Brave. Let her repair the harm she has done, by her example, which will be most efficacious, and by that power of action, with which she is endowed to a marvellous extent. By these means she will resume her power over the world, and will re-acquire that primacy amongst Christian peoples which belongs of the Great Nation beloved by Christ, as His arm and His soldier.

ADDRESS OF THE CATHOLIC UNION OF GREAT BRITAIN
TO THE HOLY FATHER.

THE following Address was presented to the Sovereign Pontiff at the
Vatican Palace, by the Deputation whose names are subjoined to it, on
a day in Holy Week :—

MOST HOLY FATHER,

More than fourteen centuries ago the greatest of the Fathers' proclaimed to his separated brethren that "God had established the teaching of the truth in the Chair of Unity." And your Holiness from that
Chair of Unity has declared again and again to the world how by a
singular provision of the Divine Providence the Roman Pontiff, whom
Christ appointed to be the Head and Centre of the whole Church, has
obtained a Civil Principate ; and likewise that it is your will firmly
to maintain and preserve whole and inviolate that Civil Principate
of the Roman Church, and its temporal possessions and rights which
are the property of the whole Catholic world, and as such claim the
defence of all Catholics throughout the world.   It is for this reason
that we, your Catholic children in England and Scotland, approach you
to express our abhorrence of a misdeed by which neither the rights of a
monarchy which has lasted more than a thousand years, nor the long and
pacific possessions of government, nor treaties, sanctioned and confirmed
by the whole weight of European authority, have been respected.   We
wish with one voice and one heart to adhere to this teaching of your Holiness in words which have been consecrated by that great host of Prelates
who nine years ago assembled round your throne.   With them we proclaim that we recognize the Civil Principate of the Roman See as a thing
necessary and manifestly instituted by the Providence of God, and do not
hesitate to declare that in the present state of human affairs this Civil
Principate is absolutely required for the good and free government of the
Church and of souls.   For the Head of the whole Church, the Roman
Pontiff must be no Prince's subject nor any Prince's guest, but seated in
his own domain and kingdom must be his own master, and in noble, tranquil, and benign liberty must defend and protect the Catholic Faith, and
rule and govern the whole Christian commonwealth.   There must be a
sacred place and an august See from which a great and powerful voice,
the voice of justice and of truth, favouring none above others, and obeying
no man's will, inaccessible to terror, and not to be deceived by fraud, may
be proclaimed to princes and to peoples alike.   Such a voice could not be
uttered in security if it owed a civil obedience to any man : for those
whose crimes and errors it was obliged to condemn would never allow
it to be heard with impunity.   Such a voice could not be respected by the
faithful of all nations with the obedience due to the Head of the Church,
if it were spoken by one subject to the control of any temporal prince.

Nor, again, can the Prelates of the Church, flocking to your Holiness at all times for consultation and guidance from so many different regions and nations of the world, approach you in security, if they find a sovereign ruling over your See, who may either regard their coming with suspicion and dislike, or be at enmity with their respective countries. The duties of the Christian and the citizen, in themselves distinct but not incompatible, cannot be fulfilled by Bishops unless a Civil Princedom be maintained at Rome, such as that of the Pontiffs, absolutely free from foreign control, a centre of universal concord, soiled by no breath of human ambition, touched by no desire of earthly domination.

Nor is it possible for those to devise guarantees of independence who, by a crime without parallel, have seized what is not their own. Lawless force and shameless fraud, uniting to confiscate what has been held for centuries under the consecration of all divine and human right, leave no basis for any future structure which could secure independence. The guarantee of thieves is worthless. Robbery, superadded to sacrilege, can possess no rights, and therefore can confer none. Should a victim consent to accept as a dole a portion of the plunder taken from him, it would always remain in the power of the robber to resume it, when length of time and submission had seemed to palliate the original crime. But the Vicar of Christ cannot live upon the sufferance of those who disregard, by the same act, the law of nations and the duty of Christians.

If as Catholic Christians we all require the liberty of the Pontiff-King, no less does the security of all thrones upon earth depend upon the inviolability of the throne of Peter. The safety of rulers and the freedom of nations are equally founded upon right. But the highest expression of right is in that throne. It is not merely that as a particular state no monarchy and no commonwealth can boast of rights so august, so ancient, and so sacred. It possesses a far higher consecration as the throne of the King of Justice and Peace, presiding over that temporal order which he had re-created and re-enforced. Thus it was that, when the nations of the world had learnt to acknowledge as nations the law of Christ, the throne of Peter was seen to rise in temporal sovereignty at their centre. As they were built up on the joint foundation of Christian faith and civil rights the voice of the Holy Father was heard among them, lending a lustre to the dignity of princes which it had not before possessed, because superior to them all as the Vicar of Christ. There was not a throne which did not acknowledge in his Fathership the palladium of its liberty and its strength. Through all the shocks and changes of eleven hundred years that throne has still subsisted, and in it we see not only the outward sign and symbol of Christendom, but the power which as it first created so continues to hold it together. Since the great revolt against it that power has become the centre of a wider circle, having gathered many millions in America, in Asia, and in Australia, who look to it for guidance and for truth. If it be removed, the nations as such cease to be Christian, and fall under the rule of force. If all the rights that can consecrate a throne be, in the case of this Holy See, despised and trampled under foot, what King may be secure

in his kingdom, or what Commonwealth in its territory ?   Therefore, Holy
Father, your Sacred Person, while the champion of religion, is also the representative of all civil rights in the combat which you now maintain.   Nor
is there any civil polity existing in the world at present which might not be
dissolved and broken up, if the principles of public conduct which have been
carried into effect against the ruler of the States of the Church were used
in its own case.   And as Englishmen we feel that this remark applies in
its greatest force to the British Empire.   Injustice, the higher it strikes,
the wider it spreads.   If it triumph over that one Person, whose Chair of
Teaching, because it was the root of divine authority in the Church,
became likewise the constituent cause of Christendom, and the archetype of
all just civil rule, it will in its application stalk at once over all the earth ;
nor can that be called right when done at Rome, which shall be called
wrong when done in England or in America.

Therefore, Holy Father, in approaching you as rightful Sovereign of the
States of the Church, in praying continually and labouring by all lawful
means in our power that this throne may be preserved to you as Successor
of S. Peter, Head of the Church, and Vicar of Christ, we are expressing at
once our love to you as Catholics, and our loyalty to our own Sovereign
as Englishmen.   As we should repudiate usurpation or rebellion at home,
so we abhor them abroad ; but they assume to us an aspect of universal
menace, when they combine with insult and degradation to the Church of
Christ, and with the oppression of His Vicar.

These feelings towards the Holy See and its temporal sovereignty are
enhanced by the thought that we are approaching One who, by the good
Providence of God, has more nearly than any of his predecessors reached
the years of Peter, and who during that long period of twenty-five years
has shown every gift of a Pontiff and a Sovereign which can justify the
affection and respect felt towards him by all the Faithful, and by none more
warmly than ourselves.

We desire to see established in every Catholic household a contribution to Peter's Pence, as a chief work of mercy in these times, and no
less as a mark of affection and gratitude to our common Father, and
we have taken the opportunity to bring with us some offerings for that
purpose.

It is requisite to say that many who would have been glad on this
occasion personally to lay their homage at the feet of your Holiness,
have been prevented from joining us by duties which at this season
forbid their absence from home.   For them, as well as for ourselves,
our families, and our country, we ask of your Holiness the Apostolic
Benediction.

The following gentlemen composed the Deputation :—

His Grace the Duke of NORFOLK, E.M.	Lord ARCHIBALD DOUGLAS.
The Earl of DENBIGH	Lord HENRY KERR.
The Right Hon. Lord ROBERT MONTAGU, P.C., M.P.	Viscount CAMPDEN.
	Lord HERRIES.
Lord EDMUND HOWARD.	Lord ARUNDELL of WARDOUR.
	The MASTER of LOVATT.

The MASTER of HERRIES.
The Hon. W. NORTH.
The Hon. J. DORMER.
The Hon. W. PETRE.
R. MONTEITH, Esq., of Carstairs.
W. LANGDALE, Esq.
A. LANGDALE, Esq.
F. R. WEGG PROSSER, Esq.
ED. MOLYNEUX SEELE, Esq., Chamberlain to His Holiness.
ALEXANDER FLETCHER, Esq.
CHARLES GANDOLFI HORNYOLD, Esq.
C. DE LA BARRE BODENHAM, Esq.

EDGAR HIBBERT, Esq.
HERBERT HIBBERT, Esq.
CHARLES WELD, Esq.
H. CLIFFORD, Esq.
T. FARMER BAILLIE, Esq.
W. H. SILLS, Esq.
F. W. REYNOLDS, Esq., of Liverpool.
J. KENYON, Esq.
THOMAS WALMISLEY, Esq.
RICHARD WALMISLEY, Esq.
STUART KNILL, Esq.
J. VAUGHAN, Esq.
J. BISHOP, Esq.

His Holiness was pleased to return the following reply :—

"I am filled with love, with affection, with gratitude, in answering the noble sentiments which you have just expressed in favour of the Holy See, and of the feeble individual whom God has placed upon the Throne, in times so difficult, so perverse—times in which so many have arisen against their Lord and against His Church, and in which We are obliged to maintain the cause of right, truth, and justice. I repeat that I feel myself penetrated with gratitude ; and the sight of you recalls to my mind one of my great Predecessors — who loved you well—who loved England dearly—S. Gregory the Great. I am his successor. I cannot compare myself with him in virtues, in elegance, in learning ; but I in no wise yield to him in my love for you, for your country, for England. I have done all that was possible for me to do, in order to extend, to multiply, to expand the Church in that England which was once the Island of Saints ; and until our own times has displayed [*déployé*] so much power in the world—in society. I have prayed to S. Gregory to suggest to me the words that I should say to you this morning. There are two things: I pray you to be always united ; let your impulse and energy be united with the impulse and energy which is manifested throughout the Catholic world. As at the beginning of the Catholic religion, *Credentium erat cor unum et anima una,* so I beseech you to be always united one with the other. I charge you to say this to your Bishops : be united—the Bishops with you, and you with the Bishops. If any one lags behind, it must be made known, in order that I may suggest to him to re-unite himself to the rest, and to march against the enemies of Religion and of the Church. It is not now a political war—a battle against governments, which we have to wage ; but we have even to maintain the rights of Truth, the rights of Religion, the rights which Jesus Christ has given us. Union, then, my dear children, is necessary. Courage is also necessary—the courage to speak up for and defend the rights of the Church—to defend them against her enemies, who make war upon her here in Italy and elsewhere. And this war is not made only against the Pope; there are many who will have nothing more to do with Jesus Christ, nor with the Blessed Virgin. In such a warfare let us unite all our efforts,and the gates of hell shall never prevail—*portæ inferi non præ-valebunt.* I might, my children, say many other things to you; but I will not take up your time. I accompany you with my blessings. I give them to you with all my heart. I have already said that I love England; and I repeat that S. Gregory is my superior in science and in virtue; but as to love for England, I am equal with S. Gregory. May my benedictions be with you throughout your lives; may they remain upon you and your wives, and your children, and your brothers, your lands and your possessions, so that you may live and die in the midst of these blessings. O my God! grant that the Catholic Church may flourish in England; grant that this Church may flourish. Bless all those who are here present; may every mouth here present praise Thee and exalt Thee throughout all Eternity! BENEDICTIO DEI OMNIPOTENTIS, PATRIS, ET FILII ET SPIRITUS SANCTI DESCENDAT SUPER VOS ET MANEAT SEMPER. AMEN."

Notices of Books.

Acta Sanctae Sedis in compendium opportune redacta. Fasciculus lxiv. Romæ.

OUR readers may remember a collection of documents which we published in January, 1868 (pp. 279-290), and to which we refer also in an article of this number, on the condemnation of certain philosophical tenets which had been advocated in Belgium. The Congregations of the Inquisition and Index, having been commissioned for that purpose by the Holy Father, pronounced their united judgment on these tenets ; and their judgment was one of condemnation. Their Decree expressed Pius IX.'s confirmation ; and was afterwards declared by Card. Patrizi, in the Pope's name, to have been "doctrinal" and not merely "disciplinary." The tenets in question consisted mainly of a certain modified traditionalism, set forth by four Louvain Professors in a paper which we published in April, 1869 (pp. 532-536) : but reference was also made in the Decree to statements tending in the ontologistic direction ; and to propositions, at least incautiously expressed, concerning traducianism and concerning the vital principle in man. The Louvain Professors terminated the controversy for the time by signing a formula, authoritatively proposed to them, wherein they expressed that they "fully, perfectly, and absolutely submitted themselves to the Decisions of the Holy See" recently pronounced, "and acquiesced ex animo therein."

The Vatican Council however, while condemning traditionalism in the "Dei Filius," did not specially mention that modified form thereof, which had been advocated by the four Louvain Professors ; and some of them accordingly maintained, that they were now at liberty again to hold and advocate their old opinions on the subject. The matter was referred to Rome ; and on August 7 Card. Patrizi, by command of Pius IX., issued the following Response, which we find in the number of the "Acta" named at the head of our notice.

"That by the said Synodal Constitution [the 'Dei Filius'], especially by the monitum at its conclusion, all the Decrees of the two Congregations issued on the matter have not only not been annulled or weakened, but on the contrary have been invested with new sanction."*

---

* "Occasione promulgationis secundae Constitutionis Apostolicae Sacri Concilii Oecumenici Vaticani, quae incipit 'Dei Filius,' in quâ licet Traditionalistarum eiror damnetur, doctrina tamen de necessitate aliqualis institutionis prò rationis humanae evolutione directè vel explicitè non

The "Civiltà" of March 18 (p. 721) has declared, that this Response more useful than any *treatise* "for the purpose of clearing up better a special point concerning[the extension of the Object and the Acts of the [Pope's] Apostolic Magisterium." Nor can we be surprised at this view. This monitum, as our readers will remember,* enforces the necessity of Catholics diligently avoiding those errors, which approach more or less nearly to heresy without being actually heretical; and reminds the Church's children accordingly, of their obligation to observe those various Pontifical Decrees, whereby such errors are proscribed. The Holy Father's Response then of August 7, 1870, declares in effect that the Congregational Decrees of 1867, expressing as they did the Pope's confirmation, are to be accounted Pontifical ex cathedrâ Acts.

Petri Privilegium. Three Pastoral Letters. By HENRY EDWARD ARCH-
BISHOP OF WESTMINSTER. London : Longmans.

THE Archbishop has bound up in this volume his three successive Pastorals on Papal Infallibility. "The first, which treats of the eighteenth centenary of S. Peter's martyrdom, simply affirms the doctrine of infallibility, as it has been enunciated and taught by,the theological tradition of the Church. The second traces the line of the historical tradition by which the same Catholic doctrine has been affirmed. The third states and explains the doctrine of the infallibility of the Roman Pontiff, as it has been defined by the Œcumenical Council of the Vatican." (Preface.) We have already noticed all three in due order as they appeared ; and need here only add, that their juxtaposition greatly increases the force of each one.

We may however make the same use of the occasion, as was made by our

---

videtur attingi, quaesitum est, num iam haec doctrina liberè inter doctores catholicos controverti possit. Quod quum aliqui Lovanienses Professores tuerentur, res iterum ad S. Sedem delata est ; causâque cognitâ per S. R. E. Cardinales Inquisitores Generales, Emus Card. Patrizi de mandato SSmi D. N. ad puritatem catholicae doctrinae servandam, datis litteris ad sin-gulos in Belgio Sacrorum Antistites die 7 Augusti 1870, his verbis rescripsit :

   " ' Per memoratam Constitutionem Synodalem, praesertim per monitum ' at eiusdem calcem relatum, nedum haud infirmari vel moderari, quin imo ' novo adiecto robore confirmari Decreta omnia utriusque S. Congrega-' tionis S. Officii et Indicis hâc de re edita, illudque potissimum, quod lit-' teris meis ad singulos in Belgio Episcopos die 2 Martii 1866 datis con-' tinetur.' "

   * It runs as follows:—" Quoniam vero satis non est haereticam pravi-tatem devitare, nisi ii quoque errores diligenter fugiantur qui ad illam plus minusve accedunt ; omnes officii monemur, servandi etiam Constitu-tiones et Decreta, quibus pravae eiusmodi opiniones, quae istic diserte non enumerantur, ab' hâc Sanctâ Sede proscriptae et prohibitae sunt,"

contemporary the "Tablet" in reviewing "Petri Privilegium." We may take this opportunity of commemorating the characteristic services successively rendered to the Church, by three illustrious members of the English Catholic Episcopate : Bishop Milner, Cardinal Wiseman, and now Archbishop Manning.

It was especially Bishop Milner's work, among all contemporary bishops, to stem the torrent of non-Catholic and anti-Roman thought, which then threatened the Church in England. This phenomenon was apparently occasioned by the hope then offered to Catholics, of purchasing some considerable relaxation of the chains which had hitherto bound them, at the expense of sacrificing in this or that respect the integrity of Catholic doctrine. No thought can compass the calamity which would have befallen the cause of religion, if the necessary work had not been done, of resisting these evil principles ; and Bishop Milner was the champion called to that work by the Church's Divine Ruler. He was the most powerful and effective opponent of heresy in his day, precisely because he was the most powerful and effective opponent of unsound and of nominal Catholicism.

Cardinal Wiseman continued what Bishop Milner had begun. It was he who first set himself deliberately and systematically to oppose that narrow nationalism, which claims for Englishmen some special superiority over foreigners, in "sobriety" of devotional thought and language. It was he who placed before Englishmen the idea and (so to speak) the very exhibition of Rome, as the form and standard of religious observance. It was he who diligently fostered and promoted in England the establishment and growth of "foreign" religious orders ; and the translation into English of "foreign" lives of Saints. Catholics of the present day sometimes hardly appreciate the extent of his Eminence's success, because of its very completeness. But how complete that success has been, is evidenced by the single fact. Since the Cardinal's death attempts have been made, with signal ability and profound sincerity, to revive the distinction between what is "English" and what "foreign" in Catholic devotion ; but those attempts have been simply futile and powerless, because so violently out of harmony with the sympathies of Catholic Englishmen.

And now what the Cardinal did in matters of devotion, his successor is doing in matters of doctrine. It is more obviously true of doctrine than even of devotion, that there cannot be two standards, one for Rome and another for England. It is the Pope who has been appointed by God "the teacher of all Christians" ; and the one true Christian religion is precisely that religion in all its fulness which the Pope practically teaches. The Archbishop's labour, throughout his Catholic life, has been to place this religion just as it stands before his fellow-countrymen, whether Catholic or Protestant ; and we are confident that such a course is indefinitely more persuasive even to externs, than is any paring down of Roman doctrine with a view to supposed English requirements. The Archbishop is himself such a thorough Englishman, that his adoption of this particular course is the more remarkable, and at the same time all the more effective. It is not till he has gone to his reward—may that be a very distant period !—that Catholics will fully realize the vast services he has rendered. Yet let any one compare the doctrinal standard of Catholic England at this moment with what it was even five years ago, and he will *partly* see what the Archbishop has done.

The Infallibility of the Pope explained in a Dialogue between a Priest and a Member of his Congregation. London: Washbourne.

IT is far less easy than those probably think who have not made the experiment, to write a dialogue of this kind in a telling and effective way ; nor have we ever seen the intrinsic difficulties of such composition more successfully vanquished, than in the instance before us. Take e.g. the following page, in which a cogent historical argument is expressed with the greatest simplicity and clearness.

" The Church, in all ages, believed the Pope to be infallible, and acted upon this belief. It would take too long to show you the proof of this in the history of the Church, century by century. Here are, however, certain broad facts which you will easily understand and remember :—From time immemorial it has been the constant custom both of the Eastern and the Western Churches to submit disputed questions affecting the faith to the judgment of the Holy See. Nothing is clearer in the history of the Church than this fact. And here is another fact equally clear. Whenever the Pope gave his solemn decision, it was received by all Catholics as final, and was regarded as binding on the consciences of all. For instance, in the fifth century there were certain people who spread abroad a new doctrine about grace. The matter was laid before the Pope, who condemned the new opinion as heresy. As soon as the Pope's decision was made known to the great S. Augustine, he at once exclaimed, ' Rome has spoken ! the dispute is now settled !' That is but a sample of the belief which prevailed everywhere, and at all times, throughout the Church. Immediately the Pope spoke, all true Catholics knew at once which was the right side. Now, how could this have been the case ? Would the faithful have accepted the Pope's decision as final, unless they firmly believed that he could not lead them astray—unless, in other words, they believed him to be infallible ?

" JOHN : No ; certainly. And that just answers what a person remarked to me the other day. He said that until lately the common run of Catholics hardly ever heard of the Pope's Infallibility ; and that, for his part, he could not help thinking that it was in some way a new thing altogether. But I see now he always believed it, only he did not reason with himself about it. For if any one had put forward some strange opinion, and the Pope condemned it, the person I speak of would not, I am sure, have the shadow of a doubt that the Pope was right. And, of course, that is only saying in another way that he believes the Pope is infallible.

" FATHER F. : Just so, John ; you see exactly what I mean. In fact, when you come to think the matter over, you will find that so far from the Infallibility being a new doctrine, the truth is, that the denial of it is the new doctrine. The Popes themselves have always claimed to be infallible, for they would never permit any one, bishop, priest, or layman, to question a solemn decision of theirs, or to appeal from it to any other tribunal. They simply gave judgment, and commanded every one to submit to it. And the faithful in all ages *have* submitted ; and have, both by their words and their acts, expressed their belief that the Popes were all that they claimed to be. Now, see what results from this. If the Infallibility of the Pope were not a truth revealed by Our Lord Himself, it would manifestly follow that all along the Church had believed and accepted an error ; and that, therefore, contrary to Our Lord's own express promise, the gates of hell had prevailed against her" (pp. 8, 9).

Here again are one or two points excellently put. We italicise one sentence.

" There was a man telling me the other day that he could not understand how one man alone could be infallible. He said he could see how a General Council could be infallible ; for, as he remarked, 'among the multitude of councillors there is safety ;' but to make one man infallible, seemed almost like making him a god.

" FATHER F. : Is the person you allude to a Catholic ?

" JOHN : Yes, your Reverence ; he is a kind of one.

" FATHER F. : I suppose, then, he would admit that a General Council could not possibly teach error ?

" JOHN : O ! yes, he would allow that. In fact he said he believed that God preserves a General Council from going astray.

" FATHER F. : Of course, then, he would allow that if God did not preserve it, it might teach error.

" JOHN : O ! surely.

" FATHER F. : Well, then, the infallibility of a General Council is, after all, God's work. He it is that makes the assembled Fathers infallible in their united decision. All their wisdom, and learning, and piety, would be of no avail without the assistance of the Holy Spirit. Since, then, infallibility comes from God, it is just as easy for Him to bestow the gift on one man as on an assembly of men. And so, in reality, there is no more difficulty in admitting the Infallibility of the Pope than there is in admitting the Infallibility of a General Council. Besides, we know that God has, at times, given individual men a higher gift even than that of infallibility, and that too, before Christianity existed at all.

" JOHN : I did not know that, your Reverence. I thought that no man was infallible before the time of Our Lord.

" FATHER F. : O ! yes, there were ; the writers of the Holy Scriptures, were they not inspired ?

" JOHN : Surely, all Christians allow that.

" FATHER F. : Well, what do we mean when we say they were inspired ?

" JOHN : I suppose we mean that God preserved them from error in what they wrote.

" FATHER F. : That at least, we mean, certainly. Now, what is that but bestowing on such men the gift of Infallibility—preserving them, that is, from teaching error ? Indeed, we believe that in the case of the Sacred Writers, Almighty God did more than this. We believe that He actually suggested to them what to write, as well as secured them against error in writing it. *And I never could understand why Protestants, who profess to believe in the inspiration of the Bible, should consider us so unreasonable for believing in the Infallibility of the Pope.* They believe with us, that in past times certain men were infallibly assisted by God in teaching His truth to the people. Why, then, is it absurd to suppose that God may do a similar thing now ? And mind, John, we do not by any means claim for the Pope what we claim for the Inspired Writers" (pp. 10, 11).

The great excellence which this dialogue otherwise so conspicuously displays, makes us not a little surprised at its unguarded language concerning the *extent* of infallibility ; for in several places the writer speaks as though he confined that prerogative to definitions of *Faith.* In page 7 his words even run, as though he considered that that restriction is implied in the Preamble itself to the Vatican Definition ; but we showed in our last number (pp. 188–192) how extremely far this is from being the case. The sentence in which, more emphatically than in any other, the author seems to imply the view we ascribe to him, is at pp. 13, 14. "Let any one prove," says the priest, "that a single pope ever taught the faithful, as a doctrine to be believed by the Church, anything which was not believed in from the first. Let him prove that, *and there is an end to the Catholic religion.*" This sentence is so definitely and intelligibly expressed, that it peremptorily challenges comment.

Now we have no right to assume, that the author here intends to deny the Pope's infallibility in *dogmatical facts.* Most certainly indeed it was not "believed in from the first," that Jansenius's "Augustinus" contains five certain propositions in its legitimate objective sense ; nor that certain "most holy men have cultivated scholastic theology with great benefit to the Catholic religion" (Pius VI.'s "Auctorem Fidei," n. 76) ; nor that SS. Thomas and Bonaventura did not exhibit inaccuracy and too great heat in defending the mendicant orders (ib. n. 81).* Still it does not follow, we repeat, that the present author intends to deny the Pope's infallibility on such facts, because he would probably reply that they *are* facts and not *doctrines :* though we certainly wish he had *expressed* this distinction, in order that he might save his readers from a very natural misunderstanding. But (to take only two instances out of a large number), the Council of Trent has defined that the Eucharistic Conversion is "most aptly " "suitable and properly " called "Transubstantiation " (Sessio xiii. cap. 4 and canon 2) ; and Pius IX. has declared in the Syllabus that "all Catholics are bound (debent) to hold most firmly " that " doctrine " on his civil princedom which is "clearly laid down " in six Pontifical Acts there mentioned. The author surely will not say that these doctrines were "believed in from the first " ; for in Apostolic times the word "Transubstantiation " had never been invented, nor the Pope's civil princedom thought of. But still less will the author dream of saying that "there is an end to the Catholic religion." And as we cannot doubt that a second edition will soon be called for of so spirited and timely a brochure, we hope that the author will in that edition express more accurately and intelligibly his meaning on this particular part of his subject.

---

* "In eo quod subjungit, sanctos Thomam et Bonaventuram sic in tuendis . . . . mendicantium institutis versatos esse ut in eorum defensionibus minor cæstus, accuratio major desideranda fuisset ;—scandalosa, in sanctissimos Doctores injuriosa, &c." If *injurious*, it must be *untrue*.

Infallibility in a Nutshell. BY REV. F. WEININGER, S.J. London : Philp.

NOTHING can be more clearly expressed than this little tract ; and indeed its author had already done important service, in familiarizing both English and American Catholics with the theological grounds of the dogma which has now been defined.

" *Question I.*—What does the infallibility of the Pope mean ?

" Does it mean : That whatever the Pope does is right, and that he cannot commit any mistake or any sin ? No, it does not.

" Does it mean : That the Pope cannot err in scientific or political matters ? It does not.

" Does it mean : That the Pope, in theological discussions, writing books, or preaching, cannot err ? It does not. What then does it mean ?

" *Answer.*—It means : That the Pope, when addressing the whole Church on matters of Faith, [that is, in other words, when] teaching or defining what is to be believed by all Christians, cannot err. It is therefore not a personal, but an official prerogative of the Head of the Church, which is the kingdom of truth."

We think however that the excellent author, at the end of his tract, over-states the unanimity with which this dogma has been *explicitly* believed by Catholics of every age.

The Theology of the Parables. By HENRY JAMES COLERIDGE, S.J. London : Burns, Oates, & Co.

MANY are the intellectual desiderata of Catholics at this time. Among the foremost is an exposition of Scripture, which, while remaining faith ul to traditional principles and based on the admirable existing Catholic commentaries, shall also make full use of the vast light which has been thrown by modern criticism on the sacred text. We have more than once expressed an opinion, that no English writer is so competent to this task as F. Coleridge ; and we are delighted therefore to receive this first instalment (see note at p. 2) of his complete Commentary on the Gospels which is in preparation. Our only regret is, that the instalment is so small, and that the Commentary will presumably appear only by such slow degrees.

To criticise the little volume, would be to imply that he who does so possesses ground for a competent opinion on the matters therein treated : which in the present instance is far from being the case. We shall therefore only place before our readers a general outline of the view which F. Coleridge develops.

A critical period of our Lord's life on earth, according to the sacred historians, was His beginning to teach by parables. Now it is most difficult

2 I 2

to suppose, argues our author, that the change of teaching on which so much stress is laid was merely a change of *form* ; for the parabolic form of teaching was by no means used by our Blessed Lord for the first time at the period so emphatically indicated by the Evangelists (pp. 2–4). And again the *reason* He gave for beginning to teach by parables, was a reason which applied not to a new *form* but to a new *matter* of teaching (pp. 5, 6). F. Coleridge then suggests (p. 9) that this new matter of teaching is "God in His dealings with His creatures and especially man."

This theme, F. Coleridge suggests (ib.), was that which throughout attracted to itself " the tenderest devotion and most constant attention of the Sacred Heart of the Incarnate Son." In the earlier part of His teaching, the mention of His Father was " characteristically prominent " (p. 10) : but in proportion as there sprung up an organized and formal opposition against Him on the part of the Jewish authorities, there was less mention of His Father in His explicit lessons. Our author illustrates this in some degree (p. 10) by a comparison between the Sermon on the Mount, recorded by S. Matthew, and the Sermon on the Plain, recorded by S. Luke ; which we entirely concur with him in accounting two different discourses. But after the later of these discourses, a far more extensive development took place of this malignant opposition (p. 13) ; and so it happened (p. 15) that just when the time was come for His teaching the people more fully about His Father's dealings with mankind, it became less possible than it had even been at a former period to do this explicitly. Being debarred then by His very love for men from such direct utterance, " He was fain to pour forth, in some form analogous to the highest song, the thoughts to which the possession of all the knowledge concerning God with which the Sacred Humanity was endowed, gave birth " (p. 15). Moreover, apart from the circumstances of that particular time, there is something in the parabolic method of teaching especially appropriate for the declaration of God's dealings with man.

" When we consider Who God is, and how infinitely His attributes and nature are above our comprehension, it must be obvious at once that His government of the universe must be, as a whole and in its parts, very far above the ken of our mental faculties, though at the same time it is equally true that in nature and in Providence, as well as in the supernatural order, He distinctly reveals Himself, and intends us to learn about Him from His works and ways. He is the one great object of the study and contemplation of all created intelligent beings, and at the same time He must, as it were, break the knowledge of Himself to us tenderly, He must raise us on high and add fresh power to our eyes before we can gaze on Him. If we could fully understand Him and His ways, He would not be our God ; if we could know nothing about Him and about them, we should not be the creatures He has made us, and our life here would not be a preparation for the blessedness which He intends for us hereafter, and of which we even now enjoy the partial foretaste. The very first thing that we know about Him is a mystery to us in the common sense of the word. For the first great mystery in the providence of God—in which we may include the creation as well as the government of the world—is that permisson and tolerance of evil which follows as a necessary consequence from the planting of free creatures in a state of probation. Let us never underrate this. It has its answer, but not all can see it.* Those familiar with the difficulties which practically beset and bewilder no inconsiderable number even of Christian and Catholic souls to whom the world is a puzzle and a riddle, will hardly question the importance of this difficulty, which pushes itself, if we may so say, in so many different directions."

"All these difficulties have, then, their answer in the knowledge of God and of His character, His attributes, and His ways with men ; and most of them are touched by the remark of St. Augustine, that God chooses rather to bring good out of evil than not to permit evil. Others, again, are met as St. Paul usually, in the first instance, meets difficulties about providence and predestination, by a consideration of the absolute lordship and dominion of God over His creatures, whom He may place under whatever conditions He will, consistently, as whatever He wills must be consistent, with His justice and His holiness. And after this consideration of the absolute authority and ownership—so to speak—of a Creator over His creatures, there naturally follow others which are required also for difficulties of another kind, as well as for those of which we have spoken—considerations of God's immense and boundless goodness, His tender care over His own, His mercy and long-suffering and indulgence to those who oppose themselves to Him, His ever-ready grace, His fatherly attention to prayer, and the like. Another great head of what we may call in general the mystery of God's government contains the whole chain of His dealings with man in respect of his fall and redemption, the arrangements made for his recovery, the manner in which it is brought about, and the special laws of the new kingdom which is its organ, and through which its blessings are administered. Here we come to what in a more restricted sense may be considered as the "mystery" of God's Kingdom—the Divine "economy" of grace which is worked out through the Incarnation by means of an exquisite system, full of beauty, gentleness, and tenderness ; the principles and many of the details of which will be found, on close inspection, to be figured in the parables. All these things are what they are in detail on account of something which may be known and reflected on concerning God, and they cannot be understood and valued unless with respect to Him, and as reflecting His goodness or holiness, or mercifulness or justice.

"This is a very imperfect as well as a very general description of the sort of truths which may be conceived as forming the more substantial points in the teaching by parables—the points to which other things are subordinated, and with reference to which those other things are best to be understood" (pp. 20–21).

F. Coleridge then proceeds to go through the various parables, with this clue to their signification. It is evidently impossible, unless we were writing an article, to follow him on this further ground ; and here therefore we close our notice. We hope we have said enough to indicate our warm admiration of the essay.

---

* If F. Coleridge implies that a really *satisfactory* answer can be given to this difficulty, he would do a singularly great service by referring to the books which contain such answer.

On the Genesis of Species. By St. George Mivart, F.R.S. London: Macmillan & Co., 1871.

THE reception which Mr. Mivart's book on the Darwinian theory of the Origin of Species has received from the most able part of the periodical press cannot but be gratifying to those who, like ourselves, are anxious to defend Revelation and at the same time to do full justice to Science. For apt learning, for clearness of exposition, for force of proof combined with the utmost courtesy and good temper, there is certainly no work on the subject that can be compared to the compact volume now before us. When we add that the author points out with proper severity of language, the unreasonable conceit of the physical philosophers in supposing that their method or their facts can prove or disprove anything at all in the supernatural or hyperphysical order, the reader will not fail to perceive what a valuable contribution to real science is here provided.

It was thought by some, when Mr. Mivart's book appeared, that it would have been timed better if he had waited for Mr. Darwin's expected work, in which he was to apply his theory to the origin of Man. That work has now appeared.* But it does not appear that such objections as Mr. Mivart puts are met in it; on the contrary, some of the difficulties proposed by him seem to be admitted, and Mr. Darwin may be said to have in great measure given up his distinctive views. But of this book we say no more here, as it is our hope to be able to give an article in our next number on the whole subject of Natural Selection in relation to Faith. Meanwhile we will attempt to give our readers some idea of Mr. Mivart's welcome and masterly book.

The originality of Mr. Darwin's famous theory of "Natural Selection" does not consist in the formulating of the fact that the weak die and the strong survive. Such a truth as this could hardly be missed by the first intelligent compiler who proceeded by his own natural light to give science to the world before scientific method was born. Neither was he the first to maintain the view that Species are produced by "development" from pre-existing species. De Maillet (1734), Lamarck (1801), and Dr. Erasmus Darwin, the grandfather of Mr. Charles Darwin himself (1794), had already expressed, with greater or less precision, the theory that there is continuous development in organic nature. But Mr. Darwin's great feat has been to discover, or to announce that he has discovered, that an organism develops solely *on account of* the action of external circumstances; that an infinitesimal change in an individual, if it be for the better, will be preserved,—if it be for the worse the individual will probably perish; and that thus the process of "evolution" has for its unvarying law "the survival of the fittest." It is but justice to Mr. Darwin to allow that the apparatus of observation and fact with which he has at once illustrated and demonstrated his theory gives him a title to rank among the very first natural philosophers of the

---

* "The Descent of Man, and Selection in Relation to Sex." 2 vols. With illustrations. (Murray.)

age. It is a pity he is so pretentiously opposed to Revelation, and so absurdly apprehensive that priests and others are always jealously endeavouring to get him put down ; for we are inclined to believe that the greater part of what he makes any show of *proving* (we do not mean what he asserts or suggests) is so far from being atheistic that it will be found to be positively useful to Revelation. But we reserve this point for a future occasion.

Mr. Mivart's position is not one of absolute antagonism to Mr. Darwin. He states it clearly in a very few words. His object, he says, is " to maintain the position that ' Natural Selection' acts, and indeed must act, but that still, in order that we may be able to account for the production of known kinds of animals and plants, it requires to be supplemented by the action of some other natural law or laws as yet undiscovered. Also that the consequences which have been drawn from Evolution, whether exclusively Darwinian or not, to the prejudice of Religion, by no means follow from it, and are in fact illegitimate" (chap. i. p. 5).

Mr. Mivart, then, does not oppose the theory of Evolution. Neither does he deny that Natural Selection has much to do with Evolution. But he maintains that Natural Selection is only one among many causes and occasions of Evolution. The interest of his book consists chiefly in the patient and skilful labour with which he has marshalled an array of scientific phenomena which he asserts (and we think most of his readers will agree with him), are inexplicable on the theory of Natural Selection alone. In order to give an idea of the contents of the work, we will shortly summarise the principal classes of objections, at the risk of doing injustice to the clear and convincing language of the author. The first difficulty that Mr. Mivart notices is one that concerns the very essence of the Darwinian Natural Selection. It is well known that Mr. Darwin considers the changes which, in his view, have resulted in the infinitely varied species that people the world, to have been slight, minute, and insensible. A pigeon-fancier or a scientific gardener might easily awake and find himself the possessor of a monstrosity in pigeons or an unheard-of variety of dahlia. But it is very different, in the Darwinian theory, with natural and undomesticated species. They vary, not suddenly, but only by small inherited variations. Now, Mr. Mivart, whilst admitting that minute variations *may* often be preserved, maintains that there are a great many species of living things that could never have been developed at all merely by a process of continual slight changes. He would not deny that an extra tenth of an inch in a hawk's claw, or an additional wing-power in the bird it was pursuing, would have some tendency to survive in the struggle for life. But a single fact or class of facts that this theory of minute change would render impossible would of course be sufficient to upset the theory altogether. Mr. Mivart mentions several such classes of facts. Passing over what he says so ably about the neck of the giraffe, the beginnings of protective mimicry, the heads of flat-fishes, the origin and the constancy of the limbs of the higher animals, the whalebone (baleen) of whales, the colours of certain apes, the hood of the cobra, and the rattle of the rattlesnake, we will cite, at once to illustrate his style and to show the force of his reasoning, what he says of the " infant kangaroo."

There is another very curious structure, the origin or the disappearance of which it seems impossible to account for on the hypothesis of minute indefinite variations. It is that of the mouth of the young kangaroo. In all mammals, as in ourselves, the air-passage from the lungs opens in the floor of the mouth behind the tongue, and in front of the opening of the gullet, so that each particle of food as it is swallowed passes over the opening, but is prevented from falling into it (and thus causing death from choking) by the action of a small cartilaginous shield (the epiglottis), which at the right moment bends back and protects the orifice. Now the kangaroo is born in such an exceedingly imperfect and undeveloped condition, that it is quite unable to suck. The mother therefore places the minute blind and naked young upon the nipple, and then injects milk into it by means of a special muscular envelope of the mammary gland. Did no special provision exist, the young one must infallibly be choked by the intrusion of the milk into the windpipe. But there is a special provision. The larynx is so elongated that it rises into the posterior end of the nasal passage, and is thus enabled to give free entrance to the air. for the lungs, while the milk passes harmlessly on each side of the elongated larynx, and so safely attains the gullet behind it.

Now, on the Darwinian hypothesis, either all mammals descended from marsupial progenitors, or else the marsupials sprang from animals having in most respects the ordinary mammalian structure.

On the first alternative, how did "Natural Selection" remove this (at least perfectly innocent and harmless) structure in almost all other mammals, and, having done so, again reproduce it in precisely those forms which alone require it, namely, the cetacea?' That such a harmless structure *need not* be removed, any Darwinian must confess, since a structure exists in both the crocodiles and gavials, which enables the former to breathe themselves while drowning the prey which they hold in their mouths. On Mr. Darwin's hypothesis it could only have been developed where useful, and therefore not in the gavials (!) which feed on fish, but which yet retain, as we might expect, this, in them, superfluous but harmless formation.

On the second alternative, how did the elongated larynx itself arise, seeing that if its development lagged behind that of the maternal structure, the young primeval kangaroo must be choked; while without the injecting power in the mother it must be starved? The struggle, by the sole action of which such a form was developed, must indeed have been severe !

It will be seen from this extract that Darwinism has no contemptible antagonist in Mr. Mivart. He handles his science with as much ease as efficacy. 2. His second argument is taken from the phenomenon called Homology; that is to say, the co-existence of closely similar structures of diverse origin. He contends it is impossible—or so improbable as to be practically impossible—that two exactly similar structures should ever have been produced by the action of Natural Selection *only*. Why, for instance, should the flying instrument in birds be feathers, and in bats be a membrane spread out over bones ? Why did the pterodactyle develop only one finger of his bat-like paddles ? And why have not the aerial spiders, who have floated in the air at the end of their own threads surely quite long enough to have developed something or other—why have they not an apparatus for flight? Still interrogating Mr. Darwin, we may ask him what he makes of such a wonderful coincidence as the independent evolution of a highly complex auditory organ in the vertebrate animals and in their very far away molluscous cousins, the cuttle-fish ? " It would be difficult," says Mr. Mivart, "to calculate the odds against the independent occurrence and conservation of two such complex series of merely accidental and haphazard variations " (p. 75). 3. The third difficulty is that experience seems to show that natural development is sometimes not minute and gradual, but sudden and marked. It certainly seems a very weak point in Mr. Darwin's theory that whilst forced by his senses to admit sudden and considerable change in plants and animals *under domestication* he should most dogmatically assert that the same thing never happens in a state of nature. 4. The assertion of the old idea of Specific Stability forms the subject of the author's fifth chapter, and is his fourth argument. In the "rolling" state of things which Evolution seems calculated to produce to the simple mind, it is a comfort to find such good grounds for believing in stability of any kind. 5. Mr. Mivart proceeds, in a very interesting chapter, to propound several difficulties arising from Geological Time (chap. vi.). If minute transition has been the law during incalculable ages, how is it that the specimens of organic life which have escaped utter destruction by becoming fossilized present us with so few examples of *transition ?* Taking the whole earth's surface together, we should expect to find, for instance, not fifty *megatheria*, all as like each other as fifty cart-horses, but fifty, or say twenty-five, gradually differing animals each a link in a slowly developing series. But this is what we never find—never, that is to say, to such an extent as to be any proof of Darwinism. That we generally find the contrary—that we find remains either violently different or with quite sufficient difference to show they belong to one family—

Qualis decet esse sororum,—

is a difficulty against Natural Selection in Mr. Darwin's sense which he may palliate, but which must be very hard to explain. It is still harder to admit such enormous lapses of time as seem necessary for the gradual development of the existing species. To evolve an elephant out of a tadpole, to use Mr. Mivert's instance, must require more time than either Physics or Astronomy, according to Sir William Thompson, seems able to allow. 6. Under a sixth head we may class a variety of difficulties against Mr. Darwin's hypothesis that are not indeed singly insuperable, but still are formidable when considered all together. The chief of these arises from the geographical distribution of animals. When, for instance, the first Englishmen who colonized New Zealand found its crabs and its salmon to bear a most agreeable resemblance to the corresponding English species, they probably regarded the occurrence more as a tribute of Providence to the general perfection of everything English than as a startling scientific fact. But philosophers, other than Epicureans, have often wondered how this came to pass ; and critics ask Mr. Darwin how it is probable that identical development should have taken place at one side of the world and at the other ? He may reply that these are not independent developments, but members of the same family, now separated by upheavals of continents, sinkings of the earth's surface, volcanic action, glacial periods, and other extensive changes, which, to tell the truth, he is a little too liable to call in to his assistance. And when he has " supposed " any number of these natural convulsions, and reinforced their action by millions of " supposed " enemies, ancestors, and connecting links, most reasonable people will still think Natural Selection highly improbable. And they will be confirmed in their obstinacy by the interesting array of facts which Mr. Mivart presents in the chapter we are considering.

Mr. Mivart is not content with striking heavy blows at Darwinism ; he makes some attempt to substitute a positive view of his own. He admits, as we have already said, that Inheritance, Reversion, Atavism, Natural Selection, &c., play a part not unimportant in the Genesis of Species. But he maintains that an *internal* force or tendency interferes, co-operates, and controls the action of external conditions, and that such internal power is a great, perhaps the main, determining agent. Mr. Herbert Spencer, who, in his "Principles of Biology," adopts a sort of modified Darwinism, has already declared his belief in some such "innate" force. Mr. Wallace, when he admits, in his "Malayan Archipelago," that a "superior intelligence" must have "guided the development *of man* in a definite direction," abandons the all-sufficiency of Natural Selection, and admits that external circumstances are not everything. And, finally, Mr. Darwin himself, having already in the fifth edition of his "Origin of Species" come down so far as to allow that Natural Selection has not been the exclusive means of development, repeats the confession in his new book, "The Descent of Man, thinking it "probable that he has exaggerated its power," though not that he is mistaken in having made its power to be very great.

Catholics are tempted to look upon scientific theories which pretend to deal with Creation and the Soul of Man as idle nonsense, rather to be put down than argued with. And it is only at the end of our remarks that we mention the word Theology. Reserving for a future number a fuller consideration of "Theology and Evolution," we may say that the author's chapter on this subject contains, as far as we can see, nothing to object to ; but, on the contrary, much useful truth and careful reading. He shows that with creation, absolutely considered, physical science has nothing to do. He then explains how, primary creation being granted, no fresh creation of material substance is thenceforward considered necessary by Theology. The common expression of many Fathers and Theologians is, that Almighty God, in His first creative *fiat*, created all things *virtually* or *potentially*. It must be different, however, with the human Soul ; and he shows how, here again, Physical Science must be silent, and Reason and Revelation allowed to speak.

From what has been said above, however, it will been that Mr. Mivart by no means admits that mere Evolution has been the developing cause of even material substance. He expressly endorses, and carries much further, Mr. Wallaces's conclusion, that "even as regards man's body, an action took place different from that by which brute forms were evolved" p. 278.

We conclude these remarks on a book that is as full of solid learning as of excellent spirit by expressing the hope that it may be extensively used by all who care to have enlightened views on subjects on which views of some kind must be held by all educated men.

Contemporary Review. February, 1871. Article by Archbishop Manning on the relation between thought and will.

THIS paper is in no sense contentious and hardly controversial : but it states, with much freshnesss, vigour, and clearness, the various phenomena bearing on the psychological question which it treats. It is a great treat to read so straightforward and telling an essay, after the metaphysical subtleties, which no writers more largely inflict on the world than those who *denounce* metaphysics.

We must not omit once again to thank the Editor for inserting a Catholic contribution. The "Academy" is now following suit, and has inserted two able essays by F. Dalgairns on the Vatican Definition. Catholics have thus a far better opening than has been hitherto afforded them, of making themselves heard by thoughtful Protestants ; and we trust they will not fail to take advantage of the opportunity.

Reasons for returning to the Church of England. London : Strahan.

THE author of this volume submitted himself, as he considered, twenty-five years ago to the Catholic Church : in thirteen years from that time he ceased to profess Catholicity ; and now he returns to his old position as a clergyman of the Establishment.

The most consoling circumstance evinced by his autobiography is, that he was never really a Catholic at all. It was five years from his reception before he knew it to be the Catholic doctrine, that "the Catholic possesses an absolute certainty as to the truths of revealed religion which are taught him by an infallible Church" (p. 57). He never found himself able (as we understand him) to accept that doctrine ; and after eight more years (p. 167) "felt it was no longer possible for him with a good conscience to profess himself the adherent of a system based" thereon. At no period of his life then— neither when he was externally received into the Church nor ever afterwards —did he consider himself to possess absolute certainty on the truths of Faith. Last July we pointed out (p. 190) that, according to the "Dei Filius," no Catholic can lose the light of faith except by his own grievous sin. We added however, that "as it seems to us, the case is abundantly possible,—perhaps not infrequent,—of a person fancying himself a convert to Catholicity, who has in real truth never accepted the Church's authority with divine faith. Such a man's defection," we said, "is no real apostasy, and does not therefore perhaps fall under the words of the canon." We confess that, when we wrote that sentence, Mr. Ffoulkes was in our mind : we are most glad however to think that a similar exemption from the Church's sentence may apparently be pleaded for the present writer.

We are bound to say that he writes temperately and without a particle of bitterness. Again, his reasoning throughout is direct, straightforward and intelligible ; presenting a marked contrast to the tortuous course, whether of those unsound Catholics who minimize the Church's extent of infallibility, or of those merely nominal Catholics, who with incredible audacity claim that title while rejecting the Vatican Definitions. But though it is thus straightforward and direct, nothing can be shallower and more trite. Enemies of the Church may possibly enough make capital of his volume ; as we observe indeed that Dean Stanley calls it "truly remarkable" : but we cannot imagine it really influencing any one whatever. To the uneducated it does not appeal ; the educated must see through it.

It has become of late the fashion for misbelievers to make a great show of large-mindedness, by admitting that even among Roman Catholics there is to be found much candour and intellectual ability. Yet we have been amused with observing, that these same men endeavour to combine the pleasure of bigotry with the credit of liberality ; and carefully confine their praise to those Catholics, who are more or less disaffected to the authorities placed over them by God. For our own part, we do not see how it is more illiberal to say that no candour or intellectual power is to be found among *Catholics*, than to say that no such excellence is to be found among "*Ultramontanes.*" Yet with our author (p. 106) "the more candid" "school" means the "anti-ultramontane" ; it is *they* alone who "desire to promote the interests of science, of historical inquiry, and of general cultivation" ; while their opponents hold "that the good of the Church requires that everything shall be concealed or misrepresented, which may compromise the interests of the clergy or the autocratic supremacy of Rome." Among Catholics, it is only the "anti-ultramontanes" who regret every *needless* interference with liberty of thought"* ; who "are not blind to the practical abuses either of the past or the present" ; who hold that "between religion and science there can be no real contradiction." Similar thoughts occur throughout.

Now in many places the author laments how little Protestants understand Catholicity, and how little *pains* they ordinarily take to understand it. But we protest loudly, that no fanatical and bigoted Protestant ever took less pains to understand Chatholicity, than he (the writer of this book) has apparently taken to understand what he calls "Ultramontanism." His remarks on the "Ultramontane" school betray just the same superficial and contented ignorance, which is so commonly evinced by the most vulgar Protestants in their criticism of Catholicity in general. He has evidently not the faintest notion, what are in truth the theological, philosophical, historical principles of those whom he so names.

---

* What an extraordinary expression ! Newton "interfered" largely with "liberty of thought" when he proved gravitation. Was this "a *needless* interference?" If not, why not ? Of course the larger the amount of truths which the Church is commissioned to teach, so much the more (thank God !) must she "interfere" with "liberty of thought." Liberty of thought, so far it implies ignorance of truth, is not a blessing but an evil : often inevitable, but always an evil.

From cover to cover, we can find only three reasons given for the author's change of conviction on the truth of Catholicity. The chief is that to which we have already referred in a different connection. The Catholic doctrine on the certainty of faith is, in his view, as self-evidently false (p. 59), as is " the notion that two and two do not necessarily make four." His language however on this subject is so singular as almost to preclude argument. In pp. 56-7, he says that, when he considered himself a Catholic, he accounted the truth of that religion to " rest *on a high degree of probability* and nothing more." Yet he adds in p. 77 that the conviction of Catholics rests " precisely on the same kind of grounds on which they believe that Augustus Cæsar was once emperor of Rome, that George the Third was once king of England, and that there is such a country as China in the far East." Well, but does he not believe these three facts with *certitude?* Is it to him only a *probable* opinion, that there is such a country as China? or that Augustus and George the .Third existed? By his own account Catholics possess such evidence for the truth of their religion, as legitimately to exclude all doubt. The only objection then, among those enumerated in p. 57, on which he can intend to insist, is that the Church regards faith as the " supernatural gift of God." Of course he does not himself hold this verity: but we ask him, what is there in it contradictory to *reason?* We are far from denying, that plausible philosophical objections *can be alleged* against the Catholic doctrine on the supernaturalness and the pre-eminent firmness of faith ; though such arguments admit of most satisfactory reply. But *the author before us* has not adduced one single intelligible objection, against the verity which he so intensely dislikes.

Another of his arguments is a reply undoubtedly to his own previous course of thought, but in no respect whatever to the reasoning ordinarily put forth by Catholic controversialists. He urges (p. 51 et alibi) that there can be no legitimate à priori presumption, as to how much or how little light God will give to man, even on the hypothesis of His making some revelation. We heartily concur : but Catholic controversialists do not ordinarily *build* in any way on any such à priori presumption. We are writing at the moment without access to books ; but we may be allowed to mention some remarks of our own on the historical grounds of Catholicity : Jan. 1867, pp. 116-17. We have referred to these remarks with a view to the present pamphlet, and we find no reference in them whatever to such an à priori presumption as the author supposes.

The author's third argument is founded (p. 103) on the dogma of Transubstantiation. It is the merest parrot-like repetition of the well-worn Protestant allegation ; and we need only mention the repeated answers which it has received from Catholic controversialists.

In his final chapter the author protests against what he calls "Ultramontanism in England"; i. e. in the Anglican Establishment: meaning that "clericism", as he calls it, which would deny to men absorbed in physical science the prerogative of deciding on their own authority the true sense of Scripture. This chapter gives us more insight than any other part of the volume, into those implicit evil principles, which seem to have involved the author in his spiritual calamities. Putting aside for the moment all reference to the Church's authority in teaching,—we must maintain earnestly that there are momentous portions of Scriptural and theological exposition, which cannot be duly apprehended except by persons of mortified and un-worldly life; by persons who live (so to speak) in the invisible world. To say that men, whose predominant interest in life is the discovery of physical truth, can be trusted to determine the true sense of the Gospel, is surely not less intellectually contemptible than morally and spiritually odious. But we have opened a very large subject, which must be reserved for future elucidation and development.

A Letter from Dr. Döllinger to the Archbishop of Munich, dated Munich, March 28, 1871.

WE take for granted, as authentic, a translation of this letter, published in the " Guardian " for April 5th. It appears therefrom, that Dr. Dollinger definitively refuses submission to the Vatican Definitions.

What is the doctrinal stand-point on which this refusal is based ?

In the first place he denies the Pope's *supremacy*, no less than the Pope's *infallibility*. This is expressed throughout. He protests no less indignantly against the third, than against the fourth, chapter of the " Pastor Æternus."

As to infallibility, he makes it clear that he denies, not only the infallibility of the Pope speaking ex cathedrâ, but of the dispersed Ecclesia Docens. This view has been consistently maintained throughout by the singularly feeble writer, who does theology for the "Saturday Review," and who represents himself as an ardent admirer of Dr. Döllinger : and the latter theologian has now shown that this is no misrepresentation of his opinions. In the early part of his letter he admits the Syllabus to have been issued ex cathedrâ by Pius IX.; and no one has ever doubted that the said Syllabus has received the assent of the Episcopate : and yet Dr. Döllinger expressly denies its infallibility. Now we pointed out in January, 1870 (p. 220), how distinctly it was admitted by the keenest *French* opponents of Papal infallibility, that the dispersed Ecclesia Docens is most indubitably infallible. " A conciliar definition clothed with Pontifical assent," says the "Correspondant," " or *a Pontifical proposition corroborated by assent of the Episcopate*—infallibility *is there or it is nowhere.* The Holy Ghost speaks by that double organ, or He never speaks at all : a Catholic owes them his submission, or *he ceases to merit that name.*" We must say for ourselves, in conformity with this view, that we consider Dr. Döllinger to have been no more truly a Catholic *before* the Vatican Council, than he has been *since*. In fact, with him, the Immaculate Conception is no dogma of the Faith ; Jansenism, Febronianism, quietism, have received no infallible condemnation ; the " Unigenitus" and the " Auctorem fidei " are but non-obligatory expressions of a Pope's doctrinal opinion.

He recognizes infallibility then only as residing in an Œcumenical Council. But here a further question is opened, which his present letter does not enable us to solve more than partially : *what are those Councils which he accounts Œcumenical?* His disciple in the "Saturday," if we remember rightly, excludes from that category all which have been held between the Eighth and the Tridentine. Dr. Döllinger has nowhere, so far as we happen to know, expressed his full views on this matter. But in a paper which he published during the Vatican Council, and of which we gave a translation in April, 1870, he distinctly says (p. 508) that the Council of Florence was not Œcumenical.* And in the present letter he implicitly makes the same statement concerning the Fifth Lateran : for he denies infallibility to the "Unam sanctam"; and it is a well-known fact that the Fifth Lateran republished that Bull as dogmatic.

Now Dr. Döllinger lays much stress on the allegation, that as regards *liberty of discussion* there is a most broad contrast between the Vatican and every "true Œcumenical Council." But he forgets that there is a preliminary question to be considered : viz., which *are* the true Œcumenical Councils. Will he count in this number e.g. the Council of Ephesus? The Ephesine Fathers declared that they condemned Nestorius, because they were "compelled" thereto "by the sacred canons, and *through the Letter of the Most Holy Father.*" They were not permitted then any great "liberty of discussion." Again does Dr. Döllinger admit the Council of Chalcedon as "truly Œcumenical?" For Father Newman, as we have more than once pointed out, gives this account of what was there done. "A doctrine," he says, "which *the whole East refused as a symbol,* not once but twice, patriarch by patriarch, metropolitan by metropolitan, first by the mouth of a hundred then of above six hundred of its bishops . . was *forced upon the Council* . . by the resolution of the Pope of the day, acting through his legates and supported by the civil power." Now we refer our readers to the testimonies cited in our last number (pp. 175-177) from the Archbishop of Westminster, the Bishops of Birmingham and of Beverley, who were all present, as to the singular "freedom of speech" allowed and encouraged at Rome on the recent occasion. It is very evident, that if Dr. Döllinger denies the Œcumenity of the Vatican Council, far more confidently must he in consistency deny that of the Ephesine and the Chalcedonian. And a very impartial judge, the "Spectator" newspaper, speaks even more generally. "How he intends to prove that the Vatican Council was not free, without proving that the earlier Councils were *none of them* free, we cannot imagine." (April 8.)

When Dr. Döllinger proceeds to contrast favourably men's "*self-gained*

---

* In the present letter he speaks of "two General Councils" having been held "in the fifteenth century ;" and as this expression necessarily includes the Florentine, we can only suppose that he uses the word "General" as *distinct* from "Œcumenical." We presume that, in his present reference to that Council, he intends to make capital out of his ridiculous interpretation (we can use no milder word) of the clause with which the Florentine Decree closes.

understanding and discernment " with the humble and loving obedience of faith, he shows, more clearly perhaps than in any other part of his letter, how fundamentally anti-Catholic are his first principles of religious thought. It is true that in words he confines himself to denying the Œcumenicity of the Vatican Council ; but his whole drift implies, that there is *no authority whatever* which has so much influence over his convictions that, in deference to its pronouncement, he would surrender the conclusions at which he has arrived by his independent historical studies. We should add that, as is usually the case with such confident thinkers, his *history* is as shallow as his *theology*. His knowledge of *facts* is very large, but his historical *science* very shallow. We do not deny that he possesses various excellent intellectual qualities, and that before now he has put them to excellent service : but he has always been the very opposite to a scientific or philosophical thinker.

He accounts some of his quondam sympathisers a very unprincipled lot; for he says : "up to this day not a single one, *even of those who have signed a declaration of submission,* has said to me that he is really convinced of the truth of " the defined " theses." Let us hope he is under some delusion ; for we cannot without clearer evidence ascribe such sacrilegious mendacity to men otherwise respectable.

It may be, that Dr. Döllinger's open separation from the Visible Church will plunge him into even worse misbelief ; or it may be, that it will cause him to "enter into himself," as spiritual writers say, and so arouse him to a sense of his dreadful position. But as regards the well-being of *the Church,*—among the vast benefits of every kind which will accrue from the Vatican Definitions, not the least is, that they will render impossible, to such thinkers as Dr. Döllinger, the continuance of an empty and delusive profession of Catholicity. "Nominal Catholics," says the Archbishop of Westminster, "are our weakness and vexation ; our scandal and our shame ; *sometimes our greatest danger.*"

Familiar Instructions on Mental Prayer. By the Abbé Courbon. Translated from the French by E. F. B. Edited by William T. Gordon, of the London Oratory. Parts I. and II. London : Burns, Oates, and Co.

THE number of foreign spiritual books which one after the other are acclimatized amongst us in our own tongue is matter for much congratulation. The French language is certainly much more commonly understood in England than Italian, Spanish, or German. Nevertheless there are numbers of simple souls, thirsting for whatever can help them on in the ways of God, who are shut out from some of the best spiritual works for want of this acquisition. To many such souls the translation of Courbon's "Familiar Instructions on Mental Prayer" will be a real boon.

Though the Abbé Courbon's life has left so little trace that his French editor the Abbé Montaigne was obliged reluctantly to acknowledge that his researches had failed in obtaining any details of his history, his works hold a high place amongst those of a whole cluster of writers who adorned the Church of France in the seventeenth century—the century of Lallemant, Surin, and Boudon. Father Gordon mentions in the Preface to the present translation that this treatise in particular " was much valued by the late lamented Father Faber," and that " it was one of a number of foreign spiritual works which he had the intention of publishing in English if his life had been spared."

The Abbé Montaigne's edition united two originally distinct works—the one on the first degree of Mental Prayer or Meditation, the other on the four subsequent degrees, viz., Affective Prayer, Active Recollection, Passive Recollection, and the Prayer of Union. We observe that the present translation neither stops short at the Abbé Courbon's first work on Meditation, nor comprises the whole of the Abbé Montaigne's volume, but embraces the two first degrees of prayer, viz., Meditation and Affective Prayer. We venture to hope that this is only an instalment, and that the rest of the book is intended to follow. No doubt what F. Gordon has now edited will have the widest practical application ; and those who will chiefly need the rest, such as directors of souls and religious, will be able to avail themselves of it in the original. But a certain knowledge even of the higher kinds of prayer, like much in the lives of the saints which reveals the dealings of God with exalted souls, may be a help and an encouragement to many who themselves will never rise above affective prayer. We should be sorry that such a help should be permanently withheld from them.

If we may venture to offer our own judgment on the " Familiar Instructions " themselves, the reader will find them full of encouragement, simple and clear in language and arrangement, unexaggerated, and marked by a breadth and liberty of spirit which never loses sight of the end in anxiety about the means, and which lays singularly little stress on systems of method by which some souls are scared and repelled from the practice of mental prayer.

Perhaps, however, the most important feature in this little treatise is the prominent place given in it to the instruction on Affective Prayer as distinguished from Meditation, and on the gradual transition from the one to the other. Many books comparatively lay down guidance for the practice of Meditation; few, suited for popular use, speak expressly or at length of Affective Prayer. Here devout souls will find detailed instruction as to the time and manner of passing out of Meditation into the higher degree of Affective Prayer ; on the nature of the latter, its special fruits, the characteristic faults which beset it, the difficulties and sufferings which accompany it, and the supernatural favours which God is wont to bestow on souls engaged in it. There are probably many to whom all this will bring light and help which, consciously or unconsciously, they have sorely needed.

We presume from the initials prefixed to the translation that it is from the same hand as that of the Countess Hahn-Hahn's " Fathers of the Desert." In both cases the translator has had the very rare success of enabling us to forget that we are reading a translation, and that without any sacrifice of fidelity to the original. We can heartily congratulate both translator and editor on their work.

Macmillan's Magazine.   March, 1871.   London : Macmillan.

WE are induced to say one word on the third article of this number, for
the purpose of illustrating what every Catholic constantly observes ;
viz., how little trouble is taken, even by the most pronounced anti-Catholics,
to understand even the most elementary doctrines of the creed which they
oppose. The article in question is by Dean Stanley ; and it is written in
praise of the miserable man, who was once called in religion Father Hyacinthe.
According to the Dean's frank admission (p. 405), this person holds that the
Church in communion with Rome is only one portion of the Catholic Church :
yet on the other hand the Dean declares (ib.) that the said person " has not
renounced his priesthood or his Church " ; and that the Pope could, " by one
stroke of his pen " (p. 404) restore him " to his sacerdotal functions." Why
the Trinity and the Incarnation are not more essential articles of the Roman
Catholic Faith, than is the dogma that the Catholic Church is one visible
society in communion with Rome. Dean Stanley might as well have said of
any Catholic priest who has turned *Unitarian,* that he has not renounced
either his priesthood or his Church ; and that the Pope might by one stroke
of his pen restore him to his sacerdotal functions.

Essays Theological and Literary. By RICHARD HOLT HUTTON, M.A.
London : Strahan.

WE had fully hoped to place before our readers the present quarter, a
full review of this most interesting collection ; but we have been
prevented from doing so by our contributor's severe illness. We fully hope
we may be able to fulfil our design in July. Meanwhile, however, we are unwilling to pass such a book without some remark ; though our notice will be
not only much briefer but indefinitely less satisfactory than we had hoped.

Indeed Mr. Hutton is a writer to whom it is singularly difficult for a
Catholic to do justice. He exhibits certainly great depth and accuracy of
philosophical thought, considerable power of historical criticism, and rare
literary accomplishments. His philosophical reading is evidently very extensive, and he has studied the New Testament with a completeness and intelligence which deserve the warmest recognition. He writes moreover in a
spirit of deep earnestness, which is unusual and most attractive ; and (which
is still more unusual) he unites hearty devotion to truth with candid appreciation of those who differ from him most widely.

And yet, as we have said, he is a writer to whom it is difficult for a
Catholic to do justice. We are well aware that the very same phenomena
have a most opposite significance, accordingly as they occur (so to speak) in
a thinker's upward or downward course ; and Mr. Hutton (see p. 235) has risen,

as he considers, to belief in the Incarnation, having been educated an Uni
tarian. Still there the phenomena *are* all the same. Thus in his masterly
defence of the Fourth Gospel against Baur, he deals with the sacred text in
a way at which Catholics stand aghast. He transposes verses ; he decides
that this or that verse is spurious; he pronounces that this or that other verse
is genuine indeed, but exhibits in the Evangelist deplorable error and superstition : and he does all this apparently without the faintest suspicion that
there may be thinkers as able and sincere as himself, who are scandalized
and distressed beyond measure at such methods of criticism. Turning to
quite another subject, he considers himself (as we have said) to hold the
doctrine of the Incarnation ; and yet (p. 260) he thinks that on the one hand
" *infinite* power and knowledge *can* be given by the Father to the Son ;" but
on the other hand that " they can be *limited* as *He wills.*" We are amazed
that, as a mere matter of philosophy, Mr. Hutton can acquiesce in such a
view ; as to theology, we take for granted that he has never carefully
studied the Church's definitions on the subject.

It requires far greater breadth and elasticity of mind than is possessed by
the present writer, to appreciate equitably an intellectual position of which
he has never had the faintest experience. He confesses that he finds himself
entirely baffled in his attempt to grasp it. We can only hope that in our
next number greater justice will be done to Mr. Hutton's first volume ; and
we will say little more in this part of our notice, beyond expressing a wish
that the author had included in his collection the singularly cogent argument
which he published in " Macmillan" a year or two ago, in reply to Mr.
Herbert Spencer's theory on the origin of moral judgments.

One final remark, however, on the first volume. The argument for
God's Existence, founded (pp. 40–42) on man's combined intuition of moral
obligation and moral freedom, is (to the best of our knowledge) quite
original and very striking. " Unable as man is to affect in the smallest
degree either the laws of his body or the fundamental constitution of his
mind . . . . he finds this almost constant pressure remarkably withdrawn,
at the very crisis in which the import of his action is brought home to him
with the most vivid conviction." To what can this be ascribed except to
the agency of some Being who is carrying man through a *moral probation ?*
" The relaxation of constraint comes simultaneously with a deep sense of
obligation ; *as the child is instinctively aware, when the sustaining hand is
taken away, that the parent's eye is all the more intent on his unassisted movement.*" This last illustration impresses us as among the very happiest which
we have ever seen.

In the volume of " Literary Essays," we have a collection of critical writings of singular value and interest. The thoroughness and cultivation of
Mr. Hutton's mind, its finely poised fairness, and his very rare power of
according perfect appreciation even where he is without sympathy, are as
evident and even more diversely displayed than in his theological papers.
The first essay, on Goethe, is the most masterly, and the most completely
original. We are not acquainted with any other, upon the comprehensive
subject of the great German poet, which places him before the reader in so
true, so fine, so just, so melancholy a light. Mr. Hutton's *aperçu* is more

2 K 2

sound and complete than Mr. Lewes's by all the difference in the spiritual perceptions of the two writers, and the concluding paragraphs of the essay contain an epitome of the subject well worthy alike of its grandeur and its gloom.

Wordsworth, Shelley, Keats, and Clough are discussed in a spirit so discerning, with taste so pure, with intelligence so keen that the reader seems to see the genius of each surrounded with a new radiance, and will certainly taste the beauty of their works with a more educated palate when he returns from the critic to the poet. In his essay on Browning, Mr. Hutton fulfils a twofold office. There are many readers to whom the sweetness of the kernel enclosed in the very rugged and cordy nut of Browning's versification is not sufficiently proven or desirable to induce them to take the trouble of cracking the husk. The critic persuades such indolent loiterers to set a higher value on the fruit, and even to confess the grandeur of its rough envelope. He half reconciles Browning's public to him,—that public which does not withhold honour and admiration from him, but mixes them up with some vexation and resentment because he will not let them have his gems of thought on easier terms. He interprets him, in his sterner and more puzzling moods, after he has done justice to the spirit and the freshness of his simpler, freer poems. He disentangles his skeins of thought, finds the word of his enigmas, smooths out his wrinkles, and does not make us feel so very much ashamed, though we are convicted of never having quite understood Browning before. There is, however, one point in this essay on which we venture to differ from Mr. Hutton. It is in his interpretation of the short, strong, rugged, melancholy poem which he quotes, and which, we think, is entitled "After a Year." He sees in it the lament of a girl for the change in her lover. We see in the puzzled, baffled, heartsick complaint, a curiously subtle study of the disappointed romantic hopes of a wife, and we think the poem loses meaning, and much of its originality, if otherwise interpreted.

In an admirable essay on " George Eliot," we find several passing allusions to other novelists, which are gems of criticism. For instance, Mr. Hutton's definition of the attitude of the " drawing-room novelist " towards spiritual things,—a definition in which he sketches Miss Austen with a few light, dexterous touches, and explains by a brief but perfect analysis, the origin of the hopelessness and the emptiness into which the wit and wisdom of Mr. Thackeray resolve themselves. His criticism of the writings of the author of " Adam Bede " is masterly in its discernment, as well as generous in its praise. Nothing can be more true, or more finely expressed than his explanation of the sense of loss, of incompleteness in her genius, arising from her absolute want of faith ; and his demonstration of the false philosophy of her " Jubal." In discussing " Romola," we think Mr. Hutton has hit to a nicety the cause of its lesser popularity, and discerned the features of its superior merit, while, in his analysis of her peculiar and somewhat cumbrous humour, of its unsatirical, uncynical character, and in the instances he selects in support of his theory, he exhibits discernment equal to her own.

The Life of Sir Walter Ralegh; based on Contemporary Documents, &c. ; together with his Letters, now first collected. By EDWARD EDWARDS. Macmillan & Co. 1868.

THERE is some affectation in spelling Sir Walter's surname in the archaic form which Mr. Edwards adopts. Modern usage universally makes it Raleigh, and there is no better reason for leaving out the *i* than there would be for spelling it in a variety of other ways. Sir Walter's contemporaries did their spelling (when they could do it at all) on irregular phonetic principles, as they understood them. The very pronunciation of the name is doubtful. An epigram quoted by another Sir Walter (Scott) in the Notes to "Kenilworth," would lead one to think that the first syllable was pronounced *Raw.* The name was often written Rawleigh, and sometimes Rawley or Rauley. On the other hand, the Venetian resident in London at the court of James I. writes of the hero as "Ser Vat Ralle ; " a pretty fair indication that the surname was pronounced then as it is now, and also that it was so familiar in men's mouths that the Christian name was popularly reduced to an affectionate diminutive.

To simplify matters, however, we shall in this notice write the name as Mr. Edwards does. The retention or omission of the third vowel will not make or mar the fame of one of the most extraordinary Englishmen that ever lived. To him more truly than to the man of whom they were written do the poet's lines apply :—

" A man so various that he seemed to be
Not one, but all mankind's epitome."

At all events, there was hardly a career of earthly distinction in which his native talents did not fit him to shine, and, in whatever pursuit he was for the time engaged, his aptitude was so conspicuous that he seemed formed for that exclusively. All the elements of England's later greatness, " ships, colonies, and commerce," were thoroughly understood by him, and were to him matters of constant interest. When he left Oriel, at sixteen, to fight for the Huguenots in France, he had probably as much learning in his head as most of the less adventurous youths who remained at college to qualify themselves for quieter careers. When he stood some years after on the floor of the House of Commons, he was as well versed in points of order, as when, on the deck of galleon or galley, he gave commands to his sailors in points of seamanship, and shaped his skilful course through storm or through calm. Poet and chemist, soldier and merchant, sailor and agriculturist, statesman and adventurer, patriot and traitor : such were the apparently irreconcilable elements not inharmoniously united in this extraordinary man. Yet, great as he was, he is seldom thought of now, even by one of the many thousands of educated gentlemen who know that they are indebted to him for a not unpalatable part of their dinner and for the fragrant " weed " which helps them to digest it.

The romantic incidents and strange vicissitudes of Ralegh's career are
known to even youthful students of English history. How he first came
under Elizabeth's notice is uncertain, but that he stood for a time very
high in her favour is indisputable. We will talk "no scandal" about
her ; but there is no doubt that she was greatly attracted by handsome
men, especially if they were able to present themselves to her in rich and
tasteful apparel, and, above all, if their intellectual gifts were equal to their
personal graces. All these conditions were fulfilled in Ralegh. He was
about six feet high ; his hair dark and full ; his complexion, in early years
at least, bright and clear. His bearing was manly and dignified. All his
portraits represent him as magnificently attired ; and the Flemish Jesuit
Drexaleus, by whom he is described as "ille apud Anglicanam Cleopatram
nimis gratiosus homo," says that his very shoes were so studded with
jewels that they were of fabulous price. His influence in the royal
councils was at one time so high that it was even thought possible that the
Queen would confer on him the permanent tenure of that beautiful hand
which every one so much admired, especially the owner. And it might
have been so, if the youthful Essex had not come in the way about the
time when a new lover would find the changes of the royal fancy propitious
to his advances. Even then some calculating courtiers thought that
Ralegh might have aspired to an alliance, if not with royalty, at least with
the royal blood ; and but for the extreme youth of Arabella Stuart, a
marriage might have taken place that would have altered in some important
respects the whole course of English history.

Mr. Edwards's book throws considerable light on parts of Ralegh's
history that are less generally known, and perhaps more interesting to the
serious student. He first came into Parliament for his native county of
Devon in 1585. He afterwards sat for Cornwall, of which county he was
not only the representative in Parliament, but also Lord Lieutenant, holding besides the office of Lord Warden of the Stannaries. He was a hard-
working committee-man (though railway bills were then undreamt of), and
took part in all the principal debates, going at once to the heart of the
business that happened to be in hand, and giving in a few pregnant sentences the results of matured study and careful thought. The theory of
constructive treason was ably combated by him in a debate upon a bill
for suppressing the Brownists (April 4, 1593). "In my conceit," said he,
"the Brownists are worthy to be voted out of a Commonwealth. But
what danger may grow to ourselves, if this law passes, were fit to be
considered. It is to be feared that men not guilty will be included in it.
The law is hard that taketh life, or sendeth into banishment, where men's
intentions shall be judged by a jury ; and they shall be judges what
another man meant. But that law that is against a fact is just. Punish
the fact as severely as you will."

It will be new to many to learn that there were free-traders in Parliament in the first year of the seventeenth century. Ralegh was a free-
trader, and anticipated many of the arguments which the Anti-Corn-Law
League made familiar some thirty years ago. The subject of discussion
(November 4, 1601) was *An Act for Sowing Hemp.* Ralegh objected to

the compulsory principle which it involved. He compared it to the Tillage Act, under which holders of land were compelled to plough a third of what they held, in the idea that this secured the country against the danger of famine. But Sir Walter told the House that France had offered to supply the Queen with corn in Ireland at a rate which would not have paid the English farmer. " The Low Countryman and the Hollander," he added, "who never sow corn, have by their industry such plenty that they serve other nations. I think the best course is to get corn at liberty, and leave every man free, which is the desire of a true Englishman." Every one knows that the Cecils of our time have been stanch Protectionists. The late Marquis of Salisbury was in the Derby Cabinet of 1852. The late Marquis of Exeter held a high office in the household at the same time,—a fact which Catholics have some cause to remember. Their illustrious ancestor met Ralegh's argument with this remark : " Whosoever doth not maintain the plough destroys the kingdom." Ralegh, as we have said, was a free-trader of the period. But we have not met with any free-trader, even of the present time, who is for free trade in everything. They all stop short at some point or other. Ralegh was all for free trade in corn, but he did not approve of "unrestricted competition" in tin. In the very same month and year (November 20, 1601) there was a famous debate on monopolies, in which Sir Walter took strong Conservative ground. The reason was, he had a royal patent, the same as that always held by the Dukes of Cornwall for the monopoly of tin. His speech had important consequences, for it not only saved his privilege and his pocket for the time, but had considerable influence on the fact that the Prince of Wales enjoys the same privilege to this day. There is not free trade in tin. It is forbidden to send the ores out of Cornwall unmelted.

Mr. Edwards justly defends Ralegh's right to be considered as the author, in the strictest sense of the word, of his " History of the World," written during his long imprisonment in the Tower. Isaac D'Israeli, in the "Curiosities of Literature," treats it as a joint-stock production, in which, though Ralegh had all the renown, he had by no means all, if the chief part, of the labour. He ascribes a large share of the work to Ben Jonson, Thomas Hariot, Serjeant Hoskins, and Dr. Robert Burrel, or Burhill. The last (who was rector of Northwald, in Norfolk, and had been Ralegh's chaplain) was the only one of those named who had given any very material assistance. He was a good Hebrew scholar, and supplied information upon the books of the Old Testament and the lore of the Rabbins, which Ralegh did not himself possess. Ben Jonson had nothing to do with the work. Hariot, who was a man of great ability and learning, was often consulted upon questions of chronology, geography, and mathematics. Hoskins was a man of cultivated taste, who revised what Ralegh had written before it went to press, and probably sometimes improved the style.

Admitting that Ralegh had many heroic qualities, it cannot be denied however, that his present biographer's hero-worship is sometimes a little' extravagant. We have not much fault to find with his argument that the execution of Ralegh was unjust. He had undoubtedly invaded Spanish territory, and James I., as the ally of Spain, might without any injustice have handed him over to be dealt with by the Spanish authorities. But his execution on a charge of treason, which had been virtually condoned if he was guilty, and which in fact had not been sufficiently proved, was a judicial murder. Ralegh died bravely, and his death made him a political martyr. It had in the event an indirect, though plainly-linked, effect upon the death of Charles I. The truth is that Ralegh seldom showed any moral greatness except in adversity, and that chiefly in the latter years of his life. While he was successful, he gave as few symptoms of possessing a conscience as Bacon or Cecil. His native manliness preserved him from being as base as Bacon and as coldly selfish as Cecil. But all these men, and most other great men of that time, so highly gifted with all the qualities that lead to worldly success, were what we call in plain English arrant rogues. That was the immediate and inevitable effect of that awful moral revolution which historians think proper to call the Reformation.

To give one instance out of several in which Mr. Edwards permits his prepossessions to blindfold his judgment, we will take his comments on a letter written by Ralegh to Cecil, which referred to rumours (perfectly well-founded) of Ralegh's marriage with Elizabeth Throgmorton. That better and fairer Elizabeth had drawn Ralegh away from his equivocal attachment to her royal namesake ; but, rightly dreading the lengths to which *spretœ injuria formœ* might impel his jealous sovereign, Ralegh was anxious to temporize, and to keep the rumour of his marriage from the Queen's knowledge as long as possible. He therefore wrote to Cecil, who was his particular friend, as court friendship goes, but who was still more the Queen's most servile minister, in these terms :—

"I mean not to come away, as they say I will, for fear of a marriage, and I know not what. If any such thing were, I would have imparted it to yourself before any man living ; and therefore I pray you believe it not, and I beseech you to suppress, what you can, any such malicious report. For I profess before God, there is none on the face of the earth that I would be fastened unto."

Words cannot be plainer than these. Ralegh calls the report of his marriage " malicious," and swears that there is no one " on the face of the earth " that he would indissolubly unite himself to. It being undeniable, however, that the report was perfectly true, and that Ralegh either had been, or was immediately to be, " fastened unto " the lady in question, in what he thus wrote to Cecil, he simply swore hard to a lie. Mr. Edwards is very hard set to whitewash him ; for which purpose he amiably but very weakly conjectures that the word " rather " should be inserted before " fastened unto." The meaning then would be, that there was no woman on the face of the earth whom Ralegh would rather make his wife than the lady with whom a "malicious report " had connected his name!

Notwithstanding such blemishes, however, these volumes give the best biography of Ralegh that has been, or is likely to be, written. Mr. Edwards has collected his materials carefully ; and, though his conclu-

sions are often disputable, the grounds upon which he has formed them are
fairly stated. It was due to so great a personage that a fitting monument
should be raised to his memory ; and though the gilding is laid on too
thickly, and the inscription is unduly complimentary, we are glad to see
the effort made, though tardily, to give honour to one who was undoubtedly
a great Englishman and a great man.

Good English ; or, Popular Errors in Language. By EDWARD S. GOULD,
Author of "Abridgment of Alison's Europe," &c. &c. New York.

MR. GOULD treats the speaking of English as a fine art, which he
desires to see highly cultivated, and from the practice of which he
wishes to remove trickery and clumsiness, conventionally permitted care-
lessness, and inaccuracies which he does not admit to be trivial. His book
is the result of keen and close study, and is as curious and interesting as it is
calculated to be useful. Probably there is not one of Mr. Gould's readers
who will not be forced to recognize certain customary blunders of his or her
own, in the familiar instances of bad English which he quotes, and we do not
think any one can read these essays without feeling surprised at the general
acceptance, in the educated classes, of slovenly and inaccurate speech. The
" spurious words " which he exposes and condemns come home more strongly
to the taste and conscience of his countrymen than to ours ; they are chiefly
of American invention ; but his catalogue of " misused words," with proofs
that they are misused, is a boon of which we hope writers and speakers will
avail themselves. Hardly the first authors of the time are guiltless of one
error which he cites as frequent in newspaper composition, viz., the misuse of
the verb " to stop," in the sense of to stay, or to remain. It is noticeable
that Irish writers rarely make this mistake, or confound the adverb of place
"directly," with the adverb of time, "immediately," which is almost invariably done by English writers. Mr. Gould tells us that "immediately"
is not used in America, but the more correct phrase, " as soon as."

" 'General Grant and his family have arrived in town, and are *stopping* at
the Fifth Avenue Hotel.'
" On reading such an announcement, one is tempted to inquire, ' When will
General Grant *stop* ' stopping ' ? '
" Stopping is not a continuous process, like *going, living,* &c. To stop is
to do a single act which terminates the prior action."

This is a golden precept ; and we are also pleased to find a caution against
an equally common, if less annoying error, the substitution of " you are mistaken" for " you mistake." Many of Mr. Gould's instances are very ingenious
and droll, his reasons are all emphatic and convincing. He is strong in
argument, and hard-hitting in controversy, and it must be acknowledged
that he has demolished Dean Alford, and that he hits the Dean's critic, Mr.

Washington Moon, in his turn, very neatly and very hard, in the following sentence : "Mr. Moon has shown great critical acumen in detecting the errors of *The Queen's English*—pity that he could not have presented them to his readers in what he so confidently assumes that he himself has mastered, namely, *pure* English."

We especially recommend to the reader's attention Mr. Gould's strictures on Webster's orthography, a system which we have always regarded with aversion, and which we have had reason to fear, of late, is making inroads on the language as written on this side of the Atlantic. The arguments are admirable, and the satire is very amusing. Let us hope that no further attempts will be made to cut off our *ll's*, and make us spell centre, *center*.

Mr. Gould would probably be shocked by our use of so hackneyed a phrase, but, as we really do mean that his book is one " which no gentleman's library should be without," we make bold to employ it, and, going farther, to assert that it ought to find a place among the books for ready reference of every writer who desires to adhere strictly to good English.

The Chieftain's Daughter ; a Legend of Sybil Head, and other Poems. By EDWARD HENEAGE DERING, author of " Gray's Court," and " Florence Danby." London, Dublin, and New York : Richardson & Son.

IN this small volume of poems, partly romantic, partly religious, the utterances of a thoughtful, contemplative, refined mind are heard. Similar characteristics are manifested in Mr. Dering's prose works, but we think he has found the poet's task the more congenial. His fancy luxuriates in the legendary lore of the past, and his feelings are happily engaged in representing the sunny and sympathetic aspects of the Faith. He tries to show that there is no separation between the pure and lofty human sentiments wherein poets seek their inspirations, and the precepts and law of the Catholic Church.

Mr. Dering has caught the true character of Irish scenery and legend, in his poem, " The Chieftain's Daughter," with its wild, woful ending, and its delicate, tender portraiture of a woman's constancy and courage.

" The Pedigree of Persuasions " consists of a prologue, in which the author speaks, in his own person, and a first part, in which a dramatic dialogue is carried on between Adam and Eve subsequent to their expulsion from Eden, with an invisible chorus of angels and evil spirits. Adam is supposed to be sensible of their contending influences, and, swayed about by their opposing counsel, indicates the perplexities of the spiritual life in the future of mankind, while Eve, the first to sin, the readiest to repent, the first to dispute the will of God, the readiest to comprehend and make submission to His purposes, warns and entreats him. Brought back by conviction, by fear, by the solemn certainty that there was nothing to save them, but that they should

> "Now at this crisis of a free-willed fate
> Seek Him, whose loss no gain can compensate:
> Seek Him, who can our souls invigorate ; "

the woman thus putting forth the first fruits of Redemption, declares for God, in the strife, and rejects the devil. Adam, " mildly contentious, and well-meaning," hesitating, doubting, persuaded, not convinced, inaugurates the strife, never determined, never ceasing, between good and evil, because he could not make the first act of his free will a sacrifice of renunciation. Then comes the chorus of the mocking spirits, and the last word of the angels :—

> " A woman yet shall crush the Dragon's head—
> The Word of Life shall save the Living Dead :
> The Godhead will descend in form of man,
> He will in mercy, who in power can."

The second part of the poem is devoted to the development of the results which have accrued from this fatal indecision. Persuasions have ever since held opposing sway over man, endowed with free will. Mr. Dering defines their prototypes, and traces their descent, in verses which possess point, subtlety, and elegance.

Among the shorter pieces included in Mr. Dering's volume, we particularly admire the lines " To a Wife," and a poem, entitled " Guidance." From this we gather that to Dr. Newman the writer is indebted for the instruction and support which guided him into the sure and tranquil harbour of the Church. The verses in which he acknowledges the debt of gratitude, and repays it by reverent affection, are as admirable in themselves as their motive is touching and praiseworthy.

The Ordinal of King Edward VI. Its History, Theology, and Liturgy. By DOM WILFRID RAYNAL, O.S.B. London : Richardson & Son ; New York : H. Richardson. 1871.

IF the Ritualist party and the High Church generally are not too much prostrated just now with the crowning disaster of the Purchas decision to be able to feel the more endurable misfortune of a very effective controversial attack, we should expect that Father Raynal's book must rouse up some Lee or Haddan to a reply. " Anglican Ordinations " is a subject of which most men have abandoned all hope of seeing the end. Of all " dreary " subjects it is one of the most dreary. It is a controversy that exemplifies, as well as any other, the practical necessity of an authority with power to decide in questions of dogmatical fact. Historical disputes, if they are in the least degree complicated, can never be set at rest ; that is to say, they can never be so clearly and convincingly settled one way or the other as that the settlement should have any force in practically controlling the actions of men who have never gone through the demonstration. The question whether the ministers of the Anglican establishment are priests or not cannot be settled by an appeal to history. Not that we do not think that history, as far as it speaks, decides clearly enough in the negative. But the dispute will never be, and cannot be, closed, as a mere historical dispute. Perhaps, then, no method of raising doubt, or of bringing doubt to a head, could be found so effective, and at the same time so concise, as that followed by F. Raynal in the treatise before us.

The author's object may be expressed in a word. The Anglican ordinal, he says, for a hundred years had no valid Form of Orders. This, of course, though a fatal objection if it can be sustained, is not a new one. But F. Raynal has treated it very completely, and to some extent originally. His point is, that no Form of Orders can be valid which does not contain the " expression of the ministerial act which determines the special character conferred by the imposition of hands. . . . . All charges which destroy this expression of the ministerial act vitiate the Forms and render them null and void." (p. 106.) Neither Kenrick nor Williams can be said to duly treat this important question. Kenrick, it is true, has a chapter on the Ordinal of Edward VI., and he treats the very point expressed in the words just quoted. But besides that Kenrick only touches it very briefly, there are several reasons why it could not, when Kenrick wrote, be considered so satisfactorily as it can now. In the first place, Kenrick wrote before the Ritualist revival, and when even the Tractarian views had hardly made their way outside the walls of Oxford. At that time, therefore, disquisitions on the validity of a sacramental form, and more especially of a form for Holy Order, would have been almost thrown away. In the next place, the question of the validity of the Form was confused by theories about the " porrection of the instruments," and even about the necessity of " unction " ; whilst now it has been narrowed to the single point of the words that accompany and specificate the imposition of hands.

F. Raynal, then, proves, as we think incontrovertibly, that in the Ordinal of 1549 the act of imposition of hands is not specificated, that is, the name of " bishop" or " priest," or its respective equivalent, is not expressed in any sufficient proximity to the act of imposition. This would be enough to any one with orthodox ideas about the Sacraments. Even granting, however, that such a reticence as this only rendered the form *doubtful*, F. Raynal has another argument in reserve. He goes at some length into the history of the Ordinal, and shows how its framers were possessed by one predominating spirit and had one great object, viz., to deny the Real Presence and to abolish all vestiges of the Mass. This recital serves two purposes. It shows, indirectly, that the absence of all " sacerdotal " specificating words from the Forms was not an oversight, but was deliberately meant. And it shows, in the second place, that if the Forms are allowed to be doubtful, as far as their bare letter is concerned, they must have been framed and *used* with heretical *animus* and intention, and that therefore they were null and void at least in a great many instances.

Perhaps the most interesting and the newest part of the author's labour is the very full collation of Forms of the East and of the West, which he has given for the purpose of showing how every orthodox form without exception contains that which the Anglican forms want. We recommend the book as containing in a handy and effective shape nearly all that can be profitably said about "Anglican Orders."

The Old Religion ; or, How shall we find Primitive Christianity. A journey from New York to Old Rome. By W. LOCKHART, B.A., Oxon, Priest in the diocese of Westminster. Reprinted from *Catholic Opinion.* (Burns & Oates.)

THIS volume seems to us to justify the extraordinarily high character given of it by the Bishop of Newport and Menevia. "It is entertaining, convincing, adapted to our actual times, and altogether the most valuable work of dogmatic instruction for general readers which has issued from the press for many years." It was originally intended for publication in the *Catholic World*, a well-known magazine in America, and this no doubt is the reason why the *dramatis personæ* are Americans rather than English. But we do not know that this is really to be regretted. The tendencies of English society are the same as those in America, only they are prematurely ripened on the other side of the Atlantic. And if this is the case with political and social matters, it is still more so with religious, because the natural tendency of the English mind has been checked among ourselves by the influence of the Church Establishment, and by the political relations which it has introduced even into religious matters. It is, however, certain that all this belongs to a state of things which is rapidly passing away. A foreigner who now for the first time became acquainted with England and English society, would, no doubt, be most forcibly struck by the senseless prejudice against the Catholic Church which still exists, and by its obviously political, rather than religious, character. But any one who can remember what English society was, in this respect, only twenty years ago, must be at least equally struck by the immense change for the better which has already taken place. We cannot doubt, therefore, that the tendency of the English mind as to religious matters is the same which has already been developed in the United States. There, practical people are feeling every day more and more strongly, not indeed that the Catholic religion is the exclusive truth (that is a privilege granted only to those to whom has been given the inestimable gift of Faith), but that, true or false, it is the Christian religion, and that to call any form of Protestantism Christianity, is merely to usurp an old name for a new thing. The volume before us is devoted to develop the grounds of this conviction ; and it is at least as much needed (we think a great deal more so) in the " old country " as in the new.

The scene opens in America, with a dialogue between a respectable Protestant, who is disturbed and unhappy at the recent conversion of his son to the Catholic Church, and his nephew, the supposed author of the book, who had himself been a Catholic a short time before, and who comforts his uncle by assuring him that the son's change is by no means a mere vagary, such as makes people turn followers of "Joanna Southcote, Joe Smith, and the rest," but a sober conviction; for it is shared by so many cool judging men. "You and I know a dozen sensible, first-rate men who have turned Catholics—no fanatics, but cool-headed men of business, good neighbours, good husbands, and honest men. There is Mr. A., Judge B., General C., within the last few months. They are not men to make a serious change, which they knew would set every one talking and criticising them, unless they knew well what they were about, and could give reasons for the change, and stand a little criticism." This leads to a discussion of the reasons; which the young man, named Philp, says may be summed up on the statement that "the Catholic religion and Primitive Christianity are identical." The subject is for some time discussed between these characters and an old American Episcopal clergyman. The heads of the chapters show the matters talked over. "Early Christianity," "The Testimony of the Disciples of the Apostles," "Protestant Christianity," "The Bible, and the Bible only," "The Bible only and the Church," "The Bible and the Church." Then comes a new person on the scene—"a Live Parliament Bishop," who is supposed to be travelling in the States (we imagine the author would not find it easy to show that any one ever did, but that only makes the book safe from the charge of personality), and he brings in a friend of his, Father Holden, the head of a Catholic college. Between them the primacy, supremacy, and infallibility of the Pope are discussed, then "the Ancient Irish Church," and the question of the "Gallicans," and the "Orientals." Chapter XV. is devoted to the discussion of "Corporate Reunion," and seems to us specially valuable. What it shows is, that even the Anglican supporters of corporate reunion do not really mean what the words imply. They do not suppose, for instance, that the Low Church, or the Broad Church, but only their own party, would join the Catholic Church, so that, as Father Holden sums up the motto :—"Then I understand that by Corporate Reunion you do not mean the reunion of the Established Church with the Church Catholic, but the union of a section of the Church, divided by their own secession, or that of their opponents, from the rest of the Anglican Communion." Then the Anglican bishop is compelled to admit :—"I do not know that I could reckon on any of the Bench of Bishops, at present. Certainly the great body of the bishops would not stir, or rather, would be actively opposed to the movement." This is, as the Father urges, a "startling difference between the position of the [Anglicans who desire corporate reunion] and that of the Greeks of Florence. The Greeks were a real corporate body, animated by an internal principle which bound them together. The bishops represented the whole body of their Church. They could treat in the name of the Church, and could be treated with. If one or two Greek bishops and a section of their flocks had offered at Florence to treat for a reunion, it would have been as a seceding body that they would have come before the Council, not as the representatives of the Eastern Church. Still there is no doubt the Church would have accepted and met their advances. But here is another difficulty. The Greeks were united on the principle of the Primacy. They did not deny that, in the normal state of the Church, the See of Peter was the divinely-appointed centre of unity and rightful supremacy over all the Churches." We should add, that the other salient difference had already been discussed between the parties, namely, that the Greek orders were unquestionably valid, while the Anglican orders could never be so. "The utmost that could ever be granted would be that, in order to meet scruples on both sides, orders given to Anglican clergymen should be conferred conditionally ; always supposing, what I believe to be impossible, that you would make out a probable case for the consecration of your bishops."

Next we have a new character introduced, the Superior of the Fathers at New York, "Father Dilke, one of the most remarkable men of the Catholic Church in the States. A convert, and a man of large means and sympathies, so that he was better able to enter into the scruples and difficulties of religious Protestants in their first contact with Catholic doctrines and Catholic worship." He discusses with our heroes "Catholic worship," "God and the Saints," "the Communion of Saints," and "the Sacrifice." By this time the party, with the addition of several new characters, are on their way across the Atlantic (leaving F. Helder behind them). Next they discuss "Catholic Christianity as the greatest historical fact in the world"—the nature of the evidence on which the Christian revelation rests—the supernatural. In this chapter we have the remarkable words in which Napoleon, at St. Helena, pointed out the contrast between the history of our Divine Lord and that of all the great men that have ever lived. In several following chapters we have an outline of the proofs of the Divine authority of Christianity. The 28th chapter contains a capital allegorical sketch, called "The Story of the Old Ship," which we would heartily recommend to the study of those excellent persons who contrive to believe that the Anglican Communion is really Catholic. It is an agreeable variation of the usual gravity of this book, and a capitally written satire. The fact is, the notion is one which it is not very easy to discuss quite seriously.

After arriving in Liverpool, a great part of the company keep together, and discuss "Infallibility," "where is the visible Church" "the Church a visible Body with a visible Head." Some of the Protestant members of the party now declare themselves convinced. Then follow four chapters, headed "The Threshold of the Church," in which, as the authority of the Church is already supposed to be admitted, its teaching on the fundamental doctrines of Christianity is rapidly sketched, and the last chapter conducts the new converts to old Rome. Thus the pilgrimage is at length concluded.

We have given this outline of the subjects discussed because they are exactly those which it is important to have brought before seriously-minded men, who are looking for a sure guide to the truth. We will only add that the arguments throughout are clearly and strikingly stated, and (what we especially value) that the spirit is one uniformly charitable and loving. We do not think there is anything in the volume which can give offence to any Protestant. That there is nothing that can give pain is more than we could say, for we can hardly believe that any thoughtful Anglican can read it with tolerable fairness, without having the pain of feeling that, as far as argument goes, there is really nothing to be said against the writer's conclusion. Alas ! we know too well, that does not necessarily imply conversion to the Catholic Church, for, over and above the conviction of the reason, the will has to be influenced, and who shall do that save God only ?

When we remember the great services rendered to the Church in England by Dr. Milner's " end of controversy," we cannot help contemplating a somewhat similar career for the book before us ; and that it will, for years to come, be the means of bringing conviction to thousands, both in England and America. We will therefore suggest that at present it bears too manifest marks of its having at first appeared in a newspaper. The press has not been corrected with sufficient care. There is a great want of a good table of contents ; and we would suggest, in addition, a list of *dramatis personæ*, because, although a reader who goes carefully through the volume, from beginning to end, will have no difficulty on this score, it is to be remembered that many will want to see the way in which some one particular subject (in which they are specially interested) is treated, and such readers will be puzzled by finding themselves suddenly introduced into the society of these worthy Americans, without so much as knowing which of them are Catholics and which Protestants. This is an awkwardness which comes upon us often enough in real life but to which none of us will willingly be subjected, when we can help it.

The Rule of the Pope-King weighed by Facts and Figures. A Letter to the Legislators of Great Britain. By EDWIN ROPER MARTIN, Priest of the Diocese of Shrewsbury, some time Scholar of the Roman College. London : Washbourne. 1871.

THIS pamphlet begins by an address to British Legislators, as having again and again interfered when injustice has been done in other countries. It first gives, from page 7 to 15, a sketch of the historical origin of the Sovereignty of the Popes. Next it says, " The Pope is a king. But there are kings who rule with rods of iron, kings who rule with reins of silk, and kings who do not rule at all. The Papal Sovereignty might have been what we call a tyranny, or might have been so light that it was not felt at all. In truth, however, it is neither of these ; it is a real sovereignty, without being tyrannical."

Next, it gives an account of the state of education in the Pope's dominions from page 18 to 34. Next it answers the objection, " that even if the Sovereignty of the Pope-King gives means for a liberal education, it offers no chance of a career to a young man of promise when he has finished his education." " I reply," says the author, " that there is more chance of a career in the State of Rome than in England, and I prove it ; first by the educational statistics already given, which establish incontestably the fact that poverty is not, as in England, a ban to a liberal education, and a liberal education is the ordinary starting-point of all careers. I prove it, secondly, by facts." He then mentions the different careers, "the ecclesiastical career," and the " State career" for laymen, p. 34 to 39. The medical profession, 39 ; literary career, 39 to 41 ; commerce, 41 to 44 ; agriculture, 44 to 50.

" The next count is taxation. Is the subject of the Pope-King unfairly taxed by a drain upon his gains or his revenues, which can hardly fail to lame his work in life ?" The answer to this, giving an account of the state of taxation in the States of the Church, occupies from 50 to 56. From 56 to 58 there is a comparison of the condition of the States subject to the House of Savoy in this respect.

" The next count is justice. Are the laws and the machinery of the tribunals such as to promise a subject of the Pope-King redress of wrongs and a fair trial, if accused of wrong-doing ? "

The answer to this question occupies from 58 to 64. The author then adds :—

" I may also be permitted to give other statistics of the Italian Kingdom," pp. 64–65.

Next follows an account of the administration of the States of the Church. " The ministers who compose the Cabinet are, the Foreign Secretary, who, as in Prussia and Austria, is also Prime Minister ; the Home Secretary ; the Secretary at War ; the Minister of Finance ; the Minister of Public Works and Commerce, and the Director-General of Police and Minister of Justice." Of each of these, and his functionaries, is given an account in p. 66 to 68. In 68 to 74 an account of the different checks and limitations on the power of the ministers.

The last few pages notice the unscrupulous character of the attacks and charges made.

Lastly, the author meets the statement that the plebiscite proves the desire of the Pope's subjects to throw off his government. The facts about this are so important, that although they have already been published, *e.g.* in the *Tablet*, we think that the author does right in calling attention to them ; and we are ourselves glad to put them on record.

" I know not with what force any honest man can take his stand on the plebiscitum as an argument against the temporal sovereignty of the Popes, after the following paragraph, which appeared in a Roman newspaper a few weeks since :—

" A distinguished mathematician of our city has compared the number of votes said to have been given in Rome, on the 2nd of October, with the length of time the voting lasted, and the number of urns placed to receive the votes, and so made a calculation as to how many persons a minute, must have given their votes to produce the total return. The *Si* were returned as 40,785 ; the *No* at 46—total, 40,831. The voting lasted 10 hours, from 8 A.M. to 6 P.M. There were 12 urns in all, so at least the official gazette informs us. 10 hours = 600 minutes × 12 urns = 7,200; now, 40,831 divided by 7,200 gives us 5·67 votes per minute. To get the published result, therefore, it was necessary that the voting should have gone on during the whole ten hours at the uninterrupted rate of 5½ votes a minute for each urn. This seems impossible on the face of it ; but its impossibility is clear when we consider how the voting proceeded. The voters had to mount up steps to the polling booths, to present a ticket of admission, and in most cases to select, there and then, the *Si* or the *No* presented for choice. Now, it is a fact that for the first two hours the voters presented themselves very sparely and at intervals, for directions had been given to vote as much as possible in trade companies. Eye-witnesses affirm that during the afternoon hours the booths remained almost deserted. A person has himself assured us that he remained watching the booths on the Piazza Navona (a most public square in the heart of the city) for more than an hour, and that during that time he saw only four persons put in a vote. So long as the eminent junta can give us no official solution of this enigma, we shall be compelled by the evidence to maintain, that the number of 40,831 votes is a pure invention, or that the votes were poured into the urns by the pailful. We therefore call on the gentlemen of the ex-junta, in their own defence, and to satisfy a very natural curiosity on the part of the Romans, to publish, if they can, the names, both Christian and surname, of the 40,831 voters—all Romans."

This is important. We much doubt whether there is any one of the "Napoleonic ideas" which Europe has more just cause to execrate than this of the plebiscite, by which any man who can by force or fraud get possession of a city or parish is entitled to set up balloting-urns, and in virtue of the papers which he pretends to have been thrown into them, claim to be the legitimate possessor of the place. Mr. Martin gives a valuable protest against the application of this vile principle by its inventor.

" This brings forcibly to my mind the language with which Signor Lorente-Robaudi, Deputy for Nice, on the 12th of April, 1860, protested before the house against the value of the impending plebiscitum for the people of Nice. ' What guarantees,' he asked, ' shall we have for the urns, when they are taken to the town-hall and there left to remain till to-morrow under the care of those who want the separation from Italy ? What guarantees will you give us that these urns shall not be changed in the night for others full of votes put there by our enemies' hand ? And from such votes as these you are going to decide the nationality of a country, our will to become Frenchmen instead of remaining what we are.'

" And three days later he said of the votes already taken, ' Is it possible to get a vote in two or three days. The Government, after having insulted Nice for many months, is now mocking it and laughing at it. You cannot ask a country to vote and arrange the electoral lists in two or three days. Europe cannot take such an act as the free vote of a free people '" (p. 81).

And true as this is of Nice, we need hardly say it is ten times more true of Rome. The fact is, that odious as was the system of open violence, by which Napoleon I. annexed so many states, it was at least less hypocritical than the system now for ever identified with the name of the hero of Sedan— the plebiscite.

The appendix contains testimonies of Italian liberals and unbelievers to the temporal power, and gives quotations from Pietro Verri, Foscolo, Bianchi-Giovini, Carlo Botta, Carlo Denina, Galeotti, Buoncompagni, Capponi, Gioberti, Giordani, and Napoleon I. No. II. contains the numbers in detail of the eight plebiscites, by which the existing kingdom of Victor Emmanuel was constituted. No. III. shows the small number of Italians who vote for representatives in the existing Parliament of Florence.

We believe we give the most accurate idea of this pamphlet by the foregoing analysis of its contents, and will only add that the author seems to us to have had good means of obtaining information, and to have used them with care and exactness.

The Liturgical Year. By DOM PROSPER GUÉRANGER, Abbot of Solesmes. Translated by DOM LAWRENCE SHEPHERD. Paschal Time. 3 vols. Dublin and London : Duffy. 1871.

THE English translation of this admirable work has now advanced to the ninth volume. The three volumes we now notice are entirely taken up with the great feasts and offices that occur from Easter to Pentecost inclusively. The Resurrection, the Forty Days, and the mystery of Pentecost naturally suggest to the author a very wide field for the devotion of the faithful. In former volumes, what we may call the personal element seemed to prevail ; there was the contemplation of Our Lord in the various circumstances of His blessed life, and there was joy or mourning for personal grace or personal sin. But with Easter, Dom Guéranger begins to treat of the Church. And these three volumes, in which the Risen Jesus, the Holy Spirit, and the Church are the principal figures, seem to us the finest of the whole series. In addition to the liturgical prayers, which as usual are printed at length and translated, each week of the Paschal Time has its appropriate list of subjects, and almost every day has a separate devotional view drawn out at some length. There could not be more appropriate spiritual reading and meditation for those fifty days of " Paschal Remission," for which, strangely enough, it does not always seem easy to find either spiritual reading or meditation. In Easter week itself it is natural that the chief attention should be given to our Lord's sacred Humanity, now immortal and impassible. But it is interesting to observe how the author does away with anything like vagueness or mere generality by introducing such topics as the Resurrection of the Flesh and the devotion to the Holy Sepulchre. The second week is taken up with further contemplation of the glorified Body of our Lord, and with His relations to those concerned in His Resurrection, as for example, the Holy Souls, the unfortunate Jews, and those whom He calls His " brethren." The third week, beginning with the Sunday of the " Good Shepherd," is devoted to the Church—to her Chief Pastor, her Bishops, her people, her visibility, her teaching power. The following week continues the same class of subjects, such as Revelation, the Gift of Miracles, Preaching, Infallibility, and Faith. The fifth week is given to the Sacraments. During Whitsun-week, in addition to much other matter, we have a really eloquent and touching devotional commentary on each of the seven Gifts of the Holy Ghost. Here is a short extract from the Abbot's words on the Gift of Understanding.

" The gift of *Understanding* consists in a supernatural light granted to the mind of man. This light does not remove the sacred obscurity of Faith ; but it enlightens the eye of the soul, strengthens her perceptions, and deepens

2 L 2

her view of divine things. It dispels clouds, which were occasioned by the previous weakness and ignorance of the soul. The exquisite beauty of the mysteries is now revealed to her, and the truths which hitherto seemed unconnected, now delight her by the sweetness of their harmony. It is not the face-to-face vision which heaven gives, but it is something incomparably brighter than the feeble glimmer of former days, when all was mist and doubt. The eye of her spirit now discovers analogies and reasons, which do something more than please,—they bring conviction. The heart opens under the influence of these bright beams, for they feed faith, cherish hope, and give ardour to love. Everything seems new to her. Looking at the past and comparing it with the present, she wonders within herself, how it is, that Truth, which is ever the same, has a charm and power over her now which once it had not. The reading or hearing of the Gospel produces an impression far deeper than formerly ; she finds a relish in the words of Jesus which, in times past, she never experienced. She can understand so much better the object of the institution of the Sacraments. The holy Liturgy with its magnificent ceremonies and sublime formulas is to her an anticipation of heaven. She loves to read the lives of the Saints ; she can do so, and never feel a temptation to carp at their sentiments or conduct ; she prefers their writings to all others, and she finds in these communications with the friends of God a special increase of her spiritual good. No matter what may be the duties of her station in life, she has in this glorious Gift a light which guides her in each of them. The virtues required from her, however varied they may be, are so regulated that one is never done to the detriment of another ; she knows the harmony that exists between them all, and she never breaks it. She is as far from scrupulosity as from tepidity ; and when she commits a fault, she loses no time in repairing it. Sometimes the Holy Ghost favours her with an interior speaking, which gives her additional light for some special emergency." (" Paschal Time," vol. iii. pp. 429–30.)

It may be said that no writer of the present day has done so much to promote the exercise of the great Gift of Understanding as the Abbot of Solesmes. The peculiar obstacle to Faith in our day is what may be called the un-Christianizing of the intellect. Secular science, which in itself might be a means of promoting the supernatural, generally has the practical effect of blinding the mind and hardening the heart. Dom Guéranger has not, as a rule, addressed himself to the infidel or the sceptic. His work has been to magnify the kingdom of God to the children of the kingdom ; to promote the exercise " of the supernatural in the operations of a Christian intellect " (in F. Faber's words) ; to teach his fellow-Catholics calmly and devotionally what they have in the Pope, the Church, and the gifts of the Holy Ghost. The Liturgy (to confine ourselves to the present work) is one of those overpowering manifestations of the supernatural that cannot be properly attended to but it is sure to make a difference to the mind. It may cause gnashing of teeth, as the presence of our Lord did formerly in the possessed ; or it may cause increase of faith and affection ; but it cannot be inoperative. We are not of those who think that the time has come for " popular devotions " to take the place of the Liturgy. Vernacular hymns, confraternity prayers, and " fancy " services are excellent, no doubt ; they are adapted to the people, and they fill up in the very best way time that would not otherwise be given to God. But the Litany, the Mass, Vespers, the ritual of the B. Sacrament, are first and most important. They are not so easily intelligible at first, and therefore not so immediately impressive ; they are the growth of ages, the fruit of many inspirations, the reflection of many minds, the expression of mighty things. Therefore it is that the minds of the people have to be elevated and instructed to appreciate them. We thank Dom Guéranger and his translator, F. Shepherd, for this Paschal instalment of the best of all companions before the altar. There are few of our readers, we should think, who have not provided themselves with these volumes for use during the rich Liturgical season that is now in its course.

WE are informed, by an Anglican reader, that our notice of Blunt's "Plain Account of the English Bible," in our last number, was in error where it stated that the author of that work was an ex-Professor of Cambridge.

" Catholic Opinion."

THE Editor of this weekly periodical sends us regularly a copy. We cannot but be struck by the vigour and spirit with which it is conducted, and which are most remarkable considering its low price. It must do very important service in disseminating sound Catholic doctrine among numbers to whom from circumstances the more costly Catholic periodicals are inaccessible.

Correspondence.

To the Editor of the DUBLIN REVIEW.

SIR,—In your last number you have noticed my pamphlet on the meaning of the late definition on Infallibility, and have accused me of making "a most gratuitous and unfounded attack" on Archbishop Manning. You say that I have censured him "for introducing such terms as the personal, separate, independent, and absolute infallibility of the Pope." As I am confident that you would not intentionally misrepresent any one, however much you may differ from him, I rely on your sense of justice to allow me to point out your mistake, and to print this letter in your next number.

I have not said, nor did I mean to insinuate, that Dr. Manning first used those terms. He expressly denies having done so in his last Pastoral ; and I regret that my words should have seemed to convey even a doubt upon the point. It is very probable that the interpretation which Archbishop Manning insists upon, requires the use of those terms in order to be fully understood : and it is quite certain that he has himself adopted every one of them as not merely proper, but necessary. It is undeniable that you think so, because in the very same number (p. 197) you say that the Archbishop "sums up his argument" by asserting "the privilege of infallibility to be—1. personal ; 2. independent ; 3. absolute ; 4. separate, *i. e.* (as I have stated in my pamphlet) in the sense of *distinct.*"

The passage which I have quoted from the Archbishop's Pastoral, and protested against, is his declaration of what the acceptance of that particular interpretation, which invents terms no trace even of which is to be discovered in the decree, obliges us to believe.

I am, Sir,

Your obedient servant,

March 2nd.   W. MASKELL.

[We have much pleasure in inserting Mr. Maskell's letter, and must thank him for his courteous language to ourselves. Of course we heartily accept his explanation, and entirely retract the remark which was founded on our misconception of his meaning.

At the same time he can hardly be *surprised* at that misconception. "There is another" interpretation, he had said, of the Vatican Decree, besides those he had already mentioned, "which invents terms of which not a trace is to be found in the Decree itself" (p. 15) ; and he had proceeded to identify this interpretation with the Archbishop's. We naturally therefore understood him to say, that the Archbishop had "invented the terms" on which he commented.

The Archbishop stated in his Pastoral (p. 93) that the formula of "personal, separate, independent and absolute infallibility" had repeatedly been ascribed to "promoters of the present Definition," but quite mistakenly. "After repeated search, not only was the formula as a whole nowhere to be discovered, but the words of which it is composed were, with the exception of the word 'independent,' equally nowhere to be found." We would point out therefore to Mr. Maskell, that not only the formula in question was not "invented" by *the Archbishop*, but that neither was it invented by *any* promoters of the Definition. Since however it had been mistakenly *ascribed* to them, it became their business (acting on the defensive) to consider in what sense they could, and in what sense they could not, accept it.]

INDEX.